Henry Clay and
the War of 1812

Henry Clay and the War of 1812

QUENTIN SCOTT KING

McFarland & Company, Inc., Publishers
Jefferson, North Carolina

Library of Congress Cataloguing-in-Publication Data

King, Quentin Scott, 1924–
Henry Clay and the War of 1812 / Quentin Scott King.
p.   cm.
Includes bibliographical references and index.

ISBN 978-0-7864-7875-0 (softcover : acid free paper) ∞
978-1-4766-1390-1 (ebook)

1. Clay, Henry, 1777–1852.   2. United States—History—War of 1812—
Biography.   3. United States. Congress. House—Speakers—Biography.
4. Legislators—United States—Biography.   5. United States.
Congress—Biography.   I. Title.
E340.C6K56 2014   328.092—dc23   [B]   2013039323

British Library cataloguing data are available

On the cover: *Harry of the West* (the painting depicts Henry Clay at
the Signing of the Treaty of Ghent in 1814), oil on canvas, ca. 1965,
William P. Welsh (courtesy Transylvania University Photographic Archives)

Manufactured in the United States of America

*McFarland & Company, Inc., Publishers
Box 611, Jefferson, North Carolina 28640
www.mcfarlandpub.com*

To those who believed
in the ultimate accomplishment
of this work —
my father and my wife

TABLE OF CONTENTS

PREFACE

There must be a reason why anyone is motivated to write a book. My motivation to write this particular book began one night when I was unwell and wanted something to read as I rested in bed. I checked out my excellent personal library of books on history. There I found a lightweight but enjoyable book on the life of William Henry Seward, secretary of state for Abraham Lincoln. *The Man Who Would Be President*, by Earl Conrad, includes coverage of 1849–1850, the years when Seward was a United States senator from New York.

While reading the book, my attention was drawn to his colleagues in the Senate, whom the book casually mentions. They were Henry Clay, Daniel Webster, John C. Calhoun, Thomas Hart Benton, Jefferson Davis, Stephen A. Douglas, Sam Houston (and before the session ended), John Charles Frémont, along with several men who became famous later as a chief justice, vice presidents, or candidates for president or vice president. And the presiding officer, Millard Fillmore, became president during the session.

What a massive collection of famous men in possibly the greatest Senate ever known. I was intrigued by these men who passed the Great Compromise of 1850, in effect, postponing the Civil War more than a decade, giving the North time to grow in strength enough to win that war and sustain the United States as a nation and thus pave the way to become the greatest power in the world.

I considered who was colossus among these giants, and came to an easy answer: Henry Clay! On my next trip to two or three local Washington D.C. area libraries, I looked for his biography. I was stunned to discover there wasn't one.

Next, I went to the manuscripts division of the Library of Congress, many years ago, and asked to see some Clay papers. In those days, such requests were easily fulfilled. What I got was a box of old Clay letters which I then perused. I was startled to hold the handwritten challenge, from Clay to Senator John Randolph of Virginia, to fight a duel. At the time — in early 1826 — Clay was the secretary of state under John Quincy Adams. The duel was fought and both survived two shots.

Eventually, with greater research, I became convinced Clay was the greatest political personality of the early 19th century. So why no biography? I don't know the answer to that. Clay was Lincoln's great idol, and though never a Republican, he was the founder of the Whig party and staunch opponent of Democrat Andrew Jackson. Perhaps the lack of a biography is politically based.

Who was Henry Clay, to stand so high in my eyes, and be unknown to most Americans today? Clay was born near Richmond, Virginia, in April 1777 (and thus 10 years Jackson's junior). He was poorly educated until he moved to Kentucky when he was 20, and pursued a career in the law and was soon a member of that state's house of representatives.

In 1806, when he was 29 years old, while a member of the House, he was called on by former Vice President Aaron Burr to defend him before two sittings of a grand jury. Believing the man innocent, Clay defended Burr successfully in the first encounter. Between the sittings, the incumbent U.S. senator from Kentucky resigned his seat with a session to continue till March 4, 1807. (Clay would not be a Constitutionally-eligible 30 years old until that April 12.)

Nevertheless, the legislature elected Clay to fill the brief un-expired term. Before the second grand jury sitting, Clay asked Burr for a written statement denying any complicity to treasonable activities in the Louisiana area. Burr was again acquitted. Clay took the document with him to Washington City in late December, where he visited President Jefferson at the White House and showed him Burr's statement. Jefferson showed Clay a sheaf of papers verifying Burr's guilt. Clay wrote home that he had been duped.

By the time Clay was 34, he had continued in the Kentucky house where he was briefly its speaker, served another brief un-expired U.S. Senate term, and fought a duel with a member of the Kentucky house. In November 1811, as a freshman member of the U.S. House of Representatives, he was elected Speaker in the first hour of his membership. He was to serve in that capacity longer than any other Speaker in U.S. history, except for Sam Rayburn. At that time his political power was second only to that of President James Madison. In this position, Clay was probably better known than Jackson (though 10 years younger), and Clay labored hard for the wherewithal to put the nation in an "ardor for war." The following year, he supported the declaration of war against Great Britain — indeed urged its enactment.

By 1814, Madison named Clay to be one of five prominent men, including John Quincy Adams and Albert Gallatin, to be commissioners to meet with British representatives to negotiate a treaty of peace — all before Jackson won his battle at New Orleans and became a military "hero," a sobriquet that carried him to the presidency.

In the ensuing years, Clay served in the House until 1831, when he went to the Senate for the remainder of his very long life of service, and was still a senator at age 75 when he died in 1852. Regarding his historic place in that body, the members of the Senate, in 1957, voted for the five greatest past members of their "club." Clay was one of them and it was said at the time, that if they had needed to vote for the single greatest senator of all time, it would have been Clay. It was during his Senatorship that he authored the historic 1850 Compromise at age 73.

During his earlier eventful House years, he authored the Missouri Compromise, the American System, and advocated for internal improvements (great 19th century highways, and canals, etc.). He was one of four candidates for the presidency in 1824 — the others being Jackson, John Quincy Adams and an ailing William Crawford. As the eliminated candidate, but Speaker of the House, where the final election was held, Clay was able to influence that body to elect Adams to the White House. Adams, in turn named Clay to be his secretary of state, which ruffled the feathers of Jackson supporters, who called it a "corrupt bargain." After all, Clay and Adams had worked hard together in writing the peace treaty, and Adams was well aware of Clay's diplomatic skills.

It was in 1832 that Clay lost the presidential election to Jackson. He was to lose the Whig nomination to William Henry Harrison in 1840, and another election to Polk in 1844, and again the nomination to Taylor in 1848. Well, he was ambitious — not exactly a rare trait for politicians of either party.

Clay had 11 children. All six of his daughters died in his lifetime. Of his five sons, one was killed in the Mexican War, which Clay opposed. Another of his sons had an accident as a teenager and Clay was warned that the boy would eventually go insane, and indeed he did at age 27. He was then committed to an institution where he lived until his 70s. Clay's wife's brother, when a prisoner of war, was brutally slain by Indians working for British soldiers early in the War of 1812.

Having worked on Capitol Hill as a reporter and a congressional press secretary, I simply could not resist researching and writing Clay's life and believe he is easily a three-volume personality in comparison to Jackson's life as a single-volume. Jackson was of no note politically after 1837, while Clay was still running for president (or its nomination) three times after Jackson left office, but meanwhile continued to make his greatest marks in the U.S. Senate for another 15 years.

Since I am no academician, the reader is cautioned not to expect deep analyses of Clay's historical position in American biography. I am merely attempting to put his name, service, and his times before the Americans who are interested in the history of their country. Some will find my story (I am part journalist and part story-teller) too detailed. For those who are interested in the little details, they are here. As I state at one point, Clay was, after all, a legislator, and the words he spoke in the halls of Congress were the basis of his great fame.

1

YOUTH

The united states were at war. Though they were united in purpose and their representatives "In General Congress assembled" had declared "That these United Colonies ought to be free and independent states," the truth of that claim was yet to be proved in April of 1777. Not until the victory at Yorktown in 1781 and the signing of the peace treaty in Paris in 1783 was independence assured. The Constitution, written in 1787 and placed in operation in 1789, gave a lasting formality to the name, "The United States of America."

Henry Clay, probably the first great American to be conceived in the liberty of independence, was born on April 12, 1777, about the time that General George Washington and his courageous army were greeting spring at Monmouth, New Jersey. Six days later would be the second anniversary of "The shot heard 'round the world" when men who yearned for freedom died on the village green of Lexington, Massachusetts, and others stood against "the world's greatest army" at "the rude bridge that arched the flood" at Concord.

In the intervening days between the opening shots of the American Revolution and the birth of Henry Clay, event poured over event. The patriot army of Massachusetts had shamed the British General Thomas Gage at Bunker Hill. The Virginia farmer, George Washington, had left his seat in the Second Continental Congress to take command of the Continental Army at Cambridge outside Boston. Former bookseller Henry Knox and his troops dragged and pulled the guns of Fort Ticonderoga from Lake Champlain over the snowy Berkshire Mountains to Dorchester Heights to give Washington the power to force the British from Boston. In a document drafted by Thomas Jefferson, Benjamin Franklin, John Adams, Roger Sherman, and Robert Livingston, the 56 delegates to the Continental Congress in Philadelphia had pledged their lives, their fortunes, and their sacred honor in the cause of independence. The British had won a series of battles in the New York City area forcing Washington and his army to retreat across the New Jersey farmlands into Pennsylvania. And Washington had struck back with a surprise crossing of the ice-filled Delaware River on Christmas day of 1776 to dislodge the British from the snow-covered towns of Trenton and Princeton.

These were the times that were trying men's souls. It was the crisis when the summer soldier and the sunshine patriot would shrink from the service of his country. But it was also the time that Henry Clay was born in Hanover County, Virginia, to take his place in the new America and become the first great American who was never a subject of the crown of Britain. He was never to shrink from service to his country. His first allegiance was to no other country nor, in fact, to any section of his own country.

Henry Clay was the seventh of nine children born to the Reverend John Clay and Elizabeth Hudson Clay. The earliest tracing of Henry Clay's family goes back to the remote days of the first English colonization in Virginia. Captain John Claye, son of Sir John Claye of Wales, landed in America in 1613, only six years after John Smith founded Jamestown. Claye suffered through the hunger and despair that twice reduced the colony's population to less than 60 people and he was one of only 350 English subjects living in America in 1616.

Captain Claye and his wife, Anne, who waited

10 years to join her husband in Charles City, Virginia, had four sons. The youngest of these sons, Charles, born 1638, married Hannah Wilson, daughter of John Wilson of Henrico County, Virginia. Charles was a soldier in Bacon's Rebellion of 1676. Of the seven children of Charles and Hannah, the fifth child (the third son), Henry, was the great-grandfather of the future American statesman.

This ancestral Henry was born in 1672 and died at 88 on August 3, 1760. In 1708 or 1709 he married Mary Mitchell, the daughter of William and Elizabeth Mitchell. They had four sons followed by two daughters. The third son, Charles, was father of two outstanding men — the Reverend Eleazer Clay and Green Clay, a delegate to the Virginia convention to ratify the U.S. Constitution, and the father of General Cassius Marcellus Clay.

Little is known of Henry's youngest son, John, of Dale Parrish, Chesterfield County. By his father's will John was to receive "the plantation whereupon he now lives and all my land on the north side of Swift Creek and the upper side of Nuttree Run: Also jointly with his brother Charles, the Grist Mill on Nuttree: Also his wife's plantation after her death." John Clay died between November 15, 1761 (the date of his will) and the following November when it was probated. He did not survive his mother who died at age 84 on August 7, 1777 (four months after the birth of her illustrious great-grandson).[1]

The three children of John Clay of Dale Parrish were John (often called Sir John, probably a reflection of his Welsh ancestry), Edward, and Fanny. Sir John and his cousins Eleazer and Green were raised in Chesterfield County. John was for a time a dancing master but later followed Eleazer into the ministry as a Baptist preacher. During the years leading to the Revolutionary War, Baptist clergy were frequently oppressed and imprisoned on charges of "breach of the peace and good behaviour." Eleazer, born in 1744, was pastor of the Chesterfield Church from 1775 to his death in 1836 and was believed to be worth $100,000, though it is not known how he came by such wealth. As he was a rich and socially prominent citizen of the county the authorities did not interfere with him even though he frequently aided fellow ministers who were imprisoned.[2] In later

years he served for a long period as moderator of his church's district. He died at 91 in 1836.

The Reverend John Clay also came to the support of those Baptist preachers, who were found guilty, by giving bond in May 1773 for John Weatherford and John Tanner who had been arrested for "preaching and assembling the people together in this and other counties of the colony without license for so doing." Clay was also confined in jail at one time.[3] Weatherford, like many other imprisoned preachers, continued exhorting his congregation by preaching through the grates of his prison windows. Authorities built a brick wall topped by broken glass bottles to prevent his followers from hearing the messages from the imprisoned clergy. But the people were not to be denied. They raised a handkerchief on a pole and held it above the wall as a signal that they were present and ready to hear the word. Weatherford's voice was strong and sufficient to reach the crowds beyond the wall.[4] Among the legal minds that defended many Baptist preachers in these years was the nephew of a Baptist minister, Patrick Henry of Hanover County to the north of Richmond.

It was to Hanover County that the Reverend John Clay, our statesman's father, moved in 1777 and established Black Creek Church in the lower part of the county near "the New Kent line."[5] The Baptists of Hanover County claimed the Reverend Clay as their chief apostle. He was a man of great vigor of character, of exemplary virtue and manners, and of a nice and high sense of the decorums and proprieties of the social relations.[6]

It appears that Elder Clay, as the Baptist congregation called their pastors, while still preaching in Chesterfield County, met and married Elizabeth Hudson of Hanover County in 1765 when she was only 15 years old. Her parents were George and Elizabeth (Jennings) Hudson. George Hudson, an inspector of tobacco in Hanovertown and a staunch Tory during the Revolution, was one of 11 children of Elizabeth (Harris) and John Hudson, a gentleman of English descent who had settled in Virginia.

Elizabeth (Hudson) Clay was described as rather below medium in stature and a woman of rare beauty, with dark hair and eyes and ruddy complexion. She had great determination and was industrious and economical. She was engaging in manners, entertaining in conversation, and a great favorite in social circles. Her individuality was striking and impressive. She was animated and genial in spirit, and readily won the confidence and esteem of others. She spoke with the authority of self-conscious right, yet always with disinterested sympathy in all that concerned her friends. She was not only respected but also loved by those who knew her intimately. In her home life she was hospitable and kind to all, and sympathetic and responsive to every call of need among her neighbors. Though somewhat strict in her discipline with her children and servants, she was just and kind, and both paid her the tribute of obedience with respectful devotion. The mother of Henry Clay was marked by such traits of mind, force of will, and strength of character which made her not only equal to every occasion, but in emergencies, superior to environment.[7]

The first six Clay children were born in Chesterfield County, unless the family lived for a time in Henrico County. Only George, the second child, and John, the sixth, lived to manhood. The third child, Henry, died in childhood but passed on his name to the great brother he never knew. After the birth of the famous Henry (the family's seventh child, born April 12, 1777), only one of the next two children survived — Henry's younger brother Porter.

The union of the Reverend Clay and Elizabeth Hudson brought some land and several slaves from the wills of both their parents. Materially, the family must have anticipated a normal, peaceful life in the service of the church. So, in the spring of 1777, John Clay and his family settled in the section of Hanover County, Virginia, known as "the slashes" because of its marshy terrain. The Reverend Clay began building the congregation of the infant Black Creek Church. At the home, Elizabeth Clay tended to the needs of her infant son, Henry Clay.

Far to the north, soldiers of the infant nation continued the struggle to insure that the Declaration of Independence was a living document rather than a death certificate for its signers. General Washington's army found British General Sir William Howe at Brandywine Creek in Pennsylvania and lost a battle that gave Howe the freedom of Philadelphia. Washington's failure to dislodge Howe in the battle of Germantown

forced the Continental Army to suffer through the terrible winter at Valley Forge. But still farther north, in central New York State, American General Horatio Gates defeated General Johnny Burgoyne at Saratoga. An engagement at Monmouth, New Jersey, in mid–1778, created something of a stalemate in the north. But now the Americans were living under the Articles of Confederation and had an alliance with France.

Thwarted in the north, the British army turned for success to the southern "Colonies," striking at Savannah at the close of 1778 and spending the next two years under Lord Cornwallis winning some battles and losing others as they pushed steadily northward through the Carolinas. In May 1781, Cornwallis marched into southeastern Virginia to support the traitor, Benedict Arnold, then at Norfolk.

As the threat of war drew closer to the home of 4-year-old Henry Clay, another fear stalked the family hearth. During the preceding November the Rev. John Clay drew up his will affirming "In the Name of God Amen, I John Clay of Hanover County, being very sick & weak but of a disposing mind and sound memory, do make and Ordain this to be my last will and testament..."[8] Whatever his affliction, he died during the last week of May 1781.

On the 29th of May young Henry Clay saw his father laid to rest and the following day saw war come across his family's land. Earlier in the year, as Lord Cornwallis moved into Virginia from the south, the 24-year-old French general, the Marquis de Lafayette, marched down to Richmond from the north, with a lesser force under his command. Noting his weak posture, he wrote his American commander, General Washington, on May 24, "Were I to fight a battle I should be cut to pieces, the militia dispersed, and the arms lost. Were I to decline fighting, the country would think itself given up. I am therefore determined to skirmish, but not to engage too far, and particularly to take care against their immense and excellent body of horse, whom the militia fear as they would so many wild beasts." He added, "I am not strong enough even to get beaten."

As Cornwallis ordered his forces to cross over to the north bank of the James River to attack Lafayette, the British general wrote Sir Henry Clinton, his commander facing Washington in

New York, "I shall now proceed to dislodge Lafayette from Richmond, & with my light troops to destroy any magazines or stores in the neighborhood which may have been collected either for his use or for General Greene's army." In another letter to Clinton, Cornwallis wrote of Lafayette, "The boy cannot escape me."[9] But Lafayette retreated northward past the area of the Clay home.

On the day after the Rev. Clay's burial, Cornwallis moved to Hanover Court House on the Pamunkey River and found several French 24 pounders which had been spiked and pushed into the river by an American artillery unit under the command of Lt. Francis T. Brooke, who was later to become a life-long friend of Henry Clay. On this same day, "Bloody" Colonel Banastre Tarleton and his green-clad 23rd Dragoons, the "body of horse" so feared by the Virginia militia, stormed onto the Clay homestead still in mourning.

Warned of the approaching troopers, Elizabeth Clay engineered the escape of the only adult white male present, the plantation's overseer. On their arrival, the soldiers unceremoniously entered the house and began wantonly destroying the widow's property and taunting her with brutal jibes and insults. They ransacked the kitchen and larder, and satisfied their hunger. They then turned their attention to the destruction of the furniture and to general pillage. Bureaus were chopped to pieces, trunks and chests were broken open, and every room and closet ransacked for such articles of value as were portable. Other property which the vandals could not well carry off was wrecked and scattered about the house. After breaking up the bed frames, the roistering troopers ripped open a half dozen feather ticks and emptied their contents out the window.

Leaving the house in chaos, the raiders continued their plunder in the yard by killing and stealing scores of chickens and turkeys and even used their bayonets to poke into the freshly turned graves of the Rev. Clay and Henry's recently deceased grandmother, possibly suspecting they instead contained hidden stores. As the soldiers left the heartsick widow and the terrified 4-year-old Henry Clay, they took with them many of the family's slaves, leaving the fatherless home with only the small family to work the farm.

When Tarleton, himself, appeared at the house,

Mrs. Clay complained about the villainous treatment by his troopers. He asked her to point out the guilty and he would have them punished. She was furious and reprimanded him roundly, telling him he knew it was impossible for her, during so much confusion, to point out the guilty: they were all strangers to her and dressed alike. Tarleton then said, "Madam, you shall be paid for your losses," and at once had a sack of coins emptied on a table nearby. She was afraid to openly refuse the money, but when the British colonel left, she scraped the money off into her apron and cast it into the fire, saying her "hand should not be polluted with British gold."

Years later, in relating these accounts to neighbors, the flush of resentment would animate the features of Henry Clay's mother and her eyes would flash as she recalled the memories of the desecrations enacted at the home and over the remains of her so-recently dead husband and her mother. She related one incident with more than usual pathos. Among the things of value of which her chests were rifled, was her wedding dress, made of white satin and richly trimmed. It was a relic treasured with a tenderness of sentiment and pride and beyond all earthly price to her alone. The ruffian who stole the endeared gown was an officer. He threw it across his saddle and mounted. The last view Mrs. Clay had of her beautiful robe was as the marauder rode away.[10]

Tarleton and his troopers rode on west in search of Virginia Governor Thomas Jefferson and the fleeing Virginia legislators. But their mission failed when a "rebel" American, Jack Jouett, caught a glimpse of the British horsemen as they rode through Louisa, Virginia. Jouett struck out on an all-night ride over little-used trails to Charlottesville to warn the governor and the lawmakers. Among the half-dozen or so legislators who lingered too long and were eventually captured was one Daniel Boone.

As the summer wore on, all of Cornwallis' army, backed up into the area around Yorktown, was placed under siege by Washington (who had marched south to take command of Lafayette's meager army), and finally surrendered to the Americans on October 19, 1781, when the British general found his escape by sea blocked by a French fleet in Hampton Roads.

Washington's victory meant peace and independence for the United States. But for the devastated Clay home, it meant remolding the life of the family to till the land and provide for sustenance of all those under the widow's care. The oldest child, George, was no more than 13. In the Reverend Clay's will of November 10, 1780, he disposed of property in Hanover County and "his plantation Euphraim in Henrico County" to the south. In addition, his will named his wife, six living children, and a "child my wife is now pregnant with, if it should live." A child named Betsy and an earlier Henry had died previously. The Reverend Clay apportioned to his survivors at least 22 slaves. Following the abductions by Tarleton's Dragoons, it is not known if any of these slaves remained to help with the plowing and care of the land, but the tax records of 1782 show Elizabeth Clay as the owner of 16 slaves and records of the following year list her possessing 464 acres.

By 1785 the tax records report Elizabeth Watkins as owning one slave and others are listed under the name of Henry Watkins. Though it is not known precisely when the widow Clay married Captain Henry Watkins, a grandson of this marriage stated that his father, John Watkins, born in Virginia in 1785, was the oldest child of this union. There were to be six more children born to the couple—16 in all by Henry Clay's mother. It is presumed that Elizabeth Clay, at age 31 in 1781, after giving birth to nine children, remained an extremely attractive and engaging woman, for her second husband's will several times suggests the possibility of her re-marriage. And indeed Henry Watkins was about 9 years her junior. Some years before their marriage, Henry Watkins' older brother, John, had married Elizabeth's older sister, Mary Hudson.[11]

On the death, about May 1781, of Elizabeth Hudson, the widow of George Hudson and the mother to the two girls who married into the Watkins family, the Hudson plantations were divided between the two daughters and through them to the Rev. Clay and John Watkins. Prior to his own death that same spring, the Rev. Clay negotiated purchase of John Watkins' portion of the land. Some years later, in a friendly court action, Elizabeth and her new husband, Henry Watkins, won the right to complete the purchase from their own brother and sister, giving them a larger inheritance.[12]

Despite the availability of slaves, young Henry Clay, in his formative years, worked the fields. He reminisced in later years of his youthful plowing and how, when he unharnessed the horses at noon to feed them and get his dinner, he used, in warm weather, to go to the creek (where the French guns had been dumped), water the horses, and while they were feeding, cool himself by bathing. "I then thought the creek a monstrous stream," he said, "and indulged not a little self-complacency that I dared plunge into it, and stem its rapid current. But what was my surprise and disappointment, when I visited it, to find it nothing more than a small branch! It was one of the largest streams I had then ever seen." Clay also remembered a hickory tree which stood by and shaded the spring from which he used to drink, and was anxious to see the tree and get some nuts once more from it, as well as to drink again at the spring, but was disappointed on finding the tree had decayed, and like many of his "early friends and companions, had fallen. The fountain, however, still bubbled its cool and delicious waters."[13]

The youthful Henry Clay also had the chore of transporting the grain from the field to a mill to be ground to meal. From this childhood task would come the nickname, "Mill Boy of the Slashes," which constituted a part of every public political pageant of the Whig party during the presidential campaign of 1844. The political descriptions of the campaign told of Clay dutifully going to and from on the road between his mother's house and Mrs. Darricott's mill on the Pamunkey River. A bag of grain thrown across the back of a pony served as his saddle and a rope was the bridle.

While there were other things for Henry Clay to learn, his early education was most likely at the knee of his mother. During the late 1780s, when the young nation's leaders were writing a new Constitution and forming a new government under President Washington, Henry Clay was supplementing his mother's tutoring by no more than three years in a typical schoolhouse of the period. The structure was made of logs with no floor but earth. The entrance served for door, window, and air vent, being always open. The instructor, Peter Deacon, was an Englishman who came to America under questionable circumstances and had a proclivity for much drinking.

Henry Clay revered the teacher in speaking of him years later, yet told of an occasion when Deacon, in a fit of anger, struck the student leaving a mark which he carried for a long time.[14]

Besides reading and writing, Henry's formal education "went forward in arithmetic as far as 'practice,' a rule which, in the old style of teaching, was just far enough from 'units under units, and tens under tens,' to enable the pilgrim among figures to 'see through the book.'" Clay spoke of his education as "neglected but improved by his own irregular exertions, without the benefit of systematic instruction."[15]

What material wealth Henry Watkins brought into the life of Henry Clay is obscure, but there is no doubt as to Watkins' fondness for his stepson and he was attentive to the boy's success. In 1791 Watkins procured a clerkship for his stepson at Denny's store near the old market in Richmond.

The date of Henry Clay's move to Richmond is unknown, but if it were early in the year, it is possible that he was present on his 14th birthday, or the few days before, to see President George Washington in his visit of several days to the Virginia capital.[16] Richmond, at this time was a thriving city of about 8,500 inhabitants and more than 300 houses. On Shockoe Hill a large new and elegant Capitol building had been erected.

The duties of the new clerk at Richard Denny's store included measuring yards of silks and muslins for the ladies and selling imported books, fine wines, and expensive clothing to gentlemen. Among his experiences at the store, clerk Clay was once reproved by Denny for wasting too much string. Henry thereafter saved every scrap he could get and tied the pieces together. Denny then explained that using this sort of string might be offensive to the customer, as it made the packages look untidy by reason of so many knots. Henry Clay still wished to please his boss. So he consulted with a sailor who showed him how to splice strings to eliminate knots. From that time he spent his leisure hours making short strings into a continuous cord. When Denny discovered his young employee's ingenuity he was so pleased that he had all strings saved and turned the task of splicing them over to the clerk with the result that his enthusiasm rapidly evaporated.[17]

Store clerking was not Henry Clay's only interest in Richmond. Since succeeding Williams-

burg as Virginia's capital in 1770, the city had become the focal point of the state's political activity. It is possible that Clay had occasion to hear the future Chief Justice John Marshall during his membership in the 1791 session of the Virginia House of Delegates. In later years he spoke of hearing and admiring the great oratory of Patrick Henry.

His reading of the newspapers of the day told of plans for building a Federal City just above President Washington's home on the Potomac River. The new national capital was destined to become the seat of a new two-year-old Government which was operating under a Constitution drafted only four years before Henry's arrival in Richmond. French Colonel Pierre L'Enfant had been selected to lay out the street design and the placement of the Capitol on Jenkins Hill and the President's House about two miles to the northwest near the swampy estuary of Tiber Creek. And by the end of 1791 ten Amendments to the Constitution, known as the Bill of Rights, were adopted.

From overseas, repercussions continued from France where the monarchy had been overthrown and it appeared another people were intent on following the American example of government by the people.

As these political events stirred the interest of storekeeper Clay, his observant step-father, who had ambitions of his own, used his influence to start the young man on his life's career. Captain Henry Watkins was a close personal friend of Colonel Thomas Tinsley, a member of the House of Delegates from Hanover County. Tinsley's younger brother, Peter, was clerk of the Virginia High Court of Chancery. The older brother not only suggested to Peter that young Henry Clay should be given a desk job in the clerk's office, but when the younger Tinsley said there was no opening, the colonel said, "Never mind, you MUST take him in."[18] So, Henry Clay was employed to work at a desk in the clerk's office copying long legal documents.

On his first day at his new job Henry appeared in clean, well-starched linen and a suit of rustic "figinny," a homespun Virginia cloth, probably made by his mother. He was awkward in manner and immediately became the object of jibes and practical jokes by the other clerks in the office.

But his quick wit and repartee soon convinced the other boys that Henry Clay was a formidable antagonist. He rapidly gained the respect of both his co-workers and his superiors. While he enjoyed their companionship, he also used his leisure hours to improve his education by reading to perfect his daily duties and by developing correctness and clean writing. Blots, misspellings, and interlineation were not tolerated in the clerk's office.[19]

Though pay was meager under Peter Tinsley, Henry Clay was now practically on his own at 15. Henry's older brother George was still living in the area, but in the spring of 1792 his mother, step-father, and his other brothers and sisters succumbed to the lure of Kentucky to the west. In doing so, Henry's parents followed their own brother and sister — Mary and John who had followed a Watkins sister and her husband — all who sought a prosperous life in this state which entered the Union on the first day of June.

By 1793 Henry Clay became acquainted with the chief officer of the High Court of Chancery — 67-year-old Chancellor George Wythe. The chancellor, approaching the closing days of a long and distinguished career, was unable, by this date, to write because his right hand was affected with gout or rheumatism. Clay's excellent writing skill won him a position as the chancellor's occasional amanuensis, and eventually his permanent secretary, while still technically attached to Tinsley.

Though left a fortune when he became an orphan in childhood, Wythe squandered both his money and his talent until he was 30 years old. He caught hold of himself, studied law, and was a member of the Virginia House of Burgesses between the French and Indian War and the start of the Revolution. In this body he took an independent lead in petitioning the King to repeal some of the odious acts passed by Parliament. Wythe next served in the first two Continental Congresses at the outbreak of the war and was a signer of the Declaration of Independence. That same year he participated in revising the laws of Virginia in transition from colony to state. In 1777 Wythe was appointed judge of the Virginia High Court of Chancery and later became sole chancellor, a post he held for 20 years. He was a member of the Constitutional Convention, frequently acting as chairman, but left before signing the document when his wife became seriously ill. Wythe was for a time, during his Williamsburg days, a professor of law at William and Mary College and at various times had as his pupils, Thomas Jefferson, James Monroe, John Marshall, and many other outstanding men of a rising generation.

Henry Clay's association and work with Chancellor Wythe was best described in his own words in a letter he wrote in 1851. Clay wrote,

Upon his dictation I wrote the report of many of his leading cases. I remember it cost me a good deal of labor, not understanding a single Greek character, to write some citations from Greek authors which he wished inserted in copies of his reports sent to Mr. Jefferson, Mr. Samuel Adams of Boston, and to one or two other persons. I copied them by imitating each character as I found them in the original word. Mr. Wythe was one of the purest, best, and most learned men in classical lore that I ever knew. His personal appearance and his personal habits were plain, simple, and unostentatious. His countenance was full of blandness and benevolence, and I think he made in his salutations of others the most graceful bow I ever witnessed. A little bent with age, he generally wore a grey coat and when walking carried a cane.

In that same letter of 1851 Clay described what he knew of the unnatural and somewhat mysterious circumstances surrounding the death of his elderly mentor in 1806. Though stating that he had written the chancellor's will at Wythe's dictation, certain provisions suggest the final will was drafted after Clay's departure from Richmond. Nevertheless, Wythe planned to leave the greatest portion of his estate to his great nephew, George Wythe Swinney, the grandson of his sister. The remainder was to go to his three liberated slaves — a man, a woman, and a boy whom he had taught to read and write. Swinney, indignant at Wythe's kindness to the Negro boy and intent on poisoning the youngster, put arsenic in the coffee pot not expecting the chancellor to come to the table and have his breakfast drink. The paper containing the arsenic was later found on the kitchen floor.

As Clay related,

The coffee, having been drank by the Chancellor and his servants, the poison developed its usual effects. The Chancellor lived long enough to send for his neighbor, Major William DuVal, and got him to write another will for him, disinheriting the ungrateful and guilty grand-nephew, and making other dispositions of his estate. An old Negro woman, his cook, also died under the operation of the poison, but I believe that his other servants recovered. After the Chancellor's death it was discovered that the atrocious author of it had also forged bank checks in the name of his great uncle, and he was subsequently prosecuted for forgery, convicted and sentenced to the penitentiary.

The new will Clay spoke of mentioned the death that morning of the Negro boy.

After a full life of his own and 45 years after the death of Wythe, Clay still expressed his deep fondness for the chancellor when he added in that 1851 letter, "To no man was I more indebted by his instruction, his advice and his example, for the little intellectual improvement which I made, up to the period when, in my twenty-first year, I finally left the city of Richmond."[20]

Indeed, Henry Clay owed much to George Wythe. During the years 1793–97, the relationship between the two men — generations apart — provided a real education for Clay. As a companion to this outstanding tutor of political giants and a participant in the founding of a new nation, Clay had an education far beyond the scope of many who daily occupied a classroom desk. Not only did he gain a familiarity of the Constitution from a man who helped draft it, but Wythe also instructed his aide in the classics, in history, and in polite literature.

Shortly after Clay began his service to George Wythe, the elderly chancellor renewed his connection with national politics and used Clay in writing to the country's leadership. The French Revolution was developing full steam. King Louis XVI had been tried and lost his head to a guillotine early in the year and, by April, a month after Washington began his second term as President, word reached across the Atlantic that France was at war with Britain and Spain. Waves of enthusiasm flooded over the United States in support of the French Republic. Some pro–French elements in the country urged Washington to honor the Franco-American treaty of alliance and join them in the war.

But Wythe and Secretary of State Thomas Jefferson, both strong backers of the new French Republicanism, favored neutrality and were especially disturbed by the undiplomatic activities of Citizen Edmond Charles Genet, the new French Minister to the United States.

Already political factions were developing between the Federalists on the one hand behind Alexander Hamilton, who favored a strong central government and leaned to Britain as a friend — and the Republicans on the other hand behind Jefferson, who favored a more democratic rule by the people and leaned to France as a friend. The Federalists were more concentrated in the north while the south and western frontier was largely Republican.

Genet came into America at Charleston, South Carolina, and took a month to make his way to the capital, then in Philadelphia. All along the way his reception was tumultuous. A few days after Genet left Charleston, Washington issued his proclamation of neutrality. This did not deter Genet and he continued to entreat Americans to engage in acts of war against the British and even threatened to go directly to the people over the head of the American government.

Many of the more thoughtful pro-French Republicans in the United States, chagrined at Genet's boldness, attempted to divorce themselves from him while supporting his government. At the suggestion of James Madison, Republicans organized meetings in several cities approving the conduct of Washington in the affair, which finally included asking the recall of the Minister. George Wythe presided over the meeting held in Richmond that summer. He wrote to Jefferson, forwarding resolutions of the meeting to be handed to the President paying tribute to "His watchful attention to his own duty and the welfare of his country by his Proclamation."[21] Henry Clay probably wrote the expansive cover letter which Wythe sent along with the resolution. Washington replied to Wythe's letter with "affectionate acknowledgements."[22]

At about the same time that these community meetings were organized in various cities, a number of pro-French admirers founded "Democratic Societies" — the first started in Philadelphia. Another was initiated in Lexington, Kentucky (not far from the new home of Clay's parents), under the presidency of John Breckinridge, a former pupil of Wythe. Still another society sprang up in Richmond attended enthusiastically by 16-year-old Henry Clay.

Among his companions in the debating society were Edwin Burrell, John C. Herbert, Bennett Taylor, Edmond W. Rootes, and Thomas B. Robinson. But there were others who achieved more renown such as Walter Jones, Philip N. Nicholas, and Littleton W. Tazewell.[23] Jones, the son of a Congressman, married the daughter of Charles Lee, Attorney General under Washington and Adams, and later became the U.S. Attorney for the District of Columbia. Nicholas, son of a member of the Virginia House of Burgesses, became Attorney General of his home state but had even more illustrious brothers, two of whom became Congressmen and one an outstanding leader in Lexington, Kentucky. And Tazewell, another of Wythe's students and the son of a U.S. Senator, went on to serve in both houses of Congress, was a commissioner in the cession of Florida to the United States by Spain, and was a Governor of Virginia.

Issues other than the Genet affair were not long in coming up for debate by the members. Following the decapitation of former French Queen Marie Antoinette in October 1793, the "Reign of Terror" under Robespierre witnessed a steady parade of victims to the guillotine. In Pennsylvania, the "Whiskey Rebellion," against an excise tax on distilled spirits, was put down by the state militia. The 11th Amendment, denying suits against a state by citizens of another state or a foreign nation, was tacked on to the Constitution as a result of the Supreme Court's decision in *Chisholm vs. Georgia.*

But the topic of greatest importance to many members, and especially to Henry Clay, was the Jay Treaty with Great Britain. In Virginia, the treaty was strongly opposed for its provision settling war debts to Loyalists, much of it owed by Virginia; silence on slaves stolen by the British armies (such as those taken from the Clay household); and failure to resolve the Indian agitation west of the mountains (where Clay's family now lived).

Resentment over the treaty flowed over to the Richmond leadership where another meeting was chaired by Chancellor Wythe in 1795. At the recommendation of the meeting a letter was sent to President Washington describing the treaty as "Insulting to the Dignity, Injurious to the Interest, Dangerous to the Security, and Repugnant to the Constitution of the United States."[24] This message did not meet with the same happy reception by the President as had the previous communication from the Richmond citizens. And Washington signed the treaty.

It was also in 1795 that Wythe published a volume with the lengthy title "Decisions of Cases in Virginia by the High Court of Chancery, with remarks upon Decrees, by the Court of Appeals, reversing some of those decisions, By George Wythe, Chancellor of Said Court." This work was a sharp jab at the Judge of the Court of Appeals, Edmund Pendleton, who had so often overturned Wythe's opinions. Henry Clay, as Wythe's amanuensis, had taken the dictation on these long cases.

In 1796, Henry Clay left the employ of the Court of Chancery and moved into the home of Robert Brooke to spend the next year in the study of law. Brooke had studied in Great Britain and was captured during the Revolution on his voyage home. He was returned to England but eventually succeeded, on another voyage, in reaching America in time to fight and be captured again in an engagement near Richmond. It was Brooke's younger brother, Francis, who commanded the artillery unit that dumped the French guns in the creek near Clay's boyhood home. They had an older brother, Laurence, who had served as surgeon under Captain John Paul Jones on the *Bonhomme Richard* in the battle with the *Serapis* and other battles. After the war Robert Brooke was a member of the Virginia House of Delegates, was Governor of the state from 1794 to 1796, and was Attorney General at the time he tutored Clay in the law.[25]

Sometime in 1797, Henry Clay's older brother George died leaving the 20-year-old alone in the Richmond area with no family. On the completion of his year of studies under Attorney General Brooke, Clay obtained his license to practice law from the Virginia Court of Appeals on November 6, 1797. He could practice law in his native state but decided to follow his family to Kentucky.

2

KENTUCKY LAWYER

Reflecting on his migration to Kentucky, Henry Clay told a Lexington audience, on June 6, 1842, of his circumstances on leaving Virginia in 1797. At an entertainment in his honor on the occasion of his "retirement" from the U.S. Senate, Clay reviewed his 45 years at the center of the nation's political arena. He said of his legal beginnings,

> I obtained a license to practice the profession, from the judges of the court of appeals of Virginia, and established myself in Lexington, in 1797, without patrons, without the favor or countenance of the great or opulent, without the means of paying my weekly board, and in the midst of a bar distinguished by eminent members. I remember how comfortable I thought I should be if I could make one hundred pounds, Virginia money, per year, and with what delight I received the first fifteen shilling fee. My hopes were more than realized. I immediately rushed into a successful and lucrative practice.[1]

There is, however, evidence that Henry Clay's early plight was not as grim as he painted it in later years. His step-father's sister, Elizabeth (Sallie) Watkins, had married Edmund Wooldridge, a Missionary Baptist preacher, and had followed her husband to Kentucky in the late 1780s.[2] They in turn were followed by Henry's aunt and uncle, Mary and John Watkins, who settled in Woodford County, a few years later. In 1792, John Watkins, one of the founders of the town of Versailles, was a delegate to the Kentucky Constitutional Convention at Danville, and was later a representative in Kentucky's first legislature. That same year Henry's mother and step-father moved to Versailles and established a tavern which became a celebrated hostelry and the rendezvous of great lawyers and statesmen of the day. Furthermore,

it is believed that Henry Clay made a visit to his family's new home each summer before he finally established himself in nearby Lexington. He probably took in the social life of Versailles and developed many friendships during his visits there.[3] In addition, his association with George Wythe and Robert Brooke undoubtedly provided him with substantial credentials.

There is little question that Henry Clay's connections in Richmond were such that he would have had no problem in succeeding there as well as he was later to do in Kentucky. Yet there was an overpowering lure to Kentucky that was decisive. To be near his family must have been important, but he did not settle where they lived. Instead, he made Lexington his home. Most likely the frontier was as stimulating to Henry Clay as it has been for multitudes of Americans for generations.

The strange magnetism of Kentucky was best described by Moses Austin in the journals of his travels from Virginia to Louisiana in the winter of 1796–97, one year prior to Clay's migration.

> I cannot omit noticing the many distressed families I passed in the wilderness nor can anything be more distressing to a man of feeling than to see women and children in the month of December travelling a wilderness through ice and snow, passing large rivers and creeks without shoe or stocking, and barely as many rags as covers their nakedness, without money or provisions except what the wilderness affords. The situation of such can better be imagined than described. To say they are poor is but faintly expressing their situation. Life — *What is it, or what can it give* to make compensation for such accumulated misery? Ask these pilgrims what they expect when they get to Kentucky. The answer is LAND. "Have you any?" "No. but I expect I can git it." "Have you any-

thing to pay for land?" "No." "Did you ever see the country?" "No, but everybody says its good land." Can anything be more absurd than the conduct of man, here in hundreds travelling hundreds of miles they know not for what nor whither except its to Kentucky, passing land almost as good and easy obtained, the proprietors of which would gladly give on any terms? But it will not do. It's not Kentucky. It's not the promised land. It's not the goodly inheritance, the land of milk and honey. And when arrived at this Heaven in idea, what do they find? A goodly land I will allow, but to them forbidden land. Exhausted and worn down with distress and disappointment, they are at last obliged to become hewers of wood and drawers of water.[4]

The historic developments prior to the arrival of Henry Clay west of the Appalachian Mountains, and particularly Kentucky, form a colorful entanglement of diplomatic intrigues, speculative adventures, Indian wars, and dauntless pioneering. Woven into this fabric are two strong threads on which hung Henry Clay's two careers. The conflicting land claims in the Western Country provided the base for his legal career. A four-sided scramble of intrigue and diplomacy west of the mountains gave him a base for his political career.

From the earliest days of discovery and exploration, Spain laid claims to the lands of the Gulf Coast from Florida through Texas and deep into the mountain interior of the west. French explorers, followed by trappers, moved inland along the valley of the St. Lawrence, through the vast region surrounding the Great Lakes, and laid claim to the huge Mississippi Valley. Meanwhile, the British landed colonists along the Atlantic Seaboard from Plymouth to Savannah and granted charters which claimed land "from sea to sea." It was obvious that overlapping claims would result in great-power disputes over the Mississippi drainage sparsely inhabited by numerous tribes of Indians, the original "owners."

With the Treaty of Paris terminating the French and Indian War on February 10, 1763, France ceded to England all her possession east of the Mississippi River. Secretly France had previously transferred her western claims to Spain. However, the immense territory that stretched back toward the Appalachian Mountains contained only a few scattered forts and trading posts and became an additional lure to Spain. Otherwise, most of the area was peopled by the ancient claimants — the

Indians. Among these were the Shawnees in present-day Ohio and the Creeks and Cherokees in what is now Tennessee. The territory between, where great fields of cane grew, was known as Kan-tuc-kee. The ghosts of mound builders who lived and disappeared long before the 18th-century Indians brought the region another name, "The Dark and Bloody Ground." The Indians regarded this land with superstitious awe believing it filled with the souls of a strange race of people long since exterminated. No tribe, since the mound builders, was known to settle permanently in this wilderness.[5]

Even so, the Kentucky woods were a paradise for the Indian hunters, and as soon as the white man discovered the profusion of game — buffalo, bear, elk, and deer, etc.— they, too, were drawn to the hunt. But the terms of the 1763 Treaty of Paris forbade the incursion of white settlements beyond the crest of the Alleghenies until the Indians agreed on boundaries. While sale agreements were technically in the hands of government, private companies and even individuals took it upon themselves to negotiate with the tribes for land and soon speculators were carving out extensive tracts for sale to anxious settlers in the Western Country.

Among the leading speculators ignoring the Proclamation Line was Richard Henderson, a judge from the backwoods of North Carolina. Along with others, such as Thomas and Nathaniel Hart and Jesse Benton, he formed the Transylvania Company to buy up lands from any Indians and sell at large profits to the settlers who dared to defy both the government proclamation and other Indian tribes which refused to recognize the sales of "their" hunting grounds. With the help of long hunters — Daniel Boone, Simon Kenton, and John Finley — the wilderness was opened up to a steady flow of adventurers and later farmers. Bloody clashes between whites and Indians, with atrocities perpetrated by both, failed to stem the tide.

By the opening shot of the Revolution, the proclamation was practically obsolete and numerous settlements had risen among the canefields and salt licks of Fincastle County, Virginia. Around June 5, 1775, while on a sojourn from Harrodsburg, a group of long hunters (including Robert Patterson, Simon Kenton, Michael Stoner,

John Haggin, John and Levi Todd, and others) rested for the night on the north bank of the Kentucky River. As they munched on the inevitable jerky (or dried meat) and parched corn, they talked with enthusiasm of the beautiful country they had seen. Delighted with the spot on which they were encamped, they resolved to build a settlement there. Here they found broad rich acres that were fat and fertile with bluegrass pasture and abundant game. At once they began discussing an appropriate name for the settlement. The names of "York" and "Lancaster" were offered, but both were discarded with a shout for "Lexington!" as the conversation turned to the exciting news that had slowly crept through the wilderness. For they had just heard how "King George's troops, on the 19th of April, had called Americans "rebels," and shot them down like dogs at Lexington, in Massachusetts colony.[6]

During the Revolution the influx of settlers subsided, but those Kentuckians already there added the British to their Indian enemies. With peace in 1783, a flood of families flowed over the mountains into the "promised land" and renewed the building of towns and the clearing of land for farming. Following the Declaration of Independence, Fincastle County became Kentucky County. In 1780, this was divided into Fayette, Lincoln, and Jefferson counties. Fayette, named for the Marquis de LaFayette, amounted to more than one-third of present-day Kentucky. From 1785 to 1798, other counties, including Woodford, were formed from Fayette.[7]

Lexington was made the county seat of Fayette in 1781, though it was not incorporated until the following spring. At the first U.S. census in 1790, Lexington had a population of 850. When Kentucky became a state in 1792 the first session of the Kentucky legislature was held in Lexington but the capital was moved to Frankfort for the session beginning in November 1793. Five years later, Lexington numbered about 200 houses, a few of them brick, many of them frame, but most of them log with chimneys built on the outside.[8] The "Athens of the West" surpassed in size and importance the small villages of Cincinnati and Louisville.

This, then, was the land to which Henry Clay migrated in November 1797. Yet getting there was not an easy task in those days. There were possibly three major routes from the east into central Kentucky. One was across southern Pennsylvania by pack horse, and later wagon, to Pittsburgh where everything had to be transferred aboard flatboats or keel barges for the dangerous voyage down the Ohio River. This route was frequently under attack by the Indians from the north bank of the river. Another route was across the Blue Ridge Mountains and through present-day West Virginia.

But the usual route for Virginians trekking west to "the promised land" was through southern Virginia and the Cumberland Gap. Prior to the penetration by the white men, huge herds of buffaloes tramped through the canebrakes and salt licks and over mountain passes creating trails or "traces" by their sheer bulk and weight. They seemed to find direct routes for their migratory habits. These traces became part of the Wilderness Road opened to wagon traffic only in 1796. Henry Clay probably rode horseback over this route.

On settling in Lexington, 20-year-old Henry Clay was an inch over six feet tall. He was slender and broad-shouldered without being bulky or fleshy. He was to keep this fine figure throughout his long life. His normal stance was erect, but became even more pronounced when engaged in debate. His long limbs seemed to act in synchronization with his captivating voice. The awkwardness of his youth soon disappeared and in its place he developed an easy nonchalant air of a man accustomed to the ways of the world.

An interesting description of Henry Clay was given by his executor, a man who knew the statesman intimately from 1820 on. He wrote that

> Mr. Clay's complexion was fair, so fair, indeed, that I had supposed that his hair, when a young man, must have been of a sandy or yellowish tint; and on expressing that opinion to Mrs. Clay, several years after his death, I was greatly surprised by her prompt reply, "You were never more mistaken; he had when a young man the whitest head of hair I ever saw."
>
> His eyes were gray, and when excited were full of fire; his forehead high and capacious, with a tendency to baldness; his nose prominent, very slightly arched, and finely formed. His mouth was unusually large without being disfiguring. It, however, was so large as to attract immediate notice; so large, indeed, that, as he said, he "never learned how to spit"; he had learned to snuff and smoke tobacco, and but for his unmanageable mouth he would probably have learned to chew also.[9]

It is reasonable to assume that Henry Clay made the acquaintance of John Breckinridge soon after his arrival in Lexington since both had been pupils of George Wythe and both were members of the early "Democratic Societies." Fledgling lawyer Clay attended meetings of the group and probably dreamed of the day when he would be in court advocating some great cause. On one occasion during the club's debates, a question that was under discussion (very possibly the XYZ Affair that was the controversy of the day) was about to be put to a vote when Clay, who until then had never taken any part in the debates of the organization, was heard to say in a low voice, that he did not think the question was exhausted. Immediately, several members who heard his remark rose to call on the chairman, "Don't put the question yet. Mr. Clay will speak." With all eyes turned upon the new member, and possibly embarrassed at speaking out of turn, he was, nevertheless, obliged to rise and speak. "Gentlemen of the Jury," Clay blurted and at once appeared confused. But encouraged by the politeness of the chairman and his fellow members, he began again only to repeat, "Gentlemen of the Jury." Undaunted, at last, he seized control of his emotions and spoke to the question to the delight and admiration of the club and was cordially and loudly cheered. One member later described the long-since evaporated speech as the best Clay ever made.[10]

On March 20, 1798, still a few weeks short of his 21st birthday, Henry Clay, on his own motion before the court, obtained his permit to practice law in Fayette County, Kentucky. A few days after that birthday, he made his first public pronouncement, but cloaked it in the form of a printed statement in the Lexington paper, *The Kentucky Gazette*, and under the pseudonym of "Scaevola." The use of a concealed identity was common practice in this period. Such form was used by Hamilton, Madison, and Jay in the publication of *The Federalist Papers*. Several others used similar disguises in reply to Clay's argument, in which we have the first public expression of his views on any subject.

The 1792 Kentucky Constitution gave the voters a five-year grace period to judge its workability, after which time the desirability of a convention for revision might be considered. During the probationary period, opposition grew among the common people who cried out against the "aristocracy" of the large landowners and slaveholders. Despite Clay's likely friendship with colleagues of Wythe and Brooke, such as John Breckinridge and George Nicholas, he gave his support to the more radical elements in the controversy. Since it was many years later that one of his biographers revealed that Clay was "Scaevola," he played a safe game in attacking the economic threshold of his powerful friends.

Clay stressed two points for change in the constitution. But initially, he countered the argument that the convention should not be called because the constitution was too young to be touched. "Its infancy is a powerful reason for amending before it (acquires) that strength, that maturity, which will enable it to resist the efforts of reformation. The first dawn of disease is the moment for remedy." He rebutted the charge that it would be a "convention of the most wicked and ignorant, shaking government and attacking property" by stating that the members would be chosen by the people and suggesting that those who opposed a convention distrusted representative government. But when the election of delegates drew near, he complained that the poor, "who were too busy with their every day tasks to attend," were excluded.

On substance, Clay called for the gradual emancipation of slavery professing,

All America acknowledges the existence of slavery to be an evil, which while it deprives the slave of the best of heaven, in the end injures the master too, by laying waste his lands, enabling him to live indolently, and thus contracting all the vices generated by a state of idleness. If it be this enormous evil, the sooner we attempt its destruction the better.

With emotion, he said,

Can any humane man be happy and contented when he sees near 30,000 of his fellow beings around him, deprived of all the rights which make life desirable, transferred like cattle from the possession of one to another; when he sees the trembling slave, under the hammer, surrounded by a number of eager purchasers, and feeling all the emotions which arise when one is uncertain into whose tyrannic hands he must next fall; when he beholds the anguish and hears the piercing cries of husbands separated from wives and children from parents; when in a word, all the tender and endearing ties of nature are broken asunder and disregarded; and when he reflects that no gradual mode of emancipation is adopted either for these slaves or their posterity, doubling their number every 25 years. To suppose the people of Kentucky, enthusiasts as they are in the cause of liberty, could be contended and happy under circumstances like these, would be insulting their good sense.[11]

In advocating gradual emancipation, he enlarged on his reasoning in another "Scaevola" letter nearly a year later when he said, "Thirty thousand slaves, without preparation for enjoying the rights of a freeman, without property, without principle, let loose upon society would be wretched themselves, and render others miserable."[12] He was learning to compromise with himself before fathering great compromises on national issues.

The second constitutional change Clay urged was the elimination of the state senate — more than 150 years before the U.S. Supreme Court called for the reapportionment of many state senates on nearly the same basis. Clay said,

> the division of the legislature into two chambers has been founded upon the principle of two classes of men, whose interests were distinct, living under the same government. It was necessary that the rights of the nobility and commonalty should be guarded and protected by a body of legislators, representing each. These distinctions not existing in America, the use of the senate has ceased.

Henry Clay's first public speech came unexpectedly on an entirely different subject. In the summer of 1798 the Federalist administration, under President John Adams, secured the passage of four bills which became known as the Alien and Sedition Acts. While the three alien laws — permitting imprisonment or deportation of questionable aliens and altering the naturalization requirements were onerous, the one sedition law raised the greatest hackles. Among other provisions, this law made it a crime to publish "any false, scandalous and malicious writings against the Government of the United States or either House of Congress, or the President, with intent to defame them, or bring them into contempt or disrepute." Something later politicians might have longed for.

Protest meetings were held throughout Kentucky during the summer of 1798. One of these

meetings, scheduled for August 13 at the Lexington Presbyterian Church, was moved outdoors to Cheapside, the town's public square, when a throng of 4,000–5,000 persons assembled, making it the largest gathering of people in one place in Kentucky up to that time.[13] George Nicholas — a Transylvania College law professor, a leader in writing the Kentucky constitution and a former politician — opened the meeting. He was described by one writer as "a distinguished man and powerful speaker," but by the local newspapers as "a little, indolent, drunken lawyer, of some talent, but no principle." In his long and vehement address he denounced President Adams as a "perjured villain, and a traitor."[14] He declared "that he then felt more serious apprehensions for the liberties of the people, than he did in the year 1779 when our armies were dispersed, his family were taken prisoners and the enemy possessed all the strongholds of his native country."[15]

At the end of Nicholas' fiery speech, he was greeted with the most enthusiastic cheers. But from within the crowd came a shout of the name "Clay." It was picked up and spread through the assemblage until the young newcomer to Kentucky was brought forward and hoisted to the speakers' platform. No record remains of the words spoken by Henry Clay on the occasion, but an eyewitness to the event recalled later that the young man

> resumed the subject of government usurpation, which had been discussed by Nicholas, and set it in new and more striking light, until indignation came like a dark shadow upon every countenance, The flame that burned in his own heart, was caught up and lighted in every other. He ceased, but there was no shout. The feelings of the gathered multitude were too wild and deep for applause.

Two Federalists rose to rebut the views of Nicholas and Clay. The first, William Murray, was allowed to speak when his opponents stilled the crowd in his behalf, but the people refused to give ear to a McLean who followed and both Federalists were forced to quit the scene. The throng, in near frenzy, took Clay and Nicholas upon their shoulders, put them in a carriage and drew the Republican heroes through the Lexington streets to shouts and applause.[16]

The effect of Henry Clay's exertion may have

been negligible in the total picture of objection to the Alien and Sedition Acts, yet there were some interesting results nevertheless. Under the influence of Nicholas and the legislative initiative of Breckinridge, the Kentucky legislature drew up a set of ten resolves which were sent to the U.S. Congress and became known as "The Kentucky Resolutions of 1798." Among the resolves, the claim that "each party has an equal right to judge for itself, as well of infractions as the mode and measure of redress,"[17] was to raise its head again years later in the dispute over nullification and States' Rights. Vice President Thomas Jefferson collaborated with Breckinridge in drafting the Kentucky Resolutions. James Madison aided in a somewhat similar document adopted by the Virginia legislature. Despite these efforts, the Federalist-controlled Congress blocked any attempt to repeal the laws before their March 3, 1801, expiration date.

While the laws were in force, 25 persons (though none in Kentucky) were prosecuted, ending in 10 convictions — all of whom were Republican editors and printers. The greatest sentence was a fine of $200 and nine months imprisonment. But the general feeling of the people seemed to be expressed in the re-election of Congressman Matthew Lyon of Vermont who campaigned from his jail cell to which he had been sent for four months added to a $1,000 fine. That popular sentiment also lent itself to the defeat of the Federalist administration in the national election of 1800.

As for Clay, he was now acclaimed with Nicholas and Breckinridge among Kentucky's leading Republicans. It was to give impetus to his law career and prestige in the matters of heart. For in the city was a young lady named Hart. On the day before his 22nd birthday, Henry Clay married Lucretia Hart at her father's home on Mill Street. They moved into a house next door.

Eighteen-year-old Lucretia became the perfect wife for Henry Clay. She was no beauty, but she always attracted attention and inspired respect which she maintained with great dignity. She quietly and patiently endured long absences of her statesman husband and managed a large household until his return. She was to bear him 11 children and share with him several family tragedies until even his death was heaped on others. Through the long years of political and personal struggles, she was a constant source of great strength and calm support for her husband.

At the time she married Clay, she was a slender, sprightly active girl but gracefully formed with beautiful hands and feet. Her complexion was fair, her features delicate, her eyes blue, and she had a wealth of radiant auburn hair. In later years, according to her daughter-in-law,

> her character was strongly marked, and all who knew her were impressed by the simplicity and sincerity of her nature. Unlike her illustrious husband, she was reserved in manner and undemonstrative. But beneath a seemingly cold exterior was a warm and loving heart, full of generous impulses and ready sympathy. She had a nature, too, of rare unselfishness, and a wonderful amount of self control.[18]

Lucretia Hart was the seventh child (the fourth daughter) of Thomas Hart, He was one of the first pioneers in Kentucky and later became an energetic businessman and prominent citizen of Lexington. Hart's father, also named Thomas, came from England at age 11 and the family settled in Hanover County, Virginia (before the Clays moved there). Lucretia's grandfather died in 1755 leaving his widow, Susanna (Rice) Hart, with six children, some who had reached maturity. Two years later they all moved to the region of Hillsborough (Hillsboro), North Carolina, and within a few years some of the five boys had purchased land. Thomas (Lucretia's father) soon owned a mill and had an interest in a store. He quickly expanded his business and created a large estate with two plantations which he called Grayfield and Hartford.

By 1764, Thomas and his brother, Nathaniel, had joined Richard Henderson in forming the Transylvania Company and had "engaged a very poor man but excellent 'long hunter,' Daniel Boone, to act as confidential explorer for the company in the western wilds." The Hart brothers were present in 1775 at the signing of "The Great Treaty" by which Henderson used merchandise to purchase huge tracts of land from the Cherokee Indians. From this transaction Thomas Hart acquired more large claims, this time in Kentucky. In 1782, Nathaniel was ambushed and killed by Indians near Boonesborough.

Though the Harts had been loyal to the Crown until the Revolution broke out and had served in the North Carolina assembly, Thomas and his family began to suffer depredations on his property at the hands of Torys when Cornwallis' army moved through the Carolinas in 1780. On the advice of General Gates, he moved north to Hagers Town, Maryland. Here he continued to prosper in business in association with Nathaniel Rochester, who later founded the city of that name in New York. Here, in the Maryland town, on March 18, 1781, his daughter, Lucretia, was born.

When Thomas Hart left North Carolina, he entrusted all his business to a younger man named Jesse Benton who lived on the Hartford plantation. Benton had married Ann Gooch, Hart's niece. While Ann was still a child, her mother (Thomas' sister, Ann) and father (James Gooch, brother of a Virginia Royalist governor) had both died. Thomas took Ann into his home to raise her until she married Benton. The year after Lucretia was born, Ann Benton became the mother of a son whom she named Thomas Hart Benton. He was to become one of the greatest senators from Missouri and a frequent political foe of Henry Clay.

But Jesse Benton, who bought Hartford in 1786, was a poor business manager and eventually fell deeply in debt. When he died, about January 1, 1791, he left Ann with a large and embarrassed estate. Years later, Thomas Hart (who had moved to Lexington, Kentucky, in June 1794) re-purchased Hartford when a judgment was brought against the estate. Then, through his agents he turned over all the property, including slaves, to his niece.

In Kentucky, Thomas Hart started a general store selling dry goods and groceries, both wholesale and retail, and established factories making nails, tin goods, and hemp ropes. He became a leading citizen of the community and a promoter of Transylvania Seminary, later renamed Transylvania University.[19]

In addition to the wealth and prestige Lucretia brought to her marriage with Henry Clay, there were still other family connections of note. Her cousin, Susanna, the daughter of Nathaniel Hart, married Isaac Shelby, who became Kentucky's first governor. Lucretia's sister Ann (Nancy) married James Brown who became a senator from Louisiana, a minister to France, and a lifelong friend of Clay. James had two older brothers — Samuel,

a prominent Lexington doctor, and John, the first U.S. senator from Kentucky and grandfather of an unsuccessful candidate for vice president in 1872.

Henry Clay was now only 22 years old and was clearly in a magnificent position to step boldly into the affairs of the community as a young lawyer. Civil law suits, principally consisting of land claims, poured into his law office and paved his road to affluence. Frequently, in winning the case for his client, he became the owner of good farm land in fee payment. Among his earliest clients in these cases were: Francis Brooke of Virginia, who made Clay his attorney for land sales in Kentucky; Thomas Hart, his father-in-law; William Taylor, a Baltimore merchant; Ninian Edwards, a future chief justice of the Kentucky Court of Appeals; and several other prominent persons of that area and that time who are unknown today.

But probably his most influential promoter was John Breckinridge. Another native Virginian, Breckinridge was denied a seat in the Virginia House of Burgesses, to which he had been elected in 1780, because he was only 19 years old. In 1792, he was elected to the U.S. House of Representatives but never served; instead, he removed to Kentucky. In this new environment Breckinridge was the state's attorney general from 1795 until about the time Clay came west from Virginia. For the next three years he was a member of the Kentucky House of Representatives and was the Speaker of that body during the last two years. Meanwhile, he was the leading figure in the revision of the Kentucky constitution in 1799, even though he had opposed calling this convention which had been successfully urged by Clay.

At age 39, Breckinridge was a tall and striking individual of a spare and muscular build. His hair, a rich chestnut-brown inclining toward auburn, was brushed straight back and reached his shoulders. His eyes were variously described as hazel, reddish-brown, and chestnut. He spoke with an easy but dignified air which was natural with his habitual reserve. His exterior personality exhibited a sternness and a touch of gravity that was ignored by his friends who found him gentle and expressed delight at his return from absences and pain at his departure.[20]

Yet his sternness was real, and his comings and

goings were probably felt differently by his slaves as indicated by his own instructions to the overseer of his plantation prior to one trip to Washington.

> You are to keep good authority among my ne-groes, and keep them close at home. They are not to leave my plantation without your leave. Visit their houses frequently at unreasonable hours of the night, and punish all strange negroes that you find on my plantation after sunset, unless they are sent on business.[21]

For reasons unknown now, Breckinridge turned over eight of his law cases to young Henry Clay in February 1800, about the time he would have been free of the duties of presiding over the Kentucky House, though it is believed his health was a problem at this time. Shortly after taking the speaker's chair in November 1800, Breckinridge was elected by the Kentucky legislature to the U.S. Senate term beginning March 4, 1801, to succeed Federalist Humphrey Marshall. Before leaving for Washington, he turned over the rest of his portfolio of cases to Clay. With Breckinridge's departure from Kentucky, along with the death of George Nicholas in July 1799, Henry Clay became the leader of the Republicans in the Bluegrass state.

Records and correspondence amply reveal the scope and success Henry Clay enjoyed in handling so many civil law cases that rushed to him in his early Kentucky years. But only brief descriptive accounts by his early biographers unveil the skill and style he practiced to sway juries in criminal cases. It was these cases which attracted the public eye and did most to add to the renown and prestige he first gained as an opponent of the Alien and Sedition Laws. Clay's distant cousin, Cassius Marcellus Clay (son of Green Clay, cousin of Henry's father), wrote that Henry Clay never lost a criminal case,[22] while other biographers settle for the claim that none of his clients ever suffered the death penalty.[23] Nevertheless, these early writers were either motivated by political admiration for their subject or were unaware of the result in Clay's first capital case.

In August 1799, a farmer, Henry Field of Woodford County, was brought to trial in Frankfort (in Franklin County) charged with murdering his wife. Henry Clay, his counsel, obtained a permit to practice law in that city on August 6 (the day after the trial began). Despite his efforts, a verdict of guilty was brought on the 10th and the judge sentenced Field to be hanged on September 19. Clay filed a motion for arrest of judgment stating three grounds — among them that Field was charged with killing Sarah Field while his wife "was called and known by the name of Sallie Field." On the 12th, the court held that the grounds were insufficient and Field was hanged near the public jail on the appointed day. It is interesting to note that the county records reveal no other indictment for murder or manslaughter until July 1814.[24]

Still, other counties had their criminal offenses, and during the next few years Clay was employed as a defender of accused persons. One of these, in August 1801, was Mrs. Doshey Phelps, the wife of a respected farmer of Madison County. She was charged with murdering her husband's unmarried sister, an attractive and pleasant young lady. A dispute over the disappearance of some money arose between the two women and other members of the husband's family at the home of the accused. In support of their argument both women resorted to the use of sticks. When Mr. Phelps' sister refused to relinquish her stick, the farmer's wife seized a musket to force the surrender. Another sister intervened. But, in the emotional stress of the moment, Doshey fired the weapon "and lodged the contents of one bullet and ten buckshot in the body of her antagonist, who expired in two hours after."[25] In her dying anguish the victim was later quoted as saying, "Sister, you have killed me!"

The trial, in the Lexington Court House in September 1801, drew large crowds of spectators who were intensely sympathetic for the poor farmer who had lost a sister and had a wife indicted for a heinous act. The circumstances surrounding the killing precluded a verdict of innocence. A jury decision of murder in the first degree would cost Mrs. Phelps her life while a decree of manslaughter would send her to the penitentiary. Though the counsel for the prosecution was an able lawyer, Henry Clay dwelt on the high respect and good character by which his client was regarded in the community prior to the shooting. And he noted that her husband had forgiven his wife for the awful deed. Clay excited pity and compassion by his moving eloquence and succeeded in mitigating her punishment to the lowest degree permitted by law. The crowning feature of Clay's defense of Mrs. Phelps was her "temporary insanity," a novel legal devise to attorneys of that time.[26]

Not long afterward, Clay was asked to defend two Germans, father and son, who were accused of murder. During the five-day trial held in Harrison County, north of Lexington, Clay directed his efforts, not toward excusing the crime, but only toward saving the lives of his clients. In this, he succeeded when the jury rendered a verdict of manslaughter. But Clay pressed on and moved for an arrest of judgment, as he had in the Field case. This time, following another full day of argument, he prevailed, and the prisoners were discharged without any punishment for a crime in which a jury had found them guilty.

The early Clay biographers color this trial with an amusing postscript. Throughout the proceedings an old, ill-favored German woman, mother of one prisoner and wife of the other, sat unmoved and probably uncomprehending the language of the lawyers. With the verdict pronounced, a gentleman near her whispered in her ear that her kin were acquitted. Her countenance changed and with sudden joy she leaped from her seat, rushed through the crowd and over the bar to where Clay stood, and "bounced upon him with irrepressible emotion," to smother him with many kisses. It presented a ludicrous picture, with the handsome young advocate the recipient of the affection of a disheveled old lady. Afterward, recalling the event in which the woman had tendered her thanks by throwing her arms around his neck and clinging to him, Clay mused that it was the longest and strongest embrace he ever encountered in his professional practice.[27]

In another case, tried in Lexington, a man named Willis was accused of committing a murder "under circumstances of peculiar cruelty and cold bloodedness." Testimony presented to the jury left little room for doubt as to the prisoner's guilt. Yet Clay, by a mighty effort, created enough doubt in the minds of some jurors to secure a division among them. At the next session of the court, the attorney for the Commonwealth prosecuting the case, moved for a new trial. Clay offered no opposition to this motion and it was granted. When his turn came to address the new jury, Clay told them that whatever opinion they might hold as to the guilt or innocence of Willis, it was now too late to convict him, for he had been once tried. The law, Clay reminded them, forbade that a man should be twice put in jeopardy for life or limb for the same offense. This approach startled the Court and the judge ordered Clay to refrain from pursuing this course. In a dignified and respectful manner, Clay remarked that if he were not permitted to argue the whole case to the jury, he had nothing more to say. Making a formal bow to the Court, he gathered up his books and papers, put them in his green bag, and with great pomp and noble posture strode from the court room — his associate counsel trailing in his wake.

The Court was dumbfounded. The judge, left with continuing the case without a defense lawyer, and unsure of the law, soon sent a messenger to Clay's lodging inviting him to return and assuring Clay that he might proceed in his own way. Of course, the defense pressed its point with utmost vehemence to establish that once tried, the man must now be acquitted without regard to any other testimony. The jury agreed.[28]

This case, also, had a sequel. The defendant, Willis, was far from being a good citizen and was frequently seen quite drunk. On one occasion, when in this condition, he met Clay on a Lexington street. "Here comes Mr. Clay, who saved my life," Willis said. "Ah, Willis, poor fellow," Clay replied, "I fear I have saved too many like you, who ought to be hanged."[29]

This was not the only case in which Clay was unhappy with his own success. He had tried once to procure the office of prosecuting attorney for a friend, but when the court refused to name the friend to the post, Clay reluctantly accepted it himself, and was afterward able to transfer the office to his friend. Meanwhile, he was called upon to appear at the bar against a negro slave — a proud and faithful servant who had been treated well by his master. But one day in the master's absence, a young passionate overseer horsewhipped the slave for some slight or imagined offense. Unaccustomed to such chastisement, the slave, in fury, seized a weapon and killed the overseer. Clay realized that such an act committed by a white man would have been declared manslaughter, but the negro was indicted for murder. It was clearly Clay's responsibility to sustain the indictment. He argued that the slave did not have the rights of a white man in similar circumstances, but that it was his duty to submit to punishment. It is probable that Clay could have taken a different tack that would have resulted in a verdict prescribing imprisonment. But Clay's personal drive demanded that he press his argument to the fullest.

In this case, the consequences were the conviction and the execution of the negro slave. The black man went to the gallows with great pride and character. Asked if he were anxious that his life might be spared, the prisoner replied, "No, I would not live a day longer, unless in the enjoyment of liberty." Clay did not witness the hanging, but remarked that he regretted the part he had played in the conviction of the slave more than any other act of his professional career. And he resigned his commission as prosecuting attorney in disgust.[30]

Three of Henry Clay's chief personal characteristics — courage, competence, and cunning — can be illustrated from episodes in seven other cases in which he acted as defense attorney in these days before stepping onto the national scene.

Physical courage was a strong element of Clay's makeup. In a backwoods area of Kentucky a rough, lawless, gang of men who termed themselves "Regulators," governed their own affairs and struck fear into anyone who stood in their way. A poor Irishman named Russell, who lived near one of the gang's haunts, offended them in some way designed to curtail their lawlessness. Much on the order of the notorious western gangs of later years, the Regulators forced Russell and his family from their home and destroyed their property. On hearing of the episode and learning that the family was witness to the depredations, Clay took a case in Russell's behalf in which the Irishman obtained damages against the gang. Risking personal harm and possible death, Clay not only stood against the ruffians but brought an end to their villainy.[31] In later life, Clay's physical courage was to lead him to the field of honor on two occasions.

In the realm of moral courage was a suit brought against one of the region's most dynamic legal powers, Joseph Hamilton Daveiss, the district attorney of the United States. Daveiss, of whom more will be heard later, struck a tavern owner in Frankfort during an argument. The victim of the assault, Philip Bush, had no trouble bringing the suit, but was then repeatedly turned down in his search for a lawyer to take his case. No lawyer in the vicinity dared to provoke the towering indignation of which Daveiss was capable of inflicting upon his opponents. When about to despair gaining a hearing, a friend suggested he apply to Henry Clay. He wrote the Lexington attorney detailing the wrongs he had suffered at the hands of Daveiss and the frustrations he had passed through in search of counsel. Without hesitation Clay agreed to plead Bush's case.

At one point in the trial, Daveiss, acting as his own attorney, was unusually cruel and severe in his verbal attacks on the tavern keeper. Clay would let no man, no matter how distinguished nor powerful, abuse his client with impunity. On this occasion he retorted with a sharp blast that so incensed Daveiss that the district attorney warned Clay in a note, possessing the air of authority, not to indulge again in such offensive language. Immediately, Clay responded that he was the plaintiff's attorney and he would manage the cause according to his own judgment without taking advice from anyone, and least of all from his client's antagonist.

It was afterward reported that Daveiss, in stinging resentment to Clay's reply, sent him a call "to single combat." It is believed that the challenge was accepted and would have been carried out except for the vigorous intervention of friends.[32] Still these two men would meet again in court room battle when the whole nation would be roused to attention by the notoriety of the central party — Aaron Burr.

Two episodes are related by early biographers which give examples of the competence Clay possessed and used in his legal practice.

Henry Clay was engaged with another distinguished attorney in a case involving a difficult question of law that was being argued in the Fayette Circuit Court. Very early in the trial, some situation arose that required Clay's attention outside the court and he was forced to leave the entire case in the hands of his associate. For two days the lawyers for both sides wrangled over the complex points which were to govern the court's instructions to the jury. Clay's associate was defeated each time in his effort to secure favorable grounds for his client. Toward the end of the second day's discussion Clay returned to the court. He had heard none of the testimony nor any of the argument that ensued. At this point Clay consulted briefly with his associate, drafted a statement on the form in which he wished the instructions to follow, and added a few of his own observations to his petition. So novel and apropos were his suggestions that the judge granted them without hesitation — and in less than a half hour after Clay re-entered the court house a positive verdict was rendered for Clay's client after all seemed lost.[33] He had demonstrated his amazing ability of going to the heart of an issue to render his appeal to the agreement of the court and the benefit of his client.

In still another important case, where much was at stake, Clay employed an assistant who became anxious that Clay was giving too little attention to the proceedings. At the next convenient moment for private conversation — while riding in the saddle to court in another county — Clay agreeably took the occasion to look through the file of papers relating to the case. One by one, he briefly scanned the documents and then returned them to the saddle bag commenting, "That'll do." There was no further discussion of the case as they rode on to the county seat where the case was to be tried the following day. As time for the trial approached, Clay was observed enjoying the repartee of friendly conversation to the growing distress of his colleague who became convinced the case would be lost for lack of proper attention.

Yet great was the astonishment of the assistant as he watched Clay gain complete mastery over the argument in which he was possessed of every point. Indeed, he was victorious in the case.

"How is this?" the assistant inquired of Clay. "I never could see when or how you studied the case, and I expected to lose it."

"Why," Clay responded, "if you ever want me to help you, you must let me have my own way."[34]

Throughout his long life Henry Clay demonstrated in numerous incidents his astounding capacity to absorb the essential elements of a situation, subject, proposition case, or debate and also to retain in his illustrious mind and recall after long years names, faces, and circumstances which would have been long forgotten by the average person.

We have seen in the case against Joseph Hamilton Daveiss how Henry Clay handled his legal antagonist. In the following three court trials we see how he manipulated witnesses, jurymen, and judge.

One of Clay's clients had been sued for non-payment of debts — or, at least, extreme slowness in making payment. One witness, a neighbor of the accused who knew his friend's malingering habits, was being pressed hard by the creditor's counsel to make a convicting statement. Yet, unwilling to injure his neighbor more than was necessary, the witness responded only that "He is slow." Clay's opponent pressed again for a stronger assertion but was met by the same answer, "He is slow."—"And sure," Henry Clay blurted out loud to tantalize the witness. "Yes, sir," was the ready reply of the surprised witness. Unable, thereafter, to alter his testimony, the witness had provided evidence that the debtor, though lazy in the repayment of his obligations, was "certain" to fulfill them. This was by no means the actual fact of his habit, but Clay's little trickery was the means of victory.[35]

In many cases there are those single adamant jurors who stand against the decision of the other eleven and thus impede a verdict. In one such situation where Clay was certain of the resolve of all but one man in the jury box, the lawyer concentrated his forensic arts and legal skills on the doubtful listener hoping to sway him. While, at one point in an impassioned passage of his argument, Clay stopped abruptly. Standing, as usual, as close to his audience as possible, Clay, in a graceful sweeping motion, brought his long finger to bear upon the face of the obdurate juror, and, calling him by name, requested "a pinch of snuff, if you please." The startled old man was so entranced by the sudden regard of the distinguished lawyer that he was able only to explain, "I don't snuff, Mr. Clay, but I chaws." We don't know if Clay got his snuff or took a chaw. But the twelve jurors rendered a verdict that was unanimous.[36]

The judges in early Kentucky were seldom to be classed as legal giants and Henry Clay was undoubtedly well aware of that fact. Sometime between January 1803 and 1806, when court was temporarily held in the old Rankin Meetinghouse following a fire that had destroyed the old Fayette County Court House, Clay used still another tactic in freeing his client. In the presence of the court he demanded the right to study the warrant and found in it certain defective and illegal ingredients. Turning to the prisoner at the bar, Clay advised, "Go home, sir!" Stunned, the client hesitated, since the judge ruled the court. Clay, in a thundering shout repeated, "GO HOME!!" Without further delay, the man sprang from his seat and departed the court room in haste to the silent and inert astonishment of everyone — audience, sheriff, jury, and judge — except Henry Clay.[37]

Though Clay achieved spectacular success as a Kentucky lawyer, he was not considered by some of his contemporaries to possess a great legal mind. Daniel Webster was one of these. Apparently speaking of Clay some time within the few months which separated the deaths of these great legislative sparring partners — since he used the past tense — Webster confirmed some of Clay's self analysis but also included his own views when he told Peter Harvey,

> With a great deal of native talent, and a little smattering of law — less than that possessed by mere office boys in some large offices — Mr. Clay went into the wilderness of Kentucky; and with a good address, natural eloquence, perseverance, boldness and all those qualities that are admired by a new people, he became an influential man. In Kentucky, while there was no lack of talent in the legal profession, neither the judiciary nor the bar could be called learned. In that State, therefore, Mr. Clay became almost supreme as an advocate. He early went into public life, of course without having had much opportunity to study, and thus make up for the deficiencies of his early training. Going to Washington with a brilliant reputation, he was naturally employed in a great many cases in the Supreme Court. He was not, however, adapted by training or education to the class of cases that were tried before that tribunal. There were no juries there; it was all dry law, all logic.

"In the course of my professional life," Webster continued,

> it has happened many times that I found myself retained in the same cause with Mr. Clay. He was my senior by several years, in the profession and in age. That fact gave him the right to speak first in all such cases. Often, before beginning my argument, I have had to labor hard to do away with the effect and impression of his. Some of the most laborious acts of my professional life have con-

sisted in getting matters back to the starting point after Clay had spoken. The fact is, he was no lawyer. He was a statesman, a politician, an orator; but no reasoner.[38]

On the other hand, John C. Calhoun is reported to have said, "Clay is a great lawyer, but no statesman."

Nor did Webster's appraisal correspond with one expressed by a justice of the Supreme Court before which Clay pleaded many cases. Justice Joseph Story, a New Englander like Webster, wrote in 1823 to one of his bench colleagues, Justice Todd of Clay's state of Kentucky, "Your friend Clay has argued before us with a good deal of ability; and, if he were not a candidate for higher offices, I should think he might attain great eminence at this Bar. But he prefers the fame of popular talents to the steady fame of the Bar."[39]

There was no question that Clay's formal education and legal training were meager. Though he had an astute ability to drive to the heart of an issue and apply well-reasoned principles, the finer technicalities of the law were often circumvented or ignored. He was not one to delve deeply into the sources of the law as did his mentor, George Wythe. Nor was he known to spend much of his free time in reading and studying. He preferred the companionship of good friends and the stimulation of pleasant conversation. In this area he became the master and achieved a success that carried him farther than he might have gone with greater attention to precedent and jurisprudence.

His genius was in his style. His oratory soared to the heights when allowed to roam, when accentuated by boldness, and when governed by originality. No one, not even his greatest political opponents — and there were to be many — ever uttered a word to deny that Clay was probably the most eloquent man of his time. His manners, his graciousness, his deep melodious voice, and his charm captured the hearts of men and moved women to tears, and probably swayed more masses of people to love an American politician than any other man in the 19th century, with the possible exception of Abraham Lincoln. This power over the emotions of people he used consistently in the political career on which be was to embark shortly after the opening of that century.

3

KENTUCKY LEGISLATOR

It was debated whether the year 1800 was the first year of the 19th century or the final one of the 18th century. Regardless of that decision, the year was an important watershed in national affairs and it marked the first faint flow of two major streams in the personal life of Henry Clay.

Early in January, news crept over the Appalachian Mountains that on December 14, 1799, George Washington, the great hero of the Revolution, the president of the Constitutional Convention, and as the first president, the guiding light of the infant American nation, died at his home of Mount Vernon on the banks of the wide Potomac River. As is so often spoken, "An era in history had ended. The world would not look upon his like again."

In Washington's honor and memory, an infant city was growing a few miles north of his estate. By the year's end, it was to host the national government to its wide muddy streets; the president's wife, Mrs. John Adams, was to hang her wash in the East Room of the incomplete "President's Palace"; and the president himself was to be observed in the ranks of fire fighters conveying water to extinguish a blaze at the Treasury Building.[1]

While Henry Clay enhanced his prestige before the Kentucky bar during the first half dozen years of the new century, he also nurtured the beginnings of his family and his political career. In June 1800, he earned the endearing title of "father," but within a year he would suffer the heartache of seeing his first daughter, Henrietta, laid to rest in a Kentucky field.

A month prior to Henrietta's birth, the young lawyer announced that he was a candidate for the office of clerk of the Kentucky Senate. In this first campaign for elective office, he failed. The post, voted by the senate in November, went, on the third ballot, to Christopher Greenup who was to become governor four years later. (Greenup was 50 years old and already had a long and distinguished military and political career behind him.)[2] It was at this same time, Clay's friend, John Breckinridge, was elected Speaker of the Kentucky House of Representatives, and then went to the U.S. Senate.

On the national scene the presidential campaign of 1800 pitted Federalist President John Adams of Massachusetts and his running mate, Charles Cotesworth Pinckney of South Carolina, against the team of Vice President Thomas Jefferson of Virginia (for president) and Aaron Burr of New York (for vice president). Jefferson and Burr were candidates of the Republican Party, also called the Democratic in certain sections of the country, thus giving rise to the combined name of Democratic-Republican.

Henry Clay played little part in the year's national politics except for "an elegant oration" in support of Thomas Jefferson delivered at a July 4th celebration in Lexington.[3] Nevertheless, some attention should be paid to this election because of its consequences, the personalities involved, and the similar political gyrations which would be generated in a later election in which Clay was to play a prominent role.

The presidential electors cast their votes in December 1800. As the results gradually became known, something of a Constitutional crisis arose when it was learned that there were 73 votes each for Jefferson and Burr, 65 for Adams, 64 for Pinckney, and one vote for John Jay. By the provisions of the Constitution the candidate with the greatest number of votes was to be elected president, with the vice presidency going to the man with the second highest vote. Apparently the Founding Fathers had not anticipated that a man running for vice president might actually win the presidency instead. In this election the voting arrangement was such that four, rather than two, men were, in reality, running for the presidency.

With the official opening of the ballots still in the future, and aware that responsibility of deciding the election would devolve upon the House of Representatives, that body enacted a set of rules to govern the coming event. In addition, the lame duck Federalists members, in numerical control, agreed, with a few defections, to support Burr for president. They had opposed Jefferson's Republican philosophy for too long to elect him without a struggle. Most Republicans, on the other hand, had begun to develop strong misgivings about the character of Aaron Burr and were determined to support Jefferson.

The election by the House was to be exercised with each state voting as a unit casting one vote each. Since 16 states were then in the Union, the Constitutional requirement for a majority to elect, demanded that a candidate gain the vote of nine states to win. On February 11, 1801, the electoral ballots were officially opened and counted at a joint session of the Congress in the Senate chamber on the ground floor of the new elegant north wing of the Capitol building standing in solitude on a Hill in the infant city of Washington. The expected results were announced by Vice President Thomas Jefferson and the House members immediately adjourned to their own chamber one floor above and facing west toward the "President's House." They proceeded then with the first ballot in the election of a president. Again, the results were as expected.

Jefferson won eight states (one less than the number needed to elect). He carried New York, New Jersey, Pennsylvania, Virginia, North Carolina, Georgia, Kentucky, and Tennessee. Burr collected New Hampshire, Massachusetts, Rhode Island, Connecticut, Delaware, and South Carolina. Vermont's two votes and Maryland's eight votes were divided evenly and failed to count. It is interesting to note that 24 Federalist members from New England were able to give Burr only four states while just four Republican members from Kentucky, Tennessee, and Georgia gave Jefferson three States. A Federalist member from each of Maryland and New Jersey voted for Jefferson. Had they voted for Burr, the indecision would still exist but in a dead heat.

Since there was no election on the first ballot, 18 more were taken that day with identical results. Nine more ballots were taken on February 12th, one on the 13th, four on the 14th, and one each after noon on the 16th and 17th — with no change occurring.[4]

With the next ballot ordered to be repeated at one o'clock on the 17th, the Federalist held another caucus at the call of the single member from Delaware, James A. Bayard (with whom Henry Clay would be intimately associated in years to come). Bayard had finally concluded that Burr could not be elected. For the past several weeks Bayard and other Federalists had received letters from former Secretary of the Treasury Alexander Hamilton, Federalist from New York, expressing in some detail his belief that Jefferson was the lesser of two evils.

Yet Hamilton gave succinct appraisal of the two men in a letter dated December 26, 1800, to New York Senator Gouverneur Morris, who would not be involved in the election. He wrote that

> Jefferson ought to be preferred to Burr. I trust the Federalists will not finally be so mad as to vote for the latter. I speak with an intimate and accurate knowledge of character. His elevation can only promote the purposes of the desperate and profligate. If there be a man in the world I ought to hate, it is Jefferson. With Burr I have always been personally well. But the public good must be paramount to every private consideration.

To Bayard he described Burr "as unprincipled and dangerous a man as any country can boast — as true a Catiline as ever met in midnight conclave."[5]

As the House prepared to cast its 36th presidential ballot, Bayard dropped a bombshell on his fellow Federalists, when he finally decided to take it in his hands to change the Delaware vote to Jefferson and thus be the catalyst for his election. He also determined to seek some political assurances from the prospective administration. With this end in view, Bayard applied to John Nicholas, a House member from Virginia, and brother of the late George Nicholas of Kentucky, suggesting that he could accept a Jefferson administration if "subordinate public officers employed only with the execution of details ... shall not be removed from office on the ground of their political character." He particularly referred to collectors of ports in Philadelphia and Wilmington. When Nicholas stated that he was certain that this was acceptable to Jefferson, Bayard replied that he insisted on a firmer commitment from Jefferson himself. Nicholas refused to go further than to offer his opinion of Jefferson's sentiments. Bayard next made a similar proposal to General Samuel Smith, a congressman from Maryland. Smith conferred with Jefferson but only stated that some Federalists were concerned with the status of certain specific customs officials. Without realizing the import of the conversation, Jefferson indicated that the government employees were safe in their jobs. Smith relayed Jefferson's comments as an authorization from him.

On the basis of these assurances Bayard informed the Federalist caucus of his intentions. Some supported him. But representatives of four New England states refused to go along, and the meeting broke up in great confusion and bitter acrimony only minutes before the 36th ballot was taken. However, the acquiescence of three other delegations made it unnecessary for Bayard or any other pro–Burr Federalists to vote for Jefferson. Casting the lone Delaware vote, Bayard and the entire South Carolina delegation voted blank ballots. Also voting blank ballots were the Federalists of Maryland. The Vermont Federalist did not vote at all, thus giving Maryland and Vermont to Jefferson by virtue of the Republican votes cast by half of those latter two delegations. The single Vermont vote was, in fact, cast by Matthew Lyon, the congressman who had been imprisoned under the Sedition Act. (He later settled in Kentucky.)

There was a sequel to this episode which was similar in some respects to the future election involving Clay, but then would have tragic consequences. In the late days of his term, President Adams offered Bayard the post of minister to France. Following his part in the election, Bayard was wise to write Adams,

> The service which I should have rendered by accepting the appointment, would be under the Administration of Mr. Jefferson and having been in the number of those who withdrew themselves from the opposition to his election it is impossible

for me to take an office the tenure of which would be at his pleasure.[6]

In the wake of this election, the 12th Amendment to the Constitution was passed by Congress and sent to the states to be ratified before the next election. Henry Clay would participate in the ratification process. The Amendment called for the electors to vote separately for president and vice president. It also provided for the three candidates with the highest number of electoral votes to be chosen by the House of Representatives in the event none had a clear majority of the votes cast.

It is impossible to know how much Clay ever learned of the maneuvers which took place in the 1801 election. Yet it is unlikely that he went into the 1824 election blind to the turmoil that can surround a House election. He would work with Bayard at the Treaty of Ghent in 1814–15. He also had that family connection, through his wife to the Brown family of Frankfort — and John Brown was a member of the U.S. Senate during those election days of 1801.

Throughout most of 1801 and 1802 Clay continued to build his law practice and provide for his growing family. (His son Theodore Wythe was born on July 3, 1802. But through an unfortunate accident in childhood, this boy would bring heartache to his parents in their later years. His doctor forecast that the young man would become insane when in his late 20s. And so, in fact, it happened. He was to die in his 70s in a lunatic asylum.) In payment for some of his legal fees, Clay continued to come into possession of more property in and around Lexington. He was soon negotiating for construction of a home on Mill Street built to his specifications which cited styles in other homes in the community.

In the closing weeks of 1802 and the early weeks of 1803 a series of developments merged to revive Clay's passion for politics. His Federalist legal adversary, Joseph Hamilton Daveiss, announced through a newspaper statement that he was a candidate for Congress from Kentucky's 4th District.[7] This did not include Fayette County, but Clay was provoked by Daveiss' assertions of friendship to the Republican philosophy.

Using his old "Scaevola" nom de plume, Clay charged that Daveiss had commenced his career in deceit and "will end by betraying" in pledging himself to a faithful observance to the political terms recently espoused by Jefferson. With reference to Adams' departure from office and Jefferson's ascent, Clay remarked, "I am well aware, sir, that it is natural for some characters to worship the rising sun; but I do not therefore conclude that it is generous to kick at the fallen." He asked Daveiss to clarify his position on several issues in which he had previously supported the Adams administration.[8]

Daveiss wrote in response that he would air his political philosophy in public speeches to reach more voters and to avoid

> entering into newspaper controversies with impertinent and calumniating scribblers whose opposition is manifestly personal, not political, and who delight in traduction and abuse, so long as their fictitious names secure them from responsibility.[9]

How much Henry Clay influenced this election is unknown. But Daveiss was never elected to Congress.

A couple months prior to Daveiss' announcement, international politics, centering on the lower Mississippi Valley, grew to a storm which cast its clouds over Kentucky. The mountain barrier that stood between the eastern seaboard and the Bluegrass country forced trade between the two regions to use the Ohio and Mississippi waterways and exit through Gulf ports, as a cheaper and easier, though longer, route to transport western grain and tobacco and other goods to eastern markets. The free transit of these waterways and ports was vital to the economic well-being of Kentucky and its neighboring states. Yet ever since the Revolution, Spain had controlled the entire southern and western water outlets of the United States and the movement of merchandise out of the Western Country.

While Spain hoped to separate this region from the rest of the United States, and dealt covertly with some of its influential residents to achieve this objective, the American government dreamed of one day gaining control of Spain's coastal possessions. With the rise of Napoleon in France, Spain's power gradually diminished, and for many months the French First Consul secretly pressured King Charles IV of Spain to return the vast Louisiana territory to France. However, France's disastrous military campaign against pestilence and Toussaint L'Ouverture, Negro slave leader of Haiti, and the picador-style diplomacy of Don Manuel Godoy (Prince of Peace), the prime minister of Spain, kept Napoleon's repossession of Louisiana at bay for nearly three years.[10]

President Jefferson believed he could deal with the French Republic on friendlier terms than had the pro–British Federalist administration. But he soon found that Napoleon's foreign minister, Talleyrand, was speaking "with a forked tongue," especially regarding French ambitions in the Mississippi delta. Although Talleyrand denied that Spain was ceding Louisiana to France, Jefferson learned negotiations were in progress. On May 26, 1801, Jefferson wrote to James Monroe (then governor of Virginia), "There is considerable reason to apprehend that Spain cedes Louisiana and the Floridas to France. It is a policy very unwise in both, and very ominous to us."[11] The joint control of the Gulf ports and the west bank of the Mississippi River by two great European powers was unthinkable to the United States and could have dire consequences to the future of the western states. Talk of war spread across the land.

Through the long months of French-Spanish negotiations over the vast unexplored territory west of the Mississippi, Jefferson moved slowly hoping for a peaceful arrangement. Finally, on October 15, 1802, in Barcelona, the King of Spain signed the order delivering Louisiana to France. But Spain retained East and West Florida.

On the following day, far across the Atlantic Ocean and the Gulf of Mexico — several weeks away from word of the retrocession — the Spanish Intendant in Louisiana, Don Juan Ventura Morales, closed the port of New Orleans to American shipping and their previous right of deposit. He based his action on a change in British-Spanish relations which freed Spain from continuing the open-port policy that had been granted in October 1795 for a 3-year term.

It was more than a month before this startling information reached Lexington, Ky., the distribution point for all of Kentucky and parts of Tennessee, Ohio, Indiana, and Illinois. But it wasn't long before a business stagnation was felt throughout the region as large quantities of tobacco, hemp, butter, pork, and beef piled up in warehouses and were ruined. Merchants cut their prices and demanded "cash only." Mass meetings were held and appeals for help were sent to

called on Clay to come to him. The man exhibited all the characteristics of a seasoned hunter — buckskin breeches and hunting shirt, coon-skin cap, black bushy beard, below which hung a huge powderhorn across a bare and brown chest. From his belt hung the indispensable knife and hatchet. He stood there leaning on a rifle and regarded Clay with an all-knowing expression.

"Young man," the hunter challenged, "you want to go to the legislature?"

"Why, yes," Clay responded. "Yes, I should like to go, since my friends have seen proper to put me up as a candidate before the people, I do not wish to be defeated."

"Are you a good shot?" the rifleman asked.

Clay was somewhat surprised at this turn in the questioning, but quickly replied, "The best in the country."

The old man persisted. "Then you shall go. But you must give us a specimen of your skill. We must see you shoot."

In defense Clay tried an excuse, "I never shoot any rifle but my own, and that is at home."

It was useless. The hunter said, "No matter, here is old Bess. She never fails in the hands of a marksman. She often sent death through a squirrel's head at one hundred yards, and daylight through many a redskin twice that distance. If you can shoot any gun, you can shoot old Bess."

Clay had no choice but to comply. "Well, put up your mark, put up your mark," he said reluctantly but with assurance. The target was arranged at about 80 yards. Clay steadied himself, shouldered the weapon, squeezed the trigger, and his bullet pierced the target near the center.

"Oh, a chance shot! A chance shot!" shouted several of his political opponents. "He might shoot all day and not hit the mark again. Let him try it over," they challenged.

"No," Clay answered in defiance. "Beat that, and then I will." He went unchallenged further and it was considered that he had given proof of his marksmanship. It probably gained him the vote of most hunters and other self-styled marksmen present and elsewhere. Clay later admitted, "I had never before fired a rifle, and have not since."[18]

The election of early August 1803 sent three other Fayette County representatives to the Kentucky legislature along with Henry Clay — namely, William Russell, James Hughes, and James True. Before the 26-year-old legislator began his service he again became a father, Thomas Hart Clay was born on September 22.

On November 12, 1803, the Frankfort newspaper, *The Palladium,* carried a brief report that the Kentucky General Assembly opened its session on the 7th of the month at the three-storied statehouse topped by its ornate cupola. The house and its new member, Representative Clay, met on the second floor and proceeded to elect John Adair of Mercer County to be the speaker. The senate, meeting on the floor above, named Clay's distant cousin, Green Clay, to be its speaker.

Of more importance to the legislators and the Kentucky community were two other items which appeared. in that same issue of *The Palladium.* A report dated October 21 from Washington City announced, "Yesterday at about 5 o'clock P.M. the Senate ratified the LOUISIANA TREATY; Twenty four votes in the affirmative, and seven in the negative."

The second report gave rise to speculation over the certainty of the huge land sale, for it stated "that France has declared war against Portugal, and has an army of 200,000 men in motion, to effect its conquest," and "that Great Britain has declared war against Spain, for suffering the French army to march through that country against Portugal." Would the Treaty of retrocession be abrogated somewhere along the line?[19]

Since the closing of the port of New Orleans in late 1802 and the rumored transfer of Louisiana from Spain to France, Jefferson strove to purchase "New Orleans and the Floridas" from Napoleon. In January 1803 the president called on James Monroe to go overseas to aid the U.S. minister to France, Robert R. Livingston, who had helped Jefferson draft the Declaration of Independence in 1776 and later rendered the oath of office to the first President of the United States in 1789. Monroe's mission was not so much to accomplish the purchase as it was to quiet agitation at home, for Monroe was highly respected throughout the country. Jefferson's true expectations were that Napoleon would not yield to sell the port until there was a war between France and England — an event not then immediately anticipated.[20]

But the situation changed abruptly. In mid–

April Jefferson received word from the Spanish minister that the right of deposit and transit was to be restored at New Orleans relieving the tension in the Western country. About the same time, Napoleon came to the conclusion that the disaster in Haiti had destroyed a key point in France's supply route to Louisiana and that possession of the entire territory was no longer vital to his goals as it once had seemed. Indeed, his ambitions were in Europe and his demand that England cede Malta to him raised the threat of renewed war. He saw in the sale of the entire Louisiana territory the liquidation of a difficult possession to hold and a source of finances to prosecute his war.

So it was that an unpredictable Napoleon ordered Talleyrand to offer all of the vast land to the American diplomats, Livingston and Monroe (who had just arrived in Paris). The Americans were stunned. Yet within a month the French had signed over Louisiana to the United States for 80 million francs ($15 million). But nowhere in the sale document were the boundaries spelled out. Talleyrand said they were the same as when the land belonged to Spain and he did not know what they were — except that the Floridas were not included. These boundaries and the acquisition of the Floridas were to concern Henry Clay in years to come.

Through the greatest real estate deal in history the United States nearly doubled its territory with a rich land that was far beyond the value it surrendered in dollars. France gained $15 million for a land on which she had hardly spent a cent in occupation. But a third party created a complexity in this gigantic transaction. Spain still possessed, garrisoned, and administered the territory. No delivery had actually been made to France. And in the retrocession agreement with France, Spain had obtained a solemn pledge from Napoleon never to alienate Louisiana. Spain was aghast and protested to France in the strongest diplomatic language of that day, complaining that the action eliminated "a strong dyke between the Spanish colonies and the American possessions" and, with some vision, expressing the fear that "the doors of Mexico are to stay open to them."

Late in the summer of 1803 Jefferson began getting hints that Spain objected to the French sale of Louisiana and might refuse to follow through

with the cession. By the time Congress met in special session on October 17, to ratify the Treaty with France, Jefferson was so disturbed that he issued a call to governors of western states and territories to furnish certain numbers of troops, including 4,000 from Kentucky and 2,000 from Tennessee, to be prepared to march on New Orleans by December 20.[21]

Reacting to the call for troops by Kentucky Governor James Garrard, Representative Henry Clay offered his services and, on November 21, wrote to his good friend, John Breckinridge in Washington, to describe the affairs in Kentucky.

> Our assembly commenced its session on the day appointed by law. And various new projects were very soon suggested. But the arrival of the News from Washington, relative to the Expedition to New Orleans, has called the public attention from every other object & placed it on this great National concern. Armies, Sieges and Storms completely engross the public mind and the first interrogatory put on every occasion is Do you go to New Orleans? If all who answer in the affirmative should really design to go, Government will find it necessary to restrain the public Ardor, instead of resorting to coercion to raise the 4000 called for. You will have heard that General Hopkins is appointed commander in chief, and Generals Adair and Russell his Brigadiers.... Having been honored by Genl. Hopkins with the appointment of one of his Aids I shall go with the croud (sic) to endeavor to share the glory of the expedition.
>
> The accounts from Tennessee are not so flattering. Rumour says that the Governor of that State has lately become disgraced in the public estimation in an affair with Genl. Jackson and has made such unpopular appointments that no Volunteers can be had.[22]

The reference to Tennessee related to a quarrel between ex–Senator Andrew Jackson (then a judge of the Tennessee Supreme Court) and Governor John Sevier (an old pioneer of the Daniel Boone style), over charges of fraud in land speculation and on other grounds. Jackson had issued a challenge, but Sevier's reputation was damaged by his refusal to fight in his own state. No duel resulted.

Early in the 1803 session of the Kentucky General Assembly, freshman Representative Henry Clay was appointed to a committee "to lay off the State into Electoral districts."[23] The committee's bill prescribed that the state be divided into two districts for the purpose of choosing electors for president and vice president. With some exceptions, the Kentucky River formed the basic dividing line. On the basis of the 1800 census, which found Kentucky's population rising to 220,955 from the 1790 territorial figure of 73,677, the state's representation in the U.S. House of Representatives rose from two to six. Thus, with the two senators, Kentucky had eight electoral votes. The two districts would each select four electors. By this arrangement Republicans thwarted the chances of the Federalists from obtaining a single vote. There was a growing apprehension that the Federalist element was reviving in Kentucky.[24] It was a purely political gerrymander—though Elbridge Gerry, father of the term, had not yet concocted the weird alinement of counties in Massachusetts for which he has derived his greatest fame.

In addition to this act, the Kentucky legislature reapportioned the representation in the lower house and struggled several days over the appointment of a new registrar of lands. A payment rate was set on debts due from settlers south of the Green River—a subject that would come up in a later session to be used by Clay as a political weapon. And in the senate, the Federalists blocked a house-passed measure giving a bounty of 150 acres of vacant land to each soldier volunteering for the Louisiana expedition."[25]

Henry Clay exhibited his eloquent style in this session in his appeal to remove the state capital from Frankfort to Lexington. Frankfort, sliced in two by the Kentucky River, had been described as "sunk down, like a huge pit, below the surrounding country, and environed by rough and precipitous ledges." Clay told his colleagues, "We have the model of an inverted hat—Frankfort is the body of the hat, and the lands adjacent are the brim. To change the figure, it is natures greatest penitentiary; and, if the members of this house would know the bodily condition of the prisoners, let them look at those poor creatures in the gallery." As he spoke, his long slender finger tracked the movement of several figures wandering about the gallery possibly in search of seats or at least a vantage point to observe the actions of the legislators below. On becoming the observed, rather than the observers, the "creatures" hastened in mock terror to seek shelter behind posts and pillars to the uproarious amusement and merriment of the new spectators—the lawmakers. As usual, Clay won his point and the house considered the change of venue. But Lexington was not the choice of the majority and the bill failed by a 31 to 29 vote—and Frankfort remains the seat of the Kentucky government.[26]

The General Assembly had intended to adjourn on Christmas eve but remained in session until the 27th to receive and ratify the 12th Amendment to the Constitution, which changed the manner of choosing the president and vice president. Henry Clay was on hand for the close of the session. He had not marched on New Orleans.

The purpose for the military expedition ended on November 30 when the Spanish intendant formally handed over the Louisiana Territory to the new French prefect, Pierre Clement Laussat, who ruled until December 20. Then in an elaborate ceremony in New Orleans, the French Tri-color was lowered from the top of the staff, and paused briefly at mid-staff where it was met by the Stars and Stripes ascending on another halyard. After Laussat presented the keys of the city to the new American territorial governor, William C. C. Claiborne, the residents listened with some skepticism as Claiborne proclaimed a new freedom for them. They had seen their homes transferred back and forth for years among the powers of the world. Would this time be different?[27]

On December 30, 1803, Clay expressed his feeling about the new peace in a letter to Breckinridge. "I am happy to learn that the conduct of Kentucky has raised her in the estimation of our Eastern friends. It would have given me individual pleasure to visit New Orleans, but I nevertheless sincerely rejoice that the affair has terminated pacifically."

Clay went on in this letter to suggest, "You must no doubt be considerably perplexed in adopting a government for our newly acquired territory."[28] Both he and Jefferson were indeed perplexed. Jefferson wrote months before to Breckinridge suggesting that a Constitutional Amendment might be required to legalize the purchase. Breckinridge turned a deaf ear to this proposal but did make suggestions that only the lower part of the territory be opened for settlement while the upper regions might be a fit land to transfer those Indian tribes still east of the Mississippi River. Nevertheless, Breckinridge recognized the historical significance of the administration's achievement when he wrote Jefferson the previous September. While at first he was apprehensive over the failure to buy the Floridas, he became convinced that the Louisiana Purchase "was one of the most important events we have ever witnessed."

Breckinridge went on to say in his September 10, 1803, letter to Jefferson,

> The magnitude of the acquisition is not less important than the manner in which it was acquired. To add to our empire more than two hundred millions of acres of the first portion of the earth, without a convulsion, without spilling one drop of blood, without impairing the rights or interest of a single individual, without deranging in the slightest degree the fiscal concerns of the country, & without, in short, the expence of a single dollar (for the port of Orleans will of itself reimburse the 15 millions of dollars in the 15 years) is an achievement of which the annals of no country can furnish a parallel.
>
> As to the Floridas, I really consider their acquisition as of no consequence for the present. We can attain them long before we want them, & upon our own terms,

And Breckinridge added to these prophetic remarks, other thoughts that were directed at Henry Clay's generation,

> We certainly discharge the duty imposed on us, and have nothing to answer for to our posterity by seizing every occasion to advance the present prosperity of our country & by leaving remote and, to us, incalculable events to be governed by those whose immediate duty it becomes to watch & to direct them.[29]

Going back to the letter which Henry Clay wrote to Breckinridge at the end of 1803, the freshman legislator sought political patronage from his influential friend in behalf of his older brother.

> If in the distribution of offices in New Orleans it should happen that one could be procured for John Clay, I should be much indebted to you. His residence in that place for three years — his knowledge of the French language and acquaintance with the inhabitants and their manners may give him some claim to a subordinate post.[30]

John Clay had migrated to Kentucky in 1792 with his parents and eventually settled in Lexington where he engaged in the merchandising busi-

ness. However, he did not possess the genius for making money that Henry had. In May 1800 he sold some Lexington property to Henry and that summer moved to New Orleans still in debt. Throughout 1804, while for a time serving as an unpaid government inspector of flour, salt provisions, and hemp,[31] John appealed to Henry to intervene with his Washington contacts to obtain a federal job in Louisiana. Henry petitioned Breckinridge in several letters passing on John's preference for the position of surveyor of the port.[32] It is not certain what arrangements came to pass, but in March 1805, Lucretia Clay's brother-in-law, James Brown (who had ventured to New Orleans in the summer of 1804, and was soon appointed secretary of the territory of Orleans), wrote Henry Clay,

> I am happy to find my friend John Clay so completely cured of every wild and extravagant idea as he is at this time — His steady habits, industry, and obliging temper are gaining him many friends, and I beg of you to use your influence to gain him the confidence of the people of Lexington — I think they will find him every thing they can wish — .[33]

Nevertheless, John Clay was to have financial difficulties for many years and often called on his younger brother for help.

After the departure of Henry's brother John to the south, he was still left with the local companionship of his younger brother, Porter. This youngest living child of Sir John and Elizabeth Clay spent his early years in Lexington as a cabinet maker. In March 1803 his shop was destroyed by fire but he re-established himself in his trade[34] and continued in it until 1815 when he obtained a license to practice law. In this profession he was appointed by the governor to be the state's auditor of public accounts, an office he held for 14 years. He then entered into still another profession, that of Baptist minister in the steps of his father. When Porter Clay died in 1850, his distinguished older brother wrote that he had passed his life "in the full enjoyment of the Christian hope." Henry also referred to his younger brother as "the greatest man I ever knew."[35]

As summer came to 1804 Henry Clay continued to prosper both politically and financially. In August, he won re-election to the Kentucky House of Representatives, and in September be purchased 125 acres of land on the outskirts of Lexington where he had plans to build a new home.

Nationally, it was another presidential election year. Jefferson stood for re-election to his office and was given the unanimous approbation of his party at a congressional caucus held in the Capitol in Washington on February 25, 1804. But Aaron Burr's attitude in the 1800 election continued to rankle Republicans. The caucus refused to give him a single vote for vice president. Six others were considered. Scoring second for this office with 20 votes was Kentucky's John Breckinridge, giving the first faint recognition of the growing political power of the west. Named as Jefferson's running mate was New York's perennial governor, George Clinton, who won the support of 67 caucus delegates from the 108 voting. The Federalists held no caucus and remained strangely silent as to their candidates until the November election when the electors in three states gave votes to Charles Pinckney and Rufus King, a former diplomat from New York.[36]

Burr, finding the door closed to his re-election to the vice presidency, sought Federalist support for the governorship of New York. But in this he had to contend with the state's party leader, Alexander Hamilton. Needless to say, Hamilton blocked Burr's effort, and in private continued to blast the vice president as "a dangerous man." The castigations reached Burr, a challenge was issued, and on July 11, 1804, on the Palisade bluffs of Weehawken, New Jersey, Burr mortally wounded Hamilton in America's most famous duel. The repercussions of this duel, which altered the direction of Burr's ambitions, were later to have a major impact on Henry Clay's career.

The November election was won easily by the Jefferson-Clinton team. On the 5th of that month Clay returned to the Kentucky General Assembly in Frankfort and met Felix Grundy who, after a year's absence from the house because of his move to Nelson County, was all fired up to open the fight against the Kentucky Insurance Company. Grundy was of ordinary stature but inclined to portliness. His face had a ruddy complexion. His hair was light brown with a reddish hue. He had blue eyes. He had an even temperament and was quite popular, making few enemies and many friends. His manners and graciousness were akin

to those of Henry Clay who was his senior by only five months. Like Clay, Grundy was born in Virginia, but in the western mountains. As small children they both saw their homes plundered and laid waste by marauders — Indians in the case of Grundy. And each obtained his law license the same year, but Grundy preceded Clay into the political cauldron. In 1799, Grundy served in the Kentucky constitutional convention, which had been partly the fruit of Clay's labor. In 1800, he began a three-year tenure in the Kentucky legislature.[37]

On the opening day of the 1804 session of the Kentucky General Assembly, following the election of William Logan as speaker of the house, Clay and Grundy met in their initial test of political strength. In a contest to fill the office of clerk to "the committee of privileges, and elections, and propositions and grievances," Clay's nominee, William Waller, was elected over Grundy's candidate, Lyne Starling. Both Clay and Grundy were then appointed to a committee of four members "to prepare and report a set of rules for the government of this house." The next day this report was presented to the house, which then listened to a speech by Kentucky's new governor, Christopher Greenup, who had defeated Clay for the senate clerkship in 1800. On succeeding days Clay and Grundy were appointed to serve together on several other committees before their first major skirmish on November 15.[38]

The U.S. senatorial term of John Brown of Frankfort was due to expire on March 3, 1805, and it became the duty of the Kentucky General Assembly to elect an incumbent for the next 6-year term. Henry Clay naturally supported and even nominated Brown to return to Washington. Grundy put forward the name of John Adair. A third candidate was Buckner Thruston. Under the provisions of a resolution offered by Grundy, the candidate with the least number of votes was to be dropped from contention after the first ballot. Clay made two attempts to amend this method before he succeeded in getting the entire resolution substituted for one of his own permitting the house to cast six ballots before making a cut in the number of aspirants. The individual senate votes were to be added to those of the house.

Had Grundy's resolution stood, Thruston, as

the lowest man of the first ballot, would have been eliminated. By virtue of Clay's tactics, his friend Senator Brown was turned out of office by being the lowest on the 6th vote. On the 7th ballot, with Clay voting for Thruston, the house deadlocked 31–31. However, the senate's ballot made Thruston the new senator by a one-vote margin.[39]

A poor-spelling witness to the scene, Jack Jouett, who had galloped out to save Jefferson from capture by Colonel Tarleton in 1781, wrote to Breckinridge in Washington,

> Adair, after having nearly as good an interest as both the others got work'd out of his election by the artful management of H. Clay. You have no gues [sic] how much he was mortified. Clay has proved intirely two hard for Grundy.[40]

Henry Clay played a leading role in the passage of four other pieces of legislation which (1) compelled certain Lexington property owners to pave their frontages on Main Street, (2) provided for construction of canals and locks at the falls of the Ohio River, (3) granted the Fayette Circuit Court an additional term, and (4) requested the Kentucky congressional delegation to urge the extension of the Federal Circuit Court to Kentucky.[41]

But the greatest battle of the 1804 session was fought over an attempt by Felix Grundy to repeal the banking privileges of the Kentucky Insurance Company. It was clearly evident to the public that two very able orators were locking horns in the house chamber of the old state capitol in Frankfort. As stated in the *Kentucky Gazette*, "It is a very comprehensive field for the display of eloquence."[42] Each day that this subject was up for debate, the galleries were filled to standing-room-only capacity and the house members were host to senators and even jurists who left their court rooms to attend.[43]

Grundy's friends in the senate pushed through a repeal measure that was blocked by the house on December 6. But Clay's attempt to close off further discussion also failed and a new provision was brought forward by Clay on the 14th. His amendment to the charter would limit the company's notes to the value of its assets, or, in the event larger amounts were issued, the company's "president and directors shall be liable therefor out of their private individual fortunes." This amendment passed.

Grundy then tried again to repeal the banking

privileges, and when this failed, he endeavored to include the stockholders (of which Clay was one) in the company's liability. This, too, lost on a 30–28 vote. The entire measure, as amended, was sent to the senate the following day and Clay announced to the house on the 18th that the senate had agreed. The new arrangement was later approved by Governor Greenup.[44]

On learning of the results, James Brown, Clay's friend, linked by marriage, wrote from New Orleans, "I am happy that the bank has had the means of resisting the attacks of that unprincipled demagogue Grundy, and of defeating the villainous speculations of the nest of rascals who have fattened under the auspices of Morrison's office."[45] James Morrison was supervisor of the federal land tax that had placed many land owners near bankruptcy. Hatred of the tax and its collectors so aroused the citizenry that Morrison and his deputy, George Mansell, were burned in effigy in Paris, Kentucky. Mansell was nearly murdered but "got off with no other injury than his clothes being torn off."[46]

On the action of the insurance company in regard to this land tax, an anonymous correspondent, writing in the *Kentucky Gazette* over the signature of "A Poor Farmer," said,

> The late humane and benevolent conduct of the Kentucky Insurance Company, is an incident so singular in itself that it deserves to be announced to the world. Individuals have sometimes been found, whose charities have had extensive influence upon the State of society; & their names have been enrolled among the benefactors of their country. But when a corporate body, whose functions are generally limited by the rules of caution, steps forward, from motives of humanity, to rescue the property of a *whole state*, from the fangs of a set of merciless speculators, it exhibits such a moral attention to justice, that the transaction assumes a shape very different from that of common charities, and is justly classed among the most distinguished deeds of patriotism.

The "Poor Farmer" also wrote that in the house debate, Grundy had "led his adherents by the nose, at will," and the farmer described them, as "too ignorant to comprehend one word that fell from the Leader and too wise to utter a single sentence themselves."[47]

One further description of the contest between Clay and Grundy was penned to Senator Breckinridge by Judge Harry Innes (who had left his chambers to witness the encounters).

> Grundy made a violent attack on the Lexington Insur. Co. (as it was also called since its offices were in that town), his object was to destroy the system. Clay defended it very ably & the result will I think prove beneficial to the institution as it adds apparently additional security to the payment of the notes issued.[48]

Grundy's growing prestige and political stature disturbed some of Senator Breckinridge's friends who advised that "the indefatigable Felix" might oppose the senator in the future. During the next year Breckinridge made an attempt to get his potential opponent out of Kentucky politics by appointing him to an office in the new Louisiana territory. But the post was filled before Grundy had a chance to accept, and he continued to challenge Clay in Kentucky rather than Breckinridge in Washington.[49]

With the dawn of 1805, Clay returned to Lexington, contracted for the construction of a home on his country land, became the father of Susan Hart Clay on February 14, and resumed his legal practice in which he acquired money "as fast as you can count it" (so heard his friend James Brown).[50] Meanwhile, his friend, Breckinridge, remained in Washington where he sat on the impeachment of Justice Samuel Chase. The senate, sitting as a court, was presided over by lame duck Vice President Aaron Burr, a man under warrant for murder in New Jersey. Both Breckinridge and Burr were to travel separately to Kentucky after Chase was acquitted and the 8th Congress adjourned. Burr passed through the state in May. and returned to Lexington on August 20 amid much public speculation as to his intentions and purposes in traveling through the old southwest section of the country. He informed inquirers that he traveled for amusement and information.

About the time of Burr's return visit to Kentucky, Breckinridge received a letter from President Jefferson inviting him to join his cabinet as the United States Attorney General. Breckinridge accepted the offer and opened the door to another battle in the Kentucky legislature to name someone to complete Breckinridge's senate term ending in March 1807.

The 1805 session of the Kentucky General Assembly convened on November 4. Immediately

following William Logan's re-election as speaker of the house, Felix Grundy moved to re-open the attack on the Kentucky Insurance Company. Parliamentary procedure placed this issue in abeyance until after the election of a new United States Senator. The contest this year produced no pyrotechnics. Former house Speaker John Adair, supported by Grundy, won easily on this second try over one-armed John Pope, Clay's candidate.[51]

The collision over the insurance company was something else. Two elements had combined by November 1805 to electrify the atmosphere surrounding the second battle between Clay and Grundy over the company's fate. The havoc wrought by the direct federal land tax, causing the sale of millions of acres of land to pay the tax, was well known by lawyer Clay and he resolved to give all his support to the insurance company in its effort to protect the remaining land owners. On the other hand, Grundy and his followers saw the bank as a "monied aristocracy." They also pointed a finger at the eight-percent profit earned for the company's shareholders in a six-month period.[52]

In addition to the influence of the land tax, Grundy came into the 1805 session of the legislature with majority support behind him in both houses. His principal backers came from that part of the state lying south of the Green River. And this group was to become directly involved in the bank controversy.

When Grundy's motion came before the house on November 21, he argued that

> Banks were inimical to a free Government as they indirectly tend to draw the balance of wealth out of the hands of the people and that the law establishing a bank in Lexington was unconstitutional, as it gave a certain class of individuals an exclusive privilege, by lending out their paper and money, or rather their credit and money, and recovering their debts on motion.

Clay countered "that it was unconstitutional to repeal the laws, because the law had vested certain rights, and that it was unconstitutional to repeal a law that had vested rights." He also advocated the policy of banking.[53]

Despite Clay's eloquent plea to his colleagues, Grundy's majority support was too much for the Clay forces and the bill amending the company's charter preamble passed the house decisively, 37–19. The amendment read that so far as it authorises said company to establish a bank, it is considered hazardous to the interest of the people of this commonwealth and unfavorable to that spirit of independence which ought ever to be encouraged in a republican government.

Two days later the senate passed, and sent to Governor Greenup, the bill, which, in effect, repealed the company's banking privileges.[54]

But Governor Greenup saw the company's rights in like mind as Clay. On December 5th, he returned the measure to the house with his veto and a message questioning the standards of a state

which erects a corporation, vests it with certain privileges and powers, engages expressly that it shall continue thus privileged and vested for fifteen years — invites her citizens to participate in its concerns — gives for two succeeding years additional assurances until thousands are vested, and then in violation of her express undertaking to the contrary, and of the confidence reposed, and to the great injury, if not the entire ruin of many individuals, prostrate the institution.[55]

Grundy's political troops were furious at executive interference and were unhearing to his plea. One day later they overrode the veto with even greater strength in a 40–18 vote. The bill then went to the senate where there were easily enough votes to override the veto and kill the bank.

The survival hopes of the bank were so desperate that Dr. Samuel Brown of Lexington had given his brother, James in New Orleans, a written diagnosis that the end was near. But on December 13, with the vetoed bill still pending in the senate, Dr. Brown wrote his brother again saying, "I am still, I find, a stranger to Kentucky politics. A bill to coerce the payment of the installments due on the Green River debt has changed the state of opinion in the Senate and it is now doubtful what will be the fate of our poor little institution,"[56] the Kentucky Insurance Company.

This sudden turn for the better in the health of the bank was directly related to the potent medicine administered by Henry Clay.

In the early days of land settlement in the Green River section of Kentucky, wealthy speculators frequently bought up thousands of acres by a fraudulent scheme of using the names of their Negro slaves who could not legally own land. Many titles carried the name of Tom, Dick, or Harry with "Black" appended, so that when registered in the record books, with last name first, it was readily seen that the owners were *Black Tom, Black Dick,* and *Black Harry.*[57] The "Masters" at land speculation were to become leaders in the Kentucky legislature and in that capacity they managed to quash legislation, year after year, that would force them to pay off the enormous debts that had accrued.[58]

On the day following the insurance company's first defeat in the house, Clay quietly slipped into the parliamentary machinery a bill that would coerce the payment of the long overdue debts owed by the prominent and political leaders from the Green River area. On this issue Clay had strong support from all other sections of the state. This measure came before the house after that body had voted to override the governor's veto of the Bank repeal bill. Its consequences frightened and temporarily stunned the house members from the Green River. But on recovering their composure, they rushed headlong to the senate chamber and lobbied mightily against the measure which they had so recently supported. The senate's Green River boys fell in line and with the votes of the Clay faction, they "formed a party sufficient to lay the law asleep."[59]

Ironically, the senate meanwhile passed a bill creating a state bank with a capital of $600,000. And when this measure came to the house, Grundy was its chief advocate. His reasoning was that the state bank gave no exclusive privilege for any group. Clay opposed the bill because the notes of the proposed bank were to be issued on the credit of the state. The other house members were so confused by the technicalities of the legislation that they refused to pass the bill in any form.[60]

The battle between Grundy and Clay was clearly the high point of the 1805 session and the two men towered over their colleagues. Each possessed an ample sense of humor and as they fought with political and parliamentary weapons they did so with graciousness and courtesy. Clay, the clear winner, was at age 28 just as clearly the new leader in Kentucky state politics. Clay would soon stride on to the national scene in two steps. And Grundy would take one stop to a judgeship on the Kentucky Court of Appeals followed in short order with a second step to the seat of chief justice of the Kentucky Supreme Court — and then resign to build a new political career in Tennessee. The two would meet again.

4

In Defense of a Vice President

When James Brown left Lexington in May 1804 for the new American city of New Orleans, he vacated the seat of professor of law at Transylvania University. Records fail to show the name of a teacher for the law students over the next 17 months. Then, on October 10, 1805, the board of trustees of the institution unanimously elected Henry Clay to the post of Professor of Law and Politics.[1] Yet it appears the law students still lacked instruction until early 1806 when Clay completed his duties as a legislator at Frankfort during the closing months of 1805.

As Clay turned 29, in April 1806, he could rest assured that his position in Kentucky was secured for many years to come. He was eminent in his chosen profession of law, he was a popular legislator, and now he had established himself in the academic community. His family was growing and a new home was rising on the edge of town.

These early months of 1806 must have given Henry Clay a great sense of serenity in the quiet fertile countryside of Kentucky. He was totally uninvolved, except as a newspaper reader, with the dynamic events exploding on the other side of the Atlantic. A January paper related the death of British Admiral Horatio Nelson along with a description of the Battle of Trafalgar. A few months later Clay read of the death of William Pitt and Lord Cornwallis. A couple weeks later there was an account of the British capture of the Cape of Good Hope, and one month later there appeared a story about three British ships seizing and killing crew members of American ships entering and leaving New York harbor. By June he had an account of the Battle of Austerlitz, fought six months earlier between Napoleon's French Army and the combined forces of Russia and Austria.[2] A letter to Clay from John Breckinridge, in Washington, told of a Congressional resolution to cut off importation of British goods because of their impressment of American seamen and the violations of neutral rights.[3] But in Kentucky, interest centered on the eclipse of the sun in mid-June.

In this easy-going environment of the Bluegrass world, Clay was the principal orator at the Independence Day festivities in Lexington. It should have been a happy occasion, but he found it difficult to give his best to the speech since he had just learned of the strange death of his old friend and teacher, George Wythe. In August, along with William Russell and one-armed John Pope, Henry Clay was returned by the Fayette County voters to represent them in the Kentucky legislature.[4] His course was set to continue in the tranquil direction that had now become familiar.

Unknown to Clay, the seeds of a growing controversy had already been sown. Its tangled web was slowly reaching out and would seize him and lift him suddenly onto the national scene. Again it was the reading of newspaper stories that alerted Clay to the meandering vine of villainous charges that would touch his life.

At the beginning of July, a new paper, the *Western World*, appeared in Frankfort. With the first issue it began a serialization entitled, "The Kentucky Spanish Association, Blount's Conspiracy, and Miranda's Expedition." Despite its title, the stories dealt almost exclusively with the "Spanish Association" (more frequently termed, "The Spanish Conspiracy"). These articles had a dynamic impact on Kentucky and were reprinted in all papers of the state and many appeared in prominent Eastern papers. The accounts accused several

Republican leaders of 1806 Kentucky with secretly conspiring to separate the Western region from Virginia in the late 1780s and put the land under the control of Spain. The articles then attempted to link these Republicans with new mysterious activities unfolding in 1806.[5]

The editor of the Frankfort paper was Joseph M. Street of Richmond, where his previous experience was in commercial business. His co-editor was John Wood, described as a New York newspaper hack. Wood, the author of *The History of the Adams Administration* (suppressed in 1802 for political reasons by Aaron Burr), later journeyed to Richmond where he was an editor of *The Virginia Gazette*.[6] Wood came to Kentucky with Street, whom he had met in Richmond and for whom he had developed an unnatural admiration and affection. Secretly, they had been invited to set up the newspaper in Kentucky by Humphrey Marshall, a former U.S. senator from Kentucky.[7]

Marshall was born in Westmoreland County, Virginia, in 1760. As a youngster he went to live, and be tutored, in the home of his father's brother, Colonel Thomas Marshall. The uncle was the father of 15 children, the oldest of whom was John Marshall — soldier, legislator, diplomat (one of the X Y Z envoys), briefly secretary of state under John Adams, and midnight appointee by the second president to the seat of chief justice of the United States.[8] (The last two offices he held simultaneously for one month. And his initial day as chief justice, February 4, 1801, was the first day the Court sat in Washington, D.C.) About 1780, Humphrey Marshall and his uncle settled in Kentucky where both, as members of conventions, were active in opposition to efforts to separate the Bluegrass Country from Virginia and establish it as another state in the Union. Four years later, Humphrey took time out to marry one of John Marshall's sisters — a first cousin named Mary Anne and nicknamed Molly. When Kentucky achieved statehood in 1792, the nephew served a single term as U.S. senator from December 1, 1795, to March 3, 1801. But his Federalist sentiments were unpopular among the growing Republican population of Kentucky. He was succeeded by John Breckinridge and returned to Frankfort with something of a chip on his shoulder. There he took up journalism as the covert publisher of the *Western World* in 1806, and years

later as the author of a two-volume partisan *History of Kentucky*. He was also for a time a representative in the Kentucky legislature.[9] A genealogist of the Marshall family called Humphrey, "violent, profane, and irreligious. He had but little respect for God or man."[10] He was to use this personality liberally in his written and oral attacks on all Republicans that crossed his path. More is to be heard of him.

Thus it was that the central theme of the articles relating to the Spanish Conspiracy published in the *Western World* were to strike at the 1806 Republican leadership of Kentucky. From the earliest exposés the paper sought to pin the charge of treason on the state's pioneer political leaders who had petitioned Congress and the state of Virginia to allow Kentucky to become an independent "State." On this single word, "State," apparently hung much of the controversy. While these leaders held out that their efforts were aimed at establishing a new state as part of the United States, the editors of the paper charged that some were, in fact, in the pay of Spain and were attempting to turn the region over to that European nation after a time as an independent national State.

Without going too deeply into the morass that was the Spanish Conspiracy, the following facts can be related. In the late 1780s several conventions met in Kentucky to express the grievances of the populace as to their treatment by Congress and Virginia and to request a separation from the mother state. They were grieved by the terms of the Jay Treaty which would have closed, for 25 years, their access to the Mississippi River and the Gulf ports that were so vital to their commerce and economic well-being. They were grieved at the meager protection they received from their governments against attacks by Indians living north of the Ohio River. And they were grieved by the distance and time which separated them from the legislative and judicial bodies that controlled their affairs.

The petitions for separation were met by procrastination, indifference and buck-passing. In fact, the influential powers in New England threatened secession if political equality were granted to the western inhabitants. The statehood drive had begun when the national government was operating under the Articles of Confederation.

While the Virginia legislature agreed to the separation, they left it to Congress to set the final terms. But by this time the new Constitution was promulgated and the old Congress failed to act.

It is no wonder that some Kentuckians looked to Spain, and Spain was quick to consort with them. As we have seen, Humphrey Marshall had been a member of some of these early conventions but had been beaten in elections to attend others.[11] In his contacts he had learned of rumors and facts and had developed his own opinions along with deep animosities. These he joined in his observations to the *Western World* under the pseudonym of "An Observer."

The very first edition of the *Western World's* serialization established the purpose of its attacks, summarized the past history of the Spanish Conspiracy, and then introduced its principal victims — General James Wilkinson and former Kentucky Senator John Brown. Brown was very close to Clay through his marriage to Lucretia Hart's sister Nancy.

First charged by the paper was General James Wilkinson, a member of the Kentucky conventions in the 1780s, but named Governor of Upper Louisiana in 1806. He was described as "an intriguing and ambitious adventurer." Wilkinson had joined the continental army when only 18 and was with Benedict Arnold and Aaron Burr on the winter march to Quebec in 1775–76. Later, following participation in the Battle of Saratoga, he was involved in the Conway Cabal which attempted to substitute his commander, General Gates, as the American Army's leader over General Washington. After removal to Kentucky in 1784, he was one of the founders of Frankfort. He thereafter continued to climb the military ladder to succeed Anthony Wayne as commanding general of the Army.

The first article by *The World* noted that Wilkinson had made excursions down the Mississippi in early 1785 and again in 1786. (Still nearly 20 years before the Louisiana Purchase.) It said further that he

contacted proper emissaries in New Orleans and convinced them that he was a person of the first influence in Kentucky and the Western Country; and could command at pleasure, an army of 10–15,000 citizens.

One of Wilkinson's contacts, according to the *Western World's* account, was Manuel Gayoso, governor of Natchez. He reportedly told Gayoso that the inhabitants of Kentucky "were in a state of the greatest discontent, and even bordering on insurrection; and that they would cheerfully accept the yoke of any foreign power which would aid them in separation from the union." Gayoso forwarded this intelligence to his government in Madrid where it was leaked to the British.

The *Western World* went on to report that Spain, through its minister to the United States, Diego Gardoqui, in 1788, sounded out Senator John Brown, then a member of Congress under the Articles of Confederation. "Having discovered in Mr. Brown an accommodating disposition towards the Spanish government," the paper continued, "he (Gardoqui) directly made proposals for a separation of the state of Kentucky from the United States in favor of Spain, on three conditions related to the rights of Kentucky and its citizens, with an assurance to Mr. Brown, if they were carried into effect, he himself would be raised to the dignity of a Spanish grandee with a suitable pension for life."

The paper said the scheme came to light through a letter from Brown, dated July 10, 1788, "to Judge George Muter, present president of the Kentucky Court of Appeals," and which was published about 1789 in the *Kentucky Gazette.*

Meanwhile, the British got into the act with proposals to Wilkinson, who thereafter attempted to play off both countries for the better deal. Hoping for wider support, another British agent, a Colonel Conolly, conferred with Colonel Thomas Marshall, whom he had met while an American prisoner of war in Virginia during the Revolution. Conolly showed Marshall a copy of the Wilkinson report that had gone through the two European capitals. The *Western World*, echoing the sentiments of Humphrey Marshall, declared that Humphrey's uncle terminated that conversation stating that Kentuckians would never agree to a separation from the United States. The Colonel even went so far as to relay the contents of the meeting to his boyhood friend, George Washington.[12]

As the weekly flow of accusations by the *Western World* continued through the summer of 1806, Henry Clay undoubtedly learned of the wording of Brown's letter to Muter and discussed its contents with his friend. The letter reflected neither approval nor disapproval of the Spanish scheme. Furthermore, Brown had privately presented the same information to other leaders of the day including James Madison (then one of the principal powers in drafting the new Constitution), an unlikely confidant if treason were intended.[13] In any case, other documents show that all of Brown's efforts at a separation for Kentucky were from the state of Virginia and not from the Federal Union.

By September, the lengthy exposés were clearly attempting to link these pioneer Kentucky statesmen with ex–Vice President Aaron Burr's mysterious travels in the Western Country. Editor Street remarked that it now appeared that

> the original design of the Kentucky Spanish Association has been entirely abandoned. The views of the conspirators are no longer to unite with Spain; but to form Kentucky, Tennessee, Ohio, Indiana, the Louisiana, and the Floridas into one independent government.

The issue of September 13, 1806, carried a reference that Burr

> had arrived at Frankfort from Cincinnati on Tuesday evening last about an hour after sun set. He took his lodgings at Major Love's Tavern, the house adjacent to Mr. John Brown's, and consequently more convenient than any of the other taverns for visiting his *bosom friend* and arranging the plans of their future operations. In a few minutes after his arrival he paid his respects at the palace of Mr. Brown, and we believe spent all evening until 12 at night and the greater part of the next day in secret consultation as to the most effectual mode of preserving the secrecy of the future proceedings of the Western Association. At five o'clock in the afternoon of Wednesday he departed for Lexington; but we understand is to return in a few days.[14]

It is possible that Burr met Clay in Lexington though it is certain that they had met the previous year. While Clay might have been as mystified about Burr's wanderings as any other citizen, he was also aware that Burr had certain interests in construction of a canal at the falls of the Ohio River, that he was interested in lands owned by Philip Bastrop in Louisiana (a legitimate land negotiation for new American settlers as shown by titles and deeds accessible to Clay in the Kentucky courts), and that Burr supported armed protection of the Western Country from Spanish intrigues.

Two weeks after his visits in Kentucky, Burr was in Nashville dining and conferring on military support with General Andrew Jackson.[15]

The entire series of revelations was having a dramatic impact in Kentucky, where the "public was agitated and incensed," and nationally with many of the leading papers of the eastern seaboard reprinting or recounting the substance of the exposés noting that "persons implicated as concerned in this traitorous attempt maintain an exalted standing in society."[16] Other persons soon named in the charges included Senator Jonathan Dayton of New Jersey (a former Speaker of the U.S. House of Representatives), Judge Benjamin Sebastian of the Kentucky Circuit Court of Appeals, and Judge Harry Innes of the Federal Circuit Court in Kentucky. Still other prominent citizens would be implicated with either the old or new conspiracies, or both.

The explosive climate resulting from the commentaries incited several personal attacks and then legal indictments against editor Street. One of the first confrontations took place in the presence of Henry Clay at the Bush Tavern in Frankfort in July. Shortly after publication of the second issue of the *Western World*, co-editor John Wood began to fear the alienation of his strong emotional and affectionate ties to Street — his "real object" in working with him on the paper. The cause of his fear was the ascendancy which he saw Joseph Hamilton Daveiss and Humphrey Marshall were gaining over Street. Wood contacted Clay and apparently requested that he witness an interview with Street at the tavern. There he urged Street in vain to break off his connection with the Marshall family to whom Daveiss was now related by marriage. Though harsh language passed between the two editors, Clay aided them in a temporary reconciliation. Nevertheless, the relations again became strained and Clay advised Wood to relinquish his connections with the paper.[17] Wood did so in December after regretting much of his writing and accusations. He left Frankfort and became editor of the *Atlantic World* in Washington, D.C. Wood's revelation that Daveiss and Marshall were behind the paper must have been news to Clay.

Late in August another more violent episode

involved Street. A man named George Adams, a subscriber to the paper, told Street privately that he wished the subscription halted since Street was in the employ of one whose name was linked with the conspiracy. Street later repeated the conversation to a man named Bodley, who in turn inquired of Adams as to its truth. Angered by the betrayal of a confidence, Adams attacked Street with a bludgeon in the State House yard when they next met. Street drew a dagger to defend himself, but could not use it as Bodley, a witness to the encounter, interposed by grappling with Street. Meanwhile, Adams took advantage of the interposition, drew a pistol from his pocket, and fired at Street. The ball penetrated the editor's clothes, grazing the skin at the base of his sternum, but he was not seriously wounded. As Street rushed at his assailant, waving the dagger in his hand, Adams threw the empty pistol at Street and fled. A little while later, as Street was showing his wound to spectators, Adams returned with another loaded pistol and threatened to complete his purpose but was prevented from doing so by several persons present. In court the following Monday, Street was dismissed for his part in the episode. The grand jury brought an indictment against Adams for attempted murder, but as the result of errors in the legal paperwork, the indictment was quashed.[18]

Somewhat surprisingly, in October, Clay found himself allied with Humphrey Marshall acting in defense of libelous characterizations by the *Western World*. This time the victim was Governor Christopher Greenup who brought a suit against the paper for defamation of character. The written account had described some fictional portraits and depicted the governor in a derogatory manner as he may have appeared reading the first number of the *Western World*.[19] Street survived this suit as well as other personal assaults and went on in later years to become an Indian agent, a negotiator in the Black Hawk War, and finally spent his latter years in promoting the interests of Indians of the upper Midwest.[20]

While Humphrey Marshall and Jo Daveiss were secretly active in establishing their muckraking newspaper and feeding inflammatory copy to its editors, Daveiss was busy on another front battling against the Republicans in the West. Unknown to Clay, Daveiss was writing President Jef-

ferson a full six months before the first issue of the *Western World* came off the presses. He was trying to alert the chief executive to the new conspiracies and stated, "We have traitors among us." In his first letter, dated January 10, 1806, he went on to suggest the taint of treason reached western men in high office but gave no names other than Wilkinson. In this matter he questioned Jefferson's appointment of Wilkinson to be governor of Upper Louisiana. He advised the letter be held in strict secrecy but might be shown to Secretary of State James Madison or Secretary of the Treasury Albert Gallatin.

Receiving no reply from Jefferson, Daveiss again wrote on February 10 implicating Burr as the focal point of a current plot. With this letter he attached a list of names of suspected persons, though admitting that "many of these persons may be innocent." Names mentioned which were later to appear in the *Western World*, included Wilkinson, Sebastian, Innes, and Burr. Other names included U.S. Attorney General John Breckinridge, Senators John Adair of Kentucky and John Smith of Ohio, Congressman John Fowler of Kentucky, Indiana Territorial Governor William Henry Harrison, and Lexington lawyer Henry Clay.

When still he received no answer, Daveiss sent a third letter on March 5 requesting an acknowledgment, fearing the earlier epistles had gone astray. This time Daveiss got a lukewarm response. Throughout the spring and summer Daveiss continued the correspondence expanding on the plot each time and always bringing in new names. He offered his services to travel or to do anything else possible to break up the alleged plot. Again he had to ask for acknowledgment and suggestions as to what course he should pursue. Jefferson's September 12 reply said the letters had reached him but he gave the district attorney no advice on action.

Daveiss was later to publish this correspondence with a running account of his feelings. "Good God!" he wrote after this last letter.

> Was ever anything so astonishing! So unaccountable! That in reply to a letter so distinct, the government should still keep me profoundly in the dark, never order me to do or forbear anything, or give me one hint of their views![21]

The treasonable web woven by Daveiss might seem reasonable in some respects and in regard to some personalities. But to accuse high-ranking political friends of Jefferson — all, in fact, Republicans, when the charge came from a known Federalist — was quite enough to still any presidential action.

Who was Daveiss anyway to be the author of such a tale?

Joseph Hamilton Daveiss (whose last name is frequently spelled Daviess and whose middle name he is said to have added himself in admiration for Federalist Alexander Hamilton),[22] was born in the Blue Ridge Mountains of Virginia in 1774. When he was five, he went with his family to the Kentucky country where he grew up with the terror of Indian raids and with a sparse education obtained by firelight at his mother's knee. Following the Revolution he acquired a smattering of formal education and a good deal of military experience in which he displayed a reckless lack of fear in an encounter with Indians. At home again he studied law under Republican George Nicholas along with other young men whom he would later meet in legal combat. In fact, he was soon to win a court case against his teacher but still became the executor of Nicholas' will.

In his new profession Daveiss combined skill, daring, and ruthlessness with an assortment of eccentricities and a devotion to Federalism in the midst of a growing Republican populace. While enhancing his fame as he "rode the circuit," he dressed in weather-worn hunting garb and carried a rifle en route from one court to another. In August 1801, he went east to plead the land case of *Wilson vs. Mason* as the first western lawyer to appear before the U.S. Supreme Court, at least, in the infant capital city of Washington. Dressed in his usual rugged hunting clothes, Daveiss sat in the small Capitol room then serving as the High Court's chamber. During the early stages of the arguments Daveiss munched on food he drew from his pocket, and occasionally questioned or otherwise needled Mason's attorney. Supposing him to be some Kentucky backwoodsman come to see the progress of his case, Chief Justice John Marshall admonished him to hold his peace. But later the jurists were astonished when Daveiss stood and pled the case for plaintiff Wilson with such precise and legal ability that he won his case.[23]

Yet his victory in Washington was much greater than the legal case. He won the admiration of the chief justice, visited his home and family, and won the heart of John Marshall's sister Nancy. He married her at the home of Humphrey Marshall in Frankfort on July 17, 1803.[24]

Some writers credit John Marshall with suggesting to the president that Daveiss be appointed a Federal district attorney for Kentucky. But Marshall did not meet Daveiss until August 1801 when Republican Jefferson was president. Daveiss was, in fact, appointed by Federalist Adams in December 1800.[25] It is more likely that Daveiss had been recommended to Adams by Humphrey Marshall, at that time a U.S. senator. In any case, Daveiss was district attorney in November 1806 when Clay journeyed to Frankfort for the opening of the annual session of the legislature on November 3.

Following the re-election of William Logan as Speaker of the House, a false air of serenity and well-being was reflected in a speech to both houses of the legislature by Governor Greenup when he said America "enjoys peace and all is tranquil."[26] Yet three days later the *Kentucky Gazette* spoke of troop movements at Natchitoches in conjunction with an expected war against Spain in the lower Mississippi River area. And the paper reprinted a letter from General Wilkinson stating that "unless his or Spanish orders are countermanded within 10 days the sword will be drawn."[27]

However, military action on the Mississippi was not the explosive element. Instead, spectacular legal action detonated the simmering controversy. About noon of Wednesday, November 5, District Attorney Jo Daveiss rose in the Federal court and addressed Judge Harry Innes, one of those he had named as connected with the old Spanish Conspiracy in his letters to Jefferson. He told the court that he had "a motion to make of the utmost magnitude and extraordinary nature and which regarded the welfare of the Union at large." He then offered an affidavit charging that

> Aaron Burr hath been, is now engaged in preparing, and setting on foot, and in providing and preparing the means, for a military expedition and enterprise within this district, for the purpose of descending the Ohio and Mississippi therewith, and making war upon the subjects of the king of Spain, who are in a state of peace with the people of these United States. To-wit: on the provinces of

Mexico, on the westwardly side of Louisiana, which appertain and belong to the king of Spain, an European Prince, with whom these United States are at peace.

Daveiss told the court that his charge related only to the expedition against Mexico but that he had

> information on which I can rely, that all the western territories are the next object of the scheme — and finally, all the region of the Ohio is calculated as falling into the vortex of the new proposed revolution.

Judge Innes took the motion under advisement and set the next hearing for Saturday the 8th at 11 A.M.[28]

Meanwhile, Aaron Burr had returned to Kentucky following his conference with Andrew Jackson in Tennessee. He was at this time staying at Wilson's Tavern in Lexington with his daughter, Theodosia Alston, and her husband, the future governor of South Carolina, completing the purchase of the Bastrop lands in Louisiana. On Friday, November 7, 1806, Burr addressed the following letter from Frankfort to Henry Clay:

> Loves Inn ½ past 3
>
> Sir
>
> At nine this Morning Mr. Jordan recd. your letter in reply to one which he wrote at my request —
>
> I have just arrived, wet and something fatigued and send to inquire whether my presence in Court is *now* deemed necessary or expedient. —
>
> I pray you to consider yourself as my Counsel in the business moved by Mr. D — a more *technical* application will be made when I shall have the pleasure to see you — an early interview, at this house, would very much gratify,
>
> Yr Ob St   A. Burr
> H. Clay Esqr.[29]

The correspondence between Jordan and Clay is unknown.

We can only surmise what thoughts raced through the mind of 29-year-old Kentucky lawyer Henry Clay when he read this personal appeal of a former vice president — a man who lost the presidency less than six years earlier after 36 ballots by the House of Representatives to break a tie. Clay had only a local reputation while Burr had figured in great national events for over a quarter of a century. Clay and his assistant, John Allen, were convinced of Burr's innocence and later wrote that

when he sent us a considerable fee, we resolved to decline accepting it, and accordingly returned it. We said to each other, Colonel Burr has been an eminent member of the profession, has been Attorney-General of the State of New York, is prosecuted without cause in a distant State, and we ought not to regard him in the light of an ordinary culprit.[30]

Aaron Burr was the son and grandson of clergymen (the Rev. Aaron Burr and the Rev. Jonathan Edwards) both of whom served as president of Princeton college. In a diary, his mother described her two-year-old son as

> a little, dirty, noisy boy, very different from Sally (his sister) almost in everything. He begins to talk a little, is very sly and mischievous. He has more sprightliness than Sally, and most say he is handsome, but not so good tempered. He is very resolute, and requires a good governor to bring him to terms.[31]

But within a 13-month period, around the ages of 2–3, he lost both his parents and two grandparents. He and Sally were then raised by a stern uncle. At 10 he attempted to run away to sea but returned to his uncle on conditions he negotiated from a safe vantage point high in a ship's rigging.

With the outbreak of the Revolutionary War, Burr joined the continental forces at Boston and through that first bleak winter of war he and James Wilkinson marched with Benedict Arnold to Quebec. Burr served with distinction but broke with Arnold. He later served on General George Washington's staff but neither liked the other. Burr felt he was not given enough credit for his daring exploits, particularly during the New York retreats and again at Monmouth, New Jersey, and thereafter eventually joined General Gates in the Conway Cabal that nearly overthrew Washington during the winter of Valley Forge. Burr's health later forced him to retire from the service.

After the war Burr read law and progressed through several stages of New York politics making enemies of Alexander Hamilton and the powerful Clinton family. By adroit management he propelled his way upward to become the running mate of Thomas Jefferson in the election of 1800. His tie vote assured him of the vice presidency — in which he served as one of the best parliamentarians the office has had through the long decades that followed.

Yet there was always something suspicious

about Burr. Men could not fully trust him and many believed he was an evil man. The killing of Hamilton in the duel in New Jersey only added to the feelings so many had. And since his departure from the vice presidency his trips to the southwest and New Orleans in 1805 and 1806 were heavily cloaked in mystery.

But Clay recognized Burr as a gallant and heroic soldier, a leading American citizen, a Republican, and a man who was interested — indeed fascinated — in the development of the nation's newly acquired provinces across the Mississippi River. This small, impeccable but renowned American had called upon him, young Henry Clay, to defend him, former vice president of the United States Aaron Burr, against the vicious persecuting charges of treason leveled by embittered Federalist District Attorney Joseph Hamilton Daveiss.

When the district court convened on Saturday, Judge Innes overruled the motion made by Daveiss, calling for the arrest of Colonel Burr, stating: first, that the court was not invested with the power, and second, if the court were, that the evidence was not sufficient. Daveiss then moved for a warrant to summon a grand jury before whom he would prefer an indictment against Burr. This motion was granted by Innes and a 24-man grand jury was impaneled.

At one P.M., after the names of the grand jury had been called, Burr accompanied by his counsel, Henry Clay, entered the courtroom where they both took seats. As described by the *Western World*, Burr, after a few minutes,

rose and addressed the court in concise and impressive terms. He stated that he had been upon the eve of his departure from Lexington, when he was informed that his name had been mentioned with reproach in that court; that he made it his business to hasten to this place, and present himself before the court for investigation.

Daveiss told the court he could proceed with his charge as soon as witnesses could be summoned and these, he believed, could be in town by the following Tuesday evening and be available on Wednesday morning. Burr agreed to this timing, the court was adjourned, and Innes ordered the jury and certain witnesses to meet on the following Wednesday, the 12th, at 10 A.M.[32]

News that Burr was facing indictment, that he was in town, that Henry Clay was his counsel,

and that both might be present in court on the 12th attracted a throng of spectators who filled the courtroom to capacity, overflowing into adjacent corridors, the upper and lower state house halls, the offices downstairs, and onto the grassy public square surrounding the building. The crowd was hugely in support of the diminutive ex-vice president, and all wanted to catch a glimpse of "the great man."

The court reconvened at the appointed hour and all witnesses who had been summoned were present. As expected, Daveiss rose to deliver his charge against Burr. But to the astonishment of all, he moved instead that the grand jury be dismissed, declaring that he was not prepared to proceed with the inquiry by reason of the absence of a witness whom he deemed material to his case. Only after Judge Innes agreed to dismiss the grand jury did Burr appear in court accompanied by his counsels, Henry Clay and John Allen.

The crowded audience felt cheated. They had not seen the lively court performance or heard the expected elocution of brilliant lawyers. Daveiss was hissed, ridiculed, and laughed at. Burr had been a favorite of the throng and was now a hero. They believed the motive behind Daveiss' charge was not prosecution, but persecution. Indeed, hadn't Daveiss adopted as his middle name that of his hero, Hamilton — the Federalist struck down only two years ago by Burr's bullet? Daveiss attempted to convince whoever would listen that one witness, Davis Floyd, whom he had not summoned, was essential to his proof. Daveiss stated that Floyd had left the state to attend the legislature of the Indiana Territory which had begun its session on the 5th of the month.[33]

The disappointed crowd had very different heroes to proclaim the next day as Frankfort was visited by Meriwether Lewis and William Clark, now returning with a chief of the Mandan Indians from their epic exploration of the Missouri River Valley and the land between to the Pacific Ocean.[34] It was over two years before, that they had begun the great expedition. About this same time Zebulon Pike, under the command of General Wilkinson, had trekked westward into the Rocky Mountains and had discovered, but did not climb, the great mountain which he named Pike's Peak.

But Henry Clay still had a job to do in the

Kentucky House of Representatives. In fact, as he was acting as counsel for former Vice President Aaron Burr, Clay's name was being muddied in a bribe charge made by a member of the house. Representative Mills sought to remove a justice of the peace (William Owens of Pendleton County) for "offering Henry Clay a bribe to use his influence in the house of representatives, to obtain for him (Owens) a bill or act of divorce for the purpose of repudiating his lawful wife." But it was quickly admitted that Clay had rejected the bribe with disdain.[35]

On Tuesday November 18th, the legislature moved to the election of a United States senator for the six-year term beginning March 4, 1807. John Adair was the incumbent senator. Felix Grundy, still a member of the house, but now a candidate for lieutenant governor, nominated Adair for re-election to the Senate. Henry Clay put forward the name of General Samuel Hopkins, to whom Clay was to have been aide in the aborted expedition to New Orleans in 1803. In addition, one-armed John Pope was named a candidate.

With the senate's votes added to those of the house, Pope led on the first ballot with 38 votes to 28 for Adair and 15 for Hopkins. On the second ballot one vote moved from Hopkins to Pope, and the third ballot remained the same. The fourth ballot was between the two highest candidates and, with Clay voting for Pope, the one-armed man was elected, 45–36.[36]

The next surprise came that evening when John Adair, in anger at being displaced, penned the following to John Rowan, Kentucky's secretary of state:

18 November 1806

Sir,

Please to accept of this as a resignation of the place of Senator in the Congress of the United States which I now hold — I hope my country will not deem this the effect of ill temper. Had I been selected for the next term, every exertion of mine would have been to discharge that important duty faithfully; that not having been the case, personal motives forbid, and in my judgment the obligations I owe to the public, render it improper I should go forward the present session.

I am, Sir,
With high personal esteem,
Your most ob't serv't.
John Adair.[37]

Therefore, on the following day, Felix Grundy moved still another election to fill an interim U.S. Senate vacancy until next March 4. Logically, John Pope would be sent to his new post nearly four months early. But the Kentucky legislature did not act logically. Instead, General Hopkins nominated Henry Clay. Another member nominated George Bibb. It took only a single ballot to elect Henry Clay to the United States Senate by the overwhelming vote of 68–10.[38] That day, as Senator-elect Henry Clay resigned his seat in the Kentucky House of Representatives, one wonders if he gave any thought to the Constitutional requirement that a U.S. Senator must be 30 years of age. He would not reach that age until the following April — over a month after his short interim term was to expire.

The past two weeks had been filled with drama for Henry Clay. But now he believed he could relax from professional duties for a while as he prepared to journey to Washington City to enter a new career, brief as it was to be, in the halls of the national Congress. He must lay aside his professorship, his state legislative tasks, and his law career.

But even this respite was not to be. Only six days after Clay's election to the Senate, Jo Daveiss was back in Federal Court again to petition Judge Innes to call another grand jury for the same purpose as before. Daveiss revealed that Floyd had returned to Kentucky and would be available to testify. He stated further "that unless a decisive step was now taken, Mr. Burr would be afloat with his flotilla in a short time."[39] Burr was in Louisville when he learned of this new court motion. On November 27, he addressed a note to Clay:

Dear Sir —

Information has this morning been given to me that Mr. Davies [sic] has recommended his prosecution & inquiry — I must intreat your professional aid in this business — It would be disagreeable to me to form a new connection & various considerations will it is hoped induce you even at some personal inconvenience to acquiesce in my request — I shall however insist on making a liberal pecuniary compensation — the starting of your journey to Washington for a few days cannot be very material — No business is done in Congress till after New Year

Respectfully Yr Obt St
A. Burr

I pray you to repair to Frankfort on receipt of this —[40]

What were these charges Daveiss mentioned about Burr being afloat with his flotilla in a short time? There were other peculiar things going on. The same day that Burr addressed the letter to Clay, the Kentucky House of Representatives began an investigation into the activities of Judge Benjamin Sebastian. In fact, Senator-elect Pope, chairing the inquiry, began the proceedings by reading a letter from Governor Greenup informing the investigating committee that Sebastian had resigned. Committee witnesses then revealed that the Judge held "a pension for life of two thousand dollars per annum from the Government of Spain, expressly for personal services." Solid evidence of a conspiracy was unfolding, and on December 2 the committee agreed on Sebastian's guilt.[41]

But how deep was this treason and who was touched by it? And was Burr now linked to the old Spanish Conspiracy as the *Western World* had been saying? Clay was now a Senator-elect and a national figure. Doubts surrounded him. He now believed he must be sure of his grounds and his client. Was Burr really involved in some unsavory activity? Could such a man, who was once a heartbeat from the presidency be involved in anything treasonable? Where could Clay turn to get a personal reference of Burr? One man in Lexington knew Burr well — John Breckinridge. But the attorney general had spent much of the summer at Olympian Springs for his health. On October 22, as Breckinridge prepared to mount his horse for the expected 20-day journey to Washington over the western Virginia mountains, with a planned visit with a son in Virginia, he was stricken anew and now in late November he was lying in bed in precarious health.[42] Then on the advice of John Rowan, Clay agreed it was best to have a statement from the ex-vice president which would clarify his position. Burr was perfectly willing to provide such a note and wrote Clay as follows:

Frankfort, 1 Dec. 1806

Sir

I have no design, nor have I taken any measure, to promote a dissolution of the Union or a separation of any one or more States from the residue — I have neither published a line on this subject nor has any one through my agency or with my knowledge — I have no design to intermeddle with the Government or to disturb the tranquility of the United States, or of its territories or any part of them. I have neither issued nor signed nor promised a commission to any person for any purpose. I do not own a musket nor a bayonet nor any single article of military stores nor does any person for me by my authority or with my knowledge.

My views have been fully explained to and approved by several of the principal officers of Government, and I believe, are well understood by the Administration & seen by it with complacency. They are such as every man of honor & every good Citizen must approve.

Considering the high station you now fill in our national Councils I have thought these explanations proper as well to counteract the chimerical as to satisfy you that you have not espoused the cause of a man in any way unfriendly to the laws, the Government or the interests of his Country.

The Honble   respectfully
    Henry Clay   yr obt. Servt.
                 A. Burr[43]

This statement in black and white was a clear denial of any wrongdoing on the part of Burr. And it was clear evidence in the hands of Clay to prove that he represented Burr in good faith, if such proof were ever needed.

The next day Clay was back in Frankfort ready to renew his defense of the former vice president. When the court convened, Judge Innes read the charge to the new grand jury. His charge denied that the prosecuting attorney, Jo Daveiss, had the right, as he had claimed, to go out with the jury to examine witnesses or that the inquiry could extend beyond the limits of the Federal district. Daveiss then stated two material witnesses — this time John Adair and a man named Luckett — were absent and that he could not proceed without them.

Aaron Burr's counsel, Henry Clay, rose to tell the court that these delays were painful to such a busy man as the ex-vice president. Clay said it was "particularly irksome to be obliged perpetually to dance attendance" upon such a charge in that court.

Daveiss responded that under these circumstances the jury would go out in the absence of these important witnesses, "the charge not being proved, they, the defense, imagine themselves a triumph." Then Daveiss took another tack. "Who asked him to dance attendance?" he asked. "Who solicited his presence in court? His appearance here is entirely voluntary; and I will venture to say illegal."[44] Daveiss held that Burr's presence was "rather ostentatious than useful or proper" and that his counsel was there illegally until an indictment was brought.[45] Nothing came from the day's proceedings except a continuance to 10 A.M., Wednesday, and a growing public support and admiration of Burr.

When the court re-convened the next day, Daveiss handed the jury foreman a paper and announced, "I have an indictment against general John Adair." He said nothing about Burr except that the purpose of Burr's appearance was to stifle inquiry. But then he renewed his demand for the right to examine witnesses in the jury room stating that he saw "nothing novel, nothing out of the common mode of procedure, except the conduct of Mr. Clay." And he suggested to the grand jury that they call upon him to assist in examining witnesses.

Clay had had enough and interrupted the district attorney to contend that such a privilege was a novel one since it would convert the grand jury to a trial court and he hoped the court would not grant it. Further he argued that he cared not in what attitude he should be considered as standing; but he would instantly renounce Colonel Burr and his cause, did he entertain the slightest idea of his guilt. As to the charges exhibited against him by Mr. Daveiss, he said,

> You have heard of inquisitions in Europe, you have heard of the screws and tortures made use of in the dens of despotism, to extract confession; of the dark conclaves and caucuses, for the purpose of twisting some incoherent expression into evidence of guilt. Is not the project of the attorney for the United States, a similar object of terror?[46]

The former vice president then rose to announce that he was willing to submit to the right demanded by the public attorney as far as it was sanctioned by law. But he argued that never in his experience as a public attorney (in New York) did he exercise the right to examine witnesses before the grand jury. He followed this statement with a denial of the stories and rumors circulating as to his activities and he declared his innocence in unequivocal terms.

Further action was put off until Thursday when Judge Innes agreed with Clay and Burr but still granted the jury the right to call on Daveiss or accept his list of questions if they chose. The grand jury retired, but refused the aid of the district attorney. It was not long before they returned to report "no true bill," as far as Adair was concerned.[47]

Immediately, Daveiss handed the foreman another indictment, this time charging that Aaron Burr

> did with force and arms at the county of Fayette in said district, on the 25th day of November last past wilfully and unlawfully, and from evil premeditation, then and there set on foot and prepare for a military expedition against the dominions of the King of Spain, who is an European friend, at peace with the said United States, to wit against the provinces of said King, in North America contrary to the laws of the United States in such cases provided, and against the peace and dignity, thereof.

No direct charge of treason was issued. On receiving this indictment Judge Innes again held over proceedings an additional day.[48]

The trial against Aaron Burr was now reaching the critical point. When the court met at its usual hour on Friday, a buzz ran through the chamber that the grand jury had sent for other witnesses. Conjecture and expectation were alive, but were succeeded by astonishment, when editors John Wood and Joseph Street of the *Western World*, were brought in and sworn as witnesses. Their testimony was even more astonishing.

Street declared under oath that he could give no information relative to the indictment; that his knowledge had been derived wholly from hearsay; that he knew no one who could testify in the case! Then Wood admitted the charges were false, as were the unfounded slanders which had been uttered. Indeed, he stated that for some time he had been changing his mind concerning Burr, and ended with the amazing statement that he was persuaded that Burr had "no intentions which antagonized the laws and interests of the United States!"[49]

It is no wonder that when the grand jury returned its verdict at 2 P.M., it reported "not a true bill." But they went further than declaring him not guilty as charged, but cleared him of all suspicion. Daveiss' objections to this added exoneration were overruled by Judge Innes.[50]

The local inhabitants and Kentuckians elsewhere celebrated the acquittal of "a great American."

The next Monday an elaborate ball was held at Captain Taylor's in Frankfort in honor of Aaron Burr. It was attended by the political and social leaders of the city. One of these was Speaker of the Senate, Green Clay.[51] One person notable for his absence was the Speaker's distant cousin, Senator-elect Henry Clay. He was busy in Lexington preparing for his departure for Washington City. He advertised in the Lexington *Kentucky Gazette* to let his legal clients know that he would be absent from Kentucky for several months and he provided the names of other lawyers who could handle their cases if they preferred not to wait his return.[52]

As Henry Clay left Kentucky, the local newspapers also reported that a second ball had been sponsored by the friends of Daveiss in honor of the Union (and where the ladies were applauded for not "dancing attendance at the ball in honor of Burr"), that John Wood had left the *Western World* to edit a paper in Washington, that Burr had gone to Nashville where he was meeting again with Andrew Jackson, that Felix Grundy had been appointed to the judgeship formerly held by Benjamin Sebastian, and that U.S. Attorney General John Breckinridge had died at his home on December 14th.[53]

There was one other major news item that appeared in the papers shortly after Clay's departure. It was a proclamation by President Jefferson dated November 27, 1806, the day Burr requested Clay to act as his counsel for the second time. It said:

> Whereas information has been received that sundry persons, citizens of the U.S., or resident within the same, are conspiring & confederating together to begin & set on foot, provide & prepare the means for a military expedition or enterprise against the dominions of Spain, against which nation war has not been declared by the constitutional authority of the U.S.; that for this purpose they are fitting out & arming vessels in the western waters of the U.S., collecting provisions, arms military stores & other means; are deceiving & seducing honest & well meaning citizens under various pretences to engage in their criminal enterprises; are organizing, officering & arming themselves for the same, contrary to the laws in such cases made & provided, I have therefore thought fit to issue this my proclamation, warning and enjoining all faithful citizens who have been led to participate in the said unlawful enterprises without due knowledge or consideration to withdraw from the same without delay.

It also required all proper officials to be vigilant and search out and bring to punishment all persons so engaged, but Jefferson gave no names.[54]

5

APPRENTICESHIP FOR HIGH OFFICE

Lucretia Clay was pregnant and did not accompany her husband on his long and arduous journey to Washington City in December 1806. Henry Clay's route to the nation's capital took him northward through Chillicothe, Ohio. Here he ran into a whirlwind of popular emotion centered on the activities of Aaron Burr. Clay freely expressed his opinion that Burr was innocent and was the victim of persecution by Jo Daveiss. But Clay was flabbergasted at the strong, local sentiment against Burr.[1] He was even accused of being a partisan of Burr's because he had been counsel to the former vice president.

By the time Clay arrived in Chillicothe, Jefferson's proclamation of November 27th had also reached Ohio and Governor Edward Tiffin had acted upon its exhortations. The governor asked the Ohio legislature for authority to "arrest persons suspected to be carrying on an expedition unfriendly to the U.S. and to seize and detain any boats containing provisions, arms, or ammunition belonging to such persons." Already 10 boats, or bateaux, had been seized at Marietta.[2]

With the new knowledge at his disposal, Clay could reflect on the charges made by Daveiss that a flotilla would soon be afloat. Something was certainly afoot and the people of Ohio were outraged over the growing intrigues evolving on their soil and along their waterways. But still Clay had Burr's written denial that he was in any way involved with these preparations. And though the inhabitants linked Burr to these machinations, President Jefferson's proclamation revealed no accusation against Burr. Clay remained convinced that the popular sentiment, though highly emotional, was, nevertheless, misguided.

Clay believed their mistaken sentiment also extended to two Ohioans. He learned in Chillicothe that the temper of the populace had driven Harman Blennerhassett and his associate, Comfort Tyler, to flee the former's grandiose palace on his private river-island to escape arrest for complicity in the alleged conspiracy. Clay believed they had acted imprudently—

> but not in flying—for such was the state of public opinion in Chilicothe [sic] that innocence was no security—that accusation founded on mere suspicion, was in fact equivalent to conviction and condemnation—that a mania had seized the public mind in that place.[3]

Born in England of Irish parents in 1764 or 1765, Harman Blennerhassett grew up in Ireland, studied law, sold his extensive inherited property for a fortune, married well, and in 1796 sought new adventure in the American west. The following year he purchased most of a 170-acre island in the Ohio River two miles below Parkersburg, Virginia. On it he constructed an elaborate and very expensive mansion where he luxuriated for nearly a decade. In May 1805, Aaron Burr visited the island and was entertained by Mrs. Blennerhassett in her husband's absence. But later Burr opened correspondence with Harman which continued into August 1806 when Burr was Blennerhassett's house guest. In October 1806, the two journeyed to Lexington where they negotiated for the Bastrop lands on the Washita River in Louisiana Territory for future sale to American settlers. Clay knew this real estate venture to be the principal connection between the two adventurers, and in it he saw nothing illegal in contradiction to the sentiments of the Ohio populace.

Nevertheless, astonished by the feeling in Ohio, Senator-elect Henry Clay had much time on his hands during the next couple weeks to ponder the latest political intelligence he had acquired regarding Burr and the mysterious projects that were clearly afoot and afloat to consider the faint suggestion that his reputation might be tarnished by having defended Burr. Judging by the geographical location of Chillicothe, it can be assumed that Clay was making his journey to Washington entirely by land — avoiding the flatboat trip up the Ohio River to Pittsburgh. The water trip in December could be quite dangerous but smoother, a bit more comfortable but slower. The overland trip by unheated stagecoach was, on the other hand, a trial on one's constitution. A traveler could expect to cover about 40 miles in a jolting, bouncing, eight-hour pounding over uncertain, rutted mountain roads. The overnight inns lacked much to be desired in bed comfort though the meals were often quite good.

Clay's route took him through Wheeling, Virginia (now West Virginia), from where, on December 17, 1806, he wrote the *Western World* editor Street to send him recent copies of the paper. He wrote of traveling "amidst bad weather and wretched roads. Tho' I confess I have found them better than I expected. I still indulge the hope of dining on oysters at the _____ city on Xmas day."[4] He was too optimistic as he continued through Pittsburgh and across the Allegheny Mountains of Pennsylvania before descending to the coastal plain through the Catoctin Mountains of Maryland. Christmas was behind him as he approached the still new nation's capital by way of Frederick and the little village of Georgetown.

Down the road, new arrivals asking where Washington City was were told, "You're in it now." It had no appearance of a city. There were, to be sure, those two rows of houses already known as the six and seven buildings just three blocks west of the President's House. Not yet called the White House, the executive mansion sat behind "a low dead-wall in front" and had "an ordinary post-and-rail fence in the rear of it." To the west was the post office and on the right was the Department of State — both in ordinary brick houses.[5] On a hill, two miles to the southwest, sat two gray truncated structures separated by a large space filled with building materials for use in constructing the edifice to the right. Between this growing Capitol Building and the President's House, and lining the broad dirt road that was Pennsylvania Avenue, were double rows of Lombardy poplar trees planted on orders of President Jefferson.

The view westward from "Capitol Hill" during the first decade of the 19th century was best described (in her unique spelling of plants) by Margaret Bayard Smith, wife of the editor of the first newspaper in Washington, the *National Intelligencer*.

> Between the foot of the hill and the broad Potomac extended a wide plain through which the Tiber [Creek] wound its way. The romantic beauty of this little stream was not then deformed by wharves or other works of art. Its banks were shaded with tall and umbrageous forest trees of every variety, among which the superb Tulep-Poplar rose conspicuous; the magnolia, the azalia, the hawthorn, the wild-rose and many other indigenous shrubs grew beneath their shade, while violets, anemonies and a thousand other sweet wood-flowers found shelter among their roots, from the winter's frost and greeted with the earliest bloom the return of spring. The wild grapevine climbing from tree to tree hung in unpruned luxuriance among the branches of the trees and formed a fragrant and verdant canopy over the greensward, impervious to the noon-day sun. Beautiful banks of Tiber! delightful rambles! happy hours! How like a dream do ye now appear. Those trees, those shrubs, those flowers are gone. Man and his works have displaced the charms of nature. The poet, the botanist, the sportsman and the lover who once haunted those paths must seek far hence the shades in which they delight. Not only the banks of the Tiber, but those of the Potomack and Anacosta, were at this period adorned with native trees and shrubs and were distinguished by as romantic scenery as any rivers in our country. Indeed the whole plain was diversified with groves and clumps of forest trees which gave it the appearance of a fine park. Such as grew on the public grounds ought to have been preserved, but in a government such as ours, where the people are sovereign, this could not be done. *The people*, the poorer inhabitants cut down these noble and beautiful trees for fuel. In one single night seventy tulip-Poplars were *girdled*, by which process life is destroyed and afterwards cut up at their leisure by the people. Nothing afflicted Mr. Jefferson like this wanton destruction of the fine trees scattered over the city-grounds. I remember on one occasion (it was after he was President) his exclaiming, "How I wish that I possessed the power of a despot." The company at table stared

at a declaration so opposed to his disposition and principles. "Yes," he continued in reply to their inquiring looks, "I wish I was a despot that I might save the noble, beautiful trees that are daily falling sacrifices to the cupidity of their owners, or the necessity of the poor." "And have you not authority to save those on the public grounds?" asked one of the company. "No," answered Mr. J., "only an armed guard could save them. The unnecessary felling of a tree, perhaps the growth of centuries seems to me a crime little short of murder, it pains me to an unspeakable degree."[6]

Henry Clay took temporary lodging in the capital city and made his first appearance in the Senate chamber of the new Capitol on December 29, 1806. Only a few years earlier this building had been described as "elegant," but since then it had already acquired its critics. Earlier in the month Senator William Plumer of New Hampshire wrote that

> the north wing of the Capitol was finished in a most shameful manner. Dr. Thornton, who superintended it, knew little of architecture — was incapable of designing it properly — & was, deserving, of more censure for his gross inattention to the manner in which it was executed. This building now leaks so much that in every storm that falls, the water leaks down into every room. It not only renders it damp & unhealthy, but keeps the minds of members, during every storm, in a state of fear & uneasiness, least the wall, which is thick & high, should fall on them & either maim or kill them. I own I have sat for hours in my chair rather uneasy. The falling of water once obliged me to leave my seat. The last session at the door of the Representatives chamber, just after they passed, there fell near 500 lb. weight of plaisering [sic]. This week the members of that house have been so much alarmed for themselves, that they have suspended their business, & requested their Speaker to examine the wall, & take measures to render it secure.[7]

Young Senator Clay's 33 colleagues, from 17 States which comprised the United States Senate of the 9th Congress, would be recognized more for their anonymity than for their fame. Beside Plumer the most outstanding members were James Bayard of Delaware (who had figured prominently in the presidential election by the House in 1801), and the two members from Massachusetts — Timothy Pickering and John Quincy Adams (son of the second president). Clay's Kentucky colleague was Buckner Thruston. The presiding officer, and Vice President of the United States, was 67-year-old George Clinton of New York.

Following the retirement of Aaron Burr as presiding officer of the Senate, its decorum deteriorated. Clinton preserved very little order. Age impaired his mental powers, conversation and noise in the chamber prevented members from hearing the debate. The vice president seemed to lose track of the status of legislation before the body, declaring a bill had been read a third time after its first reading, putting questions without a motion, and declaring votes when no vote had been taken.[8]

Federalist William Plumer's memorandum for "Monday, Dec. 29, 1806," noted

> This day Henry Clay, the successor of John Adair for this session, was qualified & took his seat in the Senate. He is a young man — a lawyer — his stature is tall & slender. I had much conversation with him, & it afforded me much pleasure. He is intelligent, sensible & appears frank & candid. His address is good & manners easy. So much for the first impression — I hope a further & more intimate acquaintance, will not weaken, but add force, to these favorable impressions.[9]

The conversation dwelt heavily on Clay's defense of Aaron Burr, a former close friend of Plumer's. Clay went so far as to allow Plumer to read the note from Burr denying any wrong-doing or complicity in treasonable activities. Clay again expressed his opinion that Burr was unjustly accused and that if there were any evidence against him he had been unable to discover it. He said he was aware of Burr's interest in the Bastrop lands and that he had examined the title and thought it legal. Clay told Plumer he had asked Burr why he had not contradicted newspaper accounts against him but received the reply that such an attempt would be unavailing and that time would set all things right.

Plumer does not reveal any response of his to those bits of information. He had, however, recently obtained his own accounts from other sources, including from the president himself, that indicate that Clay saw only the tip of a giant iceberg of schemes and plots and manipulations. It is possible that Plumer advised the freshman senator to talk to President Jefferson.

It is not known when Henry Clay and Thomas

Jefferson had their first private meeting. But Clay wrote later that the president listened to his account of the defense of the former vice president and was shown the letter of denial. Then Jefferson produced his portfolio of evidence amassed from various reliable sources that left no doubt in the mind of the president that Burr was guilty of all for which he had been accused. He revealed to Clay letters in cipher sent by Burr to General Wilkinson and the investigative reports of a presidential emissary, John Graham, who had followed Burr in his expeditions into the southwest and had questioned many informed people along the way. Jefferson even had documents sent by Wilkinson in October 1806 warning the president of Burr's treasonable designs. (Something in the nature of a traitor turned traitor.)

In addition, Jefferson scotched the report that the administration supported Burr's activities. At the president's request Clay gave him the original denial note from Burr and Jefferson retained it in his possession with a copy of it returned to Clay in the handwriting of the president's secretary.[10]

It must have been a great shock to the young senator only days into his new exalted position in life after so recently having defended a man who the president now was convinced was guilty of treason. That Clay was now convinced of the guilt is revealed by a letter to his father-in-law (Col. Thomas Hart) a month later when he wrote,

> It seems that we have been much mistaken about Burr. When I left Kentucky, I believed him both an innocent and persecuted man. In the course of my journey to this place, still entertaining that opinion, I expressed myself without reserve, and it seems owing to the freedom of my sentiments at Chillicothe I have exposed myself to the strictures of some anonymous writer at that place.... It appears ... that Burr had formed the no less daring projects than to reduce New Orleans, subjugate Mexico, and divide the Union.[11]

This startling information, presented by no less than the President of the United States to a young man in his first days of a national career, might have shattered a lesser personality. But Henry Clay possessed the resilience of youth and a determination and boldness in excess quantities. He entered into his new status with more than enthusiasm and energy. He was quoted by Senator Plumer as saying he meant "this session should be

a tour of pleasure." And Plumer was able to confirm the fact when he wrote that Clay was

> very fond of amusements — gambles much. He told me that one evening he won at cards $1,500 — that at another evening he lost $600 — He is a great favorite with the ladies — is in all parties of pleasure — out almost every night — gambles much here — reads but little.

On the other hand, Plumer noted frequently that Clay was active in his senatorial duties, pointing out that the freshman senator "has talents — is eloquent but not nice or accurate in his distinctions — He declaims more than he reasons. He is genteel polite & a pleasant companion. A man of honor & integrity."[12]

Only three days after he took the oath of office, Senator Clay attended the President's levee on New Year's day 1807, along with "the Vice President, many senators, representatives, heads of departments, foreign ministers, ladies, gentlemen strangers, gentlemen of the vicinity — and several Indian Chiefs with their wives and children." That evening he attended a theater exhibition of Indian dancing. Among those present at this event, though not taking part in the exercise, was the Mandan Indian chief who had accompanied Lewis and Clark nearly 2,500 miles from the head of the Missouri River as they returned from their great exploration of the upper Louisiana territory.[13]

Despite these entertainments Henry Clay was not only on the floor of the Senate the following day, but he even went so far as to make a motion requesting that a committee be appointed to draft legislation to extend the United States Circuit Court system to Kentucky, Tennessee, and Ohio. Only four days a senator and he was recognized as "an easy graceful, and eloquent speaker," as he told his older colleagues that suits now pending in the District Court of Kentucky exceeded 400, that a majority of them were on the chancery side of the court, and that most related to titles of land.[14] His motion was adopted on the 5th, the committee brought out a bill on the 14th. The measure, setting up the 7th Circuit, was signed into law on February 24.

On January 12, he exhibited his earliest national concern for the improvements of the nation's internal transportation system when he introduced a resolution to appropriate land "towards the opening of the Canal proposed to be cut at the Rapids of the Ohio on the Kentucky shore." The resulting bill passed the Senate but later failed to clear the House.[15]

Henry Clay also lent his support to the construction of a toll bridge across the Potomac River within the District of Columbia (the south and west side of the river then belonging to the District rather than Virginia). In his "eloquent speech" Clay was animated and used bold and flowery language, was prompt and decisive, but did not "reason with the force and precision of Bayard," according to Plumer.

On the other hand, Senator John Quincy Adams, who was later in life to be called "Old Man Eloquent," noted in his diary his own travail at speaking on this same topic.

> I spoke an hour; but the subject had been exhausted by Mr. Giles, and I could only present some of his ideas in new lights. I should have done better to remain silent. My defects of elocution are incurable, and amidst so many better speakers, when the debates are to be reported, I never speak without mortification. The process of reasoning in my mind is too *slow* for uninterrupted articulation. My thoughts arise at first confused, and require *time* to shape into a succession of sentences. Hence the transition from thought to thought is awkward and inelegant, and expression often fails me to accomplish a sentence commenced; so that I often begin a thought with spirit and finish it with nonsense. The chain of my argument often escapes me, and when lost can seldom be retrieved. I then finish as I can, without producing half the arguments I proposed before I began to speak. These faults would be so overpowering that I should sink into perpetual silence, from mere impotence, were it not that sometimes in the order of debate, when my feelings are wound up to a high tone, elocution pours itself along with unusual rapidity, and I have passages which would not shame a good speaker: This is the only thing that makes me tolerable to others or to myself.[16]

On the Potomac River Bridge issue, Clay and his pro-bridge colleagues were only the first of nearly two centuries of politicians who met strong resistance from local citizens who opposed such construction in the area. Those who fought the bridge in 1807 feared the demise of a lucrative ferry service that crossed the river below the heights of Georgetown. They rallied their forces under a motion to postpone consideration of the legislation until the next Congress and suc-ceeded in their effort by a vote of 17 to 16, on January 29.

Plumer, in favor of the bill but irked by the legislative dickering, set down his feelings toward the Senate's action:

> I have seen men in a single day pass an important bill, the suspension of the Habeas Corpus — but after weeks debate postpone a bill for erecting a bridge over a small stream under the flimsy pretext of gaining more information.[17]

Toward the end of February, Clay impressed his Senate colleagues as he also spoke "with great ability and much eloquence" in favor of permitting the sale and grant of land to the Chesapeake and Delaware Canal Company to build a waterway through Delaware to connect the upper reaches of Chesapeake Day with the Delaware River below Philadelphia. But again, opponents succeeded in postponing action. In addition, Clay's name was tied to two resolutions to which he gave only lukewarm backing. One was to inquire into indemnifying citizens suffering from Indian depredations and the other was a Constitutional Amendment relating to judicial powers over land disputes between citizens of different States. Neither resolution survived the session.[18]

Meanwhile, at the beginning of February, the Supreme Court opened its session. Along with his legislative responsibilities, Clay was now engaged in arguments before the high tribunal since he had come to Washington with a purse of more than $3,000 in client fees. Another Kentuckian, Humphrey Marshall, was also in Washington to plead before the Court. In fact, Marshall and Clay opposed each other in a land case brought by Marshall and his wife against James Currie. The land was part of a military warrant claimed by Thomas Marshall, Humphrey's uncle and the father of Humphrey's wife and Chief Justice John Marshall now presiding over the Supreme Court that was hearing the case.

Clay argued that the language of the claim entry was uncertain and vague — "A *few* poles," "a *small* distance," "a *branch*." The court felt otherwise and awarded the judgment to Marshall.[19] But Clay moved unsuccessfully for a rehearing. Years later Marshall twitted Clay over this act charging that "this told me that Mr. Clay felt more on the subject than a necessary attachment to his client's interests.... There hardly remained, in fact, any form of friendship between us when we next met."[20]

This next meeting must have meant elsewhere than in Washington because Marshall had taken up lodging at Plumer's boarding house run by Frost and Quinn to which Clay had moved on January 12. With Henry Clay joining the six Federalist lodgers at Frost and Quinn's, was Republican Congressman Matthew Clay, brother of the old Rev. Eleazer Clay and Kentucky Senate Speaker Green Clay. The neat and clean house, with good bed and good table, was about 80 rods from the Capitol. All boarders ate together at one table in a large dining room. This room doubled as parlor where all met for conversation and to receive company — only at the consent of the lodgers. Though the house and its members were quiet and sober, the company, especially with the influx of boarders for the opening of the Court session, was intelligent and highly agreeable.[21]

Throughout Henry Clay's active "tour of pleasure" in Washington, his lucrative business before the Supreme Court, and his eloquent debates in the Senate chamber, one continuous topic intruded upon Clay's life and the concerns of his Senate associates. This was the unraveling saga of Aaron Burr and his grandiose designs. The first official moves against Burr by the Congress came on January 16, 1807, when the House of Representatives passed two resolutions requesting information from President Jefferson relating to the alleged conspiracy in the western country, and asking of him what measures he had taken to suppress it. This was a confused request by the House since much that was secret could not possibly remain so when placed in the hands of 140 talkative men and to do less than present the full evidence would render only a partial view of the episode. Plumer remarked that "curiosity ought not to be gratified at the hazard of our security."[22]

An example of Burr's response, when partial charges became public, is seen by his action on hearing of Jefferson's proclamation of November 27, 1806. In four days, Burr galloped 300 miles from Frankfort to Nashville to see General Andrew Jackson. Burr boldly showed Jackson a copy of the proclamation (in which no names were mentioned) and convinced the general that Burr and Jefferson had jointly agreed on the document except that the president had issued it before the set time. Thus Jackson, though kept in line with Burr's plans, was also being duped.[23]

Jefferson answered the call of the House on January 22 with a message detailing his evidence of the Burr affair. The president noted that his information was voluminous but not "under sanction of an oath, so as to constitute formal and legal evidence." Rumors mixed with facts restricted his exposure of names, "except that of the principal actor, whose guilt is placed beyond question." Jefferson dated his earliest intimations of the unlawful designs by "the prime mover, Aaron Burr," from September 1806 — this in contradiction to the numerous letters from Joseph Hamilton Daveiss earlier in the year and the muckraking of the *Western World* during the summer. As to Jefferson's open charge of guilt by Burr, ex–President John Adams wrote that he suspected his successor "had been too hasty in his Message in which he had denounced (Burr) by name and pronounced him guilty. But if his guilt is as clear as the Noon day Sun, the first Magistrate ought not to have pronounced it so before a Jury had tryed him."[24]

Jefferson remained pretty much in the dark throughout the fall months of 1806 so far as good solid information was concerned. Then on November 25th, a Lt. Col. Thomas A. Smith visited the president and extracted two letters that had been concealed between the soles of Smith's slippers. The letters, written from Louisiana Territory on October 20 and 21, 1806, by Gen. James Wilkinson, provided Jefferson with the substance on which to base his proclamation that was issued two days later. Two months later, in his January message to Congress, Jefferson described the design as follows:

> It appeared that he (Burr) contemplated two distinct objects, which might be carried on either jointly or separately, and either the one or the other first, as circumstances should direct. One of these was the severance of the Union of these States by the Alleghany mountains; the other, an attack on Mexico. A third object was provided, merely ostensible, to wit: the settlement of a pretended purchase of a tract of country on the Washita, claimed by a Baron Bastrop. This was to serve as the pretext for all his preparations, an allurement for such followers as really wished to acquire settlements in that country, and a cover under which to retreat in the event of a final discomfiture of both branches of his real design.

Continuing in his January message, Jefferson referred to the prompt response of Ohio's Governor Tiffin in seizing boats, to the premature attempts (by Daveiss) to bring Burr to justice in Kentucky; and to the subsequent support by authorities throughout the southwest as the proclamation reached their hands. The president also noted that the United States remained at peace with other powers with whom Burr meant to make war, and that indeed two of his aides were already in custody and being transported eastward for trial.[25]

Jefferson's reference to two men in custody carried the affair back to July 1806 when Burr, in Philadelphia, wrote two letters to Wilkinson in New Orleans. The first, dated July 25th, was a cover letter for the second written mostly in cipher four days later. Burr and Wilkinson, old friends since the Revolution, had been using their concocted cipher for nearly a decade. These two letters were carried to Wilkinson by a man named Samuel Swartwout (sometimes spelled Swartout), along with a third written on the 24th by Gen. Jonathan Dayton (a veteran of the Revolution, youngest signer of the Constitution, Speaker of the U.S. House of Representatives for two Congresses, a senator from New Jersey, and the man for whom Dayton, Ohio, was named). In the ciphered letter, Burr, a very cautious person in conversation and even more so in written communication, detailed the tactics of his expeditionary plans and included the statement. "Wilkinson shall be second to Burr only: Wilkinson shall dictate the rank and promotion of his officers. Burr will proceed westward 1st August, never to return: with him go his daughter; the husband will follow in October, with a corps of worthies."[26]

Dayton, in his letter, also partially in the same cipher, told Wilkinson,

> It is now well ascertained that you are to be displaced in next session. Jefferson will affect to yield reluctantly, to the public sentiment, but yield he will; prepare yourself therefore for it: you know the rest.
>
> You are not a man to despair, or even despond, especially when such prospects offer in another quarter. Are you ready? Are your numerous associates ready? Wealth and Glory, Louisiana and Mexico.[27]

Already Wilkinson had been mysteriously mixed up in the old Spanish Conspiracy of the

1780s. Already it was known that he had taken money from Spain (though denying that it was a pension, he said it was payment for business ventures). And now Aaron Burr and General Dayton were putting on paper information that clearly suggested that Wilkinson had been deeply associated with them in their current enterprise.

It took Swartwout from late July 1806 to October 8 to find Wilkinson in the southwest. Twelve days later Wilkinson was confiding what he knew in the October letters to the President of the United States. About two weeks later Wilkinson received another communication from Dayton, this time delivered by Dr. Erick Bollman, a man who had been involved in an aborted attempt to free the Marquis de Lafayette from the Olmutz prison in Austria during the period of the French Revolution.

Shortly after Wilkinson read this last letter, he received a communication, from a James L. Donaldson written October 30 from Natchez, to the effect that the whole southwest was "ready to explode — that Kentucky, Ohio, Tennessee, Orleans [then the name for the lower part of Louisiana], and Indiana are combined, to declare themselves independent on the 15th of November." Wilkinson conferred with his second in command, and on the 12th of November sent another letter to President Jefferson by Isaac Briggs (a surveyor sent to that region by Jefferson to map a road from Washington to New Orleans). The letter contained alarming suggestions of a great force descending on New Orleans. Before Briggs' departure, Wilkinson showed him the correspondence from Burr and Dayton. After an arduous journey, in the midst of a severe winter, of more than 1,200 miles, 600 of it through wilderness, Briggs arrived in Washington on New Year's Day 1807 and presented his dispatches to Jefferson the next day. On opening them the president "exclaimed with earnestness, 'is Wilkinson sound in this business?'" Briggs "replied very promptly, 'there is not the smallest doubt of it.'"[28]

The reports from Wilkinson were the evidence Jefferson showed Senator Clay to convince him of Burr's "treason." Jefferson was not overly worried about Burr's expedition by this time, believing the response to his proclamation had cut the threat to the bone.

But what about Wilkinson? He was now

maneuvering in support of the Government and against Burr's expedition. To every authority within reach he warned of thousands of armed men prepared to descend on New Orleans against his meager forces. Among these alerts were requests to the territorial governor, William C. C. Claiborne, to place the area under martial law — that is, under Wilkinson's control. Claiborne refused and his legislative counsel also refused Wilkinson's request for a suspension of the habeas corpus. This did not deter Wilkinson. He acted as if his requests had been granted and, on December 12 and 14, Wilkinson had Swartwout and Bollman and others arrested. Wilkinson personally confiscated Swartwout's watch and had him placed in chains. And before writs of habeas corpus could be issued, the general had both men on board a ship bound for Washington. These were the two men mentioned by Jefferson in his January message as being in custody and en route eastward.

By a strange coincidence, Swartwout and Bollman were brought into Washington on the same day that the Congress received Jefferson's message detailing the Burr affair. The message and the arrival of these two men spurred Senator William Branch Giles of Virginia to introduce a bill calling for the national legislature to suspend the privilege of the writ of habeas corpus for three months.

Henry Clay objected to the suspension bill believing that the occasion was not serious enough to warrant it. He probably had the same assurance that Jefferson had that current steps to dissolve the threat were sufficient — though on this, Clay and Plumer disagreed. But Clay was in a delicate position. Having been counselor for Burr twice in the Kentucky indictments, he could easily be suspected of continuing his support for this man if he should vote against suspension of the habeas corpus. To prove that he did not now countenance Burr's acts, he voted for suspension. Only three or four senators voted against the bill.[29] Its quick passage that same day gave rise to Plumer's complaint of the length of debate during the Potomac Bridge bill.

Clay's deeper feelings toward suspension were upheld three days later, however, when the House of Representatives refused to concur with the Senate. Over the weekend, between the action by the two Houses, Dr. Bollman actually received an au-

dience with President Jefferson. Yet by the end of the week the Federal District Court ordered both Bollman and Swartwout to jail, without bail, upon a warrant for high treason.[30]

Around the middle of February, Clay received a letter from his senatorial predecessor, John Adair (who had also been accused by Jo Daveiss during the second Burr trial in December). Adair wrote Clay that he had received a communication from Wilkinson during the autumn of 1806 which in substance said:

> Dear Adair, the time is now come to subvert the Spanish government — That 5000 light troops would conquer Mexico — That your military talents are requisite — That unless you fear to join a Spanish intriguer (meaning Wilkinson) come immediately — That without your aid I can do nothing.

Adair told Clay that he responded to Wilkinson telling him that he

> was too old for military service — That he was encumbered with a family — That the United States had not declared war against Spain — That he did not believe they would — and That he could not violate the laws of his country by levying war against a power in amity with it.

Adair went on to tell Clay that following the grand jury hearing in Frankfort, he had gone south to New Orleans on personal and private business accompanied by one servant. He arrived on January 14. That very evening, while at dinner, a Colonel Kingsbury, with 100 soldiers, entered Adair's lodgings with an order from Wilkinson for his arrest. He was not permitted to finish his meal or take some medicine with him. They would not even permit him to give directions respecting his horses, which had cost him $700 in Kentucky, or allow him to take all his clothing with him. Adair was hurried on board a boat, carried down a river, held in miserable conditions for six days, put on a second boat and eventually shipped on the schooner *Thatcher* to Baltimore where he arrived, under a military guard, on February 17.

During the voyage, he suffered much from sciatica, from the inclemency of weather, want of accommodations and from seasickness. He was only able to write to Clay using paper, pen and ink obtained secretly from a stranger. But in Baltimore the stranger also obtained a writ of habeas corpus for Adair and the court there freed him the day after his arrival in Maryland. Three days later the Supreme Court also freed Bollman and Swartwout. And Wilkinson was beginning to look more guilty than Burr in the whole affair. And Plumer had second thoughts on his vote to suspend the habeas corpus.[31]

But Burr was not out of it. That same week, information came to Washington that Burr had surrendered himself, on January 18, to the highest court of law in the Mississippi territory for trial. Even so, this arrest was not to hold firm as still another grand jury found

Burr has not been guilty of any crime or misdemeanor against the laws of the United States, or of this Territory, or given any just occasion for alarm or inquietude to the good people of this Territory.[32]

But this clean bill of health was not enough. Burr's great scheme was already falling apart.

The only other matter involving Clay with the Burr affair during this session of Congress was the connection of Kentucky Judge Harry Innes to the old Spanish conspiracy and the new Burr conspiracy. Innes' name was currently being dragged into the whirlwind of controversy and even in Washington there were attempts to have him turned out of office. Innes was condemned in Congress for failure to advise the government of the approaches made to him by Spanish agents years before, particularly in the light of facts which came out in the Kentucky legislature's investigation of Judge Sebastian along with his action in the two Burr indictments during the fall of 1806. There were threats of impeachment. Nevertheless, Clay wrote the judge on January 16, 1807,

You have only to bear with fortitude the present crisis, that it will pass off without affecting your official situation, and that ultimately the momentary tarnish which your character is supposed by some to have received, will be obliterated.[33]

As the short Congressional session neared adjournment, President Jefferson moved to take some of the authority away from Gen. James Wilkinson when he nominated explorer Meriwether Lewis to be governor of the Territory of Louisiana, leaving Wilkinson *only* as the commander of the army. Also nominated at this same time, as a result of Clay's bill to extend the court system, was a Kentucky friend of Clay's, Thomas

Todd, to be a justice of the U.S. Supreme Court. Todd, a brother-in-law of Judge Innes, had become the chief justice of Kentucky only in December 1806.

Despite all these activities Clay curiously wrote to a friend in mid–February,

The session of Congress has not been so interesting as I had anticipated. No questions in relation to our foreign intercourse, involving much discussion, have been agitated; every thing depends upon the result of pending negotiations, and this will not be known, it is probable, until the session expires.[34]

The negotiations referred to by Clay were being conducted by James Monroe and William Pinkney in London. Since the renewal of warfare in 1803 between Great Britain and France, both countries had attempted to prevent other foreign nations from carrying on ocean commerce with their enemy. Among other unfriendly acts, Britain had recently been engaged in stopping American vessels and seizing seamen whom they claimed were deserters from the British Navy. Monroe and Pinkney were trying to get Great Britain to abandon this tactic and also restore U.S. trade rights in the West Indies on the basis of a 50-year-old "broken voyage" principle. As predicted by Clay, the treaty that evolved did not reach the Senate before it adjourned. However, it actually reached Jefferson a day or so before the end of the session but since it lacked the stipulations he sought, he had no intention of ever submitting it to the Senate for approval.

In addition to the problems with Great Britain, Napoleon, in reprisal to Britain's declared blockage of European ports, issued his own blockade declaration of British ports to be known as the Berlin Decree. In the same letter in which Clay regretted lack of debate on foreign affairs, he stated, with great clairvoyance, "It is said that our minister at Paris has written on to Government that our commerce is not affected by it (the Berlin Decree); I apprehend. however, that it will subject it to much embarrassment."

On the night of March 3, 1807, the 9th Congress became history. Henry Clay, still only 29 years old, could be pleased with his effort in the Senate despite his disappointment in the debate. He could also give a sigh of relief that his reputation had remained untarnished despite his connection with Aaron Burr before coming to Washington. He was yet to be touched once more in 1807 by the Burr affair — which was also to grow to a climax that still shrouds his guilt or innocence in mystery — and by the international issue that was to become even more important to both Clay and the nation.

6

BURR TRIAL/BRITISH IMPRESSMENT

Again Henry Clay had before him that long, difficult, westward journey by stagecoach over the Appalachian Mountains. And again he had time to reflect on his position and goals in life. He could attempt to digest the meat of four very astonishing months just behind him. Twice he had victoriously, but regretfully, defended a former vice president charged with treason, and had for more than two months, unconstitutionally, but brilliantly, served as a United States senator. He had tasted fame and satisfaction which could make him restless in the peaceful hills of Kentucky. How much time he had to reflect on these matters is uncertain because he went briefly to Philadelphia on legal business, and was then accompanied on his return to Lexington by two young men, one expecting to practice law in Kentucky, and the other planning to enter the Transylvania University law school as one of Clay's students.[1]

Clay could regret his circuitous route home since his arrival in Lexington was not until Friday, April 17, 1807. Two days earlier, and three days after his 30th birthday, his fifth child, Ann Brown Clay, was born. He now had two boys and two girls living. The family was growing and his plans for the new home, to be called Ashland, were also growing. The meadows of his new estate were surveyed during the summer.[2]

Already Clay's interests had touched on another field — horses. During the early days of 1807, he became a partner in the ownership of an outstanding race horse named Buzzard. The great English thoroughbred won 34 races and lost only two during a seven-year racing period in the 1790s. Buzzard, purchased for $5,000, was brought to America sometime in 1804 or 1805. An ad, in- serted in the local Kentucky papers by the owners in early 1807 and again in 1808, showed well over 100 different colts sired by Buzzard as having won nearly 400 prizes in England alone from 1799 to 1806. Now the owners were offering the stud of Buzzard for $40 per season.[3]

Aside from his new "farming" activities, his teaching, and his vigorous legal exertions, Henry Clay sought and won re-election in August 1807 to his old seat in the Kentucky House of Representatives for the next term beginning in December. During the summer months, Clay was, for the most part, an uncommonly interested newspaper-reading spectator of the climax of one major national drama and of the first violent shock of another event that would slowly build to a greater national crisis.

With his vindication by the Mississippi court in early February, Aaron Burr was aware of possible attempts at assassination or capture by agents of Wilkinson, and he endeavored to make his escape across the wilderness of lower Mississippi and Alabama and into Spanish Florida and thence somehow to France. Accompanied by an aide, Major Chester Ashley, Burr left the rest of his expedition, nearly opposite Bayou Pierre (Mississippi Territory), to fend for themselves and make their own way independently to settle the Bastrop lands in the Orleans Territory. Late on February 18, while passing through Washington County, Alabama, Burr and Ashley, disguised as river boatmen, inquired of Nicholas Perkins, county registrar, as to the directions to a Colonel Hinson's home. After their departure, and his suspicions aroused by the fine boots under the disguise, Perkins reported the incident to a local sheriff and the two found Burr and Ashley at the Hinson residence. Leaving the sheriff with the two trav- elers, Perkins rode off to nearby Fort Stoddert seeking military aid. On the way back to Hin- son's, Perkins, with Lieutenant Edmund Gaines and four soldiers, met Burr, Ashley, and the sheriff (who, like Clay and other prominent men, had been seduced by Burr's flattery to believe him in- nocent and was even now aiding him in reaching his destination). On demand, Burr reluctantly ad- mitted his identity to Gaines and was placed under U.S. government military arrest and taken to Fort Stoddert where he was held until March 6. Ashley was allowed to go free.

Perkins, anxious for the $2,000 reward offered for Burr, went so far as to volunteer to escort his captive all the way to Washington, D.C., for trial. As Henry Clay was heading home from his first senatorial experience, Aaron Burr, as prisoner of Nicholas Perkins and under guard of six other civilians and two soldiers, started the long sojourn to the nation's capital. En route across unsettled lands, over unbridged rivers, through Indian country, and under cold rainy weather, they con- tinued at a fatiguing rate on horseback at 40 miles a day and slept upon the bare ground at night. While passing through South Carolina, home state of his son-in-law, Colonel Joseph Alston (fu- ture governor of the state), Burr made one attempt to escape his military guard. Jumping off his horse, though surrounded by eight other riders, Burr shouted to a group of men at Chester Court House, "I am Aaron Burr, under military arrest, and claim the protection of the civil au- thorities!" But Perkins and the soldiers swiftly re- stored the diminutive Burr to his saddle and spir- ited him away before aid could be rendered. The incident provoked Perkins to secure a carriage to transport his prisoner the remainder of the trip. In Virginia, the guard received orders to carry Burr to Richmond where trial would be held. They arrived on the evening of March 26, and Burr was lodged at the Eagle Tavern. Eventually, the persistent Perkins was awarded $3,331 for de- livery of his prominent prize.[4]

The judicial proceedings would hold the na- tion's attention for more than six months. Except for one more legal action, Clay was no longer di- rectly involved with the Burr episode as he had been during the Kentucky indictments and the senate legislation. But the enthralling trial was to be much more than a question of Aaron Burr's guilt or innocence on the charges of treason against the United States and waging war on Spain. It was a balance of power between the Re- publican President of the United States and chief accuser, Thomas Jefferson; the Federalist Chief Justice of the United States and sitting judge on the case, John Marshall; and the former brilliant Vice President of the United States and accused, Aaron Burr. Each served at the pinnacle of a branch of government. Burr himself had been a Republican candidate for high office, and, with the help of the Federalists, he almost won the presidency. Yet he had slain a distinguished Fed- eralist, Alexander Hamilton, in a duel. And Burr was first accused of treason by other Kentucky Federalists who were related by blood and mar- riage to the Judge who now presided over his fate. But it was the Republicans who brought him to bay.

And why to Virginia? Earlier in the year, during the proceedings freeing Erick Bollman and Samuel Swartwout, Chief Justice Marshall ob- served that in cases of treason,

> If a body of men are actually assembled for the purpose of effecting by force a treasonable pur- pose; all those who perform any part, however minute, or however remote from the scene of the action, and who are actually leagued in the general conspiracy, are to be considered as traitors. But there must be an actual assembling of men for the treasonable purpose, to constitute a levying of war.[5]

This was to conform to the Constitutional defi- nition of treason.

On the basis of this opinion, Jefferson and his legal advisors determined that the most obvious point of overt action in the conspiracy was Har- man Blennerhassett's island in the Ohio River where militia had attacked the gathering expedi- tion. The island was within the legal boundaries of Virginia (now West Virginia) and thus that state and its capital city were chosen as the site of the trial. But to complicate matters, this judicial jurisdiction was under Chief Justice Marshall. And since in those days the U.S. Supreme Court justices heard cases in the circuit, Marshall was to be the presiding judge.

One of America's outstanding legal minds him- self, Burr was supported in defense by six distinguished Virginia lawyers including Edmond Randolph (former attorney general and secretary of state under Washington, and governor of Virginia); John Wickham (a talent to rank with Burr); and Luther Martin ("Bulldog of the Federalists" who, with reciprocity, hated Jefferson). For the prosecution there were only two lightweight Virginia lawyers supporting the rising young orator, William Wirt.

On April 1st, at the end of preliminary trial hearings, Marshall ruled that insufficient evidence was brought forth by the prosecution to warrant a charge of high treason and set bail of $10,000 on the misdemeanor count of waging war on Spain. Bail was paid the same day and Burr was again free until May 22 when the circuit court was to reconvene. Jefferson was in a rage, now aimed more at Marshall than at Burr. The result was that Federal agents swarmed over the country seeking out evidence and witnesses that could be brought to the next trial to condemn Burr and block Marshall's "political rulings," which, in Jefferson's view, left the judiciary with no restraining check or balance. Jefferson's earlier open declaration that Burr was guilty had placed the president's reputation on trial as well as Burr's life.

The trial was resumed on the appointed date in a frenzied Richmond overflowing with curious and excited humanity. The first business was the selection of a grand jury. Burr himself objected to two jurymen but was satisfied with Marshall's selection of John Randolph of Roanoke, Virginia, as foreman. Randolph, a caustic-tongued congressman, was leader of the anti–Jeffersonian Republicans (or Quids). He was convinced of Burr's guilt but believed greater guilt was on the hands of the slippery Wilkinson, who was scheduled to be principal government witness against Burr. The final grand jury tally was 14 Republicans and only two Federalists. For days afterward, lawyers for both sides argued minor legal points before the grand jury, vying for an advantage. They addressed themselves to the issues, to each other, to the jury, to Chief Justice Marshall, to the spectators, to President Jefferson in Washington, and to the world at large through members of the press — such as Washington Irving.

By early June, the proceedings had reached an impasse while all awaited the arrival of the chief witness, James Wilkinson, now grown to mammoth prestige because of his mainspring position in this fantastic episode. While they waited, another witness for the prosecution arrived and instead of deriding Burr, this man was seen in crowds defending Burr as innocent and, in fact, excoriated President Jefferson and denounced Wilkinson. The man was Andrew Jackson. Washington Irving was to write at this point that

> we are now enjoying a kind of suspension of hostilities; the grand jury having been dismissed the day before yesterday for five or six days, that they might go home, see their wives, get their clothes washed, and flog their negroes.[6]

But throughout this interval, Burr remained calm and constantly planning his defense. And what a plan! He demanded that Jefferson himself be subpoenaed to present documents of evidence against him. This threw the court into confusion but eventually the president did supply certain papers only.

On June 13, portly General James Wilkinson arrived on the scene in full military uniform and took the stand two days later in the presence of Burr. The atmosphere was electric, but the only bolt of lightning was a shift in emphasis by Burr's counsel to bring charges against Wilkinson. For four days the grand jury heard Wilkinson's story, and tore it apart. Finally, the grand jury decided 9 to 7 against indicting Wilkinson, to the disappointment of foreman Randolph (a descendant of Pocahontas) who had hoped to scalp the general and at the same time undermine Jefferson's attack and prestige.

Throughout this intense period, the popular opinion was swaying heavily in favor of Burr. He was exalted in his journeys to and from court, though a prisoner, and was even guest of honor at several parties. At one stage during the proceedings, Samuel Swartwout, in town as a witness, publicly humiliated Wilkinson, and challenged him to a duel.

When Wilkinson refused to be drawn into a duel, Swartwout sent a letter to the *Virginia Gazette* castigating the general saying, "I could not have supposed that you would have completed the catalogue of your crimes by adding to the guilt of *treachery, forgery,* and *perjury,* the accomplishment of cowardice."[7] Wilkinson, expecting to be a hero, had become the lowest of creatures.

Yet there was to be another thunderbolt. On June 24, the grand jury returned to the courtroom and Randolph made its pronouncement. The grand jury brought in indictments against Burr and Harman Blennerhassett! Despite Chief Justice Marshall's ruling of insufficient evidence they were charged with treason against the United States and with a misdemeanor in preparing an expedition against Spain. So after four attempts over eight months an indictment was at last brought against Burr. The court trial was set for August 3. In the meantime, Blennerhassett had to be found and brought to Richmond. There also followed indictments against four other alleged conspirators, including Jonathan Dayton.

On the breakup of Burr's expedition on the Mississippi, Blennerhassett determined to return to his island mansion. He had since learned that following his hasty departure, in December 1806, the house and grounds had been the scene of a raid, with ruthless devastation resulting. Though anxious to reach home, he made slow progress northward, spending some time in Nashville, and eventually reached Lexington, Kentucky, on July 14.

In April, a Mr. Lewis Sanders had asked Henry Clay in Lexington for legal advice on how to obtain repayment for $10,000 in bills drawn by Burr in New York and endorsed by Blennerhassett. Clay provided some legal suggestions. Then, when Blennerhassett appeared in Lexington, Sanders had him arrested. Once in custody, that same day a deputy United States marshal arrived with a warrant to transport Blennerhassett to Richmond to stand trial on the treason charge. The following day, as Blennerhassett's counsel, Clay made a plea to the court that Blennerhassett be sent on to Richmond "in a manner as delicate as the nature of his situation would permit." Meanwhile, Clay helped Blennerhassett work out a suitable arrangement for the sale of his devastated island and turn over to Sanders the money due him. On July 20, under guard, Blennerhassett set out for Richmond to join Burr on trial.[8] This would end Clay's direct contact with the Burr conspiracy but certainly not his interest. There were still to be political and personal repercussions on Clay from the part he had played in this fantastic episode in American history.

The trial resumed on August 3, but selecting a jury of un-opinionated men became a colossal task and wasn't completed until August 17. Opening the case, the defense immediately argued that there was no case unless an overt act of war could be proved. When the prosecution attempted to introduce other evidence, three days later, the defense challenged their right to proceed without proving an overt act of war had taken place. For nine days more, the motion to exclude further testimony was debated and the court adjourned. On August 31, Chief Justice Marshall ruled no overt act had been proved. The next day the prosecution let the case go to the jury. That same day, they found Burr "not guilty" of treason. The misdemeanor charge was then taken up and argued until the end of October when Burr and Blennerhassett were cleared of it as well.[9]

Still the government did not give up. The administration arranged to have the two men stand trial again in Ohio on a misdemeanor charge. U.S. Attorney General Caesar Rodney, successor to John Breckinridge, asked Henry Clay to serve as the counsel for the United States against Burr and his associates. Clay replied to the request on December 5, 1807, saying,

> I am under no engagement for any of the parties, nor will I in any event appear for Col. Burr. Having deceived me last winter, when I really believed him both innocent and persecuted by Mr. Daveiss, he shall not deceive me again, now that I believe him guilty and meriting punishment. But it will not be in my power to appear at Chillicothe for the government. The Court there sits just at the moment when our Legislature (of which I am a member) and our Supreme State Court (the most crowded with business of any in the Country) will be in Session; and I could not think of disappointing those who have confided their business to me, by contracting new duties.
>   Although I have no hesitation as it respects Burr about appearing against him, I have some doubt whether I should not by doing so subject myself to the imputation of violating professional honor. Having once appeared for him, it will be supposed, that he imparted to me his projects etc. The fact is however otherwise, but this may not be known to or thought of by the world. Would it not be then said that by appearing for him I confidentially obtained a knowledge of his plans, means of execution, preparations etc.; and that, availing myself of this information, I afterwards pressed the prosecution agt. him with more effect than I could have done?[10]

This trial never convened.

With the Burr episode pretty much a closed case in American legal circles, there remained some interest in the subsequent fate of some of the actors in this gigantic drama. Jo Daveiss, in early 1807, was removed by President Jefferson from the office of Kentucky's Federal district attorney; he wrote a pamphlet expressing his anger at Jefferson's conduct in the Burr affair, and later died in the Battle of Tippecanoe. Daveiss' relative, Humphrey Marshall, and the grand jury foreman of the Richmond trial, John Randolph of Roanoke, were both to become bitter legislative and personal foes of Henry Clay. Yet to come was a great legal career for lawyer William Wirt, a great literary career for reporter Washington Irving, a great judicial career for judge John Marshall, and a great military and political career for unused witness Andrew Jackson. General Wilkinson was to be investigated by Congress, yet remained in the army to serve in the War of 1812. Blennerhassett was to die in poverty, leaving his widow to appeal to Henry Clay for financial help in her dying days.

Burr's life continued to be a bizarre series of adventures. In 1808, he sailed to England where he failed in an attempt to enlist British government aid in reviving his dreams of a Mexican conquest. He later eked out an existence in France where he lived on the edge of poverty and ran through a succession of amours, which he evaluated in a diary. He failed to win a parlay with Napoleon, and eventually returned to the United States incognito in 1812. In New York, he was befriended and sheltered by his old messenger, Samuel Swartwout. When it appeared safe, Burr opened a law office which prospered, but did so as he suffered a dual personal tragedy. His beloved 11-year-old grandson died in South Carolina. Then his adored daughter, Theodosia, dying of cancer, sailed from Charleston to spend her last days with her father in New York. But the ship went down in an Atlantic storm. One day in New York, not long after the end of the War of 1812, Burr met his former counsel and extended his hand in greeting. Henry Clay, recognizing the owner of the proffered hand, refused it firmly, and responded coldly to the former vice president's conversation.[11] Burr remarried in 1833 and was divorced three years later on the day he died.[12]

In a footnote to history that had long-range consequences, one of the spectators at the Richmond trial of Aaron Burr was less concerned and affected by its outcome than he was over the other major national event of 1807. Later in June, this young lawyer from the Richmond area heard of a naval action off the Virginia capes. It stirred his hatred of the British and resulted in the overthrow of his legal career and his enlistment in the U.S. Army where he made a career fighting in the War of 1812, led that army to victory in the Mexican War, and was the chief army officer at the start of the Civil War. His name was Winfield Scott.[13]

On the morning of June 22, two days before the Richmond grand jury brought its indictments against Burr and Blennerhassett, the American frigate *Chesapeake*, under command of Commodore James Barron, sailed out of Hampton Roads bound for the Mediterranean to relieve the frigate *Constitution*. The day before, the British frigate *Leopard* had arrived in the area with an admiral's order to seize several British deserters known to have enlisted on the *Chesapeake*. Though three of the deserters were American citizens impressed earlier by the British, there was one true British deserter on the crew of the *Chesapeake*. As the American ship proceeded on out into the open Atlantic, it was followed by the *Leopard*. Around 3:30 in the afternoon, some eight to ten miles southeast of Cape Henry, the British man-of-war hailed the *Chesapeake* and announced she had dispatches for Barron. A British officer was rowed to the American ship and gave Barron a note accompanying the British admiral's order to surrender deserters from specific British ships. The British ship *Melampus*, from which the three Americans had deserted, was not on this list and Barron replied that he could not fulfill the wishes of the *Leopard*'s Captain Salisbury Pryce Humphreys.

Forty five minutes later the British messenger was called back to his ship. As he departed, Barron ordered his crew to prepare his ship for action. This was not easy since the *Chesapeake*, already overdue in relieving the *Constitution*, had put to sea with her gun decks in some disorder and would require at least a half hour to get ready. Five minutes after the British officer left the *Chesapeake* and returned to the *Leopard*, Captain Humphreys brought his ship within 150–200 feet of the American ship and called out, "Commodore Barron, you must be aware of the necessity I am under of complying with the orders of my commander-in-chief." Twice Barron answered that he could not hear or understand Humphreys. The *Leopard* responded by firing a shot across the *Chesapeake's* bow followed by a second shot one minute later. Two minutes after that, at 4:30, the *Leopard* poured a whole broadside of solid shot and canister into the *Chesapeake*. The American ship was battered by two more devastating broadsides before a single gun could be brought into action. At 4:45, as Barron struck his colors, one American gun fired. Six Americans were killed and 23, including Barron, were wounded.

Following this action, British officers again boarded the *Chesapeake*, mustered its crew, and "recaptured" the three Americans who had served on the *Melampus*. The British did not take 12–15 other seamen pointed out as English deserters but, after a lengthy search of the ship, dragged out of a coal-hole the one true British deserter — the only impressment that gave any "legality" to the *Leopard's* action. A sentence of 500 lashes for each of the American seamen was never carried out, but a sentence of death for the British deserter was on August 31, when he was hung from a yardarm of a British vessel. When boarded, Commodore Barron attempted to surrender his ship as a prize, but was refused. His only recourse was to limp back to port in humiliation and disgrace. Barron was later to stand court martial. He was cleared in all respects except in failing to prepare for action instantly on reading the admiral's order. As a consequence of this "mistake" the court suspended him from the service for five years. On this court was Captain Stephen Decatur.[14] Barron and Decatur would face each other again in more vital circumstances and both would have future contact with Henry Clay.

Public response to the affront to the American flag was enormous. The passion roused by this piratical act was more national than any previous American emotionalism. President Jefferson later, expressing his view at the time of the attack said, "The affair of the *Chesapeake* put war into my hand. I had only to open it and let havoc loose."[15] The cry for war that now spread across the nation had turned to a new antagonist. Since the purchase of Louisiana, the American government

had been claiming West Florida from Spain and also looked to the Rio Bravo (or Rio Grande) as the western boundary of Louisiana. The threat of war against Spain — not Britain — had filled the air and was aggravated by the Burr episode. Yet Jefferson had worked diligently to maintain the peace knowing that war with Spain could mean war also with Napoleon's France. But now the war between Britain and France had reached the point where neutrals were being attacked and American blood was spilt. This, of course, was not the first impressment of seamen by the British, but it was the most violent and, indeed, involved firing on an American ship in peacetime.

Throughout the decade of on-and-off war between the two great European powers, British seamen frequently deserted from the harsh treatment aboard His Majesty's ships and often enlisted in the more pleasant seafaring life under American sails. But the British did not recognize U.S. naturalization of British seamen and would not tolerate their enlistment into U.S. merchant and naval ships. Meanwhile, neutrals, including the United States, prospered in trade between European countries and their American colonies. Until 1805 United States merchant vessels maintained a lucrative commerce in transporting supplies to France from their Caribbean island colonies. The British tolerated this shipping as long as the voyage was broken by a stop at an American port, ostensibly sending the cargo through U.S. customs. But in the summer of 1805 the British Admiralty court, in the Essex case, ruled that the broken voyage concept was illegal and that neutral cargoes bound for enemy ports could be seized.

In 1806, after increased impressments and searches by British ships, Congress, at Jefferson's request, passed a non-importation act barring imports of specific British goods into the United States. Most of these were items that America could provide for herself and were frequently products supplied by Henry Clay's part of the country. Yet the act failed to correct the situation and was shortly suspended, but not discarded. Nor did the treaty negotiated in 1806–07, by William Pinkney and James Monroe in London, solve the problem of impressment. This was the treaty Jefferson refused to submit to the

Senate in the closing days of Clay's brief term. Monroe and Pickney had little chance of negotiating a treaty that would be satisfactory to the United States because Britain saw no reason to give up concessions. They did not fear war with their former colony which had practically no standing army; its meager navy was no match for "the mistress of the sea," and the country was politically and emotionally divided by the Burr escapade. There matters stood at the time of the *Chesapeake* incident. Jefferson, still determined to keep the United States at peace, subdued the clamor for war by requesting a British explanation and apology for her acts. He gained time, through the slow transit of seagoing communications and the absence of the legislative process of Congress, then in adjournment, for any full scale American response.

As the theatrics of the Burr affair and the tension of the international crisis receded, Henry Clay resumed his old seat in the Kentucky House. He came to the session with much the same enthusiasm for pleasurable evenings in mirthful assemblies as he had while a member of the U.S. Senate.

A story related several years after his death described Clay as

> a rather wildish fellow in those days, and engaged in such freaks as the following: One night, after the bottle had circulated until a late hour, [Clay] announced his intention of finishing off the entertainment by a grand Terpsichorean performance on the table, which he accordingly did, executing a *pas seul* from head to foot on the dining table, sixty-feet in length, amidst the loud applause of his companions, and to the crashing accompaniment of shivered glass and china: for which expensive music he next morning paid, without demur, a bill of $120!

Also, during these legislative sessions, Clay appeared in several cases before the Kentucky Supreme Court. An account of his physical and mental endurance was related by the same witness who wrote of his dinner-dance. The two shared a room. Clay's companion retired early on the morning of the trial, and

> instead of finding the orator in bed, or up preparing himself for the coming struggle, found him just dismissing a large company with whom the whole night had been spent in gaiety. To his remonstrances, Clay replied only by begging him to

bring a basin of cold water and a cup of coffee; and after drinking the latter, flung himself on a sofa to snatch an hour's rest before the ringing of the court bell, requesting to be roused at that time. Clay appeared in court fresh and unjaded, and flung himself into the complicated case with a power of thought, clearness of arrangement, and an energy of delivery that, after twelve hours' struggle, bore off the verdict.[16]

Yet while Henry Clay enjoyed himself and was able to carry on his official obligations without ramifications, some justices of the peace were not so successful. Several motions were made in the House of Representatives seeking inquiries into the conduct of one justice charged with receiving a bribe, drunkenness, stealing negroes, and then living with the wife of the negroes' owner; two other justices charged with arranging a duel between each other; and a fourth justice charged with sitting on the bench while drunk and administering an oath on a wolf's scalp.[17]

Despite the gaiety and foolishness of political and judicial leaders, serious business was conducted by the legislature, which began its session on Monday, December 28, 1807. On Wednesday they heard the last annual address by Governor Greenup, and on Friday, New Year's Day, Clay was placed on a committee to draft a reply to the speech. Meanwhile, he was elected by the House as one of six directors of the Bank of Kentucky. Then on January 11, 1808, Speaker Logan resigned his House and Speaker's seat to become a judge in the court of appeals. On the third ballot in the selection of a successor, Henry Clay was elected as the House leader as two other candidates were eliminated on successive ballots. In acknowledging the honor conferred on him by the House, Clay recommended to them "the observance and preservation of good order and decorum," qualities already shown to be in short supply in early Kentucky government.[18] Governor Greenup, in his annual message of December 30, recalling the affront of the *Chesapeake* attack and other impressments, said,

> Our commerce continues to be harassed by several of the belligerent powers, our neutral rights infringed and the flag of the United States has been insulted in a most extraordinary manner, by a foreign power, who has never ceased to manifest hostility towards us, since by the valor and firmness of the American people their domination was shaken

off, and their schemes of subjugation and oppression were defeated.

He went on to point out that while the response to the aggressions were the province of the general government in Washington, he believed it prudent, through the legislature, that the people of Kentucky express their sentiments and support.[19]

Prior to Clay's election as speaker, his special committee sent a letter addressed to Greenup, and then on the day after his election, the committee brought to the House floor a resolution expressing the confidence of Kentuckians in "the present administration of the general government."[20] The letter to Greenup stated,

> We are sorry to find that Great Britain — our mother country — she who so proudly boasts of liberty, justice and magnanimity, should in contempt of compact, law, justice and humanity itself, insult our naval flag, plunder our property, enslave our citizens, and imbrue their hands in innocent and unoffending blood. We cannot repress our indignation when contemplating the acts of perfidy and murder of the British navy, and with one voice express a wish that the general government may adopt prompt and effective measures to support the insulted and degraded majesty of the American nation, and convince her lordly enemies that her rights shall not be invaded nor her dignity insulted with impunity.
>
> So far, sir, as this house is concerned, we are willing not only to express the public sentiment, but also to pledge our honor, our blood and treasure in support of such measures as may be adopted by the general government, to secure and protect the peace, dignity, and independence of the union against foreign invasion, and to chastise and bring to a state of reason our haughty and imperious foes.[21]

The House resolution was similar in character but said, among other things,

> It is acknowledged by all that unity of opinion ought to prevail at all times; but particularly at a period when foreign or domestic tyranny threatens an attack on liberty, and as we suppose the general government, situated as we conceive she is on the eve of a war with a nation that has repeatedly insulted the American flag — will not only feel a willingness but a desire to know the sentiments of every part and portion of the union.

And again the resolution reiterated the feeling that Kentuckians "are not only ready to step forth at their country's call, but are determined to risque their lives and property in her defense, and if her

liberty must expire they will expire with it."[22] However, these strong words were watered down by amendments to call merely for "the severest chastisement" which would "receive the support of our best exertions and the devotion of our lives and fortunes."[23]

About the time this measure was passed and sent to the senate, news reached Kentucky that Congress had approved Jefferson's request for an embargo on all commerce by American vessels to foreign ports. It was to have disastrous results in the coastal areas of the country and was exceptionally hated by the Federalist trading population of New England.

In conjunction with this rising international tension, a letter from Secretary of War Henry Dearborn, to Governor Greenup, was read to the Kentucky General Assembly calling for the formation of volunteer military units to be raised and trained for any emergency.[24]

In addition to these measures venting the American anger at Britain, the Kentucky Senate passed and sent to the house a bill to repeal all acts of the British Parliament on which Kentucky's legal system was based. Henry Clay stepped down from his speaker's chair and, in a committee of the whole house, took a stand that this action, despite the growing hatred of everything British, was too drastic. He offered, instead, to amend the act of repeal to apply only to those decisions rendered since American independence on July 4, 1776, letting stand all previous decisions when the States were British colonies. He preferred to retain "that system with which is associated everything valuable and venerable in jurisprudence." He denounced as barbarous the spirit which would "wantonly make wreck of a system fraught with intellectual wealth of centuries."[25]

One other matter brought before the Kentucky House was to consume many pages of the House Journal, numerous columns in the Kentucky newspapers, and a great deal of Henry Clay's attentions and emotions throughout the year 1808 and 1809. This began as a resolution introduced by Humphrey Marshall, of all Clay's antagonists, now a member with Clay in the House of Representatives. Marshall called for a congressional inquiry into the conduct of Federal Judge Harry Innes, noting again that he was tied to the old Spanish Conspiracy and also allied to the Burr affair. On learning of the resolution, Innes wrote the House in a letter addressed to Speaker Henry Clay stating,

> I did during the last session of Congress write to several members of that body, requesting through them that an enquiry might be made into my conduct. However, they dissuaded me, because in their judgment, there was no sufficient ground to justify or authorize such enquiry.

Of course, one of these congressional members to whom Innes had then written was United States Senator Henry Clay, the same to whom he now wrote as speaker of the Kentucky House. Marshall's resolution eventually passed. But he was met by a letter to the speaker from Thomas Bodley who placed charges against Marshall, and said that Marshall "ought to be expelled from his House seat" for land transaction frauds. On February 19, the select committee, empowered to look into Bodley's charges, recommended Marshall's expulsion. But the house, instead, on the basis of insufficient evidence, exonerated Marshall, 30–23 (Clay as speaker, not voting).[26]

Outside the chambers of the Kentucky legislature — in fact at Frankfort's Eagle Tavern — the Republican members met, with Governor Greenup presiding, to draft a recommendation "To the Freemen of Kentucky" to call to their attention Mr. James Madison, "presently the U.S. Secretary of State, as a proper person on whom to bestow your suffrage" at the next election for the presidential chair in 1808. Henry Clay and Green Clay both signed this memorial as leaders of their party in the two houses of the Kentucky General Assembly.[27]

7

RESTLESS POLITICIAN

With the dawn of 1808, Henry Clay was again settled into the routines encompassing his legal, legislative, and academic careers. But young Clay was still impetuous, impatient, rambunctious, and energetic. These traits mirrored themselves in many of his activities over the next few years.

Though this was the year of another presidential contest, Clay neither concentrated his attention toward the national elections nor in a campaign to renew his own position in the Kentucky House of Representatives. On the contrary, he spent more time in a newspaper debate over the gubernatorial qualifications of John Allen, his associate in the 1806 defense of Aaron Burr.

When Allen announced his candidacy in the spring of 1808, his character was attacked by Joseph Street, still editor of the *Western World*, in the paper's issue of May 5. The thrust of Street's attack was that Allen was not fit to be governor because he had been associated with the court defense of Burr in 1806 and the defense of Judge Sebastian during the legislative inquiry in the weeks that followed. The response to this "libel" came not from Allen but rather from Henry Clay writing in the *Kentucky Gazette* on May 31, under the pseudonym of "Regulus." In derision, Clay accused the paper of becoming "the humble instrument of a certain high toned Federalist and his party." This was a jab at Humphrey Marshall. Clay went on to praise Allen and ridicule Street for failing to determine whether certain information, which had been fed to him and which he had printed about Allen, was in fact really true.

In his "Regulus" response, Clay argued, first, that Allen had endeavored to obtain a fair and deliberate hearing for Sebastian who, prior to the inquiry, "had long enjoyed the honors and confidence of his country." As to Allen's defense of Burr, Clay noted that as late as December 10, 1806, most Kentuckians believed Burr innocent, the grand jury had so pronounced him, and even President Jefferson was later to state that the prosecution was premature for lack of evidence that only afterward flowed in.

Still writing as "Regulus," Clay explained the role he and Allen had in the trial, reporting as if a third person:

> That Burr's counsel knew what every body was ignorant of, his guilt, there is no evidence, nor reason to believe. That he [Burr] laboured to deceive them is manifest from a letter which he addressed to one of them, avowing, in the strongest and most unequivocal language, his innocence. And so satisfied has been the executive of the United States of their freedom from participation in this scheme, that the counsel alluded to, it has been said was solicited, long after the transactions at Frankfort, to prosecute him in behalf of the government.

This was a reference to Attorney General Rodney's request late in 1807 that Clay prosecute Burr in Ohio.

"Regulus" went on to cite his view of a defense counsel's duties by suggesting, hypothetically that had Allen believed Burr to be guilty,

> Was he therefore to refuse to appear as his counsel? The practice of law is his trade.... Would a shoemaker or tailor have been guilty of treason, if the one had made a pair of boots and the other a coat for Mr. Burr? Did patriotism or duty require that they should kick him out of their shops? The Constitution of the United States, almost all the state constitutions, tender of the rights of the accused, have expressly provided that they shall have the benefit of counsel for their defense. Did these

instruments mean to say to the unfortunate culprit, "you shall have advocates to defend you," and to those advocates, "if you appear in the defense, you shall be deemed unworthy of public trust or confidence?"

"Regulus" reminded Street that even he had counsel when he had been found guilty of publishing "a gross, scandalous, and indecent libel upon the chief magistrate of this state," when he described Governor Greenup's fictional portrait in an 1806 issue of the *Western World*.[1]

The reply to Clay's letter came not from Street but from a Dr. Anthony Hunn, editor of a paper, *The Lamp*, in Lincoln County, Kentucky. In the June 7 issue of his paper, he named Clay as "Regulus," saying that Allen, like the Grand Sultan, has his Vizier in Henry Clay, both champions of a traitor though conscious of his guilt. Hunn charged that Clay knew Burr was guilty, and that was why he and Allen would not permit Daveiss to question witnesses before the grand jury and therefore they were, "if not engaged Burrites, at least well wishers to his horrid scheme." Hunn, reflecting on Clay's analogy of the shopkeepers serving Burr, accused Clay and Allen of practicing dishonesty in their legal trade and added, "for God's sake let us not make such 'honorable' tradesmen-Governors!!!"[2]

Clay got hold of this and an earlier issue of Hunn's *The Lamp*, and answered in the Lexington *Reporter*, on June 18, this time using his old pseudonym, "Scaevola." He referred to Hunn as

> a legitimate descendant of the Goths and Vandals ... an European by birth — a physician by profession: and what you were by practice, may be inferred from the fact of your abandoning the pursuit of medicine ... and commencing the trade of slander and defamation.

To this "Scaevola" appended an anecdote "not generally known" about Hunn, accusing him of

> discharging the contents of your own pistol, in your own hat, for the purpose of creating a belief that you have been attempted to be assassinated. Clay scoffed at the fact that Hunn's hat had two holes in it that mysteriously left no hole through Hunn's head.[3]

The newspaper debate was picked up by "A Farmer" writing in the Lexington *Reporter*, on

June 11, and supporting the attack against Allen begun by the *Western World*. "A Farmer" saw nothing but collusion in Allen's attempt to postpone the Sebastian inquiry until the judge could gather documents for his defense, and for his being a defender of Burr who, in his view, "was universally looked upon as a fallen and desperate character" as early as 1805.[4]

Clay returned to the "Regulus" nom de plume to answer this latest blast with his own in the *Kentucky Gazette*, on June 21. Clay proclaimed that his newest antagonist was "one of the aiders and abettors" of the *Western World*, which Clay said, had vilified and abused "the whole Democratic Society in mass." He then pointed out that,

> One exception alone has distinguished its slanderous career, and that is that *not a federalist in Kentucky has been attacked*. No, the unsullied character of H. Marshall has never been tarnished by the columns of the *W. World*.

"Regulus" noted that Judge Innes, who only preserved decorum in the court during the 1806 Burr grand jury proceedings,

> has been charged over and over again with being accessory to his guilt, because the grand jury acquitted him for want of evidence. Chief Justice Marshall, by whose legal opinions he was actually acquitted, has never been arraigned by the editor of the *W. World*. But the Chief Justice is a staunch federalist — he is the brother-in-law of H. Marshall, and it would have been very ungrateful in Mr. Street to criticize his conduct.

"Regulus" went on in this essay to argue and defend the part Allen played in the legislative inquiry into the conduct of Judge Sebastian. He announced that he would discuss Allen's actions in the Burr trial in a later letter — which he did in the Lexington *Reporter* on July 9.[5]

In between these two letters, Dr. Hunn came back with another rebuke published in the *Reporter* on July 2. He defended his medical credentials and then stated that the contents of his earlier pronouncement had made "Mr. Clay so sorry, and Mr. Scaevola so mad!!!" But later he seemed to decide that "Regulus" and "Scaevola" and Clay were all the same person.[6] There is no evidence that Dr. Hunn enticed any further comment from Clay.

"Regulus'" July 9 letter was aimed entirely at the second half of his reply to "A Farmer" though addressed "To the People." He first publicly announced

> that no man entertains a more despicable opinion of Aaron Burr than I do. Whether his object was disunion, revolution in Louisiana, or conquest of Mexico, or all of them, there can be no doubt of his atrocious guilt. And I sincerely regret with every other good citizen that he has hitherto escaped with impunity.

"Regulus" was now asserting what no jury had proclaimed. He went on to retell the events of the two attempts to arraign Burr in 1806, recalling that prosecuting attorney Daveiss had himself called off the first trial and the grand jury had cleared Burr in the second instance and that it wasn't until "*eight to ten days after,* that the President's proclamation reached this country, and gave a different tone to public feeling and sentiment."

"Regulus" then made an eloquent statement with regard to a counsel and his client that could ring out in any instance where public sentiment is aroused and particularly when the press has printed suspicions against a person's character.

> Is suspicion to produce condemnation? Is it a ground for denying the common rights of a fair trial, which the constitution carefully guarantees to the meanest culprit? Are counsel, because a man covers with a mysterious veil his enterprises, to reject an application to defend him? The inference deducible from the reasoning of the Farmer is this, that whenever a general prejudice is excited against an individual, whenever *suspicion* has widely diffused its poison, the person implicated is to be deprived of counsel. Let me suppose a case — the *Western World* and the *Lamp* combine to destroy the reputation of a citizen. They commence their operations by assailing his political character — they proceed to attack his moral principles, and at length ascribe to him the most infamous crimes. It is in vain that he appeals to the rectitude of his former life. The region of truth is less extensive than the region of slander: the latter moves with electric rapidity, whilst the gait of the former is slow and tardy. Credulity is a common error, and we often believe, upon the slightest evidence, the blackest crimes.

With these conditions "Regulus" suggested that the public mind, biased and prejudiced, demands conviction by the jury and silence by the accused's counsel. "Upon the doctrine of the Farmer," he continued,

> every counsellor is a judge, before whom the accused is to be tried, and not until he received his acquittal there, is he to have the advantage of legal advice and assistance. And indeed if he does acquit him, and the jury afterwards acquit him, if it should even subsequently appear by evidence not before *either of them* that the party was guilty, both the jury and attorney are to be condemned.

"Regulus" closed this last argument in the presses by noting that Burr was honored by a ball in his honor attended by the leading citizens of the community including the governor of the state. Finally, he wrote,

> Fellow citizens, inquire, read, think, decide for yourselves and say whether the charges against Mr. Allen are not made from malice, unsupported by facts, and urged for base and electioneering purposes.[7]

But it all went for naught. Allen lost his election to General Charles Scott. Clay was re-elected to return to the Kentucky House of Representatives and received the warm congratulations from his New Orleans friend, James Brown. Though Brown's letter began with acknowledgment of a sad event — the death, in June, of Thomas Hart, the father-in-law to both the writer and the recipient — it revealed that Brown had soured on Republicanism. With regard to Clay's election victory, be warned, "Your enemies will be wounded. But I pray you to quit public life or muster up sufficient philosophy to bear up under all the hard names with which you will be christened in the papers." His accurate vision of the future went further when he prophesied that "you have destroyed your peace, encreased [sic] the number of your enemies, and perhaps endangered your very life which you may be forced to risque in defence of your character?"[8] These forebodings were not long in coming to fruition.

The next legislative session of the Kentucky House convened on December 12, 1808. Since the previous session, William Logan, Clay's predecessor as speaker of the house, had left his post as judge on the Kentucky high court and had returned to the legislative body. He was re-elected to his old leadership post by a vote of 36–31 over Clay's nominee, William T. Barry.[9] Though Clay was not a candidate for a renewal of the speakership job, which he had held earlier in the year, there is some solid indication that his re-election was seriously considered.

Humphrey Marshall, who had dogged Clay's recent career in the Kentucky legislature, in the U.S. Supreme Court, and in the public press, was returned to the legislature as a representative for Franklin County. The antagonism between the two men had become so intense that several of Clay's political allies concluded that Clay should not be reappointed to the speaker's chair since it would put restraints on him when needed to meet Marshall in floor debate. For this reason they withheld their support. During the weeks that followed the two men clashed frequently, with Clay usually the legislative victor since Marshall had little political support.[10]

The first skirmish occurred three days into the session when a senate resolution was re-drafted by Clay to praise Jefferson's Administration and particularly his embargo as "The only honorable expedient to avoid war" as a result of the escalating naval blockades proclaimed by both Britain and France in the Napoleonic wars. Clay's wording called for the legislature "to spend, if necessary, the last shilling, and to exhaust the last drop of blood in resisting" the aggressions of the British Orders in Council or the French Decrees. Only Humphrey Marshall opposed the resolution in the house. But the senate later watered down Clay's colorful language to pledge "their Most energetic support" to the general government.[11]

Clay's great success in this measure, dealing with the international crisis, led him to propose a drastic resolution on January 3, 1809, that

> the members of the general assembly will clothe themselves in productions of American manufacture, and will abstain from the use of cloth or linen of European fabric until the belligerent nations respect the rights of neutrals by repealing their orders and decrees as relates to the United States.[12]

To back up his words, Clay, who usually appeared in the best European-made clothing, took his place on the house floor wearing a suit of Kentucky jeans. Marshall, on the other hand, in utter contempt for his political opponent, did the reverse, outfitting himself in the finest English broadcloth instead of his usual homespun. The debate over the resolution displayed even more rancor between the two legislators than did their attempt to annoy one another by their apparel.

The verbal battle grew in intensity with each rebuttal. Eventually, Marshall replied to one of Clay's stinging rebukes with all the bitterness of his sarcastic tongue, openly charging Clay with demagoguery. His words were so offensive, reflecting on Clay's honor and motives, that they reached the point of deadly insult. Clay resented the insult on the spot and rose from his seat to attack Marshall, who sat only one chair removed from Clay.

In the scuffle that ensued, several members moved to interpose. Former Governor Garrard, now a member of the House, accidentally received a severe blow in the face by Clay as a result of his intervention. By this time the member who sat between Clay and Marshall rose to separate them. He was Christopher Riffe, a tall, muscular, and powerful German. He seized each combatant by one hand and pulled them apart saying, "Come voys, no fighting here. I vips you both."[13]

Tempers cooled long enough for Clay to apologize to the house for his conduct saying he would not have taken the liberty had his opponent been a man of honor. Marshall could not accept this backhanded apology and shouted back, "It is the apology of a poltroon!"[14]

The chamber returned to the business at hand and voted for Clay's resolution by 57–2, with Marshall gaining one adherent to his cause.

But the two angry legislators were not satisfied with the outcome. That evening Henry Clay sent to Humphrey Marshall the following note:

> SIR—After the occurrence in the house of representatives on this day, the receipt of this note will excite with you no surprise. I hope on my part, I shall not be disappointed in the execution of the pledge you gave on that occasion, and in your disclaimer of the character attributed to you. To enable you to fulfil these reasonable and just expectations, my friend Major Campbell is authorized by me to adjust the ceremonies proper to be observed.
>
> I am, Sir
> Yrs &c
> Henry Clay.

To this note, delivered by Major Campbell, Marshall replied on the same evening:

> Sir,
> Your note of this date was handed me by Maj. Campbell.—The object is understood; and without

deigning to notice the insinuation it contains as to character, the necessary arrangements are, on my part, submitted to my friend Col, Moore.

> Yours, Sir &c.
> H. Marshall.[15]

Immediately after Clay had penned his note to Marshall, and before receiving his reply, he wrote another letter to his wife's brother, Thomas Hart, Junior:

> Frankfort, 4 Jan. 1809
>
> Dr Sir
>
> On this day in the House of Representatives a dispute arose between H. Marshall and myself which terminated by the use of language on his part to which I could not submit, & I attempted to chastise him on the spot, but was prevented by the interference of the House. I have since challenged him, and there is a prospect of his accepting it. Should he do so I shall want a brace of pistols, and know of none that I can get on which I would rely, except Mortons. These I must prevail on you to procure upon any term, by purchase or otherwise. You will have some difficulty in doing it, and must conceal from him the true purpose of them, which may be done through the agency of some person, whom he will not suspect. I must, also request the favor of you to procure some of the best powder, adapted to such occasions, which can be had.
>
> Should the pistols require cleaning I will be obliged to you to get West to put them in proper order. But at any rate let the bearer return with them by tomorrow evening. or in the course of the night.
>
> I need not suggest to you the necessity of entire secrecy on this subject.
>
> Yrs
> Henry Clay[16]

As the seconds met to establish the rules to be observed in the forthcoming contest, the house, on the 5th, resolved

> That the conduct of Humphrey Marshall and Henry Clay, whilst in the service of the house of representatives on yesterday, was an indignity offered to the same and highly, reprehensible; but having made suitable acknowledgments the house think proper to accept the same, & proceed no further therein.[17]

The duel arrangements took some time to work up, and in the meantime both Clay and Marshall continued their service in the legislature which, on the 17th, appointed Clay one of six directors of the state bank. It was also on this date that the local newspapers reported the official results of the past presidential election naming James Madison of Virginia to succeed Thomas Jefferson as president on March 4 and George Clinton to succeed himself as vice president.

By the 19th of January, the seconds agreed on the following rules:

> 1. Each gentleman will take his station at ten paces distant from the other, and will stand as may suit his choice, with his arms hanging down, and after the words Attention: Fire: being given, both may fire at their leisure.
>
> 2. A snap or flash shall be equivalent to a fire.
>
> 3. If one should fire before the other, he who fires first, shall stand in the position in which he was when be fired, except that he may let his arms fall down by his side.
>
> 4. A violation of the above rules by either of the parties, (accidents excepted) shall subject the offender to instant death.
>
> John B. Campbell.
> James F. Moore.[18]

The best description of what followed on Thursday morning, January 19, 1809, is the eyewitness account related in the newspapers of the period by the two seconds:

> Conformably to previous arrangements, Mr. Clay and Mr. Marshall, attended by their friends, crossed the Ohio at Shippingport, and an eligible spot of ground presenting itself immediately below the mouth of Silver Creek; ten steps, the distance agreed on, we measured off, and each gentleman took his position. The word being given, both gentlemen fired. Mr. Marshall's fire did not take effect. Mr. Clay's succeeded so far as to give Mr. Marshall a slight wound on the belly.—Preparations were then made for a second fire. Mr. Marshall again fired without effect—Mr. Clay snapped, which agreeably to rules agreed on, was equivalent to a fire. A third preparation was made, when each gentleman stood at his station, waiting for the word. Mr. Marshall fired first, and gave Mr. Clay a flesh wound in the thigh—Mr. Clay fired without effect.—Mr. Clay insisted on another fire very ardently; but his situation, resulting from the wound, placing him on unequal grounds, his importunate request was not complied with. We deem it justice to both gentlemen, to pronounce their conduct on the occasion, cool, determined and brave in the highest degree. Mr. Clay's friend was under an impression, that Mr. Marshall at the third fire, violated a rule which required, that he who fired first, should stand in the position in which he was when he fired; but Mr. Marshall's friend being convinced that Mr. Clay had fired

previous to Mr. Marshall's moving from his position; this circumstance is considered as one in which gentlemen may be mistaken on such occasions, and is not to be noticed in this affair.

Thursday Jany 19th 1809

> John B. Campbell
> James F. Moore.[19]

Clay was taken to Louisville to have his wound attended to and there wrote another brief note to a Dr. James Clarke in Frankfort:

> I have this moment returned from the field of battle. We had three shots. On the first I grazed him just above the navel — he missed me. On the second my damned pistol snapped, and he missed me. On the third I received a flesh wound in the thigh, and owing to my receiving his first fire, &c. I missed him.
>
> My wound is no way serious, as the bone is unhurt, but prudence will require me to remain here some days.
>
> Yours,
> Henry Clay.[20]

While Henry Clay fought his duel with Humphrey Marshall, Lucretia Clay sat at their new home, "Ashland" on the outskirts of Lexington, awaiting the birth of their sixth child due sometime in February. On the day of the encounter, her sister, Mrs. Price (who had likely learned of the arrangement through her brother, Thomas Hart, Junior), came to spend the day with Lucretia, to be on hand when word of the fight became known. Lucretia revealed no awareness of the event in the conversation of the day.

In the afternoon, a messenger came to the house with a note for Lucretia. Doctor Frederick Ridgley, who attended Clay as surgeon, had written to Thomas Hart briefly describing the duel and then said,

> Tell Mrs. Clay, on my honor, 'tis only a simple wound and no danger but a few of the first days, say 4 or 5, I expect some pain & inflammation.... Mr. Clay wishes to come up in a Carriage tomorrow but I shall not assent to it.[21]

She read the note and handed it over to her sister saying, "Thank God, he is only slightly wounded." Mrs. Price read the note and in astonishment exclaimed, "Why, sister, I did not think you knew Mr, Clay had gone out to fight a duel, as you haven't said one word to me about it."[22] Lucretia Clay had again displayed the cool, well-composed personality that so well supported her husband in the many crises that were part of his outstanding life.

Henry Clay, himself, took his leg wound with a good deal of relaxed composure. Some of his friends, connected with the duel, had anticipated that Marshall would be killed, or at least badly wounded. With this expectation, they had planned to welcome Clay back to Louisville with a sumptuous dinner. Instead, he was carried to the home of a friend in Louisville where be spent several days recuperating from his wound. When Clay learned of their high expectations and subsequent disappointment he had them gather, as long as time permitted, in lengthy card parties at his recovery bed.[23]

Clay's wound healed quickly and he was soon ready to return to his duties as a much-relieved Lucretia presented her husband with another daughter. About the time that little Lucretia Hart Clay was born, and four days after Clay's return, on February 8, 1809, to his legislative seat in the Kentucky House of Representatives in Frankfort, still another child was born about 50 miles to the southwest. This youngster was to make Clay his idol. And Clay, in return, though unwittingly, was to play a strange little part in events that would lead to the boy's marriage, and through his yet-unborn wife, to higher greatness than even Clay was to achieve.

Two months after the birth of Abraham Lincoln, on February 12, 1809, near Hodgensville, Kentucky, the office of the governor of the Illinois Territory became vacant. Clay wrote to President Madison on April 10, only a little more than five weeks in the White House, and recommended his friend, Ninian Edwards, to the post. Edwards was then chief justice of the Kentucky Court of Appeals. Madison tendered the office to Edwards who accepted and moved to Kaskaskia, then the capital of the Illinois Territory.

Many years later, Edwards's son returned to Lexington to attend Transylvania University and during his studies, or more aptly during his extracurricular activities, he met and then married Elizabeth Todd of Lexington. Some time later they removed to Springfield, Illinois, where Elizabeth served as the state's First Lady for her widowed father-in-law, then serving as governor of the state of Illinois.

In 1839, Elizabeth was visited by her 21-year-old sister, Mary, and introduced her to the lanky up-and-coming Springfield lawyer, Abraham Lincoln. Mary and Abe married and made their way eventually to the White House — an ambition denied Henry Clay, but one that Mary Todd had possessed since her childhood acquaintance with, and love for, Henry Clay.[24]

Clay resumed his service in the legislature in February 1809. His activities for the remainder of 1809 were more modified and mostly routine and can be summed up in a cluster. On Saint Patrick's Day he toasted "The generous Irish character — frank, brave, and generous." On the 4th of July he was prophetically toasted as "Our next Senator in Congress — 6 cheers." In early August he was elected to another term in the Kentucky House. In December he comforted his wife, Lucretia, on the death of her brother, Thomas Hart. During the fall of 1809, he read of the suicide of Louisiana Territory explorer Merriwether Lewis, and of the intention of steamboat-inventor Robert Fulton to extend the utility of his "invention to the waters of the Ohio and Mississippi Rivers."[25]

On December 12, Henry Clay was back in Frankfort at his seat in the Kentucky House along with Humphrey Marshall. Again, William Logan was placed in the speaker's chair. Uneventful legislation consumed the members' time until after the New Year. On January 2, 1810, Kentucky's U.S. Senator Buckner Thruston resigned his seat to accept an appointment by President Madison to be an associate judge for the District of Columbia, a post which had become vacant because of a death.

Two days later, by a joint vote, the senate and house elected Henry Clay to be the new U.S. Senator, with a 30-vote majority over Speaker Logan.[26] Clay's term with the 11th Congress, already in session in Washington, would run until March 3, 1811. He resigned his seat in the Kentucky House immediately to prepare for his trip to the nation's capital.

As Clay left Lexington on January 9, he knew that he was only serving out a portion of an unexpired Senate term — this one to last two sessions. But he could not know that his service in the Kentucky legislature had come to an end for all time. Henceforth, all of Henry Clay's political and governmental service would be on the national level and it would be at this level that his greatness was to be achieved.

While his greatness was yet to be proved, his courage was not. It may have been on this trip to Washington that Henry Clay had still another confrontation with a Marshall — not Humphrey Marshall, but rather Eli Marshall, who claimed to be a cousin to Humphrey. The story of this episode remained in the local lore of Hebron, Ohio, for almost 50 years following Clay's death. It surfaced in an account by a reporter, George E. Kelley, writing for a Louisville paper in 1896. Kelley's report states that Clay was on his way to Washington in June.

For several years, around 1809, the middle counties of Ohio were terrorized by gangs of horse thieves and murderers. The leader of the Licking County gang was Eli Marshall, generally regarded as the most dangerous desperado in the West. He was a giant in stature and possessed great strength. At the time Clay passed through this region, the community of Hebron was in a state of terror. Clay was advised to accept an armed escort, but he declined. Because of a heavy rain early one afternoon he stopped for the night at the "Licking Arms," a hostelry near present-day Hebron.

Early in the evening, a large number of local farmers gathered at the tavern to pay their respects to Clay. They, also, told him about the depredations of the horse thieves and warned him of the villainous character of Marshall. Clay said he was not afraid of being molested by them and added he would not mind meeting the leader and calling him to account for his murderous thieving. Clay's comments traveled quickly and Marshall was ready to meet the request before the night was over.

About midnight, as Clay sat in his upstairs room writing letters, he heard loud voices outside followed by heavy knocking at the tavern door. The voices, joined by those of the landlord, were then heard on the lower floor. A few minutes later the landlord tapped lightly on Clay's door and inquired if he were awake. Clay admitted the pale-faced landlord and was told that Marshall and three of his gang were downstairs and demanded Clay come to see him. Clay sent word by the landlord that he never complied with demands.

Congress. Agitation swelled "for armed troops to invade the Crescent City."[12]

As part of an economic depression which began to spread over Kentucky prior to the port closing, Henry Clay's legal correspondence to William Taylor included such phrases as "such has been the demand upon this Country for money lately that it is almost exhausted of all light money (bank notes), and I fear I shall meet great difficulty in procuring notes." And, "I could procure no more bank notes and I fear I shall be unable to procure any more of this kind of money ... the country is quickly drained of notes." And in another letter to Taylor, "Having in vain endeavored to procure bank bills, the scarcity of which is increased by the inauspicious circumstances in which Commerce of our Country is placed...."[13]

These letters to Taylor, incidentally, concerned negotiation for settlement of land owned by Philip Bastrop in Louisiana. These same lands would come into dispute later in a legal case in which Clay would become nationally prominent.

With the growth of river commerce prior to the closing of the port of New Orleans, the Kentucky legislature brought forth a bill to organize a company to insure boats and their cargoes on the Ohio and Mississippi Rivers. Ironically, this bill did not pass the House of Representatives until December 16 — several days after word had been received that the port was closed. But the charter for the Kentucky Insurance Company contained a sleeper clause that permitted the issuance of certain financial papers and provided that "such of the notes as are payable to bearer shall be negotiable and assignable by delivery only."[14] The company made the freest use of this provision which gave it banking privileges, and within six months it divided an eight-percent profit.[15] During this profitable period Henry Clay became one of the company's stockholders and "an exceedingly learned counsellor."[16]

There was a slow reaction to the company's operation, but when it dawned on many Kentuckians in early 1803 that they had a bank in their midst, a storm of protest rose against it. The opposition was led by Felix Grundy, a former member of the House that chartered the Kentucky Insurance Company. Grundy had recently moved from Washington County to Nelson County, Kentucky, and would not be a member of the next

session of the legislature. Nevertheless, he traveled about the countryside charging that the company had come into being through deception and that the next legislature should declare the charter void.[17]

Friends of the "banking" institution sought out a champion to protect their cause and found him in Henry Clay. But they didn't find him in Lexington. For several weeks Clay had been at the Olympian Springs, a Bath County resort area, enjoying the fine waters said to be beneficial to one's health. Without consulting Clay, his friends put him forward as a candidate for representative of Fayette County in the Kentucky General Assembly scheduled to meet in November,

Clay was not at all pleased with this flattery. The contest would pit him against legislative veterans who were allied to influential and powerful friends. Thus, Clay made no move to advance his candidacy. Despite his absence in the early stages of the campaign, he appeared to be running well while languishing at the baths. Then as the time for voting drew near, Clay returned to the Lexington scene. He learned that his opponents had been using every charge they could conceive to accomplish his defeat. Alluding to his rest at the Springs, they reported that Clay was incapacitated for the office by ill health, that he did not desire the post, and that he would not accept it. Many voters were convinced and his chances of winning waned.

Clay's initial repugnance for office was overwhelmed by his growing anger over the slanderous attacks on him. He took to the stump and mincing few words expressed his political views to the voters, and refuted all the false statements used against him. He admitted the truth of the charge that he was young and inexperienced; that he had not proclaimed himself a candidate, nor sought the community's suffrage; but on finding his friends wished him to serve them he would be gratified to the people if they would elect him.

An anecdote from this campaign survives to illustrate Clay's early tact and ingenuity when confronted by an awkward campaign situation. While Clay was engaged in speaking on one occasion, a company of riflemen, dismissed from their military exercise nearby, lingered to hear what the young politician had to say. When Clay finished speaking, a man about 50 years old, clearly a veteran of Indian fights in the Kentucky backwoods,

Moments later, a heavy tread was heard on the steps and an instant later Clay's door was violently flung open. Marshall, swearing, strode into the room — only to be arrested by the firm voice of Henry Clay bidding him to halt. Marshall stared into the muzzle of a pistol and saw a sheath knife on a chair near Clay. Disarming Marshall, Clay ordered the desperado into an adjoining storeroom. Bolting the door, and with his pistol in hand, Clay went downstairs to face Marshall's cohorts. Pointing his pistol at them, he told them in firm but quiet tones he would kill the first one who moved. He then asked the landlord and his son to disarm them and securely bind them.

When this was done, Clay returned to his room and released Marshall from the storeroom, warning him that the slightest false move meant death for him. He was ordered to sit down and explain the object of his outrage. To the astonishment of Clay, Marshall stated he was a second cousin to Humphrey Marshall. He told Clay he heard that the reason the duel between Marshall and Clay was not finished was because Clay showed cowardice. Now Eli Marshall was determined to make Clay apologize to him for the injury done his kinsman.

On the basis of this intelligence, Clay proposed to the ruffian that they go downstairs into the large room and, at a distance of five paces, take three shots at each other, firing simultaneously. Marshall agreed and asked for his pistol. Suspecting this would only lead to his own murder, Clay refused Marshall's request until they were in the presence of the landlord and his son downstairs. There, Clay told them of the impending duel and advised them to get their pistols and hold them pointed at Marshall. If the villain made a move before the word to turn and fire was given, they were ordered to kill him. By now, Kelley related, Marshall was pale and shaking and exhibiting the character of the craven — and he refused to fight.

Clay then compelled Marshall to get down on his knees and apologize to both himself and the landlord for the outrage he had committed. Furthermore, Clay insisted that Marshall sign a paper acknowledging himself a coward. Marshall and his companions were afterward turned over to legal authorities and jailed in Zanesville. Though

they later escaped, they were hunted down and killed or driven out of the country. The exception was Marshall who reached Virginia, was captured, tried and hung near Wheeling. When his effects were divided, his sheath knife was sent to Henry Clay in Washington.[27]

No year was given for Kelley's account. However, no congressional session during Clay's lifetime began in June, though one opened on May 31. The incident, if true, may not have occurred as Clay went to Washington in 1810, since he went there in January.

While the entire story may be apocryphal, it is accepted as well within Clay's courage and character to comport himself in the fashion described.

Henry Clay reached Washington in early February 1810, and on the 5th he appeared in the Senate chamber, on the first floor of the north wing, to take his oath for the second time. The next day, the Senate resolved to hold their session in the new chamber, one floor above, beginning February 10th.[28] The Senate's membership now lacked the eloquent John Quincy Adams, who had become the U.S. Minister to Russia — a post he would hold until Clay's next personal association with him. One new member, who was to achieve considerable political stature, was William H. Crawford of Georgia. One-armed John Pope was now Clay's Kentucky colleague. On the weekend that the Senate moved into its new chambers, John Pope married the sister of John Quincy Adams' wife.[29]

Otherwise, there was no significant change in the Senate's membership except that there was no longer a William Plumer writing an enlightening diary unfolding enticing tidbits about his legislative companions. Instead, at least in Henry Clay's case, we are left with the official accounts only of the short-term senator's speaking efforts on several important subjects.

Clay is recorded in the Senate journal as having voted on minor legislation on the day he took his oath, but his name does not appear again on any vote or committee activity until a vote on the 20th. This absence is accounted for in a letter to a friend in Kentucky, dated March 14, stating that he had had "very bad health" since his arrival. Yet it is interesting to note that this reference is found in the same paragraph in which he remarked,

"Mrs. Dolly Madison has her parties every Wednesday evening. They are gay and agreeable tho' I have been but seldom to them."[30] It is probable that his attendance at the parties was after he resumed his duties late in February.

An anecdote related of Clay's first meeting with Dolly Madison (who was also born in Hanover County, Virginia) undoubtedly occurred during Clay's earlier service in the Senate while her husband was secretary of state. Clay went to the home for a courtesy call on the secretary. When welcomed by the pleasant smile of the young lady that greeted him, he gave her a kiss. At that point Secretary Madison appeared on the scene and the young lady forwarded the kiss to him. Suddenly aware of the young lady's identity, the young senator remarked, "Had I, Madam, known you were Mrs. Madison the coin would have been larger."[31]

With his health temporarily restored (he was to be absent from his Senate duties for another week and a half in late February and early March "due to very ill health")[32] Clay resumed his legislative duties on Tuesday, February 20th. Almost immediately, he was partially granted his three-year-old wish to engage in debate on foreign affairs. That same day the Senate took up a House-passed measure, later to be called Macon's Bill No. 1, which was to replace the Non-Intercourse Act expiring at the end of the current congressional session.

The Non-Intercourse Act, itself, was a lukewarm substitute for Jefferson's embargo which had been a disaster to United States commercial interests. All of these measures were aimed at avoiding war while forcing the repeal of the obnoxious British Orders in Council and the French Decrees against neutral shipping.

With the renewal of war between Britain and France, both belligerents attempted to restrict neutral trade with their enemy. British orders in 1804 and 1805 sought to curb neutrals from carrying goods from French colonies to the mother country — but allowed it to continue under the broken voyage arrangement (when clearing customs in mid-voyage in a neutral country). When the British revoked this privilege in the Essex decision in 1805, Congress passed the Non-Importation Act in 1806, closing the United States to British goods. About the same time, Britain declared a blockade of European ports from the Elbe

River to Brest, France. Napoleon countered with the Berlin decrees declaring Great Britain blockaded and authorizing the seizure and confiscation of all ships and cargo in trade with Britain. The English retaliated with two more orders that closed more continental ports to neutrals unless they passed through British ports. Then Napoleon issued his Milan Decree, which permitted further seizure of ships that had been searched and were obeying British orders, declaring the ships and cargoes were to be treated as British property. In response to these actions, Macon's Bill, drafted by Treasury Secretary Albert Gallatin, was designed to lift all commercial restriction except trade with Britain and France (though trade with those two belligerents was still to be permitted when carried only in American vessels).

No sooner had Macon's Bill appeared in the Senate than a majority of the upper house voted, but without debate, to emasculate this flabby bill by abolishing everything except a flat repeal of the Non-Intercourse Act, and the exclusion of British and French *armed* vessels from American waters. Even the title was changed.[33] Two days later, after the third reading of the bill, Clay rose to make a fiery appeal to return the bill to committee for further study hoping to breathe some life into it. He belittled the silence of his colleagues — every one senior to him — saying to them,

> When the regular troops of this house, disciplined as they are in the great affairs of this nation, are inactive at their posts, it becomes the duty of its raw militia, however lately enlisted, to step forth in defense of the honor and independence of the country.

He told the senators he did not like the bill as sent from the House of Representative. "It was a crazy vessel, shattered and leaky," he said, "but it afforded some shelter, bad as it was. It was opposition to the aggressive edicts of the belligerent. Taken from us without a substitute, we are left defenseless, naked, and exposed to all the rage and violence of the storm."

Clay went on to recall the years of effort by the government to resist the offensive measures of Britain and France. Those previous acts of Congress

> presented *resistance* — the *peaceful* resistance of the law. When this is abandoned without effect, I am

for resistance by the *sword*. No man in the nation wants peace more than I; but I prefer the troubled ocean of war, demanded by the honor and independence of the country, with all its calamities and desolation, to the tranquil and putrescent pool of ignominious peace.

He cited the causes for war with both nations but said if we could make peace with only one, he would prefer it with Britain, yet he chose that "enemy" as the one with whom he would prefer to engage in war. He challenged the argument that the treasury vaults were "vacant." Addressing the aging and often somnolent Vice President George Clinton, Clay said, "You have, Sir, I am credibly informed, in the city and vicinity of New Orleans alone, public property sufficient to extinguish the celebrated deficit in the Secretary's report." He then practically offered Canada to the Senate as remuneration. "The conquest of Canada is in your power. I trust I shall not be deemed presumptuous when I state that I verily believe that the militia of Kentucky are alone competent to place Montreal and Upper Canada at your feet."

Calling for a new "military ardor," Clay glorified "the withered arm, and wrinkled brow of the illustrious founders of our freedom," but said, "We shall want the presence and living example of a new race of heroes to supply their place." In closing, he pleaded for the Senate to return the bill to committee for more deliberation and consideration reminding them that while weak, the bill was not submission to the belligerent.

> It professes to oppose (in form, at least) the injustice of foreign Governments. What are you about to do — to breathe vigor and energy into the bill? No, Sir; you have eradicated all of its vitality, and are about to transmit back again the lifeless skeleton.[34]

Clay's sparkling voice was a shining new star in the Senate void. But it was not seen as a guiding light. The whole temper of this unexpected challenge from a 32-year-old — the body's most junior member only 17 days after taking his oath — must have stunned the other members of this quiet club. And they answered him quietly but quickly. They rejected his motion to return the bill to committee by 20–13, and then immediately passed the measure 26–7. Kentucky Senator Pope joined Clay as one of the seven opposing the "crazy vessel."

Though the Senate and the press gave little attention to this effort by Clay, it, nevertheless, stood as something of a turning point in the legislative position of Congress. Until this point, it had become increasingly evident that Congress was going down hill in prestige. With Clay's short impassioned speech, a new spirit of nationalism and patriotism began to grow. And though this new vigor was not recognized yet, Clay did win something of a victory when the House, resenting the Senate's action, refused to accept the emasculating amendments. On March 5, the House returned the bill to the Senate in its original form, got it back from the Senate demanding the House agree to the dissection, and then chucked the whole thing for an entirely new bill to be termed Macon's Bill No. 2. With much dickering between conferences of the two legislative bodies, a compromise bill was finally agreed to late on the last day of the session (May 1) with a provision authorizing the president "in case either Great Britain or France shall, before the 3rd Day of March next, so revoke or modify her edicts as that they shall cease to violate the neutral commerce of the United States," to prohibit intercourse with the nation which had not revoked its edicts."[35]

During this Senate session, Clay received a letter from his in-law, James Brown in New Orleans. Its subject matter was closely related to the international crisis growing out of the Napoleonic War in Europe. Brown told Clay that he was deeply disturbed over the great influx of French into New Orleans following the British possession of the island of Santo Domingo, noting that the territorial governor was true to Republicanism to such an extent that he submitted to the will of the French majority population in all his decisions. Brown feared that France would become "the tyrant of the Ocean" and asked Clay,

> Will she not immediately annex Cuba, the Floridas, and other Spanish American possessions to her Crown of Spain, and will not the important positions of Pensacola, Havanna, Campeche, La Vera Cruz, etc. give to the ambitious Emperor a compleat command of the commerce of the Gulph leaving the desirable and at present undefended point the Mississippi exposed a tempting and easy prey to her insatiable cupidity?

Brown made two suggestions to remedy the foreign threat to local government. First, he would permit "the inhabitants of West Florida to attach themselves to the American Government" with the hopeful result that that region would form the basis for a new state in the Union. Second, he proposed a method of encouraging new settlement of vacant lands in the area.[36]

Acting on these suggestions on April 7, Clay introduced a resolution to encourage the "emigration to Orleans Territory of American citizens, by making a suitable donation of certain portions of the public lands within said Territory."[37] Though no action resulted on this motion, he was, however, more successful in winning the adoption of his amendment to a bill to provide statehood for the Orleans Territory. In this he proposed that the official language of the state's records would be English rather than the French of the population's majority.[38] This provision was retained in the eventual bill for the state of Louisiana, but that statehood did not become a fact until 1812.

Henry Clay made one further major contribution to the debates of the 1810 Senate session. Here again, appeared the first faint signal of another of Clay's future legislative themes. During debate on appropriations for munitions of war, Kentucky Senator John Pope added an amendment requiring the Navy's purchase of "sail-duck, cordage, and hemp," etc., to be of United States manufacture. On March 26, Senator James Lloyd of Massachusetts, moved to strike this provision, and as a consequence got a speech out of Henry Clay supporting Pope's amendment, and at the same time supporting the manufacturing concern of the Hart family in Lexington. But in so doing he made his initial stand on the national scene for the encouragement of domestic manufacture over foreign imports. In urging the development of an American manufacture of clothing and redeeming "us entirely from all dependence on foreign countries," he scoffed at previous claims that "the indigence, vice and wretchedness" of Manchester and Birmingham (England) would be introduced into the United States. By comparison, he balanced American agriculture, "that first and greatest source of our wealth and happiness," with "the miserable peasantry of Poland ... and the days of feudal vassalage," to show that by taking "the black side of the picture ... every human occupation will be found pregnant with fatal objections." In reference to this amendment, Clay continued,

"Our maritime operations ought not (in time of war) depend upon the casualties of foreign supply."

Finally, summing up in one paragraph the tone of this Senate session, Clay said,

> The three great subjects that claim the attention of the National Legislature are the interests of agriculture, commerce, and manufactures. We have had before us a proposition to afford a manly protection to the rights of commerce, and how has it been treated? Rejected! You have been solicited to promote agriculture, by increasing the facilities of internal communication through the means of canals and roads, and what has been done? Postponed! We are now called upon to give a trifling support to our domestic manufactories, and shall we close the circle of Congressional inefficiency by adding this also to the catalogue?[39]

This time Clay won his argument by a vote of 22 to 9. Nevertheless, he had little success in any further senatorial efforts and had become disenchanted with the temper of the Senate. Even as the session was ending on May 1, Clay supporters back home in Kentucky were publicly urging that he serve as the direct representative of the people rather than in the Senate as an elected representative of the legislature. Leaving Washington a bit early and making excellent time in the stagecoaches of the day, Clay was home by May 14, and on that day he placed an insertion in the *Kentucky Gazette* announcing his candidacy for a seat in the U.S. House of Representatives for the 12th Congress. He said, "In presenting myself to your notice, I conform to sentiments I have invariably felt, in favor of the station of an immediate representative of the people."[40]

There was another unofficial reason for Clay's desire to leave the Senate. He expressed it in a letter to Secretary of State James Monroe later in the year.

> Accustomed to the popular branch of a Legislature, and preferring the turbulence (if I may be allowed the term) of a numerous body to the solemn stillness of the Senate chamber, it was a mere matter of taste that led me, perhaps injudiciously, to change my station.[41]

Though this letter was written after Clay's election to the House (which took place in August 1810) he still had another session to serve in the United States Senate before his House career was to begin.

8

THE WESTERN STAR

The congressional election of 1810, in which Henry Clay was a candidate for a seat in the U.S. House of Representatives, was held in Kentucky on August 6, 7, and 8. The current Congress was to expire on March 3, 1811, with a session scheduled through the winter months of 1810–11. Thus, despite his unopposed election to the House, Clay still was due to return to Washington later in the year as a senator at a time of growing national crisis.

The previous session of the 11th Congress had shown clearly a dissension, a disorganization, and a disarray within the federal government that had begun before the end of Jefferson's presidency. The Federalist party was sluggishly riding off into extinction. The Jeffersonian Republican-Democrats were disintegrating into quarrelsome factions.

Republican defections in both Houses of Congress had given birth to the Clintonians, the Quids, the Invisibles, and an unnamed group which still supported the administration. The Clintonians were principally New Englanders and New Yorkers who tended to gather the support of fading Federalists behind aging Vice President George Clinton. The Quids, mostly House members led by Virginian John Randolph of Roanoke, included a number of Pennsylvanians who tied their hopes to a renewal of the political career of James Monroe (temporarily out of office and at odds with President Madison over issues arising out of the presidential election of 1808). The Invisibles were an ever-changing coterie of senators following the guidance of Samuel Smith of Maryland in his opposition to everything touched by Secretary of the Treasury Albert Gallatin. Finally, there was the small gathering of legislators who backed Jefferson's protege, President James Madi-

son, of whom Henry Clay was an admirer. While Clay still considered himself a Jeffersonian, his sanguine call for "a new military ardor" was a far cry from Jefferson's passion for peace.

Making matters worse in Washington, the rift within the Congress was accompanied by contentions and mediocrity in the president's own Cabinet. Part of this was due to the pressure exerted by Senator Samuel Smith at the beginning of Madison's term in March 1809. By his demands, Smith was able to elevate his brother, Robert, from secretary of the Navy under Jefferson (whom he had served with credibility) into the cabinet's highest office, that of secretary of state. Madison had wished Gallatin would take State, giving Treasury to Smith. Though Gallatin dearly wanted State, he balked at the proposal recognizing that he would have to run both departments because of Smith's lack of experience in handling fiscal affairs. So Madison made Robert Smith secretary of state knowing he (Madison) would have to backstop foreign affairs. In the earlier days of Jefferson's administration Smith and Gallatin were close friends. But by the opening of the Madison presidency rancor had grown between these two cabinet members.

Meanwhile, the two bulwarks of national defense, the departments of war and navy, were managed by near nonentities. The War Department was under William Eustis of Massachusetts, an amiable man but incompetent administrator. Under him was a skimpy army of less than 7,000 men, mostly posted in the New Orleans area along with small units in posts spread out over a vast unsettled land. Yet much of this army, officially commanded by General James Wilkinson, was ravaged by disease. Then in the spring of 1810,

Wilkinson had been ordered to Washington where two congressional committees were inquiring into the debilitated condition of the troops under his command and into his "public life, character, and conduct."

The navy was only a trifle better off. It was headed by Paul Hamilton, a rice farmer in private life, who, as governor of South Carolina, had advocated military preparedness. Nevertheless, under Jefferson the navy had dwindled to only 16 ships of the line, of which seven were well-built and well-manned frigates. The other nine vessels were smaller brigs, sloops, or corvettes that provided little more defense than orange crates.

In only one other department beside treasury did Madison have an advisor of some strength. This was his Attorney General Caesar Rodney of Delaware, who had succeeded Clay's fellow Kentuckian and good friend, John Breckinridge. Rodney and Clay also formed a close friendship in the spring of 1810. In the summer of that year, an undertone of the issues to be faced in the coming session of the 11th Congress was revealed in a letter written by Clay to Rodney on the first day of the three-day election that was to send Clay to the U.S. House of Representatives.

In the letter, Clay noted recent confiscations of U.S. property by France in countries under Napoleon's control. While terming it "an act of infamous treachery, if not of open robbery," Clay told the attorney general, "I scarcely know of an injury that France could do us, short of an actual invasion of our Territory, that would induce me to go to War with her, whilst the injuries we have received from Great Britain remain unredressed."

Clay's outrage at England had been rekindled in recent weeks with word of another British attack on the high seas similar to the one on the *Chesapeake* three years earlier. This time John Trippe, captain of the brig *Vixen*, had acted in the same manner as had Barron by trying to "parley" after receiving two shots. Clay, who had fought a duel only 19 months earlier, merely because of insulting language, expressed his exasperation to Rodney saying, "A man receives a fillip on the nose, and instead of instantly avenging the insult, inquires of the person giving it what he means!"[1] Rodney had a very personal reason for anguish over the episode since his son, aboard the Vixen, had been slightly wounded in the attack. Also,

another friend of Clay's, the congressional delegate from Mississippi, George Poindexter and his family, had been placed in jeopardy as passengers on the *Vixen*. These and other incidents in the international arena during 1810 thrust themselves on an American government that was growing incohesive. Into this vacuum of leadership lame duck Senator Henry Clay was to step boldly in the months to come.

As the third session of the 11th Congress convened on December 3, 1810, President Madison's first concern was neither the politics of a divisive cabinet and an antagonistic Congress, nor the contemptuous belligerence of Britain and France (though the war between these two nations was the catalyst for his concern). Rather it was a crisis in West Florida, partially the consequences of the deterioration of Spanish power resulting from the Napoleonic conflicts, partially due to the restlessness of American settlers in the region, and partially the outgrowth of a tangle of unclear and covert diplomacy over many decades.

West Florida was a disputed region along the Gulf of Mexico, extending eastward from the Mississippi River (except for "the island of New Orleans" obtained in the Louisiana purchase) to the Perdido River, which now forms the state line between Alabama and Florida. The strip of land's northern boundary was 31 degrees north latitude. Since the early explorations of this area by Spain and France, possession was transferred among those two nations and England in public and secret treaties until the true ownership was uncertain. At one time, Spain held both the Louisiana Territory and West Florida. When cession of Louisiana was made by Spain to France, it was unclear whether West Florida was included. But all three European powers were willing to deny that it was part of Louisiana.

Briefly, at the end of the French and Indian War, France turned over to Spain what was to become the Louisiana Territory, and Spain relinquished East and West Florida to England. At the conclusion of the American Revolution, England returned both Floridas to Spain. Thus, just prior to Spain's transfer of Louisiana to France in 1803, Spain possessed both Louisiana and all of the Floridas. When the American ministers, negotiating the Louisiana purchase, asked the French foreign minister to define the eastern boundary, they were told it was the same as it was when it was ceded by Spain to France. When pressed further for a more definite answer, the foreign minister said he did not know what that boundary was. In reality, the United States did not know if Spain had ceded West Florida to France along with Louisiana (in which case the territory came to the United States with the Louisiana purchase) or if Spain had retained all of the Floridas (and therefore still owned them in 1810).

During this period of uncertainty, Napoleon had continued his European wars and had defeated the Austrians and Prussians and made peace with Russia. In 1808, he turned his attention to Portugal (England's ally in the wars). To strike at them, he deemed it necessary to cross Spain. By this time Spain, though allied with France, resisted the French armies trying to cross over to attack Portugal. Napoleon put down the resistance and forced the abdications of Spain's King Charles IV and his heir, Ferdinand. Napoleon made his brother, Joseph, King of Spain. Therefore, by 1810 Spain could not control her own government, let alone her possessions throughout North and South America. Internal revolutions began to spring up in many countries of South America. England made moves that suggested she would take control of Spanish possessions in America. If it were proved that West Florida were still Spanish, a threat appeared that England might seize a foothold in that land where several United States rivers emptied into the Gulf of Mexico. It was clear to President Madison that this could not be tolerated.

Though both Jefferson and Madison believed the United States became owners of West Florida in 1803, they allowed Spain to continue to occupy the territory. But Spain, in its weakened power, was lackadaisical in governing West Florida. Meanwhile, a sizeable number of Americans from Kentucky, Tennessee, and the Mississippi Territory settled along the numerous rivers that flowed through the disputed strip of land and emptied into the Gulf of Mexico. Following Napoleon's occupation of Spain, the settlers in West Florida watched as revolts against Spanish rule broke out in Buenos Aires, Argentina, and Caracas, Venezuela. Then, during the summer of 1810, those American settlers made certain demands of their Spanish governor. When the demands were re-fused, they attacked and captured the Spanish fort at Baton Rouge, Louisiana. On September 26, they proclaimed their independence. At the same time they wrote the government in Washington asking for recognition as a state in the U.S. Federal Union.

Since Madison believed the land was already a U.S. possession (which had not formally been handed over by Spain), he could not recognize the settlers' claim. But he could, he believed, take possession of the land in the name of the United States. This he did by proclamation on October 27, suggesting that U.S. failure to possess the territory "may lead to events ultimately contravening the views of both parties."[2] In other words, it was to forestall claims as well as the threat of possession by either Britain or France.

But Madison wanted congressional support for his action and made that request in his annual message on December 5, 1810, two days after the 3rd session of the 11th Congress convened. He asked Congress to declare the laws of the Orleans Territory (one of two sections into which the Louisiana purchase had been divided) extended eastward to the Perdido River.

Henry Clay, who brought his family to Washington for this session, did not take his seat in the Senate until the 13th of the month. Debate on the occupation of West Florida did not begin until the 27th when John Pope of Kentucky made a speech supporting Madison's action. On the following day, Senator Outerbridge Horsey of Delaware challenged Madison's authority, either under the Constitution or by act of Congress, to take possession of West Florida by force. He argued that Spain never relinquished West Florida to France and therefore it was not part of the Louisiana Purchase. He claimed that when Great Britain owned the Floridas, between the French and Indian War and the end of the American Revolution, she had set up the two regions of East and West Florida and that when Spain, following the Revolution, possessed both Louisiana and the Floridas, they were three distinct provinces. Thus, with the cession of Louisiana to France, West Florida was not included, Horsey contended. He went on to charge that the United States executed an act of war against Spain only after that country was allied with England and no longer associated with France in the European wars.

To answer the remarks made by Horsey, Henry Clay had done his homework, outlining in notes the history of the diplomatic transfer of the vast territories in question. But when he rose to rebut Horsey, Clay said he had hoped someone else would

> undertake to reply to the ingenious argument you have just heard. But not perceiving any one disposed to do so, a sense of duty obliges me, though very unwell, to claim your indulgence while I offer my sentiments on the subject.

The Kentuckian then went into great detail based on his outline. In his accounting, he pointed out that when Spain came into possession of both Louisiana and West Florida (following the American Revolution) the governing of both provinces was placed under the governor of Louisiana. He then summarized the complicated series of transfers among England, France and Spain, concluding again that the United States came into possession of the disputed territory through the Louisiana Purchase. On the basis of this, he then claimed, President Madison would have been derelict in his duties had he not taken possession of West Florida, particularly since a number of congressional acts gave him authority to do so in Clay's judgment.

Then Clay took a different tack, considering the situation from the hypothesis that Spain truly owned the territory and that now Senate opponents of the proclamation feared Spain's ally, Great Britain, might act against the United States because of the acquisition. "Is the time never to arrive," Clay reproached his Senate opponents,

> when we may manage our affairs without the fear of insulting His Britannic Majesty? Is the rod of British power to be forever suspended over our heads? Does Congress put on an embargo to shelter our rightful commerce against the piratical depredation of offending England. Is the law of non-intercourse proposed? The whole navy of the haughty mistress of the seas is made to thunder in our ears. Does the President refuse to continue a correspondence with a Minister who violates the decorum belonging to his diplomatic character, by giving and deliberately repeating an affront to the whole nation? We are instantly menaced with the chastisement which English pride will not fail to inflict. Whether we assert our rights by sea or attempt their maintenance by land—whithersoever we turn ourselves, this phantom incessantly pursues us.

Clay then boldly remarked that if the occupation of West Florida meant war with England, "I trust and hope that all hearts will unite in a bold and vigorous vindication of our rights." But Clay said he did not "believe in the prediction that war will be the effect of the measure in question." In concluding his rousing speech, he declared it was his

> hope to see, ere long, the *new* United States (if you will allow me the expression) embracing not only the old thirteen States, but the entire country east of the Mississippi, including East Florida, and some of the territories to the north of us also.[3]

Like his fiery speech during the first session of this Congress earlier in the year, his eloquence roused a lethargic nation and a dispirited government. The Republican press seized on his speech to acclaim this rising "western star." One champion of the lame duck senator wrote:

> The Senate have often witnessed an exhibition of Mr. Clay's powers in debate; and they have recently heard him with instruction and delight vindicate the rights of the nation and the wise policy of the republican administration, in taking possession of Florida. His speech on this subject, in learning, argument and eloquence, has seldom been surpassed in America.
> Bold and vigorous, inestimably convincing, the elocution of Mr. Clay seems to have been formed on the model of the celebrated Grecian orator. His style is nervous; his language correct and polished. He is not profuse of classic allusions; but his speeches are chaste in this respect. His prominent aim is to command attention and enforce conviction. The hearer is not permitted to infer anything; every feeling is assailed, no argument is left untouched, to strengthen and elucidate every position which the orator assumes. Mr. Clay is often keenly sarcastick; federalism writhed under the agonizing severity with which he adverted, on Friday last, to its excessive sensibility, whenever a measure was proposed which might possibly affect the haughty mistress of the ocean. In gesture this gentleman does not very much indulge himself; but he is infinitely superior in action to the mass of Congressional orators. If he does not *always* "suit the action to the word, and the word to the action," he takes special care not to overstep "the modesty of nature...." The voice of Mr. Clay is sometimes musical, always energetick and vehement.
> As a politician or statesman, he is all that becomes an American republican. A sacred reverence for the publick liberties; love of country; an ardent

zeal, tempered with prudence and wisdom, for its honour and welfare, are the predominant feelings of his Roman soul.

The writer of this letter to a Baltimore paper added that he had

> long looked forward to the time when Mr. Clay would be hailed as one of the brightest luminaries of his country; when the republick would greet him, as one of the most powerful champions of her liberties and independence.[4]

Of course, Clay's eloquence did not turn away all opposition to Madison's moves into West Florida. Massachusetts Federalist Senator Timothy Pickering went so far as to read to the Senate in public session a letter, written in 1804 by French Foreign Minister Charles Maurice Talleyrand to the American Minister at Paris, which denied that the United States had acquired West Florida by the Louisiana Purchase. Maryland Senator Samuel Smith then inquired whether the letter had ever been publicly communicated to the Senate. Pickering replied that indeed it was not a public paper but he questioned, "for what reason had it been communicated confidentially?" Smith pointed out that before such confidential papers could be read publicly "it was necessary that the permission of the Senate should be obtained."

At this point in the proceedings, the galleries were cleared and the Senate sat for an hour with closed doors. When the doors were reopened, Henry Clay submitted the following resolution:

> Resolved, that the public perusal in the Senate of certain papers with open galleries by the gentleman from Massachusetts, (Mr. Pickering) in his seat, without a special order of the Senate removing the injunction of secrecy, which papers had been confidentially communicated to the Senate by the President of the United States, was a palpable violation of the rules of this body.[5]

Two days later the wording of the resolution was changed slightly. Then Clay rose to say he reluctantly pressed for a decision on the resolution but believed he must do so since the Senate rule had been made

> for the precise occasion. If the Senate did not express their disapprobation, it would be inferred from their silence that they had given their approbation of the gentleman's conduct; and any individual would hereafter, if inclined, follow his example without hesitation.

After considerable debate a motion was made to remove the word "palpable" before "violation." Clay agreed to this. But then it was suggested that the word "unintentional" be inserted before "violation"; Clay responded that if it were persisted in, he should feel himself bound to move to strike out of the word the syllable "un." He was convinced that Pickering's act was intentional. Later, the debate concluded with a 20–7 vote to censure Pickering but with the resolution watered down by the absence of "palpable."[6]

Now a strange thing happened to the legislation for the occupation of West Florida. On the following day, January 3, when consideration of the bill resumed, the Senate gallery was cleared and the doors of the chamber were closed. In secret session the Senate secretary read several confidential messages to Congress from President Madison. Among these was a letter addressed to the government by Vincente Folch, the Spanish governor in West Florida. Folch stated that it was his intention to deliver up West Florida to the United States. From his note it was clear that he could no longer control "the disturbances which now afflict this province." When the Senate reopened its doors, it was moved that consideration of the West Florida bill be postponed until the next day.[7] But the measure was never to come up again.

Along with the Folch letter, President Madison also sent to the Senate a letter from John Philip Morier, the British chargé d'affaires in Washington, taking exception to Madison's proclamation to occupy West Florida at a time when England's ally, Spain, was suffering under the rule of the Bonapartes (Napoleon and Joseph). He castigated the United States, writing,

> would it not have been worthy of the generosity of a free nation like this [the United States], bearing, as it doubtless does, a respect for the rights of a gallant people at this moment engaged in a noble struggle for its liberty — would it not have been an act on the part of this country, dictated by the sacred ties of good neighborhood, and of friendship, which exist between it and Spain, to have simply offered it assistance to crush the common enemy of both, rather than wrestling a province from a friendly Power, and that in the time of her adversity?

Morier stated that sending armed forces into West Florida by the United States was "an act of hostility against Spain."[8]

Irked by British interference in Spanish-American affairs in West Florida (when even the Spaniards did not complain against American action), and in Latin America (where the British had no qualms about supporting revolution for independence against their Spanish ally), Madison secretly asked the Congress for authority "to take temporary possession" of the remainder of Florida east of the Perdido River. Fearing British conquest, as in Latin America, to spread to East Florida, Madison wrote that "the United States could not see ... any part of a neighboring territory ... pass from the hands of Spain into those of any other foreign Power."[9]

On Monday, January 7, 1811, Henry Clay, boldly assuming the role of Madison's spokesman in the Senate, reported a bill giving the president the authority to take possession of East Florida. After a few minor amendments the Senate passed the bill on January 10 and sent it to the House. By the 15th both Houses had approved the bill, but also passed a House resolution on the same subject stating that "under the peculiar circumstances of the existing crisis" and "that a due regard to their own safety" the United States could not permit that territory to pass into the hands of any other foreign Power but during a temporary occupation they were willing to negotiate its future.[10]

During all this legislative maneuvering in the Congress, American troops occupied only a portion of the disputed territory — eastward from the Mississippi River to the Pearl River, thus allowing the Spanish garrisons to remain in control of Mobile and Pensacola. Meanwhile, this newly occupied land, up to the Pearl River, was added to the Orleans Territory and together they were linked in a bill in the House of Representatives to permit the people of this combined territory to elect a convention to draft a constitution as the first step in admission into the Federal Union of States. This bill was debated in the House from January 2nd until the 15th when it was sent to the Senate — but not without hot words.

On the 14th, Representative Josiah Quincy of Massachusetts attacked the Statehood bill with the view that states could only be created out of the original part of the territory won by the United States as result of the American Revolution, that is, westward to the Mississippi River

but not including new lands acquired by purchase or conquest. He expressed the fear that new national legislators from possible western States would write laws that would overwhelm the affairs of the original states in the east. He prophesied to the House, "to me it appears that it [such a principle] would justify a revolution in this country, and that in no great length of time it may produce it." He stirred a storm of objection when he declared, as his

> deliberate opinion, that if this bill passes, the bonds of this Union are virtually dissolved; that the States which compose it are free from their moral obligations, and that, as it will be the right of all, so it will be the duty of some, to prepare definitely for a separation; amicably if they can, violently if they must.[11]

With this first spark of secession to be ignited in the Congress, Henry Clay's friend, Representative Poindexter, the delegate from the Mississippi Territory, called Quincy to order. Quincy objected to the interruption of his speech. Poindexter questioned Quincy's right to invite insurrection and a dissolution of the Union. Quincy replied that he was stating "the consequences of a measure which appears injurious." When the Speaker ruled that the latter part of Quincy's stated opinion was contrary to the order of debate, another member questioned the right of the delegate of the Mississippi Territory (who did not have a vote, as did members from states) to call a member to order. The Speaker ruled against this objection only to have the ruling appealed to the House membership. The House overruled the Speaker (56–53), thus, also, overruling Poindexter's call to order. Quincy won his battle and proceeded with his speech.[12] But he lost his war on the 15th as the House passed the bill (77–36), giving the citizens of the Orleans Territory the authority to take the first steps toward statehood. On February 7, the Senate approved the bill without a great deal of debate but with several amendments, including one "confining the suffrage in the election of the convention to free 'white' persons." The House rejected this amendment but eventually agreed to it when the Senate insisted upon it.[13]

One further major issue, rechartering the National Bank, occupied the attention of Henry Clay in the closing days of the 11th Congress. It was to have an effect on the nation's ability to wage war, should it come; and Clay's arguments against the bank were to come back to haunt him in later years.

The United States Bank (or National Bank, as it was sometimes called) was chartered for 20 years in 1791 by Alexander Hamilton and was viewed by Republicans as a tool of the Federalists who believed in a strong central government. During its existence more than two-thirds of its stock passed into the hands of British owners (though voting power rested only in the hands of domestic shareholders). Most of the remainder was controlled by Federalists. It is small wonder that the Republicans of 1811 had little sympathy for renewal of the charter.

In addition to these negative points, more than 100 state banks had been created. Henry Clay had fought hard in the Kentucky legislature for the Lexington bank and had later become a director of the Kentucky bank.

The disarray within the Federal government was more evident over the bank issue than it was around the Florida occupation. Treasury Secretary Albert Gallatin had previously been one of the strengths of Jefferson's eight years in the presidency. He had reluctantly continued at Treasury under Madison. Yet there was a subtle difference in national affairs. Jefferson's strong passion for peace fit well Gallatin's determination to maintain a balanced budget and this was done by keeping the nation's armed forces at a minimum. On the other hand, threats of war grew under Madison's presidency and his occupation of Florida was openly termed by some as an act of war. The need for revenue to support a potential war economy was urgent. But many were blind to it. Clay seemed to be one of the blind despite his militant speeches. Others merely let their antagonisms toward Gallatin surface. These included the "Invisibles," led by Senator Samuel Smith and his followers. Unfortunately, Madison gave Gallatin little support in urging the renewal of the bank's charter.

When Gallatin's request for renewal came to the Congress, the House considered it for nearly three weeks, and then on January 24, timorously voted 65–64 to postpone a decision until the Senate took a stand on the bank.

On January 30, Gallatin wrote an appeal to his strongest supporter in the Senate, William H. Crawford of Georgia. Serving his first term in the Senate, Crawford, just short of his 39th birthday, was considered by his enemies as overbearing, high-tempered, and intriguing. But still they recognized his courage was equal to Clay's and believed his intelligence was superior, though they felt he lacked Clay's charm.[14] Gallatin later wrote that Crawford "united a powerful mind, a most correct judgment, and an inflexible integrity; which last quality, not sufficiently tempered by indulgence and civility, has prevented his acquiring general popularity."[15]

Gallatin's letter to Crawford was, in reality, a follow-up of his report to Congress in March 1809, in which he urged the rechartering of the bank with the suggestion that its capital be increased from $10 million to $30 million to overcome the objection of heavy British ownership, and in which he pointed out the bank's usefulness in the event of war (a circumstance well within the realm of possibility). He advised Crawford of the distress that he believed would result to individuals and the public if the bank were allowed to fold and the banking activity of the nation were forced to depend on numerous state banks over which the Federal government had no control. He also told Crawford that the Constitutionality of the bank's charter was "not a subject of discussion for the Secretary of the Treasury," but that after 20 years of its use "by all constituted authorities of that nation" it did not appear to be unconstitutional to him.[16]

Crawford opened the Senate debate on the bank on February 11 with a long thesis on the Constitutionality of the bank, followed by a lengthy assertion that it would be unwise to rely on state banks to handle the government's revenue. He argued that three or four great commercial states along the Atlantic Coast showed a greed for dividends accruing from the deposits of federal money in their vaults. He referred to the chaos of war in Europe and its destructive effect upon American commerce and economy through the recent seizure of ships and cargoes and the impressment of seamen by the belligerents. And he praised Gallatin, though recognizing that "some members do not have a high estimate of the Secretary."[17]

Two other Senate speeches followed, one for

and one against the bank, before William Branch Giles of Virginia, one of the Invisibles, bored his colleagues by rendering a confusing two-hour monologue on the feebleness of the Republican administration in exercising the unlimited powers granted by the Constitution "to repel foreign aggressions, to assert our rights, and to do ourselves justice," but he was willing to contend that the power of bank incorporation "is not among the common, necessary and proper means of effecting" the enumerated powers in the Constitution.

Admitting that the Virginia legislature (which had elected him to the Senate) had instructed him to oppose renewal of the bank (which view corresponded to his own), Giles proceeded to assert that the legislature's instructions were only advisory and if extensively indulged in, the result might be the destruction of the Senate's power to achieve anything. He, therefore, was not compelled to vote according to its bidding (though he later voted as they advised).[18]

Like Giles, Clay had received instructions from his state's legislature to oppose renewal of the bank charter. But rather than aiming his barbs at Giles on this point, when he took the floor on the 15th, he castigated another speaker, James Lloyd of Massachusetts, for giving more weight to the pleas of lobbying groups, which Clay termed "self-created societies, composed of whom no body knows," while regarding "the resolutions of those legislatures — known, legitimate, constitutional, and deliberative bodies" as "officious." Clay questioned whether a representative was bound by instructions from his constituents, but he had no doubts that a senator was bound by his state's legislature.

Clay next ridiculed Giles' Constitutionality argument, by observing that the senator "had instructed and amused us" and then

> discussed both sides of the question, with great ability and eloquence, and certainly demonstrated to the satisfaction of all who heard him, both that it was Constitutional and unconstitutional, highly proper and improper to prolong the charter of the bank.

Clay went further to compare Giles' effort to a predicament in which Patrick Henry once found himself. Henry, in one trial, mistook the side he was retained to represent. Clay told the senators that Henry had, in error,

addressed the court and jury in a very splendid and convincing speech in behalf of his antagonist. His distracted client came up to him whilst he was progressing, and interrupting him, bitterly exclaimed, "You have undone me! You have ruined me!" — "Never mind, give yourself no concern," said the adroit advocate; and turning to the court and jury, continued his argument by observing, "May it please your honor, and you, gentlemen of the jury, I have been stating to you what I presume my adversary may urge on his side. I will now show you how fallacious his reasoning & groundless his pretensions are.

Clay noted that "the skillful orator proceeded, satisfactorily refuted every argument he had advanced, and gained his cause! A success with which I trust the exertion of my honorable friend will on this occasion be crowned."

Returning to the substance of the bank debate, Clay challenged Crawford's long theme on implied powers of the Constitution. Clay argued that if the bank were created under implied powers, it should operate only in areas laid out under a specific power and not stray from that area. He said,

> If then you could establish a bank to collect and distributed the revenue, it ought to be expressly restricted to the purpose of such collection and distribution. It is mockery, worse than usurpation to establish it for a lawful object, and then extend it to other objects which are not lawful.

He told bank supporters, "You cannot *create the necessity* of a bank, and then plead *that necessity* for its establishment."

Also in reply to Crawford, he pointed out that much of the Federal government's banking operation was conducted through state banks and that it was safer to have operations spread than to have them centralized in the event of corruption.

Against Crawford's argument that our possession of English capital must operate on those investors to influence the British Government in our favor, Clay asked,

> has it released from galling and ignominious bondage one solitary American seaman, bleeding under British oppression? Did it prevent the unmanly attack upon the *Chesapeake?* Did it arrest the promulgation, or has it abrogated the orders in council? In spite of all its boastful effect, are not the two nations brought to the very brink of war?[19]

The debate on the bank bill continued for another five days before being brought to a vote. On

February 20, a 17–17 tie vote was broken by Vice President George Clinton.[20] After a short speech (written by Henry Clay)[21] on the Constitutionality of the bank's charter, Clinton cast his vote to strike out the first section of the bank bill, thus ending its existence.

While the Kentucky press excoriated Clay's colleague, John Pope, for voting in opposition to the instructions of their state's legislature and in favor of the bank, the eastern Republican newspapers again lauded Clay's effort. One writer said the speech abounded "in strong perspicuous argument and in stubborn facts, pronounced in the most natural and emphatic manner. Such a display of forceful oratory I have never witnessed in a legislative body."[22] A Virginia paper, which criticized its own senator (Giles), prophesied of Clay, "whose shining talents and patriotic course, if persisted in, will one day raise him to the highest honors."[23]

Also praising Clay was one of the reporters who had covered the Burr trial in Richmond — Washington Irving. In a letter from the capital to his brother, Irving called Clay "one of the finest fellows I have seen here, and one of the finest orators in the Senate, though I believe the youngest man in it." But Irving noted that during Clay's bank speech, "the galleries were so crowded with ladies and gentlemen, that he was completely frightened and acquitted himself very little to his own satisfaction."[24]

While Clay was growing in popularity during this session of Congress, he was not as active in social circles as he had been during his earlier tours in Washington, principally because his family was with him, and Lucretia was pregnant again. They were now living at Mrs. Wilson's boarding house with other members of Congress, along with Samuel Harrison Smith (editor of The *National Intelligencer*) and his wife Margaret Bayard Smith.

Mrs. Smith, who referred to Clay as "the admired orator," wrote that

> I have formed habits of sociability with Mr. and Mrs. Clay only — Mrs. Clay is a woman of strong natural sense, very kind and friendly. She often brings work of an evening into our room and in the morning I go to hers — we help each other dress and she always offers us seats in her carriage when we visit together, — or go a shopping, and

her woman who has been the nurse of all her children, attends to mine whenever I wish it. With the rest I have little intercourse except at breakfast and dinner. Our parlour is as retired as if in our own house. We have our tea tables set as regularly and as comfortable as at home, and Mrs. Wilson endeavors in every way to make us comfortable. She always sends up a snack for the children and myself between dinner and breakfast, and whenever I want it for supper. After the children go to bed I generally sew and if I want company I have only to go down stairs, where there is generally a large circle. I have only passed one evening down below and that was to play chess. We have a great chess player here, Mr. Marke from New York — he is invincible.[25]

Despite the closeness of the boarding house company, Mrs. Clay did occasionally go out into society and even, as Mrs. Smith put it, "persuaded me to go to the levee" at the President's House on New Year's Day of 1811. Washington Irving also attended these levees, dinners and balls where, he said, of his first, he

> found a crowded collection of great and little men, of ugly old women and beautiful young ones, and in ten minutes was hand in glove with half the people in the assemblage. Mrs. Madison is a fine, portly buxom dame, who has a smile and a pleasant word for everybody ... but as to Jemmy Madison — ah! poor Jemmy! — he is but a withered little apple-John.[26]

Madison was only five feet, four inches tall.

Little or not, Madison displayed plenty of spunk and fire when Clay's coup de grace to the bank bill tossed a cabinet crisis into Madison's hands. It was initiated by Treasury Secretary Gallatin. While recognizing that the bank's most formidable opponent was Senator Henry Clay, Gallatin ascribed its defeat more to the combination of Clintonians (smarting from George Clinton's defeat by Madison for the presidency in 1804) and the Invisibles (angered by insinuations of unsavory financial transactions leveled two years earlier by Gallatin against the Smith brothers). With matters deteriorating weekly between Gallatin and Robert Smith, Gallatin finally wrote a letter of resignation to President Madison following the adjournment of Congress.

Observing to Madison that "a perfect heartfelt cordiality" among cabinet members was "necessary to command the public confidence," Gallatin told the president, "New subdivisions and personal factions, equally hostile to yourself and to the general welfare, daily acquire additional strength." He referred to measures defeated, operations prevented or impeded, and confidence impaired. He advised Madison that to continue at his cabinet post was "no longer of any public utility, invigorates the opposition against yourself, and must necessarily be attended with increased loss of reputation. to myself."[27]

But Madison had great admiration for Gallatin and had become increasingly irritated by the handling of foreign affairs by Robert Smith. It had been galling enough for Madison that he had to run the State Department while administering the entire Executive Branch. But gradually the president came to the realization that Smith had not only been undermining the chief executive's efforts in foreign relations, he had even been sabotaging them with false communications between the president and foreign ambassadors.

Adjournment of Congress put confirmation of a new secretary of state out of reach of Senator Samuel Smith and his friends for several months to come. And Madison had now found the ideal man to replace Robert Smith — newly elected governor of Virginia, James Monroe. Through intermediaries Madison sounded out Monroe to learn whether, if offered, the governor would accept the cabinet post — provided the two Virginians could agree to try harder to reach "an accommodation with England ... rather than hazard war."[28]

Around March 20th, Secretary Smith came to see Madison on ordinary business. During the conversation, Smith referred to a recently published account of Timothy Pickering's dismissal from office by Adams eleven years earlier. Madison turned the conversation to his intent to dismiss Smith that same day, intimating that Smith had anticipated the president's intentions.

Madison stated that there was a lack of harmony and unity within the executive branch — not in cabinet consultations "but as shewing itself in language and conduct out of doors, countering what had been understood within to be the course of the administration and the interest of the public." Smith expressed surprise at the president's comments and declared that he had given no cause for them. Nevertheless, Madison cited several incidents outside the cabinet in which Smith

had spoken against the administration's decisions, revealed confidential conversations, and even failed to carry out his normal duties as secretary (often leaving the president to write diplomatic dispatches).

To make the departure easier for Smith, President Madison proposed that the secretary take the post of minister to St. Petersburg, Russia, as "an important situation." Smith remarked quickly that "London was more so." Madison closed the door to that suggestion and Smith opened another to the Supreme Court, only to have Madison shut that one as well. Smith then alluded to his powerful friends in the Senate (where sat his brother — when in session). Madison noted that Smith "had assuredly lost ground extremely with members of both Houses of Congress."

At last Smith relented and agreed to the Russian appointment and they agreed on the first of April as the date for the change of posts. As that date approached, nothing seemed to happen and Madison called in Smith again to ask about the delay. This time, in another touchy confrontation, Smith refused the Russian mission (having been advised by friends that it was the result of intrigues against him).[29] Smith left the cabinet on the agreed date but returned to private life as president of an insurance company — but not quietly.

Writing to his senator brother, Samuel, a few days before his retirement from public service, Robert Smith gave his reasons for refusing the diplomatic post and revealed his intention to ruin Madison, saying,

> The course I have taken, I am confident, will lead to the injury of Mr. Madison and to my advantage.... Having formed my determination, I will make at this time no compromise with him. His overthrow is my object, and most assuredly will I effect it. He has already done me all the injury he presumably can. He has nothing more of malignity in store for me.[30]

Smith was wrong about Madison's overthrow. Smith disappeared into historical oblivion as Madison and his new secretary of state, James Monroe, stand great in the nation's records.

On returning to Kentucky, Henry Clay learned of Monroe's appointment and expressed his feelings on the event in an April letter to his good friend Attorney General Caesar Rodney,

The recent change in the Cabinet has excited here much attention and speculation. It is highly approved, the *Aurora* etc.,[31] to the contrary notwithstanding. It would have been gratifying to me (altho, I am aware it is hardly to be expected) that the measure was brought about, without offence to the ex-secretary and his friends. If however they choose to make the event the occasion of hostility to the administration I am persuaded, in this quarter, their efforts will be unavailing.

On an entirely different and more pleasant subject, Clay added in his letter to Rodney from Lexington, "Our journey out was better than I anticipated. We reached home several weeks ago, and since our return the event which occasioned us so much solicitude, on the way, has occurred & has put me in possession of the stoutest son we ever had, with less inconvenience to Mrs. Clay than she ever before experienced.

Henry Clay, Junior, was born on April 10—two days before Henry Clay's 34th birthday.[32]

9

MR. SPEAKER

As Representative-elect Henry Clay returned to his lucrative law practice in the Bluegrass lands of Kentucky, diplomatic moves and military events in the spring, summer, and fall of 1811 began to chart the course to be taken by the 12th Congress due to meet in December. As early as his April letter to Caesar Rodney, Clay expressed his thoughts on a possible early call of Congress to deal with the continuing indignities against American commerce perpetrated by both France and England under their obnoxious edicts.

"You enquire if I should like an extra session?" Clay asked Rodney.

> It would be personally very inconvenient to me, and yet I fear it may become necessary; for I find by information with which the mail was charged this day, that it is still questionable whether the decrees of Berlin & Milan are revoked, and I have always supposed that the call of Congress depended upon their being continued.[1]

On August 5, 1810, Napoleon reacted to Macon's Bill No. 2, in which Congress announced, in May 1810, to Britain and France that the United States would end trade with the nation that did not remove its blockading edicts. Through his foreign minister, the Duc de Cadore, Napoleon produced a letter which influenced President Madison to renew trade with France and close it to Britain. The letter which Cadore presented to the American minister, General John Armstrong, said in part,

> that the decrees of Berlin and Milan are revoked, and that after the first of November they will cease to have effect; it being understood that, in consequence of this declaration, the British shall revoke their Orders in Council ... or that the United States ... shall cause their rights to be respected by the English.

This convoluted wording was to haunt the American government for several years, and is worth reading a second time. In addition, Napoleon even had the gall (or was it Gaul?) to have his foreign minister say in this curious letter, "His Majesty loves the Americans."[2]

This information did not come to President Madison as an official French document and its wording was devious. Madison could not be certain as to its validity and waited in vain for further clarification from Armstrong. Whether or not Madison was deceived by the message, on November 2, 1810, he proclaimed trade with France renewed and non-intercourse with Great Britain restored. Madison did not believe the curtailment of trade with Britain would last long since a dispatch from William Pinkney, the American minister in London, encouraged Madison to believe the British government, under Spencer Perceval, would now terminate the Orders in Council. In March 1811, the U.S. Congress confirmed the president's actions by legislation.

During the interim, Madison got two pieces of information which added doubts about Napoleon's revocation. A newspaper account quoted a Cadore letter to Napoleon saying, "as long as England shall persist in her Orders in Council, your Majesty will persist in your decrees." Secondly, it was learned that the American brig *New Orleans Packet* had been seized in a French port.[3] It was still not clear whether these developments came under the Berlin and Milan decrees or to others not revoked.

Meanwhile, in England, Pinkney was having no success in his dialogue with the British government in his attempt to convince them that the Orders in Council should be repealed since the

French Decrees had been revoked. Pinkney was tired from five exhausting years of intense diplomatic negotiations in London and wished to return to America. For many months he had handled all the communications between the two countries since the "Erskine affair," wherein the British recalled their minister in 1809 for announcing, on his own initiative, the repeal of the orders.

By early 1811, Pinkney had instructions permitting his departure from England, if no new Minister were appointed. On this basis, he requested his leave from the British. But almost at the same time the British named Augustus Foster to fill David Erskine's Washington post. Undeterred, Pinkney left England anyway, but not before expressing his hope to the British foreign secretary that Foster would take with him to the United States instructions revoking the Orders in Council and authority to make restitution in the *Chesapeake* case.

In the ensuing weeks, relations with Britain deteriorated rapidly. On May 1, 1811, a British warship, the 38-gun frigate *Guerrière*, stopped the American brig *Spitfire* and impressed a native-born American. Five days later the U.S. frigate *President* put to sea to roam the coastline in search of the marauding British vessel. On May 16, a British ship was sighted near the site of the *Chesapeake* episode, off the Virginia capes. When it failed to identify itself in the growing dusk, firing broke out and the American warship disabled the British ship with broadsides that killed 9 and wounded 23 crew members. However, it was not the *Guerrière*, but a 20-gun corvette, the *Little Belt*.[4]

American bitterness toward Britain was again aroused, but this time with a satisfactory feeling of some retribution for the *Chesapeake* disgrace. By the middle of the summer, it was clear that diplomatic relations with Britain were no better than the naval relations. Foster and Pinkney arrived in the United States within hours of each other. President Madison and Secretary of State Monroe conferred frequently with Foster throughout July but found in him no willingness to negotiate the repeal of the British Orders in Council until France revoked her Decrees "absolutely and unconditionally." The British minister also put off talks on *Chesapeake* reparations

as a result of the *Little Belt* affair. All he wanted to discuss was British opposition to the U.S. occupation of West Florida.

With relations with Britain at a standstill and those with France unclear, President Madison issued a proclamation on July 24, 1811, summoning the 12th Congress to convene on November 4 — one month earlier than originally scheduled. As the call went out, still another grievance against the British was beginning to build to a crisis much nearer the hearth of the Clay family in the West.

In 1787, the old Congress, under the Articles of Confederation, had set up the region north of the Ohio River and east of the Mississippi River as the Northwest Territory. Under the Ordinance of 1787, the area could eventually be split into five new states. Already in 1803, Ohio had joined the Union. By 1811, the remainder was divided into Michigan, Illinois, and Indiana Territory. In 1801, William Henry Harrison, a former soldier under Mad Anthony Wayne and later under James Wilkinson, was named governor of the Indiana Territory. He had also been a congressional delegate from the territory. Over the next 10 years, he worked toward peaceful acquisition of Indian lands with the encouragement of the Federal government. In fact, President Jefferson had written to him, "Our system is to live in perpetual peace with the Indians." But his method was to entice the native away from hunting in the forests and instead develop agriculture and other domestic activities, hoping the Indians would give up the forest lands. Jefferson proposed that

> to promote this disposition to exchange lands, which they have to spare and we want, we shall push our trading uses, and be glad to see the good and influential individuals among them run in debt, because we observe that when debts get beyond what the individuals can pay, they become willing to lop them off by a cession of lands.... Should any tribe be foolhardy enough to take up the hatchet at any time, the seizing the whole country of that tribe, and driving them across the Mississippi, as the only condition of peace, would be an example to others, and a furtherance of our final consolidation.

Needless to say, Jefferson warned Harrison to consider this letter private — "it must be kept within your own breast."[5]

In 1800, the only white settlements in the Northwest Territory (exclusive of Ohio) were one settlement in future Michigan (Detroit), one in future Illinois (Kaskaskia), and two in future Indiana (Fort Wayne and Vincennes). In the next 10 years, the white population between Vincennes and Louisville, Kentucky, grew from 2,500 to 25,000 and was pressing for more land in the forests northward along the Wabash River. To the north were several disorganized Indian tribes. Some of these smaller tribes, which Harrison called "the most depraved wretches on earth," were quick to fall into Jefferson's trap of "running into debt" and were supported in this effort by the whites' illegal sale of whiskey to the Indians. From there on, murders and other acts of violence by the Indians were committed both among themselves and against the whites. To buy more whiskey, the Indians sold vast acres of the forest lands the whites sought.

Eventually, the more temperate Indians — chiefly the Shawnees — reacted. Under the leadership of two brothers, known as the Prophet and Tecumseh, they began to unite, to till the soil, and to abstain from drinking whiskey. They built a small village on Tippecanoe Creek, about halfway between Vincennes and Detroit, and called it Prophet's Town. While it all appeared peaceful, the union of the tribes disturbed Harrison. In late 1809, Harrison, by the Treaty of Fort Wayne, made one more huge land purchase from "the depraved Indians," with the consequence that other tribes in the north began to join Tecumseh's league.

By the summer of 1810, Harrison recognized Tecumseh as the true leader. Writing to Secretary of War Eustis, he said, "This brother is really the efficient man — the Moses of the family.... He is described by all as a bold, active, sensible man daring in the extreme and capable of any undertaking." Stating his claims, Tecumseh had told one of Harrison's most trusted scouts that

> The Great Spirit said he gave this great island to his red children. He placed the whites on the other side of the big water, they were not contented with their own, but came to take ours from us. They have driven us from the sea to the lakes, we can go no farther.[6]

Tecumseh informed the scout he was willing to meet with Harrison.

In August, Tecumseh, accompanied by his brother (the Prophet) and 400 fully-armed and war-painted warriors in 80 canoes, descended the Wabash and arrived at Vincennes on the 12th, despite Harrison's direction that the Indian chief should have only a small escort. It was not to be a meeting of master (Harrison) and supplicant (Tecumseh). Instead, Tecumseh took nearly three days negotiating protocol before the formal meeting took place.

Even then its beginning was inauspicious, for Harrison had himself well supported by armed troops and had "arranged" himself, like a king, ready to receive a vassal. Harrison had chairs placed on a veranda of his headquarters. His aide then told Tecumseh, "Your father requests you to sit by his side." But Tecumseh, surveying the setting and then pointing to the sky, replied, "My father? The Great Spirit is my father! The earth is my mother — and on her bosom I will recline." Thereupon, he and his warriors squatted.

At last the two men, who had heard so much about each other, now came face to face. Here was the 42-year-old Indian chief, just short of six feet tall, who lived the ways of the native American and learned of life by nature's teachings. Yet Tecumseh had learned the English language, though he never used it in formal meeting either with Americans or British. Whether speaking English or Shawnee, his eloquence was described as "nervous, concise and impressive." In his growth to leadership, he rebelled at the Indian habit of burning captives and went so far as to urge the protection of the lives of all prisoners.

On the other side of the conference was 37-year-old William Henry Harrison, the college-bred son of a signer of the Declaration of Independence. The tall, thin-faced general had given up the study of medicine for the life of a soldier. But he never took on the rough character of the western frontier fighter. He spent much of his spare time reading the histories of ancient military heroes, and in his long letters to superiors and others, he often made references to the battle exploits of Roman and Greek leaders.

The discussion between the two leaders continued for nearly a week with little result. Then on Monday, August 20, Tecumseh told Harrison that the Great Spirit intended him to unite all the tribes into one confederacy. He informed

Harrison that he was determined not only to recover the lands "illegally" sold to the whites, but also that he would kill those village chiefs who had sold the lands.

In reply, Harrison said if the Great Spirit had wanted the tribes united, he "would have taught them all to speak one language." He told the chief that the lands in dispute belonged to the Miamis when the Shawnees were driven out of Georgia by the Creeks, and the sale was no business of the Shawnees.

As Harrison's words were being translated, Tecumseh lost his temper, leaped to his feet, cast his blanket aside, gesticulated wildly, and shouted at Harrison in Shawnee. As his warriors also sprang to their feet, brandishing warclubs and tomahawks, the Americans moved to meet any violence with gun fire. Though he had drawn his sword, Harrison calmly interposed and asked for a translation. He was told Tecumseh had called him a liar and had accused the United States of cheating and imposing on the Indians. Harrison called Tecumseh a bad man and demanded the Indians return to their camp.

The next day, Tecumseh sent word to Harrison asking for a resumption of the council. Harrison agreed, but the Indians adhered to their previous position and their determination to form a confederation.

On the 22nd Harrison, with only an interpreter, went to speak to Tecumseh privately. He told the chief that the president would not agree to his demands and advised Tecumseh to relinquish them. "Well," he replied,

as the Great Chief is to determine the matter, I hope the Great Spirit will put enough sense into his head to induce him to direct you to give up this land. It is true, he is so far off he will not be injured by the war. He may sit still in his town and drink his wine while you and I will have to fight it out.[7]

Matters rested during the fall and winter of 1810–11 with Secretary of War William Eustis advising Harrison against precipitous action. But in the summer of 1811, after another outbreak of violence between whites and Indians, Harrison sent Tecumseh a note complaining of Indian consolidation and threats. Tecumseh sent back word that he would come to Vincennes again to meet Harrison. He arrived on July 27 with two to three hundred warriors. He informed Harrison that he was going south to Tennessee and Alabama to seek a union with the Cherokees and Creeks. (Tecumseh was half Creek himself.) He told Harrison that more Indians would be settling at Prophet's Town and he hoped the whites would make no attempt to settle in the disputed territory in his absence.

It is not clear why Tecumseh made the mistake of threatening Harrison and then disappearing far from his warriors for several months. Harrison recognized the absence of the Indian leader as a ripe opportunity to break up the confederation. He issued a call for support. Secretary Eustis ordered an army unit from Pittsburgh.

To the south, Henry Clay read Kentucky papers relating accounts of the Indians receiving arms and supplies from the British in Canada across the river from Detroit. They told of more tribes uniting for a general attack on the white settlements "as soon as the corn is ripe enough for food."

An editorial in the *Kentucky Gazette* read,

British intrigue and British gold, it seems, has had greater influence with them of late than American justice and benevolence. Be it so, but let England not hide herself any longer behind the curtain — let her appear to the world as she is, the instigator and protector of strange cruelties.... We have in our possession information which proves the late disturbances to be owing to the successful intrigues of British emissaries with the Indians.[8]

A few weeks later, to substantiate this opinion, the same paper reprinted from another paper,

In the year 1810, a Miami chief having received at Fort Malden his annual donation of goods, was thus addressed by Elliott, the British agent: "My son, keep your eyes fixed on me — My tomahawk is up, be you ready — but do not strike until I give you the SIGNAL."

The *Gazette* warned in an editorial in October 1811, "So some of these Indians appear to have gone to Malden, to receive the British signal and appear anxious to strike."[9]

Within days, Kentuckians answered Harrison's call for volunteers, and those wishing to enlist were advised "to send a note to Col. Daveiss in Lexington." This was Clay's old legal antagonist — Joseph Hamilton Daveiss.

Sometime in August, in the middle of the recruitment fever, Henry Clay received notice of the early call of Congress and wrote to his friend, Attorney General Rodney, that he assumed it was occasioned by "the state of our foreign affairs." He still believed that the French Decrees had been totally and absolutely revoked, but that Britain did not believe it, would not respond in kind with a lifting of her Orders in Council, and would, in fact, retaliate against the American non-importation law. Despite Indian threats nearer home, Clay's thoughts were more directed toward national problems.

In this same letter, Clay took time to discuss a prospective change of office for Rodney, which was one among several top-level government shifts during the year. At the time of Robert Smith's removal from the State Department in April and the appointment of James Monroe in his place, Smith was offered the post of minister to Russia, then held by John Quincy Adams. But Adams wished to complete a task he was pursuing there, and Smith asked instead to fill a vacancy on the Supreme Court created by the death, in June 1811, of Samuel Chase, the justice who was acquitted in the impeachment trial presided over by Aaron Burr in 1805. Madison refused the Supreme Court chair for Smith and by August Clay had heard that Rodney was "to be translated to the Bench, and Mr. Pinckney [sic] to be placed in your situation."[10] Clay was quite pleased with this prospect. However, Madison named Gabriel Duval of Maryland to the seat on the High Court. Rodney, miffed at being passed over, left the government on December 5, with Pinkney still getting his seat in the cabinet as attorney general.

Some three weeks after Rodney left the cabinet in late 1811, fellow Delawarean Senator James Bayard wrote to Rodney (in a form showing no breaks in the dialogue between himself and Paul Hamilton):

Your friend Paul Hamilton [secretary of the navy] called to make me a visit and after other indifferent conversation, I remarked to him that I had had a letter from our friend Rodney since I had seen him last, and that upon the fullest consideration since he had returned home he was wholly satisfied with the step he had taken, and what was that he asked with surprise. I refer said I to his resignation of the office of Attn General. What he exclaimed with great surprise had he resigned? I understood

from him I replied that he had communicated to you his intention before he left Washington. What has he left Washington? I never heard a word about the affair or otherwise it has entirely escaped my recollection. It is nearly three weeks Sir since he left us, and have you not known of Mr. Pickney's [Bayard had wrong spelling] being appointed to his place? Not a word of it. It has been in the newspapers for a considerable time; I have never seen it; I never knew a word about it. I am really very sorry — Rodney was a very amiable man and I had a great regard for him. How do you account for this that one member of the Cabinet should not know so long after that another was absent or had resigned? To me it is passing strange.[11]

In any case, this cabinet change denied Clay the friendship he had anticipated renewing with Rodney when he reached Washington with his family in early November 1811.

The comings and goings within the Federal government were not the exclusive province of the Executive or Judicial Branches. In fact, the wholesale transformation in the Legislative Branch was even more dramatic. In the Senate, both incumbents from Rhode Island were replaced by new members. George M. Bibb, of Lexington, took Henry Clay's old seat to represent Kentucky. Tennessee and Massachusetts also sent new senators. Clay's move for censure may have been indirectly responsible for the displacement of Senator Timothy Pickering from Massachusetts by Speaker of the House Joseph B. Varnum. But this transfer was to have a direct effect on Clay and United States history.

In the House of Representatives the "purge" was one of the greatest in the congressional chronicles. The new membership comprised 62 freshmen — fully 44 percent of the total body. That percentage or greater held for 10 of the 17 states, with New Hampshire clearing out its entire five-man delegation. Only 11 of Massachusetts' 20 members of the 11th Congress retained their seats in the 12th Congress, while six came back from Maryland's 11 members, eight from New York's 18, 10 from Pennsylvania's 19, and 15 from Virginia's 24.

As interesting as are the numbers, even more so are a few of the new personalities taking seats in the new Congress. From Tennessee came old John Sevier (one of the state's pioneers) and Felix Grundy (one of Clay's earliest antagonists in the

Kentucky legislature). One of three future vice presidents in this assemblage, William R. King, came to represent a North Carolina district. Much would be heard from William Lowndes and John C. Calhoun (another future vice president), both of whom took seats to represent South Carolina. And of course, Henry Clay was a new member from Kentucky.

These freshmen — most of them under 40 years of age — joined several veteran members of note. One of Clay's Kentucky colleagues, Richard M. Johnson, was the third future vice president in this body. Josiah Quincy of Massachusetts had already achieved national recognition by his threat of the violent separation of New England from the rest of the country. But the most outstanding and the most domineering member of the House, returning to his seat in the 12th Congress, was John Randolph of Roanoke, Virginia.

Randolph, foreman of the Burr grand jury in Richmond in 1807, was one of the most eccentric of men ever to sit in the halls of Congress. His erratic temperament sometimes verged on insanity. Yet he was a talented and learned orator who filled his speeches with cutting barbs and bitter sarcasm. His lengthy monologues often rambled far from the debated matter into "the fields of history, sacred and profane, ancient and modern, biography, poetry, and politics" wherein "he gathered and scattered fruit, flowers, precious stones, and worthless pebbles. To listen to one of his interminable harangues was at once a rich repast and a tedious task. To report him was impossible."[12] He commonly inserted long parenthetical comments into his theme, and just as often switched themes or ended them in mid-sentence.

In appearance, Randolph carried the facial traits of his Indian ancestry (he was a sixth generation descendant of Pocahontas). On entering Congress in 1799, already well over the minimum age of 25 prescribed for House members, Randolph had the guise of a mere skinny effeminate youth. When called to the Speaker's table to take the oath as a representative that first day in the House, the Speaker, Theodore Sedgwick, questioned whether his age was sufficient under the Constitution, Randolph's snapped reply, "Ask my constituents, satisfied the Speaker and, in effect, set the tone of his career."[13]

Twelve years later, when Henry Clay became his colleague in 1811, Randolph's youthful image and vitriolic tongue were still his dominant characteristics. Senator Plumer once wrote of him,

> His speeches were too personal — his allusions to brothel-houses & pig stys too course [*sic*] & vulgar — his arraigning the motives of members charging them with peculation, bribery, & corruption, were insufferable — He lashed demos & feds indiscriminately — He treated no man that was opposed to him with either respect or decency. The Speaker [Nathaniel Macon of North Carolina] ought to have called him to order — for his conduct was insufferable; but the Speaker dared not offend him.[14]

Speaker Varnum, of the 11th Congress, was no stranger in dealing with Randolph. Still, a nasty episode which occurred during the most recent session, can not be blamed on Varnum's lack of control over the members, since the incident took place after adjournment one day. As members left the chamber, Willis Alston, annoyed by Randolph and the dog at his heels, shouted at him that "the puppy still had respect shown him." For that, and possible other "offensive or foul language" (to use Randolph's phrase), Alston received a severe cane whipping over the head.[15]

This was the political and personality climate to which the 12th Congress travelled for the purpose of meeting in November 1811. The last two weeks of October provided the members with gorgeous weather to make their journey to Washington by packet, stagecoach, and horseback. Many of them arrived in the capital a day or two early. It was clear to all of the old members, and many of the new ones, that the decorum and order of the House were in disarray and its members intimidated. During the evening prior to the opening of Congress, several of the young new members, along with some of the old hands, met at a local boardinghouse to appraise the condition of the House. It was agreed that some reform was urgent. When questioned how this was to be achieved, one member replied, "By electing a Speaker who will enforce order." Varnum, the Speaker of the previous Congress, had gone to the Senate.

"Then it must be some man who can bridle John Randolph," replied another, "for he disregards all rules."

"Then" said one, "he must be a man who can meet John Randolph on the floor or on the field, for he may have to do both."

"But where is the man who can do this?" it was asked.

"I'll tell you," said Jonathan Roberts of Pennsylvania. "Young Henry Clay will be a member of the House and is the very man to do it."[16]

On Monday, November 4, 1811, the 12th Congress convened at 11 A.M. and on the first ballot in the election of a new Speaker, Henry Clay received 75 votes to 38 for William W. Bibb of Georgia and a scattering of 6 votes for others.

Though new to the House and without a day's seniority, the unprecedented action was not without strong reason. The 34-year-old freshman had already achieved renown in a defense of a vice president before two sittings of grand juries. He had been the speaker of the Kentucky House of Representatives. He had served in the "senior" body of Congress, fulfilling two unexpired terms of others, where he was acclaimed as a conspicuous orator and man of destiny. And he had stood on the "field of honor" with a political foe.

During Clay's senatorial tours, the House chamber in the south wing of the Capitol (now becoming his new political home) was still a mass of confused construction. But by 1811, it was a finished beauty. Much larger than the Senate chamber, the elliptical room, first occupied by the House of Representatives in October 1807, was surrounded by 22–24 Corinthian columns, shaded on all sides with red flannel curtains. Light entered from above through skylights of inch-thick glass. Between two pillars, and beneath a large stonecut eagle with extended wings, was the Speaker's chair surrounded with the richest scarlet and green velvets and gold fringe. The windows had rich scarlet curtains of velvet with yellow gold and gilt frames. On the Turkish carpet each member had his own well-stuffed armchair and desk of elegant cabinet work. Visitors could watch — but could scarcely hear — the representatives from a low gallery that followed the curve of the chamber opposite the Speaker's "royal" rostrum.[17]

Somewhat akin to watching a youthful prince suddenly become king before maturity, the House members and the packed gallery waited expectantly, and yet with sympathy, as the freshman Clay mounted the steps to the Speaker's chair to assume leadership over this fractious body of men. From his imposing vantage overlooking his colleagues, Clay was sworn in as Speaker by William

Findley of Pennsylvania. In brief remarks, Clay acknowledged the membership's deed of trust:

Gentlemen: In coming to the station which you have done the honor to assign me — an honor for which you will be pleased to accept my thanks — I obey rather your commands than my own inclination. I am sensible of the imperfections which I bring along with me, and a consciousness of these would deter me from attempting a discharge of the duties of the chair, did I not rely confidently upon your generous support.

Should the rare and delicate occasion present itself when your Speaker should be called upon to check or control the wanderings or intemperance in debate, your justice will, I hope, ascribe to his interposition the motives only of public good and a regard to the dignity of the house. And in all instances, be assured, gentlemen, that I shall, with infinite pleasure, afford every facility in my power to the despatch of public business, in the most agreeable manner.[18]

Despite Clay's past achievements, it was recognized by all that he was still an untested national leader. The first test was not long in coming, and it was only natural that John Randolph would conduct the test. Randolph had been astonished and irritated by the swift rise of "The Cock of Kentucky," who "strided from the door of the Hall as soon as he entered it to the Speaker's chair."[19] Within days after Clay's election as House leader, Randolph strolled into the chamber with his huge dog trailing at his heels in a bold attempt to embarrass the young Speaker. With no hesitation, Clay responded, firmly but pleasantly, with an order to the House doorkeeper to seize the dog and "Take *her* out — for she is a female."[20] The dog no longer joined the master in the chamber. No Speaker could deliver that order today.

With no intimation that he would be thrust so high so soon into the national leadership, Henry Clay had, nevertheless, come to Washington prepared to establish a pleasant rapport with the President of the United States. On his journey from Kentucky with his family, he brought with him a bottle of fine Madeira wine, cultivated in Kentucky, which he presented to Madison. An accompanying note stated that he

had the mortification to have been present some years ago at the exhibition at Mr. Jefferson's table of some Kentucky wine which, having been injured in the process of fermentation, was of a most wretched quality. The sample now sent will he flatters himself restore in some degree the credit of the wine of that State.[21]

On November 5, Madison submitted his annual report, in writing, to the Congress, accompanied by a sheaf of documents. He reported a stalemate in negotiations with Britain over the Orders in Council and noted there was no restitution from France for cargoes and property seized under Napoleon's Decrees. He told the Congress, he had sent a military force to thwart Indian depredations in Indiana, and he called for "putting the United States into an armor and an attitude demanded by the crisis" by giving the army more men.[22]

On receiving the papers, the House, while in Committee of the Whole House, agreed to break up portions of the message and assign various problems, brought forward in it, to six select committees and two standing committees for action. This arrangement, under the behest of Speaker Clay, brought fire from Randolph, who argued against the procedure. But the blaze was controlled, and Speaker Clay moved on to use his new power to appoint, as committee chairmen, members favoring war preparations. And the more important committees were heavily weighted with like-thinking representatives. Of course, his appointments irked Federalists, one of whom wrote,

Had the names of all the members been thrown promiscuously into a box, and been placed on the several Committees as they were drawn out, some of them at least would have been more respectable chairmen than those placed in that situation by the Speaker. The business however itself of the Speaker selecting at pleasure the characters composing the several committees is in itself a monstrous feature in our Government. It depends upon nothing in the Constitution but has hitherto been the usage of the House. It is not so in the Senate where the committees are chosen by ballot.[23]

When the Whole House Committee resolved "that so much of the President's message as relates to the subject of our foreign relations, be referred to a select committee," Clay packed it with War Hawks (so the Federalists charged). As chairman, he named Peter B. Porter, a second termer from Buffalo, New York. Sitting with him would be 29-year-old John C. Calhoun of South Carolina and 34-year-old Felix Grundy of Tennessee. All three of these men were expected to counter-balance the eccentricities of John Randolph.

As the House settled down to handle extraneous matters, while the several committees developed their reports, Clay was one of many to introduce petitions for the relief of certain individuals. In his case, it was for the reimbursement of the fine levied years earlier against Congressman Matthew Lyon under the Sedition Act of 1799 — the act which gave Clay his earliest popular speaking acclaim. Lyon, since released from jail for his "seditious" writings, had moved to Kentucky and represented one of its districts in the three Congresses prior to the 12th, for which he was defeated. Lyon did not live to see Congress refund the money to his heirs in 1840.

Also in the interim, as the House awaited the committee reports, the newspapers published Madison's diplomatic correspondence with British Minister Augustus Foster revealing that Britain was at last willing to pay reparations in the *Chesapeake* case, and return two of the surviving seamen impressed from the American ship. But, to use a phrase that was yet to be coined — "It was too little and too late." A Baltimore paper scoffed at it saying, "Presented at *such a time* is like restoring a hair after a fractured skull."[24] The *Lexington* (Kentucky) *Reporter* derided it, saying,

This DECEPTION is exactly what we expected and we expect a dozen more such. They cost Britain nothing — they muzzle Congress, and Britain continues in full sweep all her piracies, murders and impressments. Good God — Reparations!!!![25]

A week later, Washington's *National Intelligencer* was publishing the full transcript of the inquiry into the *Little Belt* affair and it was established, to the American viewpoint, that the British ship had fired first and rightly suffered the consequences. Less than a week after this anti–British news, came still more dire accounts of American casualties deep inland in the West to be ascribed to British aggression.

In the absence of Shawnee Indian chief, Tecumseh, Indiana's territorial governor, William Henry Harrison, had marched about 700 regulars, territorial and state militia, and other volunteers, to the woods surrounding Prophet's Town on Tippecanoe Creek. He arranged for a parlay on November 7th. But early that morning, the Indians attacked his encampment and killed or wounded

188 Americans. Harrison counterattacked, drove the Indians out of town, and burned it to the ground. In mopping up, Harrison's soldiers collected large quantities of British-made weapons and supplies.

As the battle news reached Washington, the greatest shock to Henry Clay was the death of his old legal opponent, Joseph Hamilton Daveiss, killed in action. The old Federalist had been a firm supporter of Harrison's strategy. But his in-law, Humphrey Marshall, was quick to denounce Harrison's tactics, publicly laying at his feet the blame for Daveiss' death.

The news also seemed to have a dramatic and quick effect on Congress (though probably only coincidental). For only one day after publication of the disaster — as that is what it was in terms of casualties, though not in strategic consequences or in the popular view of the average Westerner — the House Foreign Relations Committee brought out its report. It concurred with the administration's assertion that France had revoked her decrees while Britain persisted in her Orders in Council. In response, the committee noted that

the occasion is now presented when the national character, misunderstood and traduced for a time by foreign and domestic enemies, should be vindicated. If we have not rushed to the field of battle like the nations who are led by the mad ambition of a single chief, or the avarice of a corrupted court, it has not proceeded from a fear of war, but from love of justice and humanity. That proud spirit of liberty and independence which sustained our fathers in the successful assertion of their rights against foreign aggression is not yet sunk. The patriotic fire of the Revolution still burns in the American breast with a holy and unextinguishable flame, and will conduct this nation to those high destinies which are not less the regard of dignified moderation than of exalted valor.

It was a bold statement, but tempered by the recognition that the nation must prepare for war. Therefore, the committee, accepting President Madison's own words urging that the nation "be put into an armor and attitude demanded by the crisis," recommended to the House that the regular army be increased by 10,000 troops and that up to 50,000 volunteers "be organized, trained, and held in readiness" for service. The committee further called for naval vessels "not now in service," be fitted up and put in commission, and

for private merchant vessels to be allowed to arm themselves.[26]

But the feeling within the committee was even stronger than the public report. Felix Grundy wrote Andrew Jackson, of his newly adopted state of Tennessee,

Rely, on one thing, we have War or Honorable peace before we adjourn or certain great personages have produced a state of things which will bring them down from their high places. If there be honest men enough to tell the truth loudly.[27]

If the "great personage" referred to President Madison, freshman Congressman William Lowndes of South Carolina, a friend of committee-member Calhoun, gave even more specific sentiment of the president when he wrote home, that "Mr. Monroe has given strongest assurances that the President will cooperate zealously with Congress in declaring war, if our complaints are not redressed by May next."[28]

In his remarks, opening debate on the report on December 6, Committee Chairman Porter stated that it was the committee's unanimous opinion that "the American maritime rights which Great Britain is violating were such as we ought to support at the hazard and expense of a war." While Porter expressed a feeling for making war with England over its aggressions on the seas and its stubbornness in holding fast to the Orders in Council, the principal aim of the New Yorker from Buffalo, was to see American arms conquer British Canada, just across the Great Lakes from his home. He believed, with Clay, that it could be done easily. He boldly announced that

it was the determination of the committee to recommend open and decided war — a war as vigorous and effective as the resources of the country and the relative situation of ourselves and our enemy would enable us to prosecute.

Though he expected some members would oppose a course for war, he knew there were many who preferred "an immediate declaration of war." He rejected instant action in favor of preparation.[29]

As expected, the first major opposition to the "war" report came from John Randolph, who attacked it on December 9. In a brief statement he questioned the need for increasing the army and defamed the prospective troops, saying,

The people of the United States could defend themselves, if necessary, and had no idea of resting their defence on mercenaries, picked up from brothels and tippling houses — pickpockets who have escaped from Newgate, &c., and sought refuse in this asylum of oppressed humanity.[30]

Committee-member Felix Grundy was astonished that Randolph now found fault with the report after he had let it pass, without objection, through the Foreign Relations Committee and the Committee of the Whole House — both committees of which Randolph was a member. In reply to the Virginian, Grundy noted that while the committees had given due consideration to the assumed loss of American blood and expenditures of the public treasure, it had also reflected on the test which the shock of war would place on the government "our Republican institutions," and the future of "the liberties of the people." As the country "stands on the bank of the Rubicon," Grundy told the House, "the true question in controversy ... is the right of exporting the productions of our own soil and industry to foreign markets."

Turning to the subject of the recent battle of Tippecanoe, and charging Britain with intriguing and turning the Indians toward hostilities in the West, Grundy declared, "War is not to commence by sea or land, it is already begun; and some of the richest blood our country has already been shed," referring to Joseph Hamilton Daveiss. Speaking directly to Speaker Clay, he said, "You, sir, who have often measured your strength with his forensic debate, can attest that he, in a good degree, was the pride of the Western country and Kentucky claimed him as a favorite son." Grundy, continuing his speech on the subject of restrictive commercial law, in effect, issued a call for war in which success should win Canada for the North and the Floridas for the South.[31]

Randolph, renewing the debate on the 10th, questioned the authority of the Committee on Foreign Relations to report on the subject of increasing strength of the armed forces and also charged the committee with recommending "a war not of defense, but of conquest, of aggrandizement, of ambition." He wondered at the need for a Republican army against Britain now when Republicans felt no need for raising armies during the undeclared naval war with France at the turn of the century. He disputed Grundy's claim that Britain was behind the Indians in the episode at Tippecanoe. He accused the War Hawks of the West and the Great Lakes regions of potential territorial gain for preponderance in national political power. And he raised the specter of slave revolt in southern states when the army was off to the north engaged in conquest of Canada. His only feeling for raising a standing army would be in the cause of protecting Spain's American dominions against French appetite. And finally, he compared the character of France (a tyrant of the seas in event of victory over Britain) with that of Britain (the nation's mother country) favoring the latter despite his own recollections of fleeing before the plundering British trooper, Banastre Tarleton.[32]

The reference of Tarleton must have brought anguished memories to the mind of Speaker Henry Clay, who had, as a child, witnessed villainous depredations against his own family by that British officer and his soldiers. Reminder of Tarleton was certainly not conducive to encouraging Clay's support for Britain. Rather, Clay might recall the support of the French in bottling up Cornwallis' British army at Yorktown to enable Washington's victory in 1781.

On December 11, Clay's Kentucky colleague, Richard M. Johnson, praised Madison's exhortation "to put on the armor of defence, to gird on the sword, and assume the manly and bold attitude of war," and he belittled Randolph's numerous arguments against military preparedness. In cataloguing British infamies, Johnson related an account of the death, by American gunnery, of an American seaman impressed by the British to serve on the *Little Belt*. And finally, he spoke of the valor of American servicemen who died by the hands of the Tippecanoe Indians, "who were infuriated and made drunk by British traders." Johnson regretted that the Speaker was "not in my place to speak" the praise of fallen acquaintances such as Joseph H. Daveiss.[33]

The next major speech on the report was the maiden effort of a young man stepping on the national scene at the outset of a long and illustrious career. The 29-year-old South Carolinian and graduate of Yale college in the north was John Caldwell Calhoun. After college, a speech he made in his homeland hills against the British attack on the *Chesapeake* led him into two un-eventful terms in the South Carolina House of Representatives. There, Calhoun served under Speaker Joseph Alston, the son-in-law and accomplice of Aaron Burr. Alston, himself a man of ability, was quick to recognize in Calhoun a nature that would not be managed easily but also found him easy-going and of such friendly nature that feathers were not ruffled. When the six-foot, two-inch Calhoun arrived in Washington in November 1811, his face already had deep contours in the cheeks. His hair and eyebrows were both very dark and bushy. He was fashionably dressed for the times and had an erect bearing, much like Clay's. Other than these credentials, he had little to announce that he was there. What knowledge Henry Clay had of John C. Calhoun is unknown, and the Speaker's reason for putting Calhoun in the Foreign Relations Committee's second rank is a mystery.

Yet Calhoun proved Clay's confidence as justified in his well-organized initial speech in the national legislature. He succinctly reduced the question under debate "to this single point — which shall we do, abandon or defend our own commercial and maritime rights, and the personal liberties of our citizens employed in exercising them?" Calhoun rebuffed Randolph's reasoning, hammering away, refuting each point the Virginian had made, and then saying,

> Sir, I only know of one principle to make a nation great, to produce in this country not the form but the real spirit of union, and this is to protect every citizen in the lawful pursuit of his business. He will then feel that he is backed by the Government; that its arm is his arms; and will rejoice in its increased strength and prosperity. Protection and patriotism are reciprocal. This is the road all great nations have trod.[34]

It was not a long speech, but it was the prelude to many great speeches. Even with this first speech, he was recognized as a comer as a great body of members came forward to greet the young man on his successful effort. Editorially, the *Richmond Enquirer* said,

> Mr. Calhoun is clear and precise in his reasoning, marching up directly to the object of his attack, and felling down the errors of his opponent with the club of Hercules; not eloquent in his tropes and figures, but, like Fox, in the moral elevation of his sentiments, free from personality, yet full of

those fine touches of indignation, which are the severest cut to a man of feeling. His speech, like a fine drawing, abounds in those lights and shades which set off each other: the cause of his country is robed in light, while his opponents are wrapped in darkness.... We hail this young Carolinian as one of the master-spirits who stamp their names upon the age in which they live.[35]

Among the other representatives to speak out against the lonely anti-war voice of John Randolph, was George M. Troup of Georgia. He was distressed by the aim of the public debate. "Of what avail is argument," he questioned,

> of what avail is eloquence, to convince, to persuade, whom? ourselves, the people? Sir, if the people are to be reasoned into war now, it is too soon, much too soon, to begin it. If their Representatives here are to be led to it by the flowers of rhetoric, it is too soon, much too soon to begin it?

Troup objected to the open revelation of American intent, saying,

> At the very outset, we have been told the measures were intended as measures of offensive hostility; that the army was to be raised to attack Canada; nothing short of it; all the advocates of the resolution declare it. How, sir, could a more public or formal declaration of war have been made? Contrary to the practice of all nations, we declare first and make preparations afterwards. More magnanimous than wise, we tell the enemy when we will strike, where we will strike, and how we shall strike.[36]

In a last desperate effort to sway the House to his viewpoint, Randolph rose again to catalog the wrongs committed against the United States by France over the past 15 years, and then asserted his impression of the majority's call for war,

> Sir, if you go to war it will not be for the protection of, or defence of your maritime rights. Gentlemen from the North have been taken up to some high mountain and shown all the kingdoms of earth; and Canada seems tempting in their sight.... Ever since the report of the Committee of Foreign Relations came into the House, we have heard but one word — like the whip-poor-will, but one eternal monotonous tone — Canada! Canada! Canada!

It was another long, rambling speech, but it was to no avail.

Still, Randolph was wise enough to recognize in this same speech, that the old party lines between Republicans and Federalists were becoming so murky that they were nearly indistinguishable. Though the Federalists were becoming fewer in number with each election and appeared to be disintegrating into a dying breed, they still were capable of political machinations and were lining up with Republicans who no longer appeared to represent the peaceful aims of Jefferson. For these Republicans, Randolph, in effect, believed he read their eulogy when he "lamented" and "feared" that

> if a writ were to issue against that old party — as had been facetiously said, in another body, of our valiant Army — it would be impossible for a constable with a search warrant to find.... Death, resignation, and desertion had thinned their ranks. They had disappeared. New men and new doctrines had succeeded.[37]

Between December 16 and 19, the House, by huge majorities, passed the resolutions to increase the size of the army, fit-out a stronger navy, and permit commercial merchant vessels to arm. This last measure was considered a virtual declaration of war, since it would give those private ship captains the exclusive rights of battle, putting war or peace in their hands.

As the House concluded debate on the Foreign Relations report to prepare for war, sifted through some minor legislation, and prepared to begin debate on a Senate-sponsored bill, the affairs of state were set aside to hear the dreadful news of a great theater fire in Richmond, Virginia, that directly touched some members of Congress. On the evening following Christmas, with an audience exceeding 600 members of the city's leading families, a young stagehand was ordered to raise a chandelier among some backstage scenery. Though he replied that it could start a fire, he obeyed the firm command. In minutes, the whole theater was engulfed in flames.

Among those who lost a child in the flames was Henry Clay's distant cousin, Virginia Congressman Matthew Clay, who, in Washington, received the following descriptive letter:

Richmond, December 27

Sir,

I have a tale of horror to tell; prepare to hear of the most awful calamity that ever plunged a whole city into affliction. Yes, all Richmond is in tears: children have lost their parents, parents have lost their children. Yesterday a beloved daughter gladdened my heart with her innocent smiles; today she is in Heaven! God gave her to me, and God — yes, it has pleased Almighty God to take her from me. O! sir, feel for me, and not for me only; arm yourself with fortitude whilst I discharge the mournful duty of telling you that you have to feel also for yourself. Yes, for it must be told, you also were the father of an amiable daughter, now, like my beloved child, gone to join her mother in Heaven.

How can words represent what one night, one hour of unutterable horror, has done to overwhelm a hundred families with grief and despair. No, sir, impossible. My eyes beheld last night what no tongue, no pen can describe — horrors that language has no terms to represent.

Last night we were all at the theater; every family in Richmond, or at least, a very large proportion of them, was there — the house was uncommonly full — when, dreadful to relate, the scenery took fire, spread rapidly above, ascending in volumes of flame and smoke into the upper part of the building, whence a moment after it descended to force a passage through the pit and boxes. In two minutes the whole audience were enveloped in hot, scorching smoke and flame. The lights were all extinguished by the black and smothering vapor; cries, shrieks, confusion and despair succeeded. O moment of inexpressible horror!. Nothing I can say, can paint the awful, shocking, maddening scene. The images of both my dear children were before me, but I was removed by an impassable crowd from the dear sufferers. The youngest (with gratitude to Heaven I write it), sprang towards the voice of her papa, reached my assisting hand, and was extricated from the overwhelming mass that soon choked [sic] the passage by the stairs; but no effort could avail me to reach, or even gain sight of the other; and my dear, sweet Mary, with her companions, Miss Gwathaney and Miss Gatewood, passed together and at once into, a happier world. Judge my feelings by your own, when I found that neither they nor my beloved sister appeared upon the stairs. First one, and then another and another, I helped down; hoping every moment to seize the hand of my dear child — but, no, no, I was not destined to have that happiness. O to see so, so many amiable helpless females trying to stretch to me their imploring hands, crying, "Save me, sir; oh, sir, save *me*, save *me*!" Oh, God, eternity cannot banish that spectacle of horror from my recollection. Some friendly unknown hand dragged me from the scene of flames and death — and on gaining the open air, to my infinite consolation, I found my sister had thrown herself from the upper window and was saved — yes, thanks be to God, saved where fifty others in a similar attempt, broke their necks, or were crushed to death by those who fell on them from the same height.

Oh, sir, you can have no idea of the general consternation — the universal grief that pervades this city — but why do I speak of that? I scarcely know what I write you. Farewell. In haste and in deep affliction.[38]

Among the 73 persons who died in the fire were James Monroe's recent successor to the Virginia governor's chair, George W. Smith, and his wife; and Abraham Bedford Venable, a member of Congress until 1804.

The House unanimously adopted a resolution calling on all members to "wear crepe on the left arm for one month" in respect and sorrow for those who died in the fire.[39]

The catastrophic news from Richmond succeeded news of a less disastrous, but of a more wide-spread act of God. An earthquake, on December 16, centered near New Madrid, Missouri (then Louisiana Territory), was felt as far distant as Charleston, S.C.; Raleigh, N.C.; Washington, D.C.; Knoxville, Tenn.; Pittsburgh, Pa. As post riders brought reports to the Washington papers from each of these places over the ensuing weeks, they all noted that the tremors occurred at 3 A.M., and many reported another tremor around 8 A.M. Lesser tremors continued for many months, with another severe one — again felt strongly in Washington — in mid–February 1812. How devastating these quakes might have been to the west of the Mississippi River (which is said to have run northward for a time) is unknown since that vast region was unsettled. But in a letter to Clay in May 1812, a friend wrote that the population of New Madrid had dropped from 3,000 to 400 since the quake began.[40]

There is an interesting story tied in with this gigantic earthquake. It was told that Indian Chief Tecumseh was failing in his effort to influence the Creeks and Cherokees to join his federation during his visit in Tennessee and Alabama in the fall of 1811. He then told the reluctant chiefs of those tribes that the Great Spirit had sent him. As proof, he said he would return to Detroit, where, on his arrival, he would stamp his foot upon the ground and the homes of the southern tribes would fall down. The earthquake took place about the time of his arrival in Detroit, and Indian homes collapsed.

Resuming its work on preparing the nation for a possible war with Great Britain, on the final day of 1811, the House resolved itself into a Committee of the Whole House to consider a Senate-passed bill calling for the increase of the military force to 25,000 men. The Foreign Relations Committee had cut the figure to 15,000. But the Senate bill and the House committee's report retained the provision that all the officers, needed to command the entire force of 25,000 men spread through 13 regiments, were to be appointed at once. With Peter Porter, chairman of the Foreign Relations Committee, now sitting as chairman of the Committee of the Whole House, Speaker Clay sat in the chamber as just another representative. Using this opportunity to break with the tradition that kept the Speaker in silence during debate, Henry Clay rose to offer an amendment recommending that only eight regiments be officered (enough to command the amended 15,000 troops) until three-fourths of the privates of these eight units were enlisted. The Committee of the Whole adopted the amendment and moved to return to the regular House session wherein Clay would resume his seat as Speaker. But prior to this action, Clay rose again and asked the indulgence of the committee to permit him to make a few observations on the subject of the bill before them.

It was a simple step. But in taking it, Henry Clay was, in effect, establishing a new and fundamental precedent for the Speaker to be a participant in debate rather than only a silent presiding officer of the House of Representatives. He acknowledged the requirement of his silence on issues while acting as presiding officer of the House. But now he claimed his right to share in the responsibility of legislation, feeling that he owed it to his constituents to express his and their views.

On the substance of the measure before the committee, Clay agreed that the number of men to be recruited under the bill was more than needed in peace, but "too small for the purposes of war." But he noted, if Congress were to err, "They ought to err on the side of safety and vigor." Then in a hypothetical description of an invasion of Canada in time of war, he showed that even recruitment of 25,000 men was far short of that needed to prosecute a successful campaign. He told his colleagues he opposed standing armies in time of peace, but in time of war, "I *am* the advocate of raising able and vigorous armies to ensure its success."

Clay said he felt the militia of the many states could muster all the men necessary for the defense of the country even if harbors were blocked or major cities taken — even the capital — unlike the situation that would prevail in European countries where the fall of the capital "is the fall of the nation."

To those who preferred that war debate be conducted behind closed doors, Clay said, "It is impossible to conceal the measures of preparation for war." He felt the United States would gain more by war than

> by your mongrel state of peace with Great Britain....
> By a continuance of this peace, we shall lose our
> commerce, our character, and a nation's best at-
> tribute, our honor. A war will give us commerce
> and character; and we shall enjoy the proud con-
> sciousness of having discharged our highest duty
> to our country.

In response to the argument that England "is fighting the battles of mankind" against a French Emperor who was allegedly "aiming at universal empire," Clay said, "We cannot secure our independence of one power, by a dastardly submission to the will of another." After depicting the results of past submission, Clay asked, "When did submission to one wrong induce an adversary to cease his encroachments on the party submitting?" He charged that Britain's actions were due to jealousy toward the United States, saying, "She dreads our rivalship on the ocean."

Toward the close of his comments, Clay revealed a suspicion of covert political maneuverings by the Federalists, when he chided those who said,

> this government is not calculated to stand the
> shock of war; that gentlemen will lose their seats
> in this and the other House; that our benches will
> be filled by other men, who after we have carried
> on the war, will make for us an ignominious
> peace.

He couldn't believe that members would let Daviess and his associates "perish in manfully fighting our battles, while we meanly cling to our places." But he did believe the nation would support its government "even in an unsuccessful war to defend their rights, to assert their honor, the dignity and independence of the country." Clay declared, "My ideas of duty are such, that when

my rights are invaded, I must advance to their defence, let what may be the consequence; even if death itself were to be my certain fate."

In conclusion, Clay expressed the hope that he had

> fully established three positions: that the quantum
> of the force proposed by the bill is not too great —
> that its nature is such as the contemplated war
> calls for; and that the object of the war is justified
> by every consideration of justice, of interest, or
> honor, and love of country. Unless the object is at-
> tained by peaceful means, I hope that war will be
> waged before the close of the session.[41]

Whether or not he had established these three positions, Speaker Clay had, at the end of 1811, after less than two months as presiding officer of the House of Representatives, established three very important political positions of lasting significance. Within days of the opening of the 12th Congress, Clay had asserted the Speaker's political control of legislation, by naming, as chairmen of the House committees, men who would appear to confirm his viewpoint and conform to his direction. And followed this by adding enough like-thinking members to the key committees to support his aims with majority votes.

It was not long after this commanding stand that Speaker Clay demonstrated his firm hand of leadership in demanding order and decorum in the House as he brought the irascible Randolph under control. Even the quixotic Virginian was quick to recognize an adversary who would not flinch, yet would not rule the House as a despot or tyrant.

And, finally, Henry Clay established for all future Speakers the privilege — the right — to vote and to speak (at least, in the Committee of the Whole House). Unlike the traditions of the Speaker of the British House of Commons, Clay assumed that it was his responsibility and his duty to his constituents to cast his vote and to exercise his unrivalled talents as a persuasive speaker.

Henry Clay would continue these methods and expand on them throughout his tenure as Speaker to such a degree that his power, his prestige, and his influence would make him master of the House of Representatives and would raise him, and the office of Speaker, to a ranking second only to the presidency in the United States Government.

10

IRRESOLUTION AND INTRIGUE

Though Henry Clay had stepped boldly into the vacuum of congressional leadership, it happened so quickly that his newly achieved prestige was not yet fully recognized either in or out of the House of Representatives. His efforts to sway legislation in the direction he advocated lacked the weight it would eventually carry. It was still not to Henry Clay that observers turned for clues when they wished to determine the trends taking place in the transactions of national purpose. What they thought they saw was another "do-nothing Congress," a phrase not yet coined.

Throughout the waning months of 1811 the executive branch of the U.S. government had called for "putting on the armor of defence," and the legislative branch had debated and voted to increase the country's military posture. But not a dollar was spent, and not a man was recruited. Words of war from Washington had been heard by the people before, and nothing had happened. Was the 12th Congress no different from earlier assemblies?

As the momentous year 1812 came into existence, freshman Representative John C. Calhoun sensed the national mood and told the House, on January 2, that he "perceived that the public sentiment began already to doubt whether Congress was really in earnest, from the tardiness of their movements."[1]

His warning had little effect and the Congress continued to argue and pass legislation that was next to meaningless. They proposed armies without providing for enlisted soldiers, or providing for their needs once enlisted. Even Henry Clay's speech of December 31, 1811, was to no avail. The House cut to six his proposal to officer only eight regiments before the recruitment of men to fill out the units. The Senate refused the House amendments and the House in turn gave way to the Senate, thus passing a measure that all officers be appointed for 13 regiments regardless of how many of the 25,000 proposed troops the nation could enlist. President Madison, who wanted only 10,000 new regulars to serve for three years plus 50,000 volunteers for one year, signed the bill on January 11, 1812.

John Randolph ridiculed the ability of the government to raise 25,000 men for the five-year term as an impossibility, for he thought it had been "demonstrated that these men could not be raised; it would be an army on paper only."[2] There were few dissenters to Randolph's view that such enlistments would be hard to come by.

In the interim, it was proposed in another bill that Madison get his 50,000 volunteers officered according to the state laws to which the companies belonged and liable to service for one year. It was generally recognized that these would be classed as militia and that it would be unconstitutional to use such troops in the conquest of Canada or in the occupation of Florida — though these were the two major objectives of any military operation. A way out of the dilemma was suggested by South Carolina's Representative Langdon Cheves on the same day that Madison signed the bill authorizing recruitment of the 25,000 regulars. Cheves found the remedy in the Constitution's provision giving Congress the power to declare and make war. He took the stand that militia, when called to duty under national jurisdiction, took on the attributes of regular troops. And when serving in war, their use was limited only to "the objects of the war." He expressed the view that the power of the national government to repel invasion and suppress insurrection was an added authority not one that limits the power to prosecute a war.[3]

Cheves' opinions bordered on Republican heresy and were attacked from all directions. Even the Federalists, whose views came close to this idea, buckled and rejected the unlimited scope of militia service. But Cheves found an ally in Henry Clay. In a brief speech, again in Committee of the Whole House, Clay said it was his impression that

in case of emergency, the nation is at liberty to use the best security of the people, whether in the form of ordinary militia or volunteers, in any manner that may appear best calculated to preserve the public interest.

Noting that the Constitution gave Congress the power to raise armies and navies, he observed that no one would restrict their use merely because "there is no power given to the government to send them beyond the jurisdiction of the United States." Therefore, he reasoned, "why may not the same general power give the same authority with respect to the militia?" Quoting two Constitutional instructions referring to the militia in the "service of the United States" Clay took the broad view that "The service is spoken of generally, and means, no doubt, any service to which physical force is applicable."

Continuing, he said,

In one of the amendments to the Constitution, it is declared, "that a well-regulated militia is necessary to the security of a free state," but if you limit the use of the militia to executing the laws, suppressing insurrections and repelling invasions; if you deny the use of the militia to make war, can you say they are "the security of a state?"

He thought not.

Clay denied that use of the militia outside the country would be for "foreign conquest." He called it "defense." He said,

In making the war effective, conquest may become necessary; but this does not change the character of the war — there may be no other way of operating upon the enemy, but by taking possession of her provinces which adjoin us.[4]

It was for these reasons that Clay felt the 50,000 militia volunteers could be recruited and used wherever the president wished and yet permit the states to appoint the officers. Though such War Hawks as Porter and Grundy opposed

the unlimited use of militia, the decision was left in the hands of the president, or even allow the volunteers to decide if they wished to refuse to march out of the country. The bill passed the House by a large margin on January 17, cleared the Senate, despite a speech against it by Giles, and was made a law by President Madison on February 6.

One additional war measure linked Langdon Cheves and Henry Clay together. On the same day that the volunteer corps bill cleared the House, January 17, that body went into Committee of the Whole to consider a bill brought forward by Cheves, chairman of the Naval Affairs Committee. In a speech lasting parts of two days, he asked for money to build an enlarged navy to include twelve 74-gun warships and twenty frigates. He argued that commerce needed the government's protection as much as did agriculture. He said the conquest of Canada would leave the United States nowhere else to meet the enemy except on the sea. He put the cost of the Navy since 1789 at a bit over $27 million, while the Army had cost $37.5 million in the same period. And he noted the impracticability of Great Britain maintaining a blockade on the American seaports when Halifax, Nova Scotia, was their only supply and repair base on this side of the Atlantic — a base that could easily be denied them.

Talk of a navy was too much for Richard Mentor Johnson, Kentuckian and some-time War Hawk. On January 21, he went to ancient history to depict the evils of a navy, saying,

I will refer to Tyre and Sidon, Crete and Rhoades, to Athens and to Carthage. No sooner had these nations ceased to confine their naval strength to their maritime defense at home, to the protection of the sea coast, than they were engaged in plunder, piracy, depredations upon other nations, or involved in wars, which certainly accelerated, if it did not produce the downfall and destruction of those Governments. Peace and tranquility is not the natural state of a great naval power.[5]

Clay joined the debate the next day. He was surprised at the jealousy exhibited against a navy and disputed the allegation that navies were the downfall of ancient states. By such reasoning, he argued, it would as easily be shown that their devotion to liberty could have caused their demise with a "conclusion in favor of despotism."

In answer to those who feared a marine would

"produce collisions with foreign nations," Clay said, "It is the thing protected [commerce] not the instrument of protection, that involves you in war." With further analysis he could "see no just ground of dread in the nature of naval power" and said it was "free from the evils attendant upon standing armies."

Clay then suggested that

> three different degrees of naval power present themselves. In the first place, such a force as would be capable of contending with that which any other nation is able to bring on the ocean — a force that boldly, scouring every sea, would challenge to combat the fleets of other Powers, however great. I admit it is impossible at this time, perhaps it never would be desirable for this country to establish so extensive a navy.

(Yet such a Navy existed during World War II.)

"The next species of naval power," which Clay considered, was one "that which, without adventuring into distant seas, and keeping generally in our own harbors, and on our coasts, would be competent to beat off any squadron which might be attempted to be permanently stationed in our waters." While "unattainable in the present situation of the finances of the country," Clay contended, "it is such a force as Congress ought to set about providing, and I hope in less than ten years to see it actually established." He added to this thought, "This country only requires resolution, and a proper exertion to its immense resources, to command respect, and to vindicate every essential right."

Clay's "third description of force" was

> that which would be able to prevent any single vessel, of whatever metal, from endangering our whole coasting trade, blocking up our harbors, and laying under contribution our cities — a force competent to punish the insolence of the commander of any single ship, and to preserve in our own jurisdiction the inviolability of our peace and our laws. A force of this kind is entirely within the compass of our means at this time.

To those who intimated that Republicans were in contradiction to their own opposition to a navy in 1798, he cited examples how "the state of things is totally altered. What was folly in 1798 may be wisdom now." He went into detail to point out that since then the country's revenue had increased and the population had grown. The coastline had been extended 500 miles and an ex-

panded commerce needed protection. He paid particular interest in the need for protection of the Western country's commercial outlet at the "solitary vent" of New Orleans. He expressed a concern over possible occupation of Cuba and Eastern Florida by Great Britain and their consequent "absolute command of the Gulf of Mexico."

The Speaker spoke of the natural connection between a navy and commerce.

> The shepherd and his faithful dog are not more necessary to guard the flock that browse and gambol on the neighboring mountain. I consider property of foreign commerce indissolubly allied to marine power. Neglect to provide the one and you must abandon the other.

And, he stressed the importance of commerce by calling to attention the fact

> it has, with very trifling aid from other sources, defrayed the expenses of government ever since the adoption of the present Constitution; maintained an expensive and successful war with the Indians; a war with the Barbary powers; a quasi war with France; sustained the charges of suppressing two insurrections, and extinguished upwards of forty-six millions of the public debt. In revenue it has, since the year 1789, yielded one hundred and ninety-one millions of dollars.

Near the end of his speech, Clay offered an example, aimed at his reluctant western colleagues, of a vessel that sailed to Italy and named its port of origin as Pittsburgh, Pennsylvania. The ship's master had to use a map to show the Italian customs officer the reverse route to the Gulf, up the Mississippi and Ohio Rivers to the mountain city. "There," exclaimed the master, "stands Pittsburgh, the port from which I sailed!" Finally, Clay said,

> I derive great pleasure from the reflection that I am supporting a measure calculated to impart additional strength to our happy Union. Diversified as are the interest of its various parts, how admirably do they harmonize and blend together! We have only to make proper use of the bounties spread before us, to render us prosperous and powerful. Such a navy as I have contended for, will form a new bond of connexion between the States, concentrating their hopes, their interests and their affections.[6]

But it was in vain. Despite almost unanimous Federalist support, along with that of Calhoun,

Cheves, Lowndes and a couple dozen other Republicans, the plea to build the frigates was voted down 62–59. Among those helping to sink an expanded navy were western War Hawks Richard M. Johnson and Felix Grundy.[7]

Still, Clay's greatest concern, at this point, was not over the success or failure of this piece of legislation, as much as it would be over the attitude of Congress generated by the report from Treasury Secretary Albert Gallatin on the estimated cost of the war that was being urged. As early as December 21, 1811, Clay wrote a friend in Kentucky, "Our greatest difficulty will be revenue, and I do not well see how we can dispense with internal taxes. This is the delicate and trying topic, and that I fear on which we shall have the greatest desertion."[8]

He had good reason to see revenue as a "trying topic" for its success depended on survival in a tangle of domestic politics and international diplomacy. As Clay wrote of his apprehension, Gouverneur Morris and De Witt Clinton of New York were in Washington. Their effort to wrangle $7 million to build a canal from the Hudson River to the Great Lakes led Delaware Federalist James Bayard to write Clay's deposed friend, Caesar Rodney,

> A fine time for such an expenditure when we have not money eno' in the Treasury to pay the bounties to the troops we propose to raise. The characters of the two men are pretty well known, and it is rather supposed that they mean to open a road to the presidency than a canal from the lakes. Tho' a young republic we are already old in intrigue.[9]

The intrigue went much deeper than even Bayard apparently was aware, and it involved men of his own party — men who had been voting with those Republicans who were pushing so determinedly for a strong military posture. Bayard agreed with the determination of his party and the War-Hawk Republicans to arm the country to be prepared for possible war. But it is not so certain that he was aware that many of his party members were voting for war measures — not for war, but for the embarrassment and defeat of the Madison administration in the presidential elections later in 1812.

In December 1811, the Federalists, under the leadership of Josiah Quincy of Massachusetts, began organizing this dangerous political game.

Already he had taken a sounding of the Republican leadership in Congress and was able to write, "Clay, our Speaker, told me yesterday with some naivete, 'the truth is I am in favour of war and so are some others — *but some of us fear that if we get into war you will get our places.*'"[10]

Quincy's colleague from Massachusetts, Samuel Taggart, also recorded his impressions of the political climate. He was sure he saw a new star rising on the political horizon — and it was not the Western Star, Henry Clay. Taggart's star "arising in the east," was canal-advocate De Witt Clinton. He envisioned a coalition between Clinton's Republican Party supporters and the Federalists of New England and other northern states as insuring the New Yorker's election. "The Federalists here reason in this way," he wrote, "the prospect of a Federal President nominally so is hopeless." Taggart knew Clinton to be ambitious with presidential aspirations, and though a Republican, he would "make a good President" and impartial "if he comes in in part by Federal support."

As for Madison's position, Taggart observed,

> It is generally thought that the only thing that will save the administration is the repeal or modification of the orders in council, which may lead to some accommodation with Britain; that if these orders are not withdrawn, that whether we have peace or the present quasi-state, or war, the administration must sink. To go to war they dare not. To continue at peace after all their blustering and swaggering without a repeal of the orders in council, will immediately turn all who have thought them sincere in their clamour for war against them. To continue this present state of things they are persuaded will not be much longer borne. Poor fellows they are in a sad dilemma.[11]

With this attitude, Quincy, Taggart, and many other Federalists socialized easily with British Minister Augustus Foster and kept him informed of the developments transpiring within the American Government.

Foster, in turn, kept his own government informed, writing on December 11, 1811,

> The Federal leaders make no scruple of telling me that they mean to give their votes for war, although they will remain silent in the debate; they add that it will be a short war of six or nine months. To my observations on the strange and dangerous nature of such a policy, they shrug their shoulders, telling me that they see no end to

restrictions and non-importation laws but in war; that war will turn out the administration, and then they will have their own way, and make a solid peace with Great Britain.[12]

Throughout this period of late 1811 and early 1812, Foster continued to pour forth his findings to his government in London. But his reports were based on somewhat warped viewpoints. His contacts, other than with the administration, were principally with the Federalists and the old "peace" or Quid Republicans. And he invariably toned down any stern warnings from Secretary of State Monroe or President Madison with qualifying phrases or suggestions of government timidity fed him by those congressional members with whom he socialized. In late November 1811, he had written that he was unsure of U.S. policy because its language was either "insincere" or else the government was "undecided as to the line of policy they intended to pursue."[13]

In his talks with Madison and Monroe, Foster constantly reiterated the firmness of the British government in retaining their Orders in Council until the United States could prove satisfactorily that France had, in fact, repealed the Berlin and Milan Decrees or until the United States could induce France to repeal some municipal regulations under which France was still interdicting American shipping. Madison and Monroe continued to insist that France had repealed the two decrees, but in any case, any difference between the United States and France "would not be a reason for the interference of England."[14] Meanwhile, Madison hinted to Foster that the United States would not move toward war until after the return of messages carried on the *Hornet*, not due back in America until spring. He was hopeful it would bring word of the repeal of Britain's obnoxious orders. Yet when Foster allowed Monroe to read his dispatch intended for the British Foreign Office and was advised by the secretary of state to tone down Madison's warlike language, Foster interpreted this as another example of the American governments's reluctance to act with firmness.

On another occasion, in December 1811, Foster had written that his situation was "exceedingly embarrassing." He lamented the menacing language held in Congress," but was told by Monroe not to look "upon their use of angry terms as a threat on the part of the Government." He also wrote that "to any man of sound understanding, the absolute want of means in this country to make war on us is so palpable that the very idea seems almost ridiculous."[15]

He wrote again, before 1811 closed, that

it is the opinion of most of the sensible men here that this Government will not be pushed into a war with us, but that their object is to secure the support of their party at the next election of a President by obtaining the credit of having forced us to change a system by the line of conduct they have adopted.[16]

In January, after the passage of the two military recruitment bills, Foster wrote again of the embarrassing situation in the U.S. government and of his inability to assess it accurately. Nevertheless, he again attributed congressional war measures to presidential politics. And he apparently tossed off as a joke Madison's observation that "it seemed quite necessary to become a belligerent in order to enjoy the advantage of commerce."[17] By the end of the month he wrote that "I have been lately assured that many of the federal leaders mean to push their support of war measures no further" and they "have explicitly stated their intention to oppose the resolution for war when it shall be brought into Congress."[18]

At least two Federalists went even further in their consultations with Foster and possibly crossed the line of treason. His coded dispatch of February 1 (capitalizing words in strange places) said,

Two Federal leaders waited on me yesterday and after expressing their Conviction of how embarrassed I must be, to form a current opinion of the State of Things here, and to manage so, as neither to appear to laugh at the ridiculous Situation of the Government, nor yet to show so little Sagacity, as to be seriously alarmed, proceeded to explain, that the object of their visit was, to disclose to me, what they considered to be the best Course which my Government could take, in order to produce a thorough amalgamation of Interests between America and Great Britain.

The sum of these Suggestions was, that We should neither revoke Our Orders in Council nor modify them in any Manner. They said, this Government would, if We conceded, look upon our Concession as being the Effect of their own Measures and plume themselves thereon; that they only wanted to get out of their present Difficulties; and if We made a partial Concession, they would make use of it to escape fulfilling their Pledge to go to

War, still however continuing the restrictory System; whereas if we pushed them to the Edge of the Precipice, by an unbending attitude, that then, they must be lost, either by the Disgrace of having nearly ruined the Trade of the United States and yet failed to reduce Great Britain, by the System of Commercial Restrictions, or else, by their Incapacity to conduct the Government during War.[19]

Along with these Federalist assurances that they would not vote for war and that the "menacing language" of Congress was only electioneering, Foster's analysis of the economic picture was just as convincing that war was not on the horizon. He noted that "ships continue to sail to Great Britain & insurance has not risen a single dollar."[20] Furthermore, he wrote twice during January that Treasury Secretary Gallatin had been reluctant to provide Congress with estimates on the cost of the prospective war, "on the ground that if he did so it would be immediately said that the Government wanted to damp the ardor of Congress," and that any imposition of new taxes would "be very odious to the mass of people."[21] One of these notices was penned by Foster on January 11, the day after Gallatin sent a letter covering his tax reports to Ezekiel Bacon, Chairman of the House Ways and Means Committee. The letter did not surface publicly until January 20. Thus, it is possible the words of John A. Harper of New Hampshire were valid that

Foster knew of the existence of the letter two weeks before it was laid before the House, and boasted of the effect it would have with the people—If reports are true, Foster's carriage is frequently seen at Gallatin's house at such hours of the night as honest men are asleep.[22]

Senator Bayard described Foster's proclivity for socializing in a letter to his cousin, Andrew Bayard,

No person appears to receive less impression from our measures than the British Minister. He gives his dinners to Gentlemen of all Parties in the most friendly style possible. Some evenings ago he gave a grand fete. Not less than 300 invitations went out and nearly 200 persons composed the Party. The supper was very brilliant and was displayed on tables spread in four different but contiguous rooms.[23]

Even Henry Clay and other members of his "War Mess" boarding-house group, attended this grand ball in honor of the British queen's birthday. And they went so far as to invite Foster to a dinner at their mess. (On this and other occasions Foster wrote in his diary that "The Speaker was very warlike." He also quoted Clay as telling him that war between their two nations "was as necessary to America as a duel is to a young officer to prevent his being bullied and elbowed in society" and that such a duel, "when over, would probably leave them better friends than they had ever before been.")[24]

In his letter to Andrew, Bayard almost spoke Foster's words as he told his cousin,

Nothing has depressed the war spirit here more than the frightful exhibition made by Gallatin of War taxes. Many who voted for the army will not vote for the taxes and I much doubt whether any one proposed by the Secretary can be carried thro both Houses of Congress. They are not such fools at the same time as not to know that war cannot be carried on without money. And when they have arrived at the point—no money, no war—even they who are now panting after war if they can't have it without taxing the people and of course ruining their popularity will abandon the object.

I shall consider the taxes as the test, and when a majority agree to the proposed taxes, I shall believe them in earnest and determined upon war, but till then I shall consider the whole as a game of juggling in which the presidency and the loaves and fishes belonging to it are the objects they are contending for.[25]

Gallatin's tax report and private letter to Ezekiel Bacon, came to the House on January 10. When Bacon permitted the letter to become public, on a reading in the House on January 20, it roused a variety of strong reactions from several directions—anguish, anger, castigation, ridicule, and amusement but also support.

Reporting to former Senator Plumer, John Harper described the proposals by Gallatin (a native of Switzerland) as "the Genevan budget" and said, "It is a most unpopular thing here—the members are excessively irritated." Harper also accused Committee Chairman Bacon (an opponent of the navy) of publishing a private letter in time to kill the bill to enlarge the fleet.[26]

Felix Grundy was more direct with Bacon, advising him that "the question of War plainly and distinctly put shall go in front" of taxes. Grundy feared heavy taxation could become permanent in event "we do not go to war."[27] This view to delay taxes was held by others, in and out of Congress.

One of the outsiders, Gallatin's former cabinet colleague, Henry Dearborn (appointed senior major general of the army on February 12, 1812), remonstrated the treasury secretary,

Why is it necessary to check the ardour of the people at so critical a moment, why not postpone ... taxes ... until war shall have actually commenced, then the people will expect to bear such taxes as circumstances shall require.[28]

To be expected, Massachusetts Federalist Rep. Samuel Taggart scoffed at the distress of the War Hawks, saying "Gallatin's budget — is very chokey meat. I care not how much they pelt Gallatin I believe him to be a great rascal, but in this they abuse him." Taggart doubted Gallatin's recommendations would provide enough revenue "to defray the ordinary expenses of government" and he calculated "a debt of $100,000,000 at least to accumulate in a five years' war exclusive of the loss of lives and property" and with surprising vision added, "a war which conducted by a Dearborn, an acquitted Wilkinson, a Secretary Eustis ... can be only a war of defeat and disgrace but where victory would be equally ruinous with defeat."[29]

Federalist Bayard, writing to friend Rodney, was amused that Sen. Stephen Bradley of Vermont,

has no objection to go to war, but he does not mean that it shall cost anything. That he does not intend to vote any more money than just what is in the Treasury. He is against taxes, or loans, and he wished to God it was a part of the Constitution that the Government should neither tax nor borrow for the purpose of making war![30]

As is normal, newspapers also voiced their opinions loudly. The *Baltimore Sun*, referring to the "wily Genevan," said, "His abilities as a financier, by this report, sinks to its original nothingness."[31]

The *Philadelphia Aurora* opined that Gallatin's budget was "copied from the projects of Hamilton & Wolcott" and said of

the present occasion ... the same morbid feeling, the same stupefactious current of intrigue, the same selfishness and fatuity, prevails now at Washington which prevailed in this city during Adams' rule. It is impossible that confidence can long continue with the shocking schemes of private intrigue which now pervade and govern everything.[32]

A few days later in an editorial titled "The Rat in the Treasury," the *Aurora* charged "the measures of policy suggested by this man are calculated upon the same scale by which the blackest tyrannies are conducted." It went on with a long series of accusations against Gallatin.[33]

On the surface, the sole support for Gallatin seemed to come from the *National Intelligencer* (called by at least one foreign diplomat, "the official newspaper" of the U.S. Government). In an editorial it praised the "candor and perspicuity" of Gallatin's report and said, "once persecuted for refusing to withhold the truth," he is now "accused of *apostasy* and TREACHERY" for his effort."[34]

Indeed, a letter sent by Gallatin to Speaker Clay, and made public on January 23, was certainly enough to dampen even the vigorous ardor of that leading War Hawk. It revealed that in the last year of record, the value of United States exports to Great Britain was $20,308,211 compared with exports of only $1,194,275 to France over the same period.[35] How could any American justify going to war with the nation's best customer?

After its initial shock of publication, the subject of war taxes lay dormant for more than one month. In this interim, there seemed to be a period of ominous waiting — a calm in which affairs of state seemed to balance precariously with no one sure which way events would move. It was openly stated that matters waited the return of the frigate *Hornet* which had carried diplomatic messages to Europe in late 1811. There was a hope, but not necessarily an expectation, that France would give firmer pronouncement of revocation of the Milan and Berlin Decrees and/or that Britain would repeal the Orders in Council.

Meanwhile, Henry Clay took a small part in the debate over several domestic subjects (though some of these were discussed in January as well as later). He spoke briefly in Committee of the Whole House against a resolution that would have denied private citizens certain claims because of the statute of limitations. As Speaker he ruled against indecorous language in the House. And again in Committee of the Whole he voiced his confusion with a bill to tax marriages in the

District of Columbia to provide financial aid to schools. Clay said he

knew not which most to admire, the conduct of the opposer or supporter of this bill. If he understood the gentleman last up, there is at present a law taxing marriages, but no authority to collect the tax, which is the same as if there was no law on the subject. As he thought with the gentleman first up, that marriages ought not to be taxed, but promoted, he should vote with him for striking out the first section of the bill.[36]

The bill was rejected.

At last, on February 25, the House, in Committee of the Whole, took up Gallatin's tax proposals. Even today there is almost nothing in writing to show any pressure on House members to give their support to the secretary's tax recommendations. Yet Clay, as a leader of the war effort, must have used his own persuasive voice and the prestige of his position to corral the votes needed. Still, the only evidence of his stance on taxes appears in three of his letters reprinted in the *Lexington Reporter*. When Gallatin's recommendations came to the House, Clay wrote,

The Secretary of the Treasury has given us his budget. It comprises a number of taxes, and some not of the most agreeable description. But taxes must be laid, and we shall have to make a just selection amongst those suggested.[37]

On February 9, Clay wrote to the *Reporter's* editor,

Taxes are indispensably necessary in the event of hostilities. The only duty left to the representative, it seems to me, is to select those that are least burthensome to the people. That they will, when such a selection is made, be borne with cheerfulness I have no doubt. When the most inestimable interests of the country are at stake, the nation would be unfaithful to itself if it withheld the requisite supplies. Surely no man will hesitate to contribute his just *part* when *all* is at hazard.[38]

The House debate in Committee of the Whole was surprisingly light and the votes were surprisingly heavy in favor of the taxes. Of the 14 resolutions, half of them passed by more than two-thirds and none were really close except one on raising a tax of 20 cents per bushel on imported salt. At first a tax of 10 cents was rejected. Then the entire tax was voted down on a Friday, only to have it reconsidered on Monday and passed with the 20-cent figure.

Rather strangely, the third letter from Clay, dated February 28 (when only three of the resolutions had passed), was reprinted in the *Reporter* on March 7, saying,

On yesterday the House of Representatives, in committee of the whole, concurred with the Committee of Ways and Means in all the taxes recommended by them, without any change whatever. There were large majorities in almost every instance. With respect to the Still tax and the Stamp tax there can be no objection on principle, as they are proposed to be laid. The former is free from the vexatious incidents of an Excise, and the other is confined to bank notes (a very fit subject of taxation) and negotiable paper, leaving the great body of country transactions exempt from its operation. The whole system is to take effect in event only of the war into which we are about to be driven by the aggressions of England, and is limited in its duration to one year after the restoration of peace.[39]

The matters referred to in this last sentence were the subject of the final two resolutions which passed by votes of 80 to 26 and 72 to 27 — but not until March 4. Still, these were only House resolutions and would not have the effect of a law to extract revenue from the people to support a war.

British Minister Foster was surprised sufficiently by the easy passage of the resolutions, to write his Government, "There are indications of hostile Intentions and if no concession be made on the part of Great Britain, War may ensue in the course of a Fortnight." But, as in the past, he quickly tempered his warning with another letter a week later suggesting that the American government was "spreading reports of war" to induce his government "to strike the first blow and thereby ... enable this government to raise an army."[40]

President Madison also expressed his feelings on the passage of the resolutions. Writing his predecessor, Thomas Jefferson, he said, "The House of Representatives have got down the dose of taxes. It is the strongest proof they could give that they do not mean to flinch from the contest to which the mad conduct of Great Britain drives them."[41]

The peace-loving Jefferson, in reply, showed he, too, saw war on the horizon and that he supported his successor in moves to that end.

Everybody in this quarter expects the declaration of war as soon as the season will permit the entrance of militia into Canada, & altho peace may be their personal interest and wish, they would, I think, disapprove of its longer continuance under the wrongs inflicted and unredressed by England. God bless you and send you a prosperous course through your difficulties.[42]

A few days later Jefferson wrote another friend, Hugh Nelson,

I think all regret that there is cause for war, but all consider it as necessary, and would, I think, disapprove of a much longer delay of the Declaration of it. As to the taxes, they expect to meet them, would be unwilling to have them postponed, and are only dissatisfied with some of the subjects of taxation: that is to say, the stamp tax & excise.[43]

During the ominous pause in war preparations, another matter of intrigue, which bordered on the comical, interposed itself. A few days after writing Jefferson in early March, Madison sent a letter, accompanying a sheaf of documents, to the Congress. It was to create a new controversy and came close to impeachable action against the man who had been the Constitutional convention's authority on impeachment. This was the Henry affair. Or it could have been called the Crillon affair, since it is hard to say which was the greater scoundrel.

In 1808–09 John Henry, an Irishman, was sent by Sir James Craig, governor general of Canada, to spy on Boston Federalists and report back any New England feeling of support for England in the event of war with Great Britain. Henry had served in the American army during an earlier 20-year stay in the United States. But he was opposed to republics and went to Canada where he agreed to work for Craig in the plot to separate the five New England states (Maine was not then a state) from the rest of the United States. Henry felt he was near to success when the *Chesapeake* affair intervened and he returned to England. As an Irishman, he became disenchanted with the English (having seen the English maltreatment of his homeland) and sought payment of $160,000 from the British for his services to Craig. When he was turned down, Henry decided to return to the United States in late 1811.[44]

Prior to sailing for America, Henry became acquainted with a man who identified himself as the French Count Edward de Crillon. The count

claimed to be the son of the Duke of Crillon who commanded at the siege of Gibraltar. He allowed a rumor to circulate that his father had left him property in Spain, Majorca, and Chile, from which latter place he (the count) had received $10,000 for several years, till lately when this revenue ceased. For the purpose of looking after his Chilean lands, Crillon sailed from England on the same ship with John Henry.[45]

Landing in Boston without a passport, Crillon, nevertheless, managed to ingratiate himself with Republican governor of Massachusetts, Elbridge Gerry, and from him obtained a letter of introduction to President Madison for both himself and Henry. Though Gerry's letter to Madison praised both men, calling them great military characters and saying Henry was "truly respectable," he wrote again to Madison on the following day saying he was "uninformed in regard" to the count's politics since he was (to Gerry) "an entire stranger."[46]

While still in Boston, Crillon wrote the French minister in Washington, Louis Sérurier, informing him of Henry and "the treasure" in his possession. This treasure was correspondence between Henry and Craig during the spy mission. Crillon told Sérurier that Henry was willing to make these papers available to the United States government and thus create a greater chasm between the United States and Great Britain.

Henry and Crillon appeared in Washington in late January 1812. Immediately, Crillon was received at both the British and French legations and at the White House. Sérurier was cautious as to what or who he was, but received him publicly as a nobleman and gave him a residence at the Legation. British Minister Foster, who suspected Crillon of being a French agent, described him as "rather short in person with very thick legs and I thought that I had never beheld such a vulgar looking bully, being at once persuaded that he was an imposter." Meanwhile, Henry's papers were made available to Madison and Monroe, who examined them and accepted their authenticity.[47]

Then there followed a period of negotiation for an ownership transfer of the letters. Henry asked $125,000 but the American officials said they could only give him $50,000 from a special treasury fund, and Henry accepted the arrangement. Sometime during this period, Henry, having been told of Crillon's estate in France, offered to buy it from the count who gladly gave Henry its title for some of the thousands of dollars which Henry hoped to get for his papers. The papers had been given to Monroe to examine on January 20. Terms of an agreement were concluded on February 7, and Henry was issued a treasury warrant for the $50,000 dated February 1. He left Washington and sailed for France on March 10. As agreed, his papers were not published until he was to sail, though they were released on March 9.

Shortly after the United States government bought the Henry letters, Crillon wrote authorities in France that Henry was coming there and should be arrested — and he was. Meanwhile, French Minister Sérurier had also written authorities in France telling them of Crillon and of his (Sérurier's) inability in America to ascertain the count's true credentials. Crillon sailed for France in May and, on the basis of Sérurier's interrogations, was also arrested as an imposter losing all he had obtained from Henry. Some years later he hounded Henry in vain for more money, apparently in payment for an estate which did not exist. This gambling swindler's real name was Paul Emile Soubiron. He was the son of a goldsmith.[48]

On March 9, when President Madison sent the 1809 Craig-Henry correspondence to Congress, it was read that same day in the House. Rep. John Harper wrote William Plumer,

The federalists here are in the greatest agony and distress. I never before have seen so restless a set of men. Pitkin began to kick and *squirm*.... Quincy looked pale — walked the floor in haste and was much agitated.

And Harper spoke of Deacon Davenport, "On whose face I actually saw, not only great drops of sweat, but it really ran down copiously on his face."[49] Republican William Widgery commented to the House that it was "an old saying among gunners, that the wounded pigeons can be discovered by their flutterings."[50]

But with the reading of the letters ended, it dawned on the Federalists that no names had been mentioned and they realized that most of the views contained in the correspondence could have been gathered from newspaper accounts of the day. At first, the Federalists questioned the authenticity of the documents, but it was quickly

proved that the signatures of British writers were not forgeries. Josiah Quincy (who so recently had spoken of secession), regained his composure and blasted British efforts toward connecting New England with Canada. He told the House,

Whenever a dismemberment of the United States has been talked of, it has been with awe, and with a fear that the present course of public measures would lead to such an event, and not with a view to bring it about.[51]

On top of these views, which began to make Madison's actions look a little ridiculous, it very soon became known that Madison had paid $50,000 of public money for practically worthless papers. It was strange that the Federalists spoke only briefly or wrote little in private in opposition to Madison's deed. Their comments were generally entwined with assertions that it was an electioneering gimmick aimed at Governor Elbridge Gerry's re-election in Massachusetts. The most overt act on their part was a refusal to attend a White House levee.[52] Members of both parties joined in blaming the British government as the principal villain in the affair.

Massachusetts Federalist Abijah Bigelow wrote, "What provokes me most is that the demo's here neither know what to do next, or when to do it, and are whiling away the time to no purpose."[53]

This was true on the surface, if one regarded debate on domestic affairs as "whiling away the time." It was during this period that Henry Clay took the floor twice to speak on new statehood for Mississippi and Louisiana. The Mississippi bill was to permit the residents of the territory to draft a constitution in preparation for statehood. Clay offered an amendment to assure that the "West Florida" part of the proposed state would not be in contradiction to any United States negotiations over the internationally disputed land. On the bill to admit Louisiana to the Union, Clay wanted any boundary differences settled with this bill, rather than a separate one, and wanted a stipulation "recognizing the freedom of navigation of the Mississippi." His amendments passed. He followed up a few days later in support of another amendment that would give immediate suffrage to those residents in the far western portion of "West Florida, now to be a part of Louisiana, to permit them to vote on the State's new constitution." This also passed as did the bills aimed at statehood for both territories.[54]

While these and other domestic issues were consuming the time of the House in mid–March 1812, Clay was moving in private to capitalize on the national emotions of the Henry disclosures to press for administration action against British intransigence and intrigue.

11

EMBARGO

The disclosure that the administration had purchased the Henry papers for $50,000 out of the public treasury produced a potential crisis for President Madison. Republicans were angry that the papers provided no solid evidence of treason against the Federalists. And the Federalists were angry over the insinuation that they were party to disunion, and that the treasury had been bilked of a large amount of the taxpayers' money.

Only one thread of indignation united both parties — that Great Britain would employ such a scheme to dissect the Union. Yet it was utterly astonishing how quickly the young political novice, Henry Clay, was to perceive this small harmony and then move privately to capitalize on his brand new prestige. On Sunday morning, March 15, he visited Secretary of State James Monroe to discuss his ideas. Later in the day, Clay put in writing his recommendations for action and sent them to the secretary. He proposed:

That the President recommend an Embargo to last say 30 days, by a confidential message:
That a termination of the Embargo be followed by War: and,
That he also recommend provision for the acceptance of 10,000 volunteers for a short period, whose officers are to be commissioned by the president.

Amplifying his recommendations, Clay wrote,

The objection to an embargo is, that it will impede sales. The advantages are, that it is a measure of some vigor upon the heels of Henry's disclosure — that it will give tone to public sentiment — operate as a notification, repressing indiscreet speculation and enabling the prudent to look to the probable period of the commencement of hostilities and thus to put commercial vessels under

shelter before the storm. It will above all powerfully accelerate preparations for the War.
By the expiration of the Embargo the *Hornet* will have returned with good or bad news, and of course the question of War may then be fairly decided.

In the margin of his letter, Clay delineated a position on war declaration, which was to provide precedent for all future such declarations.

Altho' the power of declaring War belongs to Congress, I do not see that it less falls within the scope of the President's constitutional duty to recommend such measures as he shall judge necessary and expedient than any other which, being suggested by him, they alone can adopt.[1]

Henry Clay must have been greatly satisfied that his conference and letter to Monroe were soon to produce the desired results. That evening, he and Langdon Cheves met with Senator Bayard, who wrote, "They both assured me that war was inevitable & would be declared in a short time. Clay is certainly in confidence, & I believe both are & they spoke in entire sincerity."[2] But apparently Bayard learned nothing from Clay about an impending embargo.

Matters remained dormant for another week when the arrival in Washington of information exploded like two bombshells. One was a dispatch from the Foreign Office in London to British Minister Augustus Foster. The other was news of the burning of two American ships by the French.

Between 3 and 4 o'clock on the afternoon of March 20, "a middle-sized man with a weather-beaten good countenance" appeared at Foster's door. The man was Lieutenant Green, commander of the armed British ketch *Gleanor*, then lying off Annapolis, Maryland. Green brought with him dispatches through January 1812 from the British foreign secretary, the Marquess Welles-ley.[3] Word soon spread throughout Washington that Foster had received an important letter from London.

Later, Foster was to write back to England,

> The anxiety and curiosity of both houses of Congress to know the real nature of the dispatches was so great that some of the members on committees told me they could not get the common routine business at all attended to. The Department of state was crowded with individuals endeavoring to obtain information from Mr. Monroe, while I was questioned by all those with whom I happened to be acquainted.[4]

The editor of the *National Intelligencer*, Joseph Gales, also tried in vain to break through the cloak of secrecy. He wrote, "We have not of course learnt the nature of Mr. Foster's despatches; but we have every reason to believe they are not of a character favorable to our rights or interests."[5] Gales made an accurate guess.

On the 21st, Foster reported to Secretary of State James Monroe on the contents of his open dispatch. (He had also received two secret dispatches.) The British Foreign Office, in these three messages was responding to Foster's reports of late November 1811 in which he told his government that the United States intended to permit the arming of private merchant ships and send them under convoy. The British government, through Foster, told the United States government that such arming

> announces a System, which if carried into practice, must occasion Acts of Hostile Violence.... It is impossible to consider this System otherwise than as a plan of defence for the Merchant Traders of America against the search of British Cruizers. The General right of search cannot be surrendered by Great Britain.

Later in the dispatch, this claim was repeated and expanded.

> Great Britain cannot relinquish Her right of search upon the High Seas, and cannot recognize any power in Neutral States, to exempt their Merchantmen from that right of Search, either by arming Trading Vessels, or by affording them the protection of Convoy.

The dispatch went on to advise Foster to try to maintain peaceful relations between the two countries, but then gave an analysis of the British view of the "revocation" of the French decrees. It pointed out that France had stipulated that America "should cause Her flag to be respected, in order to entitle Herself to the benefit of that conditional repeal," and also that Great Britain must revoke her Orders in Council and renounce Her principles of Blockade. On this point the British dispatch stated, "we could not comply."

Secretly, the British instructed Foster to demand again "a copy of the instrument or public act by which the Berlin and Milan decrees are stated to have been revoked." In addition Foster's superiors gave him a diplomatic slap on the wrist disapproving his November suggestion "of a partial repeal of the Orders in Council as far as concerns their operation on the American Coasts," as being against the rules of blockade. Foster was to be firm in permitting no concessions or compromise to leave no American doubt as to British firmness. Additionally, the British government directed Foster to renew a "remonstrance" to the United States "against any attempt to seize" East Florida from Spain.[6]

Foster briefed Monroe on the British attitude toward arming and convoying ships and pressed upon him the British insistence "that the instrument should be produced by which the French had repealed their decrees." According to Foster, Monroe listened with great attention to his report based on his newest instructions. His report home that the secretary "then merely said, with, considerable mildness of tone, that he had hoped his conversations with me at the early part of the session would have produced a different result."[7]

Foster thought Monroe was impressed by British firmness. But he did not seem to realize that Britain's unyielding stand, that no further concession nor compromise could be expected from the British Government, in effect, laid down the gauntlet as far as both Monroe and Madison were concerned. In their talks, it is almost possible to hear Madison say to Monroe, "Jim, this closes the door to peace. Clay's recommendation for an embargo to be followed by war seems the only alternative. So, let's get to work on an embargo message to Congress."

The new state of affairs became known to the French minister to the United States, Louis Sérurier. With some pleasure, following a con-

ference with Monroe, he wrote back to his
Foreign Office that the American leaders

> talk boldly — and this will be most serious — of an
> embargo which will be ordered in a week, with the
> object of placing commerce out of reach of the
> first attacks of the enemy and of starving its armies
> in Spain. This measure is regarded as the indispen-
> sable preliminary to the declaration of war.

He also noted that all available troops were being
ordered to the Canadian frontier, grain was being
stored at Albany, and artillery assembled for the
defense of New York.[8]

Overnight the minister's impressions were
changed abruptly. On March 23, Sérurier again
met with Monroe and later wrote,

> I am, sir, just come from Mr. Monroe's office. I
> have never yet seen him more agitated, more dis-
> composed. He addressed me brusquely, "Well, sir,
> it is then decided that we are to receive nothing
> but outrages from France! At what a moment, too,
> at the very instant when we were going to war
> with her enemies."

Sérurier had a good idea what brought on the
secretary's rage since he had just received reports
from northeastern ports of the burning of two
American merchant ships by French warships.
However, he calmly asked Monroe what he was
driving at. Monroe showed the him a deposition
that was to be read by Representative Timothy
Pitkin of Connecticut to the full House the next
day. Monroe warned the diplomat that in Congress it would produce the most abominable effect
and perhaps entirely halt the progress of the administration.

Sérurier tried to play down the effect, whereupon Monroe, in vehemence, exploded, "Remember where we were two days ago. You know what
warlike measures have been progressively followed
up. We have made use of Henry's documents as a
last means of exciting the nation and Congress;
you have seen by all the use we have made of them
whither we were aiming; within a week we were
going to propose the embargo, and the declaration
of war was the immediate consequence of it. A
ship has arrived from London, bringing us
despatches to February 5, which contain nothing
offering a hope of repeal of the orders; this was all
that was needed to carry the declaration of war,
which would have passed almost unanimously. It
is at such a moment that your frigates come and
burn our ships, destroy all our work, and put the
Administration in the falsest and most terrible position in which a government can find itself
placed.

The French minister pointed out that the
vessels were supplying Wellington's army in the
Spanish peninsula. Monroe told Sérurier that
neutrals had the right to carry goods wherever
they could sell them. Sérurier responded that the
French warships had sailed shortly after word of
the burning of French ships at Savannah, Georgia,
and before word of American restitution. Monroe
said the answer might satisfy the cabinet, but not
the Congress.

Monroe reminded Sérurier that America's relations with Britain were strongly based on the
French declaration that their decrees had been repealed;

> that should the Executive now propose the em-
> bargo or the declaration of war, the whole Federal
> party — reinforced by the Clinton party, the Smith
> party, and the discontented Republicans — would
> rise in mass and demand why we persist in making
> war on England for maintaining her Orders in
> Council when we have proofs so recent and terri-
> ble that the French Decrees are not withdrawn.[9]

The deposition of French spoliation read to the
House of Representatives on the following day,
March 24, was a statement made on oath by Captain Samuel Chew of the American brig, *Thames*.
Chew said he had sailed, in mid-January, from
St. Ubes (near Lisbon, Portugal) bound for New
Haven, Connecticut, with a cargo of salt and
fruit. On February 2, a French squadron of three
warships stopped his ship and threatened to burn
it the following morning. Meanwhile, Chew
learned that on board the French ships were the
crews of two American ships, the *Asia* (bound
from Philadelphia to Lisbon) and the brig *Gershom* (bound from Boston to Oporto), both carrying corn and flour. They had been captured and
burned by the French on January 17 and 23, respectively. Chew inquired of the French commodore the reason for the burnings and was told
he had orders from his government to burn all
American vessels sailing to or from any enemy's
port. (British General Wellington fighting in the
Peninsula, then controlled those Portuguese
ports.) Apparently, Chew talked the French commodore out of his threat to burn the *Thames* and
instead gained the release of the other two American crews with orders that they be landed at the
Thames' first port.[10]

Meanwhile, British Minister Foster learned of

the report the day before its presentation to the House when he had a long talk with Secretary Monroe on the 23rd. Foster made use of the latest French atrocities — referring to them as "French perfidy" and "French outrages"— to ask the United States to return to a state of impartiality toward the two belligerents. To the American mind it would have to be impartiality toward "perfidy and outrages," not friendship and cooperation. Foster again renewed his demand for written evidence that France had repealed the decrees. Foster noted that Monroe "seemed much struck with the enormity of" the French action, but told Foster that Sérurier "stated his disbelief in the fact." Nevertheless, Monroe suggested to Foster that France might have some right in burning ships bound for enemy-controlled ports.

Indeed, Foster knew more than he said. Nearly six weeks earlier, he had received almost £400,000 from the British minister in Portugal, for the purchase of corn and flour to supply Wellington. He reported in February that a similar, though larger request had been received and complied with in 1811— undoubtedly using neutral American vessels for his purpose and comprising the cargoes of the *Asia* and the *Gershom*.[11]

Foster observed the congressional reaction to the French depredations at close hand on the evening of the 25th. He attended a reception at the White House. Foster noted that there were more members of Congress present than he "had ever seen before." He asked several of them

what they meant to do with us. Mr. Giles thinks there must be war. Mr. Livingstone thinks it will be declared in 30 days. He has before predicted the time and failed. Mr. Alston would be for an Embargo.... Mr. Clay (the Speaker) says if it be true the French have burnt the ships, he will be for war on France as well as England.[12]

Despite much talk in private circles of a "triangular war" involving both Britain and France, Congress did very little in these late days of March to push for war against either country. The Senate had some adjournments because of the illness of the presiding officer, Vice President George Clinton. And the House managed an adjournment — with some protest — for Good Friday, March 27.

On Easter Sunday evening, the 29th, Washington social attention centered on the first wedding in the White House. It united Dolley Madi-son's sister, Mrs. Lucy Washington (the widow of George Steptoe Washington, a nephew of the first president) to Supreme Court Justice Thomas Todd of Kentucky. The wedding came about quickly and received so little publicity, no guest list is known.

(While it would be reasonable to assume that if the guests included government leaders, Clay would have been present, there is no indication that he did attend the wedding. His high office in Washington and his long personal and professional association with Judge Todd in Kentucky should have secured him an invitation. However, British Minister Foster, in his diary, notes that he spent that evening at Monroe's — another high official who would surely have attended the wedding if ranking leaders had been invited. As for the marriage, the bride had spurned Todd's proposals until he set out for Kentucky late in March. She then changed her mind, a messenger was sent to catch Todd, and he returned to Washington only days before the ceremony.)[13]

In any case, it was the last function at the White House before the president moved on the "embargo to be followed by war." Already he had made his decision and his wife, Dolley, had written on the 27th to her other sister, Anna Cutts (wife of Richard Cutts who represented the Maine district of Massachusetts and who was engaged in commerce), "The war business goes on slowly, but I fear it will be sure. Where are your husband's vessels? and why does he not get them in?"[14]

The decision for embargo was still so secret that not even Treasury Secretary Albert Gallatin knew of it. On March 28, Gallatin told Senator Bayard, privately, that an embargo "was entirely out of the question." He said he had been in favor of it at the beginning of the session, but found the world against him and therefore yielded. But in late March 1812, Gallatin "was decidedly opposed to the measure and he knew of no one in favor of it."[15]

By now Bayard was confused enough to tell Foster on March 30 that "he could not conceive what I could write home, so difficult to get at correct accounts where nobody knows what is the opinion of others."[16]

Though Gallatin apparently knew nothing of the impending embargo and was opposed to one, he, nevertheless, had become convinced that war would come and had written to Jefferson the day after disclosure of the Henry papers, "I rely with great confidence on the good sense of the great mass of the people to support their own government in an unavoidable war, and to check the disordinate ambition of individuals." Further on in the same letter, Gallatin showed his farsighted vision, writing,

> With respect to the war, it is my wish, and it will be my endeavor, so far as I may have any agency, that the evils inseparable from it should, as far as practicable, be limited to its duration, and that at its end the United States may be burdened with the smallest possible quantity of debt, perpetual taxation, military establishments, and other corrupting or anti-republican habits or institutions.[17]

On the day after the first White House wedding, the House Foreign Relations Committee met and approved a resolution addressed to Secretary of State James Monroe saying that the committee would "be happy to be informed when, in the opinion of the Executive, the measures of preparation will be in such forwardness as to justify the step contemplated." A secret meeting was arranged for the next morning, March 31, between Monroe and the committee.

At this meeting, Monroe told the committee that Madison was of the same opinion that he had at the beginning of this session of Congress,

> that without an accommodation with Great Britain, Congress ought to declare war before adjourning, that the correspondence from Foster offered no grounds for expectation of an adjustment, and that the unprepared state of the country was the reason no immediate step was taken.

He said the period had now arrived "when some decisive system ought to be taken," and he added "an embargo not exceeding 60 days as preparatory to war had been spoken of." This doubled the embargo period suggested by Clay, but apparently met with his approval.

Monroe went on to tell the committee that the president still hoped for favorable news from France when the frigate *Hornet* returned to the United States — expected to arrive within the suggested period for the embargo. Justice in American relations with France would "increase the pressure upon England," otherwise, "we must resort to measures against her (France) also." The

secretary pointed out that "an object of the embargo will be an opportunity to merchants to prepare for defending their commerce." He said Madison would "be very glad to know the sentiment of Congress on the embargo."

Congressman John Smilie said there was a pretty strong inclination for the measure. But the committee chairman, Peter B. Porter, feared a state of war, "when we should be unable to carry on active operations, would be the most unfortunate imaginable for us, that we should sustain defeats and disgraces and public discontent." He thought it would take at least until September to prepare for a Canadian expedition and proposed a short adjournment during which time preparations go on prior to an embargo as preparatory to war.

Second-ranking committee member John C. Calhoun responded that "some decisive measure is required that would give a tone to our legislation which has not been hitherto perceived and that measure would be an embargo." He then asked Monroe if a Quebec campaign could be expected.

Monroe answered, "No," and then brought up the subject of finances — a concern of Treasury Secretary Gallatin — asking if Congress would adopt some measure that "would facilitate the attaining of money."

Calhoun replied, "We will give facilities one way or another."

Now, Monroe concluded, "The only question is whether to lay the embargo now or to defer it."

Mr. Harper asked, "Will the Executive recommend it by special message?"

Monroe answered, "If you give me the necessary assurance that it will be acceptable to the House, the Executive will recommend it." He thought war would excite the spirit of patriotism and predicted that, "Whatever injury may be sustained by a particular part of the Union (the seaboard), it will not affect the nation at large." But he added, "The Executive will not take upon itself the responsibility of declaring that we are prepared for war." He expressed some Constitutional scruple as to the president recommending an embargo, but Smilie reminded him that the "last embargo was recommended by the Executive."

At this point in the hearings, the committee,

in Monroe's presence, voted for the embargo and Chairman Porter directed the preparation of the necessary bills. Monroe then told the committee he would inform the president of what had passed and would wait upon the committee the following day to let them know the opinion of the executive. He also learned that there were 74 certain votes in the House for embargo and war.[18]

Later in the day, Monroe reported to Madison on the results of his meeting with the committee. Along with this information, the president had just received disturbing news from London — that restrictions on the authority of the prince regent of England had been removed, and that he had put his government's foreign affairs into the hands of a man "whom America does not possess a more decided enemy," Robert Stewart Castlereagh, in place of Lord Wellesley under the adamant Premier Spencer Perceval.

Due to King George III's periodic lapses of insanity, Parliament, in February 1811, made his son, the prince of Wales, regent. As it was believed the king might recover, the regent's powers were limited to one year. Throughout his early years the prince had been devoted to Whig politicians who were opposed to his father's Tory philosophy. But this latest news from England showed that he had deserted his old friends and cast his lot with those who were determined "to persevere in the execution of the Orders in Council at every hazard."[19]

Again we can almost hear Madison addressing Monroe saying, "This only confirms our decision for the embargo, Jim." This time, in more formal language the president expressed the same view to his old friend and supporter, Thomas Jefferson, "It appears Perceval, etc., are to retain their places, and that they prefer war with us to a repeal of the Orders in Council. We have nothing left, therefore, but to make ready for it."[20]

By that evening, British Minister Foster had heard talk of an embargo, but in a conversation with a General Smith (probably Senator Smith of Maryland or Congressman Smith of Virginia) who was "full of jokes, thought the embargo would not come on tomorrow because it was April Fool's day."[21]

Congressman Calhoun was on firmer ground regarding the enactment of an embargo when he confided in Josiah Quincy, that same day, saying it would certainly be done and that it was "the in-

tention of the government that it should be made public." Quincy asked if he were "authorized to communicate that intention to my constituents." Calhoun said that was his purpose in passing the information. Quincy thereupon, with the aid of another Federalist, wrote letters to Boston merchants and engaged a stage rider to deliver the dispatches to Boston in 76 hours. On April 4, the intelligence was received in Boston where "the effect was electric, the excitement produced never exceeded." Immediately, "the whole town was in motion," preparing ships for sea before the harbor was closed by the Embargo."[22]

At 1 P.M. on April 1, 1812, the President's secretary, Mr. Edward Coles, delivered his brief embargo message to House Speaker Henry Clay. It read:

> Considering it as expedient, under existing circumstances and prospects, that a general embargo be laid on all vessels now in port, or hereafter arriving, for the period of sixty days, I recommend the immediate passage of a law to that effect.
>
> James Madison.[23]

Clay suspended debate on a bill concerning post roads and ordered the gallery cleared and the doors closed for a secret session. The message was briefly considered by the Foreign Relations Committee and then brought before a Committee of the Whole House. Adam Boyd of New Jersey wanted the embargo period to be extended to 120 days, for the second time doubling the period recommended by Clay, saying 60 days was a time "much too short for the great amount of American property now abroad to return."

Adam Seybert of Pennsylvania said the proposal "came to the House in a very questionable shape" and wanted to know if "it is to be considered as a peace measure of a precursor of war."

Tennessee's Felix Grundy (of the Foreign Relations Committee) said he understood "it is a war measure, and it is meant that it shall lead directly to it." Then Silas Stow of New York wanted to know the status of the nation's defenses, if it were a war measure.

With the House meeting in Committee of the Whole, Clay was not in the Speaker's chair. Therefore, he rose to express his thoughts and warmly supported the president's message, despite the extension to 60 days. He told the members, "it is to be viewed as a direct precursor to war." He ran rough shod over the frightened arguments of the measure's detractors, saying he did not wish to hear the opinions of any man who used want of preparation as a deterrent to war, "After the pledges we have taken?" He went on to suggest that the burning of American vessels by the French did not bother him and we would combine France to the enemy we have selected, if necessary. "There was no intrinsic difficulty or terror in the war: there was no terror except what arises from the novelty." He noted that our contact with the enemy (Great Britain) was "on our own continent." He expected the support of the people "if we now proceed.... Many of our people have not believed that war is to take place. They have been wilfully blinded." In conclusion he stated that as an American and a member of the House, he "felt a pride that the Executive had recommended this measure."

John Randolph took the floor saying he could not be silent. He spoke of this meeting behind closed doors, that "the eyes of the surrounding world are upon us. We are shut up here from the light of Heaven; but the eyes of God are upon us. He knows the spirit of our minds." Randolph intimated that this measure did not originate with Madison. He agreed with Seybert

> that it comes to us in a very *questionable shape*, or rather in an *unquestionable shape*—whose ever measure it is, the people of the United States will consider it as a subterfuge for war; as a retreat from the battle. We some years ago resolved that we must have *war, embargo,* or *submission*—we have not had war or submitted—we must therefore have embargo.

Randolph did not believe the executive would "be guilty of such gross and unparalleled treason" as to take an unprepared nation into war at the end of 60 days. The embargo would be renewed, he believed. "The honorable Speaker is mistaken when he says the message is for war; it is the effect of an excitement occasioned by Ministerial, Federal, and neutral papers, and is not the wish or measure of the Executive." He argued that there were no new causes for war.

Clay responded sharply that the House need not be reminded "of that Being who watches and surrounds us." He would not be put off by the question, "What *new* cause of war?" but asked in

turn, "what old cause of war had been avenged?" Clay cataloged impressment of seamen, capture of vessels, Indian war on the Wabash, and the Henry mission to excite civil war. "Is this not a cause for war? We have complete proof that she will do everything to destroy us—our resolution and spirit are our only dependence."

Boyd spoke again to say he admired "the fire and spirit of the honorable Speaker," but still he thought it unwise "in an unarmed nation, as we are, to commence hostilities against one so completely prepared."

Then Randolph said he wished the actions in the Foreign Relations Committee on the previous day to show that the impetus for the president's message came from that committee and was not intended as a war measure. This move was objected to, but the Committee of the Whole voted to support Randolph.

During the debate, Smilie told the members he had heard but one sentiment from Madison, "which is, *that we must make war* unless Great Britain relents."

Randolph proceeded to recite his description of the previous day's hearing and concluded, "If you mean war, if the spirit of the country is up to it why have you been spending five months in idle debate?"

Speaker Clay (not in the chair) bristled at this remark and called Randolph to order for charging the House with spending five months in idle debate. The chairman decided the expression was not out of order. Wright of Maryland appealed the ruling but the committee upheld the chairman (and Randolph) by the slim margin of 50 to 49. Randolph was brief in continuing his discourse and shortly Clay resumed his seat as Speaker of the House to consider the bill for an embargo of 60 days.

A move to open the doors was voted down.

A move to continue consideration of the measure another day was defeated.

The House voted 70–41 for the embargo and sent it to the Senate. The doors were finally opened and the House adjourned—at 3 A.M.[24]

That evening, while the House continued to debate in secret session, British Minister Augustus Foster, attending an affair at the White House at the other end of Pennsylvania Avenue, found President Madison "very warlike, calls our Orders tantamount to letters of marque."[25] Though the president was still in doubt about the outcome of his embargo message, Foster had by now, through leaks, learned of the embargo proposal.

The next day, as the Senate debated the embargo message until nearly 5 P.M., Foster went to see Secretary of State Monroe and asked him how he was to "represent" the embargo to his government, "whether as a step preparatory to war or simply as a municipal measure." Monroe "put the latter construction on it and deprecated its being considered as a war measure.... Sneeringly," Foster thought, the secretary seemed to consider "it as an impartial measure toward the two belligerents and as thereby complying with one of our demands, namely putting them on an equality."

Foster appears not to have recognized the sense of finality when Monroe added that "the President would have waited for the arrival of the *Hornet* to propose the embargo, but that the news from England by the late papers up to February 27 just arrived," and Foster's subsequent communications to the American government had left the United States no hope of a change in British measures. In his delusion and characteristic habit of watering down any warning to his government, Foster added in his account of this meeting,

> Whatever measure is resorted to at this time, it is with a view to the approaching Election of a President.... Whatever will secure the re-election of Mr. Madison, be it Embargo, Non-intercourse, war, repeal of the Non-importation Act, or reconciliation, it will be recommended by the Government and many members who would otherwise be against any one of these measures will for the sake of the party vote in its favour. In this view it is not unlikely that the session may terminate favourably to our interests after all.[26]

On Friday the 3rd of April, Foster next met with Madison and expressed his pleasure in learning from Monroe "that the embargo was not a war measure."

"Oh, No!" Madison replied, "Embargo is not war." Again Foster missed the fine line of significance in this comment, which should not have given any satisfaction to the minister. It said nothing as to the embargo's successor. Foster did write his government that Madison added "that he was perfectly of opinion the United States would be amply justified in going to war with us ... for that

Great Britain was actually waging war upon them." Madison cited the British capture of 18 American ships carrying $1.5 million in cargo in less than one month. This alone was sufficient reason for the embargo, the president told the minister. Lastly, not quite as anticipated, Madison said the Congress would be in session "at the period fixed for the termination of the embargo when it would be renewed or not according to circumstances."[27]

As Foster and Madison talked, the Senate voted to pass the embargo bill. But they diluted its force by extending its duration from 60 to 90 days. On a final vote of 20 to 15 they returned it to the House that same afternoon. Again the House suspended other debate and took up the embargo.

This time, Josiah Quincy carried the burden of debate by anti-embargo forces arguing that the bill was not preparatory to war, but a substitute for war. He held that the threat of British capture of vessels was less a menace to merchants than loss to commerce by the embargo. "Which is best," he asked, "to keep them at home to certain loss and probable ruin, or adventure them abroad to possible loss and highly probable gain? Ask your merchant. Ask common sense.... Heaven help Our merchants from *embargo-protection*!"

He admitted he was one of three legislators who sent word to merchants of Philadelphia, New York, and Boston so that they might "escape into the jaws of the British lion and of the French tiger which are places of refuge, of joy and delight, when compared with the grasp of this hyena embargo."

Already Quincy had learned that when the news reached Philadelphia,

> the whole mercantile class was in motion, and all that had it in their power were flying in all directions from the coming mischief as if it were a plague and a pestilence. Look at this moment, on the river below Alexandria, Virginia. and the poor seamen, towing down their vessels against wind and tide, anxious only to escape from a country which destroys under the mask of preserving.

Quincy scoffed at the assertion that the embargo was to lead to war since there had been so little military preparation voted by Congress. (He said nothing to the effect that he had been one who had assured that no preparations had been voted.) And in reference to Henry Dearborn's army appointment, Quincy said, "Ever since you appointed a collector of a northern seaport Major General, I have been satisfied that what you intended was an army to fight smugglers and not Canadians."[28]

Randolph spoke against the embargo and urged that debate be postponed until the following Monday. James Emott of New York proposed a 30-day delay. But a call for the previous question (a vote on the embargo as passed by the Senate) passed to bring up the main vote. Clay put the question on passage and Randolph appealed. The House voted 86–17 to uphold Clay's decision and then voted 56–53 to accept the Senate's 90-day version of the embargo.

The next day, Saturday, April 4, Clay signed the enrolled embargo bill and John C. Calhoun delivered it to the Senate for the signature of Senator William Crawford (president pro-tem in the absence of ailing Vice President George Clinton). Later, during that day's House debate, Crawford, of the Joint Committee for Enrolled Bills, reported to the House that President Madison had signed the embargo measure, and it was now law.[29]

There were immediate ramifications to the embargo that were clearly politically inspired. One controversy had already come to a head in the House the day before the measure became law. Though the House had considered the embargo behind closed doors on Wednesday, April 1, its proceedings appeared on Thursday in the Georgetown newspaper, *The Spirit of Seventy-Six*, and on Friday in the *Alexandria Herald*. On April 3, a committee, headed by Felix Grundy, was appointed to look into the violation of secrecy.

The committee reported on the 6th that the editor of the Georgetown paper had received the account from a Charles Prentiss. He said he had gotten the information late Wednesday night from Nathaniel Rounsawell, one of the editors of the *Herald*. Rounsawell told Prentiss he had not inquired if the secrecy injunction had been removed, but Prentiss, nevertheless, furnished the report to the other editors. This narrowed the leak to Rounsawell. But he refused to divulge his source to the House committee except to say that he had obtained part of the information from members of the House. Since the committee could not get him to talk, he was brought before Speaker Clay who asked him the same questions and got the same response.

After the House voted to place Rounsawell in the custody of the sergeant at arms, there was a long discussion about the rights of citizens. Hugh Nelson, called it "a contest between the House of Representatives and the freedom of the press of America," but that the matter was too trivial and unwise for the House to meddle with it, for it would make Rounsawell "one of the most conspicuous characters of the present day." Nelson considered him as "too contemptuous to deserve so much notice." Still, the resolution passed easily.

On the following day, Republican member John Smilie revealed that he had related the details of the closed-door session to Delegate Jonathan Jennings, of the Indiana Territory, in the hearing of Rounsawell saying that he had heard that Randolph was threatening to violate the secrecy injunction. Jennings had become ill on that Wednesday and had left the House at mid day. Smilie now told the House that he was one of the first to come to Jennings' room after adjournment and was asked what had transpired. Smilie told Jennings of the session's actions, and only then noticed Rounsawell standing in the doorway listening. With this account before the House, the Republican members closed the affair and freed Rounsawell. No further action taken against any one.

Now, since confessions seemed to be the order of the day, Calhoun told the House that he had passed on to other members, on March 31, word that an embargo measure was about to be sent to the Congress. His reason was that Randolph had just returned from Baltimore where he had learned from the British consul there that an embargo was in the works. Calhoun reasoned that if the British knew, at least House members, not of the Foreign Relations Committee, ought to be informed as well. This cleansing brought another confession from Quincy, who admitted for the second time, that he was one of those who had sent word of the embargo by express to the northeastern ports.[30]

Still, the Federalists were boiling over the embargo and wanted to see the Madison administration defeated in the coming election.

12

POLITICS AND DIPLOMACY

Eventually, charges were to be made that James Madison may have submitted to some sort of political coercion, about the time of the embargo, in order that he might be supported for a second term as president. In return, he was to agree to terms presented by an unofficial committee of congressmen. Whether the embargo had any part in the alleged bargain is not clear. Also, at this particular time, part of the charges allude to pressure on Madison to abort a planned peace mission to London with Senator James Bayard as one of the supposed envoys. In any case, the charges did not become public for many months and then continued for many years. A central figure in the presumed coercion was Henry Clay. But since the pressure on Madison could have been split into two meetings about six weeks apart, a discussion of the charges will come chronologically after the second meeting, or the most likely time if there were only a single gathering.

Meanwhile, politics and diplomacy demanded the attention of both the administration and Congress for the next few weeks. Almost simultaneously with the passage of the embargo, some out-of-town newspapers carried rumors that Madison planned to send a peace mission to London. Since this, too, is wrapped up in the coercion charge, details of this matter will also be told later.

Despite charges that Madison was pushed into leading the nation towards war in 1812, there is solid proof that Madison needed no persuasion to convince him that war was on the horizon. His action in sending the embargo message to Congress on April 1 is one example. But another appears in his reaction to the Senate's extension of the message from 60 to 90 days.

President Madison wrote his predecessor, Thomas Jefferson, on April 24, 1812,

> You will have noticed that the Embargo, as recommended to Congress was limited to 60 days. Its extension to 90 days proceeded from the united votes of those who wished to make it a negotiating instead of a war measure; of those who wished to put off the day of war as long as possible, if ultimately to be met, and those whose mercantile constituents had ships abroad, which would be favored in their chance of getting safely home. Some, also, who wished and hoped to anticipate the expiration of the terms, calculated on the ostensible postponement of the war question as a ruse against the Enemy. At present, great differences of opinion exist as to the time and form of entering into hostilities; whether at a very early or later day, or not before the end of the 90 days, and whether by a general declaration, or by a commencement with letters of Marque and Reprisal.[1]

This private letter, to a lover of peace, does not sound like the views of a man who had been coerced by his supporters to do something he opposed. Madison had enough good reasons of his own to move at the rate he did in the direction of a war he recognized as inevitable, at least after March 31. He would want the majority support of Congress. He would want the support of the people. He would want time for military preparations to assure victories. And he would want to give England that 60 days (extended to 90 by the Senate) to face the reality of American firmness and recede from their Orders in Council.

On this latter point Madison could not know how his actions were being reported to the home office by Great Britain's minister to the United States. In fact, Augustus Foster's vision of affairs continued to be myopic. His attitude is revealed in his dispatch to London of April 23 as he commented on two editorials appearing in the *National Intelligencer* earlier in the month.

On April 9, the paper printed an editorial with the definition of the embargo heard earlier by Foster from the president's own mouth, "It is not war." Then the editorial added, "Nor does it inevitably lead to war." But this was immediately qualified by the words, "If that result is avoided, it is evident that it can only be by an honorable accommodation with the belligerents on the various and grievous wrongs which this country had received from them." The following paragraph is even more firm.

It would be dishonorable, and might be ruinous, if, without a redress of our wrongs, war did not promptly follow the expiration of the embargo. No other alternative is left to our choice. Every other expedient has been tried, and failed. A new and more solemn position is now taken, which must be maintained. We cannot retrace our steps and abandon, perhaps forever, our most important rights. Nor can we rest longer at the point at which we now pause. We must, without a redress of wrongs, advance, and war is the next step. It would be folly in the extreme to attempt to disguise from ourselves the true character of the present embargo. It is not an engine to be wielded in negotiation.[2]

Since this particular editorial aimed its fire at both Great Britain and France, it appears that it frightened the French minister, Sérurier, as much as anyone. He met with Monroe late that day. Monroe subdued Sérurier, who then wrote home,

that the embargo had been adopted in view of stopping the losses of commerce, and of preparing for the imminent war with England; he protested to me his perfect conviction that war was inevitable if the news expected from France answered to the hopes they had formed. He gave me his word of honor that in the secret deliberations of Congress no measure had been taken against France.... Mr. Monroe insisted here on his former declarations, that if the Administration was abandoned by France it would infallibly succumb, or would be obliged to propose war against both Powers, which would be against its interests as much as against its inclination.[3]

As for Foster's reaction, because both belligerents were included in this editorial, he wrote home that

the tone held towards France began to be pretty strong, but in succeeding papers the language of

complaint against that power ceased again, and Great Britain became once more the sole object of its abuse.

Foster was now referring to a second editorial that appeared on the 14th about which he said it was "a very vehement exhortation to Congress to declare war against us immediately and the sensation created by it was very great, not only here, but in the principal cities of the Union."[4]

This second editorial cited the arrival of the U.S. frigate *Hornet*, long delayed in France, as the time when a final decision would be made. But it questioned that if hope of an honorable accommodation with Great Britain was at an end while negotiations for favorable results with France were going forward,

where is the motive for longer delay? The final step ought to be taken, and that step is War. By what course of measures we have reached the present crisis, is not now a question for freemen and patriots to discuss. It exists, and it is by open and manly war only that we can get through it with honor and advantage to the country. Our wrongs have been great; our cause is just, and if we are decided and firm, success is inevitable. Let war therefore be forthwith proclaimed against England. With her there can be no motive for delay. Any further discussion, any new attempt at negotiation, would be fruitless as it would be dishonorable.

Answering the argument that the United States was not prepared for war, the editorial continued, "This is an idle objection, which can have weight with the timid and pusillanimous only. The fact is otherwise." It went on to ask, "From what quarter will it assail us?" and noted that England of late "dreaded an invasion of her own dominions from her powerful and menacing neighbor," France, and that British armies required strong support in the Spanish peninsula. The editorial scoffed at danger from Canada where 300,000 inhabitants faced seven to eight million in the United States. It belittled any ability of the British fleet to endanger coastal cities beyond the scope of wanton desolation which can be repelled by a well-manned shore battery. Finally, the editorial stated that to yield American rights to the British at this time, "the cause may be considered as abandoned. There will be no rallying point hereafter."[5] The British minister immediately attributed authorship of this strong language to "Mr. Clay of

Kentucky, the Speaker," and reported home that "For two or three days it was most confidently believed that a message recommending a declaration of war would follow without delay."[6]

But later, in his diary, Foster, recording excerpts from one of his numerous conversations with James Bayard, quoted him as saying, "He knew it for a fact positive that the President [Madison] furnished the articles for the *National Intelligencer*." A few weeks earlier Foster had noted in his diary that "Smilie is most in the confidence of the President but Jefferson is supposed to govern still. Commodore O'Brien observes Madison is a good little man, but that he goes by the long tiller at Monticello."[7]

A declaration-of-war message did not follow the editorial. And had the editorial been Clay's writing he might have forced such a resolution in the House of Representatives. But this very editorial has been found in the handwriting of Secretary of State James Monroe with all interlining and deletions of a first draft.[8]

More than 45 years later Joseph Gales, editor of the *National Intelligencer* in 1812, "recollected" those days of 1812 and revealed the following note:

From the Secretary of State to Editor

If convenient, J. Monroe will be glad to see Mr. Gales at his house precisely at five this afternoon.

Monday, (April 12, 1812)

Gales told of "successive interviews and conversations" between the two men,

sometimes at the Department of State and sometimes at Mr. Monroe's residence ... in the course of which the Secretary, with great kindness and unwearied patience, communicated to the latter the views of the Administration concerning the position and the duty of the Government of the United States under the circumstances of its present relations to the Government of Great Britain.

Monroe spoke of treatment by Great Britain ending these conversations frequently with vehement expressions such as this: *"There is no alternative*! WE MUST FIGHT, or be irredeemably disgraced in the eyes of the world, and even in our own." Exhortations of this character, coming from one so skilled in statesmanship and so identified from the beginning of the Revolution with his country's growth and history, could not but have made a deep and durable impression to whomever addressed.[9]

In an interview George Bancroft had with Madison in March 1836, Madison told Bancroft,

that "the British left no option; that war was made necessary, that under the circumstances of the negotiations with England war was unavoidable..." he knew the unprepared state of the country, but he esteemed it necessary to throw forward the flag of the country, sure that the people would press onward and defend it.[10]

Though Henry Clay may have been anxious to hasten the "resort to arms," he clearly had no need to convince President James Madison that war was inevitable. Even Secretary of State James Monroe, who had come into office on Madison's pledge to seek again a means to resolve the differences between the United States and Great Britain, had long since concluded that only in a British retreat from its Orders in Council would an honorable solution be possible. And the great peace-lover, Thomas Jefferson, was writing his successor of his support for the inevitable war.

With the embargo a simmering gripe among the Federalists, several other matters competed for the attention of Henry Clay and all of the other politicos in Washington City. Almost simultaneously with the passage of the embargo and publication of the editorials, news accounts began appearing in American papers that Napoleon had pulled out of the Spanish peninsula, had marched across northern Europe, and was on the verge of declaring war on Russia. Logic might have it that he would seek greater friendship with the United States and give support to their threat of war against Great Britain to insure some protection for France now far to the rear of his army. But another news item brought to the United States in 19 days (in one of the quickest passages to that time) reported that confidential dispatches, from the United States chargé d'affaires in London, Jonathan Russell, to Joel Barlow, the American minister to France, had been intercepted and seized by French authorities under orders from Napoleon.[11]

Barlow was still writing back that he was holding the *Hornet* with hopes of sending it home with a treaty of commerce negotiated with the French government. Madison was skeptical of his chances and wrote Jefferson that he believed Barlow was "burning his fingers with matters which will work great embarrassment and mischief here, and which his instructions could not have suggested."[12]

From Massachusetts other news came of the unexpected defeat of Elbridge Gerry in his bid for re-election as governor. The Henry papers had failed to turn the populace against the Federalists and in fact the governor's "Gerrymandering" of districts had turned the people against him instead and created a new word in the American political lexicon.

Meanwhile, in Congress, the New England Federalists attempted to push through a repeal of the Non-Importation Law to give some relief to their merchants. Not only did they fail in this move, but their opponents succeeded in closing a loophole in the embargo by passing a bill prohibiting the export of money or goods through Canadian or Florida seaports.

As for Florida, there were some strange antics carried out by a 73-year-old American general named George Mathews, a former governor of Georgia. A mild-mannered man most of his life, he now had read his instructions as authority to take over East Florida in a manner similar to that by which the United States had occupied West Florida. However, he acted without regard to the fact that the earlier occupation had been carried out under the claim by the American government that possession of West Florida was legitimate through purchase under the Louisiana Territory sale. With a troop of some 200 adventurers, Mathews invaded northern East Florida across the St. Mary's River as far south as the St. John's River and forced the surrender of the Spanish authorities in that area. Since the weakened Spanish empire was now allied with Great Britain, Augustus Foster (in the absence of a Spanish mission to the United States) sought out Monroe, on April 2, to counter American grievances against Britain with British charges of American abuses toward Spain. Monroe told Foster that Mathews "had no orders to excite an insurrection nor receive any part of Florida from any other than the local authorities in an amicable manner." and that Mathews' instructions "were dated before he [Monroe] came into office." Subsequent general instructions did permit a peaceful surrender to the United States of any part of Florida by Spanish authorities, or in case Mathews

had reason to believe that any other power [such as Britain] intended sending a force to occupy any part of the province to anticipate such attempt by lending his assistance in invading the country in question.

Of course, Foster "assured" Monroe that Mathews had no basis for his actions under either of these conditions.[13]

That Madison was upset by Mathews' venture was shown in another comment in his April 24 letter to Jefferson, when he wrote, "In East Florida, Mathews has been playing a strange comedy in the face of common sense, as well as of his instructions. His extravagances place us in the most distressing dilemma."[14] On the day before this letter, Foster was able to report home that the United States government had disapproved of Mathews' actions, had deprived him of his commission (which was given to the governor of Georgia), and ordered restitution of the Florida lands to the Spanish governor.[15] Mathews, hoping to clear himself, set out for Washington and died en route.

During this "comic" episode Foster noted in his diary a "ridiculous story" of one of Mathews' subordinates who took the surrender sword from the Spanish governor and did not return it, as is customary. "The Governor wept," Foster wrote, "when Ashley begged he would take the sword again, did not know he should return his sword to a commandant."

While Florida was the focal point of a minor military incursion, the brand new state of Louisiana was the focus of a Washington party celebrating its statehood. This dinner party, at which Henry Clay toasted "our younger sister, Louisiana," was on April 15, three days after the Speaker reached age 35, the age of eligibility for the presidency. And already he was recognized as the second most powerful man in the nation. Again Foster confided to his diary comments he picked up at the reception. He wrote, "I sat between the Speaker and Mr. Calhoun. Clay was very warlike. Calhoun had the cool decided tone of a man resolved." A desire for military service appeared from an unlikely source when Monroe told Foster two days later that he would have been glad to be made a major general.[16]

Already the top echelon of the army was taking form. By mid–April Henry Dearborn had at last accepted his commission as major general and commander in chief of the army. Foster described him as a heavy unwieldy looking man and added, "His military reputation does not rank very high, as neither does that of Mr. Thomas Pinckney." The latter, a Federalist from South Carolina had also been appointed a major general as a political SOP to the Federalists.

In secret session, Congress had also passed legislation for naming new brigadier generals, and the subsequent appointments were probably worse than their superiors. One was James Wilkinson, acquitted earlier in the year of the charges brought against him for his conduct in command at New Orleans. He was shortly to resume his command there. Another new general was Michigan Territorial Governor William Hull. Of him, Foster accurately wrote,

> he has proceeded to his government [Michigan], where his first object will be to withdraw to Detroit, a remote garrison of about 60 men who are stationed on the southern shores of Lake Michigan [the fort was misplaced in Foster's mind] and are said to be in great danger of being destroyed by the Indians.[17]

To support the army, in these early days of April, Congress passed a measure on the 10th permitting the president to call up 100,000 militia for six months. But Congress also sought all sorts of ways to get away from their legislative duties. Several of the members got permission to take a leave of absence. Among these was Rep. Peter Porter of New York (chairman of the House Foreign Affairs Committee). He was succeeded in that office by freshman Congressman John C. Calhoun. Several others tried valiantly to recess the session. In fact, the Senate twice passed resolutions for adjournment, but the majority in the House refused to go along.

Then on April 20 the chair of the Senate's presiding officer became vacant when old George Clinton, vice president of the United States, died about 8:35 in the morning. This was the first time in American history that one of the national government's two highest offices was vacant.

Ceremonies and procedures for a state funeral for one of the nation's highest officials had to be worked out overnight upon the death of the vice president. Not even President James Madison received an official notification of the death, or an invitation to attend the funeral. Madison had to suggest to a Congressman that he be included in the procession. The Congressional committee, arranging the solemnities, decided against inviting the diplomatic corps "in order to avoid questions of precedency as not fit to be discussed on such occasions." However, British Minister Augustus Foster ordered his "carriage and four" and was allowed to fall in line behind the American government leaders.[18]

On the following day, the House of Representatives passed a resolution to shroud the Speaker's chair in black for the remainder of the current session of Congress. And each member "will go into mourning, and wear black crepe on the left arm for thirty days." The House then agreed to attend the funeral at 4 o'clock.[19]

At about 2:30 P.M. the body of the late vice president was carried from Mr. O'Neals' boarding house, at which he lived and died, to the Senate chamber in the Capitol. About 4:30 P.M. the following procession formed:

1. The cavalry.
2. The marine corps.
3. The chaplains of both houses of Congress.
4. The physicians who attended the deceased.
5. The hearse and eight pallbearers (all veterans of the Revolution in which Clinton had served with distinction).
6. The family mourners.
7. The President of the United States.
8. The sergeant-at-arms of the Senate of the United States.
9. The Senate of the United States as chief mourners, preceded by their president pro-tem [William H. Crawford], and secretary.
10. The sergeant-at-arms of the House of Representatives.
11. The House of Representatives of the United States, preceded by their Speaker [Henry Clay] and clerk.
12. The heads of Departments.
13. The officers of government.
14. Citizens and strangers.[20]

Augustus Foster fit among the final group.

The shops of Washington City were shut at an early hour and the largest crowd ever to gather in the city turned out to be part of the solemnities. They were heightened by "the glistening arms and nodding plumes of the military corps ... and the solemn melody of the martial band, which attended all hearts to melancholy." The body was interred at the burial-ground near the navy yard.[21]

In the days after Clinton's funeral, Congress continued to do very little to prepare the country for war. On the contrary, most actions were of a negative nature. It was during these beautiful spring days that the House took up a request from Secretary of War William Eustis for the authorization of two assistant secretaries. He was supported by Tennessean Felix Grundy who had acquainted himself with "the business in that Department and the manner in which it was conducted." Grundy challenged his colleagues to look at the duties which Eustis had been

> compelled to perform, and those which in a state of war must devolve upon him, and ask themselves whether the man exists qualified to give general satisfaction under such circumstances? Hitherto, he has discharged the duties of Quartermaster General, Commissary General, and all those functions which properly belong to the whole staff department of the Army. He has also the claims of pensioners to attend to; and every member who has served on the Committee of Claims knows the labor this business requires. In addition to these duties, he is bound to correspond with the Indian agents in the different sections of the Union, and to superintend the land warrants issued by the General Government, which originally proceed from his office. And, sir, the great operations of organizing a large Army — in fact, the whole preparations for war — have fallen upon one man, altogether unaided by clerks of experience; for, not one of his assistants has been in the office twelve months.... He [Grundy] did not think Assistant Secretaries should be regarded as mere clerks, who render clerical services only. He [again Grundy] was of opinion that they were to aid the Head of the Department, not only with their hands, but with their minds.

On the other hand, William Widgery of Massachusetts opposed the appointments on the grounds that "they would create indecision, uncertainty, and discord in the department, and by dividing, weaken the responsibility," while another member suggested the measure was designed "to prop up an inefficient officer of Government."[22] The bill passed the House but the Senate killed it by postponing action.[23] And after an attempt in the House, on April 25, to adjourn failed, many congressmen simply went home on leave.

But even more disastrous for the ambitions of the War Hawks was the result of the treasury's at-

tempt to borrow $11 million to finance the prospective war. Authorized by the law enacted March 14, subscriptions for the loan were opened on May 1 and 2. It was a fiasco.

Years later, Henry Adams summarized the event.

> Federalist New England refused to subscribe at all; and as the Federalists controlled most of the capital in the country, the effect of their abstention was alarming. In all New England not one million dollars were obtained. New York and Philadelphia took each one and a half million. Baltimore and Washington took about as much more. The whole Southern country, from the Potomac to Charleston, subscribed seven hundred thousand dollars. Of the entire loan, amounting to eleven million dollars, a little more than six millions were taken; and considering the terms, the result was not surprising. At a time when the old six-percent loans, with ten or twelve years to run, stood barely at par, any new six-percent loan to a large amount with a vast war in prospect, could hardly be taken at the same rate.
>
> The Federalists, delighted with the failure, said, with some show of reason, that if the Southern States wanted the war they ought to supply the means, and had no right to expect that men who thought the war unjust and unnecessary should speculate to make money from it.

Adams, noted that Gallatin no longer had the United States Bank to help him and had to deal "separately with the State Banks through whose agency private subscriptions were to be received." Adams went on to say that

> after destruction of the United States Bank, a banking mania seized the public. Everywhere new banks were organized or planned, until the legislature of New York, no longer contented with small corporations controlling capital of one or two hundred thousand dollars, prepared to incorporate the old Bank of the United States under a new form, with capital of six million. [On March 27,] Governor Tompkins stopped the project by proroguing the legislature [until May 21], but his message gave the astonishing reason that the legislature was in danger of yielding to bribery.[24]

To many, Tompkins' action was totally political. While the governor was a Republican and loyal to Madison, most of his party members in the New York legislature supported their lieutenant governor, De Witt Clinton, as a successor to his uncle, Vice President George Clinton.[25] At a secret meeting in Albany, on March 16, these followers endeavored to get the younger Clinton to commit himself for the vice presidency if the older Clinton should withdraw from re-election. De Witt Clinton, however, held out for the presidency. It was 11 days after this meeting that Tompkins prorogued the legislature and a bit more than one month later that George Clinton's death removed him from the political scene.

By April 24, Augustus Foster was advising his superiors in London of the potential presidential candidacy of De Witt Clinton,

> If he succeed we shall probably have a new era in this country. He is a bold designing man and spares no means to effect his purpose. He is said to live with the most unprincipled society in New York and to make it a rule to employ people of the most abandoned characters.[26]

A similar view of Clinton was expressed by a Mr. Rutherford to Gouverneur Morris that "he is an unprincipled fellow who cares for nothing and for nobody but himself."[27]

The defection of Clinton and New York supporters was the first major split in the Republican Party of 1812. Earlier, on February 17, 1812, 140 Republican members of the Virginia General Assembly had caucused and nominated a slate of 25 electoral voters pledged to Madison. On May 7 a caucus in Pennsylvania did likewise, except they had named George Clinton to return as vice president.[28]

For the first half of May 1812, everything seemed to be in limbo. The administration still awaited the return of the *Hornet* hoping for favorable news from either England or France or both. Congress was doing almost nothing in legislation (except try unsuccessfully to repeal the embargo). More members went home. Now more than one-fourth of the House membership had left. Both politics and war waited for the unknown.

By the 13th, some faint traces of renewed activity began to appear when a motion passed the House to recall the absentees. Felix Grundy, while supporting the summons, succeeded in deleting the set date of June 1 for their return as being "an indication to our enemy."[29]

It is possible that the vague movement of political activities taking place this day, May 13, might have had their origins in the meeting between Henry Clay and others and President Madison which later led to the charges of coercion. Whether or not this is the day, the timing must have been very close to this. Still more important politics were to take place within the next few days.

In any case, Rep. John Harper, a member of the House Foreign Relations Committee, and a possible member of the ad hoc committee, wrote that day to his friend, William Plumer in New Hampshire, saying,

> The great question will undoubtedly be taken in June. The President will probably send an important and very argumentative message to Congress. A manifesto will be brought forward by the Committee of Foreign Relations and a declaration that "War exists" between the United States and the crown of Great Britain and its dependencies.[30]

In addition to this private communication, British Minister Augustus Foster also wrote his government on the 15th,

> Since the date of my last dispatch [on the 5th] the American Government have been using great diligence in spreading intimations of their having come to a final decision to declare war against England if the majority will support them.

Foster, again diluted his advisory by noting that "the idea had also been disseminated that the war with Great Britain will only be ... a quasi war" because of British advantages derived in direct trade with the United States and in trade from America to British forces in Spain and Portugal.[31]

Whether or not Clay and his committee conferred with Madison on the 13th and discussed the Presidential election or politics in general, is unknown. On May 16, the *National Intelligencer* gave notice of a caucus of Republican members of Congress for the evening of May 18. At 7 P.M. that day 82 members convened in the Senate chamber. Senator J. B. Varnum (Clay's predecessor as House Speaker) was appointed chairman and Representative Richard M. Johnson of Kentucky was named secretary. The gathering proceeded immediately to ballot for their candidate for president and gave all 82 votes to James Madison of Virginia. (The next day, John Randolph remarked to Augustus Foster that "there is something alarming in the unanimity of a caucus that was held last night at which 82 members were present." But Randolph added that "they cannot mean to declare war.")[32]

Nomination of a president was followed by balloting for vice president. John Langdon of New Hampshire, a signer of the Declaration of Independence, was given 64 votes to 16 for Elbridge Gerry, recently defeated governor of Massachusetts. No names were published for two scattered votes. It was later reported that one member in attendance had not voted and another listed as attending the proceedings was, in fact, confined at his lodgings because of ill health. Still 82 votes were cast.[33]

The health of Speaker Henry Clay closed down the House proceedings for the next two days (the 19th and 20th) after Clay suffered a fall from his horse. He returned to his duties on the 21st.[34] Though Clay's attention and actions, as well as those of the administration, were now turned almost exclusively toward the national issue of war, the political aftermath of the congressional caucus was to continue into early June.

On the day Clay resumed his Speakership duties, the New York legislature reconvened. On May 29, the Republicans met in caucus and 87, of the total membership of 95, voted for De Witt Clinton as their choice for president — the others were not present or did not vote. It was to split the Republican Party (or Democrats, as the Federalists preferred to call them) between North and South. It was also to leave the Federalists in a dilemma since they had hoped for dissident Republican support to defeat Madison in the fall. They had yet to name a candidate to carry their banner.

On May 28, the day before the New York caucus of Republicans, John Langdon wrote the congressional Republicans from his home in Portsmouth, New Hampshire, in reply to the notification of his nomination as vice president by the congressional caucus. He said he was 71 years old and that his faculties were blunted. In "declining the honorable offer of my friends," he said,

> my advanced age forbids my undertaking long journies, and renders me incapable of performing the duties of the important station of Vice President with any advantage to our beloved country, or honor to myself. To launch again into the ocean of politics, at my time of life, appears to me highly improper.[35]

On receipt of this withdrawal, the congressional caucus met a second time on the evening of June 8, Varnum again presiding. This time the defeated governor of Massachusetts, Elbridge Gerry (nearly as old as Langdon, being 67), was nominated with 74 votes against a scattering of three votes which went to unnamed candidates.

On the motion of Speaker Clay, a ballot was then opened for those not present at the earlier meeting to let them join in the vote for president. Ten more names were recorded for Madison. The congressional Republicans had been beaten in their selection of the Madison-Gerry ticket by the Maryland legislature which nominated a similar slate on the same day as the first congressional caucus.[36]

With settlement of the question of candidates for the Republican ticket in the coming election, Henry Clay and the members of his party could now turn their attention to pursuing their goal — WAR. Nevertheless, events had already occurred that might reflect unfavorably on Clay and the administration.

13

Coercion Charge

It is with some certainty that we know Henry Clay and an unknown number of like-thinking Republican congressmen met with President Madison some time in May 1812 to discuss a possible declaration of war message to be sent to Congress. Over a period of many years, members of the Federalist party spread innuendoes that at this meeting, and possibly at another in early April, Clay and his colleagues forced President Madison into doing their bidding in return for support for his re-election. All of this continues to remain clouded in a veil of mystery.

From the beginning, the charge was very muddied as to the date of the meetings, participants, the alleged demands by the congressmen, and even whether there were two meetings or only one. Because the precise date of the May meeting is unknown, and because of the lack of evidence of precise demands made on Madison, we can merely conjecture whether the delegation put only support for re-election on the line, or included support for re-nomination at the mid–May congressional caucus. The Federalist argument must also hang entirely on a supposition that Madison was too reluctant to move on his own in the direction of war, and that Clay and the ad hoc legislative committee, annoyed at procrastination, felt they had to build a fire under the president to get their war.

The basis of the alleged meeting in April was said to have been a demand on Madison for his withdrawal of plans for a special peace mission to Great Britain. At the May meeting the demand was said to have been for the president to send a message to the Congress asking for a declaration of war. This may have had to come after the nomination and would be countered by the support of the congressmen for Madison's re-election. However, the strength of "coercion" is less after nomination since there was little likelihood that the Republicans would withdraw their support from their standard bearer. Therefore, the timing of the various moves plays an essential part in determining the truth or falsehood of the charges.

The first insinuation of coercion was raised in a speech by Josiah Quincy in the House of Representatives in January 1813. A second allusion to coercion was made by Alexander Hanson in the same forum in June 1813. (Hanson was the grandson of John Hanson, a signer of the Declaration of Independence and as presiding officer of the Congress under the Articles of Confederation, the older Hanson has sometimes been called the first president of the United States.) In February 1814, Timothy Pickering wrote some letters to a man named Abraham Shepherd, from whom Pickering hoped to get the truth about the coercion allegations. This correspondence was eventually published in 1879, long after Clay's death, by Henry Adams in his biography of Albert Gallatin.

Between the time Pickering wrote his letters and their publication in the Adams book, extremely little information on the subject seeps into print, suggesting that most of the story must have passed verbally, though hints of a charge cropped up in history books for many decades.

In the late 1840s, a biography of Clay was written by Epes Sargent (with updates by Horace Greeley after Clay's death in 1852). This biography appears to have been approved by Clay. In it is a brief description of a single meeting between Clay's committee of Congressmen and President Madison, in May 1812, to discuss the war message.

The meeting appears to have been congenial with no evidence of any threats or coercion.

An 1849 book, however, contained a third-hand account claiming that the late Rep. James Fisk of Vermont had been one of the attending congressmen, and that he intimated there was coercion. About the time of Clay's death, a history of the United States appeared which made as strong a charge as any previous that intimidation of the president was involved in a meeting. But the most precise documentation of the beginnings of the coercion charges is the Pickering correspondence of 1814.

Beginning with the earliest insinuations, starting a little more than six months after war began, Josiah Quincy, on January 13, 1813, made a long speech in the House castigating the administration. In it, he told the House that

it was distinctly stated by individuals from that quarter of the country [referring to the West], under the influence of which war was adopted, that the support of the present President of the United States by their quarter of the country depended upon the fact of the Cabinet's coming up to the point of war with Great Britain.

To this, Quincy added, "without their support, the re-election of the present Chief Magistrate was hopeless."[1] Still Quincy did not refer specifically to the Southern or Western sections of the country nor name any individuals. Nor did he mention the embargo, a proposed peace mission, or a presidential nominating caucus.

Three days later Clay found the opportunity to answer. Clay's response lasted portions of two days, January 7 and 8. But only two sentences struck directly at Quincy's allegations.

The gentleman from Massachusetts, in imitation of some of his predecessors of 1799, has entertained us with cabinet plots, presidential plots, and all sorts of plots, which have been engendered by the diseased state of the gentleman's imagination. I wish, sir, that another plot of a much more serious and alarming character — a plot that aims at the dismemberment of our Union, had only the same imaginary existence.

While Clay expressed the belief that the plotters were incapable of achieving their mission, he reminded Quincy that he "cannot have forgotten his own sentiment, uttered even on the floor of this House, 'Peaceably if we can, forcibly if we must.'"[2] This referred to Quincy's 1811 speech to separate New England, in slightly different words, "violently if need be."

The next public accusation came on June 18, 1813 — the first anniversary of the declaration of war — adding more fuel to the fire. The *Annals of Congress*, referring to Rep. Alexander Hanson of Maryland, states,

Mr. H. here spoke of a self-created committee of Congressmen who called on the President and required him to send the House a message recommending war. He said the first demand was unsuccessful, but the second succeeded; when he was given to understand that his re-election depended upon his recommending war at once.[3]

The names of the committee members were not given, nor were the dates on which the demands were made. Again, neither the embargo nor the peace mission was mentioned. And again the supposed "carrot" was the president's re-election — not his re-nomination. Of course re-election was in the hands of *the people* not an informal committee of a few Congressmen.

Based on this vague comment by Hanson, a private inquiry was made by Timothy Pickering almost eight months later, on February 12, 1814. Pickering, who had held three cabinet posts, including that of secretary of state under President Washington, was by this date again a member of Congress. He wrote to Abraham Shepherd as follows:

CITY OF WASHINGTON,
February 12, 1814.

DEAR SIR, — At the last autumn session, Mr. Hanson, noticing the manner in which the war was produced, in addressing Clay, the Speaker, spoke to this effect: "*You know, sir*, that the President was coerced into the measure; that a committee called upon him and told him that if he did not recommend a declaration of war, he would lose his election. And then he sent his message recommending the declaration."

Now, my dear sir, I learn from Mr. Hanson that Colonel Thomas Worthington, Senator, on his way home to Ohio, gave you the above information, and some other or others who composed the committee. This is a very important fact, and I pray you will do me the favor to recollect and state to me all the information you possess on the subject; at what time and from whom you received it.

It will be noted in this letter that the charge, prefaced by Pickering with the words, "to this effect," does not agree with Hanson's version as published in *The Annals* in June 1813, which could not have referred to the "autumn session" mentioned by Pickering. No other account of Hanson's words, other than those quoted here, can be found. It is not clear why Pickering did not verify the exact wording with Hanson since they met daily in the same chamber. In addition, they refer again only to the declaration of war message and not to the embargo or peace mission. With his letter of February 12, 1814, Pickering pressed Shepherd for information he picked up second hand from Worthington 22 months earlier.

From his home in Maryland, Shepherd answered on February 20, 1814:

> NEAR SHEPHERDSTOWN,
> February 20, 1814.
>
> DEAR SIR,— I received your favor of the 12th instant, and observed the contents. Some time in the beginning of April, 1812, General Worthington came to my house from the city [being Washington City] to see Mrs. Worthington and children set out for Ohio; he continued part of two days at my house, within which time we had considerable conversation on the prospect of war. He insisted war was inevitable. I condemned the folly and madness of such a measure. He then told me that Mr. Bayard would first be sent to England to make one effort more to prevent the war; that Mr. Madison had consented to do so; and that Mr. Bayard had agreed to go; that he had used every means in his power with some more of the moderate men of their party to effect this object, and that he had frequent conversations with Mr. Madison and Bayard on this subject before it was effected, and that I might rely upon it that such measures would be adopted. He left my house and returned to the city [Washington]. After the declaration of war and rising of Congress, General Worthington, on his way home to the State of Ohio, called at my house and stayed a night. I then asked him what had prevented the President from carrying into effect this intended mission to England, and observed I was very sorry it had not been put in execution. He answered he was as sorry as I possibly could be, and that he had never met with any occurrence in his life that had mortified him so much. He said as soon as he returned to the city from my house he was informed of what had taken place by a set of hot-headed, violent men, and he immediately waited on Mr. Madison to know the cause. Mr. Madison told him that his friends had waited upon him and said, if he did send Mr. Bayard to England they would forsake him and be opposed to him, and he was compelled to comply, or bound to comply, with their wishes. I then asked General Worthington who those hot-headed, violent men were. He said Mr. Clay was the principal. I cannot say, but think Grundy was mentioned with Clay.
>
> I clearly understood that Clay and Grundy were two of the number that waited on the President. I did not ask him how he got his information. As I understood the business, a caucus was held and Mr. Clay and others appointed, and waited on the President in the absence of Worthington, which will ascertain when this business took place.[4]

Shepherd's comments intimate a much closer relationship between Senator Worthington and President Madison than is considered likely to have existed. In all of this it appears that feelings for or against the embargo were never an issue in the charges. After all, the Federalists did not seem to believe that the administration meant the embargo to be a prelude to war. It is clear from the correspondence, that Shepherd put an entirely different light on the accusations. Unlike Quincy's speech, Shepherd points to a meeting in April. Hanson did suggest an earlier-than May meeting.

On March 9, Shepherd again wrote to Pickering asking that Worthington's name not be used, saying, "I know he despises Clay and thinks him a bad man."

If Worthington, who later became governor of Ohio, needed a character reference, an unflattering one was given by John Quincy Adams who wrote of him,

> He is a man of plausible, insinuating address, and of indefatigable activity in the pursuit of his purposes. He has seen something of the world and without much education of any other sort, has acquired a sort of polish on his manners and a kind of worldly wisdom which may perhaps more properly be called cunning.[5]

Nowhere has it been found that Pickering used this information, despite the fact that he was so ardent in his opposition to the war that he verged on advocating disunion. That he did not use it is all the more interesting considering that Pickering would likely have been willing and happy to use any charge he could make to cut down Henry Clay. His antagonism toward the Speaker must have been towering, since it was Clay who had brought the censure resolution against Pickering in the U.S. Senate in 1810, contributing to his re-election defeat. It is possible that Pickering did not accept the validity of Shepherd's report as providing solid evidence against Clay.

The April peace mission that never was had a strange "life." Word of a peace mission first appeared in the *National Intelligencer* after some circuitous muttering in other cities. The story, printed in Washington on March 31 (the day before Madison sent the embargo message to Congress), was in the form of an excerpt from an undated letter to a member of Congress from one of his constituents. The writer said

> that he had met a few days past with a gentleman from Richmond, Va., who in turn reported that it was contemplated by the general Government in Washington "to send a minister to the Court of St. James to make one more effort for negotiation."

To establish a date for the writer's story, several additional days must have preceded its publication by the *National Intelligencer*, on March 31,

An additional twist to the publication of the rumor appears in the dates it appeared in the *New York Gazette* (April 1) and the *Philadelphia Aurora* (April 3). When considering the slow transit time for news in those days, it makes little sense that the story would be printed in New York only one day after publication in Washington — and why two days earlier in New York than in Philadelphia?

The *National Intelligencer* noted that two possible envoys on the peace mission would be Federalist James A. Bayard and Judge Henry Brockholst Livingston of New York. Nothing is known about Livingston's relationship with President Madison, but Bayard was in the swirl of political activity at this time.

If Bayard was asked by the president to be a member of a peace mission, there is no evidence of it. His correspondence reveals no intimation that such a mission was contemplated or that he

was to have been involved. As early as March 22, Bayard wrote Caesar Rodney, "I cannot be absent when the matter of war is to be decided on. But that in any event is not expected in a month."[6] Bayard's remarks to British Minister Foster on March 30 (two days before Madison sent his embargo message to Congress), were not the words of a member of a peace commission. Foster summarized Bayard's remarks as "he could not conceive what I could write home, so difficult to get at correct accounts where nobody knows what is the opinion of others." He showed that he was surprised by the embargo (after being led by Gallatin to believe there would be none).

Bayard was silent on any peace mission in a letter to Madison on April 14 from Wilmington, Delaware, but did offer the president his "humble services" in assisting judicial appointments. His words in this letter are cordial and show no feelings of a man who had, supposedly, been pulled back from an appointment to an overseas mission which his political inclinations might have supported. Writing to Madison he said,

> In conformity to your desire I have availed myself of the most fit occasion which had presented itself to intimate to Mr. [Caesar] Rodney your disposition and views respecting him in relation to the vacant place of Judge of this District.

(Rodney declined this offer.)[7] By a reading of this letter to the president, the mission appears to have had no basis.

It therefore appears clear that neither the embargo nor a ghostly peace mission played any part in an alleged coercion. But it also seems strange that the first public reference to this affair that can be found, which follows Hanson's remarks in Congress in June 1813, is in a book on the *Life of Henry Clay* by Epes Sargent, first published in 1842 — a full 30 years after the event! This biography was periodically edited and revised over the following decade, but the account of Clay's meeting with Madison was not changed in subsequent editions. It is as follows:

> The negotiations with Mr. Foster, the British chargé d'affaires [sic] at Washington, were protracted up to the period of the declaration of war. The republican party became impatient of the delay. It was determined that an informal deputation should wait upon Mr. Madison to expostulate against longer procrastination; and it was agreed

that Mr. Clay should be the spokesman. The gentlemen of the deputation accordingly called on the president, and Mr. Clay stated to him that Congress was impatient for action; that further efforts at negotiation were vain; that an accommodation was impracticable; that submission to her arrogant pretensions, especially that of a right to impress our seaman, was impossible; that enough had been done by us with a view to conciliation; that the time for decisive action had arrived, and war was inevitable.

By way of illustrating the difference between speaking and writing, and *acting*, Mr. Clay related to Mr. Madison an anecdote of two Kentucky judges. One talked incessantly from the bench. He reasoned everybody to death. He would deliver an opinion, and first try to convince that party that agreed with him, and then the opposite party. The consequence was, that business lagged, the docket accumulated, litigants complained, and the community were dissatisfied. He was succeeded by a judge, who never gave any reasons of his opinion, but decided the case simply, for the plaintiff or the defendant. His decisions were rarely reversed by the appellate court — the docket melted away — litigants were no longer exposed to ruinous delay — and the community were contented. "Surely," said Mr. Clay, "we have exhausted the argument with Great Britain."

Mr. Madison enjoyed the joke, but, in his good-natured, sly way, said, he also had heard an anecdote of a French judge, who after the argument of the cause was over, put the papers of the contending parties into opposite scales, and decided according to the preponderance of weight.

Speaking of the opposition of the federal party, Mr. Clay remarked that they were neither to be conciliated nor silenced — "Let us do what we sincerely believe to be right, and trust to God and the goodness of our cause."

Mr. Madison said, that our institutions were founded upon the principle of the competency of man for self-government, and that we should never be tired of appealing to the reason and judgment of the people.

Such deference did Mr. Madison have, however, for the opinion and advice of his friends, that shortly after the conference, he transmitted his war-message to Congress.[8]

This account clearly shows that Clay and his friends manifested irritation at "procrastination," but it suggests no coercion. Rather that the time had arrived for action, and that Madison accepted this conclusion.

The next allusion to any pressure put on Madison that is found in print was Edwin Williams'

The Statesman's Manual, published in 1849. (It contains various messages and brief biographies of the presidents from 1789 to 1849). Williams' writing changes the color of the May meeting based on an additional viewpoint of the conversation and places the time of the meeting prior to the nominating caucus. While discussing the threat that New York Republicans were about to nominate De Witt Clinton for president in place of Madison in the spring of 1812 (with no date mentioned), Williams wrote,

> In this state of things, Mr. Madison was waited upon by several of the leading republican members of Congress, and informed, in substance, that war with England was now resolved upon by the democratic party [synonymous with republican], the supporters of his administration; that the people would no longer consent to a dilatory and inefficient course, on the part of the national government; that unless a declaration of war took place previous to the presidential election, the success of the democratic party might be endangered, and the government thrown into the hands of the federalists; that unless Mr. Madison consented to act with his friends, and accede to a declaration of war with Great Britain, neither his nomination nor his election to the presidency could be relied on.* Thus situated, Mr. Madison concluded to waive his own objections to the course determined on by his political friends, and to do all he could for the prosecution of a war for which he had no taste.

An asterisk in Williams' account referred to the following footnote: "This information was derived by a friend of the writer, from James Fisk, a democratic member of Congress in 1812, and one of a committee who waited on Mr. Madison."[9] Though the tone of the meeting is changed slightly in this account, neither Williams nor his friend's political persuasion are known. In addition, this third-hand information was at least five years old since Fisk had died in 1844. It is hard to accept the account at face value considering that Fisk had been a strong supporter of Madison and had, in fact, been offered two high-ranking administration posts by the president within weeks following the declaration — not exactly an act on the president's part following a strong difference of opinion with Fisk. None of Fisk's papers are found.

Even so, a close reading of this account does not reveal coercion, but rather leans more toward a prediction of the consequences which might befall the administration in the nominating caucus or the election in the event it failed to support a call for war.

Three years after the so-called Fisk revelation, Richard Hildreth, accepting the weak Federalist view in his six volume *History of the United States of America* (copyrighted six weeks after Clay's death in 1852), wrote as follows:

> Though willing to sign a bill declaring war, Madison was very unwilling to take any further responsibility in bringing it on. But the leaders of the war party were inexorable. The war must not seem to be forced on the president; it must be, not their war — the war of a few young, hot-headed, upstart leaders — but his. A committee, headed by the imperious Clay, waited upon him with assurances to that effect. He must consent to recommend a declaration of war, or they would not support him as president. To this hard condition Madison yielded; and, the preliminaries thus arranged, the congressional caucus was presently held.[10]

Hildreth's statement is clearly anti–Clay and must have had some firmer base than the brief charge in *The Statesman's Manual*. In fact, the term "hot-headed" leaders, it will be recalled, was used in Shepherd's letter to Pickering on February 20, 1814, but apparently not made public until 1879, still another 27 years after Hildreth first appears to have applied it to Clay and his friends in a publication.

It is possible that Hildreth had by then seen the Pickering correspondence, since Pickering had died in January 1829. It is also possible that his papers might have become open to scrutiny by researchers within the 23 years that followed.

In the author's view, no coercion transpired to force a cautious president to do what he believed was an inevitable situation, but did want to know he had the full support of the Congress and the nation. Evidence indicating that Madison was already inclined to go to war, is revealed in Monroe's testimony before the House Foreign Relations Committee on March 31, and also in Madison's letter to Jefferson, dated April 3 (noted in the previous chapter).

14

DECLARATION OF WAR

While the coercion charge grew like a plant with only the seed sown in the spring of 1812 waiting to be nourished in the following year, the diplomatic struggle between the governments of the United States and Great Britain grew more visibly.

And while the Republicans settled on their party ticket for 1812, the long-awaited, much-delayed sloop of war, *Hornet*, arrived in New York on May 19. News of American Minister Joel Barlow's dispatches from France reached Washington by the 22nd. Again, according to French Minister Louis Sérurier,

> The avenues of the State Department were thronged by a crowd of members of both Houses of Congress, as well as by strangers and citizens, impatient to know what this long-expected vessel had brought.[1]

Within hours, both Sérurier and British Minister Foster had learned that the dispatches from Barlow brought no favorable news to the United States.

Sérurier wrote home that

> nothing was heard but a general cry for war against France and England at once.... I met Mr. Monroe at the Speaker's house; he came to me with an air of affliction and discouragement; addressed me with his cold reproach that decidedly we abandoned the Administration, and that he did not know henceforward how they could extricate themselves from the difficult position into which their confidence in our friendship had drawn them.[2]

Meanwhile, Foster wrote home that the American cabinet was divided "as to what measures they will now pursue, some of the members of it being still for war with England alone and non-intercourse with France, while others are for war with both Powers." Foster added that Attorney General William Pinkney was "against a rupture with Great Britain."

As for the president's views, Foster wrote that Madison's decision would no doubt be as unfavorable to Britain as he could make it,

> induced by the arguments of Mr. Jefferson who is said to have too much influence over his mind and from whom a letter has been seen this winter, as I am credibly informed, wherein he pronounced a war with England to be inevitable.

But as he had done for weeks, Foster watered down his warning of hostilities by saying it would likely take the form of letters of marque and reprisal with American ships acting only defensively. Foster went on to suspect a delay in a decision since there was a report that dispatches for Foster had left London on April 10. And these were following news already in American papers that there were disturbances in the interior of England demanding British revocation of the Orders in Council. So again there was to be a wait for dispatches.[3]

They were not long in coming. Foster received them on Monday, May 25 — though they were duplicates of notes from Foreign Secretary Castlereagh. Four were dated April 10 (Numbers 8, 9, 10, and 11) and two were dated April 17 (numbers 12 and 13). While Foster waited for the originals before having a conference with Secretary of State Monroe, President Madison sent the Barlow papers to Congress on the 26th.

The next day, Henry Clay wrote to an unnamed person in Lexington, Kentucky,

> That we shall have war, I still believe. The dispatches brought by the *Hornet* were yesterday laid

before Congress. Although not as favorable as we had a right to expect, or could have wished, they are more so than they had been rumored to be. They shew the practical observance of the repeal of the Berlin and Milan decrees, as to us. The Rambouillet spoliations, it is true, are not yet indemnified, but they are a subject of discussion and negotiation — and with regard to the recent burnings (which by the bye however execrable, they do not fall within those decrees) Mr. Barlow had presented a strong note but had received no reply. Throughout the whole of Mr. Barlow's intercourse with that government, they appear to have treated him with prompt attention and good manners at least. In short after the dispatches were read yesterday, there was general disappointment manifested at their being much better than they had been rumored to be and the universal sentiment was "we will go on in our intended course as to England, and wait a little longer with France." I think it therefore highly probable that about the time this letter will be with you, War will be declared in due form against England.[4]

There is no evidence in this letter from Clay that he knew a highly critical episode was unfolding that same day between Foster and Monroe, though there is strong evidence that Clay was aware of it before the day was over.

That same day, the 27th, Foster had received the originals of the dispatches from London and had a conference with Monroe. Castlereagh had advised Foster, at the end of his dispatch No. 8 of April 10, that the minister was "at liberty to communicate the whole, or any part of this Dispatch to the American Government" without specifying the means by which it would be presented. Foster showed it to Monroe and let him read it. Monroe asked Foster for a copy of it saying, "It might at some time or other be laid before Parliament, and it would be fair that there should be some answer made to it on the part of the United States."

Foster objected to this. He believed it "inadmissible," he wrote Castlereagh, "that a copy of a dispatch from your Lordship to me, should be permitted to remain at his office, to be perhaps, quoted from unfairly, and made use of in any way that might suit this Government." Foster was already miffed with Monroe at his failure to answer previous correspondence between the two men. Nevertheless, at Monroe's repeated requests, Foster allowed Monroe to take the dispatch to Madison with a promise that no copy would be

made of it. Foster hoped that Castlereagh's "strong and sound arguments," as well as an enclosed report from French Foreign Minister Duc de Bassano, to Napoleon, might provide Madison grounds for new and favorable discussions. The report had been published in France on March 16. Foster was certain that "the outrageous pretensions and principles advanced" in Bassano's report confirmed the continued application of the French decrees as affecting the United States.[5]

But the Americans didn't see it that way. Bassano's report was the fruition of months of futile pleading by America's minister to France, Joel Barlow, for written proof from the French of the revocation of the decrees. This was now an answer to Barlow's complaint over the French burning of American ships. The key phrase in the report stated, "The decrees of Berlin and Milan must be enforced toward Powers that let their flag be denationalized; the ports of the Continent are not to be opened to denationalized flags or to English merchandise." Madison and Monroe interpreted this to exempt the United States, believing the United States did not let its flag be denationalized.[6]

Then, when the president and his secretary of state privately studied Castlereagh's April 10 message, they were particularly alerted by the following paragraph:

America, as the case now stands, has not a pretence for claiming from Great Britain a Repeal of Her Orders in Council. She must recollect that the British Government never for a moment countenanced the idea, that the repeal of those Orders could depend upon any partial or conditional repeal of the Decrees of France. What Great Britain always avowed, was, Her readiness to rescind Her Orders, so soon as France rescinded absolutely and unconditionally Her Decrees:—*She never engaged to repeal those Orders as affecting America alone, leaving them in force against other States, upon condition that France would except singly and specially America from the operation of Her Decrees*; [emphasis by author] She could not do so, without the grossest Injustice to Her Allies, as well as all other neutral Nations: much less could She do so, upon the supposition, that the special exception in favor of America was to be expressly granted by France, as it has been hitherto tacitly accepted by America, upon conditions utterly subversive of the most important and indisputable maritime Rights of the British Empire.[7]

While the italicized words were to produce another controversy, the whole tone of the lengthy dispatch, and specifically this paragraph, was to be a determining factor in Madison's attitude towards the British government. He was to write years later that in this dispatch,

it was distinctly & emphatically stated that the orders in council ... would not be repealed without a repeal of internal measures of France.... With this formal notice, no choice remained but between war and degradation, a degradation inviting fresh provocations & rendering war sooner or later inevitable.[8]

The unyielding language from the British government, in effect, drew the line between war and peace in the eyes of Madison and Monroe. Until this last week of May, Madison could not send a war message to Congress unless he could be certain that sufficient numbers would vote for a declaration of war.

Still, Foster continued to confer with the administration. The next day, the 28th, he met first with Madison and then with Monroe only to be disappointed that Bassano's report "scarcely drew from them a single remark." In fact, Foster was shocked when Madison then told him,

That it was useless to discuss the matter further, that no case of a vessel captured under the French decrees, had occurred since November 1810; and that the projet of a treaty which Mr. Barlow had sent out, contained conclusive evidence that the decrees were repealed as far as America had a right to expect.

Foster made another attempt at conciliation bringing forward a proposition which Castlereagh had proposed in his dispatch No. 9 of April 10. Foster suggested that if America was aggrieved at the loss of trade with France, which Britain now had with their own enemy, his country was ready to enter into an agreement to share that trade. While the Americans apparently considered such commerce "as very naturally arising out of the necessities of both powers," the president rejected Foster's proposals intimating "that he did not imagine Bonaparte would let it be of long continuance."

Next, Foster offered to give up Britain's trading advantage altogether "if the United States would return to the relations of amity with Great Britain." The Americans did not see in these proposals

the faintest move on the part of Great Britain to compromise. Foster could only write home,

I am sorry to say, that this proposal met with even a worse fate than the former one, Mr. Monroe merely replying, that America could never bargain to give up her right to a direct trade with any country; that it would be no advantage to America that Great Britain should commit a kind of commercial suicide, in renouncing what commerce she could obtain with her enemy's dominions.

At Foster's meeting with Monroe on the 28th, which preceded a separate meeting between Foster and Madison, the secretary of state renewed his request for a copy of Castlereagh's dispatch No. 8 of April 10. Foster again refused since he considered the communication confidential. Monroe then asked for a note containing the substance of the dispatch. Foster agreed to this.

Two days later, Monroe sent his clerk, Mr. Graham, to ask Foster when the note could be expected. Foster said it would be a long one, but then said he would send the French minister's report (Bassano's) along with a short letter if Monroe wanted it soon. Graham replied that Monroe expected "a note which should contain the whole substance of the dispatch." Foster said he would fulfill Monroe's wishes and sent the note on Monday morning, June, 1.[9]

Foster's note, delivered about 10 A.M. on June 1, was nearly a complete copy. But Madison and Monroe recognized the important absence of the sentence quoted earlier in italics: "*She never engaged to repeal those orders as affecting America alone, leaving them in force against other States, upon condition that France would except singly and specially America from the operation of Her Decrees.*"

On June 3, Monroe sent Foster a note pointing out the discrepancy. In reply, the same day, Foster reminded Monroe that the note was confidential and that it was irregular to discuss a single point in a long note but, nevertheless, it contains "the whole substance" of the dispatch.

On the 4th, Monroe, asking for further explanation, wrote again to Foster,

As the despatch of Lord Castlereagh was communicated by you to me in my official character, to be shown to the President, and was shown to him accordingly, and as the despatch itself expressly authorized such a communication to this Government,

I cannot conceive in what sense such a proceeding could be considered confidential, or how it could be understood that the Executive was to receive one communication for itself, and transmit to Congress another, liable, in the opinion of the Executive, to a different or doubtful construction.

Foster rejected the charge of ambiguity, renewed his irritation at Monroe's silence to other correspondence, and referred Monroe, for an explanation, to publication in the newspapers of "the highly important declaration of His Royal Highness the Prince Regent." This declaration, issued April 21, as well as Castlereagh's April 10 dispatches, had their basis in the critical statement for Bassano's March 16 report. The declaration stated

> that the orders in council will be and are absolutely revoked from the period when the Berlin and Milan decrees shall, by some authentic act of the French Government, publicly promulgated, be expressly and unconditionally repealed.

Monroe replied to this lengthy note on the 6th.[10] But it was clear from his response that he recognized it was futile to get any better terms out of the British minister. Foster, too, must have concluded that negotiations were at an end, as he wrote on the 6th,

> So much trick, falsehood, and artifice is made use of by this Government that it is absolutely necessary in order not to be perpetually made a tool of to make use of some contrivance in their own way.[11]

In any case, events of the past week were rendering further haggling over the point a waste of time.

A final decision had, apparently, already been reached on the evening of May 27. For it was the next day that Madison told Foster that further discussion was useless. That Henry Clay was privy to the conclusions of Madison and Monroe was demonstrated within hours.

The following morning, May 28, Clay took a ride into the Washington suburb of Georgetown stopping by a congressional boardinghouse to chat with Rep. Joseph Lewis of Virginia. Clay told Lewis that on the next Monday (June 1) the president would send a message to Congress recommending a declaration of war against Great Britain. This information reached another of the boarders, John Randolph of Roanoke, and was to create a nasty episode between Clay and Ran-

dolph that was to last through the remainder of this session of Congress.[12]

Throughout this first session of the 12th Congress, the stresses and strains leading to war had aggravated a split already showing in the Republican Party. It produced the Clinton nomination in New York and it contributed to the disaffection of John Randolph of Roanoke. Ever since Clay had ordered Randolph's hounds out of the House chamber, at the beginning of the session, the two had managed to maintain a civil relationship. Clay had early resolved on a principle of never giving and never receiving an insult without immediate notice if in a place to give it notice. While at times they went weeks without speaking, there were other times when they extended every courtesy and attention to each other. On such latter occasions, Randolph often entered the House, approached the Chair, bowed to the Speaker, and inquired solicitously after his health.[13]

By late May, Randolph was greatly irked by the unanimous vote for Madison by the congressional caucus (which Randolph had not attended) and was frustrated by the national plunge toward war. His frustration was greatly aggravated when he tried to present his anti-war views before a House — and a Speaker — who were little interested in listening to his long and wandering harangue. What ensued in the chamber was really a class in parliamentary procedure conducted by this young, hardly experienced teacher by the name of Speaker Henry Clay.

On learning that the war message was at hand, Randolph rose in the House on May 29, impelled "to make a last effort to rescue the country from the calamities which, he feared, were impending over it." He stated that he "had a proposition to submit." For several minutes he continued to justify his action. As it appeared he would ramble on endlessly, Robert Wright of Maryland called Randolph to order saying there was no motion before the House. Speaker Clay overruled Wright declaring it was customary to permit a member to make prefatory remarks to a motion.

Randolph abused his privilege and continued unabated in an hour's "speech," detailing his proof that the French decrees were in force. But it was too much for John C. Calhoun when Randolph charged that in a war against Great Britain with the United States on the same side as Napoleon, "this Government will stand branded to the latest posterity ... as the panders of French despotism — as the tools, the minions, sycophants, parasites of France." He had also claimed "that there exists in our Councils an undue, a fatal French bias."

Calhoun called Randolph to order noting that the question of war was not before the country and that "the gentleman was therefore speaking, as he conceived, contrary to rule and without affording others an opportunity to reply."

Clay, at this time, had vacated the Speaker's chair briefly and was in conversation elsewhere and inattentive to the discourse on the floor. William Bibb of Georgia, in the chair, ruled against Calhoun's appeal. Randolph thanked Calhoun for the brief respite and resumed his monologue — for about one sentence — before Calhoun rose again to "give him another opportunity to rest himself." Calhoun now asked Randolph to submit his proposition to the Chair.

In this short interim, Clay had returned to the Speaker's chair and stated that "the proposition might be required to be submitted in writing." Calhoun so requested.

Randolph replied that Calhoun had no right to call upon him but that the Speaker, unquestionably, had the right and asked permission to go on.

Clay responded, "The gentleman will please to take his seat, the Chair having decided that his motion must be submitted before further debate."

Randolph said he had not understood the Speaker as making any such decision. Clay said he certainly had so decided.

RANDOLPH: My proposition is, that it is not expedient at this time to resort to a war against Great Britain.
THE SPEAKER: Is the motion seconded?

Randolph, or some other gentleman expressed his surprise that a second in such a case should be required.

Clay said he conceived that every motion must receive a second before it could be announced from the Chair. And he required that the motion be reduced to writing.

RANDOLPH: I then appeal from that decision.

Clay stated the grounds for his decision and read the rules requiring motions when made to be seconded before being put to the vote, and, when demanded, to be reduced to writing.

Randolph said he would only remark that this right of prefacing a motion by remarks was almost the last vestige of the freedom of debate; if it were destroyed, there would be none left but under permission of the majority.

In the debate that followed on Clay's decision, Charles Goldsborough of Maryland said the Speaker read rules which applied after a motion was made, but that there was no rule on length of prefatory remarks which on some previous occasions had gone on up to three hours.

He was answered by Wright who said,

Every gentleman has a right to be heard on a subject fairly before the House, after the House has determined to consider it. But, by a positive rule of the House, declared by the Speaker, no question can be received until it is made and seconded, and if required, reduced to writing — nor, after it is received, can any question be debated until the House agree to consider it.

But Wright went on to note that Randolph's "remarks were themselves out of order — have we not been denounced as legislating under French influence? Yes, sir, we have."

Now Randolph called Wright to order saying he had spoken hypothetically and that "if war did take place, it would be confirmation strong as proof from holy writ of an undue French bias."

This time, Speaker Clay intervened to say that since he had not been in the Chair he could not decide if Randolph had used the words (conveying an imputation of French influence) as ascribed by Wright. But that if Randolph did use such words they were highly improper. If not, then Wright was out of order in attributing them to Randolph.

Wright proceeded to quote Randolph's words and asked if they could be in order. As he started to list the "black catalogue of wrongs sustained by the outrages of Great Britain," he was again interrupted by Randolph calling Wright to order, because he was "discussing a question which the Speaker had declared should not be debated." Clay ruled in favor of Wright, who continued briefly.

Wright said he would not charge Randolph "with being under British influence, although we see the British licensed spies within this Hall to hear this *understood* debate...."

Randolph again called Wright to order, and this time got Clay's backing. The Speaker ordered Wright to take his seat.

If the Chair understood him correctly, he is certainly out of order. If he meant to say that there was an understanding between a member of this House and a foreign agent out of it, in relation to proceedings to take place in the House, he was undoubtedly out of order.

Wright answered that he meant to say that the attendance of such individuals (apparently in the gallery) seemed to imply that they had earlier been told of Randolph's intention to speak on the declaration of war. This temporarily concluded the debate as a vote was taken on the correctness of Speaker Clay's ruling. He was sustained by a vote of 67 to 42.

Randolph addressed Clay, "Then, sir, I am compelled to submit my motion in writing, and under that compulsion I offer it."

Clay responded, "There is no compulsion in the case; because the gentleman may or may not offer it at his option."

Randolph's motion was read from the Chair, "*Resolved*, That, under existing circumstances, it is inexpedient to resort to war against Great Britain." No sooner did he begin to discuss his resolution than Hugh Nelson of Virginia objected to debate on the resolution "before the House had agreed to consider it." Clay agreed with Nelson.

Again Randolph appealed from Clay's ruling and proceeded to speak on his justification for his new appeal. He charged the various rulings were depriving him of the right to speak. "Has it come to this," he pleaded,

> that members of this House shall grow gray in the service, and in proportion to their experience become ignorant of the rules of proceeding, and receive the construction of them from those who have never been familiar with them? After having been fourteen years on this floor, is a man to be told he knows nothing of the rules of this House?

Clay responded to this query by requesting Randolph to confine his remarks to the question on the Chair's decision. "Priority of seat on this floor," the Speaker advised, "gives to the senior members of this House no right to which the junior are not equally entitled." There was a very brief debate and Randolph then withdrew his appeal.[14]

Later, when giving advice to a successor to the Speaker's Chair, Clay wrote,

> *Decide — decide promptly — and never give your reasons for the decision.* The House will sustain your decisions, but there will always be men to cavil and quarrel about your reasons.[15]

But on this occasion, Henry Clay did take time to explain the reasons for his rulings. First, he noted that he became Speaker with doubts as to the propriety of the rule that the House must agree "to consider a proposition before it could be debated or decided." His doubts had since been removed by subsequent experience.

With regard to "requiring a second to a motion before it was received," he said it was the established practice of the British Parliament. "As to the alleged violation of the freedom of debate," he was sorry if there had been an abridgement since he was "a great friend to a legitimate and decorous freedom of debate," but he believed "the proceedings of the House during the present session would illustrate and attest" whether "its liberty had been infringed."

Clay went on to observe that it was an inherent right in every public deliberative body "to regulate its own proceedings ... without the existence and exercise of which it would be impossible to proceed in business at all, or to arrive at any conclusion." Therefore, since the Constitution gave the House the power to regulate its proceedings, he "could have no interest but to perform with the utmost impartiality, this trust, and in doing it he should always consult every source of information which was accessible to him."

So far as Clay was concerned, this closed the issue and he proceeded to the consideration of Randolph's resolution. The House gagged Randolph by a vote of 72 to 37. But Randolph was yet to be heard from a different forum.[16]

Randolph was enraged at being muzzled. The next day, May 30, he sent a letter to his Virginia constituents as the only means by which he could be heard. "It is now established," he wrote,

> *for the first time, and in the person of your representative,* that the House may and will refuse to hear a member in his place, or even to receive a motion from him, upon the most momentous subject that can be presented for legislative decision,

and with that introduction, he proceeded, in writing, with the speech he had hoped to make on the House floor.[17]

Some days later, Clay obtained a copy of Randolph's "fragment of a speech" that had ended up as an appeal to his constituents. On June 17, Clay wrote a reply which was printed the next day in the *National Intelligencer*. It began with his summary of the parliamentary proceedings that had occurred in the House on May 29.

Clay noted that

> two principles are settled by these decisions; the first is, that the House has a right to know, through its organ, the specific motion which a member intends making, before he undertakes to argue it at large; and in the second place that it reserves to itself the exercise of the power of determining whether it will consider it at the particular time when offered, prior to his thus proceeding to argue it.

In amplifying these two principles more fully, Clay, in regard to the first one, said it should afford "a protection against the obtrusion upon the body of the whimsical or eccentric propositions of a disordered or irregular mind, by the coincidence in opinion of at least two individuals." It was such a direct slur at Randolph that a reply was almost certain to follow.

Clay found no clear line to be drawn on the allowable extent of prefatory remarks. But in the case of Randolph's arguments, he said,

> Any man who will now read seven-eighths, if not the whole of his speech, keeping out of mind the motion with which it terminated, will, I apprehend, find it extremely difficult to conjecture that *such* was or *what* was to be the concluding motion.

Even when offered, Clay added, "the motion was believed not to be the one originally contemplated by the mover." Indeed, Clay saw Randolph's real complaint not in the parliamentary procedure but in being prevented, by a later House vote, in continuing his argument.

On the principle of "considering" a subject, Clay wrote that among the instruments resorted to by various deliberative bodies for regulating the time of transacting business "are the motions for the previous question, to postpone — to adjourn — to lie upon the table — to consider." He noted that the English use a motion "to proceed to the orders of the day," and do not use — "to consider." With the U.S. House of Representatives the reverse is true. In any case, he opened the door to new rulings from the Chair observing that "experience will, from time to time, suggest the defects in pre-existing rules and the necessity of adapting new ones to new exigencies as they arise." The instrument "to consider" was a novel one

to Clay when he first came to the House, but he found "old members clinging to it with great tenacity." He soon became satisfied of its wisdom. "Without such a rule," he said, "a mover and his second may become superior to the whole body forcing them to consider a proposition the majority does not wish to debate."

Addressing himself to the specific incident of cutting off Randolph on May 29, Clay pointed out that most of the current session of Congress had passed various laws "with the avowed purpose of war" and all had been discussed at great length. To this he added that

> more than any other member of the House is Mr. R. patiently and repeatedly heard to develop his views on that solemn question. Now, with a declaration of war inevitable, "What does he attempt?" Forestalling the friends of the measure with open doors, without disclosing his particular motion, he engages in an argument which, after consuming one hour, is now denominated a fragment only; and when required by the House, reluctantly submits the *negative* proposition that it is not expedient at this time, under existing circumstances, to go to war with Great Britain! ... out of Mr. R.'s motion, supposing it adopted, no positive act could grow. It would be as if the House should formally adopt an original resolution that they would *not* pass a particular law.

Concluding, Clay said, "The right of the House of Representatives to regulate its own proceedings is quite manifest."[18]

These comments were certainly enough to anger Randolph and stir a response from him. Nevertheless, he claimed he "did not aspire to the honor of a newspaper-contest with any man," and was "content to let the matter rest where it stood. But my friends have urged me not to permit this publication ... to pass unnoticed: lest the public mind ... should be misled by it." Thus, he answered Clay, on July 2, and proceeded to the newspaper debate.

Randolph proceeded to state his version to the sequence of calls for order and decisions from the Chair by both Bibb and Clay. But his statement of facts did not correspond entirely with the details of the episode as published in the newspaper. Next, he made a meaningless argument over Clay's assertion that there was "no discrepancy" between Bibb's and his decisions "and certainly between my own [Clay's]."

Randolph went on to suggest that it was a "mockery" to say there was no compulsion in presenting his motion. "There was no compulsion, mark you!" Randolph said, "It depended entirely upon my own pleasure to offer the motion or to withhold it and *take my seat in silence*." He derided Clay for deciding he could proceed after submitting the motion in writing and a minute later reversing himself. Randolph expressed his regret that he had withdrawn his appeal of the Chair's ruling when he thought his friend Macon was going to support the Chair's ruling only to find Macon instead had planned to support Randolph. He chided Clay for his comment that the motion "was believed not to be the one originally contemplated by the mover," by posing a rule for politicians — "put it impersonally, *it is said, it is reported, it is believed*, and he is quite safe from any such disagreeable consequences," such as *who told you?*

Next, Randolph attacked Clay's assumption that he knew of a projected war message because he was a member of the House Foreign Relations Committee. The Virginian said he derived the information second hand from one of his colleagues who had obtained the intelligence from Clay himself when on one of his morning rides to Georgetown. Randolph reported he had not been on a sub-committee of three to which the president's message was later referred.

And finally, Randolph argued that the rule *to consider* and the abuse of *the previous question* "are utterly subversive of the rights of the minority, for the preservation of which rules are chiefly instituted.... The majority by their numbers being always able to protect themselves."[19]

By the time this correspondence concluded, the House had adjourned for the session and Clay had headed home. He was upset enough by it that he wrote his friend Langdon Cheves for advice asking, "What notice ought I take to Randolph's reply?"

Cheves answered,

Certainly none — none whatever. Were you to notice it he would reply again, and it would never terminate. He [Randolph] spoke with great truth in the beginning of the last session, when he said the "Speaker of the House of Representatives was the second man in the nation"; and if this be true, as I think it is, it does not become the Speaker to enter into altercations with any member of the House, or even of the nation, in a public justification of his conduct, any more than it does the *first* man in the nation — the President.[20]

Accepting Cheves' advice, Clay allowed this first major confrontation between him and Randolph to die. Nevertheless, the seeds of rancor and hostility between them were sown in this correspondence during the closing days of the 1st session of the 12th Congress. It had all begun with that heated House session of Friday, May 29, when Randolph believed he was muzzled in his attempt to block a declaration of war message which he had learned, indirectly from Clay, was to be sent by the president to Congress on the following Monday.

As Clay had forecast privately and accurately (back on his morning ride on May 28th), President Madison, on Monday, June 1, 1812, sent his momentous message to Congress. With it he sent a sheaf of documents containing correspondence between the British and American governments for nearly a decade. Included was Foster's note based on Castlereagh's dispatch No. 8 with an intimation from Madison that an important sentence had been deleted.

The message and documents were received in the House by Speaker Clay. He ordered the gallery cleared and the doors closed for a secret reading.

Madison's message began by referring to maritime wrongs committed against the United States by Great Britain dating back to the renewal of hostilities in 1803 between Britain and France. Commenting on the seizure of American commerce and the impressment of American seamen, Madison charged that the British government honored, rather than punished, her naval commanders who violated American rights of freedom of the high seas and even in United States territorial waters.

With a tone of outrage, Madison continued,

Not content with those occasional expedients for laying waste our neutral trade, the cabinet of Britain resorted at length to the sweeping system of blockades, under the name of orders in council, which has been molded and managed as might best suit its political views, its commercial jealousies, or the avidity of British cruisers.

He complained that those orders issued in retaliation of French decrees, "should fall on the party setting the guilty example, not on an innocent party which was not even chargeable with acquiescence in it." Indeed, after announcement that the French had revoked her decrees, the British "formally avowed a determination to persist in [the orders] against the United States until the markets of her enemies should be laid open to British products"; thus placing an obligation on a neutral power to require one belligerent to encourage the trade of its enemy.

Madison went on to accuse the British of sacrificing American trade, not for supplying the wants of Great Britain's enemy (for she herself supplied France with some goods), "but as interfering with the monopoly which she covets for her own commerce and navigation. She carries on a war against the lawful commerce of a friend that she may the better carry on a commerce with an enemy."

The president cited attempts to turn Britain from her ways by means of successive modifications of commercial regulations — all to no avail. He detailed diplomatic efforts over several years to remove the blockades and odious orders in council — with no success. (These included an agreement by a British minister to the United States to resolve the issue only to have his government repudiate his action — this at the time when John Henry was employed to subvert and dismember parts of the Union.) He expressed his shock at the Indian warfare on the frontiers where neither age nor sex were respected and he noted that it was difficult to account for such activity without connecting their hostility to the constant intercourse and influence of British traders and garrisons.

"We behold," Madison wrote, "on the side of Great Britain, a state of war against the United States, and on the side of the United States, a state of peace toward Great Britain."

Finally, Madison, in effect skirting the responsibility, remarked that whether the United States should continue under "these accumulating wrongs, or, opposing force to force ... is a solemn question which the Constitution wisely confides to the Legislative Departments of the government." He closed his message with a statement that France also continued to commit outrages against American commerce but that no recommendation would be made towards that nation while waiting the result of unclosed discussions in Paris.[21]

Immediately following reading of the message, Randolph moved it be referred to the Committee of the Whole House, but was voted down. Instead, it was sent to the Foreign Relations Committee, which did not bring out its report until two days later. On June 3, freshman Representative John C. Calhoun, now chairman of this powerful committee, presented a report on the reasons for war — the manifesto rumored to be in preparation. It was read to the House behind closed doors.[22]

Calhoun's lengthy report said,

> The period has arrived when the United States must support their character and station among the Nations of the Earth, or submit to the most shameful degradation. Forbearance has ceased to be a virtue. War on the one side, and peace on the other, is a situation as ruinous as it is disgraceful.

The report emphasized that more than seven years had elapsed since the British government had begun their system of hostile aggression against the rights and interests of the United States. The report gave an account of efforts, as early as 1804, by the U.S. minister to Great Britain (James Monroe) to resolve differences. The report cited commercial restrictions against neutral trade, which Great Britain claimed as legal, "But with Great Britain, everything is lawful."

There followed a long, general discourse on the British attacks against American commerce, impressment of American seamen, blockages of the American coast, the supply and incitement of the Indians against the American West, and the attempt to dismember the American Union. "From this review of the multiple wrongs of the British Government," the report stated, "it must be evident to the Impartial world, that the Contest which is now forced on the United States, is radically a Contest for their Sovereignty and Independence."

In conclusion, the report called for

> resistance by force; In which the Americans of the present day will prove to the enemy and to the world, that we have not only inherited that liberty which our Fathers gave us, but also the will and power to maintain it. Relying on the patriotism of the nation, and confidently trusting that the Lord of Hosts will go with us to battle in a righteous cause, and crown our efforts with success, your committee recommend an immediate appeal to arms.[23]

Following the publication of this report a controversy arose over its authorship. As chairman of the committee which presented the report to the House, Calhoun has often been named as its author. However, there are claims that the phraseology in it is similar to that used in other documents by Monroe. And, years later, the editor of the *National Intelligencer* wrote that the report was in the handwriting of Monroe's private secretary. Nevertheless, there appear Calhoun's and Clay's styles, which strongly suggests that it is possible that all three of these men, and possibly others including Felix Grundy and President Madison, worked together to draft the report during the latter days of May. There were, of course, those rumors, since May 13, that a manifesto was in preparation.

At the conclusion of the reading of the "Foreign Relations Committee's report," on June 3, Josiah Quincy and John Randolph both moved to open the doors and remove the secrecy status. But they were voted down. Calhoun moved that the report lie on the table. Immediately thereafter, Calhoun introduced a bill declaring war between Great Britain and the United States. It was, as usual, read a first time, after which the House voted against another attempt by Randolph to reject the measure.

The bill was read a second time and debated in Committee of the whole House — but without the voices of the Federalists, who came to a determination not to debate a question of so much importance in secret.[24] After the second reading, the House adjourned for the day.[25]

British Minister Foster wrote two interesting observations for that day — one to his diary and one in an official dispatch to his superiors in London. To his diary he commented that he had taken a young Dutch refugee to see Madison, who looked "very pale and extremely agitated." He also noted that after dinner he went to the White House levee, where "friendly Congressmen told him that a newly arrived declaration of the Prince Regent was producing a great affect."[26]

According to Foster's dispatch to Castlereagh, the "democrats," as he called those of Clay's persuasion, were rallied again that evening at Madison's drawing room where they "attended in considerable numbers and accordingly on the following day they became so impatient that

they would wait no longer but carried the question."[27]

Though Foster's observation was second hand, since debate continued in Committee of the Whole House behind closed doors, his account was substantially accurate. Josiah Quincy tried, and failed, to get an amendment to the bill, which would repeal the 1810 and 1811 Non-Intercourse Acts, and the 1812 embargo act. After the war bill went through its third reading, three futile attempts were made to postpone a final vote on it to the following October, to the following Monday, and lastly to the next day. The House then voted 79 to 49 to go to war.[28]

There followed two long weeks of secret deliberation on the war bill by the Senate. Each day, the local newspaper referred to momentous decisions being taken by Congress, but it never told the public that a declaration of war was being discussed.

Nevertheless, those with inside sources were getting the word. As early as June 2, Benjamin Rush, father of comptroller Richard Rush, wrote ex–President John Adams from Philadelphia, "Accounts from Washington say war will be declared in a few days *in spite of the opposition* of printers, brokers, and tavern-keepers (who govern the public mind) in all the states."[29]

Probably many members of Congress wrote of their official activities in letters to family and friends outside Washington City. One of these (with words a bit premature) was written on June 7 by Sen. Thomas Worthington to his wife in Ohio.

> The measure alluded to in my last (the declaration of war) has been decided. I have done my duty and satisfied my conscience. Thousands of the innocent will suffer, but I have borne my testimony against it, and I thank God, my mind is tranquil. What comfort there is in having done ones duty conscientiously! I care not for popularity and I only desire to know that I have acted for the best. Now that the step is taken I am bound to submit to the will of the majority and use my best exertions to save my country from ruin.[30]

Nearly as easily, the prospective enemy in London, through Minister Foster and his Federalist sources, was able to learn of the House action almost as soon as it happened (except for the long sea voyage the news had to travel). But Foster's disclosure was rather amusing. His June 6 dispatch to Castlereagh was quite lengthy with a discussion of the give and take of his recent dialogues with Madison and Monroe with no indication that affairs were coming to a head. Therefore, later, as he read the message, Castlereagh must have literally leaped out of his seat when he reached Foster's closing paragraph:

> The two Houses of Congress have since been in a conclave every day and it is understood that a declaration of war against Great Britain passed the House of Representatives on the 4th of June, while it has met with a temporary suspension in the Senate.[31]

The Senate, in fact, spent a great deal more time in secret debate on the subject than the House had. They had a number of extremely close votes that nearly voted down a war. On Wednesday, June 17, the Senate agreed by a slim margin of 19–13 to go along with the House in declaring war but returned a bill with several amendments.

On the 18th, the House quickly accepted the Senate amendments and Speaker Henry Clay signed the engrossed bill and sent it to the Senate for the signature of that body's presiding officer. Later in the day, Senate president pro-tem William Crawford returned to the House to announce that the measure had been approved and signed by the president of the United States, James Madison. The president issued a proclamation to the people on June 19 telling them their country was at war with the most powerful country in the world. Then, wrote Comptroller Richard Rush,

> he visited in person — a thing never known before — all the offices of the departments of war and navy, stimulating everything in a manner worthy of a little commander-in-chief, with his little round hat and huge cockade.[32]

Two days later, Clay wrote to the *Lexington Reporter*, "Every patriot bosom must throb with anxious solicitude for the result. Every patriot arm will assist in making that result conducive to the glory of our beloved country."[33]

As for England, he wrote a friend, "Let us give, in return for the insolence of British cannon, the peals of American thunder."[34]

For the first time in the 25-year-old life of the Constitution, the United States tried out its written mechanism for going to war with another nation. But the congressional measure, which took the nation to war, passed without the overwhelm-

ing support of that nation and particularly from the maritime Northeast region — home of most Federalists. Though they had remained silent in the final debate over war, they were not the only ones. There, too, was John Randolph who would have spoken, but did not get the chance.

Years later, when reminiscing of Henry Clay's character at this time, Josiah Quincy wrote of the Speaker,

> Bold, aspiring, presumptuous, with a rough, overbearing eloquence, neither exact nor comprehensive, which he had cultivated and formed in the contests with half civilized wranglers in the country courts of Kentucky, and quickened into confidence and readiness by successful declarations at barbeques and electioneering struggles, he had not yet that polish of language and refinement of manners which he afterwards acquired by familiarity and attrition with highly cultivated men.... Such was the man whose influence and power more than that of any other produced the war of 1812 between the United States and Great Britain.[35]

Following President Madison's proclamation of war on June 19, 1812, and during the drawn-out public controversy between Randolph and Clay, the Congress still had some unfinished business necessary to make accommodation for the great new adventure the nation had embarked upon.

With Congress now very anxious to quit Washington and return home, they did some strange things in the face of war. A matter of first priority was legislating the financial means to carry on hostilities. The series of restrictive trade acts had closed a source of income in the form of duties.

Among the bills brought before the House was one calling for the repeal of the commercial Non-Intercourse Law. This action would open up trade between the United States and Great Britain, now at war with each other, when previously it was closed in peace.

Though this, in itself, was strange, so was the vote on the repeal. War Hawks and anti-war Federalists and John Randolph all joined hands to approve it. Still, they only came up with a 60–60 tie and the War Hawk Speaker, Henry Clay, had the deciding vote. According to the *Annals of Congress*, he, "took occasion to express the pleasure he felt in having an opportunity to manifest his decided opposition to the measure at this time, now that we had engaged in war.

"So the motion was lost."[36]

Then an attempt to suspend the Non-Intercourse Law was postponed indefinitely. Suspension was to have afforded "an opportunity for our citizens to get home some property in satisfaction for debts due them abroad, which might otherwise be lost."

Still, the House did pass one bill to levy additional duties and another bill to authorize the issuance of $5 million in treasury notes. However, the House postponed, until the fall session of Congress, consideration of a set of new taxes to pay for the war. These would pay for 1813, and a treasury report on expected expenses for 1812 did not anticipate that the military would need all the money already authorized for its use.

On the side of military preparation, the House voted only to authorize the president to take possession of East and West Florida at his discretion. And, though the nation had just gone to war and its defense was a matter of prime importance, the House and the administration took valuable time in consideration of the following:

> The Speaker laid before the House a letter from the Secretary of the Navy, stating that he had caused the invention of Mr. John Dickey to be tried at the navy yard, and that it had been found to answer no good purpose whatever.—Laid on the table.[37]

On July 6, a very tired and drifting Congress adjourned after a session of 245 days, just one day short of the longest in the nation's history to that time. They had put together one great Act — WAR — but did almost nothing to support it. And the nation itself remained divided with the Federalist Northeast showing great reluctance to participate in this war they opposed.

Late in June, Clay obtained a copy of the June 26 issue of the Boston *Repertory & General Advertiser*. In a vitriolic editorial, its editor, John Parke, asked his readers if they would

> submit to be the slaves of slaves of Bonaparte? ... You have before you the disasters of war — a war with a nation desirous of your friendship, and servility to a tyrant who knows no mercy; or peace, tranquility and prosperity.

Without using the words, the editorial went on to encourage the people of Massachusetts to resist and to withhold their support for the war.[38]

Clay responded in anger to this appeal to treason, calling attention to "the madness and desperation of an unprincipled incendiary," he asked the readers of the Boston paper,

> Does Dr. Parke allow himself for one moment to believe that he can persuade the patriotic people of Massachusetts to raise the paricidal [sic] arm? to imbrue a brother's hand in a brother's blood? to plunge that sword, which should be pointed against the enemies of our Country, into the bosoms of our own people? to divert the combined energies of a free people from a noble and manful vengeance upon a foreign foe, to a rash and diabolical resistance of their own government?

While Clay went on in a long letter to praise the general sentiment of members of the Federalist party who "have rallied round the standard of America," he expressed his indignation for such an appeal by the editor. But in conclusion, he doubted that the people of Massachusetts would ever condone such action. He suggested that the editor was "bereaved of his intellect."[39]

This was Clay's last public pronouncement before he and his family set out for home by way of Pittsburgh, and Chillicothe, Ohio (where he learned that General William Hull had crossed into Canada from Detroit in the first military move of the war).

Meanwhile, in this time of contention through newspaper columns, there was still another controversy during the early summer weeks of 1812. Though it began while Clay was still in Washington, it did not reach its violent conclusion in Baltimore until after Clay had returned home to Kentucky. His correspondence shows no notice he took of the events, but he surely must have read about it in the Lexington papers.

The incident began with Alexander Hanson, the same individual who led Timothy Pickering to inquire about charges that Clay and others had coerced Madison into taking the country into war against Great Britain. Hanson was the principal owner of the Baltimore anti-administration paper, the *Federal Republican*. On Saturday, June 22, it printed a provocative editorial against the war, its motives, and suggested that it was pro–Napoleon.

On Monday evening, a mob attacked the wooden building on Bay Street where the paper had its offices and presses. Not only was the equipment destroyed, the type and papers scattered, but the buildings was practically torn to pieces — as the mayor and other city officials watched. There were no arrests.

Hanson gathered together what he could and transported his "newspaper" to the friendly confines of Georgetown, something of a stronghold of Federalist support just outside Washington City.

When he was ready with a new issue, he returned to Baltimore and moved into a formidable brick house on Charles Street where his editor, Jacob Wagner (a bitter anti-war Federalist), lived. There they were joined by several companions representing some of the leading families of Maryland and Virginia. These included Revolutionary War generals James M. Lingan and Henry (Light-Horse Harry) Lee, the father of Robert E. Lee, and the author of the eulogy to Washington: "First in war, first in peace, and first in the hearts of his countrymen."

On July 27, the new paper came out with an editorial accusing the mayor, the police, the city of Baltimore, and the governor of failing to protect the freedom of the press. This editorial was received by the people with increased violence. Again a mob appeared and began stoning the fortified house. When they tried to force the door, shots were fired from within killing a doctor in the crowd. About that time, a field piece was dragged into place and aimed at the house. But just as suddenly a troop of cavalry came onto the scene and temporarily dispersed the mob.

Nevertheless, tensions continued throughout the night and by morning Hanson and his friends (about 20 men) agreed to be escorted to the local jail "for safekeeping." But the mob was not finished. That evening they struck again breaking into the jail. As the "prisoners" attempted to escape into the dark, they were picked out and all were badly beaten, clubbed, kicked, and knifed. They were left for dead in a heap.

Somehow all but General Lingan survived. As for General Lee, penknives were poked into him as he feigned death. He was burned by the drippings of a hot candle, grease was poured in his eyes, and an attempt was made to cut off his nose.

He survived six more years but never fully recovered from the attack on his life. Hanson went to the next Congress.

Clay arrived home in Lexington on July 24, and on the following Monday, the day the Baltimore riot began, he and Kentucky Senator Bibb were the honored guests at a banquet held at Postlethwaites Inn. (By contrast, Kentucky Sen. John Pope, who had voted against war, had been burned in effigy at Nicholasville and Mount Sterling, Kentucky.)

After the dinner, there were 17 pre-arranged toasts. The first "volunteer" toast was to: "Henry Clay, our immediate Representative in Congress — The course he has pursued meets the applause of his constituents — We are but the more confirmed that his heart is with his country."

Another toast was to:

Henry Clay, our worthy representative in Congress; he is not to be intimidated by the British lion's peals of thunder, though the earth quakes, but stands firm and undaunted, and speaks the sentiment of his constituents.

In response, Clay expressed his gratitude for their applause "after an absence of many months, employed in acting for them in the national legislature, on affairs of the last importance." He told those at the dinner his reasons for going to war were, "Our multiplied wrongs — the peaceful farmer bleeding beneath the tomahawk — the mariner no longer finding sanctuary under our national flag — the shackles imposed on our commerce." And he added that the government must depend upon the assistance of the citizens for carrying into execution the war which Congress had proposed.

He then made a toast to: "The great cause of our country."[40]

Henry Clay probably believed he could now relax at home and engage in his local law practice to renew his financial status. Yet the war was to come closer to him than he had anticipated, and his voice of encouragement and words of recommendation were to be required of him through the summer and fall of 1812.

15

WAR IN THE WEST

Within the week after his return home, Henry Clay was writing Secretary of State James Monroe to tell him of the enthusiasm with which the declaration of war had been met in Pennsylvania, Ohio, and Kentucky. "Indeed," he wrote on July 29 of the feeling in Kentucky, "I have almost been alarmed at the ardor which has been displayed, knowing how prone human nature is to extremes."

Clay told Monroe that the 400 Kentucky volunteers were more than he had expected but fewer than he wished. In any case, he urged that they be used soon by the government since few could be expected to remain in the service for more than six months. Still, he praised the Kentucky soldiers saying they had not stepped forward "for the mere show of patriotism but for effective service. They only ask 'Where is the enemy?'"

In conclusion, Clay told the secretary of state that Indiana Territorial Governor William Henry Harrison, the western hero of the Battle of Tippecanoe, had recently been received in Kentucky with great cordiality and had the confidence of the public. "Everywhere, I have been asked, 'how come Harrison overlooked?'" Clay suggested that the president appoint Harrison to be a brigadier general in the regular army.[1]

While it was odd that Clay should write to the secretary of state about military affairs, it was stranger that he should write Secretary of War William Eustis briefly two days later about bills of exchange in the western country. It was already clear that Clay had more faith in Monroe's military acumen than that of Eustis. But it would also be more reasonable to believe he would consult Gallatin on treasury affairs. Nevertheless, Clay did end this note to Eustis with an appeal to make use of the Kentucky volunteers. But throughout the summer, Clay made his firmest requests on military matters through Monroe rather than Eustis, probably knowing full well that Monroe's recommendations carried greater weight with President Madison than those of Eustis.

With regard to Clay's reference to Governor Harrison's visit to Lexington on June 29, it was described by the *Reporter,*

> The people of Lexington seized the opportunity afforded them to testify their respect for this highly distinguished citizen. He was met about a mile from town, and escorted in, by Captain McDowell's troop of volunteer cavalry, Capt. Hart's [Nathaniel, Henry Clay's brother-in-law] company of volunteer Light Infantry, and a large concourse of citizens. Yesterday he was invited to partake of an elegant Dinner which had been prepared to the occasion at Capt. Postlethwait's — There were about 120 persons present — The greatest hilarity and most perfect harmony pervaded the company during the whole evening.[2]

There was substantial reason for the local enthusiasm for Harrison. This region considered Harrison's "victory" at Tippecanoe the greatest act of protection for the population against Indian raids. Nevertheless, its basic intent — to break up Tecumseh's plan of Indian confederation — had not really happened. The numerous Indian tribes of the old Northwest Territory — present day Wisconsin, Michigan, Illinois, Indiana, and Ohio — were as varied in their feelings toward the white settlers as the whites were toward their own politics. The Delawares of Ohio were believed to be strong in their own friendship toward the United States while the Potawatomis of Illinois were most often accused of murdering white families in remote settlements. In between were other tribes throughout the area looking somewhat to the

Shawnee brothers, Tecumseh and the Prophet, for leadership, though the Prophet's influence had been in decline since the Battle of Tippecanoe. Most of the Indians viewed the Americans as land grabbers and therefore their natural enemies.

As the weather warmed up in the spring of 1812, Harrison received more and more detailed accounts of murders and other atrocities and forwarded these stories to Secretary of War Eustis, the superior to the territorial governor. By April, these attacks had worked their way southward through Indiana almost to the Ohio River. The safety of the territorial capital of Vincennes (50 miles north of that river) was becoming doubtful. As settlers fled into blockhouses and forts, leaving their fields unplowed, militia and rangers were scouring the countryside seeking the small Indian bands that left a trail of mutilated bodies, and disappeared with scalps.

In mid April, Harrison wrote Eustis,

I shall endeavor to ascertain the tribe to which these scoundrels belong but I have no hopes of their being delivered up. One of the most mischievous and successful of the Prophets schemes is that of destroying the influence of the Chiefs amongst the Pottowattimies and Kickapoos particularly. The young men are under no kind of control, each man does as he pleases, and we have in my opinion no alternative but War. The propriety of its being undertaken immediately and prosecuted with vigor is an opinion which pervades I believe the whole Western Country. In Kentucky and in this Territory I know that it does.[3]

By the middle of May, the Indian raids slackened. The lull enticed Harrison to write Eustis early in June,

Upon the whole Sir there is nothing in the suspension of Indian aggression for the last three weeks to induce a belief that the present is any other than one of those deceitful calms which frequently occur in Indian Warfare and which are always succeeded by increased activity in their depredations.[4]

There was firm basis for Harrison's analysis and a solid reason for the calm. On the 13th of May, Capt. Zachary Taylor wrote the governor from Fort Harrison, that the Prophet's army was growing daily. Later in the month, Taylor reported to Harrison on a grand council of the chiefs of 12 tribes meeting on May 15 at "Massassubwat" (the Miami tribe town of Mississinewa between present day Peru and Wabash, Indiana). In relaying Taylor's message to Eustis, Harrison said the Indians profess friendship and a desire to remain at peace with the United States but say nothing about the

Chiefs going to Washington [to consult with Madison at the President's request] or the delivery of the murderers — one or both of which was required by me as the only evidence that could be relied upon of their disposition to remain at peace with us.[5]

At this grand council, Tecumseh told his brothers (the other chiefs) that

the unfortunate transaction that took place between the white people and a few of our young men at our village [the battle of Tippecanoe] has been settled between us and Governor Harrison, and I will further state, had I been at home, there would have been no blood shed at that time.[6]

He went on to blame the Potawatomis, who, he said, had sold land to whites that didn't belong to them. The Potawatomis replied that some of their foolish young braves had followed the urging of the Prophet. Though the Indians came close to breaking up their meeting over these accusations, they nevertheless, stayed together and on returning to their tribes they had agreed to bond together for support while sending out their expressions of friendship for the whites. Still, Harrison felt confident enough of the situation in the middle of June to leave Vincennes on the 19th (the day of Madison's proclamation of war) to review regiments in the eastern division of the Indiana territory. He did this despite word a few days earlier of 20 Potawatomis heading down the road to Kaskaskia, Illinois, "to commit murders."[7] Of course, this became a concern of Governor Edwards of the Illinois territory.

It was on this review trip that Harrison received his hero's reception in Lexington late in June. He then went on to Cincinnati where his family was living. There he learned of the declaration of war and began a correspondence with those whose influence might obtain him a commission of major general in the regular U.S. army. A letter to him from Secretary Eustis, written July 9, gave no commission but stated, "Should offensive measures become necessary, the command within the Indiana Territory will devolve upon you, and with the consent of Governor Edwards, your military command may be extended in the Illinois Territory."[8]

Before this message reached Harrison, he wrote an appeal to Governor Scott of Kentucky requesting a recommendation be sent to President Madison to get a generalship for Harrison.[9]

A couple weeks after this request, and about the time Henry Clay was being honored in Lexington on his return home from Washington, Harrison received further word from his subordinates that Tecumseh had gone to Fort Malden, a British post in Canada across the river from Detroit. There, Tecumseh was to join the British in the war against the United States and obtain 12 horse loads of ammunition from his ally. Harrison also learned that the Prophet was at Fort Wayne, Indiana, and had received a message from his brother, Tecumseh,

> To unite the Indians immediately and send their women and children towards the Mississippi while the warriors should strike a heavy blow at the inhabitants of Vincennes, that he Tecumseh if he lived, would join him in the country of the Winnebagos.[10]

This would be in Illinois.

By late July, Harrison was back in Vincennes, where he wrote Eustis asking for instructions and hinting broadly at his desire for a regular army commission. But by August 6, he had returned to Cincinnati where he learned of ominous military news from the north.

The vision of Henry Clay and others of a quick and easy conquest of Canada was running into unexpected difficulties. A prewar plan, vaguely worked out in Washington, called for a strike from Detroit into Canada across the Detroit River and another from Niagara Falls, New York, to squeeze in a pincer the British force of less than 2,000 troops under Maj. Gen. Isaac Brock north of Lake Erie. Two Revolutionary War veterans were named to lead these attacks. The Detroit force was under 59-year-old Brig. Gen. William Hull. The Niagara force was under 61-year-old ex–Secretary of War Maj. Gen. Henry Dearborn.

Dearborn was, until February 1812, collector of the port of Boston. With his new assignment he went to Albany, New York, in May, to gather his troops. Late in the month, he returned to Boston to close out his customs duties there. Instead, he absorbed his time with arranging coastal defenses and was surprised on June 22 to learn of the declaration of war. But still he did not move, and indeed the incredible instructions to him from Secretary of War Eustis, to be written four days hence, did nothing to accelerate his motion.

Eustis wrote,

> Having made the necessary arrangements for the defense of the sea-coasts, it is the wish of the President that you should repair to Albany and prepare the force to be collected at that place for actual service. It is understood that being possessed of a full view of the intentions of the Government, and being also acquainted with the disposition of the force under your command, you will take your own time and give the necessary orders to the officers on the sea coast. It is altogether uncertain at which time General Hull may deem it expedient to commence offensive operations. The preparations it is presumed will be made to move in a direction for Niagara, Kingston, and Montreal. On your arrival at Albany you will be able to form an opinion of the time required to prepare the troops for action.[11]

Dearborn's response on July 1 expressed his continued concern over New England's preparation for war and he wrote, "I shall have doubts as to the propriety of my leaving this place until I receive your particular directions after you shall have received my letter."[12]

Eustis again instructed Dearborn on July 9 "to march immediately to Albany, or some station on Lake Champlain."[13] No mention was made of attacking Niagara to support Hull.

Eventually, Dearborn left Boston on July 22 — without an army, which he could not raise there — and on arrival in Albany, on the 26th, wrote Eustis in regard to the Niagara area, "Who is to have command of the operation in Upper Canada? I take it for granted that my command does not extend to that distant quarter."[14]

During Dearborn's procrastination, Hull took command of his troops at Dayton, Ohio, on May 25. Then during a fortnight in mid–June his force of around 1,500 men hacked their way northward through forests and brush or waded knee-deep through the swamps and marshes of western Ohio. On June 26, he received word from Eustis that war was close at hand. Hull hurried forward 35 miles to the Maumee River. On July 1, he packed his personal baggage, hospital stores, and some guard troops onto the American schooner *Cuyahoga* and sent it up the west end of Lake Erie and the Detroit River to Detroit. Unknown to him at the time, his official instructions and the master roll of his army went with the cargo.

Only the next day, when the vessel had sailed beyond recall, did Hull learn, in a dispatch from Eustis, that war was a fact. When the general reached Detroit on July 5, he became aware that the British had received word of the declaration of war on June 28, and that they had seized the *Cuyahoga* as it attempted to pass Fort Malden at the entrance to the Detroit River.

Despite these difficulties, Hull's army, after a clever feint, crossed the Detroit River with great zeal and ambition on July 12, occupied the small Canadian village of Sandwich without opposition, and was well received by the inhabitants. Wishing to avoid battle, Hull issued a proclamation to all Canadians of Upper Canada. In part, with its strange punctuation, it read:

> You will be emancipated from Tyranny and oppression and restored to the dignified station of freemen.... I have a force which will look down all opposition and that force is but the vanguard of a much greater. If contrary to your own interest & the just expectation of my country, you should take part in the approaching contest, you will be considered and treated as enemies and the horrors, and calamities of war will Stalk you.
> If the barbarous and Savage policy of Great Britain be pursued, and the savages are let loose to murder our Citizens and butcher our women and children, this war, will be a war of extermination.
> The first stroke with the Tomahawk the first attempt with the Scalping Knife will be the Signal for one indiscriminate scene of desolation, *No white man found fighting by the side of an Indian will be taken prisoner* Instant death will be his Lot.... The United States offer you *Peace, liberty,* and *Security* your choice lies between these, & *War, Slavery, and destruction,* Choose then, but choose wisely.[15]

This proclamation was to become very controversial. Contention as to authorship would depend upon whether the advocate supported or condemned Hull. It would be claimed that the administration supported it and that the peace commissioners disavowed it.

The immediate result of Hull's proclamation was to bring into his camp 50–60 Canadian deserters (mostly strongly pro–American militia of the region).

During the next few days, Hull resisted the urging of his subordinates to move on to attack Fort Malden before reinforcements arrived. Hull hoped for more Canadian desertions. Small skirmishes and minor artillery dueling at the besieged Fort Malden continued until July 28 when Hull received distressing news from much further north.

The rapid British communications, which cost Hull his supplies and papers on the captured *Cuyahoga,* also served the British outpost at St. Joseph, a large Canadian island in the waterway separating Lakes Superior and Huron. On July 8, British Capt. Charles Roberts received notice of the declaration of war sent out from the Canadian governor's office. It also advised him to take the utmost care of his party in case he must retreat. Instead, Roberts, on July 16, after pleading permission from his superior, General Brock (who was marching toward Fort Malden), attacked Fort Michillimackinac, on Mackinac Island, in the strait between Lakes Michigan and Huron.

The American commander, Lt. Porter Hanks, only then learned the United States was at war, surrendered his 88 men the next day. Hanks was permitted to go to Detroit on parole with a promise not to serve in the war again. But he was killed in Detroit in an artillery bombardment within a month.

During the first week of August, Hull gradually became fearful of a horde of Indians descending on him from the north. He, also, had reports that 42-year-old British General Brock was advancing rapidly by land and lake craft from Niagara to reinforce Fort Malden with a force that could double the enemy's strength. Already, Hull's supply line south into Ohio was being raided frequently by Tecumseh's Indians. Despite these threats, on August 7, at the pleading of his colonels, Hull announced they would attack Fort Malden. Happily the troops prepared for the assault.

Then suddenly, on August 8, Hull ordered a retreat back out of Canada to hole up in Fort Detroit. With Hull's failure to make an assault on Fort Malden followed by his retreat back across the river to Detroit, the returning troops were sullen and dispirited and grumbled against "the old man" that led them. The chagrined commanders of Hull's four regiments were close to anger and their confidence was fast disappearing.

During that same first week of August 1812, Kentucky was in a fever pitch of anxiety. And in the middle of it all was an election in which Henry Clay was returned unopposed to his seat in the U.S. House of Representatives. Also elected to office was Isaac Shelby, the state's first governor, now to return as Kentucky's chief executive on August 26. He was to succeed Charles Scott.

On learning of the surrender of Michillimackinac, Governor Scott sent an express to Cincinnati asking General Harrison to meet him in Frankfort, Kentucky. Before leaving Cincinnati, Harrison wrote Secretary of War Eustis, on August 6, warning him of the possible losses of Detroit and Chicago (then just a farming settlement along the southwestern Lake Michigan shore supported by about 50 soldiers inside Fort Dearborn at the mouth of the Illinois River).

Harrison met with Scott in Frankfort on Saturday, August 8. The next day he rode over to Lexington and dined with a party of prominent men, including Henry Clay. In the course of the conversation, Harrison related his meeting with Scott. He said Scott had shown him several documents from Governor Edwards of the Illinois Territory, "which unequivocally prove the existence of a combination amongst the Indian tribes more formidable than any previous one." Then Harrison stated his views on a proper direction military action should take. He advised moving up a force of up to 5,000 men to Fort Wayne to lend support to Hull. And he suggested erecting a string of forts on the Illinois River from the Mississippi [River] to Chicago. But, he added with respect to the situation of Chicago, "if it is not well supplied with provisions the danger must be imminent." Harrison also showed his dinner companions the July 9 letter from Eustis, which had said Harrison would command the Indiana and possibly Illinois Territories in event of offensive measures.

Harrison was urged, by those present, to communicate his views to Secretary of War Eustis. Harrison objected on the ground that it might be considered as interfering with matters which were foreign to his duty, which was confined to the defense of the territories. Clay disagreed and assured Harrison that the views would be well received by the government. But Clay and others also suggested that Harrison "not put any part of the troops in motion" until he had heard from Eustis. An exception was the few companies that had

been ordered for protection of Vincennes. On the 12th, Harrison wrote a long letter to Eustis relating his ideas as told to the Lexington gentlemen.[16]

On August 10, the day after Harrison's dinner meeting in Lexington, Clay attended a public gathering at the court house at which citizens agreed to a series of resolves supporting the war. Included was one proclaiming that the Kentucky volunteers, then on orders to rendezvous on the 14th, were competent to protect the frontiers and conquer Canada

> if they have such a man as William H. Harrison for their commander.... Their unbounded confidence in his Talents and skill will stimulate them under the severest hardships, and would undoubtedly lead them to perform feats of valor, that would do honor to our fathers.[17]

That same day, Harrison left Lexington for Louisville. En route, he stopped again in Frankfort to consult with Governor Scott. At the urgings of a Kentucky colonel, Scott decided to place Harrison in command of a regiment of volunteers destined for Vincennes and collecting at Louisville. The consultation developed further plans for a rendezvous, on September 1, of a force of cavalry and two regiments of infantry at Frankfort and a single infantry regiment each at Louisville and Henderson. Harrison was in Louisville by August 18.

On the 12th, the day that Harrison wrote Eustis, Clay also wrote a letter. But his went to Secretary of State James Monroe. In it he lavished praise for the 41-year-old Harrison. "Within these few days past," Clay wrote,

> I have had the pleasure of meeting with Govr. Harrison. The favorable sentiments I before entertained of him, and which I endeavored to communicate to you at Washington, are fully confirmed by the repeated conversations I have had with him. His merit cannot be too highly appreciated. He is full of devotion to the cause in which we are embarked. No other man in the U. States enjoys more highly the confidence of the Western people as a military character. I was the other day a passive spectator of a very large body of citizens assembled in Lexington to express their opinion on public affairs. A number of resolutions were proposed and carried. One affirmed our ability to bring the Indian war to a speedy conclusion under the guidance of W. H. Harrison. The people were all enthusiasm when his name was pronounced. It was carried by the loudest acclamation. I noticed

the fact as illustrative of general feeling and sentiment in the Western Country.

Clay said he wished Monroe could see Harrison's letter to Eustis containing his plans for military action. Clay noted that he preferred marching an army to Fort Wayne. There it

> would afford powerful assistance to Genl. Hull, as
> a covering army, by preventing indian [sic] succor,
> or carrying on offensive operations agt. the hostile
> tribes to the Westward, and if necessary by actual
> cooperation under him. It would at the same time
> be the means of protecting Chicago.

Clay recognized a command difficulty if Harrison were called upon to act outside the Indiana
Territory. If a conflict developed between his office
as the Territorial Governor and military commander, Clay wrote that Harrison would rather
relinquish the political post, and "accept a Brigadier's command, which it would be extremely
gratifying to the friends of the Administration in
this quarter." But Clay went further to suggest
that Madison appoint Harrison a brevet major
general.

Taking up the military situation in the West,
Clay wrote that he did not believe Indian attacks
would start until their corn was ripe. But "they
will then fall upon our frontier with all their fury,
unless in the mean time there is some vigorous
blow aimed at the British and themselves."

Meanwhile, believing Hull to be still besieging
Fort Malden, Clay told Monroe, "I lament the
necessity which has obliged Genl. Hull" to call
for more troops, but Clay was glad to see an

> opportunity of employment to our volunteers....
> We feel at the same time great solicitude for the
> fate of Genl. Hull's army. His suspension of offen-
> sive operations, after his bold and confident entry
> into Canada, was much to be deprecated. It will I
> fear present him in the ridiculous attitude of a gas-
> conader, whilst it affords to the enemy the sub-
> stantial advantage of assembling his before fugitive
> forces and strengthening himself in Malden.
> When we add to this the fall of the important post
> of Michilimackinack, and duly estimate the use
> which will be made of it in exciting the Indians
> against us, and drawing them down from the
> Northern extremity of Lake Michigan and the
> Westward of Detroit to the relief of Col. St.
> George [the tactical British commander of Fort
> Malden] and the annoyance of our frontiers, you
> will I think agree that our apprehensions are not
> destitute of foundation.

The detachment of 2,000 Kentucky volunteers
would of necessity, have to follow the treacherous
road carved out of the Ohio wilderness by Hull's
army. "On the line of their march," Clay continued in his long letter to Monroe,

> you will see, from a momentary glance of the map,
> there are several points at which an enterprising
> enemy might issue from Malden and attack them
> with great advantage. Should Hull's army be cut
> off the effects on the public mind would be, espe-
> cially in this quarter, in the highest degree injuri-
> ous. Why did he proceed with so inconsiderable a
> force? was the general enquiry made of me. I
> maintained that it was sufficient. Should he meet
> with a disaster the predictions of those who pro-
> nounced his army incompetent to its object will be
> fulfilled; and the Sec. of War (in whom already
> there unfortunately exists ["here" is crossed out in
> Clay's letter] no sort of confidence) can not possi-
> bly shield Mr. Madison from the odium which
> will attend such an event.

To this letter, Clay appended a postscript on
the following day with a report he had just heard
that Hull had taken Malden. Though Clay doubted
it was true, it would not be long before he was to
learn how disastrously erroneous the report was.[18]

On August 14, according to a Lexington paper,
a regiment of Kentucky volunteers, under Lt. Col.
William Lewis, rendezvoused at Lexington

> and marched to the garden of Mr. Sanders [Lewis
> Sanders, whom Clay had dealt with in a suit
> against Blennerhassett in 1807] about 2 miles on
> the road to Georgetown, where they partook of an
> elegant dinner prepared by the citizens of Lexing-
> ton, as the parting tribute of gratitude and respect
> and a farewell to these gallant defenders of their
> country.[19]

Clay spoke to the troops, but no record of his
words exists. Two days later there was a similar
gathering in Georgetown where three regiments
mustered under Brig. Gen. John Payne, a veteran
of Tippecanoe. Among these were Lewis' regiment. Another was under the command of Lt.
Col. John Allen, Clay's associate in the grand jury
defenses of Aaron Burr, and an 1808 candidate
for governor. One of his majors was soon to become Kentucky secretary of state. A Capt. John
Simpson had been speaker of the Kentucky House
of Representatives and had the week before been
elected to the U.S. House of Representatives.
Clearly, at least in the West, very prominent men
were putting their lives on the line.

Governor Scott came from Frankfort for the occasion and reviewed the troops in parade and then spoke to them. He was followed by Henry Clay who "addressed them with his usual eloquence," a writer of the day said, "and painted in lively colours, the honor which belongs to the volunteer soldier, fighting to defend the rights of his injured country."[20] Clay told the soldiers that much was expected of them from abroad. "Kentucky was fam'd for her bravery:— they had the double character of Americans and Kentuckians to support." Then Clay responded to a slander he had heard,

> The Kentuckians, by the very foe you are marching against, have been reproached as savages — Now, is the opportunity to avenge yourselves of the insult, not only by a salutary vengeance, but by showing your calumniator that you are not only brave, but humane and merciful when circumstances permit.[21]

A week after Henry Clay addressed the departing defenders of the Western Country, while the military hopes and fears were foremost in the minds of the populace, Clay read a report in the local newspaper of August 22, which, at another time, might have changed all that was transpiring. Now, it had little effect. Word had reached Kentucky that the British had, at long last, repealed their Orders in Council. Even this very belated and now worthless act came about in a peculiar way.

The British prince regent's declaration of April 21, offering a basis for repeal of the Orders in Council, reached Paris on May 1. American Minister Joel Barlow hastened to see the Duc de Bassano, the French foreign minister, to plead once more for a written proof of revocation of the French decrees. Bassano responded with a monstrous falsehood. He complained to Barlow for making such a demand telling him that the American government had possessed this document for more than a year. Bassano handed Barlow a decree signed by Napoleon and dated April 28, 1811, which declared the decrees revoked as of November 1, 1810. Bassano accused the Americans of concealing it. But later, in writing to the French minister in Washington, Bassano suggested that it might have been lost in transit. In any case, Barlow asked for a copy which he received from Bassano on May 10, the day after Napoleon left Paris

to take command of his Grand Army on the Russian frontier.

At this point, the events switch to England. Barlow sent a copy of the repealing decree to American chargé d'affaires in London, Jonathan Russell. During these recent months, the rupture in trade between the United States and Great Britain, resulting from American restrictive commerce laws and now the embargo, was causing economic distress in the English seaports and the inland manufacturing centers. Members of Parliament from these areas were flooded with petitions for the repeal of the Orders in Council. When these members joined the already vocal pro–American members, the combined strength at last forced Prime Minister Spencer Perceval to yield on April 28 in permitting a committee of the House of Commons to hear the petitions.

The hearings went on for several days, when, on May 11, the committee summoned Perceval to attend the investigation. As the P.M. entered the House a deranged and bankrupt broker named James Bellingham settled grievances against Perceval, by firing a pistol at him at point-blank range. The prime minister died instantly.

Though the hearings continued for several days, the government was at loose ends tidying up national affairs for more than a month. By the time the prince regent named the Earl of Liverpool as Perceval's successor, nothing had been done about the Orders in Council despite surprising news from abroad.

Nine days after Perceval's assassination, Russell received the purported revocation of the French decrees sent by Barlow. That same day, May 20, Russell gave it to British Foreign Secretary Viscount Castlereagh. Though the British also recognized it as a fabrication they slowly came to the view that it was a way out of the depressing dilemma into which the country was drifting. Finally, on June 16, the British government announced suspension of the Orders and on the 23rd, the outright repeal. It was too late. The United States had already been at war with Great Britain for four days!

Years later, Madison was to write about this period with emphasis on the crucial nature of Castlereagh's April 10 dispatch,

> Had Castlereagh's letter therefore been of a different tone war would not have been at that time

declared, nor is it probable that it would have followed, because there was every prospect that the affair of impressment and other grievances might have been reconciled after the repeal of the obnoxious Orders in Council.[22]

At least, here was a fundamental difference between James Madison and Henry Clay. The Kentuckian placed impressment of seamen as the controlling factor in his motivation for going to war. He was, in the next session of Congress, to get into a fierce debate with Josiah Quincy over continuing the war on that question.

But on August 22, 1812, news of the repeal of the Orders in Council gave Clay no relief for the anxiety growing over the military affairs on the frontier. Only the slow transit of news cloaked word of disasters already history. All Clay knew from the newspaper was that Hull's situation at Detroit, as of August 11, was "extremely critical."

Clay wrote to Eustis the same day (August 22) that he learned of the British suspension of the Orders in Council. He referred to Hull's "perilous condition" and expressed his "strongest apprehensions" that the detachment of 2,000 to 2,500 Kentuckians would not reach Hull in time. But his correspondence with the secretary of war was primarily aimed at getting more provisions for the local troops since only three month's supplies for only 1,500 troops were available — and no winter clothing was included.[23]

Two days after this letter, Clay and other prominent political leaders of Kentucky travelled to Frankfort for the inauguration of one-time Gov. Isaac Shelby to succeed Gov. Charles Scott on Tuesday, afternoon, August 25.

But on Monday, Governor Scott received an express message from Detroit dated August 12. It reported the evacuation of Canada and the American return to Detroit. It also said, "The greatest discontent appeared to prevail in the army with the commander in chief. All confidence in him seem to be utterly extinguished," with suggestions of dark suspicion and hints of treachery.[24]

Typical of the dire communications arriving from the north was a letter posted in Detroit on August 8 and printed in a Lexington paper on August 29:

Dear Sir — The alarming prospect before us, you can have no idea of— horror and dismay has given to every countenance, the most gloomy appear-

ance; but a few days ago we landed triumphantly on the shores of our enemy, and now we have precipitately fled, under cover of night to Detroit.[25]

On the morning of the 25th, Scott called in an impressive group to discuss the crisis. Joining him were his predecessor, Governor Greenup; his successor, Governor Shelby; U.S. Supreme Court Justice Thomas Todd; General Samuel Hopkins; Kentucky Congressmen Richard M. Johnson and Henry Clay; and Indiana Governor William Henry Harrison.

The Kentuckians agreed unanimously, and in writing, for Scott (with only hours remaining in his term) to order another detachment of the state's military quota to follow the one which had already left the state under General Payne. Joining this detachment a week later as a major, was Congressman Johnson, one of those present at this meeting. And they chose to put Harrison over the entire force. For the purpose of removing all difficulties, they recommended (and Scott obliged) to commission Harrison a brevet major general of the Kentucky militia.[26]

On this last matter there was some question of giving the territorial governor of Indiana such a commission when he was not a Kentuckian. "But," as Clay wrote Monroe that night from Frankfort, following Shelby's inaugural ceremonies,

when it was seen that throughout all parts of the W[estern] Country there has been the strongest demonstrations of confidence in him given, and when he was called for by the very army itself to be relieved, as their last hope, we could not hesitate, especially when the popular sentiment entirely accorded with our own.

Then Clay made a comparison,

If you will carry your recollection back to the age of the Crusades, and of some of the most distinguished leaders of those expeditions, you will have a picture of the enthusiasm existing in this country for the expedition to Canada, and for Harrison as the commander.

As to Govr. Harrison himself he is so zealously devoted to the country that he may be perfectly satisfied with whatever post may be assigned him. The Commission granted to him was intended only under any contingency, to ensure respect to his command, until the pleasure of the President is made known.

Again Clay revealed his lack of confidence in Eustis by adding to his letter to Monroe, "I write you this letter, instead of sending it to Mr. Eustis, to multiply the chances of information reaching you. Be pleased to make my respects acceptable to the President."[27]

However, Clay wrote Eustis the next day from his home in Lexington. In this letter he briefly mentioned Harrison's appointment referring him to "communications from Frankfort of yesterday to different branches of the Executive of the U. States."

But Clay also apprised Eustis of the local feelings toward General Hull.

> It is with regret that I have to add that reports are every where prevalent in this State & Ohio imputing to Genl. Hull more than incapacity. It is alleged, by way of color to the imputation, that his family have in several instances intermarried with the very enemy he is encountering. Confidence in him is utterly and irretrievably gone. I have endeavored at least to preventing the formation of opinions of his alleged treachery until further information is obtained. The most sober and deliberated are doubting his fidelity.[28]

The "further information" was to reach Clay only one day later, on the 27th. He then learned of Hull's operations since August 8th when the general ordered his retreat from Canada. Ensconced in Detroit and worried about Indians descending from the north, British Gen. Isaac Brock's advance from the east, and Indian raids which severed his supply line from the south, Hull sent out two different kinds of missions.

As for the first of these, Hull sent an express to Capt. William Wells, commanding at Fort Wayne, to effect the evacuation of Fort Dearborn which protected the small village of Chicago. Wells, brought up by the Miami tribe of Indians as an orphan, had later returned to the white men's life and served for several years as an Indian agent and now had the respect of both races. He reached Chicago on August 13 with a group of 30 Miamis as a neutral support. Almost at the same time, a messenger from Tecumseh arrived to tell neighboring Indians that he had joined the British. On the 15th, Wells, believing it safe, directed the evacuation of women, children, and soldiers from Fort Dearborn. But outside the fort, they were ambushed by Potawatomis and Winnebagos and were deserted by the Miamis. Most whites were slaughtered and Wells was killed, his heart cut out, and half eaten raw by the Potawatomis.[29]

Hull's other mission involved 200 Ohio militia under Maj. Thomas B. Van Horn sent south from Detroit, on August 4, to meet a supply group under Capt. Henry Brush coming north from Ohio, and now encamped on the River Raisin about 35 miles south of Detroit. The following day, the militia failed to meet the supply train and were turned back at Brownstown [now Monroe, Michigan] by a large group of Indians under command of Tecumseh. (Following this engagement Tecumseh captured papers from the camp in Detroit revealing deep dissension at the fort and passed this intelligence on to the British commander.)

This and the Chicago mission were both ordered prior to Hull's retreat from Sandwich to Detroit. On the morning after Hull's force returned to Detroit, August 8, he dispatched a force of 600 men under Lt. Col. James Miller of the regular army to meet Brush. Again, on the following day, this group was also met by Tecumseh's Indians who had been joined by a detachment of British troops that had crossed the River Raisin below Detroit. Though Miller claimed a victory in the ensuing engagement, he sent back a request to Hull for provisions, but got a recall order instead. Of this, Hull wrote to Eustis, "The blood of seventy-five gallant men could only open the communication, as far as the points of their bayonets extended."[30] Under a heavy rain this group also returned to Detroit.

By now there was very serious dissension in the ranks of Hull's army and his three Ohio militia colonels — Duncan McArthur, James Findlay, and Lewis Cass — considered deposing Hull and putting McArthur in command. But McArthur declined. Rather than take overt action, Cass wrote a note to Ohio Governor Meigs hinting at Hull's incompetence, and saying that Malden might have been seized, but that a golden opportunity had passed. And the following postscript was added, "Believe all the bearer will tell you. Believe it, however, it may astonish you, as much as if told by one of us. Even a C —— is talked of by the ——. The bearer will fill the vacancy."[31] The bearer revealed the blanks to be "capitulation" and "commanding general."

Whether or not Hull got wind of this near mutiny, he moved as if he had. On the 14th, he dispatched both McArthur and Cass, with 350 men, to reach Brush by a different route than previously taken.

Almost at the same time that this expedition marched out of Detroit, British General Brock arrived at Fort Malden. On the 15th, he sent a dispatch to Hull saying, "The force at my disposal authorizes me to require of you the immediate surrender of Detroit." He told Hull that he would not be able to control the Indians now with him once the battle should start.[32] Hull responded that he would fight. This reply was met by British artillery fire on the fort at Detroit, now overcrowded with frightened women and children. The next day, Sunday the 16th, began with more shelling. But there was a difference. About 700 of Brock's troops had followed nearly an equal number of Indians across the river at a point five miles below Detroit.

Inside the fort a scene of chaos and desperation ensued. As British shells exploded in the midst of the crowded fort, Hull's fears reached their peak. He envisioned awful scenes of Indian atrocities, the unspeakable horrors of the tomahawk and scalping-knife. Hull — cowering from the British shot, his face white with fear and his ruffled shirt stained with tobacco juice — beseeched an aide, "My God, what shall I do with these women and children?" He had tried to recall Cass and McArthur, but had heard nothing from them (though they had received his order at dusk on Saturday and marched all night toward Detroit posing a threat to the British rear).[33]

Suddenly, from a parapet, in full view of the British troops, a white tablecloth, hung on a pole, waved a "greeting" from General Hull to General Brock. The surrender of Detroit came as a shock to the American troops who were still full of fight and, in contradiction to Hull's claims, still sufficiently supplied to hold out until the arrival of Brush and more supplies.

Hours later, Cass and McArthur arrived at Detroit only to learn that they had been included in Hull's infamous surrender to Brock. They and their 350 troops had not had a chance to escape southward. Even Captain Brush and his men, who had never reached Detroit, were included in the surrender document. Though the British reached Brush under a flag of truce to demand his surrender, he had them seized and held prisoner overnight, calling them imposters. Then

Brush and his men escaped to Ohio during the night.

As the other Americans under Hull gave up their weapons in great anger at the disgrace that made them prisoners, tears flowed down their cheeks and they swore at their "treasonable" commander. Colonel Cass, exasperated beyond endurance, snapped his sword in two. Later, he expressed his anger, anguish, and chagrin in a long detailed letter to Secretary Eustis.

> Basely to surrender without firing a gun — tamely to submit, without raising a bayonet — disgracefully to pass in review before an enemy, as inferior in the quality as in the number of his forces, were circumstances, which excited feelings of indignation more easily felt than described.

Cass added that at least 500 shed tears.[34]

Cass reported that Hull had about 1,060 men at the fort, not counting 350 with McArthur and Cass and another 300 guarding the northwest approach to Detroit. Hull claimed he had less than 1,000 and was opposed by 1,800 British regulars plus hordes of Indians. In fact, British General Brock said he had captured 2,500 troops "without the sacrifice of a drop of British blood." He did this with only 770 troops including Canadian militia plus 400 Indians. He wrote his superior, "When I detail my good fortune Your Excellency will be astonished."[35]

The news of Hull's surrender, which reached Lexington and Henry Clay on August 27, created a sensation — but not of despair. Clay was to write Monroe. "It has on the contrary awakened new energies and aroused the whole people of this state."

He told Monroe,

> It is impossible to give you an adequate idea of the sensations excited in this country by the mortifying event at Detroit. Altho' our previous intelligence had in some degree prepared us for unfavorable occurrences, the disaster so far exceeded our worst anticipations, that it was som[e] time after the fact was first announced before it was credited. Of Hull's treachery scarcely a doubt is entertained in this Country. For my own part as it respects the man I do not think it worth investigation whether the act is to be attributed to treachery or cowardice. It was so shameful, so disgraceful a surrender, that whether it proceeded from the one or the other cause he deserves to be shot.[36]

Monroe, on learning of Hull's surrender, was not so sanguinary as Clay. Writing to Clay, on August 28, he said,

So far as we are informed on the subject, there appears to be no justification of it. I can not suspect his integrity; I rather suppose that a panick had seized the whole force, & that he & they became victims, of his want of energy, promptitude of decision & those resources, the characteristic of great minds in difficult emergencies.[37]

Clay's letter to Monroe was written nearly a month after Monroe's, and Clay by then had more time to assimilate more details of the debacle.

Dolley Madison was also more charitable than Clay. She and the president had just left Washington on August 28 for their mountain home, Montpelier, Virginia, when word reached them that evening of Hull's surrender. Only twice during the long Congressional session beginning in November had Madison left the White House. Now he found himself "much worn down," he wrote General Dearborn, "and in need of an antidote to accumulating bile of which I am sensible, and which I have never escaped in August on tide water."[38] The Madisons hurried back to Washington from where Dolley wrote, "Do you not tremble with resentment at this treacherous act? Yet we must not judge the man until we are in possession of his reasons."[39]

Clay's view, however, was supported from a strange source — the peace-loving Thomas Jefferson. Some weeks later he wrote Madison, "Hull will of course be shot for cowardice & treachery."[40] The feelings of Clay and Jefferson very nearly prevailed.

Despite the bitterness and anguish brought on by this military disaster, there were still those who could find some humor in the situation. A writer to a Richmond, Virginia, paper, who called himself "Falstaff," wrote,

Mr. Editor — A constant reader of your paper wishes to enquire the reason, why — (seeing the late General of the U. States' North Western Army was nothing but a Hull) — those, who were the Colonels [kernels] did not take the command, and throw the *Hull* away?[41]

Hull and his men were eventually paroled to the United States. Lewis Cass was to become the chief witness against Hull in a court-martial (and was still later to contend with Clay in a distinguished political career that included running for the presidency as a Democrat against Zachary Taylor in 1848). Hull was, in 1814, tried for treason

and cowardice. The court sidestepped the treason charge as out of its jurisdiction. It convicted him of cowardice and sentenced him to be shot but recommended leniency. President Madison then pardoned Hull on consideration of his faithful service during the American Revolution. The general lived out his life in obscurity hoping always to regain his reputation, believing he had acted justly in sparing the lives of the women and children in the fort at Detroit.

But the loss of both Detroit and Chicago (though lightly garrisoned) left a huge gap in the western defense line. The critical points now became Fort Wayne and Fort Harrison in Indiana. Monroe was so anxious over the turn of events that he wrote Clay,

I most sincerely wish that the President could dispose of me at this juncture, in the military line. If circumstances would permit, and it should be thought that I could render any service, I would in a very few days, join our forces assembling beyond the Ohio, & indeavor to recover the ground which we have lost.[42]

In a later letter to Clay, Monroe gave more details on this project.

On the intelligence of the surrender of Detroit the President expressed a desire to avail himself of my services in that quarter, & had partly decided so to do. He proposed that I shd. go in the character of a Volunteer with the rank of Major Genl. to take command of the forces. I expressed my willingness to obey the summons, altho. it was sudden, and unexpected, as indeed the event which suggested the idea was. On mature reflection however he concluded that it would not be proper for me to leave my present station at the present juncture. I had no opinion on the subject but was prepar'd to act in any situation in which it might be thought I might be most useful.[43]

Nevertheless, the correspondence between Clay and Monroe continued to reveal the activity transpiring in the Western Country to secure it from Indian depredations and British conquest. Monroe told Clay that 3,000 troops were ordered westward from Pennsylvania and Virginia, and

a large park of heavy artillery is sent on to Pittsburg [sic] to be forwarded thence towards Cleveland for the use of the army, whose duty it will be to retake Detroit & expell the British from Malden & Upper Canada.[44]

And Clay wrote Monroe that Kentucky had put 8,000 to 10,000 men in the field.

> Except our quota of the 100,000 militia, the residue is chiefly of a miscellaneous character, who have turned out without pay or supplies of any kind, carrying with them their own arms and their own subsistence. Parties are daily passing to the theatre of action. Last might 70 lay on my farm, and they go from a solitary individual to companies of 10–50–100 &c.

Clay's major concern over sending so many troops far off into the wilderness was that the Indians would elude them and "fall upon our frontiers," he wrote Monroe. "They have alre[ad]y shocked us with some of the most horrid murders. Within 24 miles of Louisville, on the head waters of Silver Creek, 22 were massacred a few days ago."[45]

Clay also wrote Monroe about General Harrison's plans to relieve Fort Wayne where hordes of Indians had descended following the fall of Detroit. But Harrison's objectives ran into more trouble from red tape than red men.

After Harrison's appointment as a major general of Kentucky militia, at the August 25 meeting with those leading citizens in Frankfort, he journeyed to Cincinnati arriving there probably late on August 26. Already in the same city was regular army Brig. Gen. James Winchester in command of a body of troops including many Kentucky militia.

Winchester, 60-years old, had commanded small units on Long Island and later at Yorktown under Washington during the American Revolution. In years since, he moved to Tennessee, fought some Indians, and settled into a life of elegant luxury and ease as a friend of Andrew Jackson. He had obtained his recent commission through the recommendation of Felix Grundy.

On August 27, Harrison sent a note to Winchester telling him of the Frankfort meeting, of his military appointment, and of the authority granted him by the president to take command of the defense of Indiana and Illinois. "I am now here for the purpose of assuming the command," Harrison wrote him. Then offering Winchester a sop, he added, "I conceive however that it remains for you to fix the destination of the regular troops." Still Harrison suggested that it would be impossible for the whole force to act effectively "without being put under my command."[46]

Winchester, of course, objected to the arrangement assuming that a regular army commission out-ranked even a higher militia commission. Furthermore, the current military actions were largely taking place in Ohio and Michigan rather than in Indiana and Illinois. The two generals exchanged two or three more notes during the day and then had a personal meeting. Winchester later wrote,

> It was agreed that General Harrison might assume the command, but entirely on *his own responsibility* ... I was determined that the public service should never suffer from a personal contention with General Harrison or any other officer, where the least doubt existed as to the legitimacy of my own authority.[47]

Clearly, a resentment existed between the two generals. Winchester returned to Lexington to resume recruiting of troops as he had before the war began.

The news of Hull's surrender, which reached Harrison at Cincinnati the next day, the 28th, was only confirmation of a previous rumor. Harrison was anxious and willing to march upon the enemy. But, as so often happens in the early stages of a war, the use of civilians for soldiers leaves much to be desired. Harrison lamented his situation to the secretary of war,

> The troops which I have with me and those which are coming on from Kentucky are perhaps the best materials for forming an army that the world has produced. But no equal number of men were ever collected who know so little of military discipline.... The confusion which exists in every Department connected with the army is such as can only be expected from men who are perfectly new to the business they are engaged in.[48]

As an example of camp laxness, some days later, Harrison made an attempt to impress the troops with the need for discipline. He addressed them briefly, read the Articles of War, and told them of the dangers ahead. He then requested those not willing to endure the life of a true soldier to leave the ranks. Only one did. His companions, suggesting he was too feeble to walk, carried him on a rail to the banks of a river and gave him a "plunge bath." The discipline improved.[49]

Harrison also wrote Clay on the 28th with the same view of affairs as described to Eustis but with more enthusiasm and in his strange capitalization.

I have an army competent in numbers & in spirit equal to any that greece or Rome have boasted of but destitute of Artillery, of many necessary equipments & absolutely ignorant of every military evolution, nor have I but a Single individual capable of assisting me in training them. But I beg you to believe my dear Sir that this retrospect of my Situation far from producing dispondency produces a contrary effect. And I feel confident of being able to surmount them all — The grounds of this confidence are reliance in my own zeal and perseverance & a perfect conviction that no such *Material* for forming an invaluable army ever existed as the volunteers which have marched from Kenty. on the present occasion.[50]

That same morning, the 29th, Harrison dispatched some of his troops northward for the relief of Fort Wayne. But on the 30th Harrison seemed to fall into a mood of despondency and some fear for the success of the prospective military operations. His emotions are revealed in another letter to Clay that day.

After having been absent from home for so many months you will no doubt think it unreasonable that you should be asked to take a considerable journey & that on an occasion entirely foreign to yr. ordinary public duties — I know you however too well not to believe that sacrifice of private convenience will be always made to render service to yr. country. Without further preamble then I inform you that in my opinion yr. presence on the frontier of this State would be productive of great advantages. I can assure you that your advice & assistance in determining the course of operations for the army (to the command of which I have been designated by yr. recommendation) will be highly useful — You are not only pledged in some measure for my conduct but for the success of the war — for gods sake then come on to Piqua as quickly as possible — & let us indeavour to throw off from the administration that weight of Reproach which the late disasters will heap upon them.[51]

With regard to Harrison's comment that Clay was pledged to his conduct and the success of the war, the general undoubtedly referred to Clay's political efforts in Congress to bring the nation to war and then to his lead at the Frankfort meeting in putting Harrison in command of Kentucky troops. Evidence that Clay's power of persuasion had their effect on the administration is revealed in a response by Monroe on the matter of a regular commission for Harrison. "You & our other friends in Kentucky," Monroe wrote Clay, "will

find that the utmost attention has been paid to your opinions & wishes, on all these subjects."[52]

There is no evidence that Clay fulfilled Harrison's plea to visit the troops at Piqua. On the contrary, various legal documents signed by Clay on intermittent succeeding days render it nearly impossible for him to have made the journey to and from Piqua between those dated signatures.

The same day that Harrison wrote Clay from Cincinnati to appear before the troops, the general left for Piqua some 80 miles further north to overtake his troops. He reached that town on September 1. A day later he received dispatches dated August 22 from Secretary of War Eustis confirming his command in Illinois and Indiana and informing him that he had been appointed a brigadier general of the regular army by President Madison (pending confirmation by the Senate when it was to reconvene in November). Though this commission would put Harrison on an equal level with Winchester, it would make him junior with respect to time in rank. He therefore wrote the secretary that he was postponing his acceptance of the commission, basically because the military situation throughout the entire Western Country had deteriorated since the commission was issued. He told the secretary that Fort Wayne was under siege, that almost all Indians had joined the enemy, and that he had decided to open offensive operations against them immediately. For that purpose he intended to rendezvous his forces at Dayton on September 15.

Harrison recognized that there was now a dual command situation with Winchester charged with support of Hull (an order that no longer had meaning). Harrison therefore wrote Eustis, "I wish to know how far I am to be subordinate to him in the main design of regaining our lost territory and retaking Malden" (which had never been taken in the first place). Tooting his own horn, he continued,

There is in my opinion a necessity of having one head in the western country to direct all military movements. It might perhaps be presumption in me to compare my military information with that of Gen'l Winchester and his extreme amiableness of character will insure him respect and esteem where he is known. But that happens not to be the case either in this state or Kentucky. The backwoodsmen are a singular people. They are susceptible of the most heroic achievements but they must be taken in their own way. From their affection and attachment everything may be expected but I will venture to say they never did nor never will perform anything brilliant under a stranger. I will venture to add another thing also. No general can act in this country without personal knowledge of the country

as there were no reliable maps. Harrison claimed the affection of the troops and knowledge of the country.[53]

Nevertheless, Harrison had come to the conclusion that he should relinquish command of his forces to Winchester and wrote him to that effect by September 5. Winchester later wrote that he received official notification from Eustis of his authority to command all forces in the Northwest. While waiting a formal change of powers, rumors of a British movement toward Fort Wayne reached Harrison. He judged it expedient to advance there rather than await in Piqua for Winchester to come up from Lexington.[54] Harrison reached Fort Wayne on September 12. Only the day before had the Indians "retreated precipitately." No British were there. For the next few days he had his troops destroy Indian supplies and crops as far as 60 miles from Fort Wayne.

General Winchester arrived at Fort Wayne on the 18th and Harrison surrendered the command to him on the following day. But not without a great howl from the Kentucky troops. One soldier wrote home,

> General Winchester being a stranger, and having the appearance of a supercilious officer, he was generally disliked. His assuming the command almost occasioned a mutiny in camp; this was prevented by the solicitations of the officers to go on.[55]

Kentucky Congressman Richard M. Johnson, only three weeks earlier appointed an aide to Harrison, wrote to President Madison,

> Let me inform you that no event is now so important to the cause of our country in this quarter as the giving Gov. Harrison command of the forces from Kentucky destined for Canada. He has capacity without equal. He has the confidence of the forces without parallel in our History except in the case of Gen'l Washington in the revolution. Gen'l. Winchester has this morning arrived & the united exertions of us all cannot reconcile them to the transfer of the command. I speak what I know & you cannot be wrong in acting accordingly.[56]

The tension in camp and threat of mutiny by many Kentuckians was so great, Harrison was forced to appeal to them through a general order to support his successor. In it he praised Winchester as "one of the Heroes of our glorious Revolution." He praised the troops who had recently "performed severe duty with scarcely a sufficiency of food to sustain them and entirely without some of the articles which constitute the ration"; and it was done "without a murmur and with the alacrity" of veteran troops. He acknowledged

> the personal attachment which the army has manifested toward him and he assures them that their welfare and glory is the first object of his wishes, and as a means of securing both he most earnestly recommends and entreats that the confidence which they have so often expressed in him may be transferred to his worthy successors.[57]

Harrison assumed command of troops in Indiana. And as a major general of the Kentucky militia he took command of all the troops of that state north of the Ohio River, excepting the army of General Winchester. He left shortly, with some of the troops, and returned, via St. Mary's, to Piqua late on the evening of September 24 — where a pleasant surprise awaited him.

Opening his mail, Harrison found a letter from Secretary of War Eustis dated two days prior to his surrender of command to Winchester. It began, "The President is pleased to assign to you the command of the Northwestern Army...."[58] It was what Harrison had been hoping and pressing for. It was what Clay and others, including Governor Shelby had been urging on the administration in Washington.

In fact, on the same day on which he wrote Harrison, Eustis also wrote Shelby responding to a letter from the Kentucky governor on September 5. "To meet existing emergencies after consulting the lawful authority vested in the President," Eustis wrote,

> it has been determined to vest the command of all the forces on the western and northwestern frontier in an officer, whose military character and knowledge of the country, appear to be combined with the public confidence. General Harrison has accordingly been appointed to the chief command.[59]

Harrison would have been delighted had he known his words were paraphrased by the secretary in stating the reasons for giving command to the vigorous governor of the Indiana Territory.

Still, Harrison did not hurry forward to resume command. Already Winchester had begun a slow and cautious march along the Maumee River toward Detroit. Not until October 3 did Harrison reach Winchester at Fort Defiance, Ohio, about 45 miles east of Fort Wayne. Again the aging Winchester turned over top command to Harrison but retained a tactical command under him. The happy troops again listened to the praise by one general for another. But an antagonism had been fixed and was to smolder for weeks. It was to affect future military operations the result of which was to bring sorrow to the Clay home.

16

BATTLE ACTION AND ELECTION

Almost as soon as General William Henry Harrison took command of the Northwestern Army for the second time, he lost one of his valued aides. Richard M. Johnson, now a colonel, had to leave the army to make the journey to Washington City for his duty as a Kentucky Congressman in the 2nd session of the 12th Congress. Also leaving Kentucky in early October 1812 was House Speaker Henry Clay. He had written to James Monroe that he intended, this time, to travel to Washington by way of the haunts of his youth, Richmond, Virginia. However, no news story or correspondence confirms that he took this routing. It is known that Lucretia and three of the children went with him.[1] What is also known is that Clay was able to proceed eastward with the exhilaration of glorious war news countering the disasters and fears in the west — especially encouraging since it came from an unexpected source. Now Clay's early vision of the war — an expectation of an easy conquest of Canada by Kentucky militia — anticipated to overshadow the threat to the East Coast by British sea raiders — was being reversed. The disasters were with the Army in the north and the triumphs were on the sea against the expected invincible British navy. Clay had no direct connection with these naval actions, except as their being a consequence of his zest to send the country to war with a strong navy. Later, though, he was again to be involved in legislation that related to the actions.

Before the start of the war, there was concern within the administration that the "mistress of the sea," the British navy, was so vastly superior to the tiny American navy it would be wisest to act strictly on the defensive. In later years it was even charged that American vessels were to be held in port and their guns be removed to channel forts. However, by the time war was declared, the naval commanders were to consider themselves "as possessing every belligerent right of attack, capture, and defense."

On the day war was declared, Navy Secretary Paul Hamilton sent an order to Commodore John Rodgers (who was, in addition, captain of the frigate *President* of 44 guns). It stated, "As it is understood that there are one or more British cruisers on the coast in the vicinity of Sandy Hook, you are at your discretion, free to strike them, returning immediately into port." Rodgers had learned of the declaration before receiving Hamilton's orders, but wrote him in the interim, that he was putting his command in the state of defense and awaiting the secretary's instructions. When the dispatch arrived on June 21, Rodgers was so prepared that he put to sea in 10 minutes and wrote that he would go out in search of a British convoy scampering home from Jamaica to England.[2]

Sailing under Rodgers' command were four other warships — the frigates *United States*, 44; and the *Congress*, 38; along with the sloop *Hornet*, 18; and the brig *Argus*, 16. Since Rodgers' cruise lasted more than 10 weeks, it was only as Clay prepared to return to Washington from Kentucky that he learned of it. But in July, while still in Washington, during the earlier session of Congress, Clay did get some misinformation about the cruise. He heard that Rodgers' ship, the *President*, had captured the British frigate *Belvidera*, 32. When the news reached Clay's boarding house, the whole mess — Clay, Calhoun, Cheves, Bibb, Grundy, and Lowndes — got up, joined hands, and danced over the floor![3]

Actually, Rodgers had chased and fired on the *Belvidera*, but in the action one of the American guns exploded breaking Rodgers' leg. In addition, vessels of those days could fire only broadsides, effectively, thus forcing the chasing ship to turn to bring her guns into action. And each turn opened the distance between antagonists. This enabled the *Belvidera* to escape rather than be sunk or captured.

Aside from this action, very little happened on Rodgers' cruise to the other side of the Atlantic and his return home. He never caught up with the Jamaican convoy and his voyage was fruitless in terms of sea fights and vessels captured. Indeed, it was considered a failure by the vocal press of anti-war New England.

Nevertheless, some press observers saw the cruise in a different light. One eastern paper said,

He has detached the enemy from our coast — he has distracted and divided the Halifax fleet — *millions* of American property has arrived safe owing to this circumstance, which would otherwise have been lost, but for his wise and prudent manoeuver.[4]

This analysis appeared in Kentucky one week after the news reports of the first major American victory of the war. Almost at the same time that Rodgers set out on his expedition, Captain Isaac Hull (the nephew of General William Hull of Detroit infamy), commanding the frigate *Constitution* of 44 guns, sailed from Annapolis. He had a quick voyage on which he was chased by a fleet of British ships. But, by remarkable seamanship, first in a calm and then in a storm, Hull managed to elude the British vessels by using the tactic of kedging, a technique by which an anchor is dropped and then the attached line is pulled in to haul a ship forward. In this case, the anchor and its line were probably carried ahead in a small boat, the anchor dropped over the side, and the crew then pulled in on the line attached to the ship.

But, after a brief respite in port, Hull, too, returned to sea to avoid anticipated orders to remain in port. His second sortie took him out of Boston, where it was almost as dangerous for him and his crew as it might be on the high seas controlled by the self-confident and ubiquitous British navy. This time, he was in search of an opponent with whom he had once wagered a cocked hat on the outcome of a future engagement.

At 2 P.M., on August 19, 200 miles off the Maine coast, the bet for the hats was about to be called. Sailing south from Halifax was the British frigate *Guerrière*, 38, under Capt. James Richard Dacres. This same ship had harassed American ships for months along the American shore. So arrogant were the British that on their sail was painted in red, "*Guerrière*, not the *Little Belt*." It took nearly four hours for the two ships to maneuver into close battle position, each seeking the greater advantage. Throughout the advance on the weaving *Guerrière*, Hull held off firing until the two ships could close to his liking.

Captain Hull, as described by a witness of the battle,

was quite fat, and wore very tight breeches. As the shot of the *Guerrière* began to tell upon the *Constitution*, the gallant Lieutenant Morris, Hull's second in command, came to the captain and asked permission to open fire. "Not yet," quietly responded Hull. Nearer and nearer the vessels drew toward each other, and the request was repeated. "Not yet," said Hull again, very quietly. When the *Constitution* reached the point 50 yards from the British adversary, Hull, filled with sudden and intense excitement, bent himself twice to the deck, and then shouted, "Now, boys, pour it into them!" The command was instantly obeyed. The *Constitution* opened her forward guns, which were double shotted with round and grape, with terrible effect. When the smoke that followed the result of that order cleared away, it was discovered that the commander, in his energetic movements, had split his tight breeches from the waistband to knee, but he did not stop to change them during the action.[5]

As the cannon sent their "messages" into the British sails and rigging, sharp shooters in the *Constitution*'s rigging peppered away at the *Guerrière*'s deck hands. Within 10 minutes, the *Guerrière*'s mizzen mast crashed over the far side. Minutes later, the *Constitution*, passing ahead of the Britisher, had its own mizzen rigging fouled by the *Guerrière*'s bowsprit. As the Americans prepared to board their opponent, the two vessels broke free — free for another American broadside that brought down both the fore and main masts of the shattered enemy, leaving it a "helpless wreck, rolling like a log in the trough of a sea, entirely at the mercy of the billows."[6]

During the battle there were two incidents of note. Much of the spirited fire of the *Guerrière* passed high through the rigging of the *Constitu-*

tion. One shot left the American flag hanging down tangled with sails and a splintered mast. An ordinary seaman, named Don Hogan, climbed into the rigging oblivious to the firing of the enemy and at the top of the mast, clinging with one hand, used his other to nail the flag to the mast so that it could never come down, unless the mast itself came with it. He soon joined his mates at his battle station among great cheers.

But not all shots went into the rigging. Some slammed violently against the ship's hull. After one of the enemy's largest shot bounced off the planking and fell harmlessly into the sea, a shout went up from many of the crew. "Huzza! Her sides are made of iron! See where the shot fell out!" The *Constitution*, before winning the battle, had won herself a new and glorious name for all time — "*Old Ironsides!*"[7]

Only 25 minutes after the close action began, Dacres surrendered his wallowing vessel. For a while it was not altogether clear whether or not the British had indeed surrendered. When a jack, that had been flying on the stump of the *Guerrière's* mizzen-mast, was lowered, Lt. George Read, of the *Constitution*, went aboard the prize and inquired of Captain Dacres, "Commodore Hull's compliments, and wishes to know if you have struck your flag?" Captain Dacres, looking up and down, coolly and dryly remarked, "Well, I don't know; our mizzen-mast is gone, our main-mast is gone, and, upon the whole, you may say we *have* struck our flag." Read then asked Dacres if his crew needed the assistance of a surgeon or surgeon's mate. Dacres replied, "Well, I should suppose you had on board your own ship business enough for all your medical officers." Read answered, "Oh, no; we have only seven wounded, and they were dressed half an hour ago."[8]

The surprises had not ended for Dacres. As the British captain came up the side of the *Constitution*, Captain Hull stood ready to receive his prisoner. Hull, in his best manner, rendered a proper salute and said, "Sir, I am happy to see you." "Ugh, Damn you," Dacres replied, "I suppose you are!" Once aboard the *Constitution*, Dacres handed his sword to Hull, who asked instead for Dacres' three-cornered hat, thus fulfilling the wager.[9]

The next day, with the British crew (including some women), as prisoners of war aboard the *Constitution*, the *Guerrière's* battered hulk was set afire and soon exploded. Writing some time after the battle, Dacres stated,

> I feel it my duty to state that the conduct of Captain Hull and his officers to our men has been that of a brave enemy, the greatest care being taken to prevent our men losing the smallest trifle, and greatest attention being paid to the wounded.[10]

Though this victory was met throughout the United States by the greatest enthusiasm, rejoicing, and the lighting of candles in the windows of homes, it got the usual backhanded compliment from a Boston paper, "The brilliancy of this action, *however we may regret the occasion that has produced it*, will excite the liveliest emotions in every American bosom."[11]

Word of this victory was followed in a week by the report of another of lesser significance — the frigate *Essex*, 32, over the British sloop-of-war *Alert*, 20. Captained by David Porter (father of a greater Civil War naval officer), the *Essex* had, in the Barbary Wars, been the ship of Edward Preble, the mentor of many 1812 naval captains. But now, in this ship, was an 11-year-old cabin boy whose fame was far in the future — David G. Farragut.

News of still another naval encounter reached Henry Clay as he arrived in Washington in early November 1812. On October 18, the American sloop-of-war, *Wasp*, 18, bested the British sloop *Frolic*, 19, in a raging sea — the tail of an Atlantic hurricane. Using an American tactic to his advantage, the *Wasp's* captain, Jacob James, fired as the ship's side was rolling downward with the waves so that her shots went either onto the *Frolic's* deck or into the hull, while the British vessel fired as the ship's firing side rose on the waves, thus throwing her shells into the *Wasp's* rigging or missing altogether. The tactic was devastating in comparable loss of life in each of the British-American engagements with equal-sized opponents. In this battle, the British crew of 107 had 90 men killed or wounded to 17 of the Americans. Unfortunately, the British 74-gun *Poictiers*, a ship of the line, hove into sight within two hours of the previous action and recaptured both the *Wasp* and the *Frolic* from Jones' command.[12]

As a result of these naval victories, the commanders were given orders more agreeable to their passions.

You are to do your utmost to annoy the enemy, to afford protection to our commerce, pursuing that course which to your best judgment may under all circumstances appear the best calculated to enable you to accomplish these objects as far as may be in your power, returning into port as speedily as circumstances will permit consistently with the great object in view.[13]

But also with Henry Clay's arrival in Washington, the encouraging news of naval success was superseded by word of new army blunders and debacles in the northeast. Most of the details and controversy surrounding these latest disasters were unfolding in the local Washington papers to greet Congress. Even accounts of stirring adventure, brought to Boston by the victorious ships, could not entice enlistments into General Henry Dearborn's army. At last, he left Boston without troops and made his way to Albany. There, on August 9, he entered into an unauthorized truce with the British governor of Canada, Sir George Prevost.[14] This took effect just at the time when General Brock and much of his Niagara command went west to capture Detroit leaving Canadian Niagara relatively unprotected — a perfect prey. When President Madison learned of the truce, on August 13, he had to tell Dearborn the armistice was not acceptable and to renew offensive operations toward either end of Lake Ontario.

Dearborn wrote, on August 25, to inform the militia commander at Niagara, Major General Stephen Van Rensselaer, that the armistice was "no longer binding." That message reached the frontier on September 1. By this time, the British conqueror of Detroit was back at Fort George across the Niagara River from the Americans. Very little happened during the month of September as Van Rensselaer hoped for more troops from Pennsylvania, but got warnings of disaster from Dearborn and a suggestion to "make good a secure retreat as a last resort" if the troops didn't come in time.

On September 29, regular army Brig. Gen. Alexander Smyth arrived at Buffalo with several units to bring the total Niagara force to about 6,000 men. He immediately notified Van Rensselaer at Lewiston, halfway between Niagara Falls and Lake Ontario. Across the Niagara River from Lewiston, on the Canadian side, was Queenstown (sometimes spelled Queenston). Both of these cities were below high bluffs looking northward over flat land extending to Lake Ontario and cut by the river. Where the river met the lake, the American Fort Niagara faced the British Fort George.

Prior to Smyth's arrival, Van Rensselaer had developed a plan for a two-pronged attack. One would cross the river from Lewiston to take Queenstown, while a second would be by boat on the lake to come ashore behind Ft. George — after the Ft. George force left to give support at Queenstown. But he had to forgo this plan when Smyth proposed that Van Rensselaer cancel his long prepared plan and support the regulars in an improvised attack at Fort Erie across from Buffalo. Smyth also noted that a general court martial had become necessary to deal with a mutiny.

On October 5, Van Rensselaer asked for a conference with Smyth and his commanders at "the earliest day possible, consistent with the business of the court martial, and other indispensable duties."[15] The only reply Van Rensselaer got was a brief note on October 10, from a Smyth aide, that his general had not set a date.

Meanwhile, units under Smyth made a daring attack across the river to seize two British ships — one being the former American brig *Adams* (captured at Detroit in August and renamed *Detroit* by the British). When word of this adventure reached Van Rensselaer and his subordinates, he was pressed to attack and felt he must in order to save his own reputation. An attack against Queenstown was set for the night of October 10–11. He wrote Smyth asking him to march to his support.

For the purpose of the attack, Van Rensselaer ordered 13 boats capable of transporting 340 men. He enlisted "experienced boatmen" and put the lead boat under a Lieutenant Sims, judged to have the greatest skill. His skill seemed to be in deception. For no sooner did he take his boat beyond the point of debarkation on the Canadian side, than he disappeared "in a most extraordinary manner," according to the general's later testimony. But to add to the general's woes, Sims took all the oars for the other boats in his boat leaving the troops standing in a violent rain storm on the opposite bank. Smyth had finally agreed to cooperate and was marching his weary troops through the middle of the night and the same vicious storm — only to be informed that the operation was canceled, and he should return to Buffalo.

Two days later, Van Rensselaer tried again and this time succeeded in getting troops across to attack Queenstown. However, his plan was to send across militia. But at the embarkation point there was another foul-up as they found the way blocked by units of regulars that had come there from the Buffalo area and under the command of Col. Winfield Scott (who had left his spectator seat at the Burr trial, in 1807, to enlist in the army at the time of the *Chesapeake* affair). Van Rensselaer let the regulars — under his cousin, Col. Solomon Van Rensselaer — carry out the attack with new plans to send over the militia as reinforcements.

The attack went fairly well, with exceptions of another apparent defection and the six wounds suffered by Colonel Van Rensselaer. The Americans captured the heights above Queenstown and were near victory when General Brock (the conqueror of Detroit) arrived from the north with his reinforcements from Fort George. General Van Rensselaer, who had come across to take charge, returned to Lewiston to order the militia across in support. But he was met by near mutiny as none would cross the river, nor would boatmen cross to save the Americans still in battle. On the Canadian side, General Brock was killed, but his subordinates moved in on the Americans and took over 900 prisoners including Colonel Scott. Colonel Van Rensselaer was taken back to Lewiston before the surrender. Two days later, General Van Rensselaer resigned his command to Smyth who took over on October 24. Smyth was not to succeed where Van Rensselaer had failed.

Such was the status of military and naval affairs when the 2nd session of the 12th Congress met in Washington on November 2, 1812. Whereas Clay was in Kentucky when he learned of the Hull debacle at Detroit and expressed his disgust in letters written to Monroe and others, he was in Washington when he read of the Van Rensselaer–Smyth fiascos. Therefore, there is no written record available of his certain vocal condemnation of these latest episodes. In the capital, he had the opportunity of stating his views personally to Madison, Monroe, and anyone else he cared to include in his comments.

However, Clay's impressions probably coincided with Jefferson's views, as they had earlier. In the same letter in which the former president

had told Madison that "Hull will of course be shot for cowardice & treachery," he added,

> And will not Van Rensselear [sic] be broke for cowardice and incapacity? To advance such a body of men across a river without securing boats to bring them off in case of disaster, had cost 700 men: and to have taken no part himself in such action & against such a general would be nothing but cowardice.[16]

At least, now, Henry Clay had his duties as Speaker of the House of Representatives to draw his attention away from military stupidity. Two days after the session began, the House received President Madison's annual message in writing. It was read to the House.

Madison began it with a summary of the debacle at Detroit, and of the alliance between the Indians and the British, and followed with assurance that the defeat had aroused the patriotic ardor of that section of the nation. Next, he referred to the attack and defeat at Niagara. He took up the refusal of New England authorities to support the war. (Madison reinforced this discussion by submitting his recent correspondence with the governors of Massachusetts and Connecticut in which they firmly refused to support his call for troops. Two days before Madison's message, news reached Washington of the death of Connecticut Governor Roger Griswold.) And finally, his summary referred to the successes on the ocean.

Madison's message noted that word had been sent to Britain regarding American terms on which the war's "progress might be arrested" — repeal of Orders in Council, and "an immediate discharge of American seamen from British ships" and an end to impressment. Though the British had already satisfied the demand for the former, prior to a U.S. offer of an armistice, they had since refused to agree to a cessation of impressment. Documents sent Congress would also explain American reasons for rejection of the British-Canadian armistice proposed during September.

Madison's mention of continued good relations with Russia, despite their alliance with Britain, was later to be personally significant to Clay.

Among his recommendations, Madison called for an increase in the number of generals and a reorganization of the military system, both regular and militia. He vaguely suggested an enlargement of the navy. He stated that Congress should have the opportunity to act as

> they may think proper in regard to forfeitures attendant to imports of British goods in American vessels which returned to the U.S. from England following the repeal of Orders under erroneous impression that the non-importation act would immediately cease to operate.

This legislation was to be referred to as *Merchants Bonds* (so titled in the *Congressional Annals*), and would become a major piece of legislation occupying much of the House's time during the rest of the year.

Madison noted that revenues were sufficient for the expenses through the remainder of the year. And he said, "the spirit and strength of the nation are ... equal to the support of all its rights, and to carry it through its trials."[17]

As usual the pertinent parts of this message were assigned by Speaker Clay to the various House committees having jurisdiction to study and report on what measures were deemed appropriate to carry the recommendations into fruition.

Since little of significance transpired visibly in Congress during these early days of November 1812, the predominating political news was the national presidential election. By the time Congress convened, some states had already cast their votes, while in others the polling came as late as November 9. In any case, the campaign had been almost non-existent compared with others of later years. In fact, it was less a two-party contest than it was a selection between two men, or even a vote for or against the war.

Both the candidate selection and the electoral vote machinery were still evolving in 1812 through the various methods toward the system it was eventually to reach. In some states, where the parties were nearly balanced numerically, conventions were held to nominate candidates and to elect presidential electors. In other states, where one party had a substantial majority, a caucus of political leaders performed these functions. Only New Jersey and Pennsylvania chose their electors by popular vote.

In some degree, the 1812 presidential election was an intra-party fight between Madison and De Witt Clinton, a renegade Republican. The Federalists, failing to come up with a candidate of their own, had to sit out this election, or support one whose motives for office even they questioned. The Federalist plight was expressed by Timothy Pickering,

> I am far enough from desiring Clinton for President of the United States. I would infinitely prefer another Virginian — if Judge Marshall could be the man. But I would vote for any man in preference to Madison. I am disposed to believe that neither Jefferson nor Madison have dared resist the will of Napoleon; because I presume they stand committed to him, and dread an exposure. Both also, with their adherents, hate England, — the country of our forefathers, and the country to which we are indebted for all the institutions dear to freemen.[18]

But John Marshall would not consent to run, and most Federalists were not too anxious to see him out of the chief justice's chair. The fact was that the Federalists saw that their own strength was too weak to win with their own numbers. But united with dissident Republicans they might win.

Not long after the declaration of war, several Federalist leaders began private consultations aimed at tying their political fortunes of 1812 to Clinton, who was being represented as a peace candidate. Early in August, a meeting was arranged between Clinton and Federalist Rufus King, John Jay, and Gouverneur Morris at Morrisania, the New York home of Morris. Prior to the meeting, these and other Federalists had drafted a set of resolutions which was read to Clinton at the conference. Clinton approved the resolutions, but asked that a plan for a peace convention be delayed four or five weeks until events, as well as time, could enable his supporters to gain further adherents. He also advised that publicity be avoided.

In effect, the Federalists granted these requests to Clinton as plans went forward for the convention. But not without King's skepticism. He looked upon Clinton's leadership as secure only so long as he expressed the views of his followers, but that they would desert him as soon as their views differed. King also was aware that a formidable portion of the leadership of the New York Republicans opposed Clinton, and would not follow him. And finally, King felt the Federalists would only tarnish their character if they submitted to control by their former political opponents.[19]

Nevertheless, 70 delegates from 11 states formed the peace convention, which met in New York on September 15. King, writing a few days later, said he attended

> chiefly because I was unwilling that my absence should by any possibility be construed to mean, what is not true in respect to my personal views.... It was in the opinion of the meeting impracticable to elect a Federal President, and that it would be inexpedient to name a Federal candidate. 2nd that it should be recommended to the Federalists to co-operate in the election of a President, who would be likely to pursue a different course of adminis-tration from that of Mr. Madison.[20]

These resolutions passed easily. But on the third day, after his opposition to them failed to gain any support, King rose to say he "could feel no dislike to Mr. Clinton on any account other than that which arose from his political character & views," but he feared "if we succeeded in promot-ing his election, that we might place in the chair a Caesar Borgia instead of a James Madison."

King also objected to one of the resolutions

> because it did not speak out and name the person, whom every one had in view, and because there was no evidence exhibited that Mr. Clinton, with the aid of the federalists, can be elected, and, if elected, that he will pursue a better system than that of Mr. Madison.

In fact, by the end of October, still before the election, King was to write that he preferred the election of Madison.

King later noted in his papers that several letters from several states were presented to the conven-tion in which his name was given as one of the preferred candidates for president or vice presi-dent.[21]

While it appeared for a while on the third day that King's effort would prevent the convention from making a final determination, Harrison Gray Otis of Massachusetts rose with hat in hand as if ready to depart — as many others wanted to do.

> Soon he warmed with his subject, his hat fell from his hand, and he poured forth a strain of elo-quence that chained all present to their seats, and when at a late hour, the vote was taken, it was al-most unanimously resolved to support Clinton.[22]

The convention did not formally endorse Clin-ton. It was believed he could be dumped and a Federalist name substituted in the electoral college in the event his slate of electors won in Novem-ber — a very strange way to treat the vote of the people.

Shortly after this convention adjourned, but still before news of it could reach Virginia, that state's Federalists met at Staunton, in the western valley, and named Rufus King as their candidate for president. As a running mate, they selected William R. Davie of North Carolina. In Penn-sylvania, Federalists added their attorney general, Jared Ingersoll, as a running mate to the Clinton ticket. The confusion of Federalists backing a Re-publican who had difficulty rousing favor among members of his own Party resulted in his support-ers being termed Federalists in one locale and Clintonians in another.

Among the varied forms of selecting electors, some states chose them through a popular vote (five by a state-wide vote, four by districts). But in New Jersey, to circumvent such support by a Republican majority among the electorate, the Federalist majority in the legislature passed a late law giving it control of the electors which would put the state in the Clinton column. In other states to the north, the Clintonians derided the Congressional caucus system which had named Madison and Gerry, but still the legislators chose electors in nine of the 18 states.

The campaigning that ensued was rather lack-luster and was largely newspaper declarations by local groups championing one candidate or the other. Occasionally, a letter or statement by either Madison or Clinton would appear in one of the major eastern papers and be reprinted in the press elsewhere. Also, local supporters would organize political rallies. Typical of these was one described by British Minister Augustus Foster in his diary of a local contest earlier in the year.

> The two candidates are invited to a barbeque of either Party for the purpose of being heard. A hole is made in the ground and burning charcoal placed in it. Stakes are fastened at each end, and between them is placed at full length a pig or shoate, split up the belly, the spine bone just slit so as not to cut the skin. Thus which he is roasted, being continually basted in the inside.... The can-didates are expected to speak in public sometimes mounted on the stump of a tree and sometimes on a beer barrel. Then after eating, they dance (often all night).[23]

The voting results of late October and early November trickled in slowly throughout the month of November and it was not until the first week of December that the press could write, "There cannot now be any doubt of the re-election of Mr. Madison, by a large majority. The whole number of votes to be given is 218 of which Mr. Clinton will have 89."[24] The total vote was actually 217 with Madison receiving 128. Clinton's vote included all of New England (except Vermont), New York, New Jersey, and Delaware. (Old Federalist ex–President John Adams had been a Madison elector in Massachusetts.) Maryland's vote (by districts) was divided six for Madison and five for Clinton making only one vote effective. All to the south went for Madison. His victory hung on the 25 votes cast by Pennsylvania.

The Clintonians won the New York vote of the Republican controlled legislature through the shrewd management of newly elected state senator Martin Van Buren — a former Madison supporter and an advocate of the war.

The election would bring to the next House of Representatives a young Federalist lawyer from New Hampshire named Daniel Webster and would exclude from its ranks that veteran Republican legislator from Virginia known as John Randolph of Roanoke. In addition, Timothy Pickering and Clay were to meet again in Congress, but this time in the House rather than in the Senate where Clay's resolution of 1811 was approved to censure Pickering.

Though the results of this election would not bring Madison into his second term until March 4, 1813, and the new Congress would not begin until that same day in March, the 13th Congress would not actually convene for business until late May of 1813.

17

POLITICAL REACTION

While the second session of the 12th Congress had to wait several weeks for the election returns to come in to establish the make up of the 13th Congress, the House gradually took up legislative issues, mostly related to the war effort. One of the first measures was a resolution proposed, on November 10, by Richard M. Johnson, fresh from the fighting front in Ohio. He sought congressional authority for "an expedition of mounted volunteers against several Indian tribes hostile to the United States." The House agreed to it without debate.[1]

Late in November, those sections of the president's annual message, which Speaker Clay had sent to committees for study, began to come to the House in the form of bills. One of these dealt with army pay, and three others with matters related to the sea. On the 20th, the House, in Committee of the Whole, took up the army pay bill. On the second day of debate, Federalist Josiah Quincy of Massachusetts rose to tell his colleagues that he had intended to remain silent through this session because,

> Seven years' experience in the business of the House, has convinced me that from this side of the House all argument is hopeless; that whatever a majority has determined to do, it will do, in spite of any moral suggestion or any illustration made in this quarter.

Quincy was not to abide by his own declaration of silence.

In this particular effort, he was attacking a section in the bill which provided for enlistment of men as young as 18-years old. He said he would consider the subject "under three aspects — its absurdity — its inequality — its immorality." Quincy gave his three-pointed view and summed up saying,

> I hope what I am now about to say will not be construed into a threat.... But pass it [the section on recruitment], and if the Legislatures of the injured States do not come down upon your recruiting officers with the old laws against kidnapping and monstrosity, they are false to themselves, their posterity, and their country.[2]

That same day, Quincy spoke on another issue dealing with merchant bonds. His approach to the subject, rather than its substance, drew comments from John Harper in a letter to his friend, William Plumer.

> Mr. Quincy commenced the debate in a speech of about 40 minutes, in which the most indecent, abusive, ungentlemanly and threatening language was made use of, that I ever heard fall from a *gentleman*, in company of gentlemen — Nothing but his being in the minority, and being considered in some degree below contempt, induced the Speaker to suffer him to proceed in his philippic. But he was severely castigated — Williams, Fisk, Troup, Johnson, and others paid him in his own coin, and with use — He was called almost everything, but an American, an honest man, a gentleman, and a man of truth. He was told that nothing but the canopy under which he sat, protected him — even Randolph, who espoused his cause, abused him severely for his rash, inconsiderate and intemperate remarks. So much did he disgust his audience, that in the lobby, I heard his Reverend colleague, the *sage* Mr. Taggart say, that he could not approve of Mr. Quincy's speech. I am apprehensive that his speech will not be faithfully reported. Gales, the only *faithful* reporter was not present all the time.[3]

(Gales was editor of the *National Intelligencer*. Even in modern days, legislators often go to the reporter's office to have unsavory language expunged from their floor remarks so that they never appear in the record. And Quincy's "unprintable words" are not printed in the *Annals*.)

The renewal of debate on the army bill in January would bring on a severe clash between Clay and Quincy.

Of the sea issues, two, directly associated with the navy, were quickly shunted aside for later debate. One of these came to the floor, on November 25, in the form of a resolution to compensate Captain Hull of the *Constitution* and his crew for the loss of prize money they would have received had they towed the *Guerrière* into port rather than sinking that British warship. On this issue Secretary of the Navy Paul Hamilton recommended awarding them $100,000. But this legislation was returned to a committee, and did not come out again for debate until mid–January.

The second sea subject, on an increase in the size of the navy, was not debated until the middle of December. But it created some controversy arising from the committee's request for information from the Navy Department. And this, in turn, resulted in a couple of social affairs that interrupted debate on the third sea matter — Merchants' Bonds, concerning private shippers dealing in international trade.

Regarding enlarging the navy, the committee had requested the Navy Department to furnish them with information demonstrating the navy's needs in size and quantity for new ship construction. To satisfy the committee with the pertinent documents, Navy Secretary Hamilton prepared an analysis of the great value of 76-gun ships of the line (more often built and referred to as 74's) as opposed to 44-gun frigates. Actually this detailed statement was written by Capt. Charles Stewart of the *Constellation* (then lying off Greenleaf's point near the Washington navy yard). Stewart's report was endorsed by Capt. Isaac Hull and lately-promoted Capt. Charles Morris, both heroes of the *Constitution's* victory over the *Guerrière*, and both at this time in Washington on navy business. (Hull, in fact, had requested and been granted relief from command of the *Constitution* for family reasons, and had since been replaced by Capt. William Bainbridge at this time at sea in that frigate.)

Undoubtedly, the supporters of the naval increase had been skeptical of the bill's chances for several days, and it languished as the House considered the Merchants' Bonds. At some earlier date one of these backers, John C. Calhoun, returned home to Mrs. Bushby's boardinghouse and suggested an idea to his fellow boarder, Captain Stewart, "of putting Congress in a better humor with the Navy." (The "war mess," where Calhoun and Clay lived the previous session at Mrs. Dawson's No. 2, boardinghouse, was broken up among several boardinghouses this session.) Acting upon Calhoun's suggestion, Stewart organized a sumptuous all-day entertainment aboard the *Constellation* for Thursday, November 26.[4] By today's reckoning, that would have been Thanksgiving Day.

November 26, "a fine day," according to the *National Intelligencer*, the House did not meet and the Senate adjourned when no quorum was present. Instead, as the paper reported,

> Many hundreds of ladies and gentlemen, previously invited, amongst whom we recognized the President of the United States and his lady, all the Heads of Departments and their ladies, very many of the Members of Congress, the French Minister, etc. assembled on board the *Constellation* between ten and twelve o'clock. The day was spent in the utmost concord and hilarity, no accident intervened to damp the gaiety of the scene. An elegant cold collation of the choicest viands and liquors, prepared under the direction of Mr. Tomlinson, was served up to the numerous guests. The old and the young mingled in the sprightly dance, and pleasure beamed on every countenance. The presence of the brave Capts. Hull and Morris, our readers may be sure, did not lessen the gratifications of the day. The company began to separate towards evening and were relanded with great safety and regularity. When the President came on board and when he parted from the ship, in a boat under the direction of Capt. Hull, salutes were fired from the ship with great effect.[5]

The departure of the secretary of the navy was less auspicious. Because of *his habit*, "he needed assistance to get out of the vessel."[6]

The next day Hamilton's letter, and Stewart's accompanying analysis of one 74 being equal to three 44's, was presented to the House by the naval committee. Still, no further action was taken on it for nearly three weeks.

While the subject of the navy's size was laid aside temporarily, the Merchants' Bonds issue was again taken up briefly on Wednesday, December 2 (the day the presidential electors met and voted in their separate states). But it was postponed one day when Langdon Cheves, chairman of the Ways and Means Committee, which had reported the bill, notified the House he could not support the measure he had been called upon to introduce.

Still before debate on this issue began in the House on December 3, Secretary of State James Monroe summoned Senate President Pro-tem William Crawford and House Speaker Henry Clay to meet with him "early in the morning, before 10 ... on an interesting subject." Monroe said he wished to avoid attention and preferred

> meeting you rather here [most likely at Monroe's home] than at the office, or at your lodgings. Mr. Eustis (I mention it in confidence) sent his resignation to the President today, & it is not improbable that the place will be offered to me. I wish to converse with you both on all the circumstances connected with this event, not as it may relate to me, but the public also. This is the time when the arrangements that are to insure success to the republican party & to free government for our country, are to be made, or which will lay the foundation of their overthrow.[7]

Throughout the summer and fall of 1812 such leaders as Clay, Gallatin, Crawford, and Monroe were becoming apprehensive over the lack of confidence and of the ineptness exhibited by Secretary of War Eustis. It may be recalled that Clay, writing to Monroe in August, spoke of Eustis "in whom already there unfortunately exists no sort of confidence."

Gallatin later wrote to Jefferson concerning Eustis, "His incapacity and the total want of confidence in him were felt through every ramification of the public service."[8]

Crawford included Secretary of the Navy Paul Hamilton in a warning written to Monroe in September, that if Madison's feelings forbade the dismissal of

> unfaithful and incompetent officers, he must be content with defeat and disgrace in all his efforts during the war. So far as he may suffer from this cause he deserves no commiseration, but his accountability to the nation will be great indeed.[9]

Monroe's own feeling toward the secretaries of those two cabinet departments was well concealed, except that in writing Jefferson some time later, he noted that "a change in both was indispensable."[10]

With these views much in agreement, Monroe conferred with the two congressional leaders, and certainly sought their advice on the place he

should take in the new cabinet arrangement. For some weeks the expectation of some urgent correction in the War Department had induced Monroe to offer his services to the president either as a general officer in the field, or as head of the department or both simultaneously. His correspondence with Jefferson shows his feelings on these points. Having frequently discussed with the president the possibility of commanding troops, Monroe told Jefferson, "I would prefer it to the Department of War" ... where ... "a man might form a plan of a campaign and write judicious letters on military operations; but still these were nothing but essays. Everything would depend on the execution. I thought that with the army I should have better control over operations and events."[11]

In addition, earlier discussions between Madison and Monroe gave rise to the opinion that Jefferson might be brought into the cabinet as secretary of state as Monroe went to the War Department. But Monroe felt he would have to leave the cabinet if Jefferson came in, since it would put three Virginians into five cabinet offices.[12]

And Jefferson, learning of this, scotched the idea, writing,

> I am past service. The hand of age is upon me. The decay of bodily faculties apprizes me that those of the mind cannot be unimpaired, had I not still better proofs. Every year counts by increased debility, and departing faculties keep the score. Last year it was the sight, this it is the hearing, the next something else will be going, until all is gone.[13]

Jefferson was only 69 years old. He would live another 14 years, during which time he had a brilliant correspondence with a former political colleague and sometimes adversary, former President John Adams.

Also, Monroe agreed that Gallatin had a fair right to claim State if Monroe went to War. But he felt Gallatin was needed at Treasury.[14]

In the final analysis Madison decided it was more expedient to keep Monroe in Washington. On the question of giving Monroe a military commission as well as the cabinet seat, the secretary of state questioned the Constitutionality of combining the two posts. Yet strangely, he was, by the end of the year, to agree to sit in two cabinet seats simultaneously, adding the Department of

War *pro-tempore* to his permanent job as secretary of state. Though Eustis was officially secretary of war until December 31, 1812, Monroe responded on December 23, to a request from the Military Committee of the Senate with lengthy "Explanatory Observations" and "Notes on Idea of a Plan of Campaign for the Year 1813." His report was from "The War Department."[15]

There is no record of Clay's views on this arrangement, but he undoubtedly gave his full support to Monroe as the strongest personality in the president's cabinet, particularly in these affairs. And it is safe to guess that Clay preferred Monroe's continuing in a cabinet post at the center of power in Washington as opposed to a military office in the field.

Later in the day of Monroe's conference over Eustis' resignation, the House began debate in Committee of the Whole House on the issue of the Merchants' Bonds. This problem grew out of a backlog of orders for British goods waiting in England for the repeal of the American non-importation act of March 2, 1811. This act had been imposed as a pressure to force England to repeal the Orders in Council. When these Orders were revoked on June 23, 1812, it was assumed by merchants that the non-importation act would thereby be withdrawn and the goods, now valued at more than $420 million could be shipped to the United States fearing no penalty. To their astonishment on arrival in the United States, the privateers found that the Act was not withdrawn because of the Declaration of War, which had preceded the revocation of the Orders by five days. Not only had the vessels and cargoes become liable to confiscation by the United States government, but they were also fair game for capture by public and private armed ships of both warring countries. Both events occurred — and all were seized and forfeited on entering U.S. ports.

Under the current law, half of the forfeiture was to go to customs officials, while the other half went to the U.S. Treasury where its secretary had the power to remit in whole or in part. Treasury Secretary Albert Gallatin dearly wanted to keep in his department's hands as much revenue as possible to ward off the threat of bankruptcy. But before he acted, several courts interfered to order customs to release the cargoes, some of which were perishable articles, on the receipt of bonds equal to their appraised value. The courts stated that the importations had been made in good faith and were now mainly American goods. This action forced the president's hand and all cargoes were released on the same bond arrangement. The net to the Treasury was $5 million in duty (up to 25 percent in value of the cargoes) plus $418 million in Merchants' Bonds — which were now in dispute.

Throughout the opening days of this session of Congress, petitions were introduced from merchants appealing for remittance of their bonds. But it seemed that the Ways and Means Committee leaned more on the report from Treasury Secretary Gallatin for guidance than from their constituents. In reporting the situation to Congress, Gallatin said,

> Considering the magnitude and unforeseen nature of the case, it was thought proper not to exercise that authority until Congress had taken the subject into consideration, and prescribed, if they thought proper, the course to be pursued.

Furthermore, Gallatin recognized that the importers would sell the goods with extraordinarily high war profit when, by the law, he said they "had no right to a profit at all." He, therefore, suggested remitting that half of the forfeitures that would go to the collectors, and exacting for the Treasury only an equivalent to cover unexpected war profits.

It was in response to Gallatin's report to the House Ways and Means Committee that the committee then reported to the full House on November 25, that they believed "it is inexpedient to legislate upon the subject" and that it should be referred back to the secretary of the treasury. On December 2, the committee's chairman, Langdon Cheves, rose in the House to say he disagreed with the report which the committee had directed him to make to the House, and stated that its support would devolve upon other committee members.

This was only the beginning of some strange twists of political alignment during this session of Congress all growing out of the non-importation act as a source of revenue, a pressure to force repeal of the foreign edicts, and a protection for American manufacturers.

First to pick up the gauntlet in behalf of the Ways and Means Committee was Richard M. Johnson, the warrior from Kentucky. On the afternoon of the resignation of Secretary of War Eustis, Johnson told the House that the committee had decided that Congress should not interpose on the matter since the secretary had the power to handle the problem, and indeed his letter to the Congress represented a fair and equitable manner of resolving it.[16]

By normal procedure each committee member had the right to speak before outsiders. And it was now Cheves turn to rebut Johnson. But he hesitated, and Samuel Mitchell of New York rose to state the case for his constituent merchants. In his brief remarks he said he believed the president, in his annual message, meant Congress to debate and render a view on the issue. He then offered a resolution to remit forfeiture for those goods shipped since June 23, the date of the repeal of the British Orders in Council.[17]

The next morning, as the debate was to proceed, Cheves contended that another committee member, Jonathan Roberts of Pennsylvania, should have the floor. Roberts, a freshman congressman, felt himself too inexperienced to take such a prominent position in the debate. William Bibb of Georgia, recognizing Roberts' reluctance, put a hand in his pocket and pulled out a silver dollar. He challenged Cheves with a "heads or tails" decision. Cheves lost and had to speak. Roberts, writing of the episode and speech afterward, said of Cheves, "In this effort, he was not usually happy. It seemed to me, he wanted the sense of a strong conviction that he was right."[18]

Cheves told the House he believed no subject "more extraordinary in its nature, and more important in its consequences," had ever been presented for consideration by Congress. He was concerned about letting one man, the secretary of the treasury, decide on his own the disposition of funds which, he said, amounted to at least $40 million. He then stated his view for full remittance of the bonds through congressional legislation. His stand was intensified by the character of his constituency — the merchants of Charleston, South Carolina, and the citizens of the seacoasts who, he said, "were distressed because they would have to pay doubly for the goods." Not only had he long opposed the restrictive commercial acts, but also he was against any form of internal taxation to raise revenue for the treasury. He wanted the government to support itself by admitting British goods under heavy import duties! In this particular case, he said the importers had already provided the treasury with $5 million in revenue and that their commercial profits would provide a source of loans to aid the treasury further. On this, he said, "We must not disgust the moneyed interest of the country...." The government "must rely on its credit for a great portion of the ways and means of carrying on a war.... The great source from which you must draw is the commercial wealth of the country."[19]

Of course, Cheves said nothing about the fact that if the bonds were forfeited to the treasury, the department would have a revenue on which they would not need to pay an interest as they would with a loan. Though Cheves did not hesitate to draw the attention of his colleagues to their preference last session to waiting until after war was a fact in order to levy taxes, he said nothing about the greater difficulty now with reports of military disasters screaming from the pages of the press.

"How are the exigencies of the government for the next year to be supplied?" Cheves asked as early as December 4.

> Is the deficiency to be derived from [internal] taxes? No! I will tell gentlemen who are opposed to them for their comfort, that there will be no taxes imposed for the next year. It was said last session that you would have time to lay them for this session, but I then said it was a mistake. You now find this to be a fact. By your indecision then, when the country was convinced they were necessary, you have set the minds of the people against taxes; but were it otherwise, you have not time now to lay them for next year.[20]

Cheves did not use the whole of the time for debate on December 4, and a reluctant Roberts had to take the floor after all. Prior to speaking, Joseph Gales, one of the editors of the *National Intelligencer*, asked Roberts if he must report his speech. Roberts felt timid and said, "No." But Gales told the congressman he would "take large notes" and it could be written out later. After speaking in support of the committee's report for about an hour, not to his own satisfaction, he was asked by his 71-year-old Pennsylvania colleague, John Smilie, if adjournment should be moved. Despite his poor showing, Roberts was unsure he could do even this well another day. He hesitated too long, and Smilie made the motion and the

House adjourned. It was the last motion Smilie ever made, as he never again appeared in the chamber, and died on December 30.

Roberts described his own next several hours.

> I went to dinner with my mind in high fermentation in my subject. I wrote out my speech from Gales' notes. At night I went to bed, but soon found I could not sleep. I rose & wrote letters, & digested my future speech. Every faculty seemed brightened. I got a clear view of my subject, & was full of it, when the House met. The morning's business had been disposed of by half past eleven; earlier than was usual by half an hour. Cheves enquired if I was ready to proceed. I answered yes. Then said he, I will call the question. He did so, & I rose & spoke the whole day. I felt no embarrassment, I wanted neither words, nor arguments. I was heard with respectful patience, by all parts of the House.

Roberts went on to express the pleasure he had from the compliments he received on his presentation. Though his speech added little to the outcome over the issue, Gales later told him, with respect to Cheves, "He had never heard a man so cut up as he was by me," Roberts wrote. Cheves himself was in distress over being lampooned and censured by his papers at home as a result of Roberts' effort.[21]

On the following legislative day, Monday, December 7, William Richardson of Massachusetts, spoke in behalf of remitting the forfeiture and concluded his remarks by saying that if gentlemen think

> we ought to enforce the payment of these bonds, because we have the power to do it, I have only to beg them to remember, that it is excellent to have a giant's strength, but it is tyrannous to use it like a giant."[22]

With the House still in Committee of the Whole, at the conclusion of Richardson's remarks, Henry Clay rose (or rather descended from the Speaker's Chair), to express his views on the subject. In reference to Cheves' attack on the restrictive system, Clay reminded the House that

> the principle of these restrictive measures ... is to create such pressure on the foreign nation as would compel it to revoke its anti-neutral edicts.... Yet we are called upon to abandon this system! We wanted firmness. We are deficient in the virtues of patience and perseverance.

Clay said he viewed the restrictive system as a powerful auxiliary of the war and he cited several areas in which it had gone badly and where "Opposition, transcending all legitimate bounds, may be carried to the very confines, themselves, of treason." But despite the inglorious surrenders and a degenerate spirit, "if you cling to the restrictive system, it is incessantly working in your favor." He believed, "if persisted in, the restrictive system, aiding the war, would break down the present [British] ministry, and lead to a consequent honorable peace."

Clay replied to Cheves' concern that the system was the cause for suffering in coastal cities saying rather that the cause of the disease "flowed from anti-neutral edicts," and, in Cheves' home state,

> from cutting off the market for the staple commodity of South Carolina. If it be true, as he has already admitted it was, that an export trade could not exist without an import trade, the converse of the proposition was no less undeniable. Suppose then the non-importation law not to have existed, how would Charleston or South Carolina have been able to sustain a trade in importation only? Cut off as she has been from a market for her cotton where would she have found the means to pay for foreign articles?

But Clay found the case for the cities to be otherwise than suffering. "Where are to be found your magnificent palaces — your splendid equipages — your sumptuous villas — all the luxury of wealth? In these same pining, desolated cities, and their vicinities."

Clay doubted that this was the time for abandoning the system. "This certainly was the period best calculated to test its value," he said. But he was quite right and quite wrong as he continued, "Perhaps, at this moment, the fate of the North of Europe is decided, and the French emperor may be dictating the law from Moscow." While the fate was truly being decided, Napoleon was not even in Moscow. The last news Clay had seen was a report of horrible battles with 12,000 to 13,000 Russians killed and the French only 25 leagues from Moscow on September 12. Though the emperor did enter Moscow three days later, he remained only until October 23 when he began his disastrous retreat. By the time Clay was speaking, Napoleon had abandoned his freezing army and was riding post-haste to the warmth of the French capital.

But to continue with Clay's remarks, he turned to the meat of his remarks — the claims of the petitioners for relief. He said he was embarrassed by the decisions to reconcile "an act of liberality to individuals with the public interest." He had no doubt that the British revocation of the Orders in Council required of the president a proclamation ending the Non-Importation Act — if the two countries had remained at peace.

Specifically, Clay thought that "in all cases where the departure of the vessels from British ports was prior to a knowledge there of the war, relief ought to be afforded." He noted that it appeared that such information was received on August 1. He acknowledged a still stronger class of cases

> which consists of purchases prior to the 2nd of February, 1811. They bought when the trade was un-restricted, and of course violated neither the prohibitory provisions of the law, nor the policy of the government. Those who shipped goods after August 1, knew they were acting contrary to law.... The state of war itself rendered the trade unlawful. It was vain to say they did not intend to violate the law. It was a palpable, wilful, undisguised violation. Remit the forfeitures in their case, and your law is virtually repealed.... The law ought to be enforced or not.

In this situation he thought a compromise dangerous and undignified. Clay told his colleagues he was for remission in the specified cases, where remission appeared to him to be due. He was for an enforcement of the law in all other cases.

Speaker Clay concluded his discussion by offering a resolution remitting forfeitures and penalties of those citizens who purchased British goods prior to February 2, 1811, and who shipped goods between June 23 and August 1, 1812 (upon payment of legal costs). "The law ought to be enforced in all other cases," he said.[23]

Clay was followed that same day by Alexander McKim of Maryland and the following day (December 8) by William Widgery of Massachusetts. In short speeches favoring the merchants, neither added much to the debate except that Widgery took the opportunity to twist Clay's comments to present him in an unfavorable light, or at least describe his means of travel. In reference to Clay's view of rich furniture and costly equipages in the so-called "distressed seaports" of South Carolina, Widgery said,

> I thought the honorable Speaker had forgotten himself, for if that was to be the criterion by which to squeeze money from the citizens, the Speaker would be squeezed very hard, for I know of no man who rolls on the wheels of luxury in more magnificent style than does the honorable Speaker.[24]

Widgery was followed on the 8th by John C. Calhoun of South Carolina. He joined Cheves in rejecting the report of the Ways and Means Committee. Calhoun objected to Gallatin's suggestion that the merchants could be taxed for making an "extra profit," saying that he had power under an act of 1797 "to mitigate or remit," but not to levy. "Is the object profit, or the execution of the laws?" He did not believe that the government had a right to the extra profit.

> If our merchants are innocent, they are welcome to their good fortune; if guilty, I scorn to participate in its profit. I will never consent to make our penal code the basis of our ways and means; or to establish a partnership between the Treasury and the violators of the non-importation law.

Calhoun went on to dispute Clay's attempt to favor two classes of merchants — purchasers before February 2, 1811, and shippers before August 1, 1812. Though he preferred "to condemn or acquit the whole," he said, "I am ready to acknowledge, that an act of grace will weaken the non-importation law; but that is less evil than the alienation of the whole mercantile class."

Calhoun also joined his fellow South Carolinian, Cheves, in opposition to the restrictive system in words that could be recalled from a different viewpoint at the time of his death in 1850.

> The non-importation, as a redress of wrongs, is radically defective. You may meet commercial restrictions with commercial restrictions; but you cannot safely confront premeditated insult and injury with commercial restrictions alone.... It sinks the nation in its own estimation; it counts for nothing what is ultimately connected with our best hopes — the union of these states. Our Union cannot safely stand on the cold calculation of interest alone. It is too weak to withstand political convulsions. We cannot without hazard neglect that which makes man love to be a member of an extensive community — the love of greatness — the consciousness of strength. So long as an American is a proud name, we are safe; but that day we are ashamed of it, the Union is more than half destroyed.[25]

As Calhoun spoke, news was flashing through the capital city, through means of an extra printed by the *National Intelligencer*, which was to intensify the pride of America. President Madison received dispatches, late in the afternoon, from Commodore Stephen Decatur presently sailing off New London, Connecticut, that his frigate, the 44-gun *United States* (carrying 54 guns), had captured the 38-gun frigate *Macedonian* (carrying 49 guns)[26] in a battle fought October 25. The British ship, only a little more than two years old, was reported to be one of the fastest ships of His Majesty's navy. Decatur was already a hero of the Barbary Wars, in which he had destroyed the captured *Philadelphia* in Tripoli harbor. He later sat on the court martial of Commodore Barron of the *Chesapeake*. Now he was one of the navy's youngest captains, but one of the most admired and respected.

Sighting each other at dawn, off Madeira Islands, the two vessels closed to cannon range by 9 A.M. After a half hour of receiving damaging round shot, Capt. John S. Carden of the *Macedonian* turned his ship to close the range hoping to board. But Decatur's crew was well trained and disciplined in accurate and rapid gunnery. They poured devastating broadsides into the enemy's hull and rigging as their captain skillfully outmaneuvered the more experienced Britisher. After an hour's fight and more than 100 rounds of roundshot on the *Macedonian's* hull, and with masts shot down, Carden, who described his ship, then, as "a perfect wreck and unmanageable log," hauled down his colors. Only moments earlier, Carden had thought the flames from the rapid firing of the American guns meant the American ship was afire. Carden thought he had won a victory. But, in fact, Decatur had pulled away to get into a raking position.

With the battle concluded, the ships closed again and Captain Carden boarded the *United States* as a prisoner of war. Handing Decatur his sword, Carden was very dejected and observed that he was a ruined man; that all his hopes of honor and fortune were blasted. When Decatur inquired as to the reason, Carden replied, "This is the first instance of one of His Royal Majesty's ships striking to a vessel of similar grade and my mortification is insupportable." It was then that Decatur informed his "guest" (as Decatur truly treated his prisoner as a guest), that the *Guerrière* had previously struck her colors to the *Constitution*. Carden's mood changed abruptly and he exclaimed, "Then I am safe."[27]

Captain Dacres, who had surrendered the *Guerrière* truly did suffer for his defeat. He was exchanged to Halifax where, it was reported, following insults by his fellow officers, he quarreled with five and fought two, killing one in a duel. He was arrested and sent home.

The *Macedonian*, as a prize of war, was sailed into New York while the *United States* went to New London, Connecticut, from where word of the battle was sent to Washington.

It so happened that as word of this third major naval victory reached Washington, a ball had previously been arranged for that evening at Tomlinson's Hotel to reciprocate the entertainment given earlier in the month on board the *Constellation*. While the newspaper of the day reported that it was in compliment to Captain Stewart of the *Constellation*, Edward Coles (private secretary to President Madison), wrote years later, that it was tendered particularly to the heroes of the *Constitution* (Captains Isaac Hull and Charles Morris, both then in Washington on business), in recognition of their victory over the *Guerrière*, and only secondarily to Stewart.

As the entertainment got underway, the city was illuminated brilliantly with candles in most windows of the homes. Guns were fired as a salute. Then as the *National Intelligencer* described it,

A large & very respectable company assembled — The scene was graced by the presence of nearly all the beauty and fashion of our city. All was joy and gaiety, such as could scarcely admit of augmentation. And yet it was destined to be increased. About 9 o'clock a rumor spread through the assembly, that Lieut. Hamilton [actually Midshipman Archibald Hamilton], the son of the Secretary of the Navy, had reached the house, the bearer of the colours of the *Macedonian* & dispatches from Com. Decatur. The gentlemen crowded down to meet him. He was received with loud cheers, and escorted to the festive hall, where awaited him the embraces of a fond father, mother, sisters! It was a scene easier felt than described. The room in which the company had assembled had been previously decorated with the trophies of naval victory — the colours of the *Guerrière* and the *Alert*, displayed on the walls, roused the proud feelings of patriotism, and had revived in every mind the recollection of the bravery which won them. The flag of the *Macedonian* alone was waiting to complete the group. It was produced and borne into the hall by Capts. Hull and Stewart and others of our brave seamen, amid the loud exclamations of the company, and greeted with national music from the band. The amusements of the evening, we need scarcely add, were suspended from the time Mr. Hamilton's arrival was announced, until the fervor of the moment had in some degree subsided.[28]

While the dancers and other guests celebrated this third major naval victory (though its glories did not rub off on Secretary Hamilton or any others of the administration) the seeds of controversy were sown. One such grew out of the parading of the *Macedonian*'s flag. In part, this episode was described in 1845 by a congressman of that period, Lemuel Sawyer of North Carolina. He boarded at Tomlinson's Hotel on Capitol Hill where the ball was held. He wrote that he had been ill and had retired early, but was kept awake by "the music, and the regular vibration of the floor to the motion of the dance.... I considered as I was thus condemned to suffer the evil of the ball, I might as well compensate myself by its gratification." He dressed and went down to join in the merriment. He noted that young Hamilton arrived about 11 P.M. The managers of the ball arranged for a grandiose entrance. "An opening was left through the crowd of spectators, from the door to the back part of the room," Sawyer wrote.

> Secretary Hamilton and his family were placed at the bottom of the passage, and in front of the door, while the President and his lady, with members of the cabinet were arranged on each side. A breathless silence prevailed. The ladies stood upon the back seats, between the columns that supported the ceiling, the whole length of the room, gazing with intense interest at the door.

When at last the procession entered, Lieut. Hamilton preceded the flag, which was borne by four captains, and went forward to embrace his mother and sisters, shake the hands of his father. "Then," Sawyer continued in his account,

> The flag was paraded and marched around the room to the tune of Hail Columbia — after which it was brought before Mrs. Madison and laid at her feet, but she did not tread on it, as some of the opposition papers alleged.[29]

Writing of the event on December 21, 1812, Federalist Congressman Samuel Taggart of Massachusetts, noting that the flag was laid at Mrs. Madison's feet, said,

> Report says, but for the correctness of which I do not vouch as I go to none of these entertainments, that she set her feet on the colours to show contempt. An Englishman in the city hearing this report basely observed that Charlotte, meaning the Queen of Great Britain, would not have done so with American colours.[30]

It should be noted that Taggart's account was based on hearsay.

To add another viewpoint to this controversy, Edward Coles, responding to the 1845 writings, said the flag

> was not spread on the floor, except the corner of the flag bourne by Capt. Stewart which fell at the feet of a lady — whether by accident or design, I know not, but I recollect it gave rise to comments both in conversation and in the newspapers.

Coles also wrote at this time, "I am very certain [Madison] did not attend the ball."[31]

Another controversy developed over a statement made at the celebration by Navy Secretary Paul Hamilton. Of the secretary, Taggart wrote on the night of the ball, his

> talents have never been estimated above mediocrity. He is much of a gentleman, very agreeable in private life especially at certain times of day, but a man whatever may be his other qualifications who rarely spends a day without being in a state of approaching intoxication, if not absolutely intoxicated, cannot be considered as one of the most fit persons for a high responsible office.[32]

Hamilton was "inebriated" at this ball as well as at the entertainment aboard the *Constellation*.

The controversy over Secretary Hamilton's part in the use of ships at the outbreak of war also came to a head in the 1845 publications. At this same time Charles Jared Ingersoll's *History of the War of 1812* was published. Captain Stewart contradicted several statements in Ingersoll's book in the letter consuming four columns as published in the *New York Courier and Enquirer* on October 18, 1845. (This is the letter answered a few days later by ex–Congressman Sawyer.)

Contrary to Coles' statement that the president did not attend the ball, Captain Stewart wrote,

The President permitted the Secretary to read aloud the despatches of Decatur, [Coles said they were not read], and then made the remark to the assembled company.... "It is to Commodores Bainbridge and Stewart that we owe these victories. It was at their instance and strong solicitation that the ships were permitted to go to sea and cruise."

Stewart went on to tell a story that, on June 19, 1812, he had left Philadelphia for Washington in the stage and had met Bainbridge en route. He had supposed Bainbridge was at his command at the Charlestown or Boston navy yard. In Baltimore, Stewart said, they learned, for the first time, of the declaration of war by Congress on the previous day. On their arrival in Washington, on the 21st, Stewart relates, they went to the Navy Department where the chief clerk, Charles W. Goldsborough, showed them a paper. On reading it, Bainbridge observed, "This blasts all hopes of the navy." Stewart went on to describe the meeting.

Bainbridge's manner, when excited, was remarkable, and on this occasion as on all occasions when his indignation was aroused, with a vehemence which impeded his utterance, he exclaimed,— 'Unto, unto,— you will ruin the navy if such be its destiny.

This paper contained the orders which had just been drawn for *Commodore Rogers* (sic) *not to leave the waters of New York with his naval force.*

Stewart's story states that he and Bainbridge then conferred with Secretary Hamilton who told them that, at Gallatin's suggestion, the president had ordered the ships to lay up in New York harbor and that their guns were to be taken ashore for defense of the city. They appealed to Hamilton to seek a change in the order and were granted an interview with the president. Madison listened to their argument that the small American navy could give a good account of itself when in equal battle. Madison appeared to them to be convinced that they could provide victories and said he would assemble the cabinet that evening. But later that same evening, waiting at Hamilton's house for a change in orders, the naval officers were informed by the secretary that the orders stood, "Mr. Monroe, being the only member of the Cabinet, on this occasion, who advocated the ships being sent to sea."

The two naval officers, according to Stewart's account, debated what should be done, Bainbridge did not want to give up and proposed a letter to Madison, since he had appeared favorable to their view during the morning. They completed a draft by 3 A.M. and retired. But Bainbridge arose and completed the copy before breakfast. They both felt the letter put their naval careers on the line. They gave the letter to Hamilton for transmission to the president. Hamilton told them certain passages were objectionable and dictatorial and advised toning down. They refused and later went on with their regular duties. Meanwhile, Hamilton did present the letter at a cabinet meeting and their proposals for sending the ships to sea were adopted.[33]

While these accounts can basically be considered to be true, the timing and other parts appear in error. In February 1812, Bainbridge arrived in Boston from commercial business abroad. He went directly to Washington where he stayed a few weeks prior to receiving command of the navy yard at Charlestown, across the river from Boston. A dispatch of his to Secretary Hamilton from Charlestown and dated June 23, 1812, states, "This day mail having brought to us there the information of a declaration of war against Great Britain,"— etc. This clearly shows that he did not meet Stewart in Baltimore on June 19th, learn of the declaration of war that day, and then continue to Washington with Stewart. It is fair to assume, however, that the two captains did meet and had the conference described by Stewart — but that it took place in the time frame of Bainbridge's earlier stay in Washington around February or March.

Stewart's article went on to refer to the discussion of Hamilton's pre-war suggestion of keeping ships in port and of its negative response. It was followed by a description of Commodore Rodgers' preparation to leave port within 10 minutes of learning of the declaration of war (all described herein at the beginning of chapter 16). Stewart then noted that on June 22 he was given command of the *Argus* and was sent to sea.

Therefore, Stewart's charge that Gallatin convinced the cabinet to hold the ships in port appears erroneous. In 1845, published correspondence between Gallatin and Edward Coles, Gallatin wrote that he had no recollection of any of the facts stated by Stewart and that such a cabinet decision would have been unusual. The only cabinet discussion relating to military/naval memos that he recalled related solely to affairs at Detroit. In a lengthy letter, Gallatin refuted Stewart on most points and expressed astonishment that under these circumstances two naval officers could wrest a different decision from the president. But one statement not refuted was when Stewart said, "That Mr. Monroe was the only member [of the cabinet] who advocated their [the ships] being sent to sea." Nevertheless, a year after the war began, Monroe wrote Jefferson,

> At the commencement of the war I was decidedly of your opinion, that the best disposition which could be made of our little navy, would be to keep it in a body in a safe port, from which it might sally only, on some important occasion, to render essential service.[34]

While the city continued its celebration of the 9th of December, Henry Clay returned to the less exciting roll of presiding over the continuing debate on the Merchants' Bonds. The issue was to hang over the House for another two weeks and Clay was to take a small part in the deliberations, again in Committee of the Whole House. On the 9th, William Bibb of Georgia, member of the Ways and Means Committee, supported its report for the House to take no action, William Lowndes of South Carolina wanted the House to act, and Silas Stow of New York called for remission of the Bonds. The next day Felix Grundy of Tennessee opposed remission and Langdon Cheves introduced a resolution for "unconditional" remission. It was voted down.

Clay followed with another resolution. He proposed that relief (upon payment of legal costs) should be granted to those merchants who purchased goods prior to February 2, 1811, and those who shipped between June 23 and August 1, 1812. This, too, was voted down. After this the Committee of the Whole House reported that they could not agree on legislation. This was debated further in the following week when Josiah Quincy of Massachusetts charged the treasury with attempting to obtain revenue through the forfeiture of the bonds and sniped, "I think a highway robbery a little higher in point of courage, and a little less in point of iniquity."[35]

As the House could make no headway on the measure, they waited for the Senate's version on the subject. It called for remission of the forfeitures on goods shipped between June 23 and September 15, 1812, provided they had not been purchased after war became known in Great Britain. In the debate on this version, Clay tried again and failed to get his December 11th resolution passed. On December 23, the House got rid of the subject, passing the Senate bill 64–61. The old war mess of the previous session split down the middle. They had not only separated physically, but also politically.

That same day, the House also voted 70–56 to increase the size of the navy. Two days earlier Clay had taken the floor briefly to state that he favored the increase, but was opposed to the building of 74-gun ships. When an amendment to prohibit their construction was rejected, Clay proposed an amendment expediting construction. It was accepted.[36] He wrote a week later that he was satisfied the 74's were retained in the measure.[37]

Before the day was over, Clay was already shifting his concerns and vision to matters relating to the army and expressed his opinion in a letter to James Monroe. Referring to Richard M. Johnson's resolution, passed by the House at the beginning of this session of Congress, Clay told Monroe he favored the reinforcement of General Harrison's troops by a recruitment of new volunteers or militia. Clay pointed out that the present term of Kentucky and Ohio detachments would end by February 20, and those from Pennsylvania and Virginia about 20 days later. If Harrison was not reinforced, his expedition to recover Detroit would have to be abandoned or, if he possessed that city by that time, it would have to be given up.

Clay recommended raising "two mounted regiments not to exceed 1,200 men." If not immediately needed on an advance toward Detroit, they could be used to

> pass over to Chicago, scour the Country thereabouts, proceed from thence to the St. Joseph's, break up the settlements there and advance from thence to Detroit or to Harrison's Headquarters. I think it very possible that the party might surprize [sic] Detroit and take it by a coup de main, from the St. Josephs.[38]

It was now logical that Clay would be directing these views to Monroe, who was at this date acting as secretary of war. (Comptroller Richard Rush was acting as secretary of state.) Though Monroe had already expressed his repugnance at keeping the war job, Rep. John Harper thought Monroe might yet consent to retain the office. On the other hand, Harper wrote his friend, ex–Senator William Plumer (now Governor of New Hampshire), "It is thought that Mr. Hamilton *cannot* retain the office of Secretary of the Navy much longer." A month earlier he had written Plumer,

> The complaints against Doctor Eustis, want of energy and decision, and for bringing forward the many federalists for officers — The complaints against Mr. Hamilton are, a *want* of energy and capacity, and the possession of a confirmed habit of intemperance.[39]

Still, President Madison made no move to remove Hamilton. On the evening that the naval legislation cleared the House, an entertainment was held at the White House, possibly attended by the Clays and described by Federalist clergyman from Massachusetts, the Rev. Dr. John Pierce:

> In the evening Mr. Reed of Marblehead called on us in his carriage to go to Mrs. Madison's drawing room. We arrived at about 7, and found a richly furnished room and a splendid company. We were first ushered into a large hall, separated by pillars, where we took off our coats and hats. We were immediately introduced to Mrs. Madison, who received us with great politeness. The President made us on our introduction very stiff and formal bows. Mrs. M., though originally of a Quaker family, was dressed very splendidly with a crown on her head. Her face and neck were obviously daubed with paint so as fairly to glisten. There were two rooms for the guests, around which were elegant seats covered with red morocco, with cushions of the same kind. On these the ladies were seated. The men generally stood, or walked about the rooms. The President paid no attention to the ladies, but was all the time engaged in conversing with the men. The officers of the navy talked with him considerably. But what was most disgusting was to see him in a long, close, and what appeared confidential conversation with Gales, the imported editor of the National Intelligencer. The President is a short and small man, with a face shrivelled with care. He is bald, has large earlocks, a club behind precisely like Dr. Osgood's. I watched him a great part of the evening, and in no instance was his face illumined with a smile. No wonder, if he soberly reflects on the evils which he has been instrumental of bringing upon his country. I was introduced to Col. Monroe, who has most of the appearance of a gentleman of any at the palace. I was next introduced to Mons. Gallatin, Sec. of the Treasury. He has quite an original countenance, a dark complexion, black hair, a bald foretop, a large and aquiline nose, black and piercing eyes. Indeed, there is in his appearance a great degree of cunning.[40]

The next day Madison, and a multitude of other Washington dignitaries, attended the launching at the navy yard of the rebuilt frigate *Adams* to be commanded by the newly promoted Capt. Charles Morris, a hero of the *Constitution*. Madison's own prestige was becoming so belittled that an example of it was later published as a minor episode during the launch. A Federalist member of Congress standing next to the president said to him, as the ship glided gracefully into the water, "What a pity it is, sir, that the vessel of *state* won't glide as smoothly in her course, as *this* vessel does!"

"It would, sir," replied the president, "If the *crew* would do their duty as well."[41]

The Federalists were not the only ones becoming disenchanted with Madison's administration. On December 29, Clay wrote his old friend Caesar Rodney,

> I have intended, my dear Rodney, twenty times to write you, but really such have been the mortifying incidents of the last Campaign on that theatre where all our strength was supposed to lay, that I have not had the courage to attempt to pourtray [sic] my feelings to you. Your agreeable favor of the 27th imposed on me an imperious duty to overcome this apathy. And however little I shall be able to impart as to the past or future satisfactory to either of us the claims of a friendship which I will never cease to cherish shall not be slighted.
>
> It is in vain to conceal the fact — at least I will not attempt to disguise with you — Mr. Madison is wholly unfit for the storms of war. Nature has cast him in too benevolent a mould [sic]. Admirably adapted to the tranquil scenes of peace — blending all the mild and amiable virtues, he is not fit for the rough and rude blasts which the conflicts of Nations generate. Our hopes then for the future conduct of the War must be placed upon the vigor which he may bring into the administration by the organization of his new Cabinet. And here again he is so hesitating, so tardy, so far behind the National sentiment, in his proceedings towards his War Ministers, that he will lose whatever credit he might otherwise acquire by the

introduction of suitable characters in their places. One of them, unfit by Nature, has resigned; the other incapable now by habit, is still permitted to hold his station to the astonishment of everyone. He will probably vacate it, if not by Mr. M's resolution perhaps by his own kindness & pity.

In that same letter, Clay recognized that the navy's achievements had been brilliant but said, "They do not fill the void created by our misfortunes on Land." Still he did not despair even in that area. "The justness of our cause," he wrote,

the adequacy of our means to bring it to a successful issue — the spirit or patriotism of the Country — the Chapter, if you please, of chances (you know Rodney that I have always paid peculiar homage to the fickle goddess) will at last I think bring us honorably out. When I speak of the Country I do not see in the result of the Northern elections any cause to distrust its patriotism. Our Land disasters and the incompetence which we have too unfortunately exhibited are sufficient to account for that result. The ensuing campaign conducted with the energy which it ought to be would bring back the heads, as I believe we now have even in that quarter the hearts of a great majority of the people. In the South & in the West the Republican cause remains firm and unshaken.[42]

Even as Clay wrote his friend, changes were in process. The night before, during a ceremonious visit by the secretary of the navy to the White House the president suggested to Hamilton that there had been complaint against the management of his department. The matter went no further that day and Hamilton left in a good humor but not heeding the suggestion.

On the evening that Clay wrote Rodney, and, as Hamilton and his family dressed to attend a large party at the Gallatins', the secretary received a note from the president requesting an interview. Hamilton went immediately to the White House. In the course of the meeting, Madison again mentioned congressional dissatisfaction over management of the department and added that "this was a government of opinion, and where the popular current set against an office he could not be useful." When Madison said that Congress would not make the department's appropriation until there was a change in it, Hamilton observed that when he came into office, the naval establishment was much deranged — that there was not a ship

in commission adequate to a twelve month voyage, that almost all the vessels had been rebuilt since his appointment — that he had in a great degree, retrenched the expenses in that Department, that since the declaration of war, the only glory which this country had acquired was from the navy, and that he felt himself fully competent to conduct its future operation.

The President replied, that the Navy could not operate without appropriations, and that he believed none would be made until there was a change in the Department — Mr. Hamilton said, "Sir, I understand your meaning, and here is my commission."

On the 30th Hamilton tendered his formal letter of resignation. Reflecting on his 30 years of public service he stated that he felt "a consciousness of having done my duty according to my best judgment and understanding." He then asked President Madison, "Whether, in your opinion, there has been anything in the course of my conduct in that station reprehensible?"[43]

On the last day of the year, as the members of Congress attended the funeral of the pro-Madison Congressman John Smilie of Pennsylvania, the president responded to Hamilton's letter. He wrote,

I cannot satisfy my own feelings, or the tribute due to your patriotic merits & private virtues, without bearing testimony to the faithful zeal, the uniform exertions, and unimpeachable integrity, with which you have discharged that important trust; and without expressing the value I have always placed on that personal intercourse, the pleasure of which I am now to lose.

Hamilton became entangled with one further minor controversy on his way out of office. The day he tendered his resignation, he felt compelled to have the information published. He went home and wrote a note containing details surrounding his purpose in resigning. After a few moments reflecting he decided it might be better to give the bare facts only and wrote another note. As he finished it, company arrived at the house demanding his presence. When the guests departed, Hamilton returned to his desk, picked up the note and sent it to the *National Intelligencer* which published it. He threw the other note into the fire. To his astonishment, the wrong note appeared in the paper, for he had thrown into the fire the note he had finally intended for publication. He was thus forced to publish an explanation and acknowledge his mistake. Rather pathetically, Hamilton added that since he could not continue in office until the return of peace, as he had hoped to do, he had the consolation to know that "still I am willing and able to shoulder my musket in defense of my country, in a war which I conscientiously believe to be both necessary and just."[44]

18

WAR EFFORT ADRIFT

As the new year of 1813 dawned, there was renewed hope that cabinet changes would make possible a more active prosecution of the war, which in turn would result in success in battles. The hope was mingled with the usual pleasures of the New Year's Day reception at the White House. And as expected it was a pro–Madison gathering with most Federalists making excuses to stay away. Dolley Madison, as always, the gracious and picturesque hostess,

> received in a robe of pink satin, trimmed elaborately with ermine, gold chains and clasps about her waist and wrists, and upon her head a white satin and velvet turban with a crescent in front, and crowned with nodding ostrich plumes.[1]

While the seeds of a nagging political controversy and explosive diatribes had already been sown, and were, for the moment, dormant, reports of further military folly had reached Washington, and were alive.

The military folly was a continuation of the disgraceful episode at Niagara in the fall of 1812. Nevertheless, it was only in late December and early January that revelation of this latest absurdity became a topic of discussion in Washington.

The news of January 2, 1813, woke Congress to the events transpiring to the north when they learned that one of their colleagues — a member in the 1st session of the 12th Congress, but not of the 2nd — had been involved in an affair of honor. This former legislator was Peter B. Porter. He had been chairman of the Foreign Relations Committee prior to his resignation from the House in March 1812 to join the army.

Not long after militia Maj. Gen. Stephen Van Rensselaer turned over his command to regular

army Brig. Gen. Alexander Smyth in mid–October, the new commander received an order from Maj. Gen. Henry Dearborn to attempt another crossing into Canada, if possible, with 3,000 men "at once."[2] Early in November, in order to stimulate recruitment, Smyth issued a proclamation, "To the Men of New York." Reprinted in Washington, in early December, it read in part:

> For many years you have seen your country oppressed with numerous wrongs. Your Government, although above all others devoted to peace, have been forced to draw the sword and rely for redress of injuries on the valor of the American people.
> That valor has been conspicuous; but the nation has been unfortunate in the choice of some of those who directed it. One army has been disgracefully surrendered and lost. Another has been sacrificed by a precipitate attempt to pass it over at the strongest point of the enemy's lines, with most incompetent means. The cause of these miscarriages is apparent. The commanders were popular men, "destitute alike of theory and experience" in the art of war.

Smyth went on in a bombastic manner to appeal to a desire for fame and renown which, he believed, the venture would bring to those who joined him.[3]

In response, the men of New York's Western District answered,

> General, we have seen your proclamation. We have seen this country not many years ago the sole habitation of the beasts of the forest and their prowling enemy. We see it the habitation of many thousand souls, rich in all the necessaries and in many of the comforts of life. Till the day that the sound of war burst on our ears from the Capitol at Washington we scarcely experienced one moment of anxiety for the safety of our persons and

property. The charm of avaricious traders and of factious office seekers trouble not our quiet.... Why should our swords be drawn in redress of injuries which we have never felt, or which if they exist are beyond our reach? Why appeal to our valor for the destruction of our own happiness or that of others?

The renown which you seek is not our renown. It is the renown of Europe not America. The wrath of God precedes it, and desolation follows in its footsteps. It delights in blood and in fields strewn with carnage, in the tears of the widow and the complainings of the orphan, perishing of want and disease. This is your glory. Ours has upon it the primeval blessing of the Almighty; our victories are victories over the unproductive face of nature; our renown is in fertile fields, in peaceful homes and numerous and happy families.

Go, General, if you will. Should you ever reach the walls of Quebec, the shade of Montgomery will reproach you for not having profited by his example, and when you fall the men of New York will lament that folly has found new victims.[4]

Like many wars of the future, there were many who disagreed with the handling of this one.

Along with about 2,000 New Yorkers, one other person who supported Smyth's appeal was his quartermaster general, former congressman Peter B. Porter. He issued a call to two western counties to support the project.

On November 17, one week after his "call to arms," Smyth issued another flamboyant charge to his "Companions in Arms," starting off with, "The time is at hand when you will cross the streams of Niagara to conquer Canada and to secure the peace of the American frontier. You will enter a country that is to be one of the United States." He promised them booty from public — but not private — captures, and praised their skills. He ended with an easily-forgotten rallying cry. "The cannon lost at Detroit or Death."[5]

On November 25th, Smyth issued a general order prescribing in detail how the men were to advance in battle three days hence with points three and four reading as follows:

> 3. At twenty yards' distance the soldiers will be ordered to trail arms, advance with shouts, fire at five paces' distance, and charge bayonets. 4. The soldiers will be *silent*, above all things, attentive at the word of command, load quick and well, and *aim low.*[6]

"Shout" and "be silent?" While his words spoke of "heroics," it was almost possible to read "fiasco" into Smyth's babblings.

In the early morning hours of Saturday, November 28, two groups of Americans, each with about 200 men, crossed the river at Black Rock (north of Buffalo). One, under Lt. Col. Charles Boerstler, was to destroy a bridge to the north, and the other, under army Captain King and navy Lieut. Samuel Angus, was to destroy some artillery to the south.

Captain King and 30 of his men were captured as the rest returned with numerous casualties and about 30 British prisoners.[7] Their only success during their few hours in Canada was the spiking of most of the British batteries. Meanwhile, three sailors crossed alone and unauthorized at another point and spent two hours in Canada burning three buildings, killed some hogs, and chickens, and returned to their own camp unmolested but with a boat full of booty.

Despite these limited achievements, General Smyth's 3,000 or so troops, only half embarked, sat around throughout the fine, mild and pleasant morning waiting to do honor for their country, and seek fame and renown "for themselves." But late in the afternoon the general ordered them "to disembark *and dine.*"[8] They did so murmuring their discontent. After consultation with his subordinates later that day, Smyth renewed his marching orders for a crossing early on Monday, November 30. Then Smyth postponed the embarkation for pre-dawn Tuesday. Again only half of the intended force was in boats by dawn, but nothing moved. This time Smyth ordered the troops not only to return ashore but also to go into winter quarters completely abandoning the invasion of Canada.

A general unrest ensued which the officers could not restrain. Many of the 4,000 men in camp fired off the muskets in every direction. It was reported that some "officers broke their swords, the men beat their muskets over stumps with rage." Crowds of troops called Smyth a scoundrel, a coward, and a traitor and menaced him. He fled to Buffalo for safe lodging. En route, he was fired at and was nearly hit and an aide was struck on a belt. In Buffalo he had to answer charges made against him by a committee of "patriotic citizens" of the western counties of New York. Still his landlord in Buffalo, hearing the threats against his guest, found it dangerous to harbor the general and asked him to leave. Smyth took refuge in camp surrounded by a strong guard of loyal soldiers.[9]

About a week later General Smyth found time to compose his official dispatch of the events to be sent to his superior, Major General Dearborn. A copy of the message came into General Porter's hands and he immediately appealed to the Buffalo newspaper to withhold its publication until he could also publish his "true" account of the episodes. In Porter's letter to the paper he ascribed "the late disgrace on the frontier to the cowardice of General Smyth."[10]

This charge brought forth a challenge from Smyth and, on December 12, on Grand Island, half way between Buffalo and Niagara Falls, the two men exchanged shots without affect. Porter then retracted his charge of cowardice against Smyth who in turn explained that his actions "were the result of irritation." Their seconds, William H. Winder for Smyth and Samuel Angus for Porter, reported in writing, "The hand of reconciliation was then offered and received." Three days later Porter published a whitewashed account of the fiasco.[11]

Porter was to return to Congress for one term after the war and later served in John Quincy Adams' cabinet as secretary of war when Henry Clay was secretary of state. In the years between holding those two offices, General Smyth was to serve with Clay in the House representing Virginia. Colonel Winder would become a general and be involved in the disastrous battle of Bladensburg which permitted the British to occupy and burn the principal buildings of Washington in August 1814. In the spring of 1814, Samuel Angus was to command the ship which was to convey Henry Clay to Europe to treat for peace with the British. Angus' career was to be star-crossed.

Accounts of these latest ridiculous army blunders came just as the House was taking up the consideration of two bills — one of which carried the timely title of "An act for the more perfect organization of the Army of the United States." The other was "to raise an additional military force."

At the request of the chairmen of both congressional military committees, acting Secretary of War James Monroe, on December 23, provided them with identical copies of information "respecting the defects in the organization of the general staff of the Army ... and ... the propriety of augmenting the present military force." He proposed a regular army force of about 7,350 to defend all the coastlines from Maine to New Orleans, with another 2,000 to protect the western frontier up to the Detroit area, and leaving 26,000 regulars for offensive purposes along the rest of the Canadian frontier. Much of this force was still only authorized and not in existence. Even so, he asked for a further increase of 20,000 troops for one-year enlistments. To stimulate this recruitment, he suggested raising the bounty to $40 for each recruit. The rest of his report centered on plans of a campaign in 1813.[12]

The chairman of the House Military Committee, David R. Williams of South Carolina, brought the two bills (based on Monroe's recommendation) to the Committee of the Whole House on December 29. The issue of the bounties was considered first. After Williams' presentation, Henry Clay rose to propose an amendment which would repeal all previous laws providing for bounties of land (160 acres) to recruits as a waste of the nation's "capital, without producing a single provident result ... it had not added an hundred men to the army." He suspected the land would, in the end, get into the hands of speculators. Now that bounties were to be increased in money, he believed this was the time to do away with the bounty in land, "on which the recruits set generally as much value as if it were located in the moon." The motion was passed on in Committee of the Whole House, but rejected by the full House the next day. The bill passed on January 2.[13]

Still, on December 29, the Committee of the Whole House also took up the other bill — to increase the army by 20,000 men, with appointment of officers below the rank of colonel to be made by the president. In opposing this provision, one Federalist, Timothy Pitkin of Connecticut, prophesied and warned,

The President of the United States has now more power than is consistent with the simplicity of Republican Government. If this Government ever be wrecked, it will be on the rock of Presidential power.... It is in time of wars and convulsions that power is improperly vested in men; and when they have thus obtained the power, it has been found difficult in peace to divest them of it.... I ask if a Burr, or a person of like disposition, had been put at the head of this immense military force, with the power of appointing all his officers, where would be the liberties of this people?[14]

These kind of fears would remain through much of the life of the country.

With these expressions by Pitkin, the bill was to take a peculiar turn and develop intense animosity in the House. On the 30th, Josiah Quincy asked for additional time to consider the great questions resulting from the measure since they "touched the whole course of the Administration; that they had a relation to the present character and future prospects of the country." James Fisk of Vermont opposed this delay, accurately predicting, "the discussion would transcend reasonable limits."[15]

For about a week the bill was debated with moderation and containing discussion clearly to the central theme of increasing the size of the army. But then things began to get a bit sticky. On January 3, Speaker Clay had to call one member to order. The next day, he called two members to order. One of these was his old nemesis, John Randolph of Roanoke. This minor collision came over Randolph's measure requesting the president to furnish all names of people in the pay of the United States government. Another member requested postponement of this subject. Randolph replied that

> the mode of doing business [in the House] was almost such as to seal the lips of every man who has not the honor to hold some prominent station in the standing or select committees of the House.... The floor of the House should be open as well to one side as the other of the House....

At this point Speaker Clay interrupted to say he did not think the remarks of the gentleman reflecting upon the House for the mode of transacting business, proper in themselves or relevant to the proposition to postpone the resolution until Wednesday. He added that "there was no difference in the opportunity enjoyed by gentlemen on all sides of the House, or submitting their motions." Randolph sat down and the House voted to postpone his proposal. They immediately resumed debate on the army bill.[16]

But the real fight on the bill began the next day, January 5, when its opponents attacked it obliquely. That day, Josiah Quincy rose to observe that the increase of the army from 35,000 men

to 55,000 was for the sole purpose of the conquest of Canada — an avowed wish of the American cabinet. And that group of men became the focal point of his assault.

Quincy's long speech was to become more important historically because of a two-day response by Clay. Since the Speaker was not to make such a major speech again for several years, and due to the great bitterness evoked by both men, more than usual of their remarks are quoted here. After all, Clay was a legislator, and what he said and did in the halls of Congress were the basis of his great fame. In addition, the two speeches display the two opposing viewpoints of the national war effort.

Quincy began by charging that whenever the cabinet wanted "any obnoxious measure" to be passed by Congress when it is loathed by a majority of the people,

> certain under-operators are set to work, whose business it is to amuse the minds, and beguile the attention of the patients while the dose is swallowing. The language always is: "Trust the Cabinet doctors. The medicine will not operate as you imagine, but quite another way." After this manner the fears of the men are allayed.

He also observed that "no scheme ever was, or ever will be, rejected by them [the men in power these eight years past], merely on account of its running counter to the ordinary dictates of common sense and common prudence."

Quincy said he could not (before the war) believe that a people 20 years at peace would enter hostilities against a people 20 years at war, "that a nation, whose army and navy were little more than nominal, should engage in a war with a nation possessing one of the best appointed armies and the most powerful marine on the globe." He thought it so absurd that it reminded him of certain Pennsylvania Germans, he had heard, consider the allegation that war exists, to be a "federal falsehood."

He laughed at the idea of an invasion of Canada.

> That the United States should precipitate itself upon the unoffending people of that neighboring colony, unmindful of all previously subsisting amities, because the parent State, three thousand miles distant, had violated some of our commercial rights; that we should march inland, to defend

our ships and seamen; that with raw troops, hastily collected, miserably appointed, and destitute of discipline, we should invade a country defended by veteran forces, at least equal, in point of numbers, to the invading army; ... in every aspect, the design seemed so fraught with danger and disgrace, that it appeared absolutely impossible that it should be seriously entertained.

Quincy's analysis of the situation encouraged him to connect those events to the election of the president then pending. It was here that he raised the charge that war was the condition "on which the support for the Presidency was made dependent." He went on, "It is now apparent to the most mole-sighted how a nation may be disgraced, and yet a Cabinet attain its desired honors. All is clear. A country may be ruined in making an Administration happy."

In an aside to his general remarks, Quincy then spoke of the cabinet as "the friends of the French Emperor," and was called to order by a member from Georgia for intimating that the members of the cabinet were friends of the French emperor. Quincy replied that he understood that the relations of amity did subsist between this country and France, and that in such a state of things, he had a right to speak of the American cabinet as friends of France, in the same manner as he had now a right to call them the enemies of Great Britain.

Speaker Clay, noting the truth in this, said he did not conceive the gentleman from Massachusetts to be out of order in his expressions. That it was impossible to prevent gentlemen from expressing themselves so as to convey an *innuendo*!

To this Quincy advised, "No Administration, no man, was ever materially injured by any mere *innuendo*! The strength of satire is the justness of the remark, and the only sting of invective is the truth of the observation."

At this point Quincy outlined the remainder of his speech considering the

invasion of Canada from three different points of view.
1. As a means of carrying on the subsisting war.
2. As a means of obtaining an early and honorable peace.
3. As a means of advancing the personal and local projects of ambition of the members of the American cabinet.

Concerning the first view, Quincy called the invasion of Canada "cruel, wanton, senseless, and wicked." Expanding on his earlier objection, he chided those American politicians who believed the injury done the United States by a corrupt ministry 3,000 miles away as "ample course to visit with desolation a peaceable and un-offending race of men, their neighbors, who happen to be associated with that ministry by ties of mere political dependence." He added that neither he nor the great mass of the population of his section of the country held communion with such men. Accusing them of seeking glory, he said,

The whole atmosphere rings with the utterance from the other side of the House, of this word "glory"—"glory" in connection with this invasion. What glory? Is it the glory of the tiger which lifts his jaws all foul and bloody, from the bowels of his victim, and roars for his companions of the woods to come and witness his prowess and his spoils? Such is the glory of Genghis Khan, and of Bonaparte. Be such glory far, very far from my country. Never, never may it be accused with such fame.

Quincy went on to degrade the character of the soldiers and their officers prophesying that after conquest they could not be "disbanded by vote," but would establish a dynasty "by the sword," and threaten to "enslave the country." He spoke with pride that his section of the country, in the invasion of Canada, was "free from the iniquity of this transgression."

On the view that the invasion would obtain an early and honorable peace, Quincy rejected the idea that Great Britain would negotiate out of fear for the fate of her colonies. Aiming a barb at the young War Hawks, he scoffed at them.

Those must be very young politicians, their pinfeathers not yet grown, and however they may flutter on this floor, they are not yet fledged for any high or distant flight, who think that threats and appealing to fear are the ways of producing a disposition to negotiate in Great Britain. Of all nations in the world, Great Britain is the last to yield to considerations of fear and terror.

Quincy claimed that the American cabinet understood this and its purpose for a larger army was "to put at still further distance the chance of amicable arrangement." He charged that the whole history of the men now in power had, since the Jay Treaty of 1794, been to reach and remain in office by artfully fomenting prejudices and antipathies against Great Britain. Quincy believed the cabinet so intent on hostilities that he was reminded

> of the giant in the legends of infancy:
>
> Fee, faw, fow, fum,
> I smell the blood of an English man;
> Dead or alive, I will have some!

Quincy believed that as he spoke "a thousand tongues and a thousand pens" were preparing to answer his remarks with "traitor," "British agent," "British gold," etc., but he could not

> hesitate or swerve a hair's breadth from his country's purpose and true interest, because of the yelpings. The howlings, and snarling of that hungry pack which corrupt men keep directly or indirectly in pay, with the view of hunting down every man who dare develop their purposes; a pack composed it is true of some native curs, but for the most part of hounds and spaniels of very recent importation, whose backs are scarred by the lash, and whose necks are sore with the collars of their former masters.

This comment led him to the charge that the Canadian invasion was for the purpose of advancing the personal ambitions of the American cabinet composed, he said, of two Virginians — and at times three — and a foreigner. Quincy noted that Virginia had furnished the president for 24 of 28 years and "that James the First should be made to continue four years longer — that James the Second shall be made to succeed, according to the fundamental rescripts of the Monticellian dynasty."

Here, Speaker Henry Clay called Josiah Quincy to order saying that really, the gentleman laid his promises so remote from his conclusions, that Clay could not see how his observation applied to the bill.

Quincy argued that it was within the scope of the debates to show that the cabinet's general policy with this bill was to aggrandize themselves. Supporting this view, Quincy unveiled the embargo of the earlier coercion charge against Clay.

> Antecedent to the declaration of war, it was distinctly stated, by individuals from that quarter of the country, under the influence of which this war was adopted, that the support of the present President of the United States by their quarter of the country depended upon the fact of the Cabinet's coming up to the point of war with Great Britain ... without their support [the Southern and West-

ern States], the re-election of the present Chief Magistrate was hopeless.

He added that the invasion of Canada represented a test of the cabinet's sincerity in prosecuting the war.

Connecting prediction of a "Monticellian dynasty" with the proposal for an enlarged army, Quincy asked,

> To be commanded by whom? The answer is in every man's mouth. By a member of the American Cabinet, by one of the three; by one of that "trio," ... who have always constituted the whole Cabinet ... the man who is notoriously the selected candidate for the next Presidency.

He considered this as "ominous to the liberties of this country."

In conclusion, he noted that the new army, under "a candidate for the Presidency," was to operate in his section of the country with one object, "to put down opposition." Therefore, if "my children are destined to be slaves" by his revelation of the cabinet's ambitions and his attempt to warn his countrymen, those children would be able to say, "*Our father was guiltless of these chains.*"

As caustic as Quincy's remarks are shown in the official reports of the day, they were softer than those heard in the House. Yet some of his "expunged" vituperation did come out in the following days. The next day John Rhea and Felix Grundy, both of Tennessee, referred to Quincy's characterization of Eastern Democrats as "reptiles which spread their slime in the drawing room," and his reference to administration supporters who haunted the Executive "like toads, that live on the spittle of the palace and the levee." Rhea commented that "such foul and undeserved aspirations have one only answer —'*Let him who is filthy be filthy still.*'"[17]

Nevertheless Quincy had support from his Massachusetts colleague the Rev. Samuel Taggart, who said Quincy

> was very severe on the Cabinet.... The bill which was then in the House was recommitted to the committee of the Whole for the ostensible purpose of making some trifling amendments which might have been as well made in the House, but for the real one of giving the Speaker, which is perhaps the most accomplished blackguard of the party the opportunity of abusing Quincy, which he did in such a strain of low vulgar Billingsgate scurrility,

as was much better adapted to a barroom after the close of an angry town meeting when the disputants were pretty well heated with liquor, than to the hall of a national legislature.[18]

Quincy had his view of the episode and, in his own memoirs, went so far as to give praise to his own efforts and briefly described what followed.

> The plainness and directness of this attack were of such a nature, that, although all the minor herd of debaters poured out their wrath upon my head, it was deemed important enough that the untamed ferocious tongue of Henry Clay should be detailed to the services of responding to and prostrating the assailant. Accordingly, the House was resolved into a Committee of the Whole, and Speaker Clay descended from the chair to the floor, for the purpose, as one of his friends informed me, *of reducing one to the alternative of a duel or disgrace.* He consequently on this occasion exceeded himself in his characteristic power of insolent vituperation of his opponent and unlimited laudation of the Administration.[19]

As described by Quincy and Taggart, the chairman of the Military Committee had risen to put the question, which would have returned the bill to the House cutting off Clay's chance to comment on it.[20] He had hoped for a different opportunity telling the committee he was unprepared to speak on this day [January 8] and he was "the more sensible from the ill state of his health." The climate within the House chamber was not to help him. "The day was chilling cold, so much so," the *National Intelligencer* reported afterwards "that Mr. C. has been heard to declare, that it was the only time he ever spoke, when he was unable to keep himself warm by the exercise of speaking."[21] With reference to the timing of the debate, Clay thought the loan bill, "which will soon come before us, would have afforded a much more proper occasion [for the opposition] to lay before the House their views of the interesting attitude in which the nation stands." He said they had the right of selection "and having exercised it, no matter how improperly," he was gratified for the latitude indulged. He claimed, in return of the House to the Committee of the Whole, "a like indulgence in expressing, with the same unrestrained freedom, my sentiments." He acknowledged his remarks might "assume too harsh an aspect" but he spoke as it struck his moral sense without intending "to wound the feelings of any *gentleman.*"

Clay then began an historical review of the events leading to war, chiding the opposition with being for war through the years. The Jeffersonian Republicans strived for peace through its series of commercial restrictive acts.

> Whilst these peaceful experiments are undergoing a trial, what is the conduct of the opposition? They are the champions of war; the proud, the spirited, the sole repository of the nation's honor; the men of exclusive vigor and energy. The administration, on the contrary, is weak, feeble, and pusillanimous. "incapable of being kicked into a war" (Quincy's words over a year earlier) and they were proud to utter the maxim, "not a cent for tribute, millions for defense."

But when it was no longer possible to abstain from it [war] ... Clay said,

> behold the opposition veering round and becoming the friends of peace and of commerce. They tell you of the calamities of war — its tragical events — the squandering away of your resources — the waste of the public treasure, and the spilling of innocent blood.... They tell you that honor is an illusion! Now we see them exhibiting the terrific forms of the roaring king of the forest. Now the meekness and humility of the lamb! They are for war, and no restrictions, when the administration is for peace. They are for peace and restrictions, when the administration is for war. You find them, sir, tacking with every gale, displaying the colors of every party, and of all nations, steady only in one unalterable purpose, to steer, if possible, into the haven of power.

Next, Clay attacked the "cunning sarcasm or sly innuendo" with which the "parasites of opposition" throw out the idea of French influence. "The Administration of this country subservient to France! Great God! how is it so influenced." He said it was not by language, jurisprudence, trade, or form of government. "But," Clay told the chairman, "I am insulting you by arguing on such a subject."

Yet amidst the opposition's "veerings and changes," Clay said it had remained inflexible in

> the application to Bonaparte of every vile and opprobrious epithet which our rich language affords. He has been compared to every hideous monster, and beast, from that of the revelations to the most insignificant quadruped. He has been called the scourge of mankind, the destroyer of Europe, the great robber, the infidel, and Heaven knows by what other names.

Clay admonished his colleagues discussing European interests and forgetting those of America. Stepping almost a decade ahead, Clay said he had more interest in the movements in South America.

Prophesying correctly, Clay next alluded to Quincy's abuse of Jefferson, at first saying Jefferson's name would "be hailed as the second founder of the liberties of these people" when Quincy is consigned to oblivion. But remembering Quincy's motion, some few years earlier, for the impeachment of Jefferson (which failed 117 to 1), Clay recalled that "the same historic page that transmitted to posterity the virtue and the glory of Henry the Great of France ... has preserved the infamous name of his fanatic assassin." And Clay gave a similar reference to Christ and Judas.

Taking up the innuendo of the coercion charge, Clay said Quincy "has entertained us with Cabinet plots, Presidential plots, which are conjured up in the gentleman's own perturbed imagination." But Clay wished "another plot of a much more serious kind — a plot that aims at the dismemberment of our Union, had only the same imaginary existence." He reminded the House of Quincy's own sentiment uttered about the time the Henry mission to Boston was undertaken. It was then that Quincy advocated separation "peaceably if we can, FORCIBLY if we must." Clay inferred that the purposes then of neutrality and eventual separation coincide with New England's efforts since the declaration of war. In turning from his attack on Quincy, Clay called him "one, whom no sense of decency or propriety could restrain from soiling the carpet on which he treads." This referred to another of Quincy's epithets expunged from the official record.

Following this comment, Clay asked the indulgence of the House to permit him to continue his speech on the following day saying, "I really am so exhausted!" Returning to the floor on January 9, Clay refuted Quincy's allegation of a Southern influence aimed at a Virginia monopoly of the presidency. This would require the consent of the electorate of many states, Clay suggested, and added that the designation of Madison as Jefferson's successor was by public sentiment.

Then Clay very concisely cited the reasons for the declaration of war — that Great Britain tried to regulate "our foreign trade" under the Orders in Council; that "she persisted in the practice of impressing American seamen"; that "she had instigated the Indians to commit hostilities against us"; that "she refused indemnity for her past injuries upon our commerce." He added, "The war, in fact, was announced, on our part, to meet the war which she was waging on her part." He added, in addition, that the causes were so undeniable when war was debated in June, "the opposition — although provoked to debate, would not, or could not, utter one syllable against it," but "wrapped themselves up in sullen silence, pretending that they did not choose to debate such a question in secret session."

With reference to France, Clay said there was too little support for a declaration of war with France at the same time as that against Great Britain, but he still wished "to God that our ability was equal to our disposition to make her feel the sense we entertain" of French injustice to the United States. Still the exceptionable handling of the French revocation of their decrees had not the effect on the cause of war as was "the unequivocal declaration of the British Government" transmitted in May by Augustus Foster. Clay referred to Castlereagh's avowal "that to produce the effect of the repeal of the Orders in Council, the French decrees must be absolutely and entirely revoked as to all the world, and not as to America alone." Clay spoke of two incidents in June, prior to the final votes for war, when Foster, undoubtedly aware of its imminence, reiterated Britain's intransigent stand. Clay denied that the revocation of the French decrees precipitated the repeal of the British Orders (that could have been done months earlier), but argued instead that repeal resulted from the inquiry by the British government "into the effect upon their manufacturing establishments, of our non-importation law, or to the warlike attitude assumed by this Government, or to both."

Clay believed war might have been declared even had the Orders been repealed earlier. "I have no hesitation in saying, that I have always considered the impressment of American seamen as much the most serious aggression." Clay went on to compare this war with that of the Revolution as "an example of a war begun for one object and prosecuted for another," a fight against taxation giving way to a fight for independence. Then he made a statement which could have come back to haunt him two years later.

> When nations are engaged in war, those rights in controversy, which are not acknowledged by the Treaty of Peace are abandoned. And who is prepared to say that American seamen shall be surrendered, the victims of the British principle of impressment?

In support of Clay's strong feeling that impressment was now the major cause of war, he attacked it from two directions — legally and emotionally. He cited Britain's claim that, to exercise a right to the services of her own subjects, she could "lawfully impress them, even although she finds them in our vessels, upon the high seas, without her jurisdiction." Clay denied Britain had the right. Continuing he said, Britain "further contends, that her subjects cannot renounce their allegiance to her and contract a new obligation to other sovereigns." He noted that all nations deny such contention and at the same time all "admit and practice the right of naturalization. Great Britain herself does." Speaking of the dual citizenship, Clay observed, "if subjects cannot break their original allegiance they may, according to universal usage, contract a new allegiance." But he said, "the sovereign having the possession of the subject would have the right to the services of the subject." The naturalized subject could serve his native sovereign if he returned on his own, Clay contended,

> but his primitive sovereign can have no right to go in quest of him, out of his own jurisdiction, into the jurisdiction of another sovereign, or upon the high seas, where there exists either no jurisdiction, or it belongs to the nation owning the ship navigating them. Still, Clay expressed his greatest anger at Britain's practice when he declared, "The naked truth is, she comes, by her press-gangs, on board of our vessels, seizes our native seamen, as well as naturalized, and drags them into her service.

Along with these arguments Clay objected to the opposition's complaint that the American government had not done enough to protect its seamen. Clay said it had done too much by providing them with "certificates of protection" which in effect resembled "the passes which the master grants to his negro slave, 'Let the bearer, Mungo, pass and re-pass without molestation.'" These certificates implored "that Great Britain has a right to take all who are not provided with them." But Clay contended, "The colors that float from the mast head should be the credentials of our seamen."

Apparently using the symbolism of an early day "female" Uncle Sam, Clay moved his listeners, saying

> the Genius of Columbia should visit one of them in his oppressor's prison and attempt to reconcile him to his wretched condition. She would say to him, in the language of gentlemen on the other side, "Great Britain intends you no harm; she did not mean to impress you, but one of her own subjects; having taken you by mistake, I will remonstrate, and try to prevail upon her, by peaceable means, to release you, but I cannot, my son, fight for you." If he did not consider this mockery, he would address her judgment and say, "You owe me, my country, protection; I owe you, in return, obedience. I am no British subject, I am a native of old Massachusetts, where live my aged father, my wife, my children. I have faithfully discharged my duty. Will you refuse to do yours?" Appealing to her passions, he would continue, "I lost this eye in fighting under Truxtun [Commodore Thomas Truxton on the frigate Constellation in the undeclared Naval war with France 1798–1800], I got this scar before Tripoli; I broke this leg on board the Constitution, when the Guerrière struck." If she remained still unmoved, he would break out, in the accents of mingled distress and despair.

> *Hard, hard, is my fate! once I freedom enjoyed,*
> *Was as happy as happy could be!*
> *Oh! how hard is my fate, how galling these chains!*

> It will not be, it cannot be, that his country will refuse him protection!

Reporting these remarks later, the *National Intelligencer* said, "It is impossible to describe the pathetic effect produced by this part of the speech ... yet there were few eyes that did not testify to sensibility excited."

With respect to the current British view of impressment, Clay quoted Lord Castlereagh's remarks to American Chargé d'Affaires Jonathan Russell just prior to his return home in September 1812. Castlereagh, in his remarks communicated by the administration to Congress in November, told Russell,

> Indeed there has evidently been much misapprehension on this subject, and an erroneous belief entertained that an arrangement, in regard to it, has been nearer an accomplishment than the facts will warrant. Even our friends in Congress, I mean

those who were opposed to going to war with us, have been so confident in this mistake, that they have ascribed the failure of such an arrangement solely to the misconduct of the American government.

Castlereagh went on to state that the error arose from Rufus King's belief that he had won over a key British Lord to the American viewpoint. Castlereagh gave evidence to Russell that this was not so and added, "Thus you see that the confidence of Mr. King on this subject was entirely unfounded."

While the issue of impressment was to come to Congress later in the session in the form of a message from the president, the next subject of Clay's lengthy speech was soon to strike his family with personal anguish. Noting the concern of the people of the West for the hardships of seamen, Clay expressed certainty that those of the East "feel for the unhappy victims of the tomahawk in the Western Country." But in reply to Quincy's representation that Canada was connected to the bordering states by "tender ties, interchanging acts of kindness, and all the offices of good neighborhood," Clay scoffed,

> Canada, innocent! Canada unoffending! Is it not in Canada that the tomahawk of the savage has been molded into its death-like form! From Canadian magazines, Malden and others, that those supplies have been issued which nourish and sustain the Indian hostilities? Supplies which have enabled the savage hordes to butcher the garrison of Chicago, and to commit other horrible murders? Was it not by the joint cooperation of Canadians and Indians that a remote American fort, Michilimackinac, was fallen upon and reduced while the garrison was in ignorance of a state of war?

Clay recognized that the sensibilities of the administration's opposition were cruelly shocked, but "all their sympathies are lavished upon the harmless inhabitants of the adjoining provinces."

To Clay, the Federalist's enemy was elusive — not Canada, not the West Indies, not the British seaman and soldier, not the sacred person of his majesty.

> Indeed, sir, I know of no person on whom we may make war, but Mr. Stephen, the celebrated author of the Orders in Council, or the board of admiralty, who authorize and regulate the practice of impressment!

Comparing the naval victories with the army disasters, Clay said, "On the one element organization, discipline, and a thorough knowledge of their duties exist, on the part of the officers and their men. On the other, almost everything is yet to be acquired." Not quite so true, he added, "in no instance when engaged in an action have our arms been tarnished. At Brownstown and at Queenstown the valor of veterans was displayed, and acts of the noblest heroism were performed." However, he could not trust his feelings on the episode at Detroit which he thought caused a delay in conquests leading to Montreal. He briefly took note of less newsworthy but more successful military actions near Peoria (in Illinois territory), at Prophet's town (in Indian territory), against the Seminole Indians (in Florida), and the destruction of two small ships in the Niagara River.

Finally, in answer to Quincy's charges that the administration was not serious in its search for peace, Clay spoke of messages through Russell to the British government immediately following the declaration of war stating that repeal of the Orders and cessation of impressment were conditions for peace. Even "an informal understanding of these points" and a prohibition of the employment of British seamen on American ships, "thus removing entirely all pretext for the practice of impressment" was "rejected as absolutely inadmissible" by the British on the shallow reason that Russell's powers to negotiate were inadequate. Despite British insults to American peace overtures, Clay maintained the administration still left the door open to negotiation. Clay declared that

> the Administration has erred in the steps which it has taken to restore peace, but its error has been not in doing too little but in betraying too great a solicitude for that event. An honorable peace is attainable only by an efficient war. My plan would be to call out the ample resources of the country, give them a judicious direction, prosecute the war with the utmost vigor, strike whenever we can reach the enemy, at sea or on land, and negotiate the terms of peace at Quebec or Halifax.... In such a cause, with the aid of Providence, we must come out crowned with success; but if we fail, let us fail like men, lash ourselves to our gallant tars, and expire together in one common struggle fighting for "*seamen's rights and free trade.*"[22]

As expected, the reaction to Clay's speech depended upon the viewpoint of the observer (or reader, as the case may be). John Harper described it in a letter to New Hampshire's Governor William Plumer.

> In committees of the whole this day, the Speaker opened all his portholes upon poor Quincy — He brought his artillery to play well. The fire on board the Constitution, the Wasp, or the United States could not have been better directed, than that of the Speaker's. But *unlike* the inanimate hulls of the British ships, Quincy could not be brought to feel it. They were made to feel and receive an impression, but Quincy, more callous than British oak, cannot be made to *feel*. Never was a man more severely castigated, or one who more richly deserved it.[23]

The praise heaped on Clay was so great that one of his own supporters was a bit uneasy. Jonathan Roberts, sometimes called Albert Gallatin's mouthpiece, wrote his brother,

> Clay made a fine speech but to hear Binns of the Philadelphia *Democratic Press* eulogizing him while deprecating Madison, Monroe, and Gallatin was disgusting. Clay could not live a week under the pressure of responsibility these men resist.[24]

Quincy made his own observations on the aftermath of Clay's speech, as well as of others.

> I do not wonder at the rage of these men. The truth is, I thrust the spear directly between the joints of the harness. I made a reply of about ten sentences, which my friends say was the best I ever made. I suppose the charm lay in its brevity. The palace and all its retainers are in a most tremendous rage.... I laid the mysteries of their power open to public inspection, and when you throw light upon an owl's nest, there is nothing like the agitation of the whole family.

Quincy's few sentences noted that he "did not pass the fair limits of parliamentary discussion" because "the Speaker himself, then presiding in this House, neither stopped me himself, nor permitted others to do it when it was attempted." With regard to reducing him to the alternative of a duel, Quincy laughed it off in a letter to assure his wife saying, "As to my *personal safety*, that is the last thing I think of. I am secured by my place in some measure." Even a warning of trouble a fortnight later was turned aside and Quincy told his wife "The storm was mere wind."[25]

Not unexpectedly, the *Boston Messenger* supported Quincy's viewpoint and happily quoted from the anti-administration Georgetown *Federal Republican* which wrote that Clay's speech appears to have surpassed in a profligate contempt of all moral sentiment, and grossness of personal abuse, all former democratic speeches.

> We have often remarked the dull malignity, and vulgar insolence of this Gentleman in debate; we have also remarked his coarse and mawkish attempts at eulogy, and we know not which a man of taste and true honour would most deprecate. His "*sign post daubery*" of those pure patriots, Thos. Jefferson and James Madison, are as indicative of his taste and moral tact, as his ribald invective against Mr. Quincy. His blasphemous compliments are infinitely more revolting, than even the "grossierte" of his manners.

> He seems for some days to have been collecting the materials for this display of his devotion to the court; and at length, like one of those shells, or carcasses charged with foetid and noisome combustibles, he burst on the floor of Congress, with no other harm, or inconvenience, than the stench that followed the explosion.

> As an orator this Speaker appears to us greatly to resemble the taylor's goose that is "both hot and heavy" — as a statesman to comprehend as much of the principles of Legislation and the various questions, growing out of our foreign relations, as ought to be expected from a man, bread to the bar of Kentucky: & a Gentleman as much courtesy, in his language & manners, as naturally belongs to one, habituated to the brawls of a Kentucky tavern, and eminently distinguished among the Honorable corps of *black legs* [a term used against Clay in later years which would result in a duel].

> Mr. Quincy's reply was dignified, contemptuous, and altogether appropriate. — It is not the first time he has been thus assailed; and he has with a magnanimity, that is highly honorable to his principle, and his station declared his disapprobation of settling controversies about principles or facts, by wager of battle.

> As Mr. Quincy's determination on this subject was well known, we cannot help thinking that the courage of Mr. Clay was stimulated to insult him by the conviction, that he was in no danger of bodily harm. We can hardly resist the impression, that the honorable speaker is, after all, a "sheep in wolf's cloathing"; and a worthy representative of the plundering scalping band of patriots, better known as Kentucky volunteers, who so well understand the "*manual exercise of heels*."[26]

The Georgetown paper itself must have delighted in the odious descriptions they had reprinted from the New England paper. They followed suit within the week by publishing their own characterizations of various members of the administration as follows:

Madison — a mind debased and capable of any thing, no matter what, if required to preserve the party.

Gallatin — the foreigner who requited the hospitality and unsuspecting kindness of his adopted country ... by stirring up insurrection, and figuring in the character of a rebel.

Monroe — this gentleman came out of political banishment, upon condition of surrendering his conscience into the keeping of his virtuous Mr. Madison, abandoning the principles he brought with him from Europe, and became an accessory after the fact to all misdeeds which have damned to everlasting fame their author.

Armstrong — is universally considered a perfidious, designing, treacherous man.

Jones — the executive touch has had the magical effect of transforming him into a virtuous and enlightened citizen.

Pinckney — rotten to the very core — touch him and he falls to pieces.

In part, Quincy won his battle, though his political wars were to end with this session. Rumors that James Monroe would succeed to the War Department followed by the presidency were only half true. While it was later made to appear that Quincy's attack on "the three Virginians plus a foreigner" drove Monroe from the War Department, Monroe's "escape" was already in the works before Quincy spoke.

Treasury Secretary Albert Gallatin, advising Madison on the succession to the War Department, wrote the day before Quincy's speech, "the office requires first abilities and frightens those who know best its difficulties. Dearborn and Mr. Monroe have shrunk from it, and so will, I suspect, Crawford." Indeed, on January 6, Crawford declined Madison's "very kind and flattering" offer claiming he was not qualified.[27]

The offer narrowed the choice to two New Yorkers — Governor Daniel Tompkins and former minister to France John Armstrong. In Gallatin's advice to Madison, he said, "I do not believe that the appointment of Gov. Tompkins would be either eligible or calculated to inspire confidence. No person thinks him equal to the place at such a time as this." The next day (January 7), Gallatin conferred again with the president and then in writing compared Tompkins and Armstrong since he was "personally acquainted with both." He placed Armstrong superior "as respects talents and military knowledge," while

Tompkins "would prove inadequate to the task of organizing the Department of the Army" though "in point of temper, Gov. Tompkins would perhaps have the advantage." Gallatin recognized that Armstrong was considered indolent but he believed

> a sense of duty & fear of disgrace may, even in a man much less ambitious than Genl. Armstrong, prevent any sensible inconvenience from that cause. And it is much more important for the head of a Department that he should think and act well than that he should work much.

Another serious factor in deciding between the two men, was that of politics. Both were New Yorkers where the Republican cause had been split by the Clinton defection in the late presidential election. All three men — Tompkins, Armstrong, and Clinton — were potential adversaries of Monroe in 1816. Armstrong stood somewhere between the other New Yorkers. Gallatin told Madison it seemed best to leave Tompkins as governor of the state rather than risk letting it fall by default into the hands of Clinton in the coming April election.

As for Armstrong's influence in the cabinet, Gallatin noted that the general had many enemies and would not bring into the administration "that entire unity of feeling, disinterested zeal. That personal attachment which are so useful in producing hearty cooperation to unity of action." He added that his department (treasury) would be "most seriously affected when perfect cordiality & disposition to accommodate do not exist." Nevertheless, Gallatin felt he must support Armstrong, who "has too much sense not to perceive that his only chance of success will depend on a cordial union with all of us. That once embarked he could not save himself if we are shipwrecked."

Gallatin added an interesting footnote to his letter the next day (January 8).

> If the choice is to fall on a man not professional, I will be ready (Mr. Monroe still refusing) to accept the War Department, with all its horrors and perils and let Tompkins take the Treasury. That, at least, would be better than to give the War Department to him.[28]

Later that day Madison sent to the Senate his nomination of John Armstrong to be secretary of war and William Jones of Pennsylvania to be secretary of the navy.[29] Though Armstrong had served several partial terms in the Senate prior to service as minister to France, he had little political support in that body in 1813. However, it was remembered that Armstrong, as an army major in 1783 had drafted the two Newburgh Addresses attacking the Continental Congress and nearly advocated a mutiny over soldiers' grievances. Only General Washington's tact and skill in handling men blunted the rising. There was doubt that he would be confirmed by the Senate, and John Harper wrote William Plumer that "he will rub hard, if he gets through at all."

On January 13, the Senate, without objection, confirmed Jones early in the day and accepted Armstrong in the evening. Though Armstrong "rubbed through" by a vote of 18–15, he would have been rejected had the two Virginia senators voted and had Samuel Smith of Maryland and Michael Leib of Pennsylvania "voted as they took pains to make others vote." James Bayard wrote Caesar Rodney, "It is the common opinion that he will soon set the Cabinet by the ears."[30]

These confirmations left Plumer with one question. "Who is William Jones?"[31] Harper replied,

> He is a citizen of Pennsylvania. In early life he was a master of a vessel or vessels in the East Indies trade. Afterwards a merchant, and formerly a member of Congress. Having acquired great wealth he retired from active business. For several years past he has been president of one of the insurance offices in Philadelphia.[32]

On the day following confirmation of the new secretaries for the War and Navy Departments, the House concluded its action on the "Additional Military Force" bill to enlist 20,000 troops for one year. The members had sat through further lengthy debate by such House powers as Randolph, Calhoun, and Cheves before passing the bill 77 to 42. The Senate approved it on January 25, and President Madison signed it into law on January 29.

19

REMEMBER THE RIVER RAISIN

Henry Clay had expressed his views on the character of the presidential cabinet in the summer and fall of 1812. After the new secretaries entered on duty — William Jones at Navy on January 19 and John Armstrong at War on February 5 — Speaker Clay said nothing more during this session of Congress regarding the actions of the administration. In fact, he spoke publicly only briefly on any subject and little of his correspondence remains of the last two months of the 12th Congress. Nevertheless, as he continued to preside over the legislation of important measures, he must have conferred privately with members of the administration on matters of national concern. But no trace of such conferences have been found even in the writings of others.

At this time, he was to rejoice in another naval victory, but be stunned by another military disaster that would strike close to the Clay hearth. And finally, he was to witness Madison's second inaugural prior to returning to Kentucky for a short interval before the 1st session of the 13th Congress.

Since December 21, the bill to provide compensation to the officers and crew of the *Constitution*, in lieu of the capture of the *Guerrière*, had remained dormant in the House Naval Committee. It was returned to the floor on January 18, 1813. That same day, Clay opposed the measure, believing "the principle unprecedented in any other country; but even if it were met, he thought it ought not to exist in this country." He thought the law would encourage the destruction of captured vessels rather than their salvage.[1] His opposition led to returning the bill to the Naval Committee where it died.

Three days later, Clay spoke only two sentences in opposition to a committee report growing out of a private petition tied to the forfeitures under the Merchants' Bonds legislation.[2] Clay's support of the petitioners led to their eventual success in a Senate substitute bill.

In mid–February a Clay motion succeeded in postponing action on a Senate bill relating to land claims in the Yazoo area of Mississippi. Early in March, in an unreported speech, Clay spoke at considerable length in favor of a measure to prohibit the exportation of certain goods in foreign ships. The bill later passed the House but was shunted aside without action by the Senate. These brief activities account for the total known endeavors of Clay in the closing days of the 12th Congress.

Yet, those two months of January and February 1813 were filled with important events affecting Clay's life and the conduct of the American government and its army in the West. Making no public comment, Clay presided over two key measures that originated with the executive. One was the subject of financing the government. The other was now the basic rationale for the war — impressment of seamen.

While still arguing the question of enlarging the army, Josiah Quincy's rival for caustic comment — John Randolph — took a swat at Albert Gallatin. The Virginian said the secretary of the treasury "has trifled with the dignity of this House" for changing his mind about the urgent need for taxation.[3] Gallatin could not damage the dignity of the House which Randolph and Quincy had already disgraced. But he did have substantial reason for his "temporary" change in attitude toward taxation.

Gallatin had always advocated a balance in

treasury revenues and expenditures. With congressional measures aimed at arming the nation for war in early 1812, the secretary pleaded for increased taxation — which the South and West were reluctant to support — but settled for an $11-million loan, which was not fully subscribed. Even with the declaration of war in the middle of the year, Congress postponed the subject of taxation to the winter session expecting patriotism and enthusiasm for the war to ignite a national zeal strong enough to take the medicine of taxation. But Congress convened in November with the smell of military debacles drifting in from the North and West. Gallatin knew a plea for taxes would get nowhere. At least he had found an unexpected source of revenue in the Merchants' Bonds affair. Though he failed to pick up $9 million in forfeitures, he still came out ahead with $5 million in duties. It was enough to tide over the treasury to the end of the 12th Congress — thus his reason for dropping the urgency for taxes and the basis of Randolph's charge of "trifling."

Since Congress was in no mood for increasing taxes, Gallatin proposed borrowing money. On January 23, 1813, Langdon Cheves, chairman of the House Ways and Means Committee, brought forward a bill authorizing a loan of $16 million. On the 26th, the bill was passed to permit the loan to be paid off at any rate obtainable over 12 years. The House then passed a second measure permitting issuance of $5 million in treasury notes for one year at 5.4 percent interest.

As reluctant as Congress was in giving authorization to the treasury to obtain money, the task of actually obtaining the funds put the treasury in a near-impossible situation. New England and New York, the principal sources for revenue, were holding back in all ways, including financing, in their support of the war effort. Those banks that were willing to help, had supplied as much as they could in the 1812 loans, which remained only partially subscribed. Eventually, Gallatin (that "foreigner" in the cabinet) found the aid of David Parish (a native of Hamburg, Germany, now with land holdings in New York), Stephen Girard (a native of France, now active in banking and commerce from Philadelphia), and John Jacob Astor (German born, now active in Canadian-American fur trade). These men used their vast influence in the international money markets to obtain the revenue needed by the United States government. Their collateral lay in expectations of a speedy peace which would re-open and stimulate international commerce. Of course, they also hoped to make huge profits from their loans. But the "foreigners" kept the United States solvent. Still, Congress postponed any discussion of taxation until a special session of the new 13th Congress, which had been called to convene late in May.

Almost at the same time that the financial measures came before the House, the members took up consideration of the president's message on "Impressment of Seamen." It came to the House in the form of correspondence to Monroe from John Mitchell, an agent in behalf of prisoners of war held by the British at Halifax, Nova Scotia. Mitchell had been blocked in his efforts to obtain the release of certain nationalized Americans among the captured seamen in an exchange of prisoners. The British admiral there, Sir John B. Warren, had informed Mitchell he could release no men without proof of nativity (which very few men could even obtain in those days). And then Warren insisted that all claims by seamen for release must come directly through their commanding officers (who refused to pass them on) and thus denying Mitchell any contact with the men.[4] Similar correspondence from Jamaica was published in *Niles Register*.[5]

The correspondence was sent to the House Foreign Relations Committee where it was tied in with Madison's annual message of November 1812, wherein he said

> there should be an immediate discharge of American seamen from British ships, and a stop to impressment from American ships, with an understanding that an exclusion of the seamen of each nation from the ships of the other should be stipulated.[6]

The committee reported to the whole House on January 29, "a bill for the regulation of the seamen on board the public vessels and in the merchant service of the United States."[7] A basic purpose of this bill was to set forth a firm provision on which a peace treaty must rest. Under it, all foreign seamen were to be dismissed from American service (at the end of the war) and all foreigners would be forever prohibited from engaging in a seafaring livelihood.

Again there is no record of Clay's attitude

toward the measure at this time, though it was, before the war ended, to become a major concern of his. But congressional objections were loud and clear. Henry Adams summed it up.

> It seemed tacitly to admit the right of impressment; it denied to one class of citizens rights in which all others were protected, and its Constitutionality was at least doubtful; it trenched on Executive function and treaty-making power; it placed American merchants under great disadvantages, depriving them of seamen, and under many circumstances making it impossible for an American ship to return from a distant port. Yet perhaps its worst practical fault consisted in pressing upon England, as an ultimatum, terms of peace which she had again and again rejected and was certain to reject.[8]

The House eventually passed the bill on February 12. The Senate modified the clause forbidding foreigners to join the American service by attaching a five-year limit to such prohibition. Practical application of the law would be next to impossible since the true nationality of so many seamen was only a matter of personal claim with no valid papers for proof.

The discord over the subject of impressment in the halls of Congress was exceeded by the bitterness aroused over its practice by the British as detailed in the public press.

Typical of these accounts was the following letter reprinted in *Niles Register*:

> *Isaac Clark*, of Salem, in the county of Essex, and commonwealth of Massachusetts, on solemn oath declare, that I was born in the town of Randolph in the county of Norfolk, have sailed out of Salem aforesaid, about 7 years; that on the 14th day of June, 1809, I was *impressed* and forcibly taken from the ship *Jane* of Norfolk, by the sailing-master (his name was Car) of his majesty's ship *Porcupine*, Robert Elliott commander. I had a protection from the custom-house in Salem, which I shewed to Capt. Elliott; he swore I was an Englishman, tore my protection to pieces before my eyes, and threw it overboard, and ordered me to go to work—I told him I did not belong to his flag, and I would do no work under it. He then ordered my legs to be put in irons, and the next morning ordered the master at arms to take me on deck and give me two dozen lashes; after receiving them, he ordered him to keep me in irons, and give me one biscuit and one pint of water for twenty-four hours. After keeping me in this situation one week, I was brought on deck and asked by Capt. Elliott if I would go to my duty—on my refusing,

> he ordered me to strip, tied me up a second time, and gave me 2 dozen more, and kept me on the same allowance another week—then ordered me on deck again and asked if I would go to work; I still persisted that I was an American, and that he had no right to command my services, and I would do no work on board his ship—He told me he would punish me until I was willing to work; and gave me the third two dozen lashes, ordered a very heavy chain put round my neck, (such as they had used to sling the lower yard) fastened to a ring bolt in the deck, and that no person, except the master of arms should speak to me, or give me any thing to eat or drink, but my one biscuit and pint of water for twenty-four hours, until I would go to work. I was kept in this situation *nine weeks*, when being exhausted by hunger and thirst, I was obliged to yield. After being on board the ship more than two years and a half, and being wounded in an action with a French frigate, I was sent to a hospital—when partially recovered, I was sent on board the *Impregnable*, a 98-gun ship. My wound growing worse, I was returned to the hospital, when the American consul received a copy of my protection from Salem, and procured my discharge on the twenty-ninth day of April last.[9]

It is worth noting that his discharge from the British service and his entire impressment period was when that nation was "at peace" with the United States.

Niles and most other periodicals of the day reprinted many similar accounts of impressment atrocities including British threats to try and hang some of these seamen as British deserters. These stories fired the anger of Henry Clay and most other Americans. But adding to the public indignation over the issue were further reports reprinted from British newspapers relating the magnanimous manner in which the American captains and their crews treated their British prisoners (though some of the crew members of British ships were impressed American seamen who had been forced to fight their own countrymen on the high-seas battles). As noted before, Captains Dacres of the *Guerrière* and Carden of the *Macedonian* both praised the generous conduct of Captains Hull of the *Constitution* and Decatur of the *United States*.

As the press continued to publish these provocative reports, and as Congress continued to harangue over Madison's proposal for a point on which peace negotiations might hang, dramatic news from Europe intervened to undermine the American hopes for a quick solution to the war.

Since early January, rumors circulated that the French occupation of Moscow was not the great victory it had seemed. By January 23, French bulletins reported that the Emperor Napoleon had left Moscow in mid–October "with a view to put his troops in winter quarters," and that a few days after his departure the French blew up the Kremlin "and finished the destruction of the proud city of the Czars, which the *Russians* themselves had begun and nearly accomplished." The accounts continued relating severe skirmishes with Cossacks, claimed as victories by the French but "dearly purchased." A week later American papers reprinted a proclamation of Czar Alexander which began,

> *Russians!* At length the enemy of our country — the foe of its independence and freedom has experienced a portion of that terrible vengeance which his ambitions and unprincipled aggression has aroused.[10]

In the same issue of *Niles,* further accounts of the events in Russia left the readers somewhat uncertain. Reprinted stories from the same British papers had earlier doubled the U.S. casualty numbers from actions around Niagara (to as much as 1,500 prisoners), leaving great doubt that reports of 200,000 French casualties in Russia could be accurate.

By February 11, Clay was reading that the British had several times reported the death of Napoleon, but French bulletins described his arrival in Paris on December 18. These same bulletins praised the French skill in extracting themselves from the Russian attacks at Moscow and continuing raids on their lines by mounted Cossacks as they returned westward to a more suitable environment for winter quarters. The French papers said, "The plan of the Russians to prevent the [French] army from reaching its winter quarters was profoundly conceived" but they attribute the defeat of the Russian plan "to the superior genius of the emperor only."[11]

While this claim of French success and Russian failure was very soon to be reversed, it is certain that Henry Clay's personal concern for the military events half a world away were obscured by others in his own country.

Throughout the fall of 1812, General William Henry Harrison had organized his northwest army for the recapture of Detroit. He wrote the secretary of war on October 13,

> If the fall should be very dry I will retake Detroit before the winter sets in but if we should have much rain it will be necessary to wait at the Rapids until the Margin of the Lake becomes frozen sufficiently to bear the Army and its baggage.[12]

The "Rapids" were on the Maumee River, which flowed into "the Lake," Erie.

Two days later Harrison wrote the secretary that he had appointed Captain Nathaniel Gray Smith Hart of the 5th Regiment of Kentucky Volunteers to be his deputy inspector. This appointment was effective on October 5. In his dispatch Harrison said, "Captn. Hart is as well qualified as any other officer amongst the Volunteers, a warm advocate of the present administration, the brother-in-law of Mr. H. Clay and nearly connected with Gov. Scott."[13] Hart was Lucretia Clay's brother. His other sister was married to James Brown, then living in New Orleans. Hart's wife was a stepdaughter of Kentucky Governor Charles Scott. They had two sons, Thomas Hart, Jr. and Henry Clay Hart. He left his own mercantile business in Lexington in the summer of 1812 to join the Kentucky Volunteers and was serving under Lt. Col. William Lewis when made inspector.

While Hart remained with General Harrison at his headquarters at Franklinton (now within the limits of Columbus), Harrison had deployed his growing forces in three groups. On the right, along the Sandusky River, were Pennsylvania and Virginia troops. In the center, at Urbana, Ohio, along the road cut earlier by General Hull, were Ohio troops under General Edward W. Tupper. And on the left, at Fort Defiance on the Maumee River, were four regiments of Kentucky Volunteers and the 17th U.S. Infantry, all serving under Gen. James Winchester. These Kentucky soldiers were the ones Clay addressed in August at Georgetown, Kentucky. They included Colonel Lewis's regiment from which Nathaniel Hart was now detached. And they included the regiment under Col. John Allen, Clay's co-counsel in the Burr trials and the man Clay had once supported for Kentucky Governor in a losing cause. These troops were Clay's good friends and neighbors.

Harrison's hope for a dry fall did not materialize.

Instead, it rained much of October, leaving the roads impassable but yet did not fill the swamps enough to permit the regular passage of boats.[14] None of the columns could move. But still worse was the failure of urgently needed supplies to get through. The troops were living in tents, fighting cold winds and rains and mud. In mid–October a brigade inspector described their condition, noting that there had been no full rations since September 8.

> Sometimes without beef— at other times without flour; and the worst of all, entirely without salt, which has been much against the health of the men.... At this time the sick amounted to 216 men...Some without shoes, others without socks, blankets, etc. All the clothes they have are linen ... worn very thin ... and some of these were literally torn to rags by the brush.[15]

In the early days of November, typhus swept the camp and there were daily burials. Though a new fort was constructed the troops moved three times down river seeking drier ground to pitch their tents and find timber to build boats to carry them on down the river toward the rapids near present-day Toledo. Still, supplies were promised but never got through. Freezing conditions came with December, but as no shoes arrived, the men made moccasins out of green hides. But even these did not prevent serious frost bites. It was not until Christmas time — when the camp was called "a loathsome place" or "Fort Starvation," and the troops were close to mutiny — that some small quantities of flour, pork, and beef got through to the camp. And a few days later some clothing arrived from Kentucky. "Our clothes and blankets looked as if they had never been acquainted with water, but intimately with dirty smoke and soot."[16]

During these same December days, Harrison was exchanging correspondence with the secretary of war regarding the political considerations of a winter assault to recapture Detroit. If such considerations could be disregarded he believed the campaign should wait till spring when "Malden, Detroit and Mackinac would fall in rapid succession." On the other hand, the best he could hope for in the winter, provided the Detroit River froze over, was to "sit down before Malden (without going to Detroit) in six days from my leaving the Rapids." If the river did not freeze, he didn't

expect to be able to take Detroit before late February or early March.[17]

In later letters, Harrison wrote of the difficulty inherent in an attack across an iced Detroit River to lay siege to Malden, considering the uncertainty of the river supply and retreat line remaining frozen. He suggested a naval force on Lake Erie and some defense to the north and west resulting from a recapture of Fort Michilimackinac guarding Indian routes of Lakes Superior and Michigan (especially the latter which "running deep into our country approaches Fort Wayne, the settlements upon the Wabash, and those of the Illinois River."[18]

By Christmas, the new temporary secretary of war, James Monroe, was reminding Harrison that "the object of your Expedition was to retake Detroit, to take Malden, with the adjacent Country, and to hold them." He then added, "the delay however which has already taken place, and which is not doubted has been unavoidable ... give the President much concern.... The President still considers the occupancy of Detroit and Malden objects of the highest importance." He believed their fall "would demolish the British power in that quarter."[19]

Monroe gave Harrison a little more leeway in that letter on making plans. Then, too, late on January 17, in response to Harrison's (January 4) go-slow proposal, Monroe advised the general,

> The President wishes you to attempt nothing in vain or at least without the fairest prospect of success.... The delay of a few months is an evil not to be compared with the failure of another expedition. Whatever ground is gained must be held, and he is content to gain it slowly, provided it be made secure, rather than to put the important interests of the Country to hazard by a rash enterprise.[20]

Early in December, Harrison sent orders to Winchester to move down to the rapids, where the whole northwestern army was eventually to gather for the attack on Malden or Detroit, and there build huts to present the appearance of going into winter quarters. As supplies never got through until Christmas, Winchester delayed the start of his march until December 30. By this time the river was frozen and boats were useless. Sleds had since been constructed but now the few horses were useless. The sleds were to be pulled by the men —five or six to each sled. Two days out the snow melted stalling the sleds. The boats were tried but were blocked by ice in the river. On January 2, snow came again and in two days was two feet deep. Eventually, after a 50-mile march, the troops reached their destination on January 10, and Winchester notified Harrison of his arrival. But two days out of their old camp, General Winchester received an order from Harrison to send back a large part of his force to Ft. Defiance. This was because Harrison had learned of a large force of Indians under Tecumseh southwest to Winchester's rear. Winchester, who had in the meantime sent a dispatch to Harrison informing him of his move to the rapids, declined to follow Harrison's orders for reasons basically centering on the fact that the rapids were a better position for him to place his troops for supply, communications, and defense.

The next day, a series of events began that was to lead to disaster. Learning of a nearby Indian camp, a small unit was sent out to chase them away. Most of the Indians escaped and ran north to a village on the River Raisin called Frenchtown (after the nationality of most of its inhabitants) and then continued to the British camp across the Detroit River at Malden. While the Indians informed the British of the presence of the Americans at the rapids, two Frenchmen from the village came to the American camp to plead for protection against the Indians. By the 17th of January more villagers had come in to report British troops assembling at Frenchtown.

Winchester counselled with his subordinates. Colonel Allen, in a stimulating address, advocated aid to the inhabitants of Frenchtown. The other officers unanimously supported an expedition to go to the village's relief.[21] The general wrote that same day to Harrison regarding the plan, noting that in addition to securing the village (which he intended to hold) he would deprive the British and Indians of flour and grain held in that area. He told Harrison he expected to encounter about two companies of Canadians and 200 Indians. And he said he had, that morning, sent out a detachment of 550 under Colonel Lewis followed by 110 men under Colonel Allen.

These troops reached the rapids the next afternoon (the 18th) by marching on the ice of Maumee Bay and the western edge of Lake Erie. At 5 P.M. they crossed the frozen River Raisin and began a fight with the enemy, dislodging him by dark, leaving the Americans holding Frenchtown on the north bank.[22]

After the battle the poorly-fed and scantily-clothed troops refreshed themselves in the houses with food and warmth giving little thought of the British encamped only 18 miles away at Malden across the frozen Detroit River. But Colonel Lewis and his other officers were well aware of their dangerous plight. Lewis sent word that night to Winchester to bring up support. Winchester learning, the next morning, of the previous day's success, wrote to Harrison, and then left with another 250 men under Col. Samuel Wells to support those already at the Raisin, reaching them late on the 20th. Harrison was already in motion to support Winchester and arrived at the Rapids the day after Winchester had left. There he learned of the battle which had taken place 38 miles ahead. He wrote Monroe to pass on the intelligence he had received, saying Winchester had acted properly in going to Col. Lewis' support. But he added, "I fear nothing but that the enemy may overpower Genl. Winchester before I can send him a sufficient reinforcement. I have however the highest confidence in the General and the troops."[23]

Harrison then sent a communication to Winchester by his deputy inspector, Capt. Nathaniel Hart (it may have been oral or else a written message has been lost) with orders to "maintain the position at the River Raisin, at any rate."[24]

On his arrival at Frenchtown, Winchester agreed with Lewis that the position was dangerous and would have retreated except for his 55 wounded. Instead, he threw out a defensive line in a sort of semi-circle around the north of the town with the river at his rear — or the rear of his line. Winchester took up lodging at the home of Col. Francis Navarre south of the river! Probably there, on January 21, he received Captain Hart and replied, in a message to Harrison, that his ground was "not very favorable for defence," but he requested his force be "increased to 1000 or 1200 effective men." As additional troops were already on the march to Winchester, Harrison waited until the 23rd for further word from the Raisin.

When Captain Hart reached General Winchester on the 21st, he found the camp in a state of excitement and apprehension. Earlier that morning two or three Frenchmen had arrived from Malden and had informed Winchester that the British were preparing an attack. But one of the Frenchmen, a man named James (or Jacques) Lasselle (or LaSalle), played down the threat. Unknown to Winchester, Lasselle was pro–British. Probably during this day Lasselle dispatched a letter by an Indian, George Blue Jacket, to British Colonel Proctor commanding at Malden, outlining the American military position. He noted that there was a gap between Colonel Lewis and his 500 men in the center and Colonel Wells and his 300 men in an exposed position on the right. Proctor was advised "that getting between them with a proper force they could be defeated in detail."[25]

To make the military situation worse on the right, Colonel Wells, according to one account, appealed to General Winchester that same morning for leave to return to the camp at the Rapids to pick up his baggage. Winchester declined the leave informing Wells that an attack was imminent. The account stated,

In the afternoon Wells renewed his request to which Winchester replied, "The spies bring intelligence that the enemy have reached Stony Creek, five miles from here. If you are disposed to leave your command in the immediate vicinity of the enemy, when a battle is certain, you can go." Wells left and went back

to Harrison's camp.[26]

A different account said Wells had begged Winchester to order cartridges to be distributed to the men and that other preparations be made, but that the general would not admit the necessity of these measures and was contemptuous of an "Indian" attack. In any case, Wells took with him a message from Captain Hart (and probably one or both of two dispatches written by Winchester to Harrison on the 21st).

Hart wrote to Harrison.

Colonel Wells will give you the news we have received. The importance of holding this post I know you have fully weighed. In the event of its loss, the people having taken an active part against the British, will be subjected to utter ruin — perhaps scalped.

Hart told Harrison that

the officers here are truly desirous of seeing you here, if it were even for a day. Many things ought to be done, which you only know how to do properly. Such, however, is the opinion they entertain of you.[27]

That evening Captain Hart rejoined his old company of the Lexington Light Infantry within the garden pickets under Colonel Lewis. Colonel Allen's units were also in this area.

The night of January 21–22 was exceedingly cold with a deep blanket of snow on the ground. Several of the army units posted guards around garden pickets but none were placed on "the road by which the enemy was expected to advance."[28] And Winchester wrote later, "Neither night-patrol, nor night pickets were ordered by me, from a belief, that both were matters of routine and in constant use."[29] There were later denied reports that Winchester retired after a frolic, and under the influence of liquor. In the denial, the writer also states that Winchester was aroused at midnight with the battle in progress though all other accounts say it began at daybreak.[30]

Around 6 A.M. on January 22 the drums beat reveille, muffling any noise of British gun-carriages moving from their overnight position five miles above Frenchtown. As the American soldiers sat down for breakfast, they were interrupted by cannon and musket fire from the woods to the north. Almost immediately Indians and British troops drove in the Americans camped in the exposed right now under Colonel Wells' subordinate. Within 20 minutes the line had been forced back to the river but tried to bend back westward to come under support of Colonel Lewis' troops. Colonel Allen took his unit forward and tried three times to halt the retreat. Colonel Lewis and General Winchester also reached the scene about this time.

In the action, Colonel Allen was wounded in the thigh and, with other wounded troops, moved back across the river south of the town only to find the Indians had cut them off behind. In this situation Allen, exhausted and suffering from his wound, sat down on a log. Some months after the battle, one of Allen's fellow officers in captivity received the following account from an Indian chief who had Allen's sword:

The chief stated that he noticed Col. Allen in the retreat, and he saw he was a brave man, and determined to save him; that he ordered his men to take him, upon which they surrounded him. The chief said he threw his gun across his lap and told colonel Allen if he would surrender he should be safe; whilst one of the warriors, unordered, advanced on him, for what purpose the chief did [not] know; upon which the colonel, with one stroke of his sword, laid him dead at his feet; another, instantly, and without orders, shot the colonel dead. The chief attributes his death to the conduct of the warrior who advanced on him, and spoke of it with regret.[31]

While some soldiers made good their escape southward by pulling off their shoes and leaving only barefoot tracks in the snow to resemble those of Indians, General Winchester and Colonel Lewis were less fortunate. By mid-morning they were captured by Indians and taken to Col. Henry A. Proctor, commander of the British forces based at Malden. The British were fearful of the arrival of General Harrison and American reinforcements, but decided on a ruse and demanded Winchester surrender with the army still locked in a struggle behind the garden pickets in the town. Proctor told Winchester that if he refused surrender, the British could not restrain the Indians. Around 11 A.M., under flag of truce, one of Winchester's aides and Colonel Proctor carried the message to Maj. George Madison, now senior American on the field. (Madison was a distant relative of the president. He died shortly after becoming Governor of Kentucky after the war.) Madison and his fellow officers knew their ammunition was about exhausted, but replied that it had been customary for the Indians to massacre the wounded prisoners after a surrender, and told the British officer, "We will not surrender without a guarantee for the safety of the wounded." The British officer haughtily responded, "Do you, sir, claim the right to dictate what terms I am to offer?" Madison answered, "No. I mean to dictate for myself — and we prefer to sell our lives as dearly as possible, rather than be massacred in cold blood."[32]

The British agreed to the terms and said they would send sleds the next morning for the wounded to take them to Malden. Almost immediately after the surrender was agreed to, several Indians began plundering the American property. Madison appealed to Proctor to "keep the Indians off." Proctor answered, "The Indians are fierce and un-

manageable. *It cannot be done.*" Madison coolly replied, "If you cannot disperse them, I will!" He ordered his men to shoulder their arms and Proctor, fearing that "charge bayonets" would follow, waved his sword and the Indians instantly withdrew.[33]

As the frustrated and angry American soldiers threw down their weapons (sometimes with such vigor as to break them), the walking wounded were ordered in line to march off to Malden. The other wounded were left behind with two American surgeons, Dr. John Todd, and Dr. Gustavus M. Bower. Todd was the brother of Robert S. Todd, a corporal in Captain Hart's company. Robert Todd, some five years later, was to become the father of Mary Todd, the future wife of Abraham Lincoln.

Among the wounded cared for by the two surgeons, at the home of a Frenchman, were several other American officers, including Captain Hart, and about 15 to 20 privates from scattered units. More wounded were at one or two other houses. As requested, to assure protection against the Indians, the British left a light guard under Capt. William Elliott (son of Colonel Elliott, the agent for furnishing weapons to the Indians prior to the war) and three Indian interpreters. Meanwhile, both Colonel Proctor and Captain Elliott promised that sleighs would come from Malden by the next morning to transport the wounded over the snow-filled roads to the British fort. To provide even more confidence in the minds of the wounded Americans was the revelation that Captains Hart and Elliott had been classmates at Princeton College and that Hart had entertained Elliott at his home in Lexington.[34]

Throughout the remainder of January 22 and into the cold night, an apprehensive peace reigned over the battered village. Almost all of the Indians had gone to Stony Creek, six miles north of Frenchtown, where it was rumored "that the British had promised the Indians a frolic that night."[35] Some may have gotten drunk there while others returned to Frenchtown and broke open barrels in a tavern. In any case, the events that followed on the 23rd have survived in accounts that differ in some details, as all such accounts do when reported by witnesses to extremely emotional scenes.

Blending several accounts and centering them on the actions of Captain Hart, it is clear that

Captain Elliott left Frenchtown either late in the afternoon of the 22nd or during the night. He may have taken two of the interpreters with him. Shortly after dawn, six or eight Indians came in the house but molested no one. After a while, more Indians, possibly between 100 and 200, came to the village and then began plundering the houses and massacring the wounded. Doctor Todd related that he then carried Captain Hart to an adjoining house. The house had already been plundered and was empty except for one Indian whom they had met the day before. The Indian inquired why the surgeons and wounded had been left. Doctor Todd said it was the wish of Colonel Proctor that they wait for transportation and Captain Hart told him that Captain Elliott was his friend and was to call for him in the morning.

The Indian replied that the British were damned rascals. He added that all the Americans would be killed. He requested Todd "to be quiet, for the chiefs were then in counsel, and 'maybe' only the wounded would be killed."[36]

Accounts now differ in saying that Captain Hart was still in the adjoining house with other wounded, was in another room of the first house, or was outside in a yard. But all agree that he had a discussion with an interpreter. One account reports that he asked the Indian to allow him "to make a speech to them before they kill us." The interpreter told him the Indians could not understand. Hart said, "But you can interpret for me." The Indian replied, "If we undertook to interpret for you, they will as soon kill us as you."[37]

Somewhere during these discussions, many accounts state that Hart offered an Indian $100 to take him to Captain Elliott at Malden. Apparently the offer was accepted and Hart was put up on a horse and taken from the scene.

Captain Hart is next mentioned in three additional differing accounts. In a brief sworn statement given three months after the battle, a surviving private stated that the recipient of the $100 and another Indian quarrelled over the money only to settle it by agreeing

> to kill Hart and plunder him of the rest of his money and effects, which they did, by taking him off his horse, then knocking him down with a war club, scalped and tomahawked him, and stripped him naked, leaving his body on the ground.

The private related,

> I was gratified in observing that during this scene of trial, Captain Hart refrained from supplication or entreaty, but appeared perfectly calm and collected. He met his fate with the firmness which was his particular characteristic. No other prisoner of our army of the United States was present to witness this melancholy scene, the death of Captain Hart.[38]

But there were two other accounts which were written much later. They appear together, but one was written by 1818 and the other as late as 1858. They both relate that Hart's captors took him to a house about 100 rods up the river and motioned for him to continue to the home of Francis Lasselle, about 40 rods further. Hart hailed Lasselle and entreated him to rescue him from the Indians.

Lasselle, peeking out a partially opened front door, told Hart it was not in his power to save him, that earlier in the day other Indians had threatened to kill him and the women and children in the house and burn all his property if he should give aid to the Americans. Lasselle advised Hart to continue another 15 rods to the home of his brother, James Lasselle (the man who had written Proctor about the American troop dispositions before the battle). Whether or not this Lasselle was in the house, five drunk Delaware Indians were. As Hart came up to that house, "one of the Indians from within, leveled his rifle at Hart and shot him in the breast. Another ran out and scalped him and tomahawked him and left his body stretched in the road almost naked."[39] So fearful were the French of the Indians' wrath and threats that they left Hart's body in the road for two days before burial.

Yet Hart's fate was not unusual. In the months and years following, survivors of the battle told grisly tales of wanton brutality, when wounded American prisoners of war were scalped alive and attacked from without when trying to escape through windows from burning houses. Even before Hart was led away from the houses containing the other wounded, men were being stripped bare in the freezing weather and forced out of doors into the 18-inch-deep snow. Many were tomahawked, scalped, and mutilated while still pleading for their lives. Others died horribly in houses set afire by the Indians. Those who survived were marched to Malden. En route to Malden, Doctor Todd met up with Captain Elliott and told him of the depredations occurring in Frenchtown and asked him to send back to rescue the wounded, especially Captain Hart. Elliott replied, "It is now too late; you may rest assured that those who are badly wounded are killed ere this." To further entreaties, Elliott answered. "Charity begins at home; my own wounded are to be conveyed first."[40]

And finally, those soldiers, who had survived near-starvation with inadequate clothing through several winter weeks, fought two battles, witnessed and suffered through an atrocious massacre and a freezing march to Malden, underwent a cruel march of 284 miles in 16 days from Malden to Niagara Falls where, at last, they were paroled. Frequently, they traveled in sub-zero weather, through snow as deep as 24 inches, with meager rations (and sometimes none for as long as two days), sleeping in unheated barns, and still poorly clad. The suffering endured by the Kentuckians that fought at the River Raisin stands equally with that of Washington's army at Valley Forge which neither fought a battle, marched in the winter, nor were prisoners of a cruel enemy. These gallant warriors of the War of 1812 are, regretfully, unheralded, despite the first use of a "Remember" phrase. The plea went out, "Remember the River Raisin!" (In later times there would be substituted, "The Alamo," "the *Maine*," and "Pearl Harbor.")

As these veterans returned to their homes, their stories were told across the nation. In Washington, and later at home in Kentucky, Henry and Lucretia Clay learned of the events in bits and dribbles for weeks to come. The earliest news they received was on January 28 — that military moves were about to take place in the northwest. By February 9, they learned of Colonel Lewis' successful attack of January 18. Two days later, news headlined "Disastrous Event" appeared in the *National Intelligencer*. It noted that Winchester had been killed, that he "had not taken the precaution of supplying the troops [with ammunition or even adequate clothing], and that they were scarcely able to fire five rounds," and that his move was without orders from Harrison.

Only on February 13 did the Clays read that Captain Hart had been on the battle scene; that

he "got to camp in advance the night before, just in time to suffer with his company." Their anxiety was enhanced by the report that,

> Out of three Kentucky regiments not a battalion remains. Only two officers that were in the engagement have got in; viz. McClanahan and Graves. Surely the Clays received word through official channels of Hart's encounter with Elliott and subsequent brutal death before it was described in the *Intelligencer* of March 9 — six days after Congress adjourned.[41]

Even so, as the tragic news reached the Clays' home, Lucretia was not alone in her mourning for her brother. Her sister Nancy, married to James Brown, had only recently arrived in Washington. On February 5, James Brown took his seat in the United States Senate as the newly elected Senator from Louisiana succeeding John N. Destréhan, who had never qualified for the seat. The two families apparently shared their grief within their own hearths.

This final month of the 12th Congress had to be a period of great mental anguish for Clay. In addition to the family's personal loss, the hopes of an easy conquest of Canada had turned into continuing disaster. Yet none of Clay's emotions are revealed in speeches or correspondence.

On the day he read that Winchester had been killed, February 11, Clay presided over the traditional opening of the electoral votes which officially confirmed that James Madison of Virginia had defeated De Witt Clinton of New York for the presidency by 128 votes to 89. And he also proclaimed that Elbridge Gerry of Massachusetts was elected vice president over Jared Ingersoll of Pennsylvania, 131 to 86. That same day also brought news that Captain Charles Stewart's frigate *Constellation* had run aground near Norfolk, but had managed to get afloat and into safety as several British ships began a blockage of Hampton Roads at the entrance to Chesapeake Bay.

The only good news to reach Clay during February was, as usual, another great naval victory. On the 20th, the *Intelligencer* reported that the frigate *Constitution*, now sailing under the command of Capt. William Bainbridge, had met the British frigate *Java* in the early afternoon of December 30, off the coast of Brazil. A week after this first announcement, Bainbridge's succinct report described the action:

At 2:10 P.M. Commenced the action within good grape and canister distance, the enemy to windward (but much further than I wished).

At 2:30 our wheel was shot entirely away.

2:40 determined to close with the enemy, not withstanding his raking — set the fore and mainsail, and luff'd up to him.

2:50 the enemy's jib-boom got foul of our mizzen-rigging.

3:00 the head of the enemy's bowsprit and jib-boom shot away by us.

3:05 shot away the enemy's foremast by the board.

3:15 shot away his main-top-mast just above the cap.

3:40 shot away gaff and spanker-boom.

3:55 shot away his mizzen-mast nearly by the board.

4:05 having silenced the fire of the enemy completely, and his colors in the main rigging being down, supposed he had struck, then hauled aboard the courses to shoot ahead to repair our rigging, which was extremely cut, leaving the enemy a complete wreck; soon after, discovered the enemy's flag was still flying — hove too to repair some of our damage.

4:20 the enemy's main-mast went nearly by the board.

4:50 wore ship and stood for the enemy, got very close to the enemy in a very effectual *raking position*, athwart his bows, and was at the very instant of raking him, when he most prudently struck his flag, for had he suffered the broadside to have raked him, his additional loss must have been extremely great, as he laid an unmanageable wreck upon the water.[42]

Bainbridge reported the *Java*'s Capt. Henry Lambert was mortally wounded and that the *Java* had at least 60 killed and 101 wounded (though a British letter stated 170 were wounded). The *Constitution* reported nine killed and 25 wounded. Some days prior to the battle, Bainbridge had recorded in his journal, and told some of his officers of a dream in which he foresaw almost every incident of the battle including the capture of a British army general. Aboard the *Java* was Lt. Gen. T. Hislop of the British army en route to his new post as governor of Bombay. On receiving the general on board the *Constitution*, Bainbridge informed a fellow officer, "That is the identical officer I saw in my dream." The *Constitution* put into San Salvador, Brazil, and Hislop and his staff were released. Whereupon the general thanked Bainbridge with a note acknowledging, "Your

very handsome and kind treatment." He then asked the American for parole of the *Java*'s officers. With this granted by Bainbridge, Hislop then troubled Bainbridge to look for "a small chest containing articles of plate," of sentimental value to the general.[43] In contrast to the grisly tales of Indian depredations and British naval acts of brutality against American prisoners of war, reports soon appeared in the American press of the magnanimous treatment Americans showed toward their captives.

The magnanimity of the conquering Americans had previously been expressed in the official report of Captain Dacres of the *Guerrière* when he stated,

> I feel it my duty to state that the conduct of Captain Hull and his officers to our men, has been that of a brave enemy, the greatest care being taken to prevent our men losing the smallest trifle, and the greatest attention being paid to the wounded.[44]

And the British Captain Carden of the *Macedonian* reported that,

> All the private property of the officers and men on board the *Macedonian* was given up; that claimed by Captain Carden including a band of music, and several casks of wine, valued at about $800, which the Commodore [Decatur] paid him for.[45]

While the British naval officers praised the conduct of their captors, the British politicians screamed at the outrages of Americans concealing the "fact" that they were using ships-of-the-line (74 guns) against the smaller British frigates (38 guns). The British press was more accurate but equally outraged — but at their navy. *The London Pilot* wrote,

> The public will learn with sentiments, which we will not presume to anticipate, that a *third* British frigate has struck to an American. This is an occurrence that calls for serious reflection, this and the fact stated in our paper of yesterday, that Lloyd's list contains notices of upwards of five hundred British vessels captured in seven months by the Americans. *Five hundred merchantmen and three frigates.* Can these statements be true; and can the English people hear them unmoved? Anyone who had predicted such a result of an American war, this time last year, would have been treated as a madman or a traitor.

The *Pilot* reminded its readers, "Yet down to this moment, not a single American frigate has struck her flag."[46]

Still before the 12th Congress adjourned, diplomacy became the key element in national affairs and held this position until after the special summer session of the 13th Congress convened.

20

DIPLOMACY RENEWED

On February 24, 1813, one week before the expiration of the 12th Congress, President Madison, in great indignation, sent to the Congress a short message accompanied by a proclamation from the governor of Bermuda. Based on a British Order in Council of October 26, 1812, the proclamation permitted that colony (and other British West Indies colonies), under a special license, to trade exclusively with the ports of the eastern states of the United States.

In his message Madison said,

> The Government of Great Britain had already introduced into her commerce during the war, a system, which, at once violating the rights of other nations, and resting on a mass of forgery and perjury unknown to other times, was making an unfortunate progress in undermining those principles of morality and religion which are the best foundation of national happiness.
>
> The policy now proclaimed to the world introduces into her modes of warfare a system equally distinguished by the deformity of its features, and the depravity of its character, having for its object to dissolve the ties of allegiance and the sentiments of loyalty in the adversary nation, and to seduce and separate its component parts, the one from the other.
>
> The general tendency of these demoralizing and disorganizing contrivances will be reprobated by the civilized and Christian world; and the insulting attempt on the virtue, the honor, the patriotism, and the fidelity of our brethren of the Eastern States, will not fail to call forth all their indignation and resentment, and to attach more and more all the States to that happy Union and Constitution, against which such insidious and malignant artifices are directed.

Madison then recommended a prohibition of any trade under such special licenses as proposed by the governor of Bermuda, and a further pro-hibition of exports from the United States in foreign ships.[1] The House acted on both proposals sending a bill on licenses to the Senate on March 1 and on exports on foreign vessels on March 3. Clay spoke at considerable length in favor of the latter measure but his comments were not published. The Senate postponed action on both bills until a special session due to meet in May.

The special session had been agreed upon by both Houses during the last week of the 12th Congress primarily to vote taxes, which the Congress, in two sessions, never had the courage to levy.

On Sunday, February 28, French Minister Louis Sérurier gave a farewell dinner honoring William Crawford, president pro tem of the Senate, and Henry Clay, Speaker of the House. Despite the recent news of British and Indian atrocities and the current debate over the British attempt to split the Union, Clay was in no mood to follow the advice of Polonius in *Hamlet*, and grapple the French to American friendship with hoops of steel.

Sérurier wrote his government that he was reproached by Clay, "always in a tone of extreme circumspection," for French failure to provide the aid the United States had hoped for in their war with a common enemy. Clay pointed out that by the time the special session convened the United States would have been at war one year — surely enough time for its friends to have declared themselves. "If it turns out otherwise, if we must give up the continental trade," Sérurier quoted Clay, "it will be necessary to shift to that which is offered us with our enemies; for we must finally have points, wherever they may be in Europe, where we may carry our products and exchange them for our needs."[2]

It was in the week after this meeting that the House passed and the Senate postponed action prohibiting trade with the enemy.

At an evening sitting, beginning at 5 o'clock on March 3, the House unanimously passed a resolution, "That the thanks of this House be presented to Henry Clay, in testimony of their approbation of his conduct in the discharge of the arduous and important duties assigned him whilst in the Chair."

In his reply of thanks, Clay said,

Amidst the momentous subjects of deliberation which undoubtedly distinguished the 12th Congress as the most memorable in the annals of America, it has been a source of animating consolation to me, that I have never failed to experience the liberal support of gentlemen in all quarters of the House. If in the moment of ardent debate, when all have been struggling to maintain the best interests of our beloved country as they have appeared to us respectively, causes of irritation have occurred, let us consign them to oblivion, and let us in the painful separation which is about to ensue, perhaps for ever, cherish and cultivate a recollection only of the many agreeable hours we have spent together. Allow me, gentlemen, to express the fervent wish that one and all of you may enjoy all possible individual happiness, and that in the return to your several homes you may have pleasant journeys.[3]

Later in the evening the House tried for two hours to obtain a quorum but no more than 64 members could be found. Meanwhile, several bills from the Senate awaited House approval. The approvals never came. At midnight the House adjourned *sine die*.

The following morning a huge crowd gathered at the Capitol for James Madison's second inaugural ceremonies. In his ride to Capitol Hill, the president was escorted to the building by the cavalry of the District of Columbia. There he was met by several volunteer corps drawn up in ceremonial array. The excitement which built, was described by an old Virginia farmer.

By and bye I heard the cannons roar; the crowd began to increase; my pulse increased, too; I would not have taken a dollar for my place. Now a tide, an *ocean* of people were moving towards me; now carriages, officers, horses, ladies, wheelbarrows of cake, Congressmen, apple-girls and pickpockets were huddled into one immovable mass. I was all anxiety and attention.

At length a carriage with four spanking grays drove like Jehu to the door [of the Capitol], and out popped a little man in black, with a powdered head. This, I was told, was the Lord's anointed.[4]

The president went in to the House of Representatives chamber where he was greeted by Chief Justice John Marshall, the other judges, members of Congress, foreign ministers, "and a great concourse of ladies and gentlemen."[5]

After acknowledging the confidence of the people in placing him in his high station for a second time, Madison observed that the United States had not declared war

until it had been long made on them in reality though not in name; until arguments and expostulations had been exhausted; until a positive declaration had been received, that the wrongs provoking it would not be discontinued, nor until this last appeal could no longer be delayed without breaking down the spirit of the nation, destroying all confidence in itself and in its political institutions, and either perpetuating a state of disgraceful suffering, or regaining by more costly sacrifices and more severe struggles, our lost rank and respect among independent Powers.

Madison spoke of the unlawfulness of the British practice of impressment and of the scrupulous regard with which America had waged war that "no principle of justice or honor, no usage of civilized nations, no precept of courtesy or humanity have been infringed." He then examined the treatment of American prisoners of war held by the British, many of whom should never be so regarded under the usages of war, and others naturalized being punished as British traitors or deserters. And he said,

They have not, it is true, taken into their own hands the hatchet and the knife, devoted to indiscriminate massacre; but they have let loose the savages, armed with these cruel instruments, have allured them into their service, and carried them to battle by their sides, eager to glut their savage thirst with the blood of the vanquished, and to finish the work of torture and death on maimed and defenseless captives.

Madison criticized the recent British efforts to dismember the Union through licensing trade with one region. He alluded to early American notice of reasonable terms by which peace could be restored. He noted that American resources were superior to those of the British to wage war.

And finally he expressed his conviction that discipline and habits in the army would soon produce triumphs to correspond to "the gallant exploits of our naval heroes."[6]

The entire speech was later printed in the papers, but for those listening, much was missed as Madison's "voice was so low and the audience so very great, that scarcely a word could be distinguished."[7] Only after the address did Chief Justice Marshall administer the oath. An anecdote later appeared in the anti-administration *Georgetown Federal Republican* that the Federalist Chief Justice had unnerved the president during his address "by a fixed and steady gaze in which scorn, indignation, and disgust were portrayed." The editor went so far as to say "a guilty suffusion spread over Madison's cheeks as he thought of the profound religious hypocrisy with which he had invited the smiles of heaven upon his western bloodletting." That newspaper did not believe the early reports coming to the capital of the Indian massacre at Frenchtown.[8]

> When I read Mr. Madison's message I supposed him to be out of his senses, and have since been told that he never goes sober to bed. Whether intoxicated by opium or wine was not said, but I learned last winter that pains in his teeth had driven him to use the former too freely.[9]

While Madison was being sworn in to the presidential office the second time in Washington, Elbridge Gerry took the oath to be vice president for his first term in elaborate ceremonies in Cambridge, Massachusetts.

Following the ceremony at the nation's Capitol, Madison was accompanied to the White House by

> every creature that could afford twenty-five cents for hack-hire.... The major part of the respectable citizens offered their congratulations, ate his ice-creams and bon-bons, drank his Madeira, made their bow and retired, leaving him fatigued beyond measure with the incessant bending to which his politeness urged him, and in which he never allows himself to be eclipsed returning bow for bow, even to those *ad infinitum* of Sérurier and other foreigners.[10]

Later that evening most of official Washington, as well as "a most lively assemblage of the lovely ones of our district," attended the inaugural ball at Davis' Hotel,[11] then on the north side of Pennsylvania Avenue between 6th and 7th streets.

At this ball, Sérurier found Madison in a different mood of recent days. The president had since learned of the death of the American minister to France, Joel Barlow. Barlow had followed Napoleon to eastern Europe in hopes of securing a commercial treaty. He had reached Vilna, Poland, on Napoleon's trail, took sick from the extreme cold weather, and lay dying in the city as the emperor rushed through it one night on his hasty retreat (or flight) to Paris from the Russian cold and Cossack armies. Now Sérurier spoke of Barlow with great sympathy. In return, Madison confided to him that he intended to nominate William Crawford as Barlow's successor.

This diplomatic move occurred almost simultaneously with a public announcement of new peace initiatives taken by the lately victorious Czar of all the Russias, Alexander I. Though Clay surely knew of Crawford's appointment and the Russian offer to mediate prior to his departure for Kentucky (about March 11), they were not to affect him at all during the weeks intervening before the next session of Congress. Even then, he was only indirectly involved. But within a year he would become a kingpin in peace negotiations.

As Clay headed back to Kentucky by way of Pittsburgh, only newspaper accounts could inform him of the latest political flap growing out of the Russian offer to mediate. On March 9, the *National Intelligencer* printed an announcement that the Czar's offer "has just been made to our government by Mr. [Andre de] Daschkoff," the Russian minister to the United States.[12] The Federalist news organ in Georgetown, referring to Madison's "character for cunning and his habitual deceit and hypocrisy," accused him of receiving and rejecting a Russian offer over a month earlier. It had obtained this story from the Danish minister who had quoted Daschkoff.[13] But Timothy Pickering, who also got the same story from Daschkoff, made a memo of the Russian's comments and it did not agree with claims of the Georgetown paper.

In fact, while Napoleon was having his greatest success in Russia (as far as was known in Washington) Daschkoff, without instructions from his government in Russia, proposed the Czar as a peace mediator. Madison asked if Daschkoff could guarantee the rights the United States claimed from Great Britain. The Russian could not. And there the early proposal ended. It was only after Russian victories over Napoleon's army that a valid offer of mediation came from the Czar. He was, by then, in a position of strength. It appeared the United States was about to lose an ally of sorts (the French) and would subsequently be forced to meet the unrestricted strength of the British Empire freed of her long-time foe. The time was ripe for the United States to consider the move seriously. On March 11, three days after receiving Daschkoff's note, Madison accepted Russian mediation. But would the British? Madison did not have the answer to that question.

Sometime around the first of April, about the time Clay arrived home in Kentucky, President Madison privately made his selection for a three-man commission to meet a hoped-for British commission in St. Petersburg, Russia. He picked John Quincy Adams, already serving as United States minister in that Russian city; Albert Gallatin, currently secretary of the treasury; and James A. Bayard, Federalist senator from Delaware.

The only controversy over Madison's choice was to arise over the appointment of Gallatin. But this did not come to a head until Congress convened in May.

A few weeks after Madison's appointment of peace commissioners became known, Monroe wrote their private instructions which reveal the administration's attitude toward the Russian offer to mediate. In mid–April Monroe wrote,

> It is not known that Great Britain has acceded to the proposition but it is presumed that she will not decline it. The President thought it improper to postpone his decision until he should hear of that of the British Government. Sincerely desirous of peace, he has been willing to avail himself of every opportunity which might tend to promote it, on just and honorable conditions.[14]

Meanwhile, through the month of March 1813, Gallatin was continuing in the distasteful task of finding money to pay for the government's spending. In 1809, he had revealed his feelings to Thomas Jefferson, writing,

> I cannot, my dear sir, consent to act the part of a mere financier, to become a contriver of taxes, a dealer of loans, a seeker of resources for the purpose of supporting useless baubles, of increasing the number of idle and dissipated members of the community, of fattening contractors, pursers, and agents, and of introducing in all its ramifications that system of patronage, corruption, and rottenness which you so justly execrate.[15]

What Gallatin hated to do in peacetime, he was forced to do in wartime.

Obtaining money to run the government had made Gallatin something of an ogre. Congress, in two sessions had refused to levy taxes he had proposed. On the day after Madison's second inaugural, Gallatin was forced to inform his chief, "We have hardly enough money to last till the end of the month."[16] He referred to the opening of subscriptions for the $16-million loan set for March 12 and 13, which eventually required the slight of hand of such wealthy men as John Jacob Aster to secure.

Also, in just the few short weeks since the latest cabinet change, Gallatin had clashed with his new colleague, Secretary of War John Armstrong. At the very time that the loan was being negotiated, Armstrong appointed to the post of adjutant-general, William Duane, the editor of the *Philadelphia Aurora*, an outspoken opponent of Gallatin. Henry Adams later described the appointment as,

> improper, and the motives to which it was sure to be attributed made it more scandalous than the unfitness of the person made it harmful to the service. Gallatin's anger was deep: "Duane's last appointment has disgusted me so far as to make me desirous of not being any longer associated with those who have appointed him."[17]

Gallatin was now tired of his lonely battles. When the opening developed for a commissioner to the treaty for peace, Gallatin wanted the job. Neither President Madison nor Secretary of State Monroe had considered Gallatin for the mission. When, some time around the first week of April 1813, Gallatin asked the president for the appointment, Madison replied that he could not spare Gallatin from the Treasury. Gallatin answered that he could be of no service there, because if the war continued another year it would be impossible to support public credit, that money could not be obtained, but if sent abroad, he might be useful to the government by the means he would employ to make peace, knowing as he did the want of means to support the war.[18]

Before Monroe learned of Gallatin's desire, the secretary of state wrote Jefferson,

I had thought that it would be well, to engage in the service of some distinguished popular man, from that portion of our country the western [Clay?], which had given such support, and suffer'd so much by the war, to secure the confidence of its people in the negotiations, & reconcile them to any result of it. But on finding that Mr. Gallatin, for whom I have always entertained a very high respect & esteem, desir'd the appointment, and that the President was willing to confer it on him, I readily acquiesc'd, tho' not without serious apprehension of the consequences.[19]

Madison told Gallatin, on April 5, that Bayard had been asked to join the mission and Bayard wrote to Monroe, on April 7, accepting the appointment. He told the secretary of state,

If the President considers that it is within the means of my abilities to render any service to our common country, it is for him to command the full exertion of them. The occasion is of that nature that I do not allow myself to enquire what is my private interest or convenience.[20]

This response is not one from a man who had been asked to serve on a peace mission and then have it withdrawn as was rumored to have occurred a year earlier.

In any case, the appointments were made public on April 15, the same day on which the $16-million loan was finally filled.

And, also, on that same day, Monroe issued the three commissioners their official instructions. Within this long and detailed document, describing the efforts of the American government to maintain peace prior to the war and restore it once war was begun, Monroe stated that "the impressment of our seamen and illegal blockades, as exemplified more particularly in the orders in council, were the principal causes of the war."

In certain paragraphs, labeled "confidential," Monroe admonished the commissioners that a part of the Treaty of 1794, permitting British traders in Canada to trade with Indian tribes within the United States, "must not be renewed." He advised them, also, that,

a good intelligence between the United States and Russia respecting neutral rights, may have an important influence in securing them from violation in any future wars, and may even tend to prevent war, to the advantage of all nations.

And Monroe apprised them of the proposal of the good offices of the Crown Prince of Sweden (the former French Marshall Jean Baptiste Bernadotte of Napoleon's army) and Madison's intention of sending a minister to Sweden "immediately after the meeting of Congress."[21] This, too, would meet with complications.

Still before their departure, Monroe gave the three commissioners further instructions providing for them to enter into negotiations with both Great Britain and Russia for treaties of commerce once the treaty of peace was obtained with England. For these consultations the three men were given additional commissions.[22] The order of seniority for the commissioners was described by Monroe to ex–President John Adams, father of one of the negotiators. With regard to the treaties with the British, they would be ranked, "Mr. Gallatin, your Son & Mr. Bayard," because these "negotiations which might be carried on at any other place, being with another power and Mr. G. being a member of the administration, it was thought correct to give him the priority." As for negotiating the commercial treaty with Russia, Monroe reversed the places of Gallatin and John Quincy Adams since the younger Adams was accredited to Russia, a circumstance which "seemed to justify the propriety of giving the priority to him."[23]

Joining the mission as aides or secretaries were: Gallatin's 16-year-old son, James; 21-year-old John Payne Todd, Dolly Madison's son by a previous marriage; 20-year-old George Mifflin Dallas, a future vice president and the son of A.J. Dallas, a Philadelphian friend of Gallatin; George P. Milligan; and Christopher Hughes.

The hurried nature of forming the mission imposed upon Gallatin an arduous task of settling his Washington affairs. For more than twelve years Gallatin had served in a Cabinet post. It would stand as the longest Cabinet term for more than 125 years. Yet he was so meticulous that prior to his departure he prepared two tax bills and an outline of a charter for a new United States Bank to be presented to the next Congress. Richard Rush, the comptroller of the treasury, was to write of him,

Few men are so thoroughly men of business as Mr. Gallatin; he left nothing in arrears when he went away, and this with skillful clerks in his office drilled by long practice, and very precise and full instructions for all matters which he left behind, will enable its common business to go on well enough, with Mr. Jones's mere signature to give it the official stamp.[24]

Such was the character of one of the men with whom Henry Clay would later be closeted for several months in the intricate and tedious task of peace negotiation. (William Jones, secretary of the navy, was to serve as acting secretary of the treasury in Gallatin's absence.)

About the time Madison finally made his peace mission appointments, in early April, Henry Clay was just reaching Lexington, Kentucky. There he found "a state of the public mind to be much regretted," he wrote a friend on April 10.

> There seems to be general dissatisfaction with the conduct of the war, without an accusation agt. anyone in particular. These discontents will, I fear, unless removed, ultimately concentrate & fall somewhere with a dreadful concussion. I do what I can to allay public feeling, and not being able to defend our Washington friends as fully as I could wish in the past, I point to the future and endeavor to place the hopes and attention of the public there.

He spoke of seeing a number of artisans at Pittsburgh who had waited for three weeks for tools from Philadelphia "which could have been as well if not better and cheaper supplied in the borough." In this same letter, Clay referred to a new detachment of 1500 Kentuckians having left Lexington under his distant cousin, Gen. Green Clay, to march to the relief of Gen. William Henry Harrison, rumored as besieged by British and Indians and "his situation highly perilous."[25]

During his short stay in Kentucky, before he would have to return to Washington for the session scheduled to begin in late May, Clay took no active part in recommending military actions to Monroe or others as he had in the summer of 1812. Instead, he involved himself principally with legal affairs touching on real estate. He was the last surviving executor of the will for his wife's father, Thomas Hart, who had died in June of 1808. Among these real estate transactions was the sale of Olympians Springs resort, which he had apparently bought into at an auction of Hart's estate. He was also attorney for several other real estate arrangements, including some involving relatives by marriage.

But the real estate venture of closest interest to Clay was the remodeling and enlarging of his home, "Ashland." During May and June of the previous year of 1812, Clay was meeting with Benjamin Henry Latrobe to review the latter's architectural plans and designs for work on buildings at Transylvania University in Lexington. At that time, Latrobe was principally engaged in work at the Washington Navy Yard. Previously, he had, under Jefferson's appointment, remodeled errors built into the north wing of the United States Capitol and designed the chamber of the House of Representatives in the south wing. He had also been architect of several Philadelphia buildings; redesigned portions of Nassau Hall at Princeton College; designed other college buildings, side wheels for steam boats along with Robert Fulton, and the Chesapeake and Delaware Canal.

Now in April 1813, Henry Clay made an agreement with John Fisher to build "at Ashland the brick part of a wing to his [Clay's] dwelling house, according to a plan of Mr. Latrobe." The agreement set Fisher's payment at $8.25 per thousand for the brick actually laid. Clay was to pay $2 extra per thousand for sand brick which was to finish the exterior of the house. The agreement described arching the windows and provided for strong foundations. Fisher agreed "that the whole work shall be done in a workmanlike manner, and that he will pay as agreed damages one hundred and fifty dollars for every fire place that may smoake."

Clay initially paid Fisher $345.89 and agreed to pay another $200 in horses in the fall, $150 when the foundation was completed, and the remainder on completion of the work. Clay agreed to board the working hands

> two meals a day, without lodging, of plain substantial dieting, whilst they are at work at Seven shillings and six pence per hand, the amount to be deducted from the two hundred dollars above mentioned which the said Clay is to pay in horses.[26]

While most of this work was to be done in June, Clay would not be on hand to see it carried out. He was due in Washington on "the fourth Monday of May," or the 24th.

21

THE DISASTROUS SPRING OF 1813

About the time Henry Clay was arranging for the new constructions on Ashland, his home in Lexington, he was learning of a new series of combats between both the American and British armies and navies. The stories would reach him in Lexington, on the road to Washington, and finally after his arrival in the Nation's capital late in May 1813. The hostilities almost blocked the sailing of Albert Gallatin and James Bayard as peace commissioners.

Clay probably heard of a February 24th U.S. naval victory before his early–May departure from Lexington. After the victory of the *Constitution* over the *Java* in December, off the coast of Brazil, the United States frigate *Hornet* (Captain James Lawrence commanding) blockaded a British vessel, the *Bonne Citoyenne*, laden with treasure, in the Brazilian port of San Salvador. The blockade was broken by the arrival of a British 74, which drove off the *Hornet*. However, in its flight the American ship captured several minor vessels over the next month.

Still, on February 24, the *Hornet* met and engaged the British brig, *Peacock*, 18 guns, Capt. William Peake commanding. In about 15 minutes, the *Hornet* blasted the British man-of-war into a slowly sinking hulk. With the captain of the *Peacock* killed, and with six feet of water in the hold, the British ship struck her colors and Americans boarded to help save the vessel. The *Hornet* had survived the battle with damage only to the rigging where her only crewman was lost. But salvation of the *Peacock* failed when it suddenly sank in about five fathoms of water along a reef. Though some members of both crews managed to survive by climbing the rigging, nine of the *Peacock's* crew and three of the *Hornet's* died in the sinking hull. A poem about Lawrence later said, "He lost more in *saving* than conquering his foe."[1]

Again the exploit was hailed on the *Hornet's* arrival in American ports. And again British prisoners of war praised the gallantry of their captors. The *Peacock's* surviving officers jointly wrote to Lawrence,

> So much was done to alleviate the uncomfortable and distressing situation in which we were placed when received on board the ship you command, that we can not better express our feelings than by saying we ceased to consider ourselves prisoners; and everything that friendship could dictate was adopted by you and the officers of the *Hornet* to remedy the inconvenience we otherwise should have experienced from the unavoidable loss of the whole of our property and clothes by the sudden sinking of the *Peacock*.[2]

The British did not display the same gallantry in their naval offensive along the American seaboard, a fact which surely burned deeper feelings of antagonism in Clay's heart. With the American frigate *Constellation*, Capt. Joseph Tarbelle commanding, already hiding in the back waters of Norfolk harbor,[3] the blockading British men-of-war gradually sailed into Hampton Roads and northward up the Chesapeake Bay during April.

Meanwhile, several other British ships appeared off Cape Henlopen, Delaware, and pointed their guns at the little village of Lewes. A demand was sent ashore for the town to furnish the British enemy with "twenty live bullocks, with a proportionate quantity of vegetables and hay, for the use of his Britannic majesty's squadron," or else the place would be destroyed.

The townspeople replied to the demand, "We

solemnly refuse to commit legal or moral treason at your command. Do your worst."[4] For 22 hours on April 6, the British lobbed 800 shot, shell, and Congreve rockets into Lewes. The Americans dug many of the shot out of the sand to send them back to the British ships through the muzzles of American guns. The next day, the Delaware farmers forced the British to give up a landing attempt. After the battle the farmers counted up their dead and wounded—"One chicken killed, one pig wounded, leg broken."[5]

Inside Chesapeake Bay the Americans did not fare as well. By the date of the Lewes episode, the British under Adm. George Cockburn, a man who would become infamous, had guided his fleet as far north as the Rappahannock River marauding either shore of the Bay enroute. By the middle of April he was between Annapolis and Baltimore at the mouth of the Patapsco River. But learning of the preparedness to meet him at Baltimore, he veered northeastward into the Elk River.

On April 29, a force of about 700 British sailors and marines went ashore at Frenchtown, a hamlet consisting of

> storehouses, a tavern, two or three dwelling houses, with a few stables and out-houses; deriving its whole importance from being the stopping place for land stages and water connections between Philadelphia and Baltimore.

The 10 or so stage-drivers "defending" Frenchtown made a gallant retrograde movement as the British burned the town and destroyed $20,000 to $30,000 in goods.[6]

Four days later the "veteran British incendiaries" stormed ashore at Havre-de-Grace to mete out their typical ruin which included the stages and baggage caught there in passage between Baltimore and Philadelphia. The only house to survive the torch was one set aside as a sanctuary for the town's women and children. This village, like the others in Maryland and Delaware, had no military importance, yet they were pillaged and destroyed. Before floating back down the Bay during the month of May, the British Winnebagoes (as they were now being called in scorn as representing the most malicious of Indian tribes), fired the Maryland villages of Fredericktown and Georgetown, as well as numerous farming communities along the Bay shore.

These attacks along the Bay and Delaware shores could only arouse in James Bayard the greatest apprehension for the safety of his family in Wilmington, Delaware. Gallatin's family, now removed from Washington, was only a little safer in Philadelphia. Nevertheless, their correspondence of this period spoke only of expectations of their negotiations and of a mixup in their passports, which had their ship leaving from New York instead of Newcastle, Delaware, as planned. This was straightened out, and on May 9, as "a great concourse of people attended,"[7] they boarded the *Neptune* at the Delaware port where they said farewell to their families. It took them two days to float down the Delaware and clear inspection by British warships blockading the channel. By mid–May they were in the Atlantic and out of sight, but not out of mind of the U.S. Senate meeting toward the end of the month.

While these activities were going on in the mid–Atlantic states, other military events were unfolding along the Canadian frontier. Almost nothing had transpired from Niagara to the coast since the declaration of war. The only action had been a minor and ineffective two-hour bombardment by the British of Sackett's Harbor, New York, in July 1812; a somewhat more successful five-day raid by Americans who struck several British ports on the north side of Lake Ontario in November; and an abortive and ridiculous incursion into Canada near Lake Champlain by General Henry Dearborn, also in November.

Now, in April 1813, Dearborn sent Commodore Isaac Chauncey's flotilla, carrying 1700 soldiers under mountain explorer Brig. Gen. Zebulon M. Pike, to attack York (now Toronto), the capital of Upper Canada (now Ontario). The attack on York, toward the west end of Lake Ontario, was contrary to the strategic plan of the secretary of war who had written to Dearborn to assault Kingston at the east end of the lake. Americans landed on April 28 with Pike in the second assault wave. They soon moved eastward along the lake shore until temporarily halted by the British at a ravine. Unknown to the American forces, the British were actually continuing their retreat and were near surrender. But first, they were in the process of destroying an ammunition magazine unseen in the ravine. The resultant premature explosion was almost as devastating for the British as it was for the Americans. The British lost 40 men while the Americans lost 38, including General Pike. The Americans also had 222 wounded.[8]

Pennsylvania Col. Cromwell Pearce assumed command and led the Americans into York, which capitulated. The troops were still under General Pike's pre-battle orders:

It is expected that every corps will be mindful of the honor of the American arms, and the disgraces which have recently tarnished our arms: and endeavor by a cool and determined discharge of their duty to support the one, and wipe off the other.... Courage and bravery in the field, do not more distinguish the soldier than humanity after victory; and whatever examples the savage allies of our enemies may have given us, the general confidently hopes that the blood of an unresisting or yielding enemy will never stain the weapons of his column. The unoffending citizens of Canada are many of them our own country men, and the poor Canadians have been forced into this war. Their property, therefore must be held sacred; and any soldier who shall so far neglect the honor of his profession as to be guilty of plundering the inhabitants, shall, if convicted, be punished with death. But the commanding general assures the troops that, should they capture a large quantity of public stores, he will use his best endeavors to procure them a reward from his government.[9]

Before the mortally wounded Pike died, he was carried to the American flagship off shore. On hearing a shout from the shore, during the afternoon, he asked its meaning and was told, "Victory! The British union-jack is coming down from the blockhouse, and the stars and stripes are going up." A little later the British flag was brought aboard and placed under his head, and thus he died, the first victorious American general of the war.

York was occupied at 4 P.M., on April 27. Capitulation terms became complicated and were not completed until late the next day. Part of this was due to the rapid and, in British eyes, disgraceful retreat of the British Gen. Sir R. H. Sheaffe, who secretly ordered a naval vessel (under construction) and stores burned as his agents negotiated with the Americans. During the next two days General Dearborn had stores of food and medical supplies made available to the town's people most in need of them. But as so often happens, many not in need got provisions under false pretence. Dearborn also permitted the town's civil authorities to retain their functions.

But on Saturday, May 1, an episode occurred which is still shrouded in mystery and which had devastating repercussions nearly a year and a half later in Washington. Despite orders by Generals Pike and Dearborn there apparently was some minor plundering and pillaging by American soldiers and sailors in retaliation for similar British acts at Ogdensberg, New York, some weeks earlier. And there were some pro–American Canadians from the surrounding area who were under no obligation to abide by British or American orders.

In any case, on that day, unknown parties set fire to the government offices containing the Parliament houses. One American officer who rode to the scene, shortly after the clouds of smoke appeared, asked citizens there how the fires started. None knew. And he wrote afterwards that, "At this time there was not in sight an American soldier."[10] On the other hand, the British claim the burning was precipitated by American soldiers angered at finding a human scalp suspended near the mace, the emblem of power in the Parliament House. The editor of the *Niles Register*, on learning of the display wrote,

Great Heavens! What clamor would be raised if such a thing were placed over the chair of Mr. Speaker Clay in the house of representatives of the United States, supposing it to have belonged to some *English woman or infant!*[11]

While the burning of the government house took place on May 1, by whatever means, Commodore Chauncey, commander of the attacking American fleet, wrote to the secretary of the navy in June,

I have the honor to present to you, by the hands of Lieutenant Dudley, the British standard taken at York on the 27th of April last, *accompanied by the mace, over which hung a human* SCALP.— These articles were taken from the *Parliament houses* by one of my officers and presented to me.[12]

Most of the American troops returned aboard their ships by May 4 in preparation for sailing south across Lake Ontario for a planned attack against Fort George at the mouth of the Niagara River later in the month. Unfavorable winds delayed departure of the fleet until May 9.

Henry Clay probably left Lexington, Kentucky, for Washington while these troops waited aboard the ships for their next military adventure. It is not known whether he learned about the capture of York while on the road or at the end of his usual 20-day trip to the nation's capital. There was still one other military engagement which took place about the time of his departure from Lexington. He had certainly heard the earliest reports of it within a day or so of his arrival in Washington since he was to comment on it in a letter written two days after the opening of the 13th Congress.

During his brief stay at home, Henry Clay knew that his distant cousin, Gen. Green Clay was advancing with about 1200 men to support Gen. William Henry Harrison at Fort Meigs, just below the rapids of the Maumee River in Ohio. In late April British Gen. Henry Proctor marched about 2500 British soldiers and Indian warriors toward Fort Meigs. By May 4, the British were bombarding the fort from the north side while the Indians, under Tecumseh, attacked on the south side. Late that evening a messenger from General Clay reached the fort and informed Harrison that the rest of the Kentuckians should arrive at the fort in 18 flat-bottom boats by the next morning.

Harrison sent a dispatch to General Clay ordering him to attack the British batteries with 800 troops. Clay complied and the maneuver was a complete success. However, the over-confident, but green, militia under Col. William Dudley remained on the field pressing for further victory, despite repeated calls to return to their boats, and were soon lured into the woods by the British. About fifty Americans were killed, another 600 taken prisoner, and only 50 escaped back to the boats and eventual safety of the fort.[13]

The fort withstood the siege and, within a few days, the British and Indians retired northward. In a strategic sense the outcome was an American victory because they not only retained the ground but also relieved the threat to the land westward to Lake Michigan and the Wabash River. But in terms of casualties it was another disaster for the Americans.

On learning of the attack by the Kentuckians against the British on the north side of the river, early in the engagement, Tecumseh brought a great number of his Indians back to support the British and cut off Colonel Dudley's troops, taking them prisoner. As the Indians and a few

British soldiers marched the Americans to the main British camp, they began stripping them of their clothes, their scalps, and their lives. The lives of the British soldiers were in equal danger if they intervened, and at least one was killed in such an attempt. Shortly, the procession approached an old deserted fort, which appeared to afford safety. But the Americans were about to face a harrowing experience — the infamous Indian gauntlet. As described by one survivor, the Indians began

> clubbing and tomahawking all they could of the terror-stricken prisoners as they made their wild, panic-race for its entrance, where they foolishly hoped to find protection and safety. To hesitate was instant death, and without further orders each made his individual dash for life through the yelling savage lines with superhuman speed and agility. Many who were knocked down gained the entrance upon all-fours with astonishing speed.

For those following it became more hazardous as they had to make their way over their mangled and bleeding companions.[14]

Once inside the fort, the massacre continued. Yet there were survivors, who later credited their salvation to Tecumseh.

But who was Tecumseh, whose bust has a special place of acknowledgment at the United States Naval Academy? There are three contemporary descriptions which differ in content, yet none seem to contradict.

The first is from Col. William Stanley Hatch.

> The personal appearance of this remarkable man was uncommonly fine. His height was about five feet nine inches, judging him by my own height when standing close to him and corroborated by the late Col. John Johnson, for many years Indian Agent at Piqua [Ohio]. His face oval rather than angular; his nose handsome and straight; his mouth beautifully formed, like that of Napoleon I, as represented in his portraits; his eyes clear, transparent hazel, with a mild, pleasant expression when in repose, or in conversation; but when excited in his orations, or by the enthusiasm of conflict, or when in anger, they appeared like balls of fire; his teeth beautifully white, and his complexion more of a light brown or tan than red; his whole tribe as well as their kindred, the Ottaways, had light complexions; his arms and hands were finely formed; his limbs straight; he always stood very erect, and walked with a brisk, elastic, vigorous step; invariably dressed in Indian tanned

buckskin; a perfectly well fitting hunting frock, descending to the knee, was over his under clothes of the same material; the usual cape and finish of leather fringe about the neck; cape, edges of the front opening, and bottom of the frock; a belt of the same material, in which were his side arms (an elegant silver mounted tomahawk, and a knife in a strong leather case), short pantaloons, connected with neatly fitting leggins and moccasins, with a mantle of the same material thrown over his left shoulder, used as a blanket in camp, and as a protection in storms.[15]

Another account by a man named English is quoted in Hatch's writings,

Tecumseh understands, or could speak our language. He did understand, and could speak nearly all the words in common use sufficiently to hold conversation on ordinary topics; but he never spoke any but his own language at any council, or when in presence of any officer or agent of any government; nor would he attempt to speak in any but his own language when in company with any one, except with those toward whom he felt very friendly, or had private intercourse, and who did not understand his own language. He always avoided speaking to any official agent of the British, or our government, except through his interpreter. He did not want to be misunderstood.[16]

And finally there is the following description which appeared in the *National Intelligencer* earlier in the year, and which disagrees as to his height.

Tecumseh is about 45 years of age, of the Shawnee tribe, six feet high, well proportioned for his height, of erect and lofty deportment, penetrating eye, rather stern in his visage, artful, insidious in preparing enterprises, and bold in their executions. In his youth, and before the Treaty of Greenville, he was one of the boldest warriors who infested the Ohio river — seizing boats — killing emigrants — leading the horses he took with the most valuable plunder, and retiring to the Wabash, where, careless of wealth himself, he soon lavished the treasure of his rapine upon the followers, which, when exhausted, he replenished by fresh depredations. Among the Indians, Tecumseh is esteemed the boldest warrior of the West.[17]

When word reached him that the prisoners were being killed, Tecumseh mounted a horse and galloped to the scene. Grabbing one Indian by the throat and another by the breast, he threw them both to the ground. He struck others about the face and shoulders with the flat of his sword,

exclaiming, "Are there no men here?" An English officer, witness to the event, said, "He was the maddest looking man I ever saw ... his eyes shot fire ... he was terrible." An American witness later wrote Tecumseh dared "any one of the hundreds that surrounded him to attempt to murder another American."[18]

"Now," Tecumseh shouted, "you want to kill all these prisoners do you?"

"Yes," they replied.

"Then you must kill me first, and then you can do as you please — maybe some of you will die in the effort." The Indians ceased their bloody task.[19]

Tecumseh then demanded, "Where is Proctor?" Finding the British general near the scene, the Indian chief asked why he had not prevented the massacre.

"Sir," Proctor said, "Your Indians cannot be commanded."

"Begone!" Tecumseh retorted. "You are unfit to command, go and put on petticoats."[20]

Stories of the massacre were to reach Henry Clay only in the weeks, months, and years to follow. But as the earliest information reached him in Washington, he wrote two days after the opening of Congress to Martin Hardin in Kentucky,

It appears that we have been destined to experience another severe loss in Genl. Clay's detachment. I am not in possession of facts to determine to whom the misfortune is attributable. My present impressions are unfavorable to Harrison. But justice requires that we shd. [should] not hastily decide.

On an entirely different subject, but one which would become a major issue within the 1st session of the 13th Congress, Clay wrote in the same letter,

The president's message is a plain temperate and sensible paper. It does not add however to the stock of information previously possessed by the public except in one particular, and that is, our commissioners are sent to Russia upon the presumption only that the enemy will accede to the mediation.[21]

Henry Clay's views on these two separate aspects of the war effort, brought together in two paragraphs of a very short letter, tend to reveal a change in his attitude toward the war. He saw in the military contest a continued series of debacles with great loss of life, particularly to his fellow Kentuckians. On the other hand, he realized that true diplomatic negotiations had little hope of beginning as long as the British armies were successful in the field.

Whatever were Clay's personal feelings about the military or diplomatic aspects of the war, his primary attention, in late May 1813, was on the convening of the 1st session of the 13th Congress. While the military and naval war efforts were on the verge of complete disaster, the actions of the extra session of Congress were close to an unmitigated disgrace.

The new House was no longer to be subjected to the caustic diatribes of Josiah Quincy of Massachusetts or of John Randolph of Roanoke, Virginia. In their place was the abrasive personality of Alexander C. Hanson of Maryland, editor of the anti-administration newspaper, the Baltimore (and later the Georgetown) *Federal Republican*, and instigator of the agitation that culminated in the Baltimore riot of July 1812. In support of their viewpoint, there came to this Congress another Federalist, but with a greater skill in oratory than theirs, and character to match that of Henry Clay. He was Daniel Webster of New Hampshire. Another New Englander returning to Congress was Federalist Timothy Pickering. As a Senator, he had clashed with Clay in 1810–11. They would meet again in the House. Now, as he journeyed to Washington in May 1813, Pickering had an amusing encounter with another political foe.

Not far out of Boston, Pickering was joined in his carriage by the new vice president, Republican Elbridge Gerry. When they reached Hartford, Connecticut, they found the town crowded with the taverns "full and running over." At the stage tavern only one double bed remained. Relating the episode to his wife, Pickering wrote,

I then told Mr. Gerry (as it was now near midnight) that I would either release my claim to the bed, or we would draw lots for it, or each take one side of it. "That is very fair," said he; "we will each take one side." So we slept in the same bed! This I related to a friend in Hartford, and so 'twas soon reported abroad, and excited no little amusement. Some gentlemen there (whom I did not know, but who knew me) said, pleasantly, "that the millennium must be near at hand," seeing Gerry and I

had lain down together. But which they would call the lion, and which the lamb, I do not know.[22]

Politics did make strange bedfellows, with the aid of travel.

The only outstanding newcomer in the Senate, joining Gerry, was New York Federalist Rufus King. But this Senate was losing two outstanding members — William Crawford of Georgia (selected by Madison to be the new minister to France) and James A. Bayard (to join Gallatin on the peace mission to St. Petersburg, Russia).

The first order of business when Congress met on May 24, 1813, was the organization of the bodies. The 148 members of the House immediately voted for a Speaker. On a single ballot, Henry Clay received 59 votes to 54 for Timothy Pitkin of Connecticut. Five votes were scattered. Clay was sworn in by William Findley, one of the House's oldest members. Returning to the Speaker's chair, Clay told his colleagues,

In returning to the station in which I am replaced by a continuance of your favor, whilst I am sensible of the honor which I have received, I am sensible also of my inability to fulfil the expectations justly raised by so elevated a distinction; but, gentlemen, the experience I have had, limited as it is, has satisfied me that, in the maintenance of the order of the House, less depends upon the presiding officer than upon the sense of the necessity of decorum being generally diffused throughout the body. Then only will a deliberative assembly be well governed, and its business agreeably transacted, when each member, identifying the reputation of the body to which he belongs in his own, shall make the preservation of its order an affair of personal and individual concern, and shall render to the Chair a candid, liberal, and unbiased support. Under the hope and persuasion that you participate with me in these sentiments, I shall proceed to administer the duties you have been pleased to assign me.[23]

The next day, both the Senate and the House received a message from President Madison. The principal content was notice of the Russian offer to mediate peace. Without naming names, he informed Congress that he had appointed two men to join the American minister in St. Petersburg to meet with counterparts he expected would be sent by Great Britain. He said that those two envoys had already left the country. They were Treasury Secretary Albert Gallatin and Senator James A. Bayard who would join Minister John

Quincy Adams in Russia. This was surprising since the Senate had not voted their confirmation.

Madison informed Congress that in addition to authorizing the envoys to negotiate a peace settlement, they were also empowered to conclude treaties of commerce with both Great Britain and Russia. He acknowledged that they had been sent on the presumption that Great Britain would accept mediation since, for that nation, "no adequate motives exist to prefer a continuance of war with the United States," and that

> with respect to the important question of impressment, on which the war so essentially turns, a search for or seizure of British persons or property on board neutral vessels on the high seas is not a belligerent right derived from the law of nations.

Madison went on in his message to criticize

> the spirit and manner in which the war continues to be waged by the enemy, who, uninfluenced by the unvaried examples of humanity set them, are adding to the savage fury of it on one frontier, a system of plunder and conflagration on the other.

The president, further, took note of the successes of the navy and the singular victory of the army at York, along with the "valor" at Fort Meigs, as hope for "greater victories" yet to come.

The message concluded with several paragraphs detailing the status of the treasury and requesting Congress to levy additional taxes — the real purpose for which this special session of Congress was called.[24]

The next day, May 26, the day on which Clay wrote of his "unfavorable impressions" of General Harrison, the newly elected Speaker appointed the several standing committees. Then, with the House in Committee of the Whole, he offered a resolution, "That so much of the message of the President of the United States as relates to the spirit and manner in which the war has been waged by the enemy, be referred to a select committee."

Clay prefaced his resolution with brief remarks to the House. He expressed his abhorrence of the "enormities" committed by the enemy

> as well as in the massacre of our citizens on the Western frontier, as the conflagration of our little towns on the maritime border.... If found to be as public report had stated them, they called for the indignation of all Christendom, and they ought to be embodied in an authentic document, which might perpetuate them on the page of history.[25]

In a discussion which followed, after the Committee of the Whole rose, after Clay was back in the Speaker's Chair, and after the resolution had been passed, Thomas Grosvenor of New York moved to reconsider the resolution, wanting to amend it to inquire also into the conduct of the United States in the war. Joseph Desha of Kentucky asked for a return to the Committee of the Whole to give Clay the opportunity to respond, but Robert Wright of Maryland objected to the insinuation on the conduct of American officers. The House then refused to reconsider the resolution, letting it stand as proposed by Clay.

Before any further substantive work was taken up by the House, Speaker Clay became involved in another minor hassle on Monday, May 31, over the seating of George Richards, a reporter for the anti-administration newspaper, *The Federal Republican*, the former public platform of freshman Congressman Alexander Hanson of Maryland. Again it was Grosvenor who brought the issue before the House when he questioned Clay's decision to exclude the reporter from the privilege he had had during the past session to report on the House proceedings. He suggested the reporter's petition be referred to a select committee. After Felix Grundy said the House, not a committee, should decide, and George Troup thought the Speaker's decision was sufficient; Hanson, Grosvenor, Wright, and others let loose in a hot debate that ranged far from the issue.

Hanson vigorously denounced the exclusion which left three Republican reporters and one Federalist reporter to cover both sides of the House debate. He compared the action to Caesar's Rome. With less heat Grosvenor said he did not question the Speaker's motives but thought he made an error in judgment by excluding Richards while admitting "three Democratic and but one Federal reporter." Wright charged that William Cobbett had told the British prince regent that the newspaper's editors (whose names were not printed in it) were in British pay.

When Wright repeated the charge of British influence, he challenged Hanson by adding that "if he had wounded the feelings of any gentleman, he knew where to seek the remedy." Speaker Clay immediately called Wright to order. Hanson called Wright's charge "groundless and false" and then said, "This is the first and last time I can bestow upon him any notice whatever." With that said, the House voted to go into Committee of the Whole where the Speaker would have the opportunity to explain his decision.

Clay observed at the beginning that in his opinion "an importance had been given to this petition which did not well comport with the dignity of the House." He then stated the ground on which the decision had been made was

> simply this. That in consequence of the recent alterations in the House, seats had been arranged for but four stenographers; and to those places he had assigned the applicants according to seniority; all of whom having been of longer standing than Mr. R., he had by this arrangement been excluded. If the House should deem it proper to admit others than those now on the floor, he hoped they would designate the stations they should occupy, etc.[26]

Among other speakers who followed Clay, Webster thought it would not be inconvenient to admit Richards to the floor. And within days of their first meeting, John C. Calhoun was already disagreeing with Webster. Calhoun thought Richards could be satisfied in the gallery. Jonathan Roberts of Pennsylvania objected to reporters being seated near the fireplace where members congregated and conversed privately "when the weather was intense" (though at the time of this discussion Washington's abominable summer heat was already making itself felt upon the members of Congress). Roberts thought they should be seated in the gallery as in England. The haggling on the resolution continued two more days during which the rights and responsibilities of the Speaker came under fire. Finally, Hugh Nelson, of Virginia, offered a resolution for the Speaker to provide additional seats for stenographers. The House agreed and then sent this resolution to a committee of seven to revise the House rules accordingly. When the issue returned to the House on June 11, it was agreed that places would be made available to reporters in the galleries, but they would not be admitted on the floor of the House.[27]

Led by Hanson, the Federalists had attacked Speaker Clay's action from many sides and his supporters defended him from many charges, some of which were never even leveled by the Federalists. Later in this summer session, Hanson would follow up on the charges made earlier in the year by Quincy that Clay had been party to coercing the president into the declaration of war.

With the reporter-Richards episode closed, a Clay habit was vaguely questioned. In a debate that arose over three separate contested elections to House seats, one of them narrowed down to the use of initials on voting rolls. It was all neatly summed up by Webster in a letter to a friend when he wrote that the question was,

> Can the name of a man be written by the initial of his Christian, & the whole of his surname. For example, if I should put at the end of this letter "D. Webster," is that "entering my name" upon it, "or not." On these knotty points, we are much divided. Speaker Clay made a vehement speech in favor of the report. He said the name must be written at full length — that both names might be given by initials as well as one. etc. etc. *Col. Pickering* ansd [answered] him. He said, it was required that all Bills etc. should be "signed by the Speaker," & he observed the constant mode of signing to be "H. Clay." He wished to know whether this was right or wrong; & if right, whether a public Law is not a matter requiring as much form as a Virginia Poll list. The Speaker spake no more.[28]

During this Congressional haggling over the inconsequential, more depressing battle news was being reported by the press. This time, the first word of a stinging naval defeat reached Washington on June 7. Late in May, Capt. Philip Vere Broke, commanding the British frigate *Shannon*, 38 (but mounting 52 guns), sailed boldly about just outside Boston's harbor. Broke had the means to know that the American frigate *Chesapeake*, idling in the harbor, was hardly fit to go to sea let alone fight a battle with a ship and crew that had been together for a few years. The American vessel had even lost a top-mast in a gale, with a loss of lives, as she entered the port after a recent cruise.

The *Chesapeake*, also 38, was now commanded by James Lawrence who, as commander of the *Hornet* earlier in the year, had received the praise of British prisoners of war for his magnanimous treatment of them in their time of trial. But the 32-year-old Lawrence had been aboard his new command only 10 days, And, through earlier encounters, the frigate had already earned an unlucky reputation. The *Chesapeake* was the same ship that had been commanded by Commodore John Barron, when he gave up members of his crew without a fight to the British frigate *Leopard* in 1807. For that act Barron was forced into banishment. Now, in 1813, at least four of Lawrence's subordinate officers were ill and were ashore (one died a few days later), leaving only two very young officers aboard. About 100 men of the crew had never before been to sea and along with some discontented Portuguese mercenaries and British deserters, the crew was poorly trained and near mutiny over claims for prize money from previous captures on the high seas. It was another disaster waiting to happen.

On the morning of June 1, a messenger from the *Shannon* landed near Marblehead, carrying a challenge from Captain Broke of the *Shannon* to Captain Lawrence. It read: "As the *Chesapeake* appears now ready for sea, I request you will do me the favor to meet the *Shannon* with her, ship to ship, to try the fortunes of our respective flags." He went on to speak of the withdrawal of other British vessels in order for the encounter to be solely between the single warship of each nation. By and large the two ships were of equal size and armament. But the character of the personnel was of a decidedly clear advantage to the Britisher. Furthermore, with more than 100 frigates in the British navy, loss of one of their ships could not alter that nation's nautical strength. Not so was the potential loss of one of the half-dozen American frigates still seaworthy. Each U.S. loss was a great disaster. Lawrence should not have accepted the challenge! But he did.

The *Shannon* stood outside the harbor waiting the acceptance of the challenge. By noon, on this beautiful first day of June, the shore lines as far as Salem were crowded with thousands of spectators hoping to witness another American naval victory. As the American frigate slowly sailed out to engage the intruder, Captain Lawrence hoisted a flag on which was written "FREE TRADE AND SAILORS' RIGHTS."

Finally, somewhere between Cape Cod and Cape Ann, beyond the view of thousands of people ashore, the two ships maneuvered until shortly before 6 P.M. when they closed to within pistol shot and commenced blasting away with broadsides for about 15 minutes. As the *Chesapeake* approached her opponent, her stern began to drift in toward the *Shannon's* midships, thus taking her guns out of play on the enemy. (These guns could not swivel like those of today that can hurl huge projectiles far beyond the horizon.) But it left the British ship in position to bring to bare a full broadside with which to rake the American with awful slaughter, forcing many to seek safety anywhere.

Yet in this now entangled attitude, Captain Lawrence gave the order for boarders to be called up. Unfortunately the negro bugler was one of those who cowered on deck behind the ship's small boat. On attempting to give the signal he couldn't make a sound come out. (Later he was court martialed and found guilty of cowardice. As punishment he suffered 300 lashes on his bare back. In those days this was not a racial matter, because there were hundreds of cases where both army and navy men were brutally punished by great numbers of lashes, or worse. For example, this author has found an incident where, under command of Washington in the Revolution — and approved by him — three men arrested for stealing from a New York farmer on a Monday, were tried, found guilty, and hanged by Friday of the same week.)

Suddenly, the battle took an altogether disastrous turn. Captain Lawrence was struck down by a mortal musket shot from somewhere in the *Shannon's* rigging. As he was carried below, the British captain rallied a contingent of sailors and marines to board the *Chesapeake*. While it was a dangerous act by Broke, it was successful, as far as victory was concerned. His men must have ventured forward with vivid dreams of prize money, but nearly three-fourths of them were killed or wounded. Broke himself was badly slashed by a sabre.

Now, a Portuguese mercenary of the *Chesapeake* opened a grating allowing the British full possession of the American ship. As the battle ended in the capture by the British, one of their lieutenants hauled down the American colors and hoisted the British flag. But the action cost him his life as he was slain by a shot from his own ship. The *Chesapeake* had lost 48 men killed and 98 wounded. The *Shannon* had lost 26 killed and 58 wounded.

The British took control of the *Chesapeake* and together they sailed to Halifax, Nova Scotia, arriving there on June 7. Captain Lawrence died of his wound two days earlier.

While there were to be several accounts published in the coming weeks, a much later review of the war by Benson Lossing gave this brief picture of the death of Lawrence: "His last words when he left the deck were in substance, 'Tell the men to fire faster and not give up the ship. Fight her till she sinks!'" Henry Adams, in his *History*, tells it bit differently, saying that Lawrence "cried out repeatedly and loudly, 'Don't give up the ship! blow her up!' He was said to have added afterward: 'I could have stood the wreck if it had not been for the boarding.'"[29]

Niles Register, in July, reported,

> The body of Lawrence was prostrate, but his spirit remained erect. He saw and felt the fortune of war was against him — yet cried out, "DON'T GIVE UP THE SHIP," though the enemy was carrying everything before him.

In the same issue it reported a "toast on the anniversary of Independence, 'May the expiring words of the illustrious Lawrence, "Don't give up the ship," be the eternal motto of every American.'" It was to be a rallying cry in a later battle of this war. The periodical also noted Lawrence's commitment "to his charge to defend *free trade and sailor's rights*," now a popular slogan throughout the land. On June 7, Captain Lawrence was given full burial honors by the British in Halifax for his previous gallantry. Several days after his death, his wife gave birth to twins.[30]

News of this naval defeat came to Washington in dribbles throughout the month of June and into early July when Lawrence's words were first hailed as a motto which was to stand forever in U.S. navy memory.

22

The Congressional Summer

How would Congress respond to the latest battle-disaster news?

On Monday, May 31, 1813, President Madison sent to the Senate two messages, both dated May 29. In one, he announced his recess nominations of Albert Gallatin and James A. Bayard (now many days at sea) to join John Quincy Adams in St. Petersburg "to negotiate and sign a Treaty of Peace with Great Britain, under the mediation of the Emperor of Russia," and to negotiate treaties of commerce with both of those nations. In the second message, Madison nominated Jonathan Russell to be the U.S. minister to Sweden, whose government had "repeatedly manifested a desire to exchange public Ministers." Both nominations were to run into trouble. While these nominations were of no immediate concern to Henry Clay in the House, within a year they would be a personal concern.

For the next several days, the Senate considered both sets of nominations separately, but concurrently in executive session. On June 1, Senator Goldsborough of Maryland, taking up Russell's nomination, submitted a resolution, which in character was to appear as well in the House the following week. He requested the president to inform the Senate

> when and by whom, the first intelligence was first officially communicated to the Department of State, of the repeal of the Berlin and Milan decrees, and at what time the first official information of the repeal of these decrees was given to the American Chargé des Affaires at Paris.

Or in late 20th century terms: "What did Madison know and when did he know it?"

Russell had been the chargé on April 28, 1811, the date now claimed by the French as that on which the repeal of the decrees was first announced. But it was not until May 12, 1812, that Russell's successor at Paris, U.S. Minister Joel Barlow, learned of the decree repeal from the French foreign minister, the Duke of Bassano. On relaying word of this apparently year-old repeal to the American government, Barlow quoted Bassano as saying the repeal had been passed on to Washington through Russell and also through the French minister to the United States, Louis Sérurier. Yet it never became public in the United States until Barlow's report in May 1812. And only then was it also made known through Russell, by this time chargé in London, to the British government, which, in July, apparently accepted it as sufficient reason to revoke their Orders in Council.

Since the British revocation came on the heels of notice of the "official" French repeal, and prior to British knowledge of the American declaration of war, the Federalists contended that earlier notice of the French repeal might have motivated the British revocation in time to prevent the war.

To this end, on June 2, the Senate agreed to Rufus King's amendment to Goldsborough's resolution requesting Madison to state

> whether any communication has been received from Jonathan Russell, admitting or denying the declaration of the Duke of Bassano to Mr. Barlow, that he had informed his predecessor of the repeal of the Berlin and Milan decrees at the date of that decree.

This resolution was sent to a committee.

That same day, Joseph Anderson of Tennessee, offered another resolution, asking the president for the correspondence between Sweden and the United States on the subject of exchanging ministers. The Senate agreed to this the following day.

Meanwhile, still on June 2, Senator King submitted three resolutions directed at the president dealing with the peace mission nominations. In these he asked for the correspondence between the United States and Russia on the proposed mediation; he asked for copies of the commissions for the three envoys; and he asked if Gallatin still retained the office of secretary of the treasury. On the latter, King wanted to know "under what authority, and by whom, the powers and duties of the head of the Treasury Department are discharged during the absence of Albert Gallatin from the United States."

On June 3, as the Senate approved Anderson's request for the Russell papers, it turned down King's first two resolutions, but wanted an answer regarding Gallatin's status.

On June 7, Madison complied with both requests. With regard to Gallatin, he briefly replied that his office was not vacated and in his absence the secretary of the navy, William Jones, would discharge the treasury duties "according to the provisions of the act of Congress, entitled 'An act making alterations in the Treasury and the War Departments, passed May 8, 1792."

Three days later, Anderson reported that he had called on the president, who did not consider the committee had authority to call on him in an official character. He contended that a committee was a subordinate part of the Senate and only the full body was a co-equal branch to treat with the executive. But he would freely meet them unofficially. This did not sit well with Anderson or the Senate, and on the 16th the Senate agreed on a resolution to be sent to Madison that the duties of the secretary of the treasury and of an envoy to a foreign power "are so incompatible, that they ought not to be, and remain, united in the same person."[1] There this subject remained for nearly a month.

As for Madison's reply to a request for the Russell correspondence, he sent to the Senate several documents from the Department of State, including a letter from Secretary Monroe to the effect that there had been no direct correspondence between the United States and Sweden, but that the latter country, throughout 1812, had been desirous of sending a minister to the United States and intimated a wish for a mutual exchange. On submitting this information to the Senate, Senator Goldsborough reported that Monroe had told him that Russell had made no official denial or admission on the truth of Bassano's allegation, but that Monroe "understood that allegation to be unequivocally denied."

Based on the information from the executive branch, Goldsborough submitted a resolution "that it is inexpedient at this time to send a Minister Plenipotentiary to Sweden." Again on June 14, the Senate put this matter in the hands of a committee to call upon the president and again the matter rested until early July.

The Senate's treatment of the president's nominations was no harsher than that of the House, which added its own controversial dialogue. On June 10, a 31-year-old freshman Federalist from New Hampshire, submitted five resolutions for consideration by that body.

The young congressman had a large head with coal black hair and deep sunk, dark eyes. His broad shoulders and massive chest in a solid frame suggested a wrestler rather than an orator. In fact, he was, in later years, still able to out-wrestle his grown sons jointly in a contest.[2] But equally well was he to be able to out-orate two of the nation's most brilliant legislators — John C. Calhoun and Henry Clay. For this fledgling representative was Daniel Webster. He had made a brief appearance in the House, noted in the previous chapter, but not in a conspicuous manner.

That was now to change as another description of this new power in the Congress illustrates. It may seem a duplication but is rather a seconding of the foregoing. Charles J. Ingersoll wrote,

> Mr. Webster's dark complexion, sunk and searching eye, prominent brow, voluminous head, and well-sized person, are a good frontispiece of his powerful intellect and oratory. Diction chaste, pure, and elegant; logic admirable; but action not animated or attractive, render his speeches less effective when delivered than as read afterwards. His greatest performances are elaborations. Evolving striking thoughts with great force, though occasionally sarcastic or ironical, he is never aggressive, personal, or rude.[3]

The first of Webster's five resolutions was quite similar to Senator Goldsborough's dealing with the timing, by whom, and in what manner, according to Webster's wording, "the first intelligence was given to this Government of the decree of France bearing date of the 28th April, 1811, and purporting to be a definitive repeal of the decrees of Berlin and Milan." The other resolutions requested correspondence between the two governments through their ministers relative to a real existence of the 1811 decree prior to communication of it from Bassano to Barlow in May 1812.

In his request for information, Webster told the House that the resolutions

> relate immediately to the cause of the present war. I may say, sir, without exposing myself to contradiction, that if the decree of April 1811, had been published at the time it purports to be dated, the war in which we are now engaged, would not have taken place. To whom it is to be imputed, that it was not so published, is the discovery sought by these Resolutions.

Webster had no doubt that any early appearance of the decree "would have produced the repeal of the British Orders in Council," which he said, "were the point upon which the question of war or peace did actually turn."

In concluding a stirring speech (of which only brief excerpts survive), the young congressman said,

> We owe it to the reputation of our Ministers abroad, we owe it to the character of our Government at home, and, more than all, we owe it to the honor of the nation to improve the earliest opportunity of making a full and free inquiry into a subject of so much importance, and wearing at the present moment so very singular an appearance.[4]

In his biography of Webster, written many years later, Charles March observed,

> The opening of his speech was simple, unaffected, without pretension, gradually gaining the confidence of his audience by its transparent sincerity and freedom from aught resembling display. As the orator continued and grew animated, his words became more fluent, and his language more nervous; a crowd of thoughts seemed rushing upon him all eager for utterance. He held them, however, under the command of his mind, as greyhounds with a leash, till he neared the close of his speech, when, warmed by the previous restraint, he poured them all forth, one after another, in glowing language.
>
> The speech took the House by surprise, not so much from its eloquence as from the vast amount of historical knowledge and illustrious ability displayed in it. How a person, untrained to forensic contests and unused to public affairs, could exhibit so much Parliamentary tact, such nice appreciation

of the difficulties of a difficult question, and such quiet facility in surmounting them, puzzled the mind. The age and inexperience of the speaker had prepared the House for no such display and astonishment for a time subdued the expression of its admiration.

> "No member before," says a person then in the House, "ever riveted the attention of the House so closely, in his first speech. Members left their seats where they could not see the speaker, face to face, and sat down, or stood on the floor, fronting him. All listened attentively and silently, during the whole speech; and when it was over, many went up and warmly congratulated the orator; among whom, were some, not the most niggard of their compliments, who most dissented from the views he expressed."[5]

Chief Justice John Marshall, writing to a friend some time after this speech, said: "At the time when this speech was delivered, I did not know Mr. Webster, but I was so much struck with it, that I did not hesitate then to state that Mr. Webster was a very able man, and would become one of the very first statesmen in America, and perhaps the very first."[6]

The above was quoted by March with a footnote:

> The friend to whom the letter referred to by March was written, was Justice Story, who adds: "Such praise from such a man ought to be very gratifying. Consider that he is now seventy-five years old and that he speaks of his recollections of some eighteen years ago with a freshness which shows how deeply your reasoning impressed itself upon his mind. Keep this *in memorian rei.*"[7]

Webster's own impressions of the day's events were revealed in a letter to Charles March that afternoon. He told his friend that the resolutions had been offered but would not be considered until a later date. (He thought it would be the next day.) He also wrote of the Senate's rough treatment of the Gallatin nomination and said, "There cannot be much sleep in the White-house about this time." Four days later, again with regard to Senate truculence, he wrote, "Poor Madison! I doubt whether he has a night's sleep these three weeks." It was only on June 19 (three days after the House finally took up debate on Webster's resolutions) that the young congressman from New Hampshire wrote again to March,

> Madison had been several days quite sick — is no better — has not been well eno [sic] to read the said Resolution of the Senate — the taxes go

heavily — I *fear* they will not go at all. They cannot raise a caucus, as yet, even to agree what they will do. They are in a sad pickle. Who cares![8]

Webster had formed a low opinion of President Madison at the very beginning of this session of Congress. On May 26, he wrote a New Hampshire friend, "I went yesterday to make my bow to the President. I did not like his looks any better than I like his Administration."[9]

He also wrote, trifling with the form for attending a White House levee.

You make your bow to Mrs. Madison, and to Mr. M., if he comes in your way, but he being there merely as a guest, is not officially entitled to your *congé*.... You stay from five minutes to an hour, as you please; eat and drink what you can catch, without danger of surfeit, and if you can luckily find your hat and stick, then take French leave; and that's going to the "levee."[10]

When the House took up Webster's resolutions on June 16, the first member to speak on them was to become one of his great adversaries over the next many decades — John C. Calhoun of South Carolina. Calhoun objected to the novelty of the form of the first resolution, which asked "when and by whom the information was received. Such form and particularity was unprecedented in such cases." Calhoun asked for "the precise object of the gentleman in giving this form to his motion. What use was intended to be made of the information called for?"

Webster replied that its use would depend on the information obtained. As to its form, the great orator of the future waffled, "It was on a subject on which he wished for particular information, of that nature which was designated by its terms."

In the debate that followed, Daniel Sheffey of Virginia came quickly to the point of the inquiry directed to the president. After stating that Bassano had told Barlow in May 1812 that the repealing decree had been communicated to the United States through two channels as early as May 1811, Sheffey said,

Either the assertion of the Duke of Bassano is true or it is not true.... It is manifest that if this decree was known to our Government in 1811, and had been known to the people, and used in the manner it ought to have been, the Orders in Council, the great cause of the war, would have been done away.

This was disputed by Calhoun who referred to the British Prince Regent's declaration of April 21, 1812, that "even if France did repeal her decrees in relation [to] us she [Britain] would not repeal her Orders in Council." Calhoun continued with great warmth in his argument saying he would prove Sheffey "guilty of falsity" if he dared to say that England would have repealed her Orders if she had been convinced France had revoked her decrees.

With this, Calhoun was called to order by Richard Stockton of New Jersey, who asked Speaker Clay if any "gentleman could be permitted to say that another dare not say any particular thing. Clay replied that he "did not understand the gentleman as having used a personal threat."

Calhoun likened his statement to the fact that no one would dare contradict the fact that two and two make four. But Calhoun insisted that the resolution be divested of an imputation "that the President had received the decree in question and had concealed it." Hanson insisted those words were the essential part of the resolution.

These arguments set the tone for debate continuing five days. The crux of the discussion centered on two points or charges: Whether the French foreign minister (Bassano) purposely lied to the American minister to France (Barlow) that the authentic repealing decree had been transmitted to the United States after April 28, 1811, through two channels (Barlow's predecessor, Russell, and the French minister to the United States, Sérurier); or whether the president of the United States, having received the decree through one or the other, or both, channels, had deliberately covered up the fact in order to lead the nation into war with Great Britain.

The ensuing arguments produced a strange juxtaposition of political faith. The anti–French Federalist were placing greater faith in the assertions of the Napoleonic ministers than were the pro–French Republicans. Luckily for the latter, they had often represented the French as only a little less treacherous than the British in their dealings with the United States.

In any case, it was clear to the Federalists that Madison had put absolute faith in the Cadore statement to Russell on August 5, 1810, that the decrees had been revoked — thus offering the ground on which the president issued his proclamation of that fact on November 2, 1810. It was also charged by the Federalists that Madison must be guilty of concealment since he had not, for one year (May 1812 to June 1813), denied the truth of Bassano's declaration that the revocation had been in the possession of the United States for one year (May 1811 to May 1812).

As the debate continued the Federalist maneuvered the Republicans into support of the resolutions by such statements as Thomas Jackson Oakley's of New York that "the friends of the Administration ought to promote the inquiry ... which must result in the vindication of its honor, if indeed it can be vindicated" and

> of repelling this foul slander on our Government.... Let the Administration tell us where the falsehood lies, and if they are innocent, let us know how they repelled the vile calumny. Let us see that they have had spirit enough to resent an imposition which they had discernment enough to detect.[11]

That same day, Grosvenor tied in the charge of concealment to its effect on a sick president. Supposing that Madison had delivered his country over to "all the miseries of an unnecessary and bloody war," Grosvenor asked,

> what maledictions can suit his conduct; what new and horrible punishment is commensurate with the bloody crime? Sir, the President is old, and the reproaches of men may concern and move him but little. But he must soon appear at the bar of Immortal Justice. If he had done this deed, how will he stand appalled before the accusing spirits of youth "untimely slain in battle?" How will his soul recoil from those bloody ravages, that wide devastation, that mess of human misery, which his own guilty conduct shall have produced!

Incidentally, Madison lived another 23 years.

Felix Grundy, continuing the debate the next day, went into great detail citing communications between the administration and the British government (through her minister, Mr. Foster) in late May and early June 1812 as securing evidence that the British would not give in on repealing their obnoxious Orders unless the United States could convince France to revoke her decrees as applied to all neutral nations, not just the United States.

When Maryland's Hanson responded to Grundy's speech he said he had hoped the debate would not open a deluge of documentary evi-

dence and would thereby deprive the Tennessean "of an opportunity to display the lawyer like dexterity, and a characteristic skill and cunning," etc., and moments later referred to Grundy as "the apologist of France."

At this point, Speaker Clay called Hanson to order saying he "could not proceed in such a course of argument — that the epithet "cunning" was not proper to be applied to a member of the House. Still more, it was out of order to use the words "apologist of France"?

Then, according to the dialogue printed in the *Annals*,

> Hanson asked if the same latitude of debate allowed to the gentleman from Tennessee would be extended to him. The Speaker replied, "certainly." If it is not, said Hanson, I must get at the gentleman in some other way, in the course of the argument. Mr. Grundy rose to explain; Mr H. said he had the floor and meant to keep it; there would be an opportunity to reply. And he proceeded.[12]

Within moments Hanson was casting allusions at Clay himself (and Clay's War Hawk friends) though not using his name, when the Marylander spoke of "a self-creating committee of Congressmen who called on the President and required him to send the House a Message recommending war." He said, "The first demand was unsuccessful, but the second succeeded; when he was given to understand that his re-election depended upon his recommending war at once."[13] This was the charge questioned six months hence by sitting Congressman Timothy Pickering where upon his informants referred to a supposed Clay-Madison meeting in early April 1812 and the documented meeting in late May 1812.

At last, on June 21, William Bibb of Georgia, chairman of the Ways and Means Committee, reported that they were now ready to present the tax bills for discussion on the following day and he expressed the hope that debate on Webster's resolutions could be concluded this day.[14]

Calhoun said he was so anxious to get at the tax measures that he would withdraw his amendments to the resolutions if Farrow's motion for an indefinite postponement was also withdrawn. Farrow agreed.[15] This abrupt end to a vigorous debate astounded Webster, who had prepared to speak on his resolutions. Later that day he wrote his friend, March,

I made no speech. When I came to the House this morning, Calhoun told me, the motion for indefinite postponement would be withdrawn — his motion to amend withdrawn — & he & some of his friends should vote for the Resolutions as they are. I, of course, could not object & considering the thing given up on their part, I forbade to speak. They have acted very strangely. A dozen motions, made & withdrawn — some pulling one way — some another. They do not manage like so many Solomons.[16]

The resolutions cleared by a large majority, and Speaker Clay thereupon named Webster and John Rhea of Tennessee as a committee to present the resolutions to Madison. This did not sit comfortably with Webster and he again wrote March the next day, "The Speaker has appointed me & *old Rhea* to carry the Resolutions to the Palace!!! *I never swear.*"[17]

This day, June 22, the committee called on Madison as described by Webster.

I went on Tuesday to the palace to present the Resolutions. The President was in his bed, sick of a fever. His night cap on his head — his wife attending him, etc. etc. I think he will find *no relief* from my prescription.

Two days later Webster again wrote,

The President is seriously sick. Not much is suffered to be said on this subject, & I am not disposed to excite alarm, but you may be assured, that he is sick — he has been sick 13 days — & has no Symptoms of convalescence.[18]

Though Webster was "not disposed to excite alarm," his fellow Federalist, Hanson, through an editorial a few days later in his news organ, the *Georgetown Federal Republican*, was not reluctant to point up the disastrous health of the government's leadership. Noting first that the "President continues dangerously ill," he added that the chairman of the House Ways and Means Committee, John W. Eppes of Virginia,

is disabled by sickness.... Gallatin has fled the treasury by same instinct that rats desert a sinking vessel. The Commander in Chief of the armies [Henry Dearborn] is reported to be at the point of death, and his resignation is announced.

And now, for one moment, reflect upon the condition of the country, should Elbridge Gerry succeed to the throne by the demise of the lingering incumbent. We might worship King Log for a while, but some dangerous designing men would use him as so much potter's clay, [an allusion to

Henry Clay] to be moulded into any shape; and when all was arranged, to take his place. A superannuated President, above eighty years of age, might be got rid of, without any other cause being suspected than old age. [If this referred to Gerry, it was incorrect as to his age since he was only 69.] Let a certain individual be once placed in the direct line of succession, and the ladder of promotion be in his way, we warrant he will mount it as rapidly as he has already ascended the heights of political distinction from the morasses and mud puddles below. There is a way some men have of removing obstructions from the course, which was not the first time introduced by the Duke of Gloucester.[19]

About this same time, Secretary of State James Monroe wrote to Jefferson to tell him that such senators as Rufus King of New York, William Branch Giles of Virginia, Samuel Smith of Maryland, Michael Leib of Pennsylvania, Obadiah German of New York, and Nicholas Gilman of New Hampshire,

have begun to make calculations & plans, founded on the presumed death of the President & Vice President, & it has been suggested to me that Giles, is thought of to take the place of the President of the Senate [as *pro tem*], as soon as the Vice President withdraws.

The line of succession following the vice president at that time went next to the president pro tem of the Senate — at this moment vacant because of the departure of William Crawford to be minister to France.

In that same letter to Jefferson, Monroe described the president's illness as

a bilious fever; of that kind called the remittent. It has perhaps never left him, even for an hour, and occasionally simptoms [sic] have been unfavorable. This is I think the 15th day. Elzey of this place, & Shoaff of Annapolis, with Dr. Tucker, attend him. They think he will recover. The first mention'd I have just seen, who reports that he had a good night, & is in a state to take bark, which indeed he has done on his best day, for nearly a week.[20]

Despite the concerns, the calculations, the rumors, and the innuendoes, Dolly Madison was able, on July 2, to write the president's secretary, Edward Coles (himself out of Washington recovering from an illness),

I have the happiness to assure you, my dear cousin, that Mr. Madison recovers; for the last three weeks his fever has been so slight as to permit him to take bark every hour and with good effect. It is three weeks now I have nursed him, night and day,—sometimes with despair! but now that I see he will get well I feel as if I might die myself from fatigue.[21]

By July 7, the newspapers reported that the president had resumed the most urgent public business.[22]

One piece of urgent business with which Madison dealt on the previous day was a matter that came to him at the instigation of Speaker Clay following more bad military news. After the capture of York by forces under American General Henry Dearborn, that expedition returned to the south side of Lake Ontario and made an assault on the Canadian side of the Niagara River on May 28. The drive ashore from the Lake was under the naval command of Commander Oliver Hazard Perry, and was spearheaded inland by Colonel Winfield Scott. With complete victory nearly at hand, Scott twice disregarded orders to give up pursuit of a fleeing enemy, but finally obeyed a third order. The British commander retreated west to the area of Hamilton. One American attack there, about a week later, netted the British two American generals as prisoners (John Chandler and William H. Winder). Then on June 23, another assault group, led by Lieutenant Colonel Charles Boerstler (the only hero to come out of the earlier Niagara fiasco), was mangled by British and Indians, and Boerstler and about 570 Americans were captured.

It was this news that reached Washington on July 6 and angered several of the War Hawks, including Henry Clay. Though little is known of it, a spirited conversation between Clay, Samuel Ringgold of Maryland, and Charles Jared Ingersoll of Pennsylvania took place in the lobby of the House of Representatives. Ingersoll found himself deputed "a volunteer," he said, to call on President Madison to seek the dismissal from command of General Dearborn (an ill man who was assumed to be the source of the latest debacles). Ingersoll later wrote that,

the President was ill abed when I called but promised an early answer, which soon followed me to the Capitol, in a message from Mr. Monroe, that General Dearborn should be removed: the order went at once.[23]

In fact, a dispatch to that effect was sent to Dearborn by Secretary of War John Armstrong the very same day on which the discussion in the House lobby had taken place. But Monroe's part in the episode is unclear. Dearborn was to question whether the order had come from the president (who assured him it had) by saying his health had been recovered. His replacement left much to be desired—for it was James Wilkinson of the Burr-affair notoriety!

Also, by this time, the House itself had finally become active in the nation's urgent business—that of levying taxes to pay for the war. On June 22, when it abruptly ended its bickering over the Webster resolutions, it began a month-long haggle over 12 tax bills reported out by the Ways and Means Committee. These were the measures put together by Gallatin prior to his withdrawal from the Treasury Department, which he had left in the hands of William Jones. Jones submitted the tax bills to Congress under his signature as acting secretary.

The 12 tax bills included three for direct taxes and internal duties, one to set up a revenue office, two on foreign commerce, one on financial papers, two on liquor or spirits, one each on salt and sugar, and one on carriages.[24] They produced protracted and dull debate with Federalists sniping at the war supporters while unwilling to aid them prosecute "their" war, and the Republicans very reluctant to impose the added financial burden on the citizenry.

Between the time the legislation was first submitted to the committee (June 10) and the date it was reported out (June 22), Clay reported on its effect to his constituency in a letter to the *Lexington Reporter*:

The Committee of Ways and Means has presented a System of Taxation contemplating the provision of a nett [sic] additional revenue of $5,600,000. It does not essentially vary from that which was before the last. Of this sum, three millions of dollars are proposed to be raised by a direct tax, of which the quota assigned to Kentucky, according to the principles of the constitution is $168,928.76. The committee has apportioned each state's quota among the several counties of which it is composed. In Kentucky, the basis of the apportionment has been the state tax paid in each county. The proportion allotted, upon principle, to the district to which I belong is $22,598.55, of which

Fayette is to pay $14,585.28, Jessamine $3,305.97, and Woodford $4,707.30.— The subject is not yet acted upon in the House, but will be in a day or two.[25]

For the most part, Clay stayed out of the debate though much of it took place in Committee of the Whole. From time to time, while sitting as Speaker, he had to call some member to order and one time voted against an amendment when there was a tie vote. The only significant effort on his part was some discussion on imposition of duty on bank notes which was debated on July 14. He proposed to confine the tax on notes "to those negotiated at banks, with a view to except from stamp duties the ordinary country transactions by notes." It was reported that Clay supported his motion "by a luminous and comprehensive view of the expediency and policy of the course he proposed." It carried without division.[26]

On July 12, two days before Clay's participation on the tax measures, the House received from President Madison his response to the Webster resolutions. Madison's message was accompanied by a long report of explanation from Secretary of State Monroe and a sheaf of diplomatic correspondence between Washington, Paris, and London. The report and the letters made it clear that the first knowledge the United States had of the French revocation of her decrees (dated April 28, 1811) was its presentation to the American minister to France, Joel Barlow, on May 10, 1812. Both Barlow and his predecessor, Jonathan Russell (by this 1812 date, the chargé d'affaires in London), wrote to Monroe that they had never before seen the revocation decrees.

In addition to these references to the French action, a letter from Russell to Monroe, dated June 30, 1812, was also forwarded to the House of Representatives. This letter was written in London after the American declaration of war but prior to its knowledge in England and just days after Great Britain repealed the Orders in Council. It contradicted the Federalist claim that the war was unnecessary because the British would have terminated their Orders on the basis of the French repeals. Though Russell wrote that the British founded their revocation on the sudden appearance of the French repeal dated April 1811, "The real cause," he noted,

is the measures of our Government. These measures have produced a degree of distress among the manufacturers of this country that was becoming intolerable, and an apprehension of still greater misery from the calamities of war drove them to speak a language which could not be misunderstood or disregarded.

Many members of the House of Commons, who had been advocates of the orders in council, particularly Mr. Wilberforce, and others from the northern countries, were forced now to make a stand against them, or to meet the indignation of their constituents at the approaching election.[27]

On receipt of these documents from the president, they were read in the House and referred to the Foreign Relations Committee. The next day the committee recommended to the House a resolution reading, "That the conduct of the Executive in relation to the various subjects, referred to in the resolution of the 21st day of June, 1813, meets with the approbation of the House."[28]

John C. Calhoun moved it to the Committee of the Whole House for the next day (July 14). The discussion on handling the resolutions presented a varied view: Some wanting to put the matter to rest with no discussion, some wanting to discuss it at the next session when all members might be present (Webster and several others had already left for home), some wanting to discuss it now in deference to the president and secretary of state who made the material available, some wanting to wait a few days during which copies of Monroe's report could be printed and members might have time to study it before debating, and some wanting to discuss it after the tax measures were out of the way.

The House finally agreed to discuss Monroe's report on July 15 (two days later). But when that day came around, an entirely new concern was thrust upon the members.

When British Rear Admiral Cockburn floated back down Chesapeake Bay in May, he joined his superior, Vice Admiral John Borlase Warren, who had been attempting to capture the *Constellation* in the back waters around Norfolk. The American ship was too far down the Elizabeth River for the British to reach it. And, thus, they turned their next assault to easier reachable targets — the northern shore of Hampton Roads and particularly the town of Hampton, Virginia. Cockburn's marines went ashore on the night of June 24 and captured the town the following day. Then followed another of Cockburn's atrocities. It was reported later that he had told his men, "That if they would take Norfolk, and burn it, they should have *twenty-five pounds a piece, three days' plunder! and all the pretty women as long as they wanted!!!*"[29]

Apparently, the admiral's consent extended to Hampton as well as Norfolk (which, in fact, the British failed to conquer). It was about the time that Clay and his colleagues wrestled with tax legislation in Washington that they began to hear of the attacks of the British soldiery on the defenseless women of Hampton. Among the stories that reached the legislators were these:

Mrs. Turnbull was pursued up to her waist in the water and dragged on shore by 10 or 12 of these ruffians, who satiated their brutal desires upon her after pulling off her clothes, stockings, shoes, etc. A married woman, with her infant child in her arms (the child forcibly dragged from her) shared the same fate.

Another, in the presence of old Mr. Hope, had her gown, etc. etc. etc. cut off with a sword and violence offered in his presence, which he endeavored to prevent, but had to quit the room leaving the unfortunate victim in their possession, who no doubt was abused in the same way. Old Mr. Hope himself was stripped naked, pricked with a bayonet in the arm and slapt in the face.[30]

Miss ____, was seen in the hands of 28 soldiers, and forced by the whole of them!!! She is now at the point of death.[31]

And in the letter reporting Cockburn's consent, the writer stated,

The Admirals, then permitted their men to strip those unhappy women naked, and with drawn bayonets, drive them through the streets before them. Most of these unfortunate females (now rendered wretched for life, by the *Bulwark of our Religion*) are well known, and are beautiful beyond description. Women were flying in all directions, with children in their arms, pursued by these savages. It is an eternal stigma on the British character.

Other accounts revealed that some of the crimes were the acts of French soldiers in British employ.

Further accounts of plunder in the homes must have brought back to Henry Clay those visions he still retained of the depredations perpetrated by Col. Banastre Tarleton at his own home 32 years before.

From Hampton, Cockburn again turned his fleet northward and sailed into the Potomac River to approach the capital city. It was this threat which pulled the legislators' attention away from taxes on July 15, though several votes were taken on those measures earlier on this hot mid-summer's day. When word reached the Capitol that the British fleet, with about 25 warships, was within 50 miles of the city, the House closed its doors at 3:30 and went into secret session.

Colonel Philip Stuart, a mild Federalist member from Maryland, introduced a resolution with a preamble that noted,

That the seat of government, from the unprepared and defenceless state of the District of Columbia, was in imminent danger if attacked; the fleet of the enemy was understood to be within a few hours sail of the capital, the immense value of public property exposed to destruction, and the great value of public records, rendered it important that invasion of the metropolis should be met with vigour and repelled.

He then called for

a distribution of such arms as were in possession of the government within the District should be immediately placed in the hands of all able-bodied men of the District, and of such members of the House as were willing to receive them, to act against the enemy in any manner not incompatible with public duties.[32]

The climate was not conducive to soft spoken discussion. As described by Charles Ingersoll, it was

one of those dry, sultry, windy, not cloudy, but misty, murky, smoky, overcast, uncomfortable dog days ... with unwholesome, enervating, sweltering, atrabilious, suffocating, languid, feverish heat, as hot as the faction within and war without ... it blew a hurricane, roaring like great guns through the dome of the House of Representatives, and struck down the flag rattling on the top. Distant artillery was audible, as was thought, from time to time, and rumours continually afloat as the enemy advanced. Debate ran high.[33]

The House became noisy with angry members when, according to Ingersoll,

The Speaker commanded silence with unusual emphasis, — "Gentlemen." said he, "if we do not arm and take the field, I am sure we shall be beat, if there is not more order kept in the ranks than in this House. I should be sorry to head so disorderly a body."[34]

However, the House acted in its true form by voting to strike out the preamble to the resolution and send the measure to the Committee on Military Affairs rather than act.

Meanwhile, out on the streets, solid news was hard to come by since the reporters and editors of the city's principal newspaper, *The National Intelligencer*, had gone down the river with volunteer companies to meet the enemy. Others, throughout the city and the neighboring communities of Georgetown and Alexandria, joined the companies and marched down to Fort Warburton (shortly renamed Fort Washington). Among those "new" troops were Secretary of War John Armstrong, Secretary of the Navy (Captain) William Jones, and Secretary of State (Colonel) James Monroe. Inside the city (except for Congress) all business ceased as citizens left the city until the troops numbered about 3,000 men under arms.

As it turned out, there was more battle between Armstrong and Monroe than between British and American servicemen. (Though Monroe came under shell fire from a British frigate while at breakfast one morning, no damage resulted.)[35] Both secretaries had their eye on the presidential chair and hoped to gain any military glory possible while denying such to the other. Therefore, when Monroe sought to command some regular troops to battle the British, Armstrong said he could have only militia. The antagonism was apparent even among the troops.

While the cabinet officers bickered on the scene (staying there three or four days), the House, on the day following the alarm, received the report of the Military Affairs Committee in secret session. The committee stated,

> That they have examined into the state of preparation, naval and military, made to receive the enemy, and are satisfied that the preparation is in every respect, adequate to the emergency and that no measures are necessary, on the part of the House, to make it more complete.

This report was ordered to lie on the table and all secrecy was removed on the proceedings of the past two days.[36]

The committee's report was accurate this time. The feeling in the Washington suburb (near the site of the present-day Old Soldier's Home) was expressed by the Clay family's friend Margaret Bayard Smith, writing to another friend on July 20. "There is so little apprehension of danger in the city, that not a single removal of person or goods has taken place." Nevertheless, some city dwellers made known to her the desire to come her way in the event the British passed the fort. To meet this danger she said her husband had

> procured pistols, etc. etc., sufficient for our defense, and we make use of every precaution which we should use were we certain of what we now only reckon a possibility. In the city and Georgetown the gentlemen who by their age or other circumstances are exempt from service, have formed volunteer companies both of horse and foot, who nightly patrol the streets. The members of Congress have determined to join the citizens, in case of an attack and there are many experienced officers amongst them.

She noted that the "affair of Hampton ... inspires us with a terror we should not otherwise have felt." Toward the end of her letter, she added that "we expect Mrs. Clay, her sister, Mrs. Brown ... and many others to come to us in case of a serious alarm."[37]

With each passing day, the apprehensions subsided until, as reported by Ingersoll,

> At last on the 27th July, it was understood at Washington that difficulties encountered by the British ships in passing a place called Kettle-bottoms, frustrated their approach to the seat of government ... and their naval force ... all turned back, sailing down the river, as was thought intending to go round to Annapolis.[38]

The work of the House of Representatives was all anti-climactic in these last hot, fretful days of July 1813. The 12 tax bills were passed by good margins.

On the same day that Mrs. Smith wrote her letter (July 20), President Madison sent a message to Congress requesting an embargo on exports. He noted that the British were combining their blockade of American ports with the issuance of "special licenses to neutral vessels, or to British vessels in neutral disguises," to obtain "exports essential to their wants" while discriminating between different ports of the United States. This clearly implied use of the ports of anti-war New England. An embargo bill was quickly drafted and the House with unusual speed passed it two days later. It was rejected by the Senate on July 28.[39]

On the final day of July, Henry Clay's lone proposal of the session, on the subject of British barbarities, was given consideration. The special committee's report was arranged under the following heads:

1. Bad treatment of American prisoners;
2. Detention of American prisoners as British subjects, on the plea of nativity in the dominions of Great Britain, or of naturalization;
3. Detention of mariners as prisoners of war, who were in England when war was declared;
4. Compulsory service of impressed American seamen on board British ships of war;
5. Violation of flags of truce:
6. Ransom of American prisoners from Indians in British service;
7. Pillage and destruction of private property on Chesapeake Bay, and in neighboring country;
8. Massacre and burning of American prisoners surrendered to officers of Great Britain, by Indians in the British service; abandonment of the remains of Americans killed in battle, or murdered after the surrender to the British; the pillage and shooting of American citizens, and burning of their houses after surrender to the British under the guarantee of protection;
9. Outrages at Hampton, in Virginia."

There followed a lengthy paragraph of evidence for each "head." With regard to the "eighth head," the British were specifically charged with being "deeply implicated in the infamy," at the River Raisin where Clay's brother-in-law was murdered and left in a road to be eaten by hogs. On this subject the report said,

> no person of this or any other nation can read the simple narrative of the different witnesses of the grossest violations of honor, justice, and humanity, without the strongest emotions of indignation and horror. That these outrages were perpetrated by Indians, is neither palliation nor excuse. Every civilized nation is answerable for the conduct of the allies under their command ... if the British officers did not connive at their destruction, they were criminally indifferent about the fate of the wounded prisoners. But what marks more strongly the degradation of the character of the British soldiers, is the refusal of the last offices of humanity to the bodies of the dead. The bodies of our countrymen were exposed to every indignity, and became food for brutes in the sight of men who affect a sacred regard to the dictates of honor and

religion. Low indeed is the character of that army which is reduced to the confession that their savage auxiliaries will not permit them to perform the rites of sepulchre to the slain. The Committee have not been able to discover even the expression of that detestation which such conduct must inspire from the military or civil authority on the Canadian frontier, unless such detestation is to be presumed from the choice of an Indian trophy as an armament for the Legislative Hall of Upper Canada.

In like manner the committee reported, under the "ninth head," on the atrocities at Hampton although these were committed since the select committee had been appointed. The evidence suggested that these latest acts were instigated by soldiers who followed the example of their officers. The committee charged that,

> For every detestable violation of humanity an excuse is fabricated or found. The wounded prisoners on the Northern frontier were massacred by Indians; the sick murdered, and the women violated, at Hampton, by foreign troops in the pay of Great Britain.... The shrieks of the innocent victims of infernal lust at Hampton were heard by American prisoner, but were too weak to reach the ears or disturb the repose of the British officers, whose duty, as men, required them to protect every female whom the fortune of war had thrown into their power.

The report noted that correspondence revealed an "equivalent to admission of the facts by the British commander," but there was no punishment of the offenders.

The committee said the president had the power to retaliate but then passed a mild resolution which must have rankled Henry Clay's ire. It read,

> That the President of the United States be requested to have collected and presented to this House, during the continuance of the present war, evidence of every departure by the enemy from the ordinary modes of conducting war among civilized nations.[40]

The House passed the resolution and sent it to President Madison. Two days later, on Monday, August 2, the Congress adjourned until December 6.

23

IN THE EYE OF A HURRICANE

As soon as the summer session of Congress ended, Henry Clay returned home to Lexington, Kentucky, with his family. It was to become his life-long desire to return to the peace of his "Ashland," though at this time it was still in the process of growing. Shortly after Clay's departure from Washington, Benjamin Latrobe, now designing new wings for Ashland, arrived in the capital.

On August 15, 1813, Latrobe answered a letter from Clay dated the 4th (contents unknown). Latrobe's letter reveals some of the new design. A kitchen was to be built on the right wing (looking toward the entrance from the front of the house). But this wing was to wait construction until the spring of 1814. Meanwhile, work was already underway on the other wing which would have bed chambers and a nursery.

Latrobe also requested information regarding renovation and construction of some other buildings owned by Clay in Lexington. The architect thanked Clay for an invitation to visit Lexington and said he would do so next spring "if I succeed in finishing my first steamboat at the season." Meanwhile, he informed Clay that mail could reach him in Pittsburgh by the middle of September.[1]

Near the end of August, Latrobe sent Clay a drawing "for the ground in Lexington" and enclosed "the design for your houses in Lexington which I hope will give you satisfaction. If not, any alteration you may desire will most cheerfully be made." Still Latrobe was confused by the placement of the kitchen and its relation to the stairs. "The Parlor which is between the kitchen & the body of the house will be affected in shape by the position of the door from the stairs."[2]

Though nothing further resulted from their correspondence during Clay's brief home visit of less than two months, he did make other contracts for continuing brick work with the builder John Fisher, amounting to nearly $900. Among documents showing Clay's method of payment for other brick work on the house is an agreement between him and Robert Grinstead and Allen Davis to pay off $1600. He included "John Dillon's note payable next fall for five hundred dollars," and he agreed "to deliver to them horses this fall not exceeding eight years old to the amount of five hundred dollars," and he turned over to them "a negro man named Joe at six hundred dollars."[3] Clay had purchased Joe (24–25 years old) from William Heron of Culpeper County in Virginia for $500 just four days earlier.[4] In addition, Clay sold some property he had owned for six years near Louisville. He was also receiving rent on several pieces of property in Lexington.

A newspaper item during his first week home notes that "at a convocation of the Grand Lodge of Kentucky at Mason's Hall in Lexington on Wednesday last [August 25] the following officers were elected," among whom was "Henry Clay, Grand Orator."[5]

Little else of Clay's personal activities is revealed during this home stay except that his meager surviving correspondence and newspaper accounts tie into news from other areas. The news seemed to come in alternating waves, first from the north and then from the south, and each wave seemed to try to exceed its predecessor in magnitude — almost like feeder bands of a hurricane. About the time Clay returned to Lexington, he wrote to Isaac Shelby on August 22, with reference to the governor's intent to lead a detachment of militia toward the Lake Erie area. Clay wrote,

As you will want a sword, I have the pleasure to inform you that I am charged by Governor Turner and Mr. Macon (both members of Congress from North Carolina where Turner had formerly been Governor) with delivering to you that which the State of North Carolina voted you in testimony of the sense it entertained of your conduct at King's Mountain. I would take it with me to Frankfort, in order that I might personally execute the commission and at the same time have the gratification of seeing you, if I were not excessively oppressed with fatigue. I shall not fail, however, to avail myself of the first safe conveyance.... May it acquire additional lustre in the patriotic and hazardous enterprise in which you are embarking![6]

Shortly after the Battle of King's Mountain, in October 1780, during the American Revolution, the North Carolina legislature voted a resolution of thanks and a gift of an elaborate sword to Shelby and several others for their heroic deeds in that battle. But somewhere along that early bureaucratic maze, the letter and the sword were never delivered. During the spring of 1813 this mistake was corrected, and Henry Clay was selected by the incumbent governor of North Carolina as the vehicle to present them to Shelby. They were, however, taken to Frankfort by a common friend, William T. Barry, who also delivered Clay's letter to Shelby.

As for the stormy military situation into which Shelby was about to march, some leading waves of the tempest had already flowed into Kentucky with news accounts arriving there about the same time that Clay wrote Shelby. After the British and Indians withdrew from the siege of Fort Meigs in early May, Col. Richard M. Johnson (an elected member of Congress from Kentucky who went to the battlefields instead of the legislative halls) marched north to join Gen. Green Clay holding that outpost. Johnson reached the fort in late June amidst fears of an enemy attack which, nevertheless, did not occur.

Still the threat remained and, on July 20, Gen. William Henry Harrison wrote Shelby from Lower Sandusky, Ohio, saying he had just received authorization from Secretary of War John Armstrong to call for militia from the neighboring states for an "operation against Upper Canada" (that area between Niagara and Detroit). But

Harrison went further in his letter. Recognizing "the present indisposition to the service which begins to prevail in Kentucky," Harrison said he believed, "it will not be impossible for you to reanimate your patriotic fellow citizens and once more to bring a portion of them to the field." Harrison hoped for 400 to 2000 men.

Continuing his request, the general wrote,

The period has arrived when with a little exertion the task assigned to this section of the union may be finished, and complete tranquility restored to our frontier. To make this last effort, why not, my dear sir, come in person, you would not object to a command that would be nominal only—I have such confidence in your wisdom that you in fact should "be the guiding Head and I the hand." The situation you would be placed in is not without its parallel. Scipio the conqueror of Carthage did not disdain to act as a Lieutenant of his younger and less experienced brother Lucius.[7]

Shelby was so moved by the appeal that on July 31 he issued a call for men to rendezvous with him at Newport, Kentucky, on August 31.[8] The 63-year-old governor replied to the general, "No apology was necessary to invite me to your standard had I more age and much greater experience I would not hesitate to fight under your banner for the honour & interest of my beloved country."[9]

But meanwhile, Harrison, three days after writing Shelby, received alarming news from Gen. Green Clay at Fort Meigs that the fort was suddenly surrounded by the enemy. Johnson and his troops were not then at the fort having been directed to the Illinois territory by Secretary of War Armstrong. However, his departure had been so recent Harrison was able to send express to countermand the order since he had received fresh orders from Armstrong to cancel the earlier one. Still, this did not help General Clay at Fort Meigs.

Expecting that the garrison would receive fresh reinforcements, the Indians around the fort put on a sham battle hoping the men inside would think it was help coming to them and now in danger of being wiped out. While the soldiers thought so, General Clay had received word from Harrison that no help could come immediately and Clay, therefore, restrained his troops from venturing outside the fort into a certain ambush.

The British pulled out on July 28. On receiving this information, Harrison anticipated an attack at Fort Stephenson at Lower Sandusky. (He was then many miles up stream.) This post was commanded by a 21-year-old nephew of George Rogers Clark, Major George Croghan. Having recently viewed the defenses of Fort Stephenson, Harrison, late on July 19, wrote to Croghan:

Sir — Immediately on receiving this letter you will abandon Fort Stephenson, set fire to it, and repair with your command this night to headquarters. Cross the river and come up on the opposite side. If you should deem and find it impracticable to make good your march to this place, take the road to Huron and pursue it with the utmost circumspection and despatch.[10]

The messenger lost his way and was more than 12 hours reaching Croghan. On receipt of the order, the major wrote back to Harrison,

I have just received yours of yesterday, 10 o'clock P.M. ordering me to destroy this place and make good my retreat, which was received too late to be carried into execution. We have determined to maintain this place, and by heavens we can.[11]

Harrison nearly exploded at this seeming insubordination and utter folly. After all Croghan had only about 160 regulars and a 6-pounder cannon. His anticipated enemy was at least 500 British regulars and 800 Indians all under General Proctor and another 2,000 Indians under Tecumseh on the road toward Fort Meigs ready to render additional support.

Quickly, Harrison had an aide pen an order to Croghan and had it delivered by Col. Samuel Wells, who was escorted by a squadron of dragoons. The order read:

The General has just received your letter of this date, informing him that you had thought proper to disobey the order issued from this office, and delivered to you this morning. It appears that the information which dictated the order was incorrect; and as you did not receive it in the night, as was expected, it might have been proper that you should have reported the circumstance and your situation, before you proceeded to its execution. This might have been passed over, but I am directed to say to you, that an officer who presumes to aver, that he has made his resolution, and that he will act in direct opposition to the orders of his General, can no longer be entrusted with a separate command. Colonel Wells is sent to relieve you. You will deliver the command to him, and repair with Colonel Ball's squadron to this place.

It was signed by A. H. Homes, assistant adjutant general.[12]

Croghan returned to Harrison's headquarters and explained to the general that he had received his order at 10 A.M., and all his subordinates agreed that a retreat in daylight "in the face of a superior force of the enemy would be more hazardous than to remain in the fort." The major then sent the message which so riled Harrison, believing it would fall into the hands of the enemy rather than reach the addressee. Harrison accepted Croghan's explanation — and writing style — and permitted him to resume command of the fort.[13]

On Sunday evening, August 1, as the British secured all escape routes from the fort, General Proctor sent Colonel [Matthew] Elliot, accompanied by Major [John] Chambers, under a flag of truce to demand surrender of the fort "to spare the effusion of blood." Croghan's representative was Ensign [Edmund] Shipp. Describing the ensuing conversation, Harrison wrote Secretary of War Eustis,

The major observed, that general Proctor had a number of cannon, a large body of regular troops, and so many Indians whom it was impossible to control; and if the fort was taken, as it must be, the whole of the garrison would be massacred. Mr. Shipp, answered, that it was the determination of major Croghan, his officers and men, to defend the garrison or be buried in it; and that they might do their best. Colonel Elliott then addressed Mr. Shipp, and said, "you are a fine young man; I pity your situation; for God's sake surrender, and prevent the dreadful slaughter that must follow resistance." Shipp turned from him with indignation, and was immediately taken hold of by an Indian, who attempted to wrest his sword from him. Elliott pretended to exert himself to release him, and expressed great anxiety to get him safe in the fort.[14]

When the discussion ended and the emissaries returned to their lines, the British began bombarding the fort with five 6-pounders and a howitzer. This continued until mid-afternoon of the following day. Meanwhile, Croghan had shuffled his lone cannon about the fort to fire from different positions to deceive the enemy into believing there were several cannon. By this time, he judged the bombardment was aimed at an assault at the northwest corner. He had his troops strengthen that part of the fort with bags of flour and sand, and then set up the cannon in a masked position to await the attack.

Around 5 P.M., the British advanced in a close column of about 350 men. Enveloped in smoke, they approached within "18 or 20 paces of the lines." The Americans "commenced so heavy and galling a fire as to throw the column a little into confusion." At the outer works the British leaped into a ditch — as anticipated by Croghan. At that moment his six-pounder was unmasked and "with a half load of powder and double charge of leaden slugs at the distance of 30 feet, poured destruction" upon the British.[15]

The following day Croghan wrote succinctly:

The enemy made an attempt to storm us last evening, but was repulsed with the loss of at least 100 killed, wounded, and prisoners. One lieut. col. (lt. col. Short) a major and a lieutenant, with about 40 privates, are dead in our ditch. I have lost but one in killed, and but a few wounded. Further statements will be made you by the bearer.

Then he added a note:

Since writing the above, two soldiers of the 41st regiment [British] have got in, who state that the enemy have retreated. In fact, one of their gunboats is within three hundred yards of our works, said to be loaded with camp-equipment, etc., which they, in their hurry have left.[16]

Transmitting Croghan's official report of the battle to Secretary Armstrong, Harrison noted,

It will not be amongst the least of general proctor's [sic] mortifications to find he has been baffled by a youth who has just passed his twenty-first year. He is, however a hero worthy of his gallant uncle (general George R. Clark).[17]

The story of this minor battle, Croghan's brief dispatch and detailed letter of August 5, and Harrison's letter to Armstrong all appeared complete in the *Lexington Reporter* of August 21, just as Clay returned home from that depressing Congressional summer in Washington. The news electrified Kentucky and would grow throughout his brief visit home.

On August 23, Clay's wife's second cousin, Thomas Hart Benton, penned a brief note to Clay. It basically concerned the transfer of some Negro slaves to Clay, but it contained one short sentence at the end which tied Benton to a character who would later become Clay's greatest antagonist over a quarter of his life, though not

mentioned in this letter. That was Andrew Jackson. The sentence read: "Mr. Jesse Benton has recovered of his wound."[18] Jesse was Thomas Hart Benton's brother.

To tell the story it is necessary to back track in time just a little. Late in 1812, Andrew Jackson, in Nashville, received authorization from the federal government through the governor of Tennessee to organize 1500 men from his state to go to New Orleans. More than 2,000 Tennessee volunteers (among them, Thomas Hart Benton, who got command of a regiment) assembled in December in deep snow, left Tennessee in January 1813, and reached Natchez in mid–February. Then, Jackson received orders from James Wilkinson to halt. Though Wilkinson gave lack of supplies in the New Orleans area as his reason for stopping Jackson and the ensuing correspondence appeared cordial, Wilkinson clearly antagonized Jackson by challenging his right to bring cavalry into the area and then demanding that he (a regular brigadier general) retain command over Jackson (a militia major general). Benton did not endear himself to Jackson by voicing his opinion in favor of Wilkinson's viewpoint.

One month later, a more devastating order reached Jackson from Secretary of War John Armstrong. Mis-dated January 5 (it should have been February 5), this message reached the general on March 15 and was curt. It read as follows:

Sir, The causes for embodying and marching to New Orleans the Corps under your command having ceased to exist, you will on receit [sic] of this letter, consider it as dismissed from public service and take measures to have delivered over to Major General Wilkinson all articles of public property which may have been put into its possession. You will accept for yourself and the Corps the thanks of the President of the United States.[19]

After so many hardships of cold and sickness endured by his gallant volunteers on the march south, Jackson's fury exploded. He wrote a harsh complaint to Armstrong and a softer one to President Madison. Despite Benton's advice to tone down the letter, Jackson told Armstrong that unless there was a mistake in the date, the letter had been written prior to his assuming office and was therefore an "unofficial act."

Further, he wrote to Armstrong,

If it was intended by this order that we should be dismissed eight-hundred miles from home, deprived of arms, tents and supplies for the sick, of our arms and supplies for the well, it appears that these brave men, who certainly deserve a better fate and return from their government, was intended by this order to be sacrificed. Those that could escape from the insalubrious climate, are to be deprived of the necessary support and meet death by famine. The remaining few to be deprived of their arms pass through the savage land, where our women, children and defenceless citizens are daily murdered. Yet thro that barbarous clime, must our band of citizen soldiers wander and fall a sacrifice to the tomahawk and scalping knife of the wilderness our sick left naked in the open field and remain without supplies, without nourishment or any earthly comfort.[20]

In less strong terms, Jackson related the same complaint to the president and added, "I cannot Beleave [sic] that you would reward thus, the tendered support of the purest patriots of America, to beleave it would be to beleave that you were lost to all sense of humanity and love of country." In reference to Armstrong's order, Jackson noted to Madison, "I cannot Beleave (this) was ever written by your direction or knowledge." He told the president he was determined to march his men to Nashville and trust they would be paid for their effort on arrival in Tennessee.[21]

However, Wilkinson's quartermaster general refused to furnish Jackson's army with supplies to get it home and another officer tried to recruit Jackson's "discharged" soldiers to enlist to serve under Wilkinson.[22] Though refusing the "invitation," they were forced to live off the countryside and endure more hardships. In addition, Jackson used his own name for credit for medicine and transportation facilities and paid for some supplies out of his own pocket. As Jackson shared the new hardships endured by his men in the trek homeward, they looked at him and said, "He's as tough as hickory," thus giving him the nickname, "Old Hickory."

On April 22, Jackson returned to Nashville where his exhausted army was greeted by happy families and flags emblazoned "Tennessee Volunteers," another name that would endure to this day. He discharged his men, but got no further aid from the federal government. On May 10, he sent Benton to Washington to plead for payment for his troops and a refund of his own expenses. In addition, he recommended Benton for a military commission.

Benton reached Washington by May 25, and then ran head on into bureaucratic red tape getting nowhere on his appeal until the middle of June. On Saturday morning, June 12, Benton delivered a "memoir" to Secretary Armstrong stating that the Tennessee Volunteers had been

> drawn from the bosoms of almost every substantial family in Tennessee — that the whole State stood by Jackson in bringing them home — and that the State would be lost to the administration if he was left to suffer.

On Monday, Benton inquired of a clerk at the war office if the secretary had responded to the memoir. Benton was told the secretary had taken the memoir home for "his Sunday's consideration." This encouraged Benton, but later that day, when Armstrong arrived at his office, the secretary said that he could do nothing — "that Congress would have to give the relief." Then Benton hit upon a scheme

> to give an order to General Wilkinson's quartermaster-general in the Southern department, to pay for so much transportation as General Jackson's command would have been entitled to if it had returned under regular order.

Armstrong agreed and the order was issued.[23]

As Benton happily succeeded in fulfilling this benevolence for Jackson, he could not know that Jackson was perpetrating a malevolence against Benton. Indeed, Benton sat down the next day and wrote to Jackson of his success. Within a week, Benton was on his way home. But on the way out of town he penned a note, from Georgetown, to his second cousin's husband, Henry Clay. He had obtained a commission as a lieutenant colonel of the 39th United States Infantry Regiment to be organized in Tennessee. He told Clay that his younger brothers had also enlisted and "they will do something, or they will perish." Benton went on to tell Clay that he believed the war would last several years and that the British hope to use it to divide the Union. He urged Clay to "press on vigorously. Spare neither men nor money: make the war successful and glorious, and the people will bear with pride the burthens it imposes."[24]

What Benton did not know was that his brother, Jesse Benton, nearly perished with the help of Andrew Jackson, on the very day that

Thomas Benton had obtained financial relief for the General. Jesse Benton had delivered two challenges from a young army officer named Littleton Johnston to a friend of Jackson named William Carroll. On both occasions Carroll refused to duel Johnston on the grounds that he was no gentleman. But Carroll then challenged Jesse Benton and appealed to Jackson to be his second. Jackson accepted and the duel was fought on the day Thomas Benton secured relief for Jackson's debts. Jesse fired first (grazing Carroll's thumb), crouched, and received a wound in the buttocks from Carroll's fire. (This was the wound which Thomas referred to in his August letter to Clay.)

Thomas Benton learned of the affair en route home. His anger spewed out in numerous public utterances against Jackson which found their way back to the general. Hardly had Benton returned to Tennessee when he received a note from Jackson, written July 19, that must have stunned Benton for its hypocrisy. After expressing surprise that their friendship had turned to reproach, Jackson wrote, "I have therefore to call upon you to say whether you did not leave my house on the 10th of May in perfect Friendship with me carrying with you a letter from me to the secretary of war to promote your welfare and your views? Have you not on your return and since spoken disrespectfully of me? Have you threatened to make a Publication against me since you left my House on the 10th of May? Has any act of my life towards you since I took you by the hand in Friendship and appointed you my Aid de Camp [sic] been inconsistent with the strictest principles of Friendship? And if any, in what did it consist? and lastly have you or have you not threat[e]ned to challenge me? I am Sir respectfully yours."[25]

Benton's reply, on July 25, was long and detailed. He noted that he had left for Washington as a friend but that on June 14, "the day on which you superintended the shooting of my brother, I was in the war office in Washington city, exerting my very poor abilities according to your wishes on a subject which lay near to your heart." Benton told Jackson he should not have been a party to the duel; should not have carried Carroll's challenge to Jesse Benton; and, once involved, he should have conducted the affair in the usual mode, and on terms equal to both parties. But Benton's strongest charge (which reveals some

character of the duel) was "that on the contrary you conducted it in a savage, unequal, unfair, and base manner. *Savage:* Because the young men were made to fight at ten feet distance, contrary to your own mode, to what is usual among gentlemen, and against the remonstrance of my brother. *Unequal:* Because the parties were made to wheel; and evolution which Mr. C. perfectly understood, but which my brother knew nothing about, and against which he earnestly objected. *Unfair:* Because you concealed the mode of fighting from my brother, put off the duel on a frivolous pretext from friday until monday [sic]; and in the mean time secretly practiced Mr. C. to whirl and fire ten feet at a small saplin, until he could strike the centre of it at every shot. *Base:* Because you avowed yourself to be the friend of my brother while giving to his adversary all these advantages over him. In consequence of all while my brother was drawn into a duel against his wishes, and fought under circumstance wherein the chances, according to Mr. Carrols [sic] calculation, and your own must have been the same, were *twenty to one against him.*

"I know your answer to all this: 'Mr. C would have it so.' To which I reply: From your known influence over M. C. you might have managed the affair as you pleased; if not, you were at least a free man, and might have quit him if you did not approve of his course. To this effect, but in language much stronger, I have expressed myself when speaking of this matter."[26]

As a further complaint, Benton referred to their dispute regarding Wilkinson's right to command over Jackson and noted that his written attempt to reconcile this difference had gone unanswered. Benton told Jackson he was not threatening him or seeking a duel but would not decline one.

A few days later, Jackson responded saying he had a right to advise his friend (Major Carroll) and that all aspects of the duel were carried out properly, and indeed all evidence appears that it was. He pointed out that Jesse Benton proved he could "wheel." And Jackson was, later, to have proof positive to his assertion that Jesse was a first-rate marksman. (One account of the duel relates that Jackson told Carroll, "You needn't fear *him,* Carroll, he'd never hit you, if you were as broad as a barn-door."[27] However, Jackson seemed to give the lie to his utterance that "It is the character of the man of honor, and particularly of the *soldier* not to quarrel and brawl like the fish woman."[28]

Despite the fact that nothing more transpired between Jackson and Benton from late July through the entire month of August, the subject rankled Jackson deeply. When, on September 4, according to Benton, the two Benton brothers came in to Nashville, they purposely lodged at the Talbot's Hotel knowing that Jackson always stayed at the Nashville Inn when in town.

During the morning, Col. John Coffee, a friend of Jackson, suggested the two of them "should stroll over to the post office." This would take them from their hotel past the Bentons' lodgings. Jackson carried with him his riding whip, a small sword, and a pistol. They were observed going to get their mail. On the return route, they saw Thomas Benton at Talbot's near a front door which opened onto a passageway. Apparently, there was a doorway from the passage into a bar room which also had a door to the street. As Jackson and Coffee approached, Jesse Benton had just entered the bar-room from the street and was coming around to the passage. According to one account, Jackson turned on Thomas Benton with his whip and said, "Now, you damned rascal, I am going to punish you. Defend yourself." Benton's account written six days later said that Jackson drew a pistol and leveled it at him. In any case, as Thomas apparently reached in his coat for his pistol (and by then Jackson did level a pistol), Jesse, entering the passage, drew his pistol as well and fired two balls and a large slug which slammed into Jackson's left shoulder shattering it. Jackson fell across the entry bleeding profusely.

Meanwhile, Stokely Hays, a nephew of Mrs. Jackson, charged into the fray attacking Jesse with a sword (which missed its mark) and then drew a dagger. With the additional help of Alexander Donaldson, they threw Jesse to the floor. Still recovering from his duel wound, he was unable to resist both men and, after receiving several minor cuts, was facing a mighty stab in the chest when a "generous hearted citizen," James Sumner, along with others prevented this and any further attack on Jesse.

As this action proceeded in one part of the passage, Coffee and Donaldson bore down on Thomas who retreated deeper into the passage until he ended his part in the fight by falling down a flight of stairs.

Jackson, the man who advised against "brawling like a fish woman," was carried by his friends back to his hotel where he soaked two mattresses before the bleeding could be stopped. It was recommended that his shattered arm be amputated, but he replied, "I'll keep my arm," and, of course, he did.

With Jackson and his friends out of sight, Jesse and Thomas Benton returned to the street denouncing Jackson as an assassin, and a defeated assassin. Colonel Benton found Jackson's small sword and made a great show in the public square of breaking it in two. He accompanied the act with defiant and contemptuous words uttered in the loudest tones of his thundering and eloquent voice, the same blasts that would later be heard often in the Senate chamber over 30 years.

In Benton's September 10th published account of the affray, he wrote,

> For my part I think it scandalous that such things should take place at any time, but particularly so at the present moment when the public service requires the aid of all its citizens. As for the name of *courage*, God forbids that I should ever attempt to gain it by becoming a bully. Those who know me, know full well that I would give a thousand times more for the reputation of *Croghan* in defending his fort, than I would for the reputations of all the duelists and gladiators that ever appeared upon the face of the earth.[29]

There is an interesting footnote to this wild skirmish between future political allies. Residing in rooms adjacent to the passage in the Talbot's Hotel were a young couple and their infant son. One of the bullets fired in the fracas penetrated the wall and passed only inches above the infant lying in his crib. The father, coming upon the scene, found a maid in hysterics and the pregnant mother had fainted across a bed. The father, later, castigated Benton, at least, for his part in the juvenile escapade. Neither man could know what destiny would have lost had the child been killed. The nation would have lost one if its greatest western explorers, and the two men would have lost in-laws. Because Benton's yet-unborn daughter, Jessie, was, years later, to marry the other man's son, John Charles Frémont.

As Jackson's friends freed themselves from caring for their wounded "hero," the Bentons began to find themselves in an intolerable situation as Jackson had gained great popularity in Tennessee and had powerful influence. Benton wrote,

> I am literally in hell here, the meanest wretches under heaven to contend with — liars, affidavit-makers, and shameless cowards. All the puppies of Jackson are at work on me.... I am in the middle of hell, and I see no alternative but to kill or be killed; for I will not crouch to Jackson.... My life is in danger; nothing but a decisive duel can save me.... I shall never be forgiven having given my opinion in favor of Wilkinson's authority last winter; and this is the root of the hell that is now turned loose against me.[30]

Benton would eventually move to Missouri and become one of that state's greatest senators and a firm Democrat supporter of his old adversary, Andrew Jackson.

On the same day that Benton published his account of the shoot-out, September 10, a larger and more glorious shoot-out occurred on Lake Erie between American and British ships. The defeat of General Hull at Detroit in August 1812, alerted the federal government for the need of a naval force on Lake Erie. For this purpose 27-year-old Oliver Hazard Perry was shifted, in February 1813, from his command of a flotilla of gunboats at Newport, Rhode Island, to command a force to be built on Lake Erie. He arrived at Presque Isle (now Erie), Pennsylvania on March 27. Before he arrived, two brigs, a schooner, and three gunboats were already under construction from timber drawn from the nearby forests.

These vessels were floated late in May only a few days before Perry left to lead the assault on Fort George. This action gave Perry possession of five more small vessels, until then sealed off by the British near Buffalo. Perry united these to his growing fleet at Presque Isle by mid–June. Work on his ships was completed by mid–July. But now he did not have enough men or officers to man them.

Perry's repeated appeals to his superior, Commodore Isaac Chauncey at Sackett's Harbor, New York, were at long last and grudgingly answered with what Perry called, "a motley set — blacks, soldiers, and boys." Yet, at Newport, Perry had earlier trained more than 100 men whom Chauncey kept under his own command in New York ballooning one ship's company to 470 men when about half that number would have been sufficient.

In addition, Perry's little fleet was blockaded behind a sand bar by a British fleet of six vessels under the command of one-armed Capt. Robert H. Barclay, a veteran of the Battle of Trafalgar.

Late in July, with the British attack at Fort Meigs and Fort Stephenson, Barclay's fleet withdrew from the neighborhood of Erie to lend naval support to General Proctor's army. It was about this time that Perry finally received some men and officers, enough to make his move. But there was still that sandbar blocking exit to the Lake.

By the use of camels (large boxes attached to poles running through the vessels' port holes), the men were able to pump them free of water, and thus raise the vessel to float over a shallow such as the Presque Isle sand bar. Perry got his two brigs (now named *Lawrence* and *Niagara*) and the rest of his fleet out into the lake on August 5. The task had taken four days. He now had eight ships with which to battle Barclay. The British commodore returned to the Erie area hours too late to catch Perry's brigs on the sand bar, and again withdrew. Perry followed him to the west end of the lake and, as Barclay went to Malden, Perry went to Put-in-Bay near the entrance to Sandusky Bay.

On August 19, General Harrison came aboard Perry's flagship in Sandusky Bay and the two Americans, with their staffs, conferred. Then for nearly a month, Perry reconnoitered the enemy and trained his men. During this time one of Perry's smaller ships returned to Presque Isle.

Finally, on September 9, with an attack expected on the morrow, Perry went over his final plans with his captains. Each was assigned an opponent and they were to move in quickly because of their shorter range armaments. At the conclusion of the conference, Perry brought out a large blue battle-flag, 18 feet by 9 feet, bearing in white letters the words, "DON'T GIVE UP THE SHIP." The Commodore said that when this flag was hoisted it would be the signal for going into action and added, "Nelson has expressed my idea in the words, 'If you lay your enemy close alongside, you cannot be out of your place.'"[31]

The next morning, September 10, Perry took his fleet out into Lake Erie to meet the enemy. The guns of Barclay's six ships, including the Brig

Detroit, outnumbered Perry's nine ships 63–54, and in long guns 35–15. They were close to equal in manpower, but about one fourth of Perry's men were sick, one fourth were soldiers from Kentucky, and one fourth were Negroes.[32]

The action began shortly before noon as the American fleet maneuvered to come up on the British at a shallow angle. The blue signal flag was run up on the *Lawrence*, and the battle was underway with the British flagship *Detroit* sending off the first shot from long distance. Before the American guns could reach the enemy, British firepower began a heavy concentration on the *Lawrence*.

For two hours, as Perry's flagship and three other lead ships in his column bore in on the enemy, the *Lawrence* continued to be the chief target suffering a brutal beating. His other ships, including the *Niagara*, with Capt. Jesse D. Elliott, second in command to Perry (and nephew of the British army captain Elliott who was involved in the massacre of Frenchtown),[33] lagged woefully behind and rendered no help to the beleaguered van.

One writer later described the fate of Perry and his flagship,

> During that tempest of war his vessel was terribly shattered. Her rigging was nearly all shot away; her sails were torn into shreds; her spars were battered into splinters; her guns were dismounted; and, like the *Guerrière* when disabled by the *Constitution*, she lay upon the waters almost a helpless wreck. The carnage on her deck had been terrible. Out of one hundred and three sound men that composed her officers and crew when she went into action, twenty-two were slain and sixty-one were wounded.[34]

There was no safety above or below decks. Wounded men, who were below decks being operated on, were sometimes wounded a second time and some men were wounded as many as three times. Even a pig with both hind legs blown off was observed eating peas spilled on a bloody deck from an overturned dining pot.[35]

About this time, a fresh breeze sprang up and the *Niagara*, at last, came forward — not to assist the *Lawrence* but to engage her assigned antagonist. This took her past the derelict flagship. Perry, with the help of his purser and chaplain, fired his last effective heavy gun; put on his uniform of rank; hauled down his pennant and the blue banner ("Don't Give Up the Ship"); gave command of the *Lawrence* to his first lieutenant, John J. Yarnell, with discretion to hold out or surrender; and then hailed the *Niagara*. In a small boat, carrying his young brother and four stout seamen at the oars, he put out for the *Niagara*. This small boat with its tiny crew and a huge hero now became the next target of opportunity for the British fleet.

> Cannon-balls, grape, canister, and musket-shot were hurled in showers toward the little boat during the fifteen minutes that it was making its way from the *Lawrence* to the *Niagara*. The oars were splintered, bullets traversed the boat, and the crew were covered with spray caused by the falling of heavy round and grape-shot in the water near.

Perry stood erect with his banner and pennant folded around him. Yet they all boarded the *Niagara* unscathed.[36]

The astonished Captain Elliott of the laggard *Niagara* asked Perry, "How goes the day?"

"Bad enough," responded Perry, whom Elliott had thought killed. "Why are the gun-boats so far astern?"

"I'll bring them up," said Elliott.

"Do so," replied Perry. And off went Elliott in another small boat to hurry them up and boarded the *Somers*. He fought gallantly the remainder of the day.[37] Nevertheless, Elliott instituted a dispute between the two men which lingered for many years.

Like John Paul Jones, Perry had only begun to fight. Now, he guided the *Niagara* and the remainder of his maneuverable fleet directly at and through the British fleet, firing broadsides to left and right. He came around in front of one British line to rake (or fire down their length) the two most important enemy ships, the *Detroit* and the *Queen Charlotte*. Within eight minutes of Perry's renewed assault, the *Detroit* surrendered and the rest of the British ships soon followed suit. British commander Barclay, lying wounded on the shattered *Detroit*, had now also lost his left arm in battle. His other ships' captains were all wounded or dead.

Taking an envelope from his pocket, Perry scratched out a brief note to General Harrison, "We have met the enemy, and they are ours: two ships, two brigs, one schooner, and one sloop. Yours, with great respect and esteem, O. H. Perry."[38]

In addition, Perry wrote a note to the secretary of the navy, saying, "It has pleased the Almighty to give to the arms of the United States a signal victory over their enemies on this lake."[39] He then had himself rowed back to the *Lawrence* where he intended to receive the surrender of his enemy.

His return to the flagship was described by its gallant doctor, Usher Parsons.

It was a time of conflicting emotions when the commodore returned to his ship. The battle was won; he was safe. But the deck was slippery with blood and brains, and strewn with the bodies of twenty-two officers and men, some of whom had sat at table with us at our last meal, and the ship resounded everywhere with the groans of the wounded. Those of us who were spared and able to walk, approached him as he came over the ship's side, but the salutation was a silent one on both sides; not a word could find utterance.[40]

About a week after Henry Clay heard of the first U.S. naval fleet victory over an entire enemy fleet, a letter appeared in the *Lexington Reporter* which tied Clay to a memento of the battle. A survivor of the engagement wrote a friend in Lexington briefly describing the action and ended with, "Will you have the goodness to pass to our friend, Mr. Clay, the nail which fastened the flag of the Commodore to his mast."[41]

About the time Henry Clay was reading newspaper accounts of the victory on Lake Erie, Gen. William Henry Harrison was organizing his forces to follow up on the new advantages he had between Niagara and Fort Malden opposite Detroit. By September 18, forces in the area under Harrison included, among other units, brigades commanded by Gen. Lewis Cass (survivor of Hull's treacherous surrender of Detroit a year earlier) and Gen. Duncan MacArthur; Gov. Isaac Shelby's Kentucky militia; and congressman-on-leave Col. Richard M. Johnson with a regiment of mounted Kentuckians.

That same day, Shawnee Indian Chief (and now British brigadier general) Tecumseh found Gen. Henry Proctor packing up with all the appearances of starting a retreat from Malden. Proctor was well aware of the disaster to the British fleet and the consequences to his supply route. But he kept this secret from the Indians. In a short but angry speech, in behalf of all the Indians allied with the British, Tecumseh told Proctor, "Father, listen to your children! You have them now all before you." He then reminded Proctor how the Indians had supported the British in "the war before this" and again in this war, and that Proctor had said he would take care of his "red children" of this garrison.

Then Tecumseh, wearing his usual close leather tunic with a large plume of white feathers overshadowing his brow, protested, saying,

Father listen! Our fleet has gone out; we know they have fought; we have heard the great guns; but know nothing of what has happened to our father with one arm [Barclay]. Our ships have gone one way, and we are much astonished to see our father tying up everything and preparing to run away the other, without letting his red children know what his intentions are.... We must compare our father's conduct to a fat animal, that carries its tail upon its back, but when affrighted, he drops it between his legs and runs off.[42]

Tecumseh said they had not been defeated on land and wished to fight. If then defeated, they would retreat with Proctor. The other Indian chiefs, yelling and brandishing tomahawks in a most menacing manner, supported Tecumseh. Eventually, Proctor prevailed on Tecumseh to assent to a withdrawal to a Moravian village about eight miles eastward.[43]

During the week that followed this council, Harrison, with the aid of Perry and his fleet, began shuttling his large army from the Ohio shore, around Sandusky, through the nearby islands toward the Canadian shore. Meanwhile, Colonel Johnson, with his mounted regiment, moved northward from Fort Meigs toward Detroit, by way of Frenchtown and the scene of the Battle of the River Raisin. Johnson's regiment reached the Raisin on September 27 and found, scattered over a wide area, the bleached bones of the victims of the January battle. During an expedition in this area in June, Johnson's men had found the bones scattered about then as well. Now, as his men again re-interred them, the effect of rage at the barbarous conduct of the enemy brought forth a desire for great revenge.

Back with the main force, prepared to land on the Canadian shore near Malden, Harrison joined Perry in a reconnaissance on board the schooner *Ariel* on September 26. Though Harrison located an ideal spot to land his troops, he could not interpret the silence on shore. Was the enemy waiting in ambush? That evening, the *Ariel* returned to the small island, almost weighted down with troops, and Harrison issued a general order for an embarkation on sailing for the next day. In considerable detail he spelled out the landing operation. This order was signed by Harrison's adjutant general, Col. Edmund P. Gaines (the captor of Aaron Burr in 1807).

Shortly before the landing, on the 27th, Harrison, on board the *Ariel*, sent out to the troops on all vessels the following exhortation.

> The general entreats his brave troops to remember that they are the sons of sires whose fame is immortal; that they are to fight for the rights of their insulted *country*, while their opponents combat for the unjust pretensions of a master. Kentuckians! remember the River Raisin! but remember it *only* while victory is suspended. The revenge of a soldier can not be gratified upon a fallen enemy.[44]

The depredations of the River Raisin produced a camp song for the summer of 1813. The following is one of the stanzas:

> Freemen! no longer bear such slaughters;
> Avenge your country's cruel woe;
> Arouse, and save your wives and daughters!
> Arouse, and smite the faithless foe!
> CHORUS.— Scalps are bought at stated prices,
> Malden pays the price in gold.[45]

On the morning of September 27, Harrison's army sailed forth on Perry's fleet, and that afternoon landed unopposed about three miles east of Malden. On reaching the British fort, he found it evacuated and burned. But General Proctor had the foresight to scour the countryside for nearly 1,000 horses and had retreated first to Sandwich (across from Detroit) and then on eastward.

Harrison had brought no horses with him and found only "a miserable French poney [sic] upon which the venerable and patriotic governor of Kentucky was mounted."[46] Harrison wrote Secretary of War Armstrong that he was compelled to await the arrival of Colonel Johnson's mounted regiment due shortly at Detroit. Harrison preceded Johnson in liberating that city, proclaiming that all previous civil officers would resume their positions. Johnson marched into the happy community on September 30 and crossed over to Sandwich to join Harrison's army on October 1. General MacArthur's brigade was left at Detroit to protect the citizenry from Indians who had not retreated with the British army. General Cass' reg-

iment was left to occupy Malden and Sandwich, but Cass, himself, went with Harrison as an aide. Another "volunteer" aide was Commodore Oliver Hazard Perry, who seems to have wanted to finalize his naval victory with an army conquest.

The chase of Proctor began the next day and caught up with the British army and their Indian allies under Tecumseh on October 4. A minor skirmish was fought that afternoon and Harrison's enemy retreated to within a few miles of Moravian town and took up position between the Thames River (which parallels the Lake Erie shore) and a large swamp parallel to the river and about two miles further north. Tecumseh and his Indians formed along this swamp looking south from thick undergrowth. About halfway between them and the river was another small elongated swamp about 300 yards north of the river. The British regulars were posted in two columns running from this little swamp to the river.

The main battle began around 2 P.M. when one wing of Johnson's mounted Kentuckians charged straight into the gorgeous autumn-colored woods, and through the British lines shouting, "Remember the River Raisin! Remember the River Raisin!" Within minutes the cavalry had thrown both lines into confusion. The Americans captured more than 600 troops while suffering only negligible losses. In his official report to the secretary of war, Harrison describing the action, said,

> The measure was not sanctioned by anything that I had seen or heard of but I was fully convinced that it would succeed. The American backwoodsmen ride better in the woods than any other people. A musket or rifle is no impediment to them being accustomed to carry them on horseback from their earliest youth. I was persuaded too that the enemy would be quite unprepared for the shock and that they could not resist it.[47]

It was at this point in the battle that General Proctor saw defeat ahead. He rushed to his carriage and, leaving his personal baggage behind, scurried away eastward so fast that an American "posse" could not catch him.

The other wing of the cavalry, led by Colonel Johnson, turned north and rode directly through the little swamp to attack the Indians. This charge was met more deliberately and the horsemen were soon forced to dismount to fight in the colorful but heavy underbrush. With the cavalry become infantry, Kentucky's Governor Shelby brought up more Kentucky volunteers and gave tremendous support at the edge of the swamp to fight the Indians, whose war paint blended with the brilliant shades of plants and trees.

However, while still on horseback, Johnson received a bullet wound in the thigh and hip. Meanwhile, Tecumseh bellowed through the battle urging his Indians to stand and fight bravely. But sometime in the confusion of the conflict, the Indian chief fell at last, probably after several wounds. Though his body could not be identified with any certainty, the rumor and the legend grew that he, in fact, had met Col. Richard M. Johnson, on horseback, and both had shot each other. In any case, Tecumseh certainly died, his Indians shortly gave up the battle, and later secretly buried their beloved leader. Johnson's fame was to grow and eventually make him vice president of the United States. His commander would later become president largely on account of his fame from the earlier battle at Tippecanoe.

On October 9, with his indifference to punctuation, Harrison wrote his report of the Battle of the Thames, to Secretary Armstrong.

> In communicating to the President through you Sir my opinion of the conduct of the officers who served under my command I am at a loss how to mention that of Gov. Shelby being convinced that no eulogism of mine can reach his merits. The Governor of an independent State greatly my superior in years, in experience and in military character he placed himself under my command and is not more remarkable for his zeal and activity than for the promptitude and cheerfulness with which he obeyed my orders.... I have already stated that Gen. Cass and Commodore Perry assisted me in forming the troops for action the former is an officer of the highest merit and the appearance of the brave Commodore cheered and animated every breast.
>
> It would be useless Sir after stating the circumstances of the action to pass encomium upon Col. Johnson and his regiment. Veterans could not have manifested more firmness. The Colonel's numerous wounds prove that he was in the post of danger.
>
> Our loss is seven killed and twenty two wounded five of which have since died. Of the British troops twelve were killed and twenty-two wounded. The Indians suffered most, thirty three of them having been found upon the ground besides those killed in the retreat.... Genl Proctor escaped by the fleetness of his horse escorted by forty dragoons and a number of mounted Indians.[48]

With the Battle of the Thames won, the United States gained control of Upper Canada, and put an end to Tecumseh's dream of a united Indian confederacy. Harrison returned to Detroit and accepted an armistice with several of the Indian tribes of the northwest, though Tecumseh's Shawnees did not participate.

24

RESIGNATION

Records indicate that Henry Clay was still in Lexington, as late as October 13, 1813, but was in Washington, Pennsylvania, by the 22nd. News of Harrison's capture of Malden was published in Lexington before Clay left there, but word of the victory on the Thames did not arrive in Kentucky until about the 19th. It had reached Chillicothe, Ohio, by the 15th and it is therefore reasonable to assume that he learned of this latest success somewhere in the vicinity of Cincinnati around the 17th. Clay surely grabbed at every morsel of news regarding the battle as he made his way eastward.

He was in Bedford, Pennsylvania, on the 26th at the same time that Benjamin Latrobe was there. But neither knew it then. Latrobe was later to write that he was sorry to have missed Clay there.[1]

The House Speaker was in Washington City by November 4, when he had a meeting with Secretary of the Navy William Jones. As agent for his late father-in-law's rope manufacturing company in Lexington, Clay met with Jones to negotiate the sale and delivery to Philadelphia, for the use of the navy, of 150 tons of "yarns made of the best top't & rooted Kentucky hemp, the yarns to be of fineness and quality equal to" yarns previously delivered by Hart & Co. for the navy. It was to be delivered by February 20 at 13 cents per pound.[2]

Clay's correspondence does not indicate whether his children accompanied him to Philadelphia but, at least, it appears that Lucretia went with him as he wrote to Thomas Bodley in December, "We spent very agreeably two weeks" there — most likely engaging in the rope-sale negotiation. A receipted account dated "Baltimore, 30th November," and a letter to his friend Caesar Rodney

place the "two weeks" in Philadelphia as somewhere between November 12 and 28.[3]

By the time the Clays returned to Washington, more successful war news — this time from the South — had been published in the East. The victory was claimed by Gen. Andrew Jackson as a retaliation for the destruction of Fort Mims. Clay probably learned of the Fort Mims disaster about one week after word of Perry's victory on Lake Erie. But it is also likely that his attention was drawn more to northern affairs and, in addition, the aftermath of Mims was not foreseen.

Between Tennessee and the Gulf of Mexico were five major Indian tribes (often referred to as "the civilized nations"). They were the Seminoles in Florida, the Choctaws and Chickasaws in present-day Mississippi, the Cherokees in northern Georgia and Alabama, and the Creeks in Alabama and western Georgia. Prior to the war (and again possibly during it) Tecumseh had visited the Creeks urging them to join the British and Indians of the north in war against the Americans. Into 1813, the Creeks were seriously divided as to which way to turn — the old chiefs for allying with the Americans, and the young warriors for warring on them. Throughout the early months of 1813, those following Tecumseh's urging received arms and supplies from the British and Spaniards at Mobile and Pensacola. Finally, they made their move at the end of August.

On the 29th, two Negro slaves, from Fort Mims (about 20 miles northeast of Mobile on the Alabama River), were sent outside the stockade to care for some cattle. After a while, they returned breathless to say they had observed 24 painted warriors in the woods. A scouting party, that checked out their story, found nothing, and the Negroes were ordered to be flogged for lying. One suffered his punishment, but the owner of the other balked at allowing his slave to be punished. Responding to this refusal, the fort's commander, Major Daniel Beasley, ordered the slave's master and his family to leave the fort the next day.

On the 30th, the master reconsidered against taking his family out and agreed to allow flogging of his slave. Meanwhile, the small fort (which "protected" 553 men, women, children, soldiers and slaves) continued its daily routine and prepared for lunch, while its two gates (at either end) were wide open. One slave was tied at the post prepared to receive his lashes. The other slave, punished on the previous day, was again in the field tending the cows. This day, he saw more warriors, but remembering his earlier treatment, he fled through the woods to another station.

As the fort's drums were beaten to summon the people to dinner, more than 1,000 Creek Indians rose from a ravine and were within 150 yards of the gate when soldiers at the fort sounded the alarm. It was too late, and the howling, screaming hordes breached the gateway, killing Beasley, who could not close the gate because of sand piled up next to it. For more than three hours the Indians tomahawked and clubbed and knifed indiscriminately. When they began to let up, their leaders urged them on, and subsequently put the torch to the fort. The slaughter continued until dusk, when more than 400 "mangled, scalped, and bloody corpses were heaped and strewn within the wooden walls. Not one white woman, not one child escaped." A few soldiers reached other forts, a large number of Negroes became slaves to the Indians, and one Negro woman (with a ball in her breast) rowed to Fort Stoddart, 15 miles away to alert the garrison there.

When soldiers finally arrived from Stoddart, they

> found the air dark with buzzards and hundreds of dogs gnawing the bodies. Major Kennedy's report said, "Indians, negroes, white men, women and children, lay in one promiscuous ruin. All were scalped, and the females of every age butchered in a manner which neither decency nor language will permit me to describe. The main building was burned to ashes, which were filled with bones. The plains and woods around were covered with dead bodies.[4]

The Creeks had interred only a few of their own dead before quitting the field.

Fear quickly spread over a wide area of the South. On September 25, Tennessee Governor William Blount called for 3500 volunteers to join the 1,500 already in service. The latter, under Colonel Coffee (who aided Jackson against the Bentons), were immediately ordered by Jackson to move south to Huntsville (in present-day Alabama, then Mississippi Territory). The remainder of the volunteers were to assemble at Fayetteville, Tennessee, on October 4. Jackson, with his arm still in a sling, was finally well enough from his wound in the Benton affair to join these troops on the 7th and join Coffee at Huntsville on the 11th. Among those now serving under Jackson was a 27-year-old bear hunter, a teller of amusing stories, a volunteer named David Crockett.

Despite the continuing lack of supplies promised from eastern Tennessee, Jackson cautiously moved south until November 3. That morning, on Jackson's orders, Brigadier General Coffee (recently promoted) encircled and destroyed the Creek Indian town of Talishatchee; killing about 200 and taking 84 women and children as prisoners. Coffee's losses were five men killed and 41 wounded. The town's prophet climbed on the roof of a house shouting encouragement to his tribe and defiance at American bullets. Though his courage attracted the attention of his fellows, it also beckoned the aim of an American soldier who promptly ended the exhortations.

There is an interesting postscript to this battle. Among the casualties, a slain squaw was found still embracing her living infant. It was brought back to camp where Jackson tried to induce some other squaw to care for the child. They refused saying his relations were dead and he, too, should be killed. Instead, Jackson ordered his aides to care for the child until the end of the campaign when he was taken to Jackson's home, the Hermitage. He was given the name Lincoyer. He carried his Indian traits in his love of the woods but survived only to age 17 and was mourned by Jackson as a real son.

About the same time as the battle at Talishatchee, more than 1,000 pro–British Creeks surrounded a fort at Talladega holding 2,000 pro–American Creeks. A beleaguered Creek, escaping through the siege lines and wearing the skin of a large hog, managed to reach Jackson on November 7, to alert the general on the fate of the "good Indians." The general was still busy writing pleading letters for supplies and erecting a fort. On learning of the plight of the friendly Creeks, Jackson wrote a General White from western Tennessee, understood to be approaching Jackson's fort, to come at once with supplies and to guard the fort as he went to the aid of the Creeks. Two mornings later, on the edge of Talladega, Jackson received word that General White had retreated toward his own base, leaving Jackson's base unsupplied and unprotected.

Nevertheless, Jackson attacked the hostile Creeks and, as in the previous engagement, the enemy was encircled and completely annihilated. Nearly 300 Indian dead were later counted. Jackson lost 17 men killed and 83 wounded.[5]

The highlights and official accounts of these actions were known to Henry Clay by the time Congress convened on December 6, 1813. Despite Jackson's successes, they may have been of little concern to Clay whose concentration must have been more on events along the Canadian frontier where Kentucky troops had done all their fighting. On this war front, the Speaker showed his frustration over the failure of an expedition to capture Montreal. He wrote to Caesar Rodney, "That event was wanted to enable the President to give to his message a finishing stroke, & why it was not permitted him to announce it I confess has not been satisfactorily explained."[6]

The explanation has the sound of another military farce. About the time that Secretary of War John Armstrong had ordered General Andrew Jackson to disband his volunteers in Mississippi in March 1813, he also ordered Maj. Gen. James Wilkinson to a new assignment on the New York–Canadian border "with the least possible delay." It took Wilkinson from March to late August to go from New Orleans, via Washington, to Sacketts' Harbor, New York, at the eastern end of Lake Ontario. He was accompanied from Washington by Secretary Armstrong who wished to be closer to the field of activity.

To the east, based at Burlington, Vermont, on the east side of Lake Champlain, was Maj. Gen. Wade Hampton, who insisted on sharing command in the north with his superior, Wilkinson.

He also insisted on taking direct orders from Armstrong rather than from Wilkinson, since they had for many years disliked each other intensely. Hampton, though probably more competent than Wilkinson, had not shown much skill since assuming his command in the north in July. He had failed to thwart numerous British raids into New York and Vermont and did no better in his own half-hearted raid into Canada in September.

As Wilkinson and Armstrong continued to disagree on objectives in a planned offensive down the St. Lawrence River, Wilkinson at last moved forward by boat on October 17. Already, Armstrong had notified Hampton to move from Vermont to meet Wilkinson on the St. Lawrence, possibly at the mouth of the Chateauguay River several miles above Montreal. Hampton replied, as usual to Armstrong, that he wanted notice of the time and place for his junction with Wilkinson. Armstrong, on October 30, relayed this request for Wilkinson to "give Hampton timely notice," etc.

Wilkinson answered Armstrong on November 1.

> You desire me to notify Hampton of the point of junction. I have written you on that subject and as he has treated my authority with contempt and has acted exclusively under your orders I wish this information could come from you that I may be saved the hazard of a second insult, for I need not say to you, who have seen service, what an outrage it is on the sensibilities of a soldier and how radically destructive to military enterprise for a subordinate to resist or neglect the orders of a superior.[7]

Wilkinson did not reflect on the fact that he acted in this same vain in his disputes with Armstrong on the military objectives of the current expedition.

Nevertheless, in a surprisingly cordial letter, Wilkinson wrote Hampton on November 6, "at the special instance of the Secretary of War," that his army would be passing Prescott that night en route to Montreal, but leaving to Hampton to determine the point of junction, hopefully about the 9th. Wilkinson went on to state that he was short of a variety of supplies. He had been informed by Armstrong that Hampton had ample supplies at Lake Champlain and therefore requested Hampton to forward two or three months' supply.[8]

Hampton responded on the 8th with an air of pleasure at Wilkinson's communication, until he came to the request for supplies. He said he brought no more than his men could carry on their backs and had hoped to be supplied by Wilkinson, which he now saw to be impossible. He did not tell Wilkinson of his own trials. Leaving Vermont on October 21, he had advanced into Canada along the Chateauguay River. On October 25, while engaging the British about 20 miles south of the St. Lawrence, he received instructions from Armstrong's quartermaster general to begin building huts to go into winter quarters. Under the circumstances, Hampton had begun to fall back and, on November 1, he wrote Armstrong, "The campaign I consider substantially at an end," and then requested the secretary to accept his resignation because, "events have had no tendency to change my opinion of the destiny intended for me, nor my determination to retire from a service where I can neither feel security nor expect honour."[9]

Wilkinson safely passed Prescott's British force, but put most of his army on the Canadian shore hoping to put an end to the constant harassment by British guns from the land. On November 10th, at least 1,000 of Wilkinson's 3,000 men were engaged at his rear by about 800 of the enemy and suffered a stinging defeat. (As Henry Adams later wrote, "The story had no redeeming incident.") Through the engagement, Wilkinson, aboard a boat, was too sick to command. Two days later he managed to reach Cornwall where he received the dispatch from Hampton that neither supplies nor manned support would be forthcoming. Wilkinson crossed the river and returned to United States territory where he, too, went into winter quarters.

The aftermath of this aborted expedition was that the three men — Armstrong, Wilkinson, and Hampton — all tried to place the blame on the other two. As for Henry Clay, back in Washington for the opening of Congress on December 6, only gradually did parts of the controversy come to him as some of the dispatches began to appear in the newspapers of early December. Clay was left again to despair over the incompetence of the regular army.

Related to the military affairs in Canada, Clay, in mid–December, wrote a Kentucky friend, Thomas Bodley, to challenge "a very unpopular opinion [which] has been attributed to me that it [the newly conquered Canadian territory] ought to be given up, as the price of peace." He reminded Bodley that,

> During the last summer when, so far from having reduced any portion of the Territories of the enemy, the enemy had possession of the Michigan Territory, I did say that if we could make a peace securing to us all the points in controversy, I should for one be willing not to give up Canada (for we had it not to give up) but to forego for the present its conquest.... But it has ever been my opinion that if Canada is conquered it ought never to be surrendered if it can possibly be retained.

Clay noted to Bodley that his views expressed in casual conversation were his own sentiments since he was

> totally unapprized of the views of the Administration on the subject.... You know however that I do not belong to that branch of the Government with which the power of making peace is lodged; and perhaps after all it is premature to say anything at present about the terms of a peace, which may not be made for years to come. The *state* of things is under going continual changes, and we must judge of the conditions of peace, when peace comes, not by the present state, but by that state of things which shall exist when it is negotiated.[10]

Clay could not possibly know how soon and how deeply he was personally to become involved in this very subject.

On the second day of the new session of Congress, both Houses received President Madison's fifth annual message. Not only could he not report an expedition aimed at Montreal, he also had to report that the British had refused the Russian offer to mediate peace. At least, he could comment on the successes obtained by Perry and Harrison and allude to their support by Congressman Richard M. Johnson and Governor Isaac Shelby. While he was able to report that peace with the Indians was at hand in the north, new hostilities had broken out with the Creek Indians in the south. Madison ascribed this new fighting to the British "in courting the aide of the savages in all quarters." He told the Congress that the British

> have not controlled them either from their usual practice of indiscriminate massacre on defenceless inhabitants, or from scenes of carnage without a

parallel, on prisoners to the British arms, guarded by all the laws of humanity and honorable war.

While on the subject of atrocities, Madison referred to another violation of human conduct being perpetrated by the British. In some of the battles in the north, the British captured some former British subjects though now naturalized Americans. The British had recently announced that 23 of these had been transported to England for trial as traitors. In retaliation the United States had taken 23 British prisoners as special hostages with notification to the British government that these "would experience whatever violence might be committed on the American prisoners of war." Rather than arrest "the cruel career opened by its example," Madison was forced to announce that the enemy had since doubled the number of Americans

> ordered into close confinement, with formal notice that, in the event of a retaliation for the death which might be inflicted on the prisoners of war sent to great Britain for trial, the officers so confined would be put to death also.

In addition, Madison reported that the British fleets and armies were instructed, "in the same event, to proceed with a destructive severity against our towns and their inhabitants." But Madison proclaimed, "It is fortunate for the United States that they have it in their power to meet the enemy in this deplorable contest," of retaliation.

Continuing his message, Madison asked Congress for certain revisions in the militia laws and agreements with friendly Powers in the reciprocal use of seaports. He gave a brief but favorable statement on the status of the treasury. In addressing the broad scope of the war's effect on the nation, the president observed that,

> If the war has increased the interruptions of our commerce, it has at the same time cherished and multiplied our manufactures so as to make us independent of all other countries for the more essential branches for which we ought to be dependent on none.

And finally he expressed the belief that "our free Government ... is strengthened by every occasion that puts it to the test," and that "the war, with all its vicissitudes, is illustrating the capacity and destiny of the United States to be a great, a flourishing, and a powerful nation."[11]

The only immediate association Clay had with the president's message was, on the following day, to question the House resolution which sent to the Naval Committee that part of the message dealing with the reciprocal use of seaports among friendly Powers. The author of the resolution agreed to Clay's proposal that since it dealt with foreign relations as well as naval matters it should be assigned to a special committee.

On December 9, Madison sent a special message to Congress requesting an immediate embargo on exports and on imports of goods originating in Great Britain. Madison believed "it is indispensable that the enemy should feel all the pressure that can be given to it," to shorten the duration of the war.[12]

For two days the embargo was debated by the House behind closed doors. There is little evidence of views expressed by Republicans. Most of the time was consumed by objections by Federalists who submitted a series of weakening amendments — all of which were voted down. Late on the 11th the House passed the embargo bill 85 to 57, and sent it to the Senate. It was returned to the House with new amendments on the 17th.

Though the House soon accepted all the Senate amendments, there was further discussion on the measure on the part of the Federalists. Argument by Cyrus King of Massachusetts reveals that on some previous occasion Clay had made some comments during debate in Committee of the Whole. Speaking on the effect of the embargo on the eastern seaboard, King said,

> But an honorable gentleman from Kentucky (Mr. Clay) has said, if provisions cannot be transported by land to a people thus situated, they must go to the provisions: they must even quit their country, their farms, and their endeared firesides, and go to a more hospitable, more favorable climate.
> [The gentleman from Kentucky here explained his observations, as having been confined to the thinly inhabited country near Mobile; that it was better that inhabitants there should suffer some deprivations, or even be compelled to leave that part of the country, than that the enemy should receive essential supplies through them or that the effective operations of an important measure should be prevented.]

King then listed 14 restrictive (he called them oppressive) laws beginning with February 18,

1806, under Jefferson's administration and including the current request. He said,

Here, sir, you have a catalogue of the restrictive acts of an American Congress, enacted ostensibly for the benefit of a free commercial people! If, sir, a parallel can be found in all the annals of ancient or modern despotism (always excepting that of France,) of equal commercial oppression, let her abettors show it. Would to God I could erase from your statute books this record of oppression, with the same facility as I now cast this schedule of acts from me, and tread it under foot.[13]

King's speech and exhibition of opposition achieved nothing. The bill cleared the House that afternoon (the 17th) and Madison signed it into law the following Monday (the 20th). There was still to be a near violent repercussion from the secret debate on the embargo. But it was not to take place until after the city welcomed the week-long visit of Gen. William Henry Harrison.

Throughout the latter days of November and early December, Harrison travelled by stage to Albany, New York City, Philadelphia and Washington. While he was feted everywhere he stopped, and elaborate illuminations (honoring him and Perry) had preceded his visits, there had been strong Federalist opposition to such celebrations in New York City. Though he was entertained unofficially by Republican Governor Daniel Tompkins, Madison's former presidential opponent, DeWitt Clinton (now mayor of New York City) boycotted the dinner and theaters attended by Harrison and his party.[14]

Harrison arrived in Washington on December 14. During his visit he must have met with President Madison on at least two occasions. One of these meetings (as well as a dinner with Henry Clay and Justice Thomas Todd on December 18) took place prior to Harrison's writing to the secretary of war on December 21.

Harrison told Armstrong, "The President is apprehensive that the enemy will make and [sic] attempt this winter to re-occupy Malden and Detroit." Though Harrison thought such an enterprise "is not very improbable," he believed some other western generals could handle the matter. He made certain suggestions for meeting such a contingency and referred to the concern of previously hostile Indian chiefs as to the former boundaries of their lands. On this, he wrote,

I have had some conversation with the President and some of the leading western members [undoubtedly referring to Clay]. Their opinions seem all decidedly to coincide with mine that the Indians ought to be made easy in this particular.[15]

Harrison's tone in his letter to Armstrong clearly shows that he believed he should receive an even higher command than his present one. One of his aides, with him in Washington, expressed the view that

The general sentiment is that Wilkinson, Hampton, Lewis [a subordinate of Wilkinson], and Dearborn should be so disposed of as to preclude their having a command of importance; and the eyes of all appear to be placed upon Gen. Harrison as the only officer in whom confidence can be safely placed. I should not be surprised if he should be the lieutenant-general spoken of in contemplation.[16]

Strangely, a young officer of Harrison's army, far off in the northwest near Lower Sandusky, more accurately divined the political atmosphere in Washington even before Harrison's visit and, indeed, was prophetic about future events. This young man, who had shared Perry's charmed experience of being unscathed on the *Lawrence* on Lake Erie, now wrote to his father,

We understand the whole matter out here. The people at Washington have got scared at Harrison's victories. They are afraid a few more might make him President! Therefore they have determined to put him out of the way. Mark my words; You will not see them give Harrison another command in the field during this war. They will simply leave him here where he can gain no more victories for the reason that there are no enemies left to whip.

So far as the folks at Washington are concerned, from the President down, this struggle from the start has been about three parts politics to one part war. I wish the English would land a force in the Chesapeake and take Washington and sack and burn it![17]

In fact, Harrison was to disagree with the president's system of communication with officers in the field. Along with Governor Shelby (and very possibly Clay), Harrison preferred a board of war to be set up in the west to provide quick communication for necessary orders. Madison insisted that orders be centered at Washington, where

much more accurate knowledge of affairs could always be had there than by any commander of a military district.... It was deemed essential that the war department should be able always to issue instantaneous commands to every post, quarter, and officer, without delaying them to pass through the hands of the commander of that military district.[18]

This summation of Madison's view, as described by Charles Ingersoll, was the basis of Harrison's future resignation from the army. Early in 1814, Secretary Armstrong ordered Gen. Benjamin Howard (governor of the Missouri Territory) to take command, under Harrison, at Detroit. This had been at Harrison's suggestion. But when Armstrong later countermanded the order directly without informing Harrison, it was too much for the vanity of the recent hero of the Thames. He sent his resignation via Armstrong to the president, possibly hoping that Madison would change the order system and refuse to accept the resignation. But Madison was vacationing in Virginia and Armstrong readily accepted the resignation in the president's behalf.

It is probable that this did not offend Madison as Harrison had already stepped lightly (though figuratively) on the president's toes. Just prior to Harrison's departure from Washington, he had, as Ingersoll states, received commands from "a handsome and highly connected lady" to meet her at Mrs. Madison's drawing room. "But that he cannot do," said the president, "because he left Washington this morning, with his horses and attendants, all at the door of this house, and must be now some twenty or thirty miles on his way to the west."

"Still," replied the lady, "he must be here, for I laid my command upon him, and he is too gallant a man to disobey me."

Madison, quite sure of himself responded, "We shall soon see whose orders he obeys."

Not long afterward Harrison proved it was not the president's wishes that came first as he presented himself in full uniform to the lady who commanded a general and triumphed over the president.[19]

Other political sparks were already flying in Washington before Harrison's departure on Thursday, December 23. Three days earlier, after President Madison signed the embargo into law, the Senate voted to remove the injunction of secrecy over their proceedings during debate over the issue. A similar motion was made in the House.

But John C. Calhoun, who had voted for it to please certain powerful men (probably both Madison and Clay), now objected to the motion. The *New York Evening Post* later reported,

> Calhoun seemed to suppose the people would consider him as acting *inconsistent*, as last session he voted against, now in favor of the embargo, and that the House ought therefore not publish the journals.[20]

There followed an angry colloquy between Calhoun and Rep. Thomas Grosvenor of New York. The *Evening Post* again reported that

> some remarks were made by Mr. Grosvenor which Mr. Calhoun took to himself— He replied rather passionately and improperly — Mr. Grosvenor attempted a reply — The Speaker interfered and prevented. Mr. G. again attempted to proceed, but was again stopped. He appealed from the decision of the Chair but after some remarks he observed he would not press the appeal as it did not respect the House, but him as an individual.[21]

Within days challenges were issued and accepted and news of a duel reached Clay. On Christmas eve, he wrote a friend, Dr. William Thornton,

> As to the duel, I have heard, with infinite regret, the rumor that such a thing is contemplated. The House of R. cannot I fear make any interference to prevent it. What prospective regulation on such subjects might be adopted is another question; but I fear, in spite of all the efforts of Legislation, we shall go on to fight, in simple combat, and go on to condemn the practice. The remedy lies deeper than legislative acts — public opinion must be corrected.[22]

Not only did preparation for a duel continue through the Christmas holiday, but Clay himself was drawn into the affair as a second for Calhoun. His other second was Senator William W. Bibb of Georgia. Grosvenor chose Senator Rufus King of New York and Philip Stuart of Maryland. The encounter was set to take place eight miles into Virginia at 1 pm of December 27.

Knowledge of the impending duel became public and excited the populace. On the morning of the affair, "magistrates and their officers" attempted to guard every avenue leading from the District into both Maryland and Virginia to arrest the parties involved. Grosvenor, his surgeon, and a few others crossed over into Virginia before dawn and he was on the ground at the appointed hour. But it is clear his party knew of the "blockade" and they were able to run it by subterfuge. His party was detained by authorities and a friend passed himself off as Grosvenor and was apparently sent to jail as the real Grosvenor proceeded to the designated spot. There he waited for his opponent — in vain!

During the same morning, Clay and the other seconds met along with a lawyer who was to gain fame as a writer of verse — Francis Scott Key. By noon, they reached an agreement to settle the affair without recourse to "single combat." Calhoun never appeared on the field and went through no danger.

Grosvenor, on the other hand, not only had gone early to sweat out emotional terror of a duel and escape the threat of arrest, but he was nearly killed or injured on his return home. His carriage was drawn by four active and refractory horses. The animals bolted, threw the driver from his seat, and ran off

> at full speed over a terrible rough and dangerous road for a quarter of a mile. They had just ascended a hill which on the other side was precipitous and dangerous in the extreme. At this critical moment a young Mr. Nelson ... at risk of his life, and after being dragged some yards succeeded in stopping them. He no doubt saved the gentleman in the carriage. More dangerous this than taking a shot at 10 yards.[23]

Reporting the following day, on this day's activities in Congress, the *National Intelligencer* stated,

> No business was yesterday done in the House of Representatives. The House was adjourned by the clerk at 12 o'clock, on motion of Mr. Findley, the Speaker being absent at that hour engaged, it is supposed, in an honorable and successful endeavor to reconcile a difference of a very serious nature between two members of the House.[24]

On the evening of this newspaper item, Rep. Daniel Webster arrived in Washington three weeks late for the congressional session. Awaiting him was a distressing letter from his wife in Portsmouth, New Hampshire. She told her husband of a fire that had destroyed 272 buildings in the town, including 108 residences. One of the latter was the Webster home. Uninsured, it was a $6,000 loss in which a valuable library was destroyed. Senator Jeremiah Mason, also of Portsmouth, wrote to Mrs. Mason at home that Mr. Webster

> is considerably agitated. He knows Mrs. Webster is with you; I have told him she had best tarry there till his return, and that I was confident it would be both convenient and agreeable to you. I see no inconvenience in it, and know you will do all in your power to render her situation as pleasant as you can. Poor Colonel Walbach [J.B. Walbach was adjutant general at the war department in Washington] is in much distress; I hope you have invited her [Walbach's wife] to take shelter with you. I think with you, that there are none of the sufferers who can have stronger claims on you than Mrs. Webster and Mrs. Walbach. You will of course do whatever is in your power for any and all of them. Some of them must be reduced to great distress and be in need of everything.[25]

Despite Webster's concern for affairs at home, he accepted his wife's advice, in her first letter about the fire, not to leave his congressional duties to return home.

Another news story, of indirect concern to Clay, appeared in the December 28 *National Intelligencer* and was expanded on the 30th. The account told of fires in the Niagara area. After Harrison's departure from Fort George, his troops went by boat to Sackett's Harbor. The commander at the fort, Gen. George McClure, learned on December 10 that a British force was advancing to attack the fort. His own militia had gone home leaving him with about 60 regulars and 40 volunteers. On the basis of a communication from the secretary of war on October 4, McClure evacuated the fort and burned the nearby town of Newark before crossing over to the American side of the river.

It was quickly noted publicly, and decried, that McClure had not stayed within the bounds of the secretary's instructions, which read,

> Understanding that the *defence* of the post committed to your charge *may* render it proper to destroy the town of Newark, you are hereby directed to apprise its inhabitants of this circumstance, and to invite them to remove themselves and their effects to someplace of greater safety.[26]

Since the fort was abandoned, it was not being "defended," by terms of the secretary's instructions, and the town should not have been burned. As soon as President Madison learned of Mc-

Clure's actions, he conferred with Secretary Armstrong (only recently returned to Washington from the northern theater of operations). He ordered the secretary to instruct General Wilkinson to pass on his disapproval to Sir George Prevost (governor general of Canada) and say frankly "that the burning of Newark was the effect of a misapprehension of the officer and not an order from the Government."[27]

Wilkinson's letter to Prevost was sent from Plattsburgh, New York, on January 28, and included a copy of Armstrong's original order to McClure. But it was far too late. Only days after Newark was burned, and even before Madison learned of the event, the British had crossed the Niagara River on December 19, and promptly carried Fort Niagara by storm, capturing or killing all but three of the garrison (who escaped); burned every building in the towns of Youngstown, Lewiston, Manchester, and Tuscarora and murdered many of the inhabitants.[28] Though the news was not to reach Washington (and Henry Clay) until many days later in January, this same day that the *National Intelligencer* published word of the fall of Fort Niagara (December 30), the British had marched into Buffalo and burned the "village" to the ground.

Wilkinson had word of the burnings of American towns before he sent off his letter to Prevost and added a paragraph regarding the British response. "The outrages which have ensued the unwarrantable destruction of Newark have been carried too far and present the aspect rather of vindictive fury than just retaliation." He hoped they were not part of Prevost's

> settled plan of policy ... for although the wanton conflagrations on the waters of the Chesapeake are fresh in the recollection of every citizen of the United States, no system of retaliation which has for its object the devastation of private property will ever be resorted to by the American Government but in the last extremity, and this will depend on the conduct of your royal master's troops in this country.[29]

Despite the new nasty tone of violent retaliation developing on the war front, an encouraging circumstance presented itself on the diplomatic front. And it was to affect Henry Clay dramatically. On that same December 30 (as the capital residents read of the fall of Niagara), the British

schooner *Bramble* docked at Annapolis under a flag of truce. That evening, a messenger delivered dispatches to Secretary of State James Monroe from the British Foreign Minister Robert Stewart Castlereagh. Over the following few days rumors as to the their contents circulated throughout Washington City. How soon Henry Clay learned of their contents is not known.

But as the city continued to speculate, officialdom engaged in the annual gaiety of the White House levee on New Year Day 1814. It is possible that Lucretia and Henry Clay attended the function. As described by the wife of an editor of the *National Intelligencer*,

> Everybody affected or disaffected towards the government attended to pay Mrs. Madison the compliments of the season. Between one and two o'clock we drove to the President's where it was with much difficulty we made good our entrance, though all of our acquaintances endeavored with the utmost civility to compress themselves as small as they could for our accommodation. The marine band, stationed in the ante-room, continued playing in spite of the crowds pressing on their very heads. But if our pity was excited for these hapless musicians, what must we not have experienced for some members of our own sex; who, not foreseeing the excessive heat of the apartments, had more reason to apprehend the efforts of nature to relieve herself from the effects of the confined atmosphere. You perhaps will not understand that I allude to the rouge which some of our fashionables had unfortunately laid on with an unsparing hand, and which assimilating with the pearl-powder, dust and perspiration, made them altogether unlovely to soul and to eye.
>
> Her majesty's appearance was truly regal, — dressed in a robe of pink satin, trimmed elaborately with ermine, a white velvet and satin turban, with nodding ostrich plumes and a crescent in front, gold chain and clasps around the waist and wrists. 'Tis here the woman who adorns the dress, and not the dress that beautifies the woman. I cannot conceive a female better calculated to dignify the station which she occupies in society than Mrs. Madison, — amiable in private life and affable in public, she is admired and esteemed by the rich and beloved by the poor. You are aware that she snuffs; but in her hands the snuff-box seems only a gracious implement with which to charm. Her frank cordiality to all guests is in contrast to the manner of the President, who is very formal, reserved and precise, yet not wanting in a certain dignity. Being so low of stature, he was in imminent danger of being confounded with the ple-

beian crowd; and was pushed and jostled about like a common citizen,—but not so with her ladyship! The towering feathers and excessive throng distinctly pointed her station wherever she moved.

After partaking of some ice-creams and a glass of Madeira, shaking hands with the President and tendering our good wishes, we were preparing to leave the rooms, when our attention was attracted through the window towards what we conceived to be a rolling ball of burnished gold, carried with swiftness through the air by two gilt wings. Our anxiety increased the nearer it approached, until it actually stopped before the door; and from it alighted, weighted with gold lace, the French Minister [Louis Sérurier] and suite. We now also perceived that what we had supposed to be wings, were nothing more than gorgeous footmen with *chapeaux bras*, gilt braided skirts and splendid swords. Nothing ever was witnessed in Washington so brilliant and dazzling,—a meridian sun blazing full on this carriage filled with diamonds and glittering orders, and gilt to the edge of the wheels,—you may well imagine how the natives stared and rubbed their eyes to be convinced't was no fairy dream.[30]

Nearly a week passed after the levee, before President Madison revealed the contents of the Castlereagh correspondence to the Congress. It is not known whether Clay learned more of it in any private discussion with Madison or Secretary of State Monroe. Then on January 6, 1814, with a cover letter to both Houses of Congress, the president sent three other letters. One dated September 1, 1813, was a copy of a letter presented by the British minister in Russian to the Russian foreign minister. The second, dated November 4, 1813, was Castlereagh's letter to Monroe. And the third was Monroe's reply to Castlereagh.

In chronological order, the first letter was from British Lord Cathcart to the Russian Count De Nesselrode. The British noted that the American ministers had arrived in St. Petersburg to negotiate for peace under the mediation of Russia. Nevertheless, the British said they preferred to negotiate directly with the Americans.

In essence, Castlereagh's letter to Monroe was similar, but more detailed and based on firmer ground as far as the British were concerned. On the day before Castlereagh penned his letter, he received official news from the continent that Napoleon had suffered a disastrous defeat at the hands of the Allied Powers at Leipzig in central Europe. Some reports said Napoleon's casualties

reached 40,000 men. The British government perceived this to be the beginning of the end for the French emperor's conquests. If so, America would then be left to struggle alone against the British Empire. Surely they would now accept peace at any price.

It is interesting to observe that within days of the dispatch of this letter, Londoners were reading of Perry's defeat of the British fleet on Lake Erie. It apparently had little effect on Castlereagh since the British papers insisted on downgrading the contest as being between Americans and the Canadian ships "wholly manned and equipped by the inhabitants of the Province." They said nothing about their fleet's commander, Robert H. Barclay, a hero of Trafalgar. One paper, which carried Perry's report to Secretary Armstrong (and not his famous succinct message to General Harrison), lacked vision by reporting that "Mr. Perry is a most bungling writer of dispatches. He does not, indeed, note the minute when the colours went up; but says it was *soon* after they had been hauled down."[31] This was in reference to the signal of surrender by Perry's battered flagship after he had left it. But since Perry so *soon* won the battle afterward, the Brig *Lawrence* was able to re-fly the flag with no surrender taking place.

How interesting it is that Perry, writing in his other dispatch, has provided a slogan, if not a catch phrase—"We have met the enemy..." that is remembered after 200 years far better than his battle achievement.

As to Castlereagh's letter to Monroe, the foreign minister, at the command of the prince regent, offered the Americans direct negotiations for peace. Though Castlereagh mentioned only London as a meeting place, both London and Gottenburg, Sweden, were named by Cathcart as sites for negotiation. But Castlereagh's letter also contained a clause which the American government could not totally accept. The foreign minister expressed the British earnest desire to negotiate "upon principles of perfect reciprocity, not inconsistent with the established maxims of public law, and with the maritime rights of the British empire."

Of course, the United States must reject the British "maritime rights" of impressment. In reply to Castlereagh, Secretary Monroe stated that the United States would treat on conditions of reciprocity consistent with the rights of both parties as sovereign and independent nations, and calculated not only to establish present harmony, but to provide, as far as possible, against future collisions which might interrupt it.

To this, Monroe added his regrets that the Russian mediation had been rejected, and then stated that the United States would agree to meet the British at Gottenburg,

> with as little delay as possible; it being presumed that His Majesty the King of Sweden, as the friend of both parties, will readily acquiesce in the choice of a place for their pacific negotiations within his dominions.[32]

With the exchange of correspondence, aimed at peace negotiations, now revealed to Congress, Henry Clay continued almost silently in his role as presiding officer of the House of Representatives. He rarely spoke on any issue but imposed himself on the body of argumentative colleagues only as an umpire to cool oratorical ardor, to state the House rules of motions, and maintain order which constantly threatened to break the bounds of propriety. Clay took no part in the discussions on the conduct of the war and the failure of the northern army; on Webster's renewed charges that the principal aim of the war was the conquest of Canada; a new controversy arising out of an 1809 episode involving the then French minister to the United States, Louis Marie Turreau; a debate on amending the Constitution in the vote for president; or legislation encouraging and extending military enlistments.

While these affairs occupied Clay in his House duties, Secretary Monroe was advising Madison on the next steps to take in regard to the negotiations for peace. There is no date on a long memo from the secretary to the president, but it bears the title, "Views Respecting the Rejection of the Mediation of Russia." A large part of the memo dealt with the diplomatic give and take on why the British turned down the Russian offer. But, one paragraph summed it all up and gave the American view of the British attitude.

> Why has G. Britain rejected the Russian mediation? Because she dreaded it. Why has she offered to treat direct with us? Because she wished to prevent a concert between the U. States & the northern powers, to prevent our affairs, as she says, being mixed with those of the continent.

It was Monroe's contention that the connection with a mediating power would bring the United States into closer friendship with a great European nation. Whereas, apart from friendship with such a nation, the United States would be at a disadvantage in treating solely with Great Britain. At least, that is how Monroe thought the enemy's thinking went.

Monroe believed negotiation in Sweden would be acceptable, but, as John Quincy Adams was both minister to Russia and a member of the proposed mission to mediation, so too should the United States have a peace commission member as a minister to Sweden, a post still vacant.

At both the beginning and the end of the memo, Monroe suggested certain names of prospective commissioners along with reasons for their selection. At the head of the memo, discussing whether there should be more than one member, he said, "With us every part of the nation ought to be represented to secure confidence. Mr. Adams the Eastern States — Mr. Bayard the middle — Mr. Clay the Western & Southern — Mr. Russell commerce."

At the end of the memo, he noted,

> The persons nominated friendly to the war. The commission will compromise: Mr. Adams & Mr. Bayard, especially the latter very friendly to peace. Mr. Clay & Mr. Russell friendly to it on just conditions — But not appoint to please the enemy. The way to obtain good peace, to fight well and appoint men known to be resolved to prosecute the war till honorable terms are obtained. Appoint *peace men*, as they are called; and G.B. will think her work is done, that she has gained everything.[33]

On Friday, January 14, 1814, President Madison, agreeing with Monroe's suggestion, sent the Senate the names of Adams, Bayard, Clay, and Russell to be peace commissioners, and added Russell again to be minister to Sweden. By the 18th, the Senate had consented, and on that day Madison signed a document granting full powers "to negotiate and conclude a settlement of the subsisting differences, and a lasting peace and friendship between the United States" and Great Britain; and a second document "to agree, treat, and consult and negotiate of and concerning the general commerce between the United States and Great Britain," and sign a treaty of commerce.[34] Somehow, there seems to be no account of how

Clay received the word (suggestion, request, or order) to become a minister to a peace treaty.

On January 19, everyone knew that Henry Clay was to vacate his seat of power. Quoting from a distinguished witness, "It was an impressive occasion." Even at Clay's youthful age, not yet 37,

he had no rival in popularity. His name was everywhere a "household word." Not only were all the members in their seats, but the House was attended by many senators and a large crowd of spectators. The war which he had been most active in hastening, and most energetic in prosecuting, he was now to close.... But sagacious far beyond his years. The hopes of the country tired of a protracted struggle, grew brighter from his appointment.... I was struck with his appearance on this occasion. There was fire in his eye, and elation in his countenance, a buoyancy in his whole action, that seemed the self-consciousness of coming greatness. Hope brightened, and joy elevated his crest. As full of confidence, gallant bearing, and gratified look, he took his seat in the Speaker's chair, his towering height even more conspicuous than usual, I could not but call to mind Vernon's description of Henry, Prince of Wales, in Shakespeare:

> I saw young Henry, with his beaver on,
> His cuisses on his thigh, gallantly armed,
> Rise from the ground, like feather'd Mercury,
> And vaulting with such ease into his seat,
> As if an angel dropp'd down from the clouds,
> To turn and wind a fiery Pegasus,
> And witch the world with noble horsemanship.[35]

Henry Clay addressed the House of Representatives as follows:

Gentlemen: I have attended you today to announce my resignation of the distinguished station in this House, with which I have been honored by your kindness. In taking leave of you, gentlemen, I shall be excused for embracing this last occasion to express to you personally my thanks for the frank and liberal support the Chair has experienced at your hands. Wherever I may go, in whatever situation I may be placed, I can never cease to cherish, with the fondest remembrance, the sentiments of esteem and respect with which you have inspired me.[36]

Immediately, upon concluding his brief speech, Clay stepped down to the floor and was at once surrounded by members "to express their great grief at his withdrawal,— mingled however, with congratulations upon his appointment, and with the expression of sanguine anticipations of the success of his mission."[37]

This same life-long friend of Daniel Webster best related the character of Henry Clay at this momentous period in the nation's history.

Certainly, no one ever presided over any deliberative body, in this country, with more personal popularity and influence than Mr. Clay. He governed the House with more absoluteness than any Speaker that preceded or followed him. It was a power founded upon character and manners. Fearless, energetic, decided, he swayed the timid by superior will, and governed the bold, through sympathy. A chivalric bearing, easy address, and a warm manner that seemed to imply a warm heart, drew around him crowds of admirers. He cultivated — what our great men too much neglect — the philosophy of manners. None knew better than he the wondrous power in seeming trifles; how much a word, a tone, a look can accomplish; what direction to give to the whole character of opinion and conduct. There seemed nothing constrained in his courtesy, nothing simulated; all his manner was simple, unaffected, ardent; if it were not genuine, he had early arrived at the perfection of art, and concealed the art.

As an orator, he was unequalled; even in an assembly that boasted of Cheves, of Lowndes, and others no less distinguished. His voice was sonorous and musical, falling with proper cadence from the highest to the lowest tones; at times, when in narrative or description, modulated, smooth and pleasing, like sounds of running water; but when raised to animate and cheer, it was as clear and spirit-stirring as the notes of a clarion, the House all the while ringing with melody.

He had a wonderful tact, by which he judged, as by intuition, when the subject, or the patience of his audience, threatened to be exhausted; and took care always to leave the curiosity of his hearers unsatisfied.[38]

Returning to proceedings in the House, even before the paramount duty of selecting a new Speaker, William Findley of Pennsylvania, the 72-year-old ranking member of the House, moved a resolution "that the thanks of this House be presented to Henry Clay, in testimony of their approbation of his conduct in the arduous and important duties assigned to him as Speaker of this House." It was not passed unanimously. There were still nine Federalists who could not bring themselves to express their thanks to a man they opposed so vehemently. However, 144 members of the House agreed to the resolution. This done, the House proceeded to select Langdon Cheves of South Carolina to succeed Henry Clay as Speaker. Cheves had the votes of 94 members against 59 for Felix Grundy of Tennessee and a scattering of 12 votes to others unnamed.[39]

On this same day of Clay's resignation as Speaker, the city of Washington enthusiastically welcomed the hero of the battle on Lake Erie, Commodore Oliver Hazard Perry. Already while awaiting the president's decision on peace negotiations, Clay had expressed to the House his personal admiration for Perry's achievements.

Speaking in Committee of the Whole House on January 4, on resolutions honoring Perry and other naval officers, Clay said (as reported in the third person by the *National Intelligencer*),

It would indeed have ill become the Representatives of the People, when every city on the continent had almost literally blazed with joy on the occasion of these victories, to have remained silent on this subject. Our ships on the ocean, commanded by the most gallant officers in the world, had already shown what American tars could do ship to ship. It remained for the Hero of Erie to exhibit to them an awful lesson of our capacity to fight in squadron, against not only an equal but superior force. If he were to relate the circumstances which in his opinion most distinguished the hero of that battle, Mr. Clay said, he should certainly refer to that mentioned by the gentleman from South Carolina [Rep. Lowndes who preceded Clay with praise for Perry in his explanation of his resolutions]. Imagine to yourself this valuable officer in the hour of peril, his vessel a wreck, her deck strewed with the mangled bodies of his dead and dying comrades — and admire, with me, the cool intrepidity and consummate skill with which he seized the propitious moment, changed his station, and, aided by his gallant second in command, and only second in merit, pressed forward to fame and victory.

Clay did not, at this time, know of the difficulties Perry experienced with his top subordinate. Nor was it probable that Clay had yet learned of the massive trials Perry had in building his fleet from green trees surrounding the Erie countryside; the difficulties Perry had in obtaining men, from his superior, to man his ships; or still less the drama of the battlescene in which Perry turned a terrible defeat into glorious victory. Continuing, Clay said,

Such an action, it has been well said, has scarcely its parallel in history. The importance of victory can be more readily realized, when we look at its consequences. It led to the victory on land, by which a territory was delivered, and a province conquered. No longer is the patriotic soldier, whose safety ought to be guarded by all the principles of honor and of modern warfare, to be delivered over in cold blood to the merciless tomahawk. No longer the mother wakes to the agonizing spectacle of her child torn from her breast, and immolated to savage brutality. Here, sir, the consequences of that victory are most conspicuous; and coming from a country in the vicinity of the scene of action, and so sensibly alive to its consequences, I could not forbear expressing my high satisfaction at giving my vote in favor of these propositions.[40]

On the 25th of January, Perry was entertained lavishly in Washington. Attending were several members of the cabinet and of Congress along with the ex–Speaker. Among the toasts of the evening was one by the new peace commissioner, Henry Clay: "The policy which looks to peace as the end of war — and to the war as the means of peace."[41]

25

IN TRANSIT TO EUROPE

Two days after toasting the gallant Commodore Perry, Henry Clay, in a letter to a friend in Lexington, expressed some of his feelings about his changed situation. He wrote,

> Having a decided preference for a seat in the House of Representatives over any other station under the government I vacated it with great reluctance. But I did not feel myself at liberty to decline a service, however delicate and responsible, which the President, without solicitation on my part, has been pleased to assign me.[1]

It was about a week later that the new commissioner finally left Lucretia and five of the children in Washington. Clay carried with him a long, detailed letter of instructions for all members of the mission from their new superior, Secretary of State James Monroe. The letter was formal and stated that the previous instructions issued for the proposed negotiation under Russian mediation still applied, but now "have gained additional weight, by the vast amount of blood and treasure, which have been expended in their support."

Taking up "the most important grounds of the controversy with Great Britain," Monroe said he had nothing new to add on impressment since the president's sentiments had undergone no change. "This degrading practice must cease; our flag must protect the crew, or the United States cannot consider themselves an independent nation." The American government was willing to exclude all British seaman, "excepting only the few already naturalized," from U.S. ships and even surrender up "all British seamen deserting in our ports in future." Under any treaty, Monroe wanted the British to pay for the services of any impressed American seaman released from British detention.

Next in point of importance was the blockade.

Though this cause of controversy seemed removed by virtue of Britain's revocation of the Orders in Council in the summer of 1812, Monroe felt there was need of a "precise definition of the public law on this subject" to be written into the treaty. In his letter of instructions of April 15, 1813, to the original peace mission, Monroe had stated that, "The impressment of our seamen and illegal blockades, as exemplified more particularly in the orders in council, were the principal causes of the war." Now he felt "a principal object in making peace is to prevent ... a recurrence again to war for the same cause."[2]

On another matter of great importance to Henry Clay, was the subject of Canada and the relations with the Indians in the old Northwest. Again in his instructions of April 1813, Monroe stated that there must be no renewal of the article in the treaty of 1794,

> which allows British traders from Canada and the North West Company, to carry on trade with the Indian tribes within the limits of the U. States.... The pernicious effects of this privilege have been most sensibly felt in the present war, by the influence which it gave to the traders over the Indians, whose whole force has been wielded by means thereof against the inhabitants of our Western States and Territories.[3]

In further instructions, issued in June 1813, Monroe suggested that Britain cede Canada to the United States, since

> the possession of it by England must hereafter prove a fruitful source of controversy which its transfer to the U.S. would remove ... that these provinces will be severed from G.B. at no distant day by their own career may fairly be presumed even against the strongest efforts to retain them.[4]

It must be remembered that both of these earlier sets of instructions were written at a time that British forces were roaming in the area of present day Toledo, Ohio, and the only control U.S. forces had in Canada was near Fort George across the Niagara River.

But when Monroe now added to these instructions, by way of his letter to the new mission in January 1814, most of Upper Canada across from Detroit all the way to the western end of Lake Ontario, was in American hands, and the Indian coalition, built by Tecumseh, had been broken. Furthermore, in the capture of General Proctor's baggage at the Battle of the Thames, the U.S. government had obtained official British documents that testified that

> the British Government has exercised its influence over the Indian tribes within our limits as well as elsewhere in peace, for hostile purposes towards the United States; and that the Indian barbarities since the war were, in many instances, known to and sanctioned by the British Government.[5]

Now in his new instructions, Monroe told Clay and his colleagues,

> Experience has shewn that Great Britain cannot participate in the dominion and Navigation of the Lakes, without incurring the danger of an early renewal of the War. It was by means of the Lakes that the British Government interfered with, and gained an ascendancy over the Indians, even within our own limits. The effect produced by the Massacre of our Citizens, after they were made prisoners and of defenceless women and children along our frontiers, need not be described. It will perhaps never be removed while Great Britain retains in her hands the government of those provinces. This alone will prove a fruitful source of controversy; but there are others. Our settlements had reached before the War, from our northern boundary, with lower Canada, along the St. Lawrence, to the South-western extremity of Lake Erie, and after peace it cannot be doubted that they will soon extend by a continued population to Detroit, where there is now a strong establishment & to the banks of the Michigan, and even of the other Lakes, spreading rapidly over all our vacant territory. With the disposition already existing, collisions, may be daily expected between the Inhabitants on each side, which it may not be in the power of either Government to prevent. The cupidity of the British Traders, will admit of no controul. The inevitable consequence of another war, and even of the present, if persevered in by the British Government, must be to sever those

provinces by force from Great Britain. Their inhabitants themselves, will soon feel their strength, and assert their independence. All these evils had therefore better be anticipated and provided for, by a timely arrangement between the two Governments in the mode proposed.[6]

On another subject, Monroe advised the commissioners on claims for spoliations that

> indemnity should be stipulated, on each side, for the destruction of all unfortified Towns, and other private property, contrary to the Laws and usages of war. It is equally proper that the Negroes taken from the Southern States, should be returned to their owners, or paid for, at their full value. It is known that a shameful trafic [sic], has been carried on in the West Indies, by the sale of these persons there, by those who professed to be their deliverers. Of this fact, the proof which has reached this Department, shall be furnished you. If these Slaves are considered as non-combatants they ought to be restored, if as property they ought to be paid for.[7]

Regarding the conduct of the British in declining the Russian mediation, Monroe gave his view that Britain dreaded negotiations carried on under the auspices of the Emperor of Russia because

> Russia, and all the other powers of the Continent, have a common interest with the United States against Great Britain.... It is believed that there is not a power in Europe that would give the slightest countenance to the British practice of impressment. Had that practice been brought into discussion under the auspices of Russia it may reasonably be presumed that it would have been treated by the Emperor, so far as he might have expressed an opinion on it, as novel, absurd, and inadmissible in regard to other Nations.... Had the British Government supported the practice on the ground of a maritime right applicable to all Nations, it would have offended and might have excited all, against Great Britain.[8]

Monroe went on to state that under Russian mediation the United States would have acted "independently of any other power" and that in treating directly with Great Britain,

> not only is no concession contemplated, on any point in controversy, but the same desire is cherished to preserve a good understanding with Russia and the other Baltic Powers, as if the negotiation had taken place under the mediation of Russia.[9]

He pointed to the selection of Russell (to be minister to Sweden) and Adams (current minister to

Russia) "to keep open the door of communication" to those nations.[10]

And finally, Monroe stressed that

you will always recollect that the object is to secure to the United States by means thereof, a safe and honorable peace, and not to combine with any power, in any object of ambition, or in claiming other conditions more favorable than those proposed, which may tend to prolong the war.[11]

On the same day that Monroe penned these lengthy instructions, another letter was written in New York, to Henry Clay, by a wealthy supporter of the administration, David Parish. Addressed to Clay, "expected at New York," it enclosed introductions for him to Archibald Gracie (a well-to-do merchant), and John Jacob Astor (fast becoming one of America's wealthiest men through his vast fur-trading ventures in the far west). Parish told Clay that he had opened credits with friends in Amsterdam, Hamburg, and London on which Clay might draw on for his expenses. Parish also suggested,

If you could take a Sum in Portuguese or English Gold Coins out with you to which there can be no possible objection in your Case, the Embargo Law to the Contrary notwithstanding the profit would be considerable, Say from 30 to 40 pct.— Spanish Dollars will answer better yet.[12]

It is unknown whether Clay took advantage of this means of profit, nor is anything known of Clay's journey from Washington to New York. He was in New York by February 13, when he wrote to Monroe. He commented on major events which became news in the short time since he left the capital. First, he referred to changes in the president's cabinet. On February 9, Madison declared the office of secretary of the treasury vacant and nominated the absent Albert Gallatin to join Clay, Adams, Bayard, and Russell on the new peace commission. On this appointment, Clay wrote Monroe, "I derive much satisfaction from that by which our mission has acquired the benefit of Mr. Gallatin's services." Madison had named Tennessee Senator George Washington Campbell to succeed Gallatin at treasury. In addition, William Pinkney resigned as attorney general and was replaced by Richard Rush, comptroller of the treasury and son of Dr. Benjamin Rush, a signer of the Declaration of Independence. His place as

comptroller was taken by Representative Ezekiel Bacon of Massachusetts.

Commenting on the international scene, Clay observed to Monroe,

Wonderful events in Europe are almost daily announced. A continental peace to the exclusion of G. Britain.— A general peace comprehending her — the revival of all the powers of Europe, as they existed prior to the French revolution, with some slight territorial modification — A Congress for a general peace, which will break up without arranging it — The defeat of Lord Wellington — and the defeat of the French force by which he is opposed, are among the occurrences which are asserted in the public prints. The *facts* are too confused, contradictory, and uncertain to authorize any speculations as yet on the subject of their effect on our own affairs.

Clay's confusion over European rumors was reasonable, since some of his information was inaccurate, while other reports (though nearly two months old) touched on events still in a formative stage. Some of the latest reports reaching him were of Napoleon's disastrous defeat at Leipzig in October 1813. But now, he would have to wait until his arrival in Europe before he was to gain a more intelligible understanding of affairs on the continent. Yet, these new events would send out their own clouded pictures.

Of more direct concern to the mission, Clay reported to Monroe that "Mr Hughes and Mr. Shaler have joined me." Christopher Hughes, Jr., of Baltimore, was to become mission secretary and a life-long friend of Clay's. William Shaler, a former sea captain and a diplomatic consul in Havana, was to act as a confidential courier and agent between the peace mission and various European governments. Clay noted further on new aides, "I understand that a Mr. Weir [Edward Wyer] is to go out with us, as consul at Riga. Are you quite sure that you have not been imposed upon in the appointment of this gentleman?"[13]

Ten days later, Clay was able to write Monroe that,

It seems that Capt. Angus having no instructions from the Navy Dept. declines admitting Mr. Wyer on board the ship, and he of course does not go out. He appears to regret it very much. I confess freely that I am not myself sorry that we have not the honor of his company. The public interest I am persuaded will not suffer by *his* absence from Riga; and if one half of what I have heard from a respectable source is true his Commission ought to be instantly revoked.[14]

Another aide, William D. Lewis, "went out" with Clay.

Captain Samuel Angus, mentioned by Clay to Monroe, was the commanding officer of the American corvette *John Adams*, assigned to transport Clay, Jonathan Russell, and the mission aides to Gottenburg, Sweden. Both Angus and his ship saw action in the undeclared Naval War with France and the fights against the Barbary pirates at Tripoli in North Africa early in the century. In late 1812, Angus was wounded in an engagement across the Niagara River from Buffalo. He took command of the *John Adams* on January 26, 1814. In a quirk of history, Oliver Hazard Perry was to die on this same ship several years later.

As Clay and the ship made final preparations for the voyage to Gottenburg, both official and private mail continued to come aboard for delivery to Europe. The marshall's office in New York had a notice published to those wishing mail to be taken across. But he advised that letters must be left open to be examined, and those allowed to go would be "under the care, and subject to the directions of Mr. Clay and Mr. Russell."[15]

At the time of his appointment as a commissioner, Russell was on a private visit on Lake Ontario, was late in replying to Monroe's notice, and had not reached New York when Clay arrived. Clay felt obliged to await Russell and meanwhile continued to receive official dispatches from Washington. Writing to Monroe again, on February 14, he acknowledged receipt of Gallatin's new commission and other government documents to be carried to Europe. He also wrote that,

I understand that, without waiting for other communications or orders from the Department, it is desired that we should take our departure with the utmost promptitude. Yet I doubt whether we shall get off before Sunday next, the 20th instant. Mr. Russell has not arrived, nor do I expect him before Wednesday or Thursday next, and I presume after he joins me he will require one or two days for preparation. So that I think that Sunday may be considered as the day of our departure.[16]

Monroe responded at once, advising Clay and his aides to depart immediately without waiting for Russell. Another vessel would be provided for him. Monroe added, "There is danger, by the delay of losing the services of Mr. Gallatin and Mr. Bayard, in the proposed negotiation, which would be cause of serious regret."[17]

On the 23rd, Clay replied,

Your surprize [sic] will not be greater than my mortification at the delay which has arisen in our departure. It terminates however today, and I derive some consolation from the assurance I have recd. here, on all hands, that owing to the state of the wind and weather we have not really lost any time.[18]

By this date, Russell had reached New York and, according to the *Niles Register* (published in Baltimore), they departed New York on the 23rd. Nevertheless, Clay, in later correspondence states that they left on the 25th. According to a somewhat error-prone account of incidents on the voyage, written years later by a new midshipman on the *John Adams*, as the vessel "proceeded down the North River" (the Hudson) on February 26, it was given an 18-gun salute by the 44-gun frigate *President* in New York harbor. Almost immediately the *John Adams*, flying under a white flag of truce, encountered a stiff gale and the harbor pilot could not be transferred to a small boat to go ashore and was carried all the way to Europe. Clay became very ill from sea-sickness and continued so throughout most of the trip. Russell, on the other hand, a native of Rhode Island, was "an old sea dog," and took the voyage in stride, according midshipman Joseph B. Nones.[19]

On February 28, the *John Adams* met the British blockade and was boarded by a detail from the English sloop of war *Sylph*. The Americans were treated with marked respect and were permitted to pass without further obstruction. On the way into the North Atlantic and for nearly two months, the *John Adams* and Henry Clay were out of communication with the world. Only some brief notes of the voyage written by Joseph Nones, and some records in the ship's log which are preserved only from March 27 on, remain to tell of the voyage.

Meanwhile, it would have been quite interesting to Clay if he could have read of his own family in accounts which turned up many years later in the *Autobiography of Amos Kendall*. Kendall became a tutor to Clay's children, during his absence from the United States, and later was a political opponent of Clay when Kendall served in Andrew

Jackson's so-called "kitchen" cabinet. (The story is also very descriptive of transportation of those days.)

Kendall, in 1814, was but 24 years old and a resident of Massachusetts, near Boston. He had decided to travel to Washington City to seek some sort of employment, further south or west. He left home on February 18 and, on the same day that Clay departed from New York for Europe (the 25th), Kendall crossed over the North River from New York into New Jersey. (His diary says nothing about hearing the frigate *President's* salute to the departing *John Adams* and the peace commissioners.) His trip south by stagecoach was over "indescribably dreadful" roads. "The road this day was worse than I have ever before seen. I and others of the passengers walked many miles." And on the next day he wrote,

> Set out from New Brunswick soon after daylight, and in consequence of the badness of the roads several of us proceeded on foot. The mud was a little frozen, so that it would bear a man, but not a horse. Through the swamp, so called, every passenger walked twelve miles, except one, and he walked eight.

Apparently, the roads improved somewhat the rest of the way and he seemed to enjoy his companions. He reached Washington on March 1 and took in the sights, including the Capitol, and even went to the White House where he met the Madisons and noted, "I felt no awe, although Mrs. Madison is a noble, dignified person, apparently more able to manage the affairs of the nation than her husband. His personal appearance is very inferior."

The following day, in the Senate chamber, Kendall was introduced by Senator Varnum of Massachusetts to Senator Bledsoe of Lexington, Kentucky. In the course of the conversation, young Kendall mentioned his desire to act as an instructor in some family. Bledsoe said he wanted a man in his family in that capacity to look after four children, the youngest being six years old. By early the following week, Bledsoe agreed to take on Kendall for $100 per year along with his board and use of Bledsoe's books. The work would be in Kentucky and Kendall arranged to leave Washington by March 9.

His journey westward was by stage to Pittsburgh, arriving exhausted on March 17. He left

there on a keel boat on March 25 reaching Cincinnati on April 5. Two days later, on the south side of the Ohio River, he began walking toward Lexington, stopping at farm houses (few and far between) seeking overnight lodging. By the time he reached Lexington, on April 12, he wrote, "I am excessively lame in my left knee, and fear it will continue some days."

It was only two day after this that Henry Clay arrived at his destination in Europe. But since his time there was centered on diplomatic affairs and there are only a few copies of letters relating to his family, the account of Kendall's association with the Clay family will be covered here before returning to Clay's activities en route to Europe.

Though Congress did not adjourn until April 18, Senator Bledsoe left Washington early and had arrived in Lexington by that date, when he was met on a street by Kendall. The Senator said he would be moving his family in town (from about 30 miles away) and would be ready in about a week to set up the arrangement previously agreed upon. Nevertheless, he suggested to Kendall that he might do better by becoming an assistant teacher in a neighboring academy. This put doubts in Kendall's mind as to the certainty of Bledsoe's pledge. He became more convinced that it would not be fulfilled as he encountered Bledsoe several more times in the ensuing days and seemed to feel the Senator was avoiding him.

Meanwhile, Kendall was staying at Postlethwaite's Inn where he established speaking acquaintance with several army officers boarding there. Through one of them, late in April, he was introduced to a man named Watkins, a half-brother of Henry Clay. (This was probably John Watkins, son of Clay's mother and her second husband, Henry Watkins, still living in Versailles, Kentucky.) On the last day of April, Kendall had an unpleasant episode in which he saw Bledsoe on several occasions, in which the younger man felt he was being ignored even when he approached the senator. Kendall, at this point, decided to have nothing more to do with Bledsoe and began to seek employment elsewhere. Some time afterward, Kendall was informed that Bledsoe was shortsighted and could not recognize anyone across the room, but had spoken highly of Kendall. They later became friends.

Now, through Watkins, he was introduced to

Mrs. Hart, the widow of Captain Nathaniel Hart, who had been killed at the River Raisin in January 1813. She had two daughters and proposed getting up a school composed of the children of the first families in Lexington, which would give him an income of a thousand dollars. This project also fell through. One reason for its failure was that the five children of Henry and Lucretia Clay lived so far from town that it would be inconvenient for them to attend. Mrs. Hart could pay him only $299 a year to live at her home and teach her two daughters, but then added, "Mrs. Clay will do more for you, and wished to see you at my house between ten and eleven o'clock tomorrow."[20]

It is not known when Lucretia Clay left Washington to return to Kentucky, but she was still in the capital on March 10 when she wrote a letter to her husband (then on the high seas). In it she mentioned her desire to be home in Kentucky, but spoke of Lexington as being "more sickly than it ever has been. Nelly Hart had twelve negroes sick." As for her husband's absence, she said, "I am very dreary here as I do not pay visits; indeed I found I could not go out without you in the evening, but I do all in my power to keep me from being melancholy."

Lucretia was already making preparations for going home, stating that,

> Mrs. Brown [her sister, Nancy, married to James Brown, now a senator from Louisiana] has at last made up her mind to go home with me and spend the summer. Judge Todd and his lady [U.S. Supreme Court Justice Thomas Todd and Lucy, the sister of Dolly Madison] have been very polite to me since you left this; the Judge called the other day to examine the light wagon we were to have got from Mr. L [unidentified], but he found it so completely worn out that I determined not to take it; we shall I hope get on without it.

In closing, she said, "Susan and Ann send their love to you. May God spare you to us. Do take care of yourself for our sakes."[21]

It was nearly two months later, on May 5, that Kendall met Lucretia Clay. She offered to give him board, the use of Clay's library, and $300 a year to teach her five children. He was at liberty to terminate the arrangement after six months. He accepted and moved into "Ashland" on May 10 and remained as a tutor to the Clay children until April 29, 1815 — just short of one year.

The Clay children in Kendall's care were two boys (Theodore Wythe, 13, and Thomas Hart, 11) and three girls (Susan Hart, 9; Ann Brown, 7; and Lucretia Hart, 5). A daughter, Henrietta, had already died. There were to be five more children. The boys had not been in Washington with their parents, but had been left at a school in a neighboring county where, according to Kendall,

> There was no regular government, either in school or at their lodgings. The consequence was that they profited very little by their lessons, and became ungovernable in their tempers. All the children, except the oldest (Theodore), were endowed with fine minds, and in that respect, the younger boy had few equals.[22]

Kendall gradually brought the boys around to being attentive to their studies and learning to control their tempers. A summary of extracts from his journal best illustrates his association with the children and Mrs. Clay, while providing a glimpse into Henry Clay's immediate family:

> *May 13th.* My two boys, I perceive have not been very well taught, and know almost nothing of Latin or English grammar. They have begun in Caesar's Commentaries, and after having recited, I make them write out a translation of the whole, which I intend they shall copy into a book.
>
> The oldest little girl [Susan] reads and writes, and bids fair to make an excellent scholar. The second [Ann] knows little of reading, and seems to be an idle, although a fine little girl. The third [Lucretia] is yet in her Abs. The whole of them are passionate, and have never been governed at all. But they are by no means unmanageable.
>
> *14th.* Thomas refused this forenoon to go to his lesson; but, on being carried into the room, he yielded.
>
> *20th.* I find the children, especially the boys under my care, have been indulged till they are almost ungovernable. The oldest, Theodore, has the most amiable disposition, but Thomas is the smartest boy. They have been accustomed to fight each other, so that, at the school which they lately attended, they could not be boarded at the same place.... This evening Thomas began to whine and growl after his usual manner, when I looked toward him with an eye which, no doubt, expressed my feelings. Mrs. Clay, observing me, said to him, that he must take care, for Mr. Kendall was just ready to speak. And then said to me with perfect good-nature, that she had many times seen me nearly out of patience; for she could tell. I blushed at perceiving my feelings were known, and made some indirect answer, which no doubt confirmed her opinion.... Thomas, however, grew worse and worse, until she was obliged to take him into a

room, and, giving him a severe whipping, she actually conquered him. I congratulated her with real pleasure.

29th. Yesterday, Mrs. Clay being absent, Thomas got into a mighty rage with some of the negroes, and threatened and exerted all his little power to kill them. I took him into the office and held him until he was cool, and then let him go. Notwithstanding Mrs. Clay had told me to do this on such occasions, I perceived by her conversation today that she did not feel exactly right about it. I was surprised, but am resolved to interfere no more unless it be to save life.

June 9th. This evening there was as large party of ladies with several gentlemen at Mrs. Clay's.... Thomas got into a great rage after the departure of the company, and at Mrs. Clay's request I dragged him, not very tenderly, into the office. He fought me like a tiger, and cursed me with all his might. "You damned Yankee rascal," cried he, "you have been trying to make yourself of great consequence among the ladies this evening." This he kept up for some time. At first I was provoked, and cuffed him once or twice, but not feeling myself authorized to whip him, I let him bawl. Finally, I went out and asked his mother what I should do. She ordered him to bed, and he readily, though unexpectedly, complied.

10th. The sequel of last night's adventure exhibits a striking characteristic of that singular boy. He would not get up until I had gone to breakfast, nor even show himself at the table. Afterwards, when alone with his mother, he burst into tears. On being asked what was the matter, he said it was because he treated me so ill last night. He then mentioned an anecdote which is told of General Washington,—how that good man having in anger abused an officer, afterwards asked his pardon. He wished to ask pardon of me, but feared the other children would laugh at him. He, however, came up with his mother, who asked pardon for him, which was readily and heartily granted. Notwithstanding his foibles, he is an admirable boy.[23]

Amos Kendall continued to work for the Clays until April 1815, but by the summer of 1814, his diary became bereft of items relating to the children and began to dwell more on accounts of his social activities and ambitions for his future which strayed from teaching to business, to law, and finally to journalism which field he followed on leaving the Clays. Though he often expressed a hope of profiting from an acquaintance with Henry Clay, he would, years later, come back into Clay's life as an opposition politician.

While Kendall was establishing himself in Lexington, Clay and the corvette *John Adams* continued northeastward in the Atlantic. By March 18, the ship was passing north of the Hebrides Islands in "boisterous weather" when many whales were sighted. According to midshipman Nones, Clay was induced to leave his "sick bed" and come on deck to see the show. Though he said he enjoyed the sight, he also let it be known that he did not feel comfortable with the huge creatures coming so near the ship. On the following day, the *John Adams* passed between the Orkney and the Shetland Islands and took course for the Norwegian coast.

They sighted this coast briefly on March 27, and then lost it in thick fog until late on the 30th. On March 31, they stood into the harbor of Rosvog, near the island of Nittiro in extremely cold weather. Two boats came out from shore, one with a pilot. He was taken aboard and, again according to Nones, "was paid $175 in Spanish milled dollars which he put in various pockets, fell overboard and drowned, his $175 contributing to his death."

The arrival of the corvette *John Adams* was a great event for the little Norwegian village. It was reported to be the only vessel of a large size to enter the port in 15 years. In celebration, the 70-year-old governor of the area came aboard with baskets of poultry and vegetables for sale but also informed Captain Angus that the town of 500 inhabitants was in a pitiful plight and the people nearing starvation. Angus was told there had not been a barrel of flour or any bread on the island for over eight months. Then, in a reversal of normal customs, instead of the ship taking on fresh provisions, the crew furnished whatever supplies they could to the welfare of those ashore.

Snow and rain delayed departure of the *John Adams* until April 8 when weather permitted getting underway as far as the outer harbor. But it was afternoon of the next day that the voyage was continued southward, again in thick fog. The *John Adams* finally reached the Swedish coast in the vicinity of Gottenburg on April 12, Clay's 37th birthday. Nones notes in his reminiscences that the ship had anchored at Massatuketts [now Masthugget] two miles from the mouth of the Gota River in Sweden, because of the shallow harbor. Other accounts reveal that the rest of the route into the city was ice bound.

Midshipman Nones relates another amusing incident aboard the ship, probably at sea prior to reaching Norway, which involved Clay and Russell. However, Nones includes John Quincy Adams in the account, though Adams did not sail on that ship until weeks later, when Clay was not aboard. Adams does mention his part in the episode in his memoirs much later, and so the story will be told in the next chapter using both Nones' and Adams' accounts.

Meanwhile, living as best he could in Gottenburg, was Commodore Barron, who, as captain of the frigate *Cheaspeake*, had surrendered up three American seamen to the British frigate *Leopard* in 1807. Following his court martial, Barron lived abroad in semi-banishment. Now, on learning of the presence of the *John Adams* off shore, he made his way to the vessel while the commissioners were still on board. There he appealed to Captain Angus and got his consent to sail on the *John Adams* on its return to the United States where he intended to seek reinstatement in the U.S. Navy. In two trips, Nones, using a small boat, brought Barron's effects on board the ship, and the commodore was delighted with his prospects.

However, still further offshore, was a large fleet of British frigates, blockading the entrance to the mouth of the Gota River, hopeful of intercepting the American privateer, *Isaac Chauncey* of 18 guns and 260 men. The British admiral learned of Barron's attempt to gain passage home to take up the sword against his country's enemy. The admiral sent word to Captain Angus that as his ship carried the white flag of truce, it could not shelter and return a naval officer to the United States with the intention of becoming a combatant and an active participant in the war with England. Of course, the entire ship's crew of the *John Adams* intended to fight the war once they were released from their diplomatic duties. The British admiral advised Angus that if he persisted,

> it would be a violation of the sacred white flag covering and protecting the Embassy for peace — And he [the admiral] would in that case, consider the *John Adams* as a combatant that would have to fight her way through his fleet and be subject to capture.[24]

Both Angus and Barron were stunned by the admiral's demand and threat. To resolve the matter, Angus called upon Henry Clay for a solution. With reluctance, Clay advised that Barron and his effects should be returned ashore. The commodore complied, but was so overcome by the distressing turn of events that he was seen shedding tears. Nones again transported Barron and his possessions to the shore, and Angus sent word to the British that Barron was no longer a passenger on the *John Adams*.

Barron's hope was not all gone. He later made similar arrangements for passage on the *Isaac Chauncey*. Sounding like a novel, one dark and stormy night, the privateer slipped out of the harbor and successfully ran the blockade. Eventually, after capturing several other vessels, in a cruise of several weeks, the *Isaac Chauncey* reached the United States and Barron was once again in his homeland.

Finally, on April 13, Clay, Russell and their aides took departure from the ship. As they prepared to leave by sleigh over packed ice for the 12-mile journey to Gottenburg, they heard the ship's cannon booming an 18-gun salute in their honor.

26

IDLING AT GOTTENBURG

On their arrival in Gottenburg, on April 14, 1814, Henry Clay and Jonathan Russell took up temporary lodging at the "Gotha Killa," described as "the crack hotel at Gottenburg."[1] That same day, they jointly wrote John Quincy Adams, in St. Petersburg, Russia, to notify him of his appointment as a member of the new mission and to advise him that they had just arrived in the city designated for the direct peace negotiations with the British. The letter was sent by ordinary mail.[2]

In addition, Clay and Russell learned that day, probably through the American consulate in Gottenburg, that the other two members of the new commission — James A. Bayard and Albert Gallatin — had left St. Petersburg and were believed to be in Amsterdam, Holland.

Not knowing that a new mission had been appointed, Bayard and Gallatin had left St. Petersburg in separate conveyances on January 25. Bayard, who was seriously ill en route, described their trials in a letter to his nephew, Andrew.

The journey was a terrific one. I started at 10 o'clock at night in a snowstorm in the most rigorous season of the year. In the first 28 days, we had 22 days of hard snowing. I think there were but two days on the road that we had even a glimpse of the sun. Nothing could be more waste and dreary than the appearance of the Country. A boundless expanse of snow. Not a tree nor house nor object of any kind to arrest the eye. The population of the Country is contained in villages and those are widely separated. We generally travelled all night, and of course slept in our carriages.

The depth of the snow rendered the roads almost impassable. With 8 horses to draw me alone I was once 13 hours coming 14 miles. We passed thro Riga, Konigsberg, Frankfort on the Oder, Berlin, Hanover, Utrecht, and many other towns

of less note, in the course of our route. We were four different times obliged to leave the post road on account of fortified towns still held by the French.

The last was Naarden, which is not more than 12 miles from Amsterdam, and which holds out with a garrison not exceeding 800 men, who frequently make incursions into the Country. The Dutch have few soldiers and those miserably armed. Those whom I have seen here carry nothing but a pike.[3]

Reaching Amsterdam on March 4, Bayard and Gallatin learned of the new mission, but only that Bayard had been appointed as one of the members, Gallatin's appointment having come after Monroe's January 8 notification to Bayard. In early April, both men travelled to England arriving there on the 8th, and reached their destination, Harwich, on the 9th.

Unaware of the details of the travels of Bayard and Gallatin, Henry Clay and Jonathan Russell, on the day of their arrival in Gottenburg, also wrote to their new associates. As in the letter to Adams, they advised Bayard and Gallatin that they had both been appointed as members of the new mission. And of course both were told of the arrival of the two-fifths of the mission at Gottenburg. In addition, Bayard and Gallatin were informed that their families were well in America when Clay last saw them prior to his departure for Europe.

This letter to Bayard and Gallatin was carried to Amsterdam by Nathaniel Shaler, who had crossed the Atlantic on the corvette *John Adams*. Also entrusted to Shaler's care was another letter from Clay, alone, which was to be taken all the way to William H. Crawford in Paris. Crawford had been appointed the American minister to

France, but was having trouble presenting his credentials to the French government. After relating news he brought from America, Clay, in his letter, referred to the circumstances in France which caused Crawford's difficulties. Clay wrote,

> If Paris has been really occupied by the allies, I presume your public character has protected you from any inconvenience. As to your success in the object of your mission, I apprehend that is not to be counted upon.

Clay also expressed to Crawford his wish to have visited France. Though he said, "I have not entirely abandoned the intention ... it is somewhat weakened by the late visit which Paris has received."[4] Clay was later to receive a personal viewpoint of the momentous events taking place in Paris by way of a letter written by Crawford a week before Clay wrote his. Nevertheless, Clay didn't receive this letter, dated April 8 by Crawford, until May 8.

Clay had only an inkling, on his departure from America, of the great drama unfolding on the continent of Europe. Since Napoleon's defeat at Leipzig, in October 1813, and subsequent retreat across the Rhine in November, the Allies had gathered strength along that waterway and offered Napoleon a peace on the basis of France's natural frontiers — the Rhine, the Alps, the Pyrenees, and the English Channel. The emperor's delay in accepting the proposal resulted in renewed fighting. He found himself driven backward into France by five armies. In the north, in Holland, was Napoleon's former field marshall, Charles Bernadotte (already crown prince of Sweden) with 102,000 men. In the center, Prussian Marshall Gebhard Lebrecht Von Blücher's 82,000 men moved across the Rhine on the last day of December 1813. On the Swiss border was Austrian Prince Karl von Schwarsenberg poised with another 200,000 men. Along the Italian border was an army of 55,000 Austrians and Italians. And driving over the Pyrenees from Spain was the British general Sir Arthur Wellesley (not yet the Duke of Wellington) with 80,000 troops.

Napoleon anticipated a spring encounter, but the Allies sprang on him in the winter. In a series of violent battles with thousands lost on each side, beginning on December 31, 1813, Napoleon, often greatly outnumbered, fought off Blücher, then Schwarzenberg, returning again to Blücher, winning battles but losing ground as each commander moved forward when Napoleon turned to attack the other. By the end of March, the Allies were on the outskirts of Paris. After they occupied the French capital on March 31, Napoleon abdicated in favor of his three-year-old son on April 6. But now the Allies insisted on an unconditional abdication with the emperor's exile to Elba. When Wellington defeated another French army at Toulouse on April 10, Napoleon accepted the Allies' terms the following day.

These dramatic events were observed and described in part by Crawford in a letter written to Clay from Paris on April 8. He reported that Czar Alexander of Russia and the king of Prussia entered Paris on March 31 "at the head of about 50,000 of the finest troops in the world." Other masses of troops were stationed north and south of the city. That evening the French Senate convened, "deposed Napoleon," and proclaimed a provisional government. A Constitution was quickly drafted and the House of Bourbon was declared restored putting royalty back on the throne in the name of Louis XVIII.

To Crawford's astonishment, Napoleon

> seems to have sunk without an effort, at least, with an effort corresponding in any degree with his former fame. Such at least is the conclusion which I draw from the facts which are communicated to the public. It is possible that these facts may be misrepresented. I believe however that it is certain that he had agreed to retire with his family to the Isle of Elba, upon a pension of six millions of Livres. From the moment that he saw it was impossible for him to reign, he ought to have died. The manner was his election. A strange infatuation seems to have influenced his conduct the last six months.

As for the French reception of Louis XVIII, Crawford remarked,

> Even now after the Senate & provisional government have declared for that dinasty [sic] there is not one man in an hundred who puts on the white cockade. On the day of the entry of the Allied Sovereigns, all the persons devoted to their ancient Kings endeavored to make themselves as conspicuous as possible, and to conceal the smallness of their numbers by continual change of place.

He noted further that "the mob of Paris ... could have been in favor of a free government" while "the men now in power would ... have preferred the succession of the King of Rome" (Napoleon's three-year-old son) "with a regency presided by the Empress." The remainder of Crawford's letter is chopped up with cipher which leaves its contents too mixed to obtain a clear understanding of the rest of his message.[5]

Though Clay and Russell did not receive this letter from Crawford until May 8, they were continually receiving accounts from other sources about the suspenseful events transpiring in France. They also learned that Bayard and Gallatin had gone on to England, where Clay sent another letter to them there on April 20, telling of his and Russell's arrival in Gottenburg. In addition, that same day, Clay and Russell sent a similar short letter to Adams by courier. And they finally sent yet another letter announcing their arrival to Secretary of State James Monroe.

The next day, April 21, Russell left Clay alone in Gottenburg, and set off for the Swedish capital, Stockholm, to present his credentials as the new minister to Sweden.

It was not until April 23, when writing again to Monroe, that Clay's views on the events in Europe are revealed. After noting briefly some of the same information he was later to receive from Crawford, Clay went on to say,

> A new epoch has thus arisen, the first effect of which will be an European peace. It will doubtless lead to totally new relations political as well as commercial. It remains for us to see if Great Britain will insist upon retaining or surrender her conquests, and admit other nations to a fair participation in the general commerce of the world.

He also wondered in writing whether the cooperation between the Allies, in reducing French power, would "continue to guide their councils, when delicate and difficult arrangements are to be made among themselves."

Clay also wrote about the newest transfer of sovereignty as the Danes, early in the year had been forced to cede Norway to Sweden following a battle won by former French Field Marshall Bernadotte, now the crown prince of Sweden. Clay remarked to Monroe,

> It will cost Sweden some trouble to possess herself of her new acquisition. The people of Norway are said to be extremely averse to the annexation, and countenanced as Sweden suspects by Denmark are preparing to resist it. From the scanty resources of

Norway I should suppose however that the resistance must be entirely ineffectual, unless the aid now covertly given by Denmark, if given at all should lead to a war between the two countries, and unless also that Great Britain in the new circumstances in which she may find herself sees it her interest to support the Norwegians.[6]

Of course, Clay was only on the fringe of all these events, learning of them second hand by newspapers, letters, rumors, and comments by individuals he had met in Norway and later in Sweden. Meanwhile, the most important matter — that of England's war with the United States — was wrapped up in an enigma. Clay could not know whether England would attempt to send large numbers of troops to America, now that the European fighting had apparently ended, or whether the aggravations of blockades and impressments could now end, paving the way for real peace negotiations.

In any case, Clay found himself, one of five commissioners to negotiate for peace, all alone in the designated city with nothing to do but wait and listen to rumors. He occupied part of the last week of April by taking a trip to Trollhattan, on the Gota River about 45 miles north of Gottenburg. He wrote Russell that "altho the weather was bad felt ourselves abundantly compensated for the jaunt in a view of the canal."[7] The canal, dug through solid rock, was two miles long, twenty feet wide and eight feet deep, as later described by John Quincy Adams. There were also waterfalls in the area to enhance the pleasantness of the scenery.[8]

Also in the latter part of April, Clay had removed from the Inn and taken rooms in a more agreeable location. Again writing to Russell a few days later, he commented that, "The good people of Gottenburg are becoming more civil to us than they were when you were here. I have dined at Count Rosen's and we have been invited to dine at several other houses."[9] Clay's companions were his aide, Christopher Hughes and possibly Col. George B. Milligan, the private secretary of James Bayard.

Milligan had just arrived in Gottenburg on the evening of April 30, bringing with him correspondence from Bayard and Gallatin in London. Since their arrival in England, both of them had done little but see the general tourist attractions in and near the city, dine informally with persons having no connections with the negotiating affairs, and observe the popular welcoming of Louis XVIII of France en route to the restoration of the House of Bourbon. On receipt of their letter, Clay was surprised to learn that his two American colleagues were staying in the enemy's capital. In separate letters to Clay from Bayard and Gallatin (dated April 20 and 22 respectively), they reported that they had already learned of Clay's and Russell's arrival in Gottenburg. But since these letters were not in response to those being carried from Gottenburg by Shaler, they still had not learned that Gallatin was to be one of the commissioners.

Bayard, writing first, congratulated his two new associates on their safe ocean passage and noted briefly his own travels from St. Petersburg, and his arrival in England, which almost coincided with the Allies' capture of Paris and Bonaparte's abdication. He said of the British,

> The intelligence completely turned the heads of all ranks who seem to have thought of nothing since but the means of manifesting their joy on the occasion. It is much to be apprehended that this great & unexpected event will have an unfavorable influence upon the state of affairs between the U. States & G. Britain.

As Bayard viewed the effect of events on the British ministry, he reported that,

> The sudden reduction of their naval & military establishments would create much embarrassment and the American war furnishes too good a pretense to avoid it and the great augmentation of their disposable force presents an additional temptation to prosecute the war. You must also know that the temper of the country is highly excited against us & decidedly expressed in favor of the continuance of hostilities.

Bayard acknowledged that these were his views since he had not communicated with any member of the British government. In fact, Foreign Secretary Castlereagh was then in Paris. In his absence, no British commissioners had been appointed, and the best Bayard could learn through unofficial sources, none would be named until the British received official notice "of the appointment of the American Commissioners & of their arrival at the place of rendezvous." Under these circumstances Bayard and Gallatin thought Clay

and Russell should "make the official communication."

On the subject of location for the meetings, Bayard recommended that a town in Holland should be substituted for Gottenburg. He added that, "You may rely upon the friendly dispositions of the Prince of Orange," who had nominated a minister to the United States as one of his first acts of government on his arrival in Holland from England in November 1813.[10]

Gallatin's letter to Clay was similar in content, except that his concurrence with Bayard on shifting the negotiation site was hedged with the realization that he still had no official notification of his appointment to the new peace mission, and also that he did not know if instructions had limited the locale to Gottenburg. He expressed the view that Holland was a friendly country and that the proximity to England would be an advantage since he expected the Americans would be "compelled to act with men clothed with limited authorities & who might at all times plead a want of instructions." On this Gallatin was to be proved far sighted.

In echoing Bayard's fear of increased British military pressure against the United States, Gallatin suggested, in addition, that "our own divisions and the hostile attitude of the Eastern States give room to apprehend that a continuance of the war might prove vitally fatal to the United States." Gallatin's negative views of peace hopes were shown in his belief that the British would not be disposed to make concessions and would not be displeased at a failure of the negotiations. He said the war was popular in England and that their national pride could not be satisfied without "the chastisement of America." He said that the mass of the people believed the Americans were the aggressors in the war as well as the Allies of Bonaparte. While Castlereagh and other British leaders might not be so hostile, they were not likely to act contrary to public opinion. Gallatin had one hope — that Czar Alexander's wishes in favor of peace with America might have influence with Castlereagh as the two powerful European leaders conferred in Paris.[11]

Both Gallatin and Bayard had a firm foundation for their apprehensions. They lived with daily evidence that public opinion and the British press were highly vocal in castigating America and both had a strong influence on the British government. Within days after the arrival of the Gallatins (Albert's son James, was with him) and Bayard in London, the city went wild for several days with cheering and illuminations in celebration of the victory over Napoleon. And *The Times* of London was quick to turn with viciousness on England's only remaining enemy.

Editorializing on April 15, *The Times* said,

> It is understood that part of our army in France will be immediately transferred to America, to finish the war there, with the same glory as in Europe, and to place peace on a foundation equally firm and lasting. Now, that the Tyrant BOUNAPARTE has been consigned to infamy, there is no public feeling in this country stronger than that of indignation against the Americans

as the United States' conduct is "so black, so loathsome, so hateful, that it naturally stirs up the indignation that we have described" and thus England must maintain the doctrine of "*No Peace with* JAMES MADISON." Hoping that the Eastern States would agree to treat separately for peace with Great Britain, *The Times* referred to them as "the most moral, the most cultivated, the most intelligent, the best in every respect," and that they were in the "thraldom of the Southern States." The paper said it referred to Madison only because he stands at the head of the list, "not but that Mr. GALLATIN may be more artful, Mr. CLAY more furious, Mr. JEFFERSON more malignant."[12]

A few days later, expressing the hope of a future victory by Wellington in America, *The Times* said, "MR. MADISON'S dirty, swindling maneuvers in respect to Louisiana and the Floridas remain to be punished."[13] Again on May 17, the paper poured out its venom on its newest arch-enemy, the "wretched tool of Bounaparte," scoffing that,

> Surely it would be the very extreme of imbecility, to stop short in the chastisement prepared for so black a traitor.... If ever there was an individual who merited the contempt and execration of two mighty nations, for his treachery to both, it is JAMES MADISON. He has calumniated, knowingly and wilfully calumniated England, and has prostituted the honour of America; he has injured both by a train of the most degrading and infamous subserviency to the dictates of a foreign Tyrant, to whom America and England were alike hateful.

They assigned Madison's motives to "venality, or malice."[14]

The following day, they connected their attack to the approaching peace negotiations, saying,

> We shall demand indemnity for the expenses of a war into which Mr. MADISON and his doctrines drew us, at the moment that he thought most convenient to himself and his patron BOUNAPARTE. We shall insist on security against any more insidious attacks on Canada; a security which cannot be obtained as long as the American frontier is within a hundred miles of the great Lakes, or within ten miles of Lake Champlain. We shall enquire a little into the American title of Louisiana; and we shall certainly not permit the base attack on the territory of our Ally in Florida to go unpunished.[15]

On the 20th, *The Times* accused Madison of going to war with Britain,

> at the very moment when BUONAPARTE crossed the Niemen, at the head of half a million of soldiers professedly to put the last hand to the Continental System, for the ruin of Great Britain. Then, when our fate (as this serpent thought) hung trembling in the balance, did he let slip the dogs of war, to seize and bring us to the ground. The scene is completely and wonderfully changed. BUONAPARTE is fallen, Madison is disgraced and discomfited, and Great Britain has the means of inflicting ample and deserved vengeance.... It is true that Negociators of great respectability have been appointed on the part of Great Britain to meet the Genevese democrat GALLATIN, the furious orator CLAY, the surly BAYARD, and Mr. RUSSELL, the worthy defender of the forged revocation of the Berlin and Milan Decrees.

But *The Times* did not expect the British diplomatists to "condescend to discuss the impudent nonsense called an American doctrine, about Impressment and Native Allegiance, which was in truth, a mere pretext for war on the part of Mr. MADISON."[16]

And finally, on June 2, when *The Times* had thought, in error, that Gallatin had already left for Ghent, the paper gave its prescription for peace, "Our demands may be couched in a single word, '*Submission*'.... We trust ere long the British flag will fly on the capital [sic] of Washington."[17]

The Courier, the government's mouthpiece, seemed only a little less vicious, but no less harsh in supporting a petition voted at a public meeting in the palace yard. It called for

Vigorous war with America! till America accedes to the following demands

A new boundary line for Canada.

A new boundary for the Indians.

The Independence of the Indians, and the integrity of their boundaries, to be guaranteed by Great Britain.

The Americans to be excluded from the fisheries on the coasts of British North America.

The Americans to be excluded from all intercourse with the British West Indies Islands.

The Americans to be excluded from trading with our East Indies possessions, and their *pretended* right to the north-west coast of America to be extinguished forever.

The Americans not to be allowed to incorporate the Floridas with their Republic; and the cession of New Orleans to be required, in order to ensure to us the due enjoyment of our privilege to navigate the Mississippi: and here it may also be a question, in how the arrangements made between Spain, France, and America, respecting Louisiana, can come into discussion.

Finally the distinct abandonment of the new-fangled American public law; the admission of the international law as it is at present received in Europe; the recognition of our "right of search."[18]

While these malevolent exhortations by the British press continued through May, the correspondence of the American peace commissioners was still lagging the British harangues as well as were historical events. Bayard's and Gallatin's letters of mid–April were written too early for them to develop any true impressions they were shortly to obtain of British feelings through these newspaper editorials. Nevertheless, the letters enabled Clay to focus on some of the many ramifications surrounding the atmosphere of negotiations in a very fast-changing political and military climate. The events would provide a sort of guide to follow the correspondence of the next few weeks. On the receipt of the April 22nd letter from the "London visitors," Clay immediately communicated his views to Russell in a letter dated May 1, and answered Bayard and Gallatin on the following day.

In his letter to Russell, Clay first broached the subject of "a change in the theatre of the proposed negotiation." He regretted extremely not having the opinion and advice of Russell and Adams, but said, "Our commissions oppose no obstacle to "a change." On this he said,

I recollect, before the Commissions were made out, asking the President if they would restrict us

to this place and his observing that they had been presented to him for his signature, so prepared, but he had ordered them to be changed, which was accordingly done to their present unrestricted form. Neither are we limited to the instructions to Gottenburg; but they certainly contemplate Sweden, as the scene of the negotiations.

Clay noted the reasoning behind Gottenburg was to facilitate correspondence through Russell and Adams with Sweden and Russia, respectively, as friends of the United States. But Clay wondered if, while a change in venue would compliment Holland and improve lines of communications, the removal of Gottenburg as the place of negotiation might create a coolness by the Swedish government. He felt Russell was the best judge of Swedish attitude. He proposed that it be made to appear that the change was at the instance of England and would so advise Bayard and Gallatin along with notifying them of his consent to the change. Of course, he could not commit Russell or Adams. In any case, he adamantly said, "I shall not consent to go to London."[19]

On the 2nd, Clay wrote a letter, to be carried by Christopher Hughes to Bayard and Gallatin, expanding on his thoughts to Russell. Acknowledging the receipt of their letters of April 20 and 22, he advised them of the absence of Russell and Adams leaving him alone to respond to their letters. As for Adams, Clay said he had no information except from Russell this very day, that Adams proposed to leave St. Petersburg about April 20 and be in Sweden (probably Stockholm) by May 1, the day before writing this letter.

Taking up, first, the matter of changing the place of negotiation, Clay described it as "a measure attended with some difficulty and requiring on our part great delicacy." He told his associates in London that both Great Britain and the United States (the latter through Russell) had, by this time, presented notes to the Swedish crown prince to advise him of the contemplated negotiations in Gottenburg and solicited his government's sanction and hospitality. Clay thought the United States "ought not lightly jeopardize the Crown Prince's friendship."

Nevertheless, Clay was willing "to give our instructions a liberal interpretation," and said that if Holland could be substituted for Gottenburg, "in such manner as that the change shall be understood to be at the instance of Great Britain, you have my consent to make it." He expressed the hope that any explanation to Sweden would not only "retain us her friendship, but cast upon the other party all the unfriendly consequences, should there be any, growing out of the measure." This could be a tricky maneuver.

On the subject of going to London, Clay was vehement and adamant (as he had been to Russell). He felt that following Britain's rejection of Russian mediation, the United States could

> have demanded that its own seat of Government should be the theatre for discussing propositions for peace. Having waived this, and acceded to one of the alternatives offered by the other party, I do not think that we ought to submit to further condescension, especially when we have yet to see the example in British history of that haughty people having been conciliated by the condescension of their enemy.

Clay was already showing that his life-long antipathy toward Britain was going to make him a very formidable negotiator on behalf of his country. He showed it further as he went on to tell his absent colleagues,

> I am deeply sensible of the magnitude of the present crisis which I have endeavored to view in all its immediate and remote consequences. And the result of my reflections is, that we shall best promote the objects of our Mission, and acquit our selves of our duty, by presenting a firm and undismayed countenance.

He believed the drama of Europe, liberated from the despotism of Bonaparte, would favor the United States in the negotiation, as the continent would not "be indifference to the enormous power and the enormous pretensions of G. Britain on the ocean." He expected the European Powers would impose limits of Britain and "if she is wise she will readily acquiesce in them."

Finally, touching on the matter of some official communication to the British of the arrival of the American mission, Clay again expressed his embarrassment at standing alone in his advice and actions. But, he said, since the British had invited them to Europe,

> That Government ought by the promptitude of is own measures to have rendered unnecessary such notification on our part. Again referring to himself as "alone, one of five who compose the Commission,"

he said he would waive the point of etiquette (regarding notification), but added parenthetically, "I certainly am not going during this negotiation to give consequence to any affair of mere etiquette."[20] Though Clay then sent his friends copies of the new commission and new instructions, it was clear again that a man who had watched the British desecrate his youthful home; had fought a duel; had put down John Randolph as a freshman congressman; and who had in large voice and quiet persuasion led his country into war with England — he would not show weakness, but be hard and demanding. He was not yet "The Great Compromiser."

Under separate cover, Clay sent a private letter to Gallatin in response to one from the former treasury secretary. Clay told him that the Senate's rejection of Gallatin's nomination the previous summer "was very generally condemned by the people, and produced a reaction highly favorable to you." He noted further that Gallatin would have been added to the new mission except that it was believed he was already on his way home to America. In a P.S., Clay told Gallatin that his nomination had been approved by all but two or three in the Senate.

Clay's main point in his letter to Gallatin was to allay his fears of trouble with that part of the United States so strongly Federalist and in opposition to the Madison administration. He told Gallatin,

> I have no doubt that a game of swaggering and gasconade has been played off there, without any serious intention to push matters to extremity. After a great deal of blustering about raising 20,000 men, and declaring the freedom of the port of Boston, a meeting of the malcontents there determined it inexpedient to take such measure during the last session of the Legislature, The truth is they want men — they want money — the principal actors want courage. Yet I would not despise these appearances. If the British Government should determine to land a considerable force in the Eastern States, avowing friendship to them, and an intention only to war with the Southern States, or with the Administration, certainly very serious consequences might ensue, though I believe they would fall far short of conquest or dissolution.[21]

Carrying the correspondence to Clay's colleagues in London, Christopher Hughes left Gottenburg on May 3, accompanied by Col. George

Milligan. On reaching England, Milligan had passport difficulties and was delayed three days at Harwich as Hughes carried the letters on to Bayard and Gallatin. While held up in Harwich, Milligan wrote a brief note to Bayard describing Clay's somewhat reluctant reactions to the proposal for a change of locale for the negotiations. He also said of him,

> His Excellency is very commodiously and handsomely established, and either dislikes the idea of moving, or thinks it will occasion delay in commencing the negotiation. He is far from believing we stand in as much need of peace, as I think, your much better judgment is impressed with: and should Mr. R. coincide with his opinions, joined to the known violent sentiment of Mr. A., I should fear but little good will be produced by an immediate meeting.[22]

Just before writing those letters to London on May 2, Clay received his first letter from Russell, having arrived in Stockholm on April 25. Russell wrote this brief note to Clay on the 26th. Their correspondence was to take five or six days to travel between the capital and Gottenburg. In addition to telling Clay what he knew of Adams's plans, Russell told Clay he expected to be presented to the king of Sweden on the 27th. Clay enclosed a transcript of Russell's note in his letters to London, and apparently had sent copies of the London based envoys' letters to Russell by way of the Portuguese consul who left Gottenburg for Stockholm on May 2. Clay's only comment to Russell on the exchange of correspondence was that, "Mr. Gallatin appears to have the subject [change of venue] so much at heart that I think it highly probable that your consent will be *presumed*." He added that he thought there could be "no comparison between this place and Amsterdam, or the Hague." Good or bad?

The only other matter of importance Clay mentioned in this letter to Russell was that he thought it might be advisable to give the Swedish government a "frank communication ... on the nature of the principal ground of dispute between G. Britain and America." This was to elicit further amicable support by Sweden for America's position in the negotiations.

Not until May 8 (as far as is known) was there any further communication to or from Clay with any of his mission colleagues, or for that matter,

anywhere else. On that date, he finally received the long letter from Crawford descriptive of the momentous events taking place in Paris and in France up to April 8. On May 9, Clay sent a copy of this letter, heavy with ciphered material, to Russell saying the key furnished him was not adapted to interpret the contents. Clay was hopeful Russell could remedy the problem.

The following day, Clay wrote a long answer to Crawford. He expressed his great surprise at the rapid and unexpected turn of affairs.

> When I left America a general peace in Europe was anticipated, but no human sagacity could then have foreseen the astonishing events which have since occurred in France — events which have put the mind more in that state of amazement which attends a deep dramatic performance, or an agitated dream, than belongs to the sober condition of real transactions.

Clay thought that on the arrival of the Allies at the Rhine, a peace would be offered Napoleon that he would find acceptable. He now hoped that Louis XVIII and the French people would accept the Constitution adopted by their Senate — which, he believed, would secure to the people "as much liberty as they are capable of enjoying."

The letter included a brief summary of American news up to this time known to Clay — that no lieutenant general had been appointed in the army, and that it appeared that Maj. Gen. James Wilkinson had been arrested because of his failure in the march on Montreal (or rather Kingston) with disaster in the Niagara area resulting. Clay then took some space to advise some friends of Crawford on some land-title disputes suggesting the other parties get what cash they can from them rather than try to possess land with an insecure title.

Finally, Clay repeated his sad refrain that, "I am here entirely alone keeping the ground until my scattered colleagues are assembled." He felt that Crawford (a former president pro tem of the Senate and a future candidate for the U.S. presidency) was as competent as himself to determine the probable issues to be considered once the negotiations were opened. Then in a tone of more confidence, Clay said,

> The general peace will doubtless have much influence upon it. I cannot but hope that the continent will provide, in the general peace, some limits to

the enormous maritime power and pretensions of G. Britain. Indeed it appears to me that the allies have matters amongst themselves to arrange not less different than the overthrow of Bonaparte, and I confess I shall not be surprised to find some who are now very good friends who were inveterate foes. Let what will happen, we must not despair of the Republic. If G. Britain rejecting the counsels of moderation, determine to persevere in the War, and to chastise America, as is imprudently proclaimed by some of her prints to be her purpose or her policy, I cannot but cherish the belief that she will find the energies of a free people equal to the crisis. I sincerely hope that she may not be thus unwise, and that our mission may terminate in the extension to America of that peace in which all Europe, it would at this moment seem, are about to participate.[23]

Over the ensuing three weeks, Clay's meager correspondence left him progressively more frustrated and embittered. As far as is known, he wrote only five letters during this time. On May 12, the cartel *Chauncey* arrived from New York where it left on April 10. It carried new instructions (with no essential change) and American news as old as April 9 from New York and April 7 from Washington. Clay summarized this news in letters to Russell on May 13th, to Crawford on the 14th, and to Bayard and Gallatin on the 16th.

Clay told his various correspondents that the president had, on March 31, recommended to Congress "a repeal of the Embargo and of the Non-importation system." In one letter, he learned that the bill had passed the House. He cited the liberation of commerce of so many friendly powers as the inducement for the recommendation. From other news tidbits, he reported that Wilkinson had not been arrested, that Federalist lost ground in a New England election, that a bill to establish a national bank was pending before Congress, and that the Canadian governor, Gen. Sir George Prevost, had proposed an armistice. (Clay could not judge the chances of it.)

By the time Clay wrote Bayard and Gallatin, he had received a letter from Russell, dated the 8th, expressing his reluctance about changing the seat of negotiations. In the letter to London, Clay quoted Russell, except for the matter enclosed in the following brackets:

The apprehension of any *serious* evil from this quarter, occasioned by our change of position, is I trust without foundation — I regret however that I had not known the opinions of Mess, Gallatin & Bayard in season to shape my communications here accordingly — Something like a retrograde movement will now be necessary and it may require some address to reconcile this Government to the new arrangement — I hope it may be in our power to throw the responsibility on the British Government [— but am somewhat afraid the original proposition will appear to have come from our Colleagues — My personal convenience & inclination are, indeed, opposed to the change but considerations of this kind must yield to those of public utility —] I am placed rather in an awkward predicament, by your communication, as the uncertainty, in which it leaves our ultimate location, disqualifies me from adapting my movements here, [with sufficient precision,] to either alternative.[24]

The same day (the 16th) that Clay wrote Bayard and Gallatin, he also wrote another short note to Russell responding to that which Clay quoted to his London colleagues. Clay took note of Russell's pleasure at his presentation to the Swedish king and queen, and then asked if the truth of an article could be obtained in Stockholm. It was to the effect that "the Allies on the 1st of March, besides the public treaties, entered into a secret stipulation with G. Britain that they would not interfere in the American controversy." Clay continued to write, "I cannot credit it. Such a stipulation would have been dishonorable on the part of any of them, disgraceful to the Emperor Alexander." Clay mentioned only one other matter worthy of note in this letter to Russell. He told of receiving news from London as late as May 6 which contained "a vague rumor ... that Admiral Gambier & some other persons were appointed to treat with us."[25]

This last piece of news was accurate and would eventually relieve Clay of his boredom — but not for another two weeks. Even as late as his next letter to Russell, written May 27, Clay still knew nothing of the developments taking place in England that would suddenly change his situation. Writing to Russell, he acknowledged receipt of two more letters (written by Russell on the 16th and 17th) but unfortunately had to respond that he was not permitted to "communicate something to you of an interesting nature about the prospects of the joint mission." Russell was to comment in a later letter, "Perhaps never was a joint mission so disjointed & scattered."[26]

Clay went on in his letter to reveal his growing depression.

> I am equally without information as to the movements of Mr. Adams, whose arrival here has been expected, on his own information, since the 10th. inst. In this state of painful ignorance and solicitude I have to put into requisition every resource to bear me up against ennui. Indeed the delay in opening the negotiation, whose result, be it what it may, is so anxiously looked for at home, is inexpressibly distressing.

Clay's foreboding was also underlying his comments that Crawford in Paris and Russell in Stockholm would not likely receive the favorable treatment previously hoped for. Though he did not say so overtly, Clay feared that both France and Sweden were fast becoming the victims of British hegemony. Sweden's position was revealed partly in a controversy arising out of the capture of 20 British prizes by the American armed privateer brig *Rattlesnake* which were then taken into Trondheim, Norway, where the captain and owner sought to have them condemned and thus obtain their value in cash. With Norway expected to become a possession of Sweden, Clay suggested to Russell, as American minister to Sweden, it was his duty to take up the matter with the Swedish government. But Clay added, "I fear however, I confess, that the relations between England and Sweden are such, in regard to Norway, that you will not be able to do any thing."[27]

Four days later, Clay's frustration and depression was to come to an abrupt end. That morning, May 31, he received two letters, one from Russell and one from Bayard and Gallatin. Russell's very brief note, written on May 25 from Stockholm, had one short sentence of exhilarating news, "I am at length able to announce to you the arrival of Mr. Adams at this place, he reached here yesterday evening —."[28]

John Quincy Adams, American minister to Russia, and special envoy to treat for peace with Great Britain, left St. Petersburg on the afternoon of April 28, detailing, in his expansive diary, all his joys and tribulations arising from his travel. Stopping only for meals and changes of horses and carriages, he rode westward for 33 hours. After one night's sleep, he continued another 19 hours, had another rest of seven hours, and ended with a three-hour ride into Reval, nearly 100 miles

west on the south shore of the Gulf of Finland, arriving before noon on May 1. He was to spend nearly three weeks in frustration similar to Clay's, anxiously awaiting the break up of ice in the Gulf to permit him to sail in the ship *Ulysses*. While stalled in Reval, he learned of the defeat of Napoleon and of the arrival of Clay and Russell in Gottenburg.[29]

At last, after a false start on May 16 (turned back by ice), the *Ulysses* finally sailed on May 20 and reached Stockholm on the 25th. After taking lodging at a tavern, Adams went to Russell's lodging and spent the evening with him, and his 12-year-old son, and Mr. Lawrence (Russell's secretary). It was during this meeting that Adams learned of Gallatin's appointment to the mission and that Bayard and Gallatin were urging the removal of the seat of negotiation from Gottenburg to Holland or England with Clay consenting conditionally to go to Holland. On the 27th, Adams moved in with Russell. After reading the many letters, dispatches, and newspapers in Russell's possession, Adams wrote in his diary, "They convinced me beyond every doubt that this mission will be as fruitless as the last, and led me strongly to doubt whether I ought to consent to go to Holland."[30]

Though Adams had become depressed, Clay was elated. The letter from Bayard and Gallatin, received by Clay on May 31, was dated May 17 in London, and was addressed to Adams, Clay, and Russell. It informed them that notice had been presented to the British government of the appointment of the five-man mission to conclude a treaty of peace and of the arrival of Clay and Russell in Gottenburg. Enclosed with their letter was a copy of this notice as well as a copy of the British response by Lord Henry Bathurst (secretary for war and the colonies), and an American reply to Bathurst.

Bathurst's note of May 16 to Bayard and Gallatin acknowledged that the Americans were prepared to meet with British counterparts and therefore gave notice that the prince regent would forthwith appoint British commissioners. His note also removed Clay's concern of changing the place of negotiations by suggesting that they "should be held at Ghent in the low countries," due to the important changes in the situation of affairs in Europe.[31] Bayard and Gallatin accepted

Ghent in a note sent the following day, the same day they wrote their colleagues in Gottenburg.

In their letter to the mission members in Sweden, Bayard and Gallatin supported the move to Ghent advising that Sweden could not "interpose any good offices on our behalf, being no longer wanted by the allies, whilst she needs the active assistance of this country [England] in order to obtain the possession of Norway." Still, they could not notify their colleagues that a British mission had yet been appointed.

Incidentally, on receipt of these two exhilarating letters, Clay sent two letters to Stockholm — one privately to Russell and the other jointly to Russell and Adams. The letters were carried by John Connell, an American residing in Europe, To Russell he wrote,

> I congratulate you most heartily upon the prospect of once more seeing Land. Indeed the passage through the North Sea was not more insupportable than my imprisonment here — My letter to yourself and Mr. Adams explains all —. I owe you ten thousand obligations for your kind and frequent letters during my residence here. They have served to sustain my spirits.[32]

To the two of them, Clay wrote that he had, just that same morning, received notice from their associates in London that the negotiations had now been transferred to Ghent and that "Admiral Gambier, Mr. Golsby and Mr. Adam [sic] are British Comm appointed to treat with us." He had not yet learned the correct spelling of their names.

Clay also informed Adams and Russell that he intended to leave the following day (June 1) and go by way of Copenhagen, thence overland "by Hamburgh [sic] and the most direct route to Ghent." Meanwhile, he had ordered Captain Angus, of the corvette *John Adams*, to be in readiness "to transport you to such port as you may think proper to direct, the moment you may arrive here." Clay was told the ship could actually sail that evening. Clay added an additional suggestion.

> If you do not choose to employ on this service the Corvette, you will have the goodness to inform Capt. Angus accordingly, and direct him to proceed to the port the most convenient to Ghent which I presume will be Antwerp or Ostend — He may in that case require some documentary protection.[33]

Clay did not repeat a P.S. he had sent in the letter to Russell on May 27, to the effect that, "Capt. Angus had been extremely ill, having violent fever with mental derangement. But he is getting better."[34]

Clay did not get away from Gottenburg on June 1, but did send a reply to Bayard and Gallatin to inform them of Adams' arrival in Stockholm, and of his pending departure, now set for June 2, saying he hoped to be in Ghent within three weeks. He expected Adams and Russell to follow as soon as possible since the *John Adams* was at their disposal.

On the same day (May 31) that Clay received the happy news from Stockholm and London, Adams and Russell received Clay's depressing letter of May 27. On the basis of it, Adams overcame his thoughts of giving up on the mission to return to St. Petersburg, and, instead, resolved to leave Stockholm, as it turned out, on the same day that Clay left Gottenburg. Russell was not yet ready to leave and stayed a bit longer in Stockholm.

Adams left Stockholm on June 2 at six in the evening. At two the following morning, "At Gran, the third post-house, I was already two hours in arrear," he wrote in his memoirs. "As I alighted from my carriage at Gran," he wrote the following day,

> I was accosted by Mr. Connell, who was going from Gottenburg to Stockholm as a special messenger from Mr. Clay to Mr. Russell and me. He gave me, together with the letter from Mr. Clay, more than thirty letters and dispatches, most of which had been forwarded by Mr. Clay.

Adams took a few minutes to read the letter addressed to him and Russell, resealed it with its enclosures (keeping only a duplicate of his powers to treat with the British), and sent it on with Connell to deliver to Russell. He verbally urged Russell to "use the utmost possible dispatch to join me at Gottenburg, or to give me notice if he should conclude to go on by land."

Adams left Gran at three in the morning — "now three hours in arrear of my time." He travelled all day, detailing in his memoirs, every cost of carriage and horse rental and the time lost at various posts where changes were required. After a night's rest, he was on his way again at five in the morning of June 4, riding all day, all that night, and continuing to the evening of the 5th, when he stopped at Trollhattan to view the canal as Clay had done late in April. Adams finally reached Gottenburg on the evening of June 6. Russell joined him on the 10th. And the next day both of them boarded the *John Adams*, receiving a 13-gun salute.[35]

It was the same day they boarded the *John Adams* that John Quincy Adams related his version of the episode of "Captain Barron" (so called by Adams) seeking passage on the corvette to the United States. In his account, Adams stated,

> I thought he could not, and had expressed the same opinion in relation to fifty or sixty American seamen who are here waiting for an opportunity of returning to America. Mr. Russell being of the same opinion, none of them were admitted.

Mr. Wyer, whom Clay had objected to before leaving the United States, made another appearance here attempting to gain passage to Ghent. Russell objected and Adams supported him. They sailed before dawn on June 12.[36]

As for Nones' version of Clay's dealings with Barron, which Nones dates as May 1814, it is most likely wrong, as it was written many years later. Of interest, and not less confusing, are two other incidents told by Nones. They, too, are probably true to a point, but mistaken in the names of those involved. He names the principal characters in both stories as Clay and Adams. Though both sailed on the ship, there is no evidence that they were aboard together at any time unless it was sometime later when the ship was in port in Holland shortly after the mission gathered there late in June or early July.

Nones related that Adams and Russell worked out a scheme "one fine day" to while "away a weary hour" and play a joke on Clay. Their plan was to have all three commissioners climb to the fore-top and there have some of the crew tie the three of them to the rigging and keep them prisoner there until they agreed to give the sailors a "horn," or some grog. Accordingly, Russell reached the fore-top "over the foot-hooks, and Messrs. Adams and Clay through the lubber hole. All arrived there, the process of tying them to the weather fore-topmast standing rigging took place, Mr. Clay struggling to oppose, the rest acquiescing." Adams and Russell promised to pay "the ransom" and were soon cut loose. But Clay "re-mained stubborn and indignant, and could not be induced to promise anything." He was left alone, tied to the rigging. After Adams and Russell were on deck, Captain Angus learned of Clay's predicament and ordered him freed.

Nones wrote that Clay "could not be pacified at the outrage perpetrated on his dignity, and could not be induced to look upon the transaction as a jest. The consequence," according to Nones,

> was that he and Captain Angus, and Messrs. Adams and Russell had a serious rupture. Time healed the incident between Mr. Clay and Mr. Russell, but not between Messrs. Adams and Clay. They were, during the rest of the voyage, at "dagger points," and it was currently reported and believed on board the Corvette, that Mr. Clay had challenged Mr. Adams to mortal combat.

Nones stated that on arrival at Gottenburg, Adams and Clay went to separate hotels.[37] The episode could not have taken place en route to Gottenburg unless someone other than Adams was involved, as he was still in Russia at the time of Clay's Atlantic crossing.

In further confusion over the incident, Nones stated that a complaint (he doesn't say by whom) was made to the secretary of the navy against Captain Angus' conduct, that he replied discourteously, was suspended, his mind later became deranged (Clay had evidenced symptoms of this in his May 27 letter to Russell), and still later committed suicide while in command of the New York navy yard. There is truth in the latter portion of this account though the argument with his superiors was the consequence of a dispute over his job assignment in the mid–1820s.

In September 1823, Angus wrote to Secretary of the Navy Samuel L. Southard, asking for command of the Philadelphia or Sackett's Harbor navy station, preferring the former. He wrote the Navy Department twice more in September and again in November when his letter was rather curt—

> Would you be pleased to order me to that command [Philadelphia navy yard], or to the command of the *Washington* seventy-four, which is now without a post captain.

Southard responded later in November that no action would be taken for the present and that there were other applicants senior to him.

Angus replied to this letter in early December saying he wished to receive equal pay with other captains. When he heard nothing further, he wrote Southard again in April 1824, this time saying,

> If you want to know my name, you will see it at the bottom of the letter. My grandfather and father were Scotchmen, and I was born in Philadelphia. I wish you to answer me directly whether you will give me the command without any further palaver; if you don't, I will, appeal to your master, the President of the United States, and my superior.

Of course, Southard was also his superior, as was President Monroe (at that date). But the tone of the letter was clearly one which would cause a superior in command to consider with care entrusting command of men to one who wrote in such a manner.

A month later, Secretary Southard sent Angus' letter to Captain Samuel Evans, commanding officer of the New York navy yard where Angus was attached, and requested Evans to inquire of Angus, in the presence of one or more officers, whether he wrote the previous letter. Evans carried out the secretary's instructions, but Angus refused to incriminate himself, though admitting he had written Southard several times. On June 6, 1824, Southard notified Angus that his latest letter was placed in the hands of the president and it was agreed that Angus should be separated from the service. Though no further letter from Angus appears in this collection, he apparently addressed one more to the president on November 30, 1824, requesting reinstatement to his rank or pecuniary relief. No further response was forthcoming until April 25, 1825, when the president wrote that there would be no reinstatement, but that Angus had a just claim for a pension, having been disabled in the line of duty. This letter was signed by President John Quincy Adams, a passenger on Angus's ship 11 years earlier.[38] Aside from Nones' sometimes inaccurate narrative, there is no known confirmation of Angus' subsequent derangement and suicide.

The second incident related by Nones supposedly took place aboard the *John Adams* when it was en route from Gottenburg to Holland — a time when only Adams was aboard. In his preface, Nones described John Quincy Adams as "an old sea dog ... always jovial and lightsome in his manner ... full of fun and frolic" and "never let a good opportunity for a joke on others escape his grasp." It is hard to find that personality in Adams' writings, however. Nevertheless, the midshipman advised that the account of this "little transaction was for the eye of my male readers solely — forbidding my lady readers for perusing this article — unless however their curiosity should exceed their prudence."

Nones began by telling of the vessel's accommodations for the crew, near the foremast, "now called water closets, then we called them 'beehives.'" He then noted that

> both Mr. Clay and Mr. Adams were walking on the weather side of the quarter deck in conversation, when Mr. Adams asked Mr. Clay if he had seen our Beehives. Mr. Clay said No — and did not know that we carried Bees or Beehives. Mr. Adams assured him to the contrary, and both started forward to see the sight. Arriving at the spot, Mr. Adams opened the door of the hive, and playfully asked Mr. Clay to look in. Mr. Clay did so, and as soon as apprized of the nature of Mr. Adams' joke, felt indignant. But nothing daunted, he was equal to the occasion. Mr. Adams, determined to be funny and stept into the closet, calling Mr. Clay's attention to some pert of it. Mr. Clay took in the situation at a glance, slammed the door of the closet and turned the batten.[39]

This time Adams was left a prisoner until one of the crew liberated him. Nones states that "Mr. Adams felt that he was sold — and felt cheap." But it cured him of further joking on the voyage. It seems hardly likely that the episode took place quite as told by Nones so many years later, or that Clay, after almost two months at sea, would not have learned of the "bee-hives."

27

GATHERING OF THE COMMISSIONERS

The mission was beginning to congeal. Though the month of June 1814 was as long as any other 30-day month, it went much faster for the five American commissioners sent to Europe to treat for peace with Great Britain. No longer were any of them fighting boredom in their long wait to serve in their appointed capacities. Now they were all on the move to the newly designated site for negotiations — Ghent, Belgium. In transit, they left less in the way of letters and other observations of their activities during the month, but these few reveal interesting experiences.

Almost nothing is known of Henry Clay's experiences in traveling from Gottenburg to Ghent. Jonathan Russell traveled with John Quincy Adams, and all that is known of their trip is described in Adams' *Memoirs* or letters. There are also accounts by Gallatin and Bayard of their experiences as they made their way from London, by way of Paris to Ghent.

In a letter to his wife, Louisa Catherine Adams (left with their son, Charles Francis, in St. Petersburg), John Quincy Adams described the voyage from Gottenburg (which he spelled "Gothenburg") to the Texel, Holland, "like a party of pleasure — a large, comfortable and fast sailing ship, excellent fare and agreeable company."[1]

The *John Adams* was off the shore of Texel at eight in the morning of June 17. Captain Angus had a gun fired for a pilot and two came aboard a couple hours later. Due to a very shallow channel, the ship could not enter the harbor until mid afternoon. As Adams, Russell, his son, and their aides made preparation to go ashore, a Dutch officer came on board and informed the Americans they could not land and proceed to Amsterdam

"until he should have written to the Minister of Marine and receive his answer, which would take four days. We pleaded our office, public character, and business." The Dutchman finally agreed to refer to his superior. He returned in less than half an hour with apologies and excuses, and an order from his superior "to give every assistance and show every due distinction to the ship, and that the Ministers should land when they pleased, and proceed by land or by water, as was most agreeable to themselves."

As Adams and Russell prepared to go ashore, Captain Angus ordered a salute to be fired in their honor with the intention of rendering another salute the following day for the local admiral and fort. Adams warned Angus that the first salute would be mis-interpreted, as it was. The admiral in the fort returned the ship's firing gun for gun.

Later, when Adams and Russell went ashore, they took the advice of Mr. Hoogland, the American consular agent at the Helder, who told them that unless they should have a particularly favorable wind, a sea voyage to Amsterdam would take three days. They decided to travel overland beginning at five the next morning. Russell hired a carriage and horses, while Adams hired six horses to draw his private carriage still on board the ship. Both Americans spent the night aboard their ship.

All through their first night in Holland, a gale blew. But by morning the wind was so fair that the voyage to Amsterdam could be made in seven or eight hours. Nevertheless, both Adams and Russell stayed with their plans to go by carriage overland. Adams' carriage was taken ashore by lighter and needed some minor work which delayed his departure three hours. Russell set out two hours ahead of his colleague, but waited for him at the next stage stop so they could breakfast together. They both reached Amsterdam by evening.[2]

Adams enjoyed the day, since the roads were good "and the country at this season is one continual garden."[3] To his *Memoirs*, he wrote,

> The meadows are clothed in their most beautiful verdure, and are covered with sheep and cattle. The canals are lively with the constant passage to and fro of the treckshuyts [a horse-drawn canal barge] and other boats, and the cleanliness of the houses and villages on the road is such as I had always seen in this country.[4]

Adams, reflecting on his previous travels, wrote his wife,

> I have revisited a country endeared to me by many pleasing recollections of all the early stages of my life—of infancy, youth, and manhood. I found it in all its charm precisely the same that I had first seen it; precisely the same that I had last left it.[5]

During the afternoon of the 21st, Clay arrived in Amsterdam, coming from Hamburg. He took lodging at the Doelen, but did not see Adams or Russell who were staying at the Arms of Amsterdam and were that evening attending an opera at the French theater. Adams and Russell left Amsterdam at six o'clock on the morning of the 22nd.

On their departure, Russell took a seat in Adams' carriage since he had arranged to leave his son in school in Amsterdam. This day's trip took them through Haerlem and The Hague without stopping. Adams continued to recall his earlier visits along the route as far back as July 1780 when he was 13 years old. Engaged in public missions in later years, he had again spent more than two years in the area. Now, writing of his feelings (like that of so many people who return late in life, to the haunts of their childhood), he said, "It was a confusion of recollections so various, so tender, so melancholy, so delicious, so painful, a mixture so heterogeneous, and yet altogether so sweet, that if I had been alone, I am sure I should have melted into tears."[6] They passed by Rotterdam late in the afternoon, spent that night at Lage Zwaluwe, and reached Antwerp, Belgium, at three in the afternoon of the 23rd.

The American envoys found the people of Antwerp were anxious to know who was to be their master, with the end of 20 years of Napo-

leonic wars. Though the money in use was French, the Belgium land had been severed from France and was now claimed in some degree by Austria, France, Holland, and even England. After settling at the Hotel of Grand Laboureur, Adams called on a Mr. Dutari with a letter of introduction and credit. Dutari apologized for not offering lodging at his house, but he already had guests — "14 English soldiers quartered upon him."

Dutari gave Adams a summary of the conditions prevailing in that part of Europe. He thought England would possess Belgium. He told Adams that the Allies had parted at Paris

> in very ill humor with one another, and all of them excessively dissatisfied with Austria; that Austria is now levying new troops, and that he thinks the Congress of Vienna will not end well; that they are daily expecting here the arrival of English Commissioners to take possession of one-third of the ships of the fleet and one-half of the materials of those upon the stocks; that the English are sending troops and taking possession of all the sea-ports on the coast; and that the Hollanders will certainly be disappointed in the expectations of having this country annexed to them.[7]

Despite these forebodings of the natives, Adams saw Antwerp from the view of a returning visitor. He wrote his wife, "Antwerp, when I first saw it, was a desolation, a mournful monument of opulence in the last stage of decay. It is now again what it had once been, a beautiful and prosperous city."[8]

On the following morning, June 24, as Adams and Russell crossed the river by ferry, they observed several ships of the line and frigates on the river and on the stocks "all of which are to be demolished and half the materials to be delivered up to the English." After a pleasant ride, in Adams sight (viewing the lovely countryside), but unpleasant to Russell (who was ill most of the day), they arrived in Ghent at four in the afternoon and took lodgings at "the Hôtel des Pays-Bas, on the Place d'Armes, the best public house in the city." On their arrival, the landlady inquired if one of them was Mr. Bayard, since Colonel Milligan had been there two days earlier to reserve rooms for him.

Throughout the 25th, the city of Ghent was in a "bustle of agitation," according to Adams, in anticipation of the arrival of the emperor of Russia and the king of Prussia. The bustle continued through the 28th. Yet these illustrious personages failed to make an appearance. Nevertheless, two other persons who did arrive in the city on the 27th and 28th received no official notice — not even from John Quincy Adams in his detailed diary. These individuals were American Peace Commissioners James A. Bayard and Henry Clay, respectively.

Clay's sole recounting of his travels seems to be a part of one sentence which began a letter from him, written from Ghent to William Crawford in Paris, dated July 2, 1814. "I reached this place on Tuesday last after a journey for the most part excessively unpleasant, and found here three of my colleagues, from one of whom I had the pleasure to receive your agreeable favor of the 10th Ulto." In addition to the letter of June 10, addressed to Clay alone, Clay was also handed three letters from William Crawford written during May and addressed to the entire American mission.

Beginning with Crawford's letter of May 13, written only six weeks after the fall of Napoleon, these four letters from Paris provided an important reading of the international military and diplomatic climate under which the American commissioners were going to be forced to negotiate. Crawford told his fellow Americans in foreign lands that he would endeavor, from time to time, to inform them of everything taking place in Paris "which can have any influence on your deliberations." As a result of his extended and relatively quick correspondence with the five commissioners, he, in effect, became a covert sixth member of the mission.

In this first letter, Crawford related his unsuccessful attempts to reach the ear of Russia's Czar Alexander, whom he referred to as the emperor. Twice, Crawford left notes for Count Karl Robert Nesselrode, the Russian minister of foreign affairs, only to be informed he was in council with the emperor. A third note to the Count went further to state his desire "to be presented to a Monarch who had given such strong proofs of friendship to the United States." This bit of flattery got him nowhere.

Eventually Crawford met with the Marquis de Lafayette, recently returned to France after the overthrow of Napoleon. He asked this long-time friend of America to try to get through to Nes-

selrode or the emperor by way of the latter's old tutor, Colonel Frederic César LaHarpe, a Swiss politician. This, too, failed. However, Lafayette did contact the Baron Karl Wilhelm von Humbolt, the Prussian minister who, according to Crawford, "has imbibed already the British misrepresentations." Crawford told his colleagues, "It seems as if there had been a settled determination to prevent the approach of every person who is suspected of an attachment to the U.S." Despite these feelings, it appears that Lafayette, at least, managed to bring the Baron to something of a neutral position, whether or not this had any future value.

Part of Crawford's fears of an alienation of the Allies towards the United States grew out of a statement in the official French newspaper *Monitor* to the effect that "the allied powers had by a secret convention engaged not to interfere in the affairs of the United States and that the King of France was to make the same engagement." Following Lafayette's efforts, Crawford hopefully wrote, "There is no reason to expect any interference on the part of the Emperor of Russia."

On the other hand, Crawford continued to have difficulties with the French over his credentials, which had been written to Napoleon's government. When the *Monitor* announced, on May 6, that on the next day the king would receive the Ambassadors "in the hall of his throne," Crawford conferred with Count René de la Forest, the French minister of foreign affairs. The count thought he should attend but denied that he was the proper person to decide the question or issue an invitation. This was the province of the grand master of ceremonies. Crawford wrote him a note, received no answer, and did not attend the function. In later conversations with la Forest, Crawford was told of observations (on the treatment of American and British vessels in French ports) made by Lord Castlereagh. The British foreign minister, while in Paris, used his huge influence to gather all the major European Powers into a coalition or, at least, a temperament against the United States. La Forest reported that Castlereagh exhibited "the most extreme hostility" to the United States.

Further evidence of this came to Crawford in the rumored appointments the British had made to the peace negotiations with America. He heard that Lord Gambier and Mr. Hamilton were appointed. Only the former was. The French newspaper account suggested that the British instructions "relative to the boundaries of Canada will make it necessary to wait new instructions from the United States." Crawford believed this was not possible and thought that if there were any material change in the boundaries to the disadvantage of the United States, the British then had "no serious intention of making a peace, which the Government can accept." However, he advised,

> If the alteration is immaterial, or advantageous, and the other conditions of the treaty shall be acceptable, you ought not to jeopardize the negociation by waiting new instructions. There are occasions when a public officer should not hesitate to jeopardize his own reputation rather than the national Interest.—This I think, would be one of them.

Yet Crawford felt that the British would not yield on the question of impressment and therefore "there is no possibility of making peace at the present moment," unless both sides would ignore their claims on the subject in the treaty.[9]

The next Crawford letter, which Clay read on his arrival in Ghent, was dated May 24. Crawford had little to add to his previous writing except to say he had sent a statement on the relations between the United States and England to Count Nesselrode by the hand of a friend and assumed it had been presented to the czar. His 16-page "Reflections" was an attempt to repel the charge of the ministers of the three Allied Powers that the United States was subservient "to the views of the Emperor Napoleon." Crawford said the ministers believed the American war was the result of this subserviency. Also in this letter Crawford reported that the king received the "same fulsome adulation" as Napoleon, and in many instances by the same individuals.[10]

The third letter, read by Clay and dated May 28, was even briefer but enclosed an interesting letter from the Marquis de Lafayette dated May 26. The Marquis had spent the previous evening in company with Czar Alexander, of whom Lafayette said, "He really is a great, good, sensible, noble minded man and a sincere friend to the cause of liberty." In response to a suggestion that there was too much political dissension in the United States, Lafayette observed to the czar that the Americans "were the happiest and free est [sic] people upon earth." On America's dispute between France and England, "the British outrages came nearer home particularly in the affair of Impressments."

When the czar spoke of "the hostile dispositions of England," Lafayette reminded the Russian leader that it was the British who rejected mediation. Alexander said he twice attempted to bring on peace. Lafayette urged,

> Do Sir make a third attempt—it must succeed—ne vous arretez pas en si beau chemin.... A protraction of the war would betray intentions quite perverse & hostile to the cause of humanity.—Your personal influence must carry the point—I am sure your Majesty will exert it.

The czar replied, "Well, I promise you I will. My journey to London affords opportunities and I will do the best I can." Lafayette spoke of the American commissioners, now gathered to meet with the British, and stated further that Gallatin was still in London.

In concluding his letter to Crawford, Lafayette said, "I think some good has been done—and upon the promise of a man so candid and generous I have full dependence." He added that the czar spoke well of Gallatin.

The rest of Crawford's letter, which enclosed the Lafayette account, spoke mainly of conditions in France and the resentment of the people over the attitude of the press in portraying the nation as conquered and the king asking mercy of the Allied sovereigns. "This is wholly indigestible to French Stomachs. You can not make a frenchman beleive [sic] that he is conquered as long as he can walk."[11]

Two days before Lafayette met with the czar in Paris, and five days before Crawford wrote this third letter to the commissioners, James Bayard left London and journeyed to Dover. On the day of Lafayette's meeting (while Clay sat depressed in Gottenburg and Adams arrived in Stockholm), Bayard endured a rough voyage from Dover to Calais. Because of strong winds and heavy sea, two-thirds of the 150 passengers aboard the 80-ton sloop were "sick and puking in all parts of the vessel," Bayard wrote in his diary. The trip took almost three hours. Bayard left Dover on May 25 and arrived in Paris on the 28th. He was soon to observe the same conditions of the French people as Crawford had described. He took in many of the usual tourist attractions in the area and spent a day with Crawford in a visit to the subterranean caverns beneath Paris.

> Passage narrow at first — entered a depository containing the bones of two million four hundred thousand persons. The bones piled so as to form a wall, interspersed with sculls [sic]. Obliged strictly to follow the guide. Many diverging passages — persons frequently lose themselves and perish. Number counted upon descending and ascending. Each person carried a candle. Emerging at the distance of a mile and half from the place of descent.

Two days after writing of his adventure under Paris on June 1, Bayard noted that the czar had left the previous day for London and that the Allied troops were quitting the city daily. Bayard continued his sight-seeing and visiting and enjoying dinner and conversation with Lafayette before departing from Paris on June 15. After a rather leisurely trip through heavily fortified countryside, where there was much evidence of past battles and remaining hostile feelings toward occupying troops, Bayard finally reached Ghent at 5 o'clock in the afternoon of June 27, and there he joined Adams and Russell. Clay arrived the next day.[12]

This left only Gallatin missing. While Bayard was visiting Paris on June 10, Russian Emperor Alexander arrived in London. Then on June 18, while all four of Gallatin's colleagues were en route by various means to Ghent, the czar granted a private interview to Gallatin and his son, James, at his lodgings, the Leicester House in Leicester Fields. That day, the streets were crowded with spectators hoping to catch a glimpse of one or more of the several sovereigns then in London who were to be feted at a banquet later in the day. The two Gallatins were accompanied through the crowds to the czar's temporary residence by Levitt Harris, a secretary to the original St. Petersburg mission. But Harris was not admitted to the emperor's presence and was furious at the slight, according to James Gallatin, who wrote of the meeting:

> There were crowds waiting for audiences. We were passed in at once. Father was presented and then presented me; then all withdrew except his Majesty. He is a splendid-looking man, was in full uniform and covered with jeweled orders and stars. He was most gracious, and said he had the most friendly feeling toward the United States. he added that he feared his intervention would be of little use — that he had made three attempts since he had been here, but that "England will not admit a third party to interfere in her disputes with you." This he said on account of our former colonial relations, which are not forgotten. He also expressed an opinion with regard to the conditions of peace saying: "The difficulty will be with England" ... Father expressed his deep gratitude to his Majesty for granting him an audience, and the gratitude of the United States for his interest and friendship he had shown. As we withdrew he patted me on the head and said, 'You are rather young to be in diplomacy.[13]

While the czar's audience, in London, for two Americans — the enemy of the British — though himself a guest in England, was close to a diplomatic insult, Gallatin went so far, the next day, to suggest in a supplementary note to Alexander, what Britain must do to obtain peace. He wrote,

> If the Br. Govt. sincerely wishes peace with America, it will not bring forward any new territorial or commercial protestations, and will confine itself to the discussion of the questions which gave rise to the war. That respecting impressment of seamen on board American vessels is the only one which presents any difficulty.[14]

On June 20, the British foreign secretary, Lord Castlereagh, informed Albert Gallatin that the British peace mission would leave for Ghent on July 1. Two days after that, the two Gallatins left for Ghent by way of Paris. They did not carry with them a great deal of hope for success in their peace endeavors. The political atmosphere in England, respecting her war with the United States, certainly dampened prospects for sincere negotiations.

Henry Clay, on the other hand, at this moment in time, still en route to Ghent, was largely shielded from much of the depressing atmosphere Gallatin had been living through daily in London. Not even the letters he read from Crawford on his arrival in Ghent could afford Clay a full inkling of the British recalcitrance, but Crawford had tried. But there was a fourth letter from Crawford addressed only to Clay, while the other letters were sent to all members of the mission. This letter, dated June 10, from the U.S. minister to France, set down his impressions of the chances for peace.

Crawford wrote, "My expectations of a happy

result are not strong. The arrogance of the enemy was never greater than at the present moment. The infatuation of that nation excludes almost the possibility of peace." Crawford did not believe the British ministry (referring to the delegation selected to treat with the Americans in Ghent, as well as their superiors in London) were as temperate and moderate as they were represented. Crawford thought the U.S. government might allow a peace treaty which ignored impressment, but believed, on the other hand, that the British would insist on "their maritime rights" to impressment — which "I trust will never be concluded" by America. Crawford said he would prefer a return to colonial relations than to submit to this condition. He then advised that any collapse of the negotiations should be on "principles which will convince the American people, of all parties, that peace can be obtained only by the most vigorous prosecution of the war." He noted proposals of an Englishman in France who was as closely pro–American as any, yet he [the Englishman] did not expect the British would agree to a suggestion that they abstain from impressment when the American vessels were in coastal trade or in foreign trade and still in sight of the American coast. He also favored a complicated scheme that allowed American sea captains to put into the nearest port for court decision on impressment cases.[15]

Clay answered Crawford's letter on July 2. He said it was his opinion that the mission's instructions did not empower them to conclude a treaty without the British relinquishing their claim of a right to impress. Still, if peace hung on this one condition, he would not hesitate to violate his instructions if persuaded such an action would be in the interest of the country. He agreed that "a more unfavorable moment than the present certainly never could occur," with respect to the timing of the negotiations. Nevertheless, he believed the 1814 military campaigns (he mentioned termination of the war against the Creeks by Jackson) were making such progress as to be unaffected by "any considerable force" thrown into America by the British and thus, "No treaty that we can now conclude can arrest the progress of this campaign."

As for affairs on the European side of the Atlantic, Clay referred to the occupation of the Low Countries by British troops as "giving occupation to a portion of that force which might be sent agt. [sic] us." In addition, he saw much that left Europe in a very unsettled condition which would probably make it necessary for England to retain large forces in the European area, though he did not state this directly.

Having discussed this, Clay returned again in his letter to the matter of impressment. On it he observed that if negotiations were brought to that single issue and that he must "without waiting to hear from America, sign a treaty, waiving the relinquishment of the pretension of impressment, I confess I should pause before I consented to a total rupture of the negotiation." He thought a short delay would be advantageous.

> I confess I am inclined to think that the British Government will have no difficulty in making a peace leaving Impresst [sic] untouched. They will doubtless set up many claims ... but rely upon it ultimately (and that even without any change here or in America) they will be content to cast us and make us go hence etc. Why shd. [sic] they not? Undoubtedly, if we say nothing about impressment, they triumph in the contest. As to acknowledging their right, our government would neither permit us to sign, nor would I ever sign, a treaty embracing such a stipulation.

In answer to Crawford's comments on the proposal calling for American sea captains putting into port for court decisions, Clay said,

> Altho' it would probably be better for the victims of this tyranny than the existing practice, my opinion is that as it respects the nation, it is not a subject of compromise — there is no midway point on which honor can rest between abandonment of the practice, and total silence in relation to it.

He agreed with Crawford that "if we can make no peace it is a solemn duty enjoined by our situations so to conduct the negotiation as to satisfy the nation that a vigorous and united exertion alone will procure it." In a final unrelated comment Clay told his friend, "this place is quite comfortable, infinitely more so than Gottenburg. But what think you of our being surrounded by a British garrison?"[16]

As the American peace commission slowly gathered in Ghent, it became apparent that aside from Russell (whose views were rather unknown) only Clay had a hope of success in the coming negotiations and was unimpressed with the dread warnings of new British military adventures in America.

No sooner had Henry Clay settled in at Ghent than he, too, was to have occasion to see the emperor of Russia. On June 29, the day following Clay's arrival, the city of Ghent was full of extraordinary activity with bells and carillons ringing. Despite a heavy rainfall, the streets were crowded with the populace hoping to see the czar. Adams described the event.

> He passed just at noon, on horseback, with a suite of fifteen or twenty officers. He was distinguished from them only by the greater simplicity of his dress — a plain green uniform, without any decoration, and even without facings. Very few of the crowd knew him as he passed. He stopped about ten minutes at one of the squares, while a Prussian regiment, drawn up there, defiled before him. He afterwards stopped again, while a French regiment of the garrison of Hamburg passed. But he went through the city and immediately proceeded on his journey to Antwerp.... He had entered it [Ghent], however in an open calèche, that everybody might have an opportunity of seeing him. His condescension and affability were, as usual, conspicuous.

Adams was more expansive about the czar's visit in a letter written on July 2, to his wife, Louisa Catherine, still in St. Petersburg.

> The Emperor Alexander may now be truly called the darling of the human race. Concerning him, and him alone, I have heard but one voice since I left his capital; not only in his own dominions, not only here and in Holland, but even in Sweden, where it was least to be expected that a Russian sovereign should be a favorite. In France, perhaps, his popularity is at the highest. Even those who at heart do not thank him for the present he has made them cannot deny his moderation, his humanity, his magnanimity. Of all the allies he was the one who had been the most wantonly and cruelly outraged. Of all the allies he was the only one who took no dishonorable revenge, who advanced no extravagant pretensions. It is well understood that he alone protected Paris from the rapacity of those who had marched with Napoleon, and shared the plunder of Moscow. He has redeemed his pledge to the world. He has shown himself as great by his forbearance and modesty in prosperity as by his firmness in the hour of his own trial.[17]

Adams went on to describe more personal aspects of the day.

> In the evening Messrs. Bayard, Clay, Shaler, Milligan, and myself went to the ball at the Hôtel de Ville. There were two or three hundred persons at the ball. The ladies not remarkable either for beauty or elegance. We stayed about two hours and returned to our lodgings before midnight.

During the afternoon the four commissioners agreed to hold their first official meeting the next morning in Adams' chamber at eleven.[18]

Adams wrote that conversation at the meeting was "desultory." They decided to send the corvette *John Adams* back to the United States. They agreed to order two English newspapers to be sent to them. They proposed to have regular meetings and keep a journal of proceedings when all five members were assembled.[19]

According to James Bayard's diary, the American Mission was completed with the arrival of Albert Gallatin and his son, James, "This evening at ½ past 6," on July 6. But James Gallatin recorded in his diary entry for July 7,

> We arrived here today and are lodged very comfortably in the Hotel d'Alcantara, corner of the Rue des Champs. Ghent looks clean and cheerful. The inhabitants speak only Flemish. All seem employed in commerce. There is an English garrison here; the uniforms make the streets very bright. They call private residences *hôtels* in this country. The house is large and all the delegates are to lodge here.[20]

The next day, July 8, Christopher Hughes and George M. Dallas joined the mission in Ghent. The 28-year-old Hughes, who was to be secretary for the mission, was from Baltimore, Maryland. In 1811, he had married Laura Sophia, daughter of General Samuel Smith, the United States senator from Maryland. Her uncle was the Robert Smith whom Madison had fired as secretary of state. Yet Hughes became a highly congenial friend of the mission members. Adams wrote of him early in August, "He is lively and good-humored, smart at a repartee, and a thorough punster, theory and practice."[21] Again, a couple years later, writing to Russell, Adams said, "Our lively Ghent Secretary, who makes laws and speeches and puns in the Maryland House of Assembly, writes me now and then a pleasant letter."[22] Even more so, Hughes became a life-long friend of Clay and they corresponded often over the remaining years of their lives. Hughes went on to have a long diplomatic career becoming chargé d'affaires in Sweden and The Netherlands.

Dallas, who became 22 two days after his arrival in Ghent, had travelled to Europe as Gallatin's private secretary. He was sent home in late August carrying important dispatches to the U.S. government. He remained in America and later became mayor of Philadelphia, a senator from Pennsylvania, a minister to Russia, and later to Great Britain, and Vice President of the United States under James K. Polk (victor over Clay for the Presidency in 1844). The city of Dallas, Texas, was named after him.

On July 12, Adams, writing his wife, said,

> Mr. Carroll and Mr. Todd ... are still lingering at Paris. Mr. Carroll is attached to the mission as private secretary to Mr. Clay, and Mr. Todd is of this legation, as he was of the former [at St. Petersburg], a *gentilhomme d'ambassade*, quite independent in his movements, and very naturally thinking Paris a more agreeable residence than Ghent.[23]

Now that the principal American members of the mission had finally assembled, it was time for them to organize in preparation for the arrival of their British counterparts. They were given time to develop a perceptive relationship with each other. Though they were all patriotic in their love of America, they brought with them strong personalities which were bound to clash.

Nearly 70 years later, in a biography of Henry Clay, Carl Schurz, Lincoln's former secretary of the interior, was able to sum up some of the characteristics of these illustrious men. Of Adams, he wrote,

> He was then forty-seven years old, with all his peculiarities fully matured,— a man of great ability, various knowledge, and large experience; of ardent patriotism, and high principles of honor and duty; brimful of courage, and a pugnacious spirit of contention; precise in his ways; stiff and cold in manners; inclined to be suspicious, and harsh in his judgments of others, and in the Puritan spirit, also severe with himself; one of the men who keep diaries, and in them regular accounts of their own as well as other people's doings.

And this has provided history with the intimate view of the inner craftsmanship of these negotiations. It is a wonder, that as a Federalist and a New Englander, he was a guiding force in these negotiations. But he was firstly an American.

Skipping Clay, whom we have followed so long, Schurz sums up the other personalities as follows:

> Russell, a man of ordinary ability, was much under the influence of Clay, while Bayard, although not disposed to quarrel with anybody, showed not seldom a disposition to stick to his opinion, when it differed from those of his colleagues, with polite but stubborn firmness. "Each of us," wrote Adams, "takes a separate and distinct view of the subject-matter, and each naturally thinks his own view of it the most important." A commission so constituted would hardly have been fit to accomplish a task of extraordinary delicacy, had it not been for the conspicuous ability, the exquisite tact, the constant good-nature, the "playfulness of temper," as Mr. Adams expressed it, and the inexhaustible patience of Albert Gallatin, a man whose eminence among his contemporaries has probably never been appreciated as it deserves. Without in the least obtruding himself, he soon became the peacemaker, the moderating and guiding mind of the commission.[24]

As early as July 8, only a day or so after the completion of the mission circle, Adams was confiding a minor controversy to his *Memoirs*. He wrote,

> I dined again at the table-d'hôte, at one. The other gentlemen dined together, at four. They sit after dinner and drink bad wine and smoke cigars, which neither suits my habits, nor my health, and absorbs time which I cannot spare. I find it impossible, even with the most rigorous economy of time, to do half the writing that I ought.

But the next day, Adams wrote that he dined with his colleagues and planned to continue to do so after, "Mr. Clay having expressed some regret that I had withdrawn from their table yesterday."[25]

While in St. Petersburg, there had been an undercurrent of ill will between Adams and Bayard. On July 11, Adams suffered "no small mortification" when Bayard remembered and toasted Adams' 47th birthday. The previous shadow of ill-will was not present as Adams wrote his wife of the occasion,

> It was however, done by him with so good a disposition that I took it as kindly as it was meant. He has uniformly been since our arrival here in the most friendly humor, and we appear all to be animated with the same desire of *harmonizing* together.

In an earlier part of the same letter, he had told his wife, "We are all in perfect good understanding and good humor with one another."[26]

On the other hand, Gallatin's son, James, had a different perspective when he wrote in his diary on July 15, "Mr. Adams in a very bad temper. Mr. Clay annoys him. Father pours oil on the troubled waters."[27] This view was contradicted by Adams' comment in another letter to his wife just one week later, when he wrote, "What you have heard of the character and temper of Mr. Clay coincides exactly with all the experience I have had of them hitherto." These words were in reply to her letter to him, written June 10, when she said, "Mr. Clay, I understand, is one of the most amiable and finest temper'd men in the world, and I am told you will be delighted with him. Young Lewis is lavish in his praise."[28]

Adams also told his wife that a "report of a public breach and misunderstanding between two other gentlemen is altogether unfounded." This may have referred to Bayard and Gallatin. The former was alluded to in this letter as Adams went on to write of the aides to the mission, probably Colonel Milligan and George Dallas.

> The junior attachés, who were last year in Russia, both wholly independent of their former *patrons*, and can therefore have no collision with them. Their pretensions are not so *salient* as they were, and their deportment is consequently more pleasing. The Colonel is not only reconciled to the *Chevalier* [Bayard], but more assiduous to him than ever. The Chevalier himself is entirely *another man*, with good health, good spirits, good humor, always reasonable, and almost always as you have seen him in his most amiable moments. Whether there was something baleful in the waters of the Neva, I know not; but our last year's visitors, all here, seem of another and much better world.[29]

Adams told of one other social contact with one of the mission members during these long days of waiting for the appearance of the British commissioners. In his *Memoirs*, for July 20, he wrote,

> I went with Mr. Clay [Please note, that these men, even in their private notes, did not refer to their close colleagues by their first name, such as, "Henry."] to the Hôtel de Ville, which was formerly the imperial palace, and we saw the ceremony of the "marriage civil," performed by the ad-joint [sic] Mayor of the city. There were about twenty couples to be married this day. We saw six or seven of them go through the ceremony, which was very short. It appeared to consist only in the calling over the names, age, and characters of the

parties and their witnesses, who were usually five or six. A short passage from the register was then read by the clerk, in Flemish, and the Mayor delivered a paper to the bridegroom — I suppose the certificate of the marriage. There was a brass box on the table, into which each of the parties put a small piece of money, and which was probably a charity for the poor. The brides were all ugly, and almost all apparently older than the bridegrooms.[30]

Adams related one further social episode before the British arrived. On August 1, the city of Ghent, in a festive spirit, celebrated the exertions of youngsters in the arts and awarded them prizes for their talents. Adams, apparently alone, attended the activities in the morning but was joined by the other mission members in the afternoon. They were invited to sit next to the mayor on the stage where they listened to several speeches,

> After which the victors were proclaimed, and the prizes given for the best works of painting, drawing, and architecture, exposed at the saloon. We were requested to take a part in the distribution of the prizes, and each of us delivered one of them to one of the successful candidates. There was a flourish of horns and clarions every time that a prize was given.... When these ceremonies were finished, we passed into another hall, and were requested, each of us, to return home with one of the pupils who had obtained a prize.... The streets in the neighborhood of where the victors lived were hung with evergreens and flowers in bloom. In the evening they were illuminated.... The boy presented to the gentleman who took him home a letter requesting his friendly assistance to get him and his father a place as clerk in some public office, or for himself in some counting-house.

The families were apparently very poor but the mission members could do little for them. That evening the members attended a ball given by the president and directors of the Society of Fine Arts.

As early as July 12, Adams wrote his wife that all members of the mission were determined to move from the inn where they were all lodged, and take a house and live together. A week later, he wrote her that they had agreed unanimously to live together,

> yet when it came to the arrangement of details, we soon found that one had one thing to which he attached a particular interest, and another, and it was not so easy to find a contractor who would accommodate himself to five distinct and separate humors. It is one of your French universalists who

had finally undertaken to provide for us. He keeps a shop of perfumery, and of millinery, and of prints and drawings; and he has on hand a stock of handsome second hand furniture. But then he was brought up a cook, and he is to supply our table to our satisfaction; and he is a marchand de vin, and will serve us with the best liquors that are to be found in the city. This was the article that stuck hardest in the passage; for one of us, and I know you will suspect it was I, was afraid that he would pass off upon us bad wine, and make us pay for it as if it was the best. The bargain was very nearly broken off upon the question whether we should be obliged to take wine from him, or, if we supply ourselves from elsewhere, to pay him one franc a bottle for drawing the cork. We finally came to a compromise, and are to begin by taking wine from him. But they must be at his peril such as we shall relish; for if not, we shall look further, and draw the corks without paying him any tax or tribute for it at all.[31]

The mission members finally made their move, on July 31, from the Hôtel des Pays-Bas to their new home, carrying the name Hôtel of Baron Lavendeghem, in the Rue des Champs. Their rental was 1200 francs for the first month and 1000 francs each month afterwards.[32] However, the aides did not move with them, wishing to maintain a state of independence, and the rooms left over at the new house were not so inviting to them. Adams particularly regretted the loss of Hughes' society. Less than two weeks after settling in their new lodging, Adams again wrote his wife with further description of their accommodations,

> We have the satisfaction of living in perfect harmony; the discontents of our domestic arrangements are all with our landlord, and none with one another. Even he gives us better satisfaction than he did. Mr. Hughes and the private secretaries all dine with us every day. One of our troubles you must know was that this house was *haunted*, and its ill-fame in this respect was so notorious, that the servants and the children of our party were very seriously alarmed before, and when we first came in. The perturbed spirits have all forsaken the house since we entered it, and we hope they are *laid* for ever.[33]

The following day, August 1, Hughes received a letter from a friend in London advising that the British commissioners were expected to postpone their departure until after a grand jubilee on August 1 in commemoration of the centenary of the accession of the House of Brunswick to the English throne and the anniversary of the Battle of the Nile.[34]

During this exasperating month-long wait for the British, the American mission held numerous meetings and prepared themselves for the coming conferences, most likely in a much better manner than might have been the case had they simply come together one day and begun negotiating with the enemy the following day. After their first "desultory" meeting on June 30, they did not have another until Saturday, July 9, when Gallatin had arrived to complete their circle. On this day, they conferred from noon until four in the afternoon. They agreed to have daily meetings starting with one at noon on Monday in Adams' chambers. Adams was turned down on a proposal to send the British government official notification of their being together in Ghent. Instead, they agreed only to notify their own government advising of the change in the city of negotiation. They discussed the manner of keeping the books of the mission and the obligations of the secretary. Each member was to keep his own books, but had "a right to ask the secretary for copies of particular papers which they may want."

Monday's meeting dealt primarily with the accountability of the contingent expenses incurred by the numerous messengers carrying dispatches between the mission members while they were scattered in various cities of Europe from Paris and London to Gottenburg and St. Petersburg.

Only routine matters were covered in subsequent meetings until July 18 when they began to deliberate on the principal points of their official instructions. During a discussion on impressment, it was found that they did not have a set of laws and treaties of the United States. Bayard observed that he had a set on board the *Neptune*, then at Antwerp. These were sent for the next day. Meanwhile, on the 18th, they also tried to decide on "the best mode of proceeding with the British commissioners, whether by verbal conferences or by written communications," and "whether we should make or receive the first propositions, and whether they should be a mere summary statement of the objects to be discussed, or the formal projects of a treaty."[35]

There is no account of further meetings prior to the arrival of the British. On August 4, Jonathan Russell left Ghent for Dunkirk and did not return until the 9th, when he found the British had finally reached Ghent.

Even before the envoys of the two warring nations sat down to talk, William Crawford, sitting in Paris, wrote to Clay once more baring his anxiety over the deliberations about to begin. In a letter to Clay, early in August, he also expressed the desire to be relieved of his duties as minister to the French government, and suggested to Clay that since his connection to the House of Representatives "has dissolved," the new commissioner might consent to be Crawford's replacement in Paris once his duties as peacemaker were ended. Crawford had known Clay quite well back in Washington when serving as president pro tem of the Senate. However, Crawford's successor in Paris would be Albert Gallatin.[36]

28

SINE QUA NON

Quietly and unobtrusively, the British commissioners rode into Ghent, Belgium, on Saturday evening, August 6, 1814. They took lodging at the Hôtel du Lion d'Or, called "a fine Carthusian monastery" by James Gallatin.[1]

The following morning, the British envoys sent their secretary, Anthony St. John Baker, to the Hôtel des Pays-Bas to announce their arrival to the Americans. (Baker was a former secretary for Augustus Foster, former minister to the United States.) However, since the move of the mission members, Baker found only Colonel Milligan who directed him to the new residence of the American commissioners. Baker went on to the Hôtel of Baron Lavendeghem and, meeting with James Bayard, notified him of the arrival of the British, and proposed that the Americans meet them the next day at one o'clock at the Britishers' lodging. Bayard told Baker he would send an answer in the evening.

Thereupon, the four American diplomats (Russell was still traveling to Antwerp and Dunkirk) met at noon to decide on their approach to the British on exchanging copies of powers from their respective governments to treat for peace. At once, the Americans agreed that the British proposal, to have the meeting at their lodging, was an "offensive pretension to superiority." Adams cited a legal precedent in "Martens, book vii. chap. iv. section 3, of his Summary," noting, "the course now taken by the British Commissioners appears to be precisely that stated there to be the usage from Ambassadors to Ministers of an inferior order." Clay, Bayard, and Adams made various proposals that were discussed for about two hours. They adjourned until 3:30 P.M.

On renewing their talks, Bayard "produced the case in Ward's *History of the Law of Nations*, vol. ii. chap. xvi., of the Commissioners between Spain and England, at Boulogne, in 1600, which in almost every particular resembles the present," Adams wrote, "and at which the Spanish Commissioners made, and the English resisted, the pretension now advanced by the English." Though all members of the U.S. mission believed the British intended to put the Americans in an inferior position, both Bayard and Gallatin were reluctant to make an issue of the matter since they were averse to clogging the negotiations over a question of mere ceremony.

After another adjournment for supper, they met again and finally agreed on a proposal of Adams' to have Hughes report to the British that the Americans "should be happy to meet and confer with the Commissioners, and exchange full powers with them, at any time which they would indicate, and at any place which may be mutually agreed upon." The suggestion of "place" was Gallatin's substitute for Adams' original expression of "any place other than their own lodgings." This removed the sharper tone which previously reflected Adams' and Clay's pique at the British pretensions. Hughes carried the message to the British and at ten in the evening, Baker returned to inform Bayard, and somewhat later, all of the American mission meeting in Clay's chamber, "that the British Commissioners agreed to meet us at the appointed hour, and at the Hôtel des Pays-Bas."

It was a very minor victory for the Americans considering the fact that the British had agreed to meet where the Americans had previously lodged and where their aides still lodged. Adams noted in his diary that Bayard had gone so far as to propose to Baker that the meeting should be at the Americans' home, offering "to show him an excellent room" for the meeting. But Baker declined even looking at the room.[2]

On the following day, August 8, 1814, the American mission members met briefly at noon to consider the proper manner in which to proceed with the British. At one o'clock, the first joint meeting took place. Representing the British government were: Baron James Gambier, Admiral of the Fleet; Henry Goulburn, a member of Parliament and under-secretary of state; and William Adams, a doctor of civil laws. (And it now becomes necessary in the story of the negotiations to differentiate between the American John Quincy Adams, and the British William Adams. However, the Britisher may be called "Dr. Adams.")

Gambier, the oldest at 57, was the nominal head of the British mission. He began service in the British navy at the age of 11, serving on a ship commanded by an uncle. During the "revolt of the Colonies," he was promoted to a command in American waters, but the ship, the *Thunderbomb*, was captured by the French. After being exchanged, he participated in the capture of Charleston, South Carolina, in May 1780. After that war, he continued to rise quietly in navy rank with ship commands and posts ashore at the admiralty until, as a vice admiral, he was named governor of Newfoundland and commander-in-chief of naval forces in that region. Gambier's first important notice came in September 1807, when in concert with the army under Lord William Schar Cathcort, the British bombardment of Copenhagen forced the surrender of the city and the Danish Navy. It brought Gambier a peerage. His greatest notoriety came 18 months later when he was involved in another naval episode at Basque Roads (off the Gironde estuary along the French Biscay coast). He was then commander of the Channel Fleet, but was subjected by the admiralty to act under command of a junior officer, Thomas Cochrane, who was also a member of Parliament. Cochrane had convinced the admiralty board to approve an attack with fireships on the French fleet at Basque Roads. Gambier, a deeply religious man, opposed this method of warfare and gave only partial support to the attack, thus thwarting its full success. A few weeks later, when a vote of thanks to Gambier was proposed in Parliament, Cochrane, as a member there, opposed the motion stating that Gambier was unworthy of the merit for failing to destroy the French fleet. That summer, Gambier applied for a court martial. It was packed with his friends, including William Bligh, the "dispossessed" captain of the HMS *Bounty*, later a vice admiral, who had commanded one of the ships under Gambier at the battle. The court acquitted Gambier and he received his vote of thanks from Parliament the next year. He left the navy in 1811, but in his late years, was promoted to Admiral of the Fleet.[3]

At the end of the first week's talks, the American Adams had a chance to converse with Gambier on more personal affairs. The former British admiral related some of his experiences in American waters during the Revolution. He told Adams he had known the American's father as well as other Bostonians. Gambier said that while he was a vice president of the English Bible Society, he had correspondence with the Bible Society in Boston, of which Adams replied he was a member. Gambier "expressed great satisfaction at the liberality with which they had sent a sum of money to replace the loss of some Bibles which had been taken by a privateer as they were going to Halifax."[4] Some weeks later Bayard described Gambier as "a wellbred, affable and amicable man."[5]

Next in age, at 42, was Dr. Adams. He was an admiralty lawyer with a reputation as a master of legal details. Until 1814, he served on several important commissions, though none with the importance of the peace mission. In fact, this was to be his major claim to fame. As with Gambier, John Quincy Adams enjoyed an early personal conversation with William Adams. The American learned that the Britisher's family had originally come from Wales, but some four or five generations back they had resided in Essex. They once possessed considerable estates in Wales, but none had descended to William. The two Adamses decided they were not cousins.[6]

Again, Bayard commented on this commissioner observing that "Dr. Adams has the reputation of possessing much dry wit, is shrewd and cynical."[7] In one of his first letters, after commencement of the negotiations, Bayard wrote to William Crawford of a conversation with William Adams regarding the tardy appearance of the

British. Bayard said he had been a long time waiting at Ghent wishing to make a personal acquaintance with him. Adams, replied, "Why it is some time since we have been riding at single anchor, ready to cut and make sail upon receiving orders." Bayard told Crawford, the British "have not excused nor in any manner explained the tardiness of their arrival at the appointed rendezvous. In truth I doubt whether they were made acquainted with the causes of their detention."[8]

The youngest of the British negotiators was 30-year-old Henry Goulburn. He had become a member of the House of Commons in 1808. Two years later he was appointed under-secretary for the home department. By 1812, he was under-secretary for war and the colonies. Still ahead of him was an undistinguished career in which he served briefly as home secretary and twice for longer periods as chancellor of the exchequer under the Duke of Wellington and later under Sir Robert Peel.[9] (Goulburn was the only commissioner to have his family with him, which included a 16-month-old son, though Russell's son soon left school in Amsterdam and joined his father at Ghent. And Gallatin's adult son was present throughout the negotiations as an aide.) Possibly assuming that this youngest member of the British mission was the least important, John Quincy Adams penned no early characterization of Goulburn. However, Bayard again had a comment, calling the young man, "Smooth, polite, and well informed."[10]

After the first day of negotiation, James Gallatin wrote of his father's estimate of the British delegates, being unimpressed with

> men who have not made any mark and have no influence or weight. He attaches but little importance to them as they are but the puppets of Lords Castlereagh and Liverpool. Father feels he is quite capable of dealing with them.[11]

In selecting the British mission, the prime minister, the Earl of Liverpool, had hoped to send a single negotiator, preferring "a Man of legal mind & of a very accurate Understanding" and believing one well-known man could operate more skillfully than a group.[12] Not only did he fail to find one man possessing all the qualifications he sought, but instead, he sent three men who could not embody those qualifications. They were not a worthy combination to contend with the skill and experience of men with the stature and ability of John Quincy Adams, Albert Gallatin, James A. Bayard, and Henry Clay. They might have been the equal only of Jonathan Russell.

There was possibly one man who could readily match the talents of the Americans. That was Lord Castlereagh himself. Yet this would mean sending a man standing at the government level with Secretary of State James Monroe. The British could not do the Americans such honor when they felt superior morally and militarily. In any case, Lord Castlereagh was wanted elsewhere. Within a few weeks of the opening of negotiations at Ghent, the British were going to participate in a much longer conference and, to them, infinitely more important, to be known as The Congress of Vienna. This meeting of the leadership of the Great Powers of Europe was charged with resolving the restoration of peace and stability to the entire continent following the long years of the war with Napoleon. It was to attract the primary attention and effort of foreign offices of all the nations concerned. It was to this Congress that Castlereagh was to go in person and give most of his thought and energy. The Ghent mission was, at best, secondary.

Under these circumstances, the negotiations for peace began at Ghent at one o'clock on August 8, 1814. The Americans found the British waiting for them at the Hôtel des Pays-Bas. After a ceremony of introductions, the two missions took seats around a table. Then, as described in a journal that Clay began at this time,

> Lord Gambier, the first named British Commissioner, proceeded to state the regret which the British Nation felt at the existence of the war between the two countries, and the sincere desire which the Prince Regent had for its termination; That he felt himself, as did his colleagues, no less anxious for this disirable [sic] object; and that he hoped we should be able to put an end to a state of things so contrary to the interests of the two Nations, and restore again those amicable relations, which he hoped under the blessing of divine Providence might advance the happiness of both nations. The other British Comms stated that Lord Gambier had expressed their sentiments.

Both sides then exchanged documents attesting to their full powers to treat for peace.[13]

Adams responded for the Americans,

making similar assurances on our part, expressing the high satisfaction with which we received theirs, and the promise for myself and my colleagues to bring to these discussions the disposition to meet every sentiment of candor and conciliation with the most cordial reciprocity, concurring, as we did, with the utmost earnestness and sincerity, in the hope that we might eventually have the happiness of reconciling two nations whose true interests could best be promoted by peace and amity with each other.[14]

Goulburn then told the Americans that his colleagues had given him the responsibility of presenting the issues which they believed would become matters of discussion in the negotiations. He suggested that if the Americans felt any were unnecessary to be discussed, they should say so, or if the British should omit any which the Americans thought ought to be discussed they could supply the omission. He

added the most explicit declaration that nothing that had occurred since the first proposal for this negotiation would have the slightest effect on the disposition of Great Britain with regard to the terms upon which the pacification might be concluded.[15]

Then, according to the brief "Journal" kept by Clay, Goulburn proposed the following:

The 1st point which they supposed would arise respected the forcible seizure of marines and the claim incident to it of the King of Great Britain to the allegiance of all his native born subjects.

2dly. Great Britain was disirous [sic] that the peace to be made should embrace their Indian allies and that, in order that the peace with them should be equally permanent as the peace with her, there should be fixed a boundary for the Indians, which should not be liable to be encroached upon; and this, they were instructed to say was a *sine qua non* [an essential element] to the conclusion of any treaty of amity and peace.

3dly. That a partial revision of the boundary between the Provinces of Great Britain and the U. States should take place, with a view to such modifications & alterations as would be mutually accommodating.

4. He observed that it was necessary in candor to add, that the privilege which had been accorded to the U. States by the treaty of peace [ending the American Revolution], so far as it depended upon the treaty, relative to the fisheries, would not be continued to the U. States, without an equivalent.[16]

At the conclusion of these remarkable demands, Adams inquired of Goulburn, "If I understand you ... G. Britain thinks the impressment of seamen and the incidental claim of allegiance which she asserts a point proper for discussion."

Goulburn replied,

No ... G. Britain does not think it a point necessary to be discussed; but it was impossible not to advert to that subject in stating the subjects of discussion which we supposed were likely to come up in this negotiation.[17]

In reply to a question by Bayard on the subject of a boundary between the United States and Canada, Goulburn said, "Great Britain did not contemplate an acquisition of territory."[18]

After further minor questioning and explanations, Adams told the British he would like to confer with his colleagues on the points proposed and on those the Americans would propose. Goulburn rather insistently asked for an immediate answer on whether or not the Americans were instructed on the Indian issues on which the British had been directed to make a *sine qua non*. But Adams insisted more so on consulting with his companions. The British finally agreed to meet again the next day at eleven o'clock and also agreed to hold the meetings alternately at each other's lodgings — so that the conference on the 9th would be at the Americans' rooms. The British admitted they were not well accommodated at their lodgings but later in the day entertained the Americans for a short visit.

Through the rest of the afternoon and after dinner, the Americans went over their intended reply to the British. It's hard to imagine that there was no shouting of angry words across the room — not at each other, but at the presumption of the British to interfere in American relations with Indians on their own territory, when the British had enlisted the Indians to fight against them at the Seige of Detroit and the River Raisin Massacre, about which Clay certainly had much to say. Could they really tolerate a demand on any subject for a *sine qua non*? The question of fisheries must have rankled Adams.

They prepared to address their adversaries as follows:

1st. That we were instructed as to the first point [on impressment] to discuss the subject.

2. That we had no instruction on this point [the Indians]; but that we had reason to believe our Government had taken measures and actually appointed Commissioners to treat of Peace with the Indians; but that at all events the War with them would fall with the war with Great Britain.

3. That we were instructed on this point [the boundary with Canada].

4. That we had no instructions whatever on this point [the fisheries].

In addition, they decided to suggest to the British,

> as subjects proper to be brought into the discussion, 1st. A definition of Blockade and as far as can be agreed upon other neutral and belligerent rights, and 2dly. Certain claims to indemnity arising from captures both before and since the war.

Furthermore, the Americans wanted to abridge the points of discussion as much as possible in the preliminary talks, presenting only "those we deemed essential, and to the end of making peace if possible." They would also let the British know that they were instructed on several minor points which might be brought forward later or during negotiation of a treaty of commerce on which they were also empowered to negotiate.[19]

During the course of the evening, new dispatches arrived from the commissioners' superior, Secretary of State James Monroe, having been forwarded by William Crawford in Paris. Adams, Gallatin, and Christopher Hughes worked until 1 o'clock in the morning deciphering the messages. These latest instructions were dated June 25 and 27 and took into account new knowledge of the dramatic changes in the power structure of Europe following the abdication of Napoleon. However, they produced no need for the Americans to alter their mode of address to the British at the next meeting.[20]

In his letter of June 25, Secretary Monroe observed that the changed political climate of Europe might well increase British demands and make it more difficult to obtain a provision on impressment in the peace treaty. In that case, he said the commissioners could agree to an article in that treaty referring the subject "to a separate negotiation" along with commerce. For this purpose Monroe subjoined a draft of such an article. It further noted that "by the peace in Europe, the essential causes of the war between the United States and Great Britain, and particularly the practice of impressment, have ceased," thus making possible a separation of this subject from the peace treaty. Monroe reminded the mission that the United States had "resisted by war the practice of impressment, and continued the war until that practice had ceased by a peace in Europe," and that while the nation's object had been essentially obtained, the United States wanted to assure that the practice would not revive in a new European war.

In a final paragraph in the June 25 letter, Monroe advised,

> Information has been received, from a quarter deserving attention, that the late events in France have produced such an effect on the British Government as to make it probable that a demand will be made at Gottenburg to surrender our right to the fisheries; to abandon all trade beyond the cape of Good Hope; and to cede Louisiana to Spain. We cannot believe that such a demand will be made. Should it be, you will of course treat it as it deserves. These rights must not be brought into discussion. If insisted on, your negotiations will cease.[21]

These assertions were crucial to the envoys' mission.

In his letter of June 27, Monroe referred again to Gottenburg, approving the commissioners' move from there to Ghent, but also cited the British delay in sending a mission to the original place of negotiation as "proof of a dilatory policy." In addition, Monroe stated that

> you may omit any stipulation on the subject of impressment, if found indispensably necessary to terminate it [the war]. You will, of course, not recur to this expedient until all your efforts to adjust the controversy in a more satisfactory manner have failed.

On allowing the treaty to be silent on impressment, it was important that the omission not have the effect of permitting a continued claim to the practice by Great Britain or suggest that the United States had relinquished their claims in opposition. "An acknowledgment of the right in Great Britain is utterly inadmissible."[22]

With renewed support of their government, so recently at hand, the American envoys gathered in Bayard's chamber at ten o'clock on August 9th to spend an hour solidifying their position for the next meeting with the British who came to the American residence at eleven. Adams informed them on the points his colleagues had agreed to present the night before. The Americans, he told them, "Presumed it would excite no surprise with the British at finding the Americans uninstructed upon two points, which had never heretofore formed any subject of controversy between the two Countries." (These points pertained to the Indians and the fisheries.) It was only natural that their instructions were confined to subjects of difference on which the war originated.

Clay added to this that the American government could have anticipated no such propositions from the tenor of Castlereagh's proposal for negotiations, and that up to their most recent instructions (just received) "they had not the remotest expectations of any such points." Goulburn replied that it could not be expected that Lord Castlereagh would, in that proposal, enumerate the points which would become subjects of discussion. They would depend upon events occurring after the proposal and until commencement of negotiations. But in any event, Great Britain could not be expected to make peace without including her Indian allies.[23]

Adams said the Americans had no objection to hearing what the British had to say upon the topics, but since the U.S. instructions were silent on them, they could only afterward determine whether it was within the scope of their discretionary power to deal with them. Goulburn then asked if such discussions would terminate in agreeing to a provisional article, which the Americans would sign, subject to the ratification of the U.S. government. Adams answered that such an article "must of course be unauthorized," but that the Americans, nevertheless, "thought it proper, at the same time, in candor, to tell them that we did not think it likely that any provisional form whatever which they could receive would obtain for them our assent." Goulburn was later to write his superior that "Mr. Clay stated in strong terms his sense of the extreme difficulty of any article being framed on the subject which would be acceded to by the American Government."[24]

This discussion of a preliminary article related principally to the subject of the Indians. Gallatin entered the talks to say that "the United States would have neither interest or wish to continue the war with the Indians when that with Great Britain should be terminated," and that commis-

sioners had already been appointed to treat for peace with them and it might already be concluded. Gallatin observed that the U.S. policy was the most liberal and humane of any nation toward the Indians. The American envoys said their country's

> object had been, by all practicable means, to introduce civilization amongst them [the Indians]; that their possessions were secured to them by well defined boundaries; that their persons, lands, and other property, were now more effectually protected against violence or frauds, from any quarter, than they had been under any former Government; that even our citizens were not allowed to purchase their lands; that when they gave up their title to any portion of their country to the United States, it was by voluntary treaty with our Government, who gave then a satisfactory equivalent; and that through these means the United States had succeeded in preserving, since the treaty of Greenville of 1785, an uninterrupted peace of sixteen years with all the Indian tribes — a period of tranquility much longer than they were known to have enjoyed heretofore.[25]

As to the British proposal for a distinct boundary for the Indians, Gallatin said, it "was not only new, it was unexampled." No such treaty had ever before been made by any European power, he told them.

Goulburn answered Gallatin, saying the Indians were treated as sovereigns since both Great Britain and the United States made treaties with them.

Gallatin admitted there were treaties but none between the Indians and European powers defining boundaries. The Americans tried to show the British that there was an "obvious distinction between *making treaties* WITH *them*, and a treaty between two civilized nations defining a boundary FOR *them*."[26]

Bayard then asked,

> What was understood by Great Britain to be the effect and operation of the boundary line proposed? Was it to restrict the United States from making treaties with them hereafter as heretofore? [sic] from purchasing their lands, for instance? Was it to restrict the Indians from selling their lands? Was it to alter the condition of the Indians, such as it has hither to existed?

Goulburn replied "that it was intended as a barrier between the United States and the British possessions," but he did not spell out, at this sitting, the area which they had in mind. The Americans, knowing they had no power to cede any U.S. territory to the Indians, thought it unnecessary to ask where the line of demarcation was proposed to be established. Goulburn said it would not restrict the Indians from selling their lands but would restrict the United States from purchasing them. The British Adams (William) amended this to say it would restrict purchase by both the United States and Great Britain, but not a third party. He then commented that further discussion on this subject would be unprofitable unless they could see some results — such as a provisional article. He proposed a brief adjournment to allow the Americans to consult on an article.

Gallatin advised the British that it would be easy that an article might be formed, and then afterwards break off discussion when it came to details. But it was better at once to avow the full extent of U.S. objections.

At this impasse, the British proposed a suspension of the conferences until they could consult with their government. They said a messenger could be sent home that evening. This was agreeable to the Americans who expected a reply from London within four or five days. Meanwhile, the British also proposed a protocol (or summary) of the two meetings be drawn up separately by the mission secretaries and be compared to make a final record of the proceedings of both days. The Americans agreed and the conference was adjourned until noon on the 10th, when they would meet again at the Americans' lodgings.

As they parted, Adams told Gambier he hoped the British message would express the gratification of the Americans "at the candid and conciliatory manner which the British Commissioners had adopted with us." Clay added that the British "could not express themselves too strongly" on the subject. The British answered that "they should be altogether deficient in their duty if they omitted to express their sentiments in these respects."[27]

In a letter written nine days later to Secretary of State Monroe, Clay summed up his impressions of the British position during these two days, particularly on the Indian issue.

> Their proposition that the pacification should embrace their Indian allies, and that a definite boundary, separating their possessions from our territories, should be fixed in the treaty, was

brought out in a manner that betrayed much ignorance of the political nature of that relation which has subsisted between the Indians and the U. States, or more probably it was intentionally announced in obscure and ambiguous terms. It was not until after we had put many questions to them, on both of the two first days of conference, that we acquired a distinct knowledge of their meaning. It at first appeared that their design was simply not to abandon their allies, but to provide for their peace in the same instrument which secured their own; and in order to ensure its permanency to have ascertained for them a certain boundary. Thus, in answer to a question which I put on the first day, it was expressly stated by them that they meant neither accession of territory to the Indians, nor change in the attributes of Indian sovereignty. It was not until the second day's conference that the intention of a barrier was unequivocally avowed, and that, in answer to a question put by Mr. Bayard as to the operation of the contemplated boundary, it was admitted to be the design that neither the U. States, nor G. Britain were to be at liberty to purchase lands from the Indians, who were at the same time to be left free to sell them to any third party.

> This ignorance or affectation on their part was my sole motive for the willingness which we expressed to receive a communication of their views, and to discuss all the topics suggested by them as likely to come up in the negotiation. If it were the first, I hoped that we should be able, in the progress of the negotiation, to satisfy them and their government through them, that there was no such necessity for British interference between the Indians and us as, on that account, to continue the War; that the branch would fall with the trunk; and that, as a matter of course some suitable line would be established between the Indians and the U. States. If it were the last, I thought we could lose nothing by knowing precisely their whole design. We saw the proposition to sever our Country — made under the guise of a generous and disinterested attention to the welfare of their allies, — but urged in fact for the purpose of security to the British provinces — and amounting in effect to a cession of territory by the U. States to G. Britain. On such a proposition it is quite unnecessary to add that not one of us, for a single moment, harboured the idea that it was possible for us to come to any agreement. Nor will I dwell upon the absurdity, to say the least of it, of G. Britain attempting, without powers, to treat for savage tribes, scattered over our acknowleged [sic] territory, the very names of which she probably does not know.[28]

As to the fisheries, Clay wrote Monroe,

It would seem to be the British doctrine that certain privileges enjoyed by us, under the treaty of peace, in their waters and on their shores, ceased with the declaration of War, and are revivable only by convention. Whether, on the contrary, our rights in this respect do not stand on the same firm basis as that on which our Independence rests, will demand our serious examination, if we proceed in the negotiation.[29]

In this brief opening round of discussions, the Americans were clearly more successful than the British at extracting from their adversaries the basic aims and their negotiating position. But, except for Clay, the Americans had little hope for success in the final result of their talks. On the other hand, the British failure to obtain a clear understanding of American determination to resist British arrogance led them to believe the Americans would acquiesce in their demands.

That evening (still the 9th), after the second day's conference, in his letter to his immediate superior at the Foreign Office, the Earl Bathurst, Goulburn reported that he believed the Americans

are sincere in their wish to re-establish peace between the two countries. They have conducted themselves with more candour and openness than I had expected to find from them, and I might say with as much as could have been expected by any one.

But Goulburn had clearly misjudged the Americans when he wrote,

I believe that they do not mean to put forward any claim to fish within the maritime jurisdiction of the British North American territories, or to dry their nets and fish upon the shores. At least Mr. Adams, who is the spokesman of the American Commission, contented himself merely with stating that on that point they had no instructions; and as he never again recurred to the subject, upon which (if America had intended to insist) she must have instructed her Commissioners, I conclude that we shall not be troubled on that score.

In this letter to Bathurst, Goulburn revealed a character of the British which was to persist throughout the negotiations. Uncertain as to how to handle the fact that the Americans were uninstructed on the Indian issue, on which the British had placed a *sine qua non*, these colorless and light-weight commissioners began the first of many appeals to their superiors for advice, interrupting the flow of the talks. Goulburn wrote,

Whether they [the negotiations] will be continued or not must depend upon your decision whether we shall proceed to discuss our other points of difference in the uncertainty in which the Americans are with respect to Indian boundary, or whether we shall suspend all our proceedings.

Goulburn also enclosed, with his letter to Bathurst, a more detailed summary of the conversations of the two days.[30] Needless to say, the contents of these inquiries of the British to their home office, could not be known to the Americans at this time, though they might guess at what their opponents were apt to write.

Jointly, the British commissioners sent a formal dispatch to Castlereagh which was similar in most respects to Goulburn's communication to Bathurst. The formal letter included a sentence, regarding the possibility of a provisional article, reading, "Mr. Clay stated his opinion that none could be framed." To which they told Castlereagh, "It appeared to us and we so stated it to the American Commissioners, that a proposal to discuss without a prospect of some arrangement at least of a provisional kind, would be fruitless."[31]

The Americans were also busy that evening, summarizing their views of the two days of talks. Besides writing his wife, Adams was

charged by my colleagues to make the rough draft of the protocol for Mr. Hughes. I drew it up accordingly. It was corrected by Messrs. Bayard, Gallatin and Clay, and given to Mr. Hughes to make out a fair copy of it for tomorrow morning.[32]

During the evening of August 9, Jonathan Russell returned from his visit to Antwerp and Dunkirk. He would attend his first meeting with the British the next day.

At noon on August 10, the two missions met again at the Americans' lodgings to exchange copies of the protocol each had drawn up, and conclude on a single report concurred in by both sides. The British paper was less detailed than that of the Americans. Though there was little disagreement on the summary of the first day's conference, the British began at once to object to various parts of the American account of the second day.

The British wanted only a simple statement of the points proposed for discussion and of facts. They thought the American explanations on the questions of an Indian boundary and the fisheries were "argumentative." The British Adams observed that if the protocol contained the American reason for the omission of the two points from the U.S. instructions, it should also contain the British reasons for supposing that the American instructions might have provided for them. The American Adams admitted that was true, "if in fact any such reasons had been assigned by them; but they had not." In any case, the Americans admitted the protocol ought not contain reasons at large "but that important facts ought to enter into it, and that if these facts imported reasoning, that was no objection to their insertion."[33]

Goulburn replied that the proper place for such paragraphs was in dispatches to the home government. He added,

> If matter of argument were admitted on one side it must also be admitted on the other, and must eventually contain everything said at the conferences, which, if we should have many, would swell it up to an excessive volume.[34]

The Americans answered that the "paragraphs were material to unfold the full import of their proposals." Bayard put it pointedly that the British had not disclosed their full meaning, saying that the Indian boundary proposition was not intelligible. "Did they [the British] mean to take a portion of our territory and assign it to the Indians? Did they mean, in a word, to alter the condition of the Indians in relation to the United States?"[35]

The British became upset by the sharp questioning of the Americans and, according to Adams, regretted having answered Bayard so explicitly the day before. They responded by saying "they could not be expected to develop at this stage of the business, if at any time, the ultimate views and intentions of their Government." When Goulburn used the words, "Dominions and territories of the Indians," Adams remarked that the British

> must be aware the terms Dominions, Territories, and Possessions, as applied to Indians, were of very different import from the same terms as applied to civilized nations; That this difference was well known and understood ... by all the European nations.

Goulburn said it was necessary to use one of the words and preferred "Territory."[36]

On another point of contention, the American draft stated that the British "*declined* entering further into discussion" unless the Americans agreed to draw up a provisional article dealing with the Indians, and that they proposed to suspend the conferences until they could consult their government on the points now raised. The British "objected with much earnestness" to this comment being in the protocol. The Americans replied that it was not only a fact, "but a fact so material to the statement of what had actually taken place, that without it the protocol itself must be imperfect."[37]

Dr. Adams thought it too strong to say they "had *declined* entering into the discussion." Clay reminded him that they were Dr. Adams' express words. The Englishman admitted as much, but said those were remarks he had thrown out rather in the manner of friendly discussion in a spirit of candor and mutual confidence which they desired should guide the negotiations. The Americans agreed to omit the expression that they had declined further discussion, but pressed them on the fact of calling for a suspension of the talks. Still the British objected and gave the Americans a minor warning that its effect would be to seal their lips and put them upon a reserve they did not wish to assume.

Gallatin repeated that omission would leave the protocol imperfect making it appear that an American "request for further discussions had not been answered — when in fact it had." The arguments got nowhere, and finally the Americans "agreed to omit everything to which the British objected." Clay gave in his "Journal" as a reason for giving in, that

> it was clearly and distinctly understood that, the protocol notwithstanding, we were both at liberty to communicate in the fullest manner to our respective governments, what should occur from time to time at the conferences.[38]

When this session ended, the secretaries, Christopher Hughes and Anthony St. John Baker, were left with the task of preparing the final protocol from the two drafts. The American mission also assigned to John Quincy Adams the job of preparing a draft of a dispatch to be sent to Secretary of State James Monroe. Adams put off this burden until the following day.

A lull now set in during which the American

expectations of peace, never very strong, nearly vanished and an irritation with affairs grew in place of hope. It was so apparent on this final day of discussions as to prompt James Gallatin to write in his diary,

> Father finds greater difficulty with his own colleagues. The accident which placed him at the foot of the Commission [by being named last to the second mission] placed Mr. Adams at the head of it. Messrs. Clay, Bayard, and Russell let Mr. Adams plainly know that, though he might be the nominal mouthpiece, Gallatin was their leader. Clay uses strong language to Adams, and Adams returns the compliment. Father looks calmly on with a twinkle in his eye. Today there was a severe storm, and father said, "Gentlemen, gentlemen, we must remain united or we will fail."[39]

As for expectations of peace, Adams had privately expressed his view in a letter to his wife written the night before the negotiations were suspended. He told her he had "not changed the opinion which I have constantly had of the results." In addition, he inferred that a recent speech of the prince regent — which spoke of "*unprovoked oppression*" by the Americans, yet his willingness to carry on the war with increased vigor — was mild in comparison with that of the Speaker of the House of Commons. The Speaker declared that Britain "could never consent to terminate the war *but by the establishment of the maritime rights of Great Britain.*" Adams observed to his wife, "At present I do not think that the negotiation will be of long continuance."[40]

Bayard, writing to Crawford, said,

> The state of things does not auger well. A sine qua non so early and in a manner so preemptory upon a point relatively to us of so great importance, and to them so small, looks very much like an intended stumbling block in the threshold of negociation.[41]

This feeling was so strong that it was implied to the British during the conferences and stated in writing in the final draft of an informational dispatch to Monroe. On relating to him the controversy over the provisional article, the commissioners told their superior, "We added, that, as we should deeply deplore a rupture on the negotiation on any point, it was our anxious desire to employ all possible means to avert an event so serious in its consequences."[42]

Bayard expanded his views a few days later in a letter to Robert Harper. He told his friend that since it took only one party to make war but two to make peace, peace now appeared doubtful. War had now taken on a defensive character for the Americans since the British views of it

> are undoubtedly altered by the great changes which had taken place on this Continent. While the power of Bonaparte existed Great Britain had employment for all her resources on this side of the Atlantic.... At present there is no Power in this Hemisphere from which she has anything to dread. She has been vexed for many years by the disputes we have had with Her with respect to her maritime rights. She is jealous of the encreasing resources of our country, of the aptitude of our people for commerce and navigation and their prowess in naval enterprize. She sees at the present moment a state of things which may never occur again in which she is left without an apprehension of the interference of Any European Power to exert her whole strength against us. The effort will be made to crush Us altogether and if that be impracticable to inflict such wounds as will put a stop to our growth or at least retard it.[43]

James Gallatin confided in his diary that his father "fears negotiations will soon come to an end and has but little hope; he does not think the British Government wish to make peace or they would have sent more powerful delegates."[44]

Clay was more detailed in his impressions revealed in his long letter to Secretary of State Monroe. He expressed no surprise at the turn of affairs in Ghent.

> We were prepared by events which have occurred in Europe, by the temper manifested in English pamphlets and prints, and by the well known arrogance of the British character, for the most extravagant pretention to be brought forward in our negotiation. Unhappily we have not been disappointed in this expectation, as you will see from our despatch. In such a state of mind, we have been all strongly impressed that, next to our first and greatest duty of making an honorable peace, if practicable, was that of so conducting ourselves, and the negotiation, as to demonstrate that, if the War were to be continued, this calamity was ascribable to the enemy.[45]

Remarking on the British envoys' need to obtain instructions from their government, Clay envisioned a stronger American position than seen by his fellow diplomats as he wrote Monroe,

What will be their purport when they do arrive can only be matter of conjecture. I am inclined to think that the Ministry has been attempting an experiment upon us, under the supposition that a panic has seized us, and that their policy is to consume as much time as possible before the termination of the negotiation, under the hope that they will strike some signal blow, during the present campaign. If this opinion be correct the B. Commissioners will probably be instructed to insist on their sine qua non, in expectation that we will refer the subject to our Government. In that case should we determine not to make such reference, as being wholly useless, and should they not in the mean time hear of some decisive advantage gained over us, I think the Ministry will pause before they break off the negotiation on the points in question. Such a rupture, it is evident, would entirely change the whole character of the War, would unite all parties at home, and would organize a powerful opposition in Great Britain. It is difficult to believe that they should not have foreseen such a state of our instructions as we have communicated to them, and therefore if they intended a rupture on those points, I presume their Commerce would have needed no fresh instructions. It would at the same time seem somewhat improbable that they should suddenly abandon ground which, in such an early state of the negotiation, they so earnestly occupied. This they can only avoid by prevailing on us to refer the subject to our Government.[46]

Nevertheless, Clay was equally aware of the difficulties faced by America with no allies to be counted on and an England free to concentrate her military and naval energies on a single foe. Already, the American envoys had learned that British Admiral Alexander Cochrane had declared the whole American coast to be in a state of blockade and that more than 100 transports had been engaged to carry British troops somewhere — possibly as an expedition against New Orleans.[47]

In summing up the diplomatic status of Europe, it is quite surprising that the most astute analysis comes from Clay, who had so little formal education, had not travelled widely, and had only spent a couple of years as Speaker at the upper levels of the U.S. government. Most likely, the best educated and most travel-wise was Adams. Even Gallatin or Bayard might have provided greater insight to European affairs. Yet it was Clay who wrote to Monroe as follows:

If the War is to be continued, we must rely for its prosecution exclusively upon our own resources. Continental Europe is too much exhausted, and has yet too much to do to arrange its own complicated affairs to authorize the expectation of any immediate succor from this quarter. Besides, much misconception has prevailed on the Continent, particularly in Germany, of the views of our Government in declaring War. This has been owing to the activity of the British influence & the state of the press. The British side of the question has alone reached the public. We have nevertheless many friends, and our cause is daily acquiring more. Still we cannot at present calculate upon any thing but good wishes. France is occupied in consolidating her new government. She would be very unwilling to renew the War with G. Britain until she gets back her Colonies. In that Country the materials sufficiently abound for internal explosion, which will only be prevented by the difficulty of their combination. Every body is dissatisfied, but every body is wearied, and this perhaps is the best guarantee for the continuance of the present order of things. The Military is the most discontented class, and they are represented to be anxious for War. Austria is however the power upon which they wish to fall; and it is not unlikely that Louis the 18th will find, in the indulgence of this passion, the means of preserving domestic tranquility and strengthening his throne.

The prospect of renewed War is the greatest in the North; Poland the bone of contention, and Russia and Austria the great parties. The arrangement of the concerns of Germany, and the future condition in particular of Saxony, will afford serious occupation to the Congress of Vienna, and will very likely result in War. Such is the martial character, stamped upon Europe by the last twenty years, that it will be wonderful if the habits and the pursuits of peace are resumed without further struggle.[48]

While the American commissioners settled in to wait for the British to obtain further instructions from their government, Adams put together a draft of a dispatch to Monroe. He completed it on Thursday morning, August 11, and read it to his colleagues at a noon meeting. Each wanted to have a turn at making alterations and additions. It was given to Bayard first. He returned it to Adams at dinner time. Gallatin had it all day of the 12th.

That same day, at a meeting of the mission, it was decided to request Capt. Samuel Angus, of the *John Adams*, to be ready to sail for America on August 25, to carry dispatches to the U.S. government. Then occurred a heated colloquy among the envoys on a minor matter. John Connell, the

American who delivered Clay's letter to Adams traveling from Stockholm to Gottenburg in early June, had expressed the desire to return to the United States on the ship. While the ship's passport did not forbid cargo and passengers (as usual for a cartel ship), it expressly said she was to go in ballast with the passengers named, or persons carrying dispatches. Named were: George M. Dallas, John Payne Todd, and Col. George B. Milligan — but not Connell.

Clay logically proposed, therefore, that Connell should be charged with carrying dispatches. But Gallatin argued that he had promised that office to Dallas. To this, Clay suggested (and Russell concurred) that Connell might be the bearer of dispatches aboard the ship, but on arrival in America, they would be turned over to Dallas. Adams, writing in his diary, said, "I not only disapproved this, but inconsiderately said it would be a *trick* I should think highly improper. Mr. Russell, and more especially Mr. Clay, were hurt at my use of this expression." Despite the fact that all of the American envoys thought the terms of the passport were broad enough to permit Connell's passage, Adams still felt the Americans had pledged themselves not to send any passenger without the express consent of the British government. But, the introspective Adams wrote, "the use of the word *trick* was harsh and unnecessary. The correct principle in this case is to do nothing that may not be boldly avowed. I should have said this, and no more."[49]

The following morning, both Angus and Connell left Ghent. Angus returned to his ship on which Connell had failed to obtain permission for passage. Before leaving, Angus said to one of the mission aides, William Shaler, "Well, I am going home and what shall I say? The people will all be crowding about me for news — what shall I tell them?"

Shaler said, "Tell them that the day before you left Ghent you dined with the Commissioners and all the Americans in the place, and that at the dinner Mr. Adams gave for a toast 'Lawrence's last word.'"

"Why?" asked Angus, "Do you think he meant anything by it?"

"Tell them the fact," replied Shaler, "and leave them to judge of that." Adams, who mentioned this little dialogue to his wife, wrote,

It is true that Mr. A. did give the toast, but it is very strange that Shaler should have noticed and recollected it! If he had meant anything, was it not much more probable that it would have been instantly felt by Captain Angus, himself a naval officer, than by a non-combatant landsman? Angus did however finally suspect that Mr. A. meant something. What is your opinion?[50]

Continuing to write his wife on the casual pursuits of the mission, while continuing to wait for the return of the British instructions, Adams gave a brief account of his own activities while touching on those of his colleagues. After telling her of deciphering Monroe's two dispatches until the wee hours of the morning of August 9, he wrote,

This encroached something upon my hour of retirement, which is now regularly at 9 o'clock. Hitherto we have had no evenings. We dine all together at four, and sit usually at table until six. We then disperse to our several amusements and avocations. Mine is a solitary walk of two or three hours — solitary, because I find none of the other gentlemen disposed to join me in it, particularly at that hour. They frequent the coffee houses, the Reading Rooms, and the billiard tables. Between eight and nine I return from my walk, and immediately betake myself to bed. I rise usually about five in the morning, and from that time until dinner am closely engaged in writing or in other business. We breakfast separately, each in his own chamber, and meet almost every day for an hour or two between breakfast and dinner. We are not troublesome to one another, and if our landlord was not quite so anxious as he is to fatten upon us too fast, we should live with as much satisfaction as I believe would be possible at Bachelor's Hall. We pay him a very liberal and generous price; but he was to furnish the house completely and elegantly, which he has not done; and as for the boarding part we give him a fixed price by the head and the day; he requires a scolding once or twice a week to make him provide us with tolerable fare.[51]

August 13th saw the draft of the dispatch to Monroe make a little more progress. Clay received it in the morning from Gallatin, kept it only a short time, and then gave it back to Bayard for a second time. He kept it until evening when Russell had his chance to go over it. On the morning of the 15th, Russell returned the mutilated dispatch to Adams along with "a folio sheet of amendments and corrections." Adams showed his disgust writing that the amendments were capital letters, the commas and points, and the caution to spell until with only one l. Several of them, under the idea of amending the style, made a different statement of facts from that which really occurred. The amendments to the narrative of a party who was present at the transactions related, made by a person who was not present, are not very likely to improve its accuracy.

Adams was even more irked by Bayard's treatment of his original effort. Bayard brought Adams an entire new draft "in his own language, not one sentence of which agreed with mine." Adams had had enough of the nit-picking and at their meeting, later in the day, he proposed that Bayard's draft be substituted for his. This was agreed to, but a number of questions remained to be settled — principally over omission of facts in Bayard's copy which had been Adams'. As it became difficult to harmonize all viewpoints, it was finally decided to have Gallatin take Bayard's draft and make such changes in it that seemed to present an acceptance by all. It was then given to Hughes to be copied. Adams summed up the situation, writing,

There was no other way of getting a dispatch ready; for if Mr. Bayard's draft had been taken to be altered, corrected, and amended as mine was, at the end of another week we should have had twenty sheets of paper written, instead of seven, and have to begin the dispatch.[52]

Gallatin worked on the third draft until the morning of the 17th. At noon, it was presented to the mission and finally agreed to — after more amendments. The final form was signed the following afternoon, August 18.

Despite the annoyance Adams was feeling over the "desecration" of his original draft, Clay was able to write in his long letter to Monroe (which was written this very evening),

I have great satisfaction in informing you that the most entire harmony prevails between my colleagues on the subjects of our mission. No former diversity of opinion here shews itself in the smallest degree. All are deeply sensible of the solemn nature of our duty. All are animated solely by the desire of advancing the interests of our common Country. All are equally tenacious of its rights and its honor. No one, in our most free and confidential consultations among ourselves, has ventured to suggest, even as matter of consideration, the expediency of subscribing to the demands of the other party in any possible shape which could be given to them.[53]

29

RUPTURE

Overnight, Henry Clay left unsealed his letter of August 18th to James Monroe. He had summed up, for the secretary of state, the results of three days of conferences with the British, given his assessment of peace prospects, and commented on the harmony within the American delegation. The next day, he was to add an angry postscript to the letter.

To tell the story of the next two days of conferences between the British and American envoys requires a summarized blending of paraphrased comments and direct quotes from still existing documents written overnight by participants. They appear in Adams' *Memoirs* and *Writings*, Bayard's and Clay's *Papers*, a diary of James Gallatin and his father's papers, and in the great volumes of the *American State Papers*. Even papers of the British envoys and their superiors, such as Lord Castlereagh, are included.

The day that ruffled Clay's attitude began in the dawn hours of August 19, when John Quincy Adams was up, as usual, writing to Louisa Catherine in St. Petersburg. He told her that a British messenger had arrived in Ghent in the evening of the 17th. The courier had brought a dispatch from Lord Castlereagh dated August 14, written in response to the request, on August 9, for further instructions from the British commissioners.

While the exact contents of Castlereagh's letter remained unknown to the Americans, the British envoys revealed enough of it to outrage and infuriate them. It is hard to imagine either Henry Clay or John Quincy Adams controlling his temper. Castlereagh's instructions were filled with such insolence and arrogance that Americans everywhere would resent and reject their contents.

Though it was to have no effect whatever on the deliberations of the 19th, it was soon learned by the Americans that Castlereagh, himself, had arrived in Ghent on the previous evening. There was to be no contact between him and the Americans during his two-day stopover on his way to Paris and later to Vienna. Nevertheless, Adams, later writing his wife, stated that, "It is scarcely a figure of speech to say that we felt him," at the conference.[1] Castlereagh, on the other hand, referred to the non-event several days later at the beginning of a message to his superior, Prime Minister Liverpool in London. The foreign minister noted that during his recent two-day visit to Ghent,

> I did not see any of the American Commissioners. They did not call upon or desire to see me, and I thought my originating an interview would be considered objectionable and awkward by our own Commissioners.

How did he "know" the Americans had no desire to see him? There is no evidence they were ever officially notified of his presence in the city, nor any indication the Americans would be received if a meeting were requested — and why would they ask for one?[2]

During the morning of August 19, the British secretary to the mission, Anthony St. John Baker, called on the Americans to request a meeting at the lodging of the British at three o'clock.[3] In the interim, Adams, as planned, went with the mayor of Ghent to visit the public library and view some ancient manuscripts. The other American envoys had been invited but declined. Gallatin was not well and Bayard was writing to friends at home. It was at this time that he poured out his impressions, noted earlier in a letter to Robert Harper, that the United States was in a precarious position with no allies from whom help could be obtained in Europe, with the British riding high with no one to dispute their demands.

On Adams' return to the Americans' lodgings, following his library visit with Ghent's mayor, the mission met at two o'clock to haggle a bit more over the draft of a note to Monroe accounting for the delay of the departure of the *John Adams*. At the three-o'clock meeting with the British, Goulburn began by orally relating some of the contents of a letter lying in front of him — the most recent dispatch from London. He told the Americans that his government was surprised that the United States government had provided no instructions regarding "Indian pacification and boundary, as it must have been foreseen, that they [the British] could not consent to terminate the war leaving their weaker allies at the mercy of a more powerful enemy." The British thought the American government would have instructed their mission to "agree to a provisional article" on the subject. The British also thought the least they could "demand" of the Americans was that they should sign such an article, subject to the ratification by the U.S. government, "so that if it should be ratified the treaty should take effect, and if not, that it should be null and void." In addition, the British now stipulated that refusal by the Americans to agree to such an article, or to refer home for further instructions, the conferences would be suspended and "Great Britain would not consider herself bound, upon renewal of the negotiations, to abide by the terms which she now offers," and would "hold themselves at liberty to regulate their conduct by the then state of events." Yet an American request for instructions from Washington would probably take nearly three months!

In response to an American request for a more explicit explanation of the British stand on the Indian issue, Goulburn stated that the Indian territories were to be interposed as a neutral but permanent barrier between the provinces of Great Britain and the United States to prevent them from being conterminous to each other, and that neither Great Britain nor the United States should acquire by purchase any of these Indian lands.

More specifically, regarding a proposed boundary line, the British said they would be "willing to take the Treaty of Grenville for the basis, with such modifications as might be agreed upon."

They considered that, in North America, "G. Britain was the weaker power and had no desire or motive whatever for conquest or aggrandizement there," while, on the other hand, the United States had designs of conquering Canada. (Clay, in effect, was having his own boasts of conquest thrown back at him.)

On the basis of this argument the British government felt justified in requiring "the exclusive possession of the [Great] Lakes, and for their security to cession of a certain extend of territory along their southern shores." Furthermore, to avoid a contest for control of the lakes

> in peace as well as war.... G. Britain would require that the U.S. should build or retain no vessels of war on the lakes, that is from Ontario to Superior inclusive; and that they should erect or maintain no fort or military post on the shores of the Lakes; but that the military occupation thereof should be exclusively with G. Britain, who was to be under no restrictions.

The British added that "these propositions must be considered as proofs of the moderation of Great Britain, since she might have demanded a cession of all the borders of the Lakes to herself." As further proof, they said, Britain was good enough to permit commercial navigation of the lakes to remain as it had been.[4]

Still before any two-party discussion, the British made two more demands. They insisted that navigation rights of the Mississippi River should be "continued" to Great Britain "as secured to her by the former treaties." And with this they would require the line between their two countries (the United States and Canada) to be revised from Lake Superior to the Mississippi River. The second of these additional demands was that Great Britain would require a cession of part of the province of Maine (then a part of Massachusetts) to secure a communication route between Halifax, Nova Scotia, and Quebec.

As to the first of these last two demands, the British were asked if they did not mean to speak of a line from the Mississippi River to the Lake of the Woods, instead of Lake Superior. They said, "No." They apparently had little concept of the geography of the region.[5]

When Goulburn finished presenting the British demands, Gallatin asked what they intended to do about the citizens of the United States, beyond their proposed boundary line. Gallatin observed that inhabitants numbering around 100,000 had migrated and settled along with their ancestors over 100 years in the territories of Indiana, Illinois, and Michigan and that portion of the state of Ohio.

Goulburn replied that his government had not considered their situation, but, he suggested, this might be a foundation for the United States to claim a particular modification of the line. But if that were not agreed to, the people might have to move. William Adams was even more explicit, saying. "They must shift for themselves."[6]

At this point, Bayard asked if the issue of Indian pacification and boundary was still presented as a *sine qua non*. The British answered that undoubtedly it was. Then, "From the forcible manner in which the demand that the United States should keep no naval armed force on the lakes, nor any military posts on their shores, had been brought forward," according to the mission's official dispatch to Monroe, Bayard was "induced to inquire, whether this condition was also meant as a *sine qua non*?"[7] To this, Dr. Adams replied pettishly, "One *sine qua non* at a time is enough. It will be time enough to answer your question when you have disposed of that we have given you." Gallatin inquired of them if they intended to retain a navy on the lakes and forts on their shores. The British said they certainly did.[8]

Linked somewhat to the demand for cession of a part of Maine was the status of Moose Island and other small islands in Passamaquoddy Bay. The Americans had learned only recently of their capture by the British. Gallatin asked if the report was correct that they meant to keep the islands. They replied it was, that they were a part of the Province of Nova Scotia, and that their possession was not even a subject for discussion. Goulburn said he could prove they belonged to Britain and Dr. Adams added that the United States might as well contest British rights to Northamptonshire.

The American Adams then told the British he would wish further conference "before we should have received from the British Commissioners a written statement of their propositions." This was agreed to and the British also requested a written answer to their note prior to the next conference. Adams observed that the Americans might wish some verbal explanations before sending their an-

swer and assumed there would be no objection to another conference. The British Adams briefly objected, but then agreed with the others to assent to the American request.

As the hour-long conference ended, Bayard said to Goulburn, that if the conferences were suspended, he supposed Goulburn would take a trip to England. The Britisher replied, "Yes, and I suppose you will take a trip to America."

The impression resulting from the apparent rupture of negotiations is revealed in correspondence left by each of the American envoys except Russell. To his wife, Adams wrote, "Our opponents were not only charged fourfold with obnoxious substance, they threw off much of the suavity of form which they had observed before."[9] As for the British, he wrote in his diary, "Their tone was more peremptory and their language more overbearing than at the former conferences. Their deportment this day was particularly offensive to Mr. Bayard."[10]

On August 20, Bayard, in turn, expanded his views in a supplement added to his letter of the previous day to Robert Harper. He told his friend,

> At this meeting the veil with which they had attempted before to cover their designs was thrown aside. Their terms were those of a Conqueror to a conquered People. The former points of dispute have not been the Subjects of a moments consideration. Maritime pretensions have been thrown far in the back ground and concessions of the most ruinous and disgraceful description have been required.

With an eye on the political ramifications likely to result in America, and particularly in Federalist New England, when the news of the latest British demands were learned, Bayard, himself a Federalist, went on to write,

> I trust in God that when the character of the war is so totally changed and when we are not simply contending for the honor of the nation but driven to fight for its existence — the Federalists will prove themselves, what I have always believed them to be the true and faithful friends of their Country. As to the origin of the war we are all agreed. But when peace is refused upon just and moderate terms and the most extrava[ga]nt pretensions are advanced, what is left for Us but to fight manfully or submit to disgrace and ruin.

Bayard then added, "The negotiation is not absolutely ended, but little more remains than the form of closing it."[11]

Expressing the same idea, but in different words, Bayard wrote a week later to Levett Harris, the earlier mission's secretary (when Bayard was in St. Petersburg). He said,

One good effect will follow from this abortive negotiation. The people of America will become united in the defence of the rights which they are now called upon to surrender, and shew themselves a more formidable foe than England or Europe have hitherto supposed them capable of being.[12]

Adams had one more comment on the talks, in his diary, which concurred with Bayard's statement, but also showed that expectation of a rupture of the negotiations was not a view held unanimously among the Americans. He wrote, "Mr. Clay has an inconceivable idea that they [the British] will finish by receding from the ground they have taken."[13]

And finally, we come to Clay's postscript to Monroe mentioned at the beginning of this chapter. And again, he exhibited the characteristics of a seasoned diplomat, surpassing the intuition of his more educated and experienced colleagues. Clay's view was revealed in an August 19 postscript to his letter to the secretary of state, begun the day before. With it, he sent Monroe a copy of his "Journal" of the conference and said in his letter,

You will see that there is no room for comment. The prospect of peace has vanished. In the state in which their claims now appear, I should consider that it would be offering an unpardonable insult to our Government to ask them any instructions. The pretensions of G. Britain do not admit of deliberation. I ought perhaps, after what has transpired, to suppress altogether this letter, but as with my erroneous speculations relative to the course which I supposed would be taken by the B. Commsrs. there may be mixed some matter not absolutely useless. I give it to you for what it is worth. It is indeed not impossible that our decision to make no reference for instructions to our Government of the inadmissible claims which they have brought forward, and as far as depends upon us to finally terminate the negotiation, may yet occasion a pause. But the hope of their retracting their demands is to [sic] remote to warrant the smallest calculation upon it. The reliance will be much better on the firmness and energy of the American people, to conquer again their Independence.[14, 15]

Not quite so firm in his conviction of a British diplomatic retreat, Clay also wrote William Craw-

ford a few days later. With his letter, he also sent a copy of his journal. Again he said,

The prospect of peace has disappeared and ... nothing remains for us but to formally close the abortive negotiations. The regret you will feel for the continuance of the war will be mitigated, however, by the evidence you will have, that this unhappy issue is attributable solely to the extravagant demands of the enemy; and by every section and every interest in the Union, must arouse, if anything can arouse, all parties into a vigorous resistance.

But also to Crawford, Clay expressed that very faint hope that all was not lost. He wrote,

I ought, perhaps, to mention to you that throughout the whole of the negotiations I have been inclined to think the other party has been practicing upon our supposed fears, and that he would ultimately abandon his pretensions. In this impression (I will not call it opinion) what I do not yet absolutely abandon, I stand alone. If it be well founded when our paper is received and it is known that we will not refer to our government for further instructions, he may possibly yet pause.[16]

He added that they plan to sail for Cherbourg or Brest by the first of October, hoping to spend some time with Crawford in Paris in the interim. Were the sailing plans to America?

Still on August 19, after dinner, the American delegation had a brief meeting at which they agreed to write a dispatch to Monroe. Gallatin was given the unpleasant task of drafting the official message to the U.S. government. Its final form, surprisingly accepted the next morning by the whole mission with only a few alterations, detailed the day's conference pretty much as Adams and Clay had described it in their *Memoirs* and "Journal."

Gallatin's observations resulting from the apparent rupture of negotiations took a longer-range view of the probable repercussions. Writing to Monroe, on August 20, he said results were as he had anticipated except in one respect. He had supposed that the British government

in continuing the war yielded to the popular sentiment, and were only desirous of giving some éclat to the termination of hostilities, and by predatory attacks of inflicting gratuitous injury on the United States. It appears now certain that they have more serious and dangerous objects in view.

Gallatin went on to tell Monroe that he expected the British to conquer that which they wish to gain in the negotiations. In line with this, Gallatin forecast a great British effort in Canada to possess the lands around Lakes Ontario and Erie joined with the recapture of Detroit and new support for the Indians. He also predicted that the warfare on the Atlantic shore

> will be on a smaller scale than I had conjectured, and may be confined to desultory attacks made successively on several points, for the purpose principally of distracting our defensive measures and of diverting a considerable part of our force from the points of real and serious attack

Gallatin could not know that any useful warning about British attacks along the Eastern seaboard of the United States was already too late to reach the government in Washington.

While events were nearly opposite what Gallatin predicted, he was more accurate in his next forecast. He told Monroe,

> It appears to me most likely that their true and immediate object is New Orleans. They well know that it is our most distant and weakest point, and that if captured could not be retaken without great difficulty. If successful in other quarters, there is no possession which as a sugar colony, as a port in the Gulf of Mexico, and as commanding all our Western country both in a political and in a commercial view, would be more desirous of holding. If less successful in Canada than they expect, New Orleans would be a set-off, and its restitution to depend on our compliance with their demands in the North.

Gallatin supported his thoughts relating to New Orleans by telling Monroe that a British expedition expected to sail for America early in September, must have Louisiana as an object since it was too late in the season for a move in Canada or along the northern coast of the United States. He also believed that the British

> object in protracting the negotiations has been to delay their rupture to the very moment when her expedition under General [Rowland] Hill would be ready and must sail, in order to prevent, as far as practicable, our taking early alarm and making sufficient preparations to repel the attack.[17]

That same day, Gallatin recorded the same thoughts in a letter to Alexander J. Dallas (father of mission aide, George M. Dallas, the senior Dallas was to succeed to Gallatin's former treasury post within two months). Gallatin wrote,

> Our negotiations may be considered as at an end. Some official notes may yet pass, but the nature of the demands of the British, made also as a preliminary *sine qua non*, to be admitted as a basis before a discussion, is such that there can be no doubt of a speedy rupture of our conferences, and that we will have no peace. Great Britain wants war in order to cripple us; she wants aggrandizement at our expense; she may have ulterior objects; no resource left but in union and vigorous prosecution of the war. When her terms are known it appears to me impossible that all America should not unite in defence of her rights, of her territory, I may say of her independence. I do not expect to be longer than three weeks in Europe.[18]

Not long after the American mission had settled on the wording of their official letter to Monroe, they received the written note requested of the British. This note was sent along to Monroe with no comment. And no change was made in the official dispatch except that now a paragraph, placed at the end of the letter to Monroe, was struck out. It had been in Bayard's draft and had been complimentary to the personal deportment of the British.

The British note contained nothing new, but expressed the same extravagant demands and arrogant self-confidence as presented orally to the Americans in conference. Still, behind the scenes, the British commissioners were somewhat confused about the extent of their instructions. Only during Castlereagh's two-day visit in Ghent, did Goulburn learn that his government wished "to make America disarm on the Lakes and on the shores of them." This was "more agreeable" to Goulburn's feelings. But he took issue with Castlereagh on another matter.

Writing on August 21 to his immediate supervisor, the Earl of Bathurst, Goulburn pointed out that they had consistently told the Americans that in fixing an Indian boundary,

> Neither party should acquire within that boundary any territory by purchase or *otherwise*. To the word *otherwise* Lord Castlereagh objected, as he said it was not intended to preclude the Americans from conquering the Indians who might be at war with them and acquiring territory by conquest, as a restriction of this nature would expose them to invasion from the Indians, for which there would be no redress. He therefore desired that if the

point were brought into discussion, we should disclaim such a view of the subject.

Goulburn told Bathurst that to admit acquisition of Indian territory by conquest, there should be

> no difficulty in settling that question. The Americans will, I am sure, be ready to assign a boundary, if they are told that they may conquer though they may not purchase the territory within it. Causes of war will always be found, for they almost always exist; and the only difference in the situation of Canada will be, that its frontier will be laid open by a conquering American army under General Harrison, instead of by treaties for sale, as heretofore. I must own that I do not quite see the justice of Lord Castlereagh's distinction.

Goulburn recognized that America could conquer Indian territory on the grounds of punishing them for some claimed injury. But the invaded Indians would merely move on to some more remote land. He argued that the arrangement would operate unfairly against the British.

> If an American-Indian nation injures us, we cannot attack them, because they are within the limits of the United States, and remonstrance is our only mode of obtaining redress; and if we call upon the United States to punish, they may avail themselves of our requisition to conquer their territory and bring themselves on our frontier. Our barrier, therefore, will be reduced to that portion of Indian territory within our own limits which we may set apart for that purpose; and this we may do as well without a stipulation as with it.[19]

As Goulburn tried to establish firmer grounds upon which to negotiate, the Americans set about trying to form a joint consensus upon which to respond to the British note. Both Adams and Bayard prepared lengthy drafts. Clay wrote down some ideas as did Gallatin, who had taken minutes of the subjects to be treated. Adams worked on his paper throughout Sunday, August 21, but did not finish. However, about two o'clock that afternoon, the mission met and all read their copies. Adams later told his diary what he thought of the efforts.

> I found, as usual, that the draft was not satisfactory to my colleagues. On the general view of the subject we are unanimous, but in my exposition of it, one objects to the form and another to the substance of almost every paragraph. Mr. Gallatin is for striking out every expression that may be of-

fensive to the feeling of the adverse party. Mr. Clay is displeased with figurative language, which he thinks improper for a state paper. Mr. Russell, agreeing in the objections of the two other gentlemen, will be further for amending the construction of every sentence; and Mr. Bayard, even when agreeing to say precisely the same thing, chooses to say it only in his own language. It was considered by all the gentlemen that what I had written was too long, and with too much argument about the Indians. It is, however, my duty to make the draft of the dispatch, and they usually hold me to it.[20]

Adams completed his draft on the 22nd, and before breakfast, gave it to Gallatin who kept it the rest of the day to make his amendments and additions. Adams again described the early part of the 23rd.

> We had this morning a meeting of the mission, when my draft of an answer to the note of the British Commissioners, with Mr. Gallatin's corrections and alterations, Mr. Clay's two or three paragraphs, and an attempt at a totally new draft begun and not finished by Mr. Bayard, were read and discussed; and Mr. Hughes was directed to make out a new draft from the shreds and patches of them all. About one-half of my draft was agreed to be struck out; a half of the remainder was left for consideration.[21]

That evening, they relaxed (somewhat) and attended a dinner at the home of the local intendant. Also there were the British commissioners (along with Mrs. Goulburn, who was making her first acquaintance with the Americans), the mayor of Ghent, members of the intendant's family, and others for a total of 25 persons. Goulburn sat next to Clay at the dinner and afterward wrote to Bathurst that it was evident to him that the Americans did not mean to continue the negotiations. "Mr. Clay," he wrote,

> gave me clearly to understand that they had decided upon a reference to America for instructions, and that they conceived our propositions equivalent to a demand for the cession of Boston or New York.

Clay also let Goulburn know that the American reply to the British note of August 20 would be delivered in a day or two.

As the gathering broke up, Bayard took Goulburn aside requesting, "a little private and confidential conversation." Goulburn told Bathurst that Bayard began a very long speech by saying that the present negotiation could not end in peace, and that he was desirous of privately stating (before we separated) what Great Britain did not appear to understand, viz. that by proposing terms like those which had been offered we were not only ruining all prospects of peace, but were sacrificing the party of which he was a member to their political adversaries. He went into a long discussion upon the views and objects of the several parties in America, and the grounds upon which a hostile or conciliatory disposition on our part might have upon them. He inculcated how much it was for our interest to support the Federalists, and that to make peace was the only method of supporting them effectually; that we had nothing to fear for Canada if peace were made, be the terms what they might; that there would have been no difficulty about allegiance, impressment, etc.; but that our present demands were what America never could or would accede to. This was the general tenor of his conversation, which I did not think it necessary to make much reply, and which I only mention to you in order to let you know at the earliest moment that the negotiation is not likely now to continue.

Goulburn added a postscript to this letter to Bathurst that gives a fair indication of how blind that delegation was to what their demands were doing to the cause of peace. He told his superior, "I cannot let it go without adding that it has made not the least impression upon me or upon my colleagues to whom I have reported it."[22] Bayard was aware that he had made no impression on Goulburn and so told Gallatin. Clay also let Gallatin know that he had let Goulburn know that the Americans intended to await further instructions.

August 24, 1814, was a sort of early American "Day of Infamy." To the American envoys in Ghent, they may have felt this was a dark day because of the collapse of the negotiations for peace. What they could not know, nor would know for more than a month, it was even more a day of national humiliation as the capital city was invaded and its most honored buildings were burned and desecrated by the enemy.

The American diplomats could also not know how the British expectations of this event could be a factor in the arrogant posture taken by their commissioners in Belgium.

Though the disaster in America occurred simultaneously with the apparent rupture of the peace talks, this story seems to be more appropri-

ately told in the time frame in which it became known to Henry Clay and his colleagues, so that their growing awareness of the extent of the debacle can be related as part of their personal lives and their consequent dealings with their British counterparts in light of the apparent advantage now in the hands of their opponents.

On that morning of August 24, the American mission met again in Ghent to consider a new draft of the intended answer to the British note of the 20th. Bayard was absent and Russell wanted to make a revision before the paper was even discussed. Therefore, the meeting was adjourned until after dinner. Then they "sat until eleven at night, sifting, erasing, patching, and amending, until we were all wearied, though none of us was yet satisfied with amendment," according to Adams.

> Of the part of my own draft which had been left for consideration, two-thirds were now struck out. The remnant left of mine certainly does not form a fifth part of the paper as finally settled, and it is patched with scraps from Mr. Gallatin, and scraps from Mr. Bayard, and scraps from Mr. Clay, all of whom are dissatisfied with the paper as finally constructed. Each of us takes a separate and distinct view of the subject-matter, and each naturally thinks his own view of it the most important. The peculiar difficulty with Mr. Bayard is, that his view is always exclusive. My draft contained a view of the law of nations as applied to the relations between settlements of European origin in America and the Indians. I thought it important, because the article proposed to us by the British Commissioners as a *sine qua non* would produce a total change of the public law in that respect, and because Lord Castlereagh had pledged the faith of his Government not to ask anything contrary to the established maxims of public law. Almost the whole of what I had written on this subject has been struck out; and when I stated that the right of civilized nations to settle upon lands where Indians had been was explicitly recognized by Vattel, Mr. Bayard called upon me to produce the passage, and was perfectly unaware that I could produce it much more strongly than I had stated it.[23]

The opening of Adams's draft was similar to that which eventually comprised the mission's official reply to the British. They both observed that Castlereagh's letter to Monroe, in November 1813, had pledged the British willingness to open discussions "upon principles of *perfect reciprocity*, not inconsistent with the established maxims of public law, and with the maritime rights of the British Empire." Since maritime affairs were the only subject expressly mentioned by Castlereagh, the Americans felt the British ought not to have expected the U.S. mission's instructions to contain authorization for them to treat respecting the Indians.

Following this line was general wording drawn from Bayard's draft. It observed that the differences which led to the war "were wholly of a maritime nature" arising principally from the British orders in council in relation to blockades, and from the impressment of mariners on board American vessels." Bayard's views (entered into the official note) said the United States could not have anticipated "the novel pretensions" advanced by the British (or as Bayard had phrased it, "suddenly and unexpectedly brought forward and declared in the treshhold of the negotiation to constitute a *sine qua non.*"

Despite the American indication that maritime matters should be the chief point of negotiation, they used most of this note arguing against the British demands for an Indian barrier territory. Adopting some of the thoughts from Adams's draft, the mission stated in the official note that "no maxim of public law had hitherto been more universally established" by European Powers (including Great Britain) "than that of suffering no interposition of a foreign Power in the relations between the acknowledged sovereign of the territory and the Indians situated upon it" ... and that such Indians "cannot be considered as an independent Power."

In line with this statement, but failing to be incorporated into the final draft, was Bayard's perfectly appropriate view that Indians, living within Great Britain's American dominions, were not viewed by the British Government as an independent and sovereign people nor had they ever been so regarded by any European Power.

The Americans went on to observe that the British, by the Treaty of 1783, had acknowledged U.S. sovereignty over the territory they now demanded as a barrier state under Indian control. Yet no mention was made of Indians in that treaty. In fact, the Americans told the British that the Greenville Treaty of 1795, and all subsequent ones, confirmed "that the Indian tribes shall quietly enjoy their lands, hunting, planting, and

dwelling thereon so long as they please, without any molestation from the United States," but when the Indians decided to sell the lands "they are to be sold only to the United States." Meanwhile, the United States would protect the Indians from all U.S. citizens and intrusion by all other white persons. The Americans charged that the British stipulation

> In prohibiting Great Britain and the United States from purchasing lands within [the latter's dominions] while it professes to take from Great Britain a privilege which she had not, it actually deprives the United States of a right exclusively to them.

On the basis of past treaties, the American envoys charged "there is no reciprocity in the proposed stipulation" of the British, and it "is also utterly unnecessary for the purpose of obtaining a pacification for the Indians residing within the territories of the United States."

In his draft (but excluded from the official text) Adams had asked the British where was their authority to treat independently with the Indians. They had shown the Americans no powers to treat for them. Also absent from the final draft was Adams' contention that a denial of the right to sell their lands was an injustice to the Indians because "the only value of lands to the Indian State of Society is their property as hunting grounds," and that the Indians will sell "for a liberal compensation to the hand of tillage, the soil which can no longer yield to him, either the pleasures, the profits, or the substance of the chase."[24]

But the official note did include Adams' reference that "an uninterrupted peace had subsisted" from the year 1795, between the United States and the Indians "for a longer period of time than ever had been known since the first settlement of North America." Continuing to copy from Adams, the note said further that with the Indians, the United States had "neither interest nor inclination to continue the war," and, in fact, peace with them might already be restored. In any case, the note insisted, the United States government would instantaneously reject a provisional article such as the British proposed to surrender nearly one third of the territorial dominions of the United States to Indians numbering no more than 20,000. Bayard had pointed out in an unused portion of his draft that there were more American citizens than Indians in the proposed barrier state.

He stated that "the chief effect of the proposed Boundary would be to arrest the course of civilization and the extension of Christianity."[25]

After noting that "this extraordinary demand" for an Indian barrier territory had "been made a *sine qua non*, to be admitted without discussion," the Americans said, "it is accompanied by others equally inadmissible." They were

at a loss to discover by what rule of perfect reciprocity the United States can be required to renounce their equal right of maintaining a naval force upon [the western] lakes, and of fortifying their own shores, while Great Britain reserves exclusively the corresponding rights to herself.

The Americans, while believing Great Britain to have greater armed superiority on the lake frontiers, could not believe the British would accept such demands if made by the United States.

Regarding the cession of U.S. territory west of Lake Superior and in Maine, the Americans viewed it as a British "desire of aggrandizement," and advised their counterparts that they had no authority to cede any territory nor would they subscribe to any stipulation to that effect.

The American said the conditions proposed by the British had no relation to the subsisting differences between them, were inconsistent with acknowledged principle of public law, and were not founded on reciprocity. The conditions

would inflict the most vital injury on the United States, by dismembering their territory, by arresting their natural growth and increase of population, and by leaving their northern and western frontier equally exposed to British invasion and to Indian aggression.

The conditions were

dishonorable to the United States, in demanding from them to abandon territory and a portion of their citizens; to admit a foreign interference in their domestic concerns, and to cease to exercise their natural rights on their own shores and in their own waters.

Such a treaty, they said, would only be an armistice and that it could not

be supposed that America would long submit to conditions so injurious and degrading. It is impossible, in the natural course of events, that she should not, at the first favorable opportunity, to recur to arms for the recovery of the territory, of her rights, of her honor. Instead of settling existing

differences such a peace would only create new causes of war, sow the seeds of a permanent hatred, and lay the foundation of hostilities for an indefinite period.

America "wishes for peace; but she wishes for it upon those terms of reciprocity honorable to both countries, which can alone render it permanent."

The Americans told the British that with the end of the European war, the causes of the war between their two countries had disappeared and that the United States had no desire "to continue it in defense of abstract principles." They were instructed to agree to a "solid and permanent" peace which restored whatever territory had been taken and reserve all their rights regarding their respective seamen.

The Americans deeply regretted "that other views are entertained by the British Government, and that new and unexpected pretensions are raised, which, if persisted in, must oppose an insuperable obstacle to a pacification." They found it unnecessary to refer such demands to their government for instructions and were fit for deliberation only "when it becomes necessary to decide upon the expediency of an absolute surrender of national independence."[26]

The glum mission members, meeting on the morning of August 25, agreed on the final wording of their note and signed it. As Christopher Hughes delivered it to the British, Adams wrote in his diary, it "will bring the negotiation very shortly to a close."[27]

More expansively, he gave his views to his wife in a letter written the next day.

Yesterday we sent our answer to the British note, and shall, as we expect, have nothing more to write to our adverse party on the substance of our business. The forms of parting will be all that remains after their reply. Of this, however, I cannot speak positively until their reply comes. We might have had that now, for it might be a card *pour prendre congé* [to take one's leave]. But as they could not well send us that until after the dinner to which they have invited us tomorrow, they may perhaps be waiting to get that over. As however we have given them some reasoning to dispose of, they may perhaps furnish us with some of the same commodity in return. In that case we shall find it necessary to rejoin and may be kept here a week longer. From what has already passed it is impossible that the negotiation should succeed.

Turning to a discussion of news from home, Adams wrote Louisa Catherine,

> We have no news from America of any importance since the taking of Fort Erie and the affair of Niagara. That was a brilliant action upon our side, but as usual, not followed up by any thing else. When our landsmen have struck one lucky blow, they seem to think they have conquered the world, and have nothing left to do but to slumber upon their laurels. The English accounts from Halifax are to 1 August — nothing worth telling. Could I but hope the same for the next six months, how many heartaches I should be spared! It is a painful process that I am going through; but it is some consolation that the part I am doomed to perform in the prolongation of this tragedy has never required an instant of hesitation with respect to the path pointed out by my duty, and that in this respect there has not been a shadow of difference of opinion between any one of my colleagues and me.[28]

The mission had only to wait for the expected terminating reply from the British.

The Niagara affair, mentioned by Adams, was a resumption of the dormant operations along the river that drains waters northward from Lake Erie and over the falls to Lake Ontario. The British held the Canadian peninsula formed by the eastern end of Erie with the western part of Ontario. By July 1814, U.S. forces under Maj. Gen. Jacob Brown, had arrived at Buffalo and, pursuant to orders from Secretary of War Armstrong, had crossed the river and seized Fort Erie from the British. Over July 4 and 5, they fought two bitter battles with the surprised British over the occupation of Chippawa, opposite present-day Niagara Falls, New York, not quite to the falls (which in those days was a single torrent farther down river than today's double falls around Goat Island).

Only skirmishes persisted for the next two weeks before the Americans again moved north to what is now Niagara Falls, Ontario, and attacked the British, now nearly double the Americans' strength, This battle, on July 25, took the name of Lundy's Lane. At one point in the engagement, General Brown ordered a Col. James Miller, "Take your regiment, storm that work, and take it." (A battery of cannon.) "I'll try, sir," responded Miller, and immediately moved forward to the perilous task. Miller had served at Tippecanoe and at the surrender at Detroit by General Hull.

In the violent hand-to-hand fighting that ensued, the British were compelled to abandon their artillery, ammunition wagons, and everything else. Their attempts to drive the Americans from the hill were twice repulsed. Some of the British soldiers taken prisoners of war called it "the most desperate thing we ever saw or heard of." When American General Brown next met Miller, he declared, "You have immortalized yourself! My dear fellow, my heart ached for you when I gave you the order, but I knew that it was the only thing that would save us."

Unfortunately, a very strong body of reinforcing British troops came on the scene and recaptured the terrain. The Americans fell back to Chippawa, and then to Fort Erie by the end of July.[29] As to immortalization, Colonel Miller is forgotten. So is Lundy's Lane. And the War of 1812 is nearly forgotten!

30

NEGOTIATING TO NEGOTIATE

T   *he author wishes to preface this chapter with some personal comments. After a dreary month of haggling with the British, it appeared to the American envoys on August 24 and 25, 1814 (indeed, the days that the British captured Washington City), that the peace negotiations were at an end. We know historically that they continued into late December. For the average reader, the continuing disputes over the same issues, day after day, can become quite boring and monotonous. Most popular accounts of these days are summarized to the bare bones without permitting the reader an opportunity to grasp the full sense of exasperation and stress the American negotiators lived through.*

Yet there is an historical need for this kind of detailed accounting of the problems besetting these Americans. And since Henry Clay was a principal personality in these negotiations, this is a proper place for details. Even so, the author has eliminated as much fluff as felt possible while conveying the sense of frustration felt in Ghent. This may also give the reader a better understanding of what any negotiators, at any time in history, must endure in trying to make a peace treaty.

One must also realize that these men were acutely aware that every day that the talks continued might cost a family at home the life of a loved one, and the costs of the war continued to plague the nation's finances — a fact that must have weighed heavily on Albert Gallatin, U.S. secretary of the treasury for the first 12 years of the century.

Since this is a life of Clay and his participation in the events of his days, it is again important to place his training, experience, personality, and character in contrast with the qualities of his colleagues. Despite the dearth of his personal papers at this time, we see him through the eyes of others, possibly a better viewpoint than by his own words. We have now seen how he consorted with this group of highly talented men after nearly a month in very close association. Henry Clay clearly exhibited an equality of negotiating skill to that of his companions who came to the table with much better formal education and much longer years of high level experience in government.

It is worth reflecting again on the character and ability of these five Americans sent to Europe to engage the British in a mental battle for peace. While the three British envoys were not career diplomats and were regarded by the Americans as lightweights, they had the relative advantage of quick written support of superiors in London (or wherever Castlereagh might be on the continent).

Aside from Jonathan Russell, Clay could easily have sensed a great feeling of inadequacy with his meager education, short experience in high level government, lack of worldly travel, and a scarce understanding of the ways of diplomacy. There is no evidence that this emotion existed in his personality.

Look again at his other three colleagues. Here was John Quincy Adams, the son of the patriot John Adams who was a graduate of Harvard, lawyer who defended the British soldiers of the Boston massacre, leader in the Continental Congress, one of the drafters of the Declaration of Independence, first ambassador to England (where John Quincy studied), first vice president of the United States and then second president. All along, John Quincy grew up in this household, student at Harvard, and served his father in his diplomatic travels and was, himself, a U.S. Senator and then envoy to the Czar of all the Russias, when Clay was only learning the ways of governing in the rude wiles of early Kentucky politics.

There was Albert Gallatin, the "wily Genevan," born in Europe (Switzerland, where he graduated from college), and an immigrant to America. He was a soldier in the Revolution and a teacher at

Harvard before becoming an early pioneer in southwestern Pennsylvania, a member of Congress from 1795 through 1801, and then, for 12 years, one of America's most sagacious secretaries of the treasury, serving in the cabinets of Thomas Jefferson and James Madison.

James Asheton Bayard, a graduate of Princeton, a Federalist second, but an American first, was not only a member of the House of Representatives, which chose Jefferson over Aaron Burr to be the third president of the United States, but he was, indeed, the principal individual who made the difference in that election in February 1801, again when Clay was only learning politics at the local level. Bayard was to continue government service as U.S. Senator for several years prior to his appointment to aid John Quincy Adams in Russia.

Even Jonathan Russell, the light-weight member of this contingent, presented substantial credentials compared with Clay's. Russell, a graduate of Brown University, was in the diplomatic service in France, Britain, and Norway/Sweden, prior to his appointment to this group.

It is unclear where Clay developed the skills he brought as the leader of the nation's highest parliamentary body, where he became the mast of its membership. In reality, Clay, with no college and little other education, was an upstart with a temper, a strong ego, and a brilliant mind that seemed to absorb everything of importance about his world, and he was able to bring it to bear in a convincing and orderly manner. He brought with it exuberance, insight, and intuition, which was needed in spades in these discouraging days.

It is hoped that these pages will give the reader a taste of the clash of personalities within the American mission in their resistance to repetitive demands by the British delegation to surrender rights and lands that were never in question before the war.—QSK

Except for an occasional letter to Secretary of State James Monroe and to American minister to France William Crawford, accounts of Henry Clay's personal views and activities at Ghent are almost non-existent. These are his only personal writings found during the remaining days of the negotiations, which were now in suspension. The remaining story of his involvement appears in the writings of his colleagues (or even those of his adversaries) or in joint correspondence to others.

In his last letter to his wife, which he composed as the talks were falling apart, John Quincy Adams mentioned two matters involving the American delegates. In Adams' letter of August 26, to his wife in St. Petersburg, he referred to a dinner yet to be held by the British mission, and he commented on the "affair of Niagara" back in America.

While the military action termed the "affair at Niagara" was, in effect, a hard-fought draw, Adams' fears of future disasters, resulting in "heartaches," were already a fact as he wrote his wife on August 26, 1814. The British had entered Washington City, and by this date had even left the city in flames. Aside from this event, which the commissioners would not learn of for more than a month, there was little other battle news from America.

Until early August, the only other battle ac-

counts of significance which Henry Clay and his colleagues learned of in Europe were of General Andrew Jackson's conquest of the Creek Indians in the Mississippi Territory (in present-day Alabama). On March 29, at Horseshoe Bend, Jackson had won a decisive battle over the "Red Sticks," a warrior tribe of Creeks. In that battle one of Jackson's young ensigns gallantly led a charge despite bullet and arrow wounds. His name was Sam Houston. He was to be heard from later. For his conquest, Jackson was commissioned a major general in the U.S. Army and took command of the 7th District. He would, also, be heard from again — soon.

Still, this news made only a ripple in the affairs at Ghent. The commissioners were trapped in their own state of suspended animation. As for that Saturday evening dinner, American envoy James Bayard wrote in a memorandum, dated August 27, that he had a conversation with one of his British counterparts, Henry Goulburn, about the terms of the last British note.

I told Mr. G. that not ten men in America could be found who would agree to them. He stated their only object to be security to Canada. That country would always be in danger if the U.S. maintained a military force on the lakes and retained their settlements on the present line. I answered that the U.S. could not consent to secure Canada by exposing her whole frontier, and by a sacrifice of territory more considerable than the

Provinces. He observed that our terms conceded nothing, and that we seemed to expect to retire from the war and return to the same state we were in before it commenced. This G.B. could not be expected to agree to, as she might then look forward to fresh hostilities with the U.S. as soon as she should be involved in any European War. I told him that it was sufficient mortification upon our part after having declared the war with the professed object to attain certain points to be compelled to retreat from it without gaining one of these points. G.B. [Great Britain] retaining the same ground she held before the war.

I enquired if we should shortly receive their reply which I presumed would terminate the negociation. He said that was likely to be the result, that as they had caused us some delay already they would certainly not unnecessarily encrease [sic] it.[1]

With more pessimism than that shown by Adams, Bayard elaborated on his feelings the next day (the 28th) as he again wrote Levett Harris, secretary of the earlier aborted mediation mission in Russia.

No peace will be made, but on the contrary I believe a foundation will be laid of a protracted war. The terms now proposed and insisted on by G.B. must be withdrawn or the present generation will not see the end of the contest. One good effect will follow from this abortive negotiation. The people of America will become united in the defence of the rights which they are now called upon to surrender, and show themselves a more formidable foe than England or Europe have hitherto supposed them capable of being.... I do not expect to remain in Ghent more than a few days longer. We have been talking of sending our ship to Cherbourg or Brest, and travelling through France to join her. This will enable our friend from Kentucky [Henry Clay] to see Paris before his return to the United States.[2]

Now even Clay was falling under the expectation of closure. During the course of that Saturday dinner (at which the British envoys brought family members who were in the city), Clay extracted a promise from Goulburn to provide passports for himself and Henry Carroll (his private secretary) in order to return to America in the United States ship *Neptune*. Clay renewed this request in writing on September 5 and added the names of Christopher Hughes, secretary to the mission, and William Shaler, "attached to the mission."[3]

The expected collapse of the talks left the American envoys in a quandary as to their plans for the immediate future. On the same day (the 26th) that he wrote his wife, Adams talked to Gallatin and Russell about "the expediency of my returning to St. Petersburg by way of Vienna." These two companions favored the idea, but Adams saw reason both for and against it, and the subject was renewed on the 27th. This time Adams

declared my readiness to go, if the mission would authorize me to communicate to the Emperor of Russia the official documents of the negotiation. Mr. Gallatin and Mr. Russell were willing to give me this authority, but Mr. Clay thought it must be left to my discretion. Mr. Bayard was not present, but will certainly be of Mr. Clay's opinion. I wished for an immediate decision, that I might have an opportunity of writing to Mr. Crawford on the subject, and receiving his answer before we go; but, as there is not only a diversity but an equal division of opinion upon the proposal, I could not press it any further.[4]

Adams clearly was unsure of himself on making this decision on his own and was probably reluctant to do it even with the consent of the mission when he argued with himself that their opinion was "an equal division," though he only guessed at Bayard's response.

Part of the dilemma under which the Americans lived, as they awaited the British reply, was over the relatively insignificant matter of their lodging. Adams, in his letter to Louisa, on August 26, had noted, "With the house itself we are now so well satisfied that we should certainly keep it for another month if we had any prospect of staying so long here. Our landlord now gives us tolerable satisfaction."[5]

Two days later he wrote in his diary (later printed as his *Memoirs*), following an afternoon meeting with his colleagues,

We ... concluded upon leaving this house at the expiration of our month, the day after to-morrow. As we shall certainly not have occasion to stay here more than a week or ten days at the utmost, we had proposed to Lanmeier [the landlord] to remain, paying the rent not for the whole month, but in proportion to the time we shall stay. But, although his partner had yesterday agreed to this proposal, they sent us this morning a joint letter, stating that they paid their rent by the month, and had other contracts of the same kind, and making appeals to our generosity. We therefore determined not to enter upon the second month.

However, the next day, Adams wrote,

Upon further consideration with our landlord, Mr. Lanmeier Quetelet, we have concluded to remain here without removing until our departure from Ghent, and to pay him rent for half a month, at the rate of twelve hundred francs the months, as probably some of us will be at least ten days longer here.[6]

That same day (the 29th) Adams wrote to William Crawford in Paris apologizing for not answering his letter of July 12, but noted,

I have been the less scrupulous in performing it sooner, because I have known that some of our colleagues were more punctual, and particularly that our excellent friend Mr. Clay had kept you well informed of the progress of our negotiation.

Again Adams expressed his deep disappointment at the failure of their mission by which, he said,

Great Britain has opened to us the alternative of a long, expensive, sanguinary war, or of submission to disgraceful conditions and sacrifices little short of independence itself. It is the crisis which must try the temper of our country. If the dangers which now hang over our heads should intimidate our people into the spirit of concession, if the temper of compounding for sacrifices should manifest itself in any strength there will be nothing left us worth defending. But if our countrymen are not all bastards, if there is a drop of the blood flowing in their veins that carried their fathers through the Revolutionary war, the prolongation of hostilities will only be to secure ultimately to us a more glorious triumph. I have not so ill opinion of them as to believe they will succumb immediately in the struggle before them; but I wish the real statesmen among us may form, what I fear few of them have yet formed, a true estimate of our condition. I wish them to look all our dangers in the face and to their full extent. The rupture of this negotiation not only frustrates all hope of peace for the present year, but at least also for the next. All the present preparations in England are calculated for operation the next campaign. The forces they have sent out already, and those they are about to dispatch are so large, and composed of such troops that they *must* in the first instance make powerful impressions and obtain brilliant successes.... We must expect to pass through the career of British triumph and exultation at our calamities, before we can lead them to the result that they bring our enemy no nearer to his object than his defeats.[7]

On the 31st, Anthony Baker, the secretary of the British mission, came to the lodging of the American delegation and asked for their secretary, Christopher Hughes, who was not in. Instead, Baker spoke to Gallatin and advised him that in consideration of the great importance of their reply to the Americans' note, the British envoys had decided to refer it to their government in London for instructions and that it would cause only a delay of a few days. Adams noted in his *Memoirs* that Baker

did not say when they had sent their note to England; but on Saturday [the 27th] Mr. Goulburn had told Mr. Bayard that they should reply without delay and without referring to their Government. Mr. Gallatin thinks they sent our note to Brussels, to Lord Castlereagh, and that he has chosen to refer it to England.[8]

Gallatin was correct.

Unknown at the time to the American envoys, Henry Goulburn (acting as the spokesman for the British, despite the fact that Admiral James Gambier had apparently been the nominal chairman of their delegation) sent a message to London on the day that the Americans had handed the British the note expected to terminate their negotiations. This message, wrongly dated August 24th, went to Earl Bathurst, British secretary of War and the Colonies.[9] With it Goulburn sent the note from the Americans saying it "appears to render your instructions necessary to our further proceeding," adding that the Americans' instructions didn't provide for refusal to agree to territorial status as of the time of peace. The British envoys wanted to be certain that their superiors concurred with them prior to a complete break in talks. They also wanted to allow the Americans time to receive new instructions believed to be then on the way to Europe from Washington.

Goulburn observed that the Americans' part in the negotiation had only been "a dictation to Great Britain," that peace could be made based only on the territorial status ante bellum, and that America's purpose in going to war was to annex British dominions and they would not agree to anything which would make annexation difficult in the future. Goulburn did not even want to reply to an American projet, believing that disclosure of British terms would merely give the Americans a better case for rupture of the negotiations. In an after note, he requested a map showing "a river called the Passamaquoddy," the present boundary between Maine and New Brunswick, Canada.[10]

On the 26th, Goulburn wrote Lord Castlereagh (now in Paris) saying, "I will write Lord Bathurst today." (He had not told Bathurst that he was writing the foreign secretary.) Again, Goulburn enclosed a copy of the American note and also a proposed reply by the British. Goulburn stated that he and his colleagues were "a little embarrassed" by finding in the American note that

> the words "perfect reciprocity," said to be contained in your letter to Mr. Monroe of the 4th November, 1813, do not actually occur in the document from the Foreign Office, dated the 30th October, 1813, with which we were furnished as containing a copy of that letter.

He asked Castlereagh for his clarification and said they were also asking the foreign office for a correct copy of the letter of November 4.[11]

When Castlereagh received Goulburn's communication, he replied on the 28th that he was forwarding his papers to London, and advised the envoy to notify the American mission verbally that their note had been referred to the government there. The foreign minister added,

> You will feel that your answer will acquire rather than lose weight from this interval, and from your being enabled to speak under the special sanction of your court, and that no time will in fact be lost, as you could not break up the conference and return home without express authority.[12]

The American mission would certainly have been interested in knowing of this last statement, or of the remainder of Castlereagh's communication to London.

In referring the American note to his superior, Castlereagh sent the enclosure along with a cover letter to the Earl of Liverpool, the British prime minister. It was at the beginning of this letter that Castlereagh told of his failure to meet with the Americans in Ghent.

Castlereagh, told the prime minister that the British commissioners

> inferred ... that the American Commissioners were disposed both to treat and sign on the frontier and Indian arrangements. No surprise or repugnance was at the moment disclosed to any of the suggestions.

What the British envoys read in American silence as approval, was more likely stunned incredulity. They were more in a mood to see how far the British would carry this nonsense.

Castlereagh went on to tell Liverpool that had he been writing the original note handed to the Americans, on August 19, he would

> have been inclined to state the proposition as to Indian limits less peremptorily; but the Commissioners appeared to attach so much importance to the not weakening, in this stage of their discussions, the ground which they had previously taken up upon this point, that I acquiesced in the expression "it is equally necessary," etc., which is very strong. I cautioned them, in reasoning on the words purchase or *otherwise*, not to commit themselves without further authority, to mean thereby to negative the possibility of conquest in a war justifiably declared, however open such a principle might be to evasion. The absence of any such right of acquiring territory being at this moment the state in which Great Britain and America stand mutually with respect to each other's Indians, each power would repel any attack, and follow the Indian enemy within the lines of the other State, would extinguish the tribe if possible, and destroy their towns, but their right of war would not extend to acquisition of territory beyond their own boundary. It is a right of reprisal rather than a perfect right of war. The whole seems a question of expediency, and not of principle, as the American Commissioners have endeavored to make it.

Continuing, Castlereagh wrote,

> It is extremely material to answer fully the American note, as it is evidently intended to arouse their people upon the question of their independence.... The substance of the question is, are we prepared to continue the war for territorial arrangements? and if not, is this the best time to make our peace, saving all our rights and retaining the fisheries, which they do not appear to question (in which case the territorial questions might be reserved for ulterior discussion), or is it desirable to take our chance of the campaign, and then to be governed by circumstances?
>
> If the latter is advisable, we have the means of doing so, as the American Commissioners give us no room to expect any pacific stipulation whatever in favour of what they call their Indians, without now putting the war solely and avowedly on a territorial principle, which I think it would be imprudent to do; on the other hand, if we thought an immediate peace desirable, as they are ready to waive all the abstract questions, perhaps they might be prepared to sign a provisional article of

Indian peace, as distinct from limits, and relinquish their pretensions to the islands in Passamaquoddy Bay, and possibly to admit minor adjustments of frontier, including a right of communication from Quebec to Halifax across their territory.

Castlereagh noted in conclusion that he would be leaving Paris that evening for Dijon en route to Vienna for the great Congress of European governments meeting to establish the peace of Europe following Napoleon's defeat and exile to Elba.[13]

On receipt of Castlereagh's correspondence, Liverpool replied on September 2, writing,

> Our Commissioners had certainly taken a very erroneous view of our policy. If the negotiation had been allowed to break off upon the two notes already presented, or upon such an answer as they were disposed to return, I am satisfied the war would have become quite popular in America. I was the more surprised at this circumstance as I never read a paper more easy to answer, as to its reasoning, than the paper of the American Commissioners; and I think it is of the utmost importance that the rupture of the negotiation, if it is to take place, should be thrown upon the American Commissioners, and not upon us.

Again, would not the Americans have rejoiced at reading this part of Liverpool's response? And on what a thin line was continuation of the negotiations to hang. Where was blame for rupture to lie?

Continuing his letter to Castlereagh, Liverpool noted,

> If the campaign in Canada should be as successful as our military preparations would lead us to expect, I do not think we should be justified in conceding more at present than we have done, especially after the demands already made.... If our commander does his duty, I am persuaded we shall have acquired by our arms every point on the Canadian frontier which we ought to insist on keeping.

He added,

> We cannot expect that the negotiation will proceed at present, but I think it not unlikely, after our note has been delivered in, that the American Commissioners will propose to refer the subject to their government.[14]

September 2 continued to be an active day for British correspondence. Goulburn, in Ghent, received a reply to his letter of August 25 to Bathurst. The secretary of war's letter to the envoy is not found, but Goulburn's response to Bathurst revealed his view of the Americans' reaction to sending their note to London.

> They pressed for the earliest possible answer, yet they had nothing to say to this communication. Some one or the other of them have called daily since to know if we had got an answer. Indeed, their only anxiety appears to be to get back to America. Whenever we meet them they always enter into unofficial discussions, much of the same nature as the conversation with which Mr. Bayard indulged me: but we have given no encouragement to such conversations, thinking that they are liable to much misrepresentation, and cannot lead to any good purpose. All that I think I have learnt from them is this; that Mr. Adams is a very bad arguer, and that the Federalists are quite as inveterate enemies to us as the Madisonians.[15]

Whatever Adams' ability as an "arguer" might be, Goulburn got a good taste of it the day before. Adams preserved this long conversation both in his diary and in a fairly close duplicate in the form of a message to Secretary of State James Monroe. He told the secretary that he was convinced that the "sole object" of the British envoy's request for approval by their government "was to give a greater appearance of deliberation and solemnity to the rupture." An answer from London was expected by Sunday, September 4.

To Goulburn, Adams expressed the hope that their superiors would reconsider the U.S. proposals. Adams wrote of Goulburn's reply,

> He did not think it probable, and in the whole tenor of his discourse I perceived a spirit of inflexible adherence to the terms which we have rejected; but, under the cover of a personal deportment sufficiently courteous, a rancorous animosity against America which disclosed there was nothing like peace at the heart.

In his diary, Adams wrote, "The more I conversed with him the more the violence and bitterness of his passion against the United States disclosed itself."

Throughout the discussion, Goulburn continually argued that an "Indian boundary and the exclusive military possession of the Lakes by the British, was necessary for the security of Canada." He believed that it had been the intention of the United States to conquer Canada and "that nothing had saved it but the excellent dispositions and military arrangements of the Governor who commanded there." The barrier was to prevent future encroachment by either country. "The Indians are but a secondary object," but as allies of Great Britain they should be included in the peace, Goulburn contended. Disarmament on the lakes also served as security to Canada. "Why should [America] object to disarming there where they had never before had a gun floating?"

Adams responded

that the conquest of Canada had never been an object of the war on the part of the United States; that Canada had been invaded by us in consequence of the war, as they themselves had invaded many parts of the United States — it was an effect, and not a cause, of the war; that the American Government never had declared the intention of conquering Canada.

Of course, in the pre-war days, Henry Clay had boasted that the Kentucky militia could alone conquer Canada. But his comments were made in the halls of Congress and were not necessarily the opinions of the president who represented "The American Government."

But Goulburn cited General Hull's proclamation on crossing into Canada at the beginning of hostilities. Adams replied that the U.S. government was no more responsible for that "than the British Government was answerable for Admiral Cochrane's proclamation which his Government had disavowed." The two men argued this point whether or not their governments had disavowed officers in the field. And this argument spread into the use and meaning in Cochrane's proclamation of the word "free," Adams saying that in the United States it clearly referred to negroes — who had been encouraged by Cochrane to revolt, and as such had been a practice of British naval officers. Goulburn "manifested some apparent agitation" at the impugning of these officers whose character, he said, "was universally known, their generosity and humanity could never be contested." What contradictory arguments could have been employed by the many American prisoners of war caught under the jurisdiction of such officers!

Returning to the subject of the Indians, Adams disputed an earlier reference to the Indians being allies of the British in the same way as Portugal. He opined that those Indians within the boundaries of the United States who had taken the British side in the war should be treated in the nature of an amnesty rather than be considered as British allies. But Goulburn cited the fact that the United States had made treaties with the Indians, such as are made between nations.

Adams did not believe the Indians could settle permanently within set boundaries, telling Goulburn,

Their habits, and attachments, and prejudices were so averse to any settlement that they could not reconcile themselves to any other condition than that of wandering hunters. It was impossible for such people ever to be said to have possessions. Their only right upon land was a right to use it as hunting grounds; and when those lands where they hunted became necessary or convenient for the purposes of settlements the system adopted by the United States was by amicable arrangement with them to compensate them for renouncing the right of hunting upon them, and for removing to remoter regions better suited to their purposes and mode of life.... To condemn vast regions of territory to perpetual barrenness and solitude, that a few hundred savages might find wild beasts to hunt upon it, was a species of game law that a nation descended from Britons would never endure. It was as incompatible with the moral as with the physical nature of things.

Adams had few dissenters from this view at that period in American history.

To Adams it was impossible to prevent future generations of Americans, as they grew in numbers, to be excluded from cultivation of the soil of those vast western regions as indeed proved true. Such an exclusion by treaty would only foster new wars with Britain. Adams said, "It would be an outrage upon Providence, which gave the earth to men for cultivation, and made the tillage of the ground the condition of his nature, and the law of his existence."

"What!" said Goulburn, "is it then in the inevitable nature of things that the United States must conquer Canada?"

"No," Adams replied.

"But what security then can Great Britain have for her possession of it?"

Adams answered, in part,

If Great Britain does not think a liberal and amicable course of policy towards America would be the best security, as it certainly would, she must rely upon her general strength, upon the superiority of her power in other parts of her relations with America,

suggesting the power of British naval forces to strike at more defenseless areas of the United States than there were such of Canada. Adams could not convince Goulburn that to leave the lakes defenseless, by treaty, would be humiliating to the United States as the reverse would be to Great Britain. The suggestion by Britain to disarm on the lakes seemed to operate as a warning to the United States to remain armed there when they probably would not have considered the idea had it not been advanced by the British.

In his letter to Monroe, Adams summed up his conversation with Goulburn, noting that the strangest feature was "the inflexible adherence to the proposed Indian boundary line." But the pretext upon which it was based (the future security of the Indians) "was almost abandoned — avowed to be a secondary and very subordinate object. The security of Canada was now substituted as the prominent motive." But Adams added that the great and real motive

> was no other than a profound and rankling jealousy at the rapid increase of population and of settlements in the United States, and important longing to thwart their progress and to stunt their growth.[16]

There was still occasion for levity and pleasure in the midst of these ponderous and rancorous conversations. That same evening, the American envoys hosted a dinner which included a number of local Belgian dignitaries and members of their families along with the American aides to the envoys. In all, 30 persons were present and a band played throughout the evening. After the meal, several of those present spent the rest of the evening playing cards.

Adams, again noting almost everything in his diary, wrote,

> The party broke up about midnight, and, after they were gone, Mr. Clay won from me at a game of all-fours the picture of an old woman that I had drawn as a prize in the lottery of pictures in which we had all taken tickets. He also won from Mr. Todd the bunch of flowers which Mr. Russell had drawn, and which Todd had won from Mr. Russell.[17]

Still, as the envoys of both nations awaited the reply from London, the antagonism continued.

James Gallatin, son of the envoy, wrote in his diary, on September 3, "Father is much annoyed with Mr. Goulburn. He saw him today. The latter said, 'I don't think you have the slightest intention of making peace.' Father answered, 'Surely you cannot mean this! Why should I have taken the long journey to Russia in 1813 and given up everything else in the hope of making peace?'" On the following day, James wrote, "Father is quite convinced that Mr. Goulburn has made some serious mistakes and that he has been reprimanded."[18]

Finally, on September 5, the British envoys in Ghent received their instructions from London. As noted earlier, Clay, on this date, renewed his request to Goulburn for a passport for himself and aides of the American mission to return home. It is not known at what time during the day he handed Goulburn his note. But it may be surmised that it was late in the day. For Adams noted in his diary that during the morning the British sent in the reply to the American note of August 25.

What the Americans received was a final compilation of suggestions by the three British commissioners, comments of Castlereagh sent to London, and the basic wording as proposed by Bathurst and Liverpool.

There is some confusion on the date of transmission of the British response. Their note is dated, "Ghent, September 4." And Goulburn dates a letter to Bathurst on the 5th, saying they had delivered the note "yesterday morning," whereas Adams states in his diary of the 5th that it was received that morning.

There is also considerable difference between the note proposed by the Ghent envoys and the final note handed the Americans. (Castlereagh's proposals are not found, though they are mentioned in British correspondence.) The final draft is written in more polished diplomatic language than that of the three commissioners. By reading the two versions, it is quite evident why Adams characterized these men as he did a few days later in his diary. The envoys' draft began with a statement that they had expected American instructions would have provided for a discussion of the Indian boundary. They continued to dwell on the Indian problem throughout their draft.

On the other hand, the final copy, as sent to

the Americans, began with a minor comment that the British, "with so much frankness" had disclosed "all the objects of their Government while those which the American Government had in view were withheld." But then they shifted to the security of Canada against American conquest.

Noting that it was the United States which had declared war "upon the pretense of maritime rights," the British note, embracing Goulburn's contentions, said, "It is notorious to the whole world that the conquest of Canada, and its permanent annexation to the United States, was the declared object of the American Government." The British charged that that government had been influenced

> by a spirit of aggrandizement not necessary to their own security, but increasing with the extent of their empire, has been too clearly manifested by their progressive occupation of the Indian territories, by the acquisition of Louisiana, by the more recent attempt to wrest by force of arms from a nation in amity the two Floridas, and lastly, by the avowed intention of permanently annexing the Canadas to the United States.[19]

(At this time, only a small part of "The Floridas," around the Mobile area, had been annexed by the United States as a declared portion of the Louisiana Purchase from France. The rest of that Florida peninsula was obtained from Spain five years later, in 1819.)

The British also complained that America's declared policy for making war was neither for self defense nor to settle grievances, "real or pretended."

The message was not well received by the U.S. delegation. Adams noted, "Mr. Bayard pronounced it a very stupid production. Mr. Clay was for answering it by a note of half a page. I neither thought it stupid nor proper to be answered in half a page." Each member wanted several hours to study it and "Mr. Gallatin proposed to make an analysis of its contents, to minute what would deserve to be noticed in our answer, to which we all agreed."[20] (Personally the author agrees with Bayard and Clay, but Adams was probably correct.)

In his diary, James Gallatin, the commissioner's son, noted his father's comment on the Indian issue, "The pith of it is that it would be more be-

coming on the part of the United States to agree to surrender the Lakes to England and the North-West Territory to the Indians."[21]

The American envoys may have differed in the severity of contempt for the British notes or in the manner they were to be answered. Yet they were quite united on holding firm to their own principles and in defying the British attempt to seek a virtual surrender of American territory and rights. Their attitude led Adams to write his wife, still in St. Petersburg, "We are still perfectly unanimous." He expected their actions to receive the approbation of the American public. He went on to tell her,

> We are in the first place severe judges upon one another, and setting aside your correspondent, [which he should not have] everyone of his four associates is, to say the least, a match for the brightest of our opponents.

Continuing in this same letter, Adams wrote of the British envoys,

> They are certainly not mean men, who have been opposed to us; but for extent and copiousness of information, for sagacity and shrewdness of comprehension, for vivacity of intellect, and fertility of resource, there is certainly not among them a man equal to Mr. Gallatin. I doubt whether there is among them a man of the powers of the Chevalier [Bayard].[22]

After a hasty review of the contents of the latest British note, the American envoys agreed to let Gallatin take the note the rest of the day to analyze it and make a list of points requiring a response. (That evening Adams went to a theater to see a play in Flemish and promptly fell asleep. He was a morning type.)

At their meeting on the afternoon of the 6th, they discussed Gallatin's summary and agreed that he should draft an answer to their opponents' note. In the discussion that followed, Bayard thought the Americans might permit some sort of arrangement in the matter of the Indians, but both Adams and Clay were opposed to any consideration of the Indians being part of a treaty. As to the defense of Canada, Adams reiterated his earlier views as expressed privately to Goulburn before this note came in, that goodwill and the British naval superiority should protect Canada. Gallatin suggested referring to Washington, the matter of disarming of the lakes. Adams produced their instructions which gave no allowance for such action. Finally, Gallatin suggested that, if the talks were ended, the U.S. might maintain ministers in Europe for any renewal.

On the 7th, Gallatin presented his draft, which was taken by Clay who would then give it to Bayard later that evening for study. Adams would get it in the morning, and then turn it over to Russell. Adams added a proposal, probably with Clay's strong endorsement. He wanted a provision charging the British with "employment of savages as contrary to the laws of war."

Before going to bed that night, Adams got the papers from Clay. Then on rising on the 8th, he heard Clay's companions just breaking up from their card games. As he went over the work of the others, Adams struck much of his own writings in preference to Gallatin's. He drafted his proposal on the Indians and when they all met at noon, his ideas were accepted though amended in part.

They sat until dinner time consolidating the various drafts into a single firm proposal. This was handed to the secretary, Christopher Hughes, to be put in final form for presentation to the British, and copies to be made for dispatching to Washington, and additional copies for each commissioner.[23]

In their completed note, the Americans countered the British contention that if the U.S. envoys were unwilling to discuss certain subjects, from the British note of the 4th, they must ascribe the reluctance of the undersigned (a term used throughout the document) to the nature of the proposal as being out of line with the basis on which the talks were originally authorized by Secretary Monroe and Foreign Minister Castlereagh in late 1813. And whereas the British charged that the Americans withheld subjects from the British, by contrast, the British did not advance some topics until their third meeting.

This latest American note opposed the British insistence on security of Canada by disarming on the lakes, and in fact placing the lakes totally within the territory claimed by the British, and their further demands for an Indian buffer state consisting mostly of the old Northwest Territory, which now boasts the great states of Wisconsin, Michigan, Illinois, Indiana, and Ohio. (What would such a territory look like today? Where would be Chicago, Detroit, and Cleveland, the great industrial cities of the American bread basket that gave victory to the North in the Civil War and supported the allied cause in World War II?) The American proposal stated that the Louisiana Purchase, the Florida provinces, and Indian lands were all obtained by peaceful negotiations and did not represent a threat of conquest to Canada. To this, Adams added that the British navy offered greater protection to Canada, but that the best security would be "found in an equal and solid peace, in a mutual respect for the rights of each other, and in the cultivation of a friendly understanding between them."

The Americans also questioned the right of the British to count as allies those Indians living within the boundaries of the United States and to insist that they be part of a treaty. To illustrate their point, the Americans cited a long list of British treaties with the Indians going back to the earliest days of colonial rule in America, arguing that at no time did they ever grant Indians the national status they now wished to in order to obtain rights the U.S. was unwilling to surrender. As to peace with the Indians, it would follow peace with Great Britain, and "no provision in the treaty to that effect is necessary."

There followed a statement on the use of Indians by the British, which might well have come from the hand of Henry Clay, who still carried the memories of the Battle of the River Raisin which took the life of his wife's brother.

> The employment of savages, whose known rule of warfare is the indiscriminate torture and butchery of women, children, and prisoners, is itself a departure from the principles of humanity observed between all civilized and Christian nations, even in war. The United States have constantly protested, and still protest, against it, as an unjustifiable aggravation of the calamities and horrors of war. Of the peculiar atrocities of Indian warfare, the allies of Great Britain, in whose behalf she now demands sacrifices of the United States, have during the present war shown many deplorable examples. Among then, the massacres in cold blood of wounded prisoners, and the refusal of the rites of burial to the dead, under the eyes of British officers, who could only plead their inability to control these savage auxiliaries, have been repeated, and are notorious to the world.[24]

The American proposal was long and detailed and written in highly diplomatic language, and has been rudely abridged in this telling. But where in the negotiations is there any mention of the odious Orders in Council or the impressment of seamen, issues that brought the United States to the brink of war? Only in this latest reply do the Americans mention the British aid and support given Indians living within the boundaries of the United States, to perpetrate depredations on frontier settlements, creating a class of traitors.

Again, the Americans were temporarily relieved of their arduous and frustrating burden of responding to the odious British insults and demands. Though they still expected rupture to follow, it had not happened after their previous proposal when they were more certain of its occurring. Now they began to suspect that the British were determined that the responsibility of a breakdown in negotiations must be placed on the shoulders of the Americans, and they in turn could not let this happen over the question of Indian rights.

This waiting period also provided the opportunity for Adams to catch up on his diary and his correspondence. Among the latter were letters to his wife, his mother, and the Marquis de Lafayette, then in Paris. It was in his letter to Louisa on September 9 that Adams wrote of the harmony among his colleagues. On the 10th he wrote to his mother, Abigail, of the uncertain status of the negotiations and then commented on the negative views of some Americans over the inclusion of Clay and Russell on the negotiating team.

> Whoever imagined that it [the negotiations] would be defeated by the appointment of Mr. Clay and Mr. Russell mistook altogether the views and wishes of those gentlemen. We have all been equally anxious for the success of the mission, and all equally determined to reject the bases proposed to us by the British ministers. They have entirely changed the objects of the war, and begun by requiring of us, as a preliminary to all discussion of what had been the points in controversy, concessions which with one voice and without hesitation we refused. In the course to be pursued by us there has not been the slightest diversity of opinion between us, and as the unfortunate circumstances under which we were called to treat have rendered it impossible that the peace should be made, we have had the only satisfaction which could be found in missing the great object, that of having constantly harmonized among ourselves.[25]

In his letter to Lafayette, Adams expressed his regret that he had not been free to visit Paris and

have "the pleasure of meeting you once more, after so long and so eventful an interval since I had last the happiness of seeing you." Adams noted that he expected the talks to end shortly, but that he would then be required to return to St. Petersburg. He added, "Our country must now rekindle in defence of her rights with that ardor which you witnessed and shared in the days of our Revolution."[26]

On September 10, the day after the Americans sent their note to the British, The prince of Orange, the ruler in Holland, visited Ghent and the whole town turned out to celebrate. He invited the Americans to see him after they had dined. The visit lasted only about 15 minutes and he spent much of that time talking to Gallatin about his native country of Switzerland. But he also recognized Adams and spoke to him of an earlier meeting and about their families. Then all attended the theater for what Adams called a wretched performance.[27]

There was still another occasion for a large dinner, on the visit to Ghent by the Dutch secretary of state on the 15th. This time the Americans gave the reception to more than 30 guests, including the British mission. During the evening, Lord Gambier asked Adams if he should be returning immediately to St. Petersburg. Adams' response was, "Yes; that is, if you send us away." Gambier's reply was that he hoped they would become friends again. Also during the evening, Goulburn told Clay that they had sent the American note to London the same day that they had received it, and expected an answer the next Monday or Tuesday. Goulburn "had no doubt it would terminate our business, and said we must fight it out."[28]

While the American note was still being analyzed in London, Goulburn sent a letter, on September 16, to the war secretary, divulging contents of the conversation he had with Clay at their last joint dinner. It was Goulburn's understanding that the American ministers would not

consent to the definition of a permanent boundary to the Indian territory within their limits ... our proposition to this effect is even more offensive to them than that for the military occupation of the Lakes. Mr. Clay stated his belief that even if America were to accede to our proposition, and if the Eastern States were cordially to unite with

Great Britain in endeavoring to enforce it, their united efforts would be inadequate to restrain that part of the American population which is to the westward of the Alleghany from encroaching upon the Indian territory and gradually expelling the aboriginal inhabitants. Their objection is ... upon its invading the right which they claim to extend their population over the whole of the unsettled country.

Goulburn added that in other conversations, Clay and Bayard

consider the mere conclusion of a peace to be the only security which is necessary. Our national feeling respecting the abandonment of the Indians and the aggrandizing spirit of America draws nothing from them but an expression of regret at the existence of such a feeling.[29]

Between these two dinners, Adams again wrote Louisa, on the 13th, expressing his expectations on the British strategy and their stay in Ghent.

I suppose they mean to give us another dissertation of sixteen pages, and ... it will be like the last, giving up in one sentence what they adhere to in another, scolding like an old woman, insulting in one paragraph and compliant in another.

He added to his view of the British method,

Never was anything more explicit than their conference with us the day Lord Castlereagh was here, and their note dated on the same day. "Will you, or will you not?" was the word. Never was anything more explicit than our answer, "We will not."[30]

On the 14th, writing to William Crawford in Paris of their current status, Adams became a bit visionary, somewhat akin to his father's thoughts of future July 2nds, saying,

I cannot imagine a possible state of the world for futurity in which the United States shall not be a great naval and military power.... I fear it is also certain that we never shall lay the foundation of a great military power but in a time of war. It must be forced upon us.[31]

In another letter to Louisa, on the 16th, Adams referred to "hints" in a British newspaper that there had been irritating language exchanged in the conferences. He wrote,

Irritating things were one day said by them, and our notes have undoubtedly contained expressions irritating to them; but ours were necessary and theirs were not. On neither side has there been, or will there be, any apology for them.

The truth of British handling of affairs at Ghent was not to be known publicly for many years. But after the initial official exchange of terms, the British envoys became mere puppets. They would receive the American correspondence, send it to London, where Prime Minster Liverpool and War Secretary Earl Bathurst (along with Castlereagh corresponding from Vienna, or wherever he might be) would draft a reply to be returned to Ghent and, some 10–11 days after they got the American note, they would render an obnoxious response. In addition, the formal conferences between the two missions ceased on August 9.

Thus it was, on Tuesday, September 20, that the latest British note was handed to Adams. It contained the same old demands done up in different language. After a quick review of its contents, Adams wrote in his diary an incisive characterization of the mood of his colleagues.

The British note is overbearing and insulting in its tone, like the two former ones, but it abandons a great part of the *sine qua non*, adhering at the same time inflexibly to the remainder. The effect of these notes upon us when they first come is to deject us all. We fondly cling to the vain hope of peace, that every new proof of its impossibility operates upon us as a disappointment. We had a desultory and general conversation upon this note, in which I thought both Mr. Gallatin and Mr. Bayard showed symptoms of despondency. In discussing with them I cannot always restrain the irritability of my temper. Mr. Bayard meets it with more of accommodation then heretofore, and sometimes with more compliance than I expect. Mr. Gallatin, having more pliability of character and more playfulness of disposition, throws off my heat with a joke. Mr. Clay and Mr. Russell are perfectly firm themselves, but sometimes partake of the staggers of the two other gentlemen.[32]

On September 15th, prior to delivery of the British note, Gallatin's son wrote in his diary,

Father is getting despondent, but only shows this to me, keeping a cheerful demeanor before the others. The Indian Territory question is a great difficulty. Father says if the Indians were included in the peace — and to be in the same position as they were — our Government would break off negotiations. He was of opinion that it would be folly to break up negotiations on that account. England could not now retreat from the position she had taken up with regard to the Indian Territory with dignity.[33]

What was it that was so disheartening?

The British note began with a strange tone, saying they had "no intention to make comments ... tending to create irritation." They expressed surprise that the Americans claimed as inadmissible any discussion of ceding any of Maine (then part of Massachusetts) to the British so that Canada would have a clean line of attachment between Halifax and Quebec, despite American instructions not to discuss changes in boundaries. They also wondered why the Americans had no new instructions since January, despite the peace that now changed affairs in Europe. (How would they know what or when instructions came to the Americans?)

But the main thrust of this note (shorter than the 16 pages expected by Adams) was another call for Indian boundaries for the protection of Canada. The British rejected the American catalog of colonial treatment of Indians as having no relevance in the present talks. In fact, they said the Indians objected to their "protection" by the American government as a reason why they sought protection from the British. And so, the British claimed that the old Treaty of Greenville of 1795 (between the Indians and the U.S. government) was now abrogated. This line of argument was reaching the absurd.

(The Treaty of Greenville was the result of a campaign under General "Mad Anthony" Wayne to rid a part of the old Northwest Territory of several tribes of Indians doing the will of the British in preventing the settlement of these lands obtained by the peace treaty of 1783 between the U.S. and England. Wayne had won the Battle of Fallen Timbers near present day Fort Wayne, named in his honor. By that treaty, the Indians were given an annuity.)

Yet after all of this, the British had the effrontery to say they were "willing to sign a treaty of peace with the United States on terms honorable to both parties. It has not offered any terms which the United States can justly represent as derogatory to their honor." They added that they "are instructed not to sign a treaty of peace ... unless the Indians are included in it.... From this point the British plenipotentiaries cannot depart."

And finally, they said they "have never stated that the exclusive military possession of the lakes ... was to be considered as a *sine qua non* in the negotiation." But they said the Indian issue was a *sine qua non*.[34] In addition, the British note was accompanied by copies of the proclamations issued by General Hull at Detroit in 1812 and General Smith at Niagara in 1813, in which both indicated that it was the intention of the United States to conquer Canada.

Like on receipt of the previous communication, it was given first to Gallatin for analysis for the next day's meeting. Several of the members were for keeping the answer short, but Adams opposed this and he urged Gallatin "to spare neither his paper nor the time of our adversaries and to be careful to leave nothing important unanswered." Adams also proposed an article in the nature of an amnesty to the Indians in exchange for one from the British to the Canadians who fought on our side. This was left for further consideration.

At their meeting on the 21st, Gallatin offered his analysis of the British note and "his minutes of the proposed answer." In the evening, as they returned from a card party, Clay told Adams of "his satisfaction at finding Mr. Bayard was now so strong in sentiment with us. Of Mr. Gallatin he had always been sure." Where there had been a difference is not clear. (It's interesting to note that after all this time working together, they still refer to each other as "Mr."; at least Adams does even in his personal writings.) Again that night, Clay played cards till his guests left after Adams had arisen in the morning.

On the 22nd, Adams felt obliged to draft a response, though Gallatin already was doing so. By the time of their 2 o'clock meeting, both had completed their drafts. Though they were about the same length, they differed materially in content. Gallatin argued against the demands for ceding any Maine territory, and about the "condition of the Indians."

Adams' view of how his draft was received is interesting.

> My arguments on these topics were very short, but I had replied at large to the accusatory matter of the British note, had retorted pointedly upon the Britons their own charges, and insisted on the moral and religious duty of the American nation to cultivate their territory, though to the necessary extinction of all the rights of the savage tribes, by fair and amicable means. I had also the proposal for the article of amnesty to include the Indians. It was agreed to adopt this article, though with

objections to almost every word in which I had drawn it up. This is a severity with which I alone am treated in our discussions by all my colleagues. Almost everything written by any of the rest is rejected or agreed to with very little criticism, verbal of substantial. But every line that I write passes a gauntlet of objections by every one of my colleagues, which finally issues, for the most part, in the rejection of it all. I write and propose a great deal more than all the rest together, Mr. Gallatin excepted. I have in the end, I believe, not more than my fifth part in the papers, as we dispatch them. This must be, in great measure, the fault of my composition, and I ought to endeavor to correct the general fault from which it proceeds.[35]

Adams wrote to Louisa on the 23rd, before their completion of the answer to the British, and again on the 27th, after their note was finished and given to their adversaries. In both letters, he wrote of Gallatin's expectations that this note would end the conferences, but Adams was not so sure, since their firm replies in the past had not stopped them. On the 27th, Adams told his wife,

It appears to me to be the policy of the British government to keep the American war as an object to continue or to close, according to the events which may occur in Europe or in America. If so they will neither make peace, nor break off the negotiation, and the circumstances may be such as to detain us here the whole winter.

He then noted that

our conferences have been suspended ever since the 19th of last month — nearly six weeks; and that all we have during that interval been discussing is merely preliminary, whether we shall or shall not treat at all upon the former differences between the two nations. We have not yet come to the real objects of negotiation.

He added that "we are still unanimous in the grounds we take."

Continuing, Adams made some observations on their counterparts.

In truth we have to deal not only with the three plenipotentiaries, one of whom was amply sufficient for five American negotiators, but with the whole British Privy Council, who have taken cognizance of every one of our communications, and have prescribed the answer to them.

As to the actions of his colleagues, Adams said that he and Gallatin compose drafts, with

the other gentlemen altering, erasing, amending, and adding to what we write, as they think proper.

We then in a general meeting adapt together the several parts of each draft to be retained, discard what is thought proper to be rejected, criticize and retouch until we are all weary of our conduct, and then have the fair copy drawn of to be sent to the Chartreux, the residence of the British plenipotentiaries.

Adams wasn't through with his comments,

In this process about seven-eighths of what I write, and one half of what Mr. Gallatin writes is struck out. The reason of the difference is that his composition is argumentative, and mine is declamatory. He is always perfectly cool, and I, in the judgment of my colleagues, am often more than temperately warm. The style of the papers we receive is bitter as the quintessence of wormwood — arrogant, dictatorial, insulting.

He went on to say that when he writes he indulges in his feelings that may be inflammable, but the talks take that out of the final drafts.

The result of all this is, that the *tone* of all our papers is much more tame than I should make it ... [with] all this winnowing and sifting.... I consider its principal advantage to be that it effectually guards against the ill-effect of my indiscretions. Mr. Gallatin keeps and increases his influence over us all. It would have been an irreparable loss if our country had been deprived of the benefit of his talents in this negotiation.[36]

Adams had different comments in his diary. At one point during the last day in preparation of their note, there was a squabble over a paragraph relating to the Floridas. Adams insisted on a statement that the U.S. was fully justified in their actions on Florida and produced their instructions confirming his view. However, Gallatin argued that he had "for a whole year" opposed what the U.S. had done. Adams, indeed, threatened to withhold his signature to the paper unless his view carried. Clay agreed with Adams, "though he thought the Government perfectly justifiable, did not perceive any necessity for saying so." They ended up taking Adams' paragraph with changes.

They also fought Adams on his wording

repelling an insolent charge of the British ... of a system of [the U.S.] of perpetual encroachment upon the Indians under the pretense of purchases, I had taken the ground of the moral and religious duty of a nation to settle, cultivate, and improve their territory.

While Gallatin approved the argument, he

was afraid of ridicule.... But the terms God, and Providence, and Heaven, Mr. Clay thought were canting,[37] and Russell laughed at them. I was obliged to give them up, and with them what I thought the best argument we had. My proposal of the amnesty passed more smoothly, almost without alteration.

(Was Adams' mood affected by the fact that this argument occurred on a Sunday?)

In the note, as finalized on the 26th, the Americans were "happy" that the British wished to "avoid unnecessary discussions, especially such as may have a tendency to create irritation," but they added that they thought it unnecessary to allude "to transactions foreign to the negotiation, relating to the United States, and other independent nations." This regarded the Louisiana Purchase, of which the British were notified and expressed satisfaction at the time, and "the solemn sanction of Spain." On the matter of the Maine District, they observed that those boundaries were spelled out in the treaty of 1783 and amended in 1794. Clearly the British weren't interested in revising the lines. They wanted land. For that, the American had no instructions to discuss.

On the question of an Indian boundary, the American refusal to agree to one was not because such a line would limit westward progress, but rather because the Indians were inhabitants of land within the U.S. possessions as established in treaties with Great Britain. In any case, the American people would not agree to a

> system of arresting their natural growth within their own territories, for the sake of preserving a perpetual desert for savages.... To recognize those Indians as independent and sovereign nations would take from, the United States, and transfer to those Indians, all the rights of soil and sovereignty over the territory which they inhabit ... and place them effectually and exclusively under British protection. Such a provision would not "differ from an absolute cession by the United States of the extensive territory in question.

The Americans further corrected the British on their comment that the Treaty of Greenville was abrogated when the Indians sought protection from the British. Their protection by the U.S. had not come by way of that treaty, but rather as "a necessary consequence of the sovereignty and independence of the United States. Previous to that

time, the Indians living within the same territory, were under the protection of His Britannic Majesty, as its sovereign" ... and Great Britain "has no right to consider any person or communities, whether Indians of others, residing with those boundaries, as nations independent of the United States."

As to the proclamations of two U.S. generals, the mission denied that they were authorized or approved by their government, unlike that of British Admiral Cochrane whose proclamation was an attempt to excite "rebellion and treachery" of slaves, and was not refuted by his government (though diplomatically, the words were "a portion of the population").[38]

Excerpts from the official diplomatic note show that the language differs from the normal writing of the envoys, such as in Adams' letters to Louisa. The formal communication consisted of several hundred words in its entirety.

On the 26th, the Americans signed the final draft during their two o'clock meeting, and Mr. Hughes immediately took it to the British. The next morning, Mr. Goulburn came to the Americans' lodging and excused their mission from a Thursday evening affair because they were leaving immediately to visit Antwerp. Had they even taken time to look at the note before it was sent off with Goulburn's brother who left that morning for London?

Two days later, Adams' brother-in-law, George Boyd, arrived with dispatches from Washington as "recent" as August 12. There was also a newspaper article that the U.S. had made a new "treaty at Greenville, 16th July, with almost all the Indians who have been such a stumbling-block in the way of our negotiation." Clay wanted to send a note to the British with an extract of the newspaper article. (This was agreed to the next day, though it was only a newspaper item and there was nothing about it in their official mail.) Also, in this mailing, there was a letter from Lucretia Clay telling her husband that he had been elected again to the next Congress.

There was also news that the United States government was having difficulty with British Admiral Cochrane in getting official clearance for ships to take documents to their envoys treating for peace. It appears they had to send them by British vessels. How secure was this?

That Thursday evening, the Americans had their big tea- and card-party with about 130 of the principal people of the city invited. "Our garden was illuminated with the variegated colored lamps, and there was an inscription of eight poor French verses over the central gate," Adams noted.

On Friday, the 30th, Henry Clay and Christopher Hughes left with "a party of pleasure to Brussels, to return next Monday." While they were gone, Mr. Shaler arrived with news from a London paper announcing the arrival of Admiral Cochrane in the Chesapeake on August 15th. Adams had predicted, "The next news will be of the taking of Washington or Baltimore."[39] He was half right.

31

WASHINGTON UNDER ATTACK

A *gain, the author wishes to make a few personal remarks. We cannot know how the details of the attack on the capital city of Washington came to Henry Clay and his colleagues in Ghent, what the stories included, or how long it took for the pieces to become known publicly or privately. We must assume that the revelations occurred as those of more recent times have — bit by bit over many years and still incomplete.*

While we have had close to 200 years to learn about the burning city — or for that matter, any of the other battle actions of that war — Clay had less than 40 more years to pick up anecdotes from far fewer sources than are available to us telling of his war.

Yet Clay had one source still denied us — his casual conversations with witnesses and participants. On his return to Washington, I'm sure he privately picked up emotional stories from Madison himself, as well as from Monroe, both of whom were leaders with access to papers and conversations, and were participants on the scene of action. One other conversation I would love to have been privy to is Dolley Madison's private recounting to Clay of her experiences of that dramatic night.

So, knowing that Clay only learned snippets of the events while in Europe, we will tell as much as we can which would come to him in those little stories over many years. — QSK

In the past several days, the American commissioners had been getting disturbing news of British naval activities. There was the denial by British Admiral Cochrane of a passport for official communications. Then there was word that his forces were in Chesapeake Bay again with renewed threats of hostilities along those inner shores — including against the capital.

During the first few months of the war, the aggressiveness of the small American navy had kept most of the Atlantic seaports open. It wasn't until December 1812 that the British declared a blockade of the Chesapeake and Delaware Bays, and it was pretty much an actual fact by February 1813. The blockade was extended to include New York and all southern ports by May. By bottling up Stephen Decatur in the frigate *United States* in June in New London, the British had, in effect, extended their blockade to southern New England.

Still, Boston was open and it became the major funnel for foreign goods entering the United States. It was also the political center of the most vicious anti-war activity. While some goods trickled in legally from non-belligerent countries, much was smuggled in or brought in from captured ships. The goods were then sold throughout the United States at exceedingly high prices bringing wealth to New England. Boston financial circles were soon able to control, and undermine, the nation's ability to finance the war.

When the federal government authorized war loans, the Federalists attempted to prevent New Englanders from subscribing to these loans. When they could not, they demanded the government provide large bonuses for the loan certificates. In addition, many loyal New Englanders were afraid to lend money for fear of public abuse, despite the efforts of the government's agents to assure that the names of the subscribers would be held in "perfect secrecy."

This merely aggravated the opponents of the war and excited the venom of the "Peace Party." One member of the party said,

Money is such a drug that men against their consciences, their honor, their duty, their professions and promises, are willing to lend it secretly to support the very measures which are both intended and calculated for their ruin.

Another said,

How degraded must our Government be, even in her own eyes, when they resort to such tricks to obtain money which a common Jew broker would be ashamed of. They must be well acquainted with the fabric of the men who are to loan them money when they offer that if they will have the goodness to do it their names shall not be exposed to the world.[1]

Eventually, Boston financial interests demanded payment on notes they held from New York banks which had to call on funds from Philadelphia banks, which in turn called on those from Baltimore creating something approaching a panic wave. As a result, financial supporters of the government were left short of subscribing to loans or fulfilling their promises. Some New Englanders obtained British government bills and sold them to capitalists in New York, Philadelphia, and Baltimore at rates they could not resist. By doing so, they supported the efforts of their British enemy.

With the government facing a financial crisis, the war effort also took on a bleak aspect. The Army was finding it next to impossible to obtain new recruits, and the limited number of men under arms in 1814 made it extremely difficult to defend but a few fortified points. And the navy was effectively bottled up by the British blockade.

It was in this dreary setting that Napoleon surrendered and made it possible for the British to begin the shipment of Wellington's seasoned troops to America. Of course, the British recognized that the predicament of the U.S. government improved their position at the Ghent diplomatic table. They were also aware that their planned military campaigns could practically win the war for them.

Though Gallatin had written Secretary of State Monroe on August 20 rightly warning of possible British ventures in the area of New Orleans, his letter could have no immediate effect. It was already too late to warn against the major British

attack of the summer — one aimed at the center of the nation. Anyway, Gallatin's estimate was wrong on this point. He had written,

It is not improbable that their warfare on our Atlantic shore will be on a smaller scale than I had conjectured, and may be confined to desultory attacks made successively on several points, for the purpose principally of distracting our defensive measures and of diverting a considerable part of our force from the points of real and serious attack.[2]

Gallatin's letters to Monroe earlier in the year were more accurate and effective when they counted most. The earliest inkling of new military disasters looming over the horizon reached President Madison late in June 1814. Attorney General Richard Rush wrote later in the year that "Impressions of danger appeared to acquire new force" on June 26 when the president received a letter from Albert Gallatin and James Bayard written from London in early May.

In their letter of May 6, actually addressed to Secretary Monroe, the diplomats told their superiors in Washington that the end of the war between Great Britain and France and the exile of Napoleon had entirely changed the state of affairs in Europe. They observed that the redeployment of Great Britain's army "put at the disposition of [that] government the whole of their force heretofore employed against France." They advised that the British might be reluctant to reduce suddenly their armed forces and that a great portion of that force "will be employed in America." They further reported that the popular excitement over their European success "has been attended with a strong expression of resentment against the United States." The writers then alluded to some of the extravagant claims and demands which were eventually put forward at the negotiating table in Ghent in August. But they said nothing specific about British military aims.

Weeks later, on October 15, Rush wrote that Madison had expressed his strong belief "that the entire liberation of British military power from European conflicts, created a corresponding probability that portions of it, unexpectedly formidable, would be thrown upon our shores." He also dwelt upon the probability of an attack upon Washington, enforcing his opinion on the grounds, among others, "of its own weakness, and the eclat that would attend a successful inroad upon the capital, beyond the intrinsic magnitude of the achievement." He spoke of the immediate necessity of preparing for its defense.[3]

It is possible that Rush had mis-timed Madison's apprehensions. Another letter written by Gallatin on June 13 gave Madison greater warning. But the transit time of mail in those days was a minimum of 20 days and often as long as five weeks. Madison could hardly have received it earlier than the first week of July. He may have received other correspondence which has long since disappeared. Still, Gallatin's June 13th message warned,

> The armament fitted against America will enable the British besides providing for Canada, to land at least 15 to 20,000 men on the Atlantic coast. Whether the Ministry be nevertheless disposed for peace a few weeks will determine. It may be intended to continue the war for the purpose of effecting a separation of the Union, or with a view of promoting the election of a President of the Federal party, or in the hope of imposing conditions which will curtail the territory, the fisheries, and diminish the commerce of the United States; but even with the intention of a speedy and equal peace, the pride and vindictive passions of the nation would be highly gratified by what they would consider a glorious termination of the war, by an expedition that may console them for the mortification of naval defeats, retrieve the disgrace of the campaign in the Chesapeake, and cripple the naval and commercial resources, as well as the growing manufactures, of the United States. To use their own language, they mean to inflict on America a chastisement that will teach her that war is not to be declared against Great Britain with impunity.... I think it probable that Washington and New York are the places the capture of which would most gratify the enemy, and that Norfolk, Baltimore, and the collected manufacturing establishments of the Brandywine and Rhode Island are also in danger.

Gallatin's letter went on to warn that the British would undoubtedly engage in plunder and predatory warfare, that America would be forced to rely on her resources alone as Europe would give no assistance, that no maritime issues would find a place in peace negotiations.[4]

Regardless of the timing of the receipt of these two letters from London, Madison, on June 30, called a meeting of his cabinet for the following day. When the heads of the various departments met at noon on July 1, Madison reviewed for them the growing threat of harsher war as the consequences of the liberation of British armies in Europe. As he had told some of them privately, he told all now that he believed Washington was a target for those troops to be transported across the Atlantic. While they did not object to this view at the meeting, most of the cabinet members later revealed their doubts as to the danger to the capital.

Madison, almost as a suggestion, proposed a plan for a force to be called into the field immediately, and an additional force to be kept in readiness to march, without delay, in case of necessity, and that some position should be taken between the Eastern Branch of the Potomac and Patuxent Rivers, with two or three thousand men, and that an additional force of ten or twelve thousand militia and volunteers should be in readiness in the neighboring states, including the militia of the District of Columbia. There was virtually no discussion or objection to the president's views. The secretaries of war and navy briefly detailed the status of the forces under their commands and the meeting broke up.[5]

On July 2, Madison created a new 10th Military District embracing Maryland, the District of Columbia, and Virginia (between the Rappahannock and Potomac Rivers) and gave command to Brigadier General W.H. Winder. His appointment was due more to convenience than to abilities, as the consequences were to prove. The nephew of the anti-war governor of Maryland, Winder was a lawyer who had held some state political offices before entering the army as a colonel prior to the start of the war. In November 1812, he was in charge of one of the lesser fiascos on the Niagara frontier. The following May, and some miles away in the same general vicinity, Winder was taken prisoner by the British on the Canadian side of the river in the same battle in which Oliver Perry first demonstrated his daring leadership. In the spring of 1814, Winder was paroled and was simply available with credentials to influence support from the Maryland governor when Madison needed a new commander for the defense of Washington and Baltimore.[6] Winder would have been more successful if he could have influenced Secretary of War John Armstrong.

The forces brought together under General Winder's command were a motley gathering. Totaling no more than 4,000 men, the command consisted of elements of the 36th and 38th army infantry regiments, light dragoons, Maryland and District militia (both stationed at the Washington Navy Yard), Baltimore militia (not much more than a mob under Brigadier General Tobias E. Stansbury), the 5th Maryland volunteer militia under Lieutenant Colonel Joseph Sterett, a battalion of riflemen, two batteries of light artillery and a collection of sailors supported by a company of marines detached from the Washington Navy Yard.

The latter group was aboard a flotilla of 26 gunboats under the command of an old naval officer of heroic stature, Commodore Joshua Barney. He had positioned his boats in Chesapeake Bay at the mouth of the Patuxent River. They had already engaged the vastly stronger British naval vessels. In June, Barney had battled the British who had to fight him from barges in order to chase him into the river's shallows. The net result of these inconclusive actions was that Barney was bottled up in the river, but he occupied British Admiral Cockburn enough to force him to suspend some of his depredations against the towns and farmlands along the Bay shore. But Barney was not a prisoner of the situation. He was a fighter who would be heard from again.

Secretary Armstrong's order putting Winder in command of the new 10th Military District was sent from Washington on July 2, and addressed to Winder in Baltimore. The secretary asked Winder to come to Washington for a conference. By July 9, Winder had returned to Baltimore and wrote a long letter to the secretary warning that the British forces, in the Chesapeake for over a year, knew the terrain so well that they could be "within three hours' rowing and marching of Baltimore; within less of Annapolis; and upon arriving off the South River, can debark, and be in Washington in a day and a half." He stated that reinforcements — such as could arrive from Bermuda or elsewhere — could be in any of those cities in four days after entering the Bay near Norfolk. Even allowing "for all causes of detention, he [the enemy] can be in either of those places in ten days from his arrival." Winder wanted to know how the forces to be brought in from afar could be gathered, supplied, and deployed in time to meet a strong enemy. He asked Armstrong to call out 4,000 militia without delay and proposed placing them between South River and Washington, and in the vicinity of Baltimore. Each of these forces could assist the other once the enemy's destination was determined. Winder then said he would leave the next day for Annapolis, and thus began nearly a month of vigorous travel throughout the area of his command seeking possible points of resistance to any British invasion on the western side of Chesapeake Bay.

On July 16, Winder wrote Armstrong from Annapolis warning that British 74s were at the mouth of the Potomac. On the 17th, writing from Nottingham, he believed the enemy was advancing up the Patuxent River in considerable force. On the 20th, he reported from Annapolis that the enemy had landed at Hunting Creek, committed depredations, and left. Winder went on, the next day, to Baltimore.

On the 23rd, he wrote the secretary from Upper Marlboro asking for supplies for 3,000 troops called up by his uncle, the governor of Maryland, and urging the drafting now of Pennsylvania militia. He wrote from Woodyard later that day and, on the 25th, from Fort Washington on the Potomac across from Alexandria. He continued sending notes from various other locations into early August. His correspondence nearly evaporated with letters to Armstrong on August 13, 19, and 21.[7]

Winder got very little response from the secretary. Those brief notes sent by Armstrong on July 18, 28, August 19 (two letters) and 22, were forced to ride around for days trying to catch up with the swift-riding general. It was really astonishing that any military defense was developed at all. Armstrong was so certain that there was no danger to Washington, that he scoffed at such fears.

One of the strangest complaints against Armstrong came from General John P. Van Ness, commander of the District of Columbia militia. Ever since the British incursion up the Potomac in the summer of 1813, Van Ness had been urging the strengthening of Fort Washington across from Alexandria. Armstrong consistently failed to follow through with the necessary orders to make anything happen.

While the events at Washington were still a burning memory, Van Ness penned a blistering account of the action — or inaction — by government leaders and their generals prior to the British attack. Van Ness summarized his disturbed thoughts in a report to a committee of Congress. His views are reported more fully in the next chapter after the British had departed for further depredations elsewhere.

But at this point it is possible to note that Van Ness made repeated attempts, before the British attack on Washington, to obtain some urgent preparations for defense of the city. He had encountered flabby resistance in conversations with Secretary of War Armstong, President Madison, and even Secretary of State Monroe. Yet Van Ness received no satisfaction.[8]

Meanwhile, the British fleet had only recently nearly doubled with the arrival from Bermuda of Admiral F.T. Cochrane with more than 50 ships — warships and transports carrying 3500 to 4500 of Wellington's veterans from the Napoleonic wars, now serving under General Robert Ross. Even at this late date, Navy Secretary William Jones was also reluctant to visualize any danger to Washington. He thought the British force in the Bay was "entirely Naval and apparently very satisfactorily engaged in conflagrating farm houses, and depredating upon slaves and tobacco, on the shores of the Patuxent. In this sentiment I was not alone," Jones wrote to the Congressional investigating committee in October 1814.[9]

Admiral Cochrane and his fleet, containing General Ross and his troops, left Bermuda on August 3, sailed into Chesapeake Bay on the 15th, and anchored off the mouth of the Patuxent River on the morning of the 17th. Cochrane had preceded the troopships by a couple of days and had even reconnoitered the Maryland countryside with Cockburn under escort of a battalion of British marines. On the morning of the 17th, they conferred to put together their plans to invade the area with the new army now at hand.

It is probable that the maneuvers of the two admirals, accompanied by some support forces, was interpreted by Washington as a British landing. On the morning of August 18th, Secretary Monroe visited the president at the White House. Madison informed the secretary "that the enemy had entered the Patuxent in considerable force and were landing at Benedict." Monroe expressed the belief that their objective was Washington and Madison agreed. Monroe then

> offered to proceed immediately to Benedict, with a troop of horse, to observe their force, report it, with my opinion of their objects, and, should they advance on this city, to retire before them, communicating regularly their movements to the Government.

Madison accepted Monroe's plan of action.[10]

The secretary was likely reminiscing about his thrilling experience as a young man leading some of Washington's advance troops into Trenton, New Jersey, that bitter, cold, snowy Christmas morning in 1776 after the crossing of the Delaware. But as he wrote a friend, George Hay, a few weeks later, in 1814,

> My hope was to rescue the country from the reproach impending over it, and I trusted, if I failed to do it, that I should at least, place my own conduct, in its just light, before the nation. I had a horror, at remaining inactive here, to be involved indiscriminately in the censure, which would attach to others, and which so eminently belonged to the Secry. of War.[11]

Later that day Monroe sent a note to Secretary Armstrong requesting the troop of horse through an order to General Van Ness. In his November report to Congress, Van Ness wrote that he furnished Monroe "with two small troops of horse."[12] Van Ness, himself, began having troubles that same day when General Winder wanted the remainder of Van Ness' troops. They disputed who was then to command and appealed to both Armstrong and Madison, both of whom seemed unable to make a decision. Van Ness made the decision. He resigned his commission. The resignation was refused — officially nearly three months later.

Meanwhile, Monroe set out about 1 P.M. on the 19th, with a detachment of 25–30 dragoons under the command of Captain Thornton. At eight the next morning, they arrived at Butler's Mill, four miles from Benedict, but found no enemy there. However, Monroe learned that the enemy had landed in force only on the 19th, and had advanced their pickets to within a mile and a half of the mill. By 10 P.M., Monroe was closer to Benedict, and from a height overlooking the Patuxent, he viewed their shipping about three miles distant. By 1 P.M. the next day, Monroe was seven miles from Benedict at Acquasco Mills from where he sent the above information to the president. He also gave his opinion that Washington was the object of the British army and suggested that "The Best Security against this attempt is an adequate preparation to repel it."[13]

For the next few days, it is almost possible to follow the moves of the American and British armies through the adventures of two individuals of very different ranks — the American secretary of state, James Monroe, and British army Lieutenant George Robert Gleig.

At this date, Gleig was only 18 years old. The son of a Scottish bishop, he entered the army at age 15 and served under the Duke of Wellington in the Peninsular campaign (in Spain) until peace with the French came in the spring of 1814. Without even a leave to go home to the British Isles, his unit, the 85th regiment, was transported, during June and July, via the Azores, to Bermuda where they came under the command of General Robert Ross. He was aboard the transports that left Bermuda on August 3 and entered Chesapeake Bay on the 15th. He and his companions were still aboard ship, by now in the Patuxent, on the 18th, when Monroe was requesting permission of Madison to go to Benedict to observe the British movements. Gleig was to continue in the British battles in America beyond this attack on Washington. After his wars, he returned to school and carved out a distinguished career in the work of the church and rose to the rank of chaplain-general of the armies and then became a prolific writer producing historical, biographical and theological works, including "*A Subaltern in America,*" published in 1836. It is from this book that the British army can be followed.

It was at dawn of the 19th, as Monroe prepared to leave Washington, that the main body of the British army — and Gleig — debarked from their transports at Benedict, Md., without any American resistance. The British spent much of that day bringing ashore supplies, organizing their forces, reconnoitering the surrounding area, enjoying the pleasure of land under their feet, and finally bivouacking for the night just north of Benedict. It was not until 4 P.M. on Saturday, the 20th, three hours after Monroe had written Madi-

son of viewing British shipping at Benedict, that Gleig's unit moved north. The soldiers, only a day ashore from three leisurely months on ships, and now heavily laden with camp equipment and armaments, advanced in extremely hot weather over dry dusty roads. Gleig described his "accoutrements" — his saber, sash, belt and pistol — and all that he carried on his back, front and sides — clothes, food, powder horn and other equipment.

They marched six miles in the direction of Nottingham, with American Commodore Barney's flotilla as an immediate objective. (Oddly, at this time Gleig's regiment was under the command of a Colonel Thornton, as Monroe was escorted by dragoons under command of a Captain Thornton.) Monroe quartered that night near Charlotte Hall, and reported nothing, in his dispatch the next day to Madison, of a noisy thunder and brilliant lightning storm which disturbed the rest of the British troops, giving them a thorough soaking.

Early Sunday, the 21st, Monroe again climbed the heights above Benedict to view the British shipping, and reported to Madison that he counted 23 square-rigged vessels and very few barges, suggesting to him that the British had moved up the Patuxent to attack Barney's flotilla. He told Madison he would proceed immediately to the town of Nottingham, where the secretary stayed until evening.

That same day, Gleig wrote of marching through forests, which held the threat of enemy ambush. Yet it was only late in the day that the British were interrupted by a minor skirmish with a party of American riflemen on patrol near Nottingham. Monroe sent off another note to Madison, and then watched as the advanced column of the enemy entered "the rear of the town. He wrote later,

> I concluded, [they] had passed from Benedict by a road near the river, moving in concert with the barges.... I went immediately to Mr. Oden's, where I met Colonel Beall, whom I had before seen at Nottingham. He had taken a view of the enemy's column from a commanding height contiguous to the town.

They estimated the British force at between 4,000 and 5,000 men, plus an additional 1,000 with the barges. Monroe learned that General Winder was supposed to be at the Woodyard and, as darkness fell, he proceeded there. He reached the Woodyard (about 12 miles west of Nottingham) after midnight and reported what he had observed to General Winder. Also present was Gen. Walter Smith, commander of the troops in this area. On the basis of Monroe's information, Smith returned to his camp about 2 A.M. and had his troops aroused and placed in readiness. There they waited, without sleep, until sunrise of the 22nd.

Gleig and his companions had already entered Nottingham, finding it was completely deserted of its 1,000 or so inhabitants. Meanwhile, the British learned that Barney's flotilla had retreated further up the Patuxent. As Gleig and his friends settled in for another night, he again described the landscape and even the hum of insects at dusk and the fire-flies. He and the rest of the British troops spent the night in tobacco fields and barns using large leaves as bedding and pillows.[14]

At 5 A.M. that Monday, August 22, as Winder ordered his troops to advance toward Nottingham, Lt. Col. J. Lavall's cavalry set off with Monroe, Winder and their suite of aides, and soon met the enemy a mile in advance of Mr. Oden's. Monroe dashed off a note to Madison stating,

> The enemy are advanced six miles on the road to the Woodyard, and our troops retiring. Our troops were on the march to meet them, but in too small a body to engage. General Winder proposes to retire till he can collect them in a body. The enemy are in full march for Washington. Have the materials prepared to destroy the bridges.

Monroe held the note and then appended, "*Monday, nine o'clock.* You had better remove the records."

During this activity, the Americans had remained under cover until the British had advanced within 300–400 yards. Winder and his troops retired westward through the Woodyard and then northwestward to a place called Long Old Fields (now Forestville) which covered equally Bladensburg, the bridges over the Eastern Branch of the Potomac (now called the Anacostia River), and a road to Fort Washington (below Alexandria, but on the Maryland side of the Potomac).[15]

Meanwhile, Monroe and Dr. Hanson Catlett (surgeon of the 1st regiment) galloped off toward Upper Marlboro. About noon, they began to hear a series of heavy explosions and saw smoke rising from the direction of Barney's flotilla of gunboats. The commodore was blowing them up to prevent their falling into British hands. During the afternoon, Monroe and Catlett were overtaken by some American vedettes who warned of enemy horsemen in the area. They immediately headed for the Woodyard where they met with General Winder, and then retired with the bulk of the army to Old Fields where they were to spend the night.[16]

Meanwhile, Gleig wrote of that day, the 22nd, that his unit did not move forward until about 8 A.M. He described the road over the 10-mile march, as remarkably good, hard, dusty, and having a sound bottom. Running through the heart of thick forests, it was sheltered from the sun's rays. There was no cultivation until they approached Upper Marlboro

> in a country not more fertile than beautiful. The ground ... was broken into the most graceful swells, generally cleared of wood to within a short space of the summits, and then crowned with hoary ... and venerable forests. The village itself lies in a valley, formed by two green hills; the distance from the base of one hill to the base of the other, may be about two miles, the whole of which was laid out in fields of corn, hay, and tobacco; whilst the slopes themselves were covered with sheep, for whose support they furnished ample means. [In] Marlborough, the houses are scattered over the plain, and along the sides of the hills, at considerable intervals from one another, and are all surrounded by orchards and gardens, abounding in peaches and other fruits of the most delicious flavour. To add to the beauty of the place, a small rivulet makes its way through the bottom, and winding round the foot of one of these ridges, falls into the Patuxent, which flows at its back.[17]

There was virtually no skirmishing during the day's march, but the British troops were startled by the same series of heavy explosions heard by Monroe, caused by the destruction of Barney's flotilla of gunboats.

While Gleig and his companions had a long restful night and even most of the morning of the 23rd, the American camp continued to be one of frenzied activity. During the evening of the 22nd, President Madison, along with Secretary of War Armstrong, Secretary of the Navy Jones, and Attorney General Richard Rush came to Old Fields to meet with General Winder. And, of course, Secretary of State Monroe joined this gathering later in the evening. Also joining the camp was Commodore Barney with about 500 of his flotilla men.

A false alarm in the middle of the night resulted in rousing the entire American army to stand by their arms. By sunrise, a rumor circulated that the enemy was moving toward Annapolis. This was not proved false until noon.

About that time, on the enemy's side in Upper Marlboro, British General Ross appeared in camp and his troops were ordered to fall in. Throughout the morning, a rumor had circulated among the rank and file that an advance was to be made on the city of Washington. In addition, word had reached into the lowest ranks of the British officer corps that General Ross and Admiral Alexander Cochrane had determined, by insulting the capital itself, to retaliate for what was called "excesses committed by the American army upon frontier towns of Canada."

The intent of the British leadership was more than rumor. On August 18, while the British troops were still aboard their ships and Secretary Monroe was only planning to ride out from Washington, Admiral Cochrane wrote a letter to Monroe. Eventually, Monroe received the letter and replied on September 6. But it is not known when, between these two dates, the American secretary of state received the message.

In it Cochrane said he had been asked by the governor general of Canada to aid him in "retaliation against the inhabitants of the United States for the wanton destruction committed by their army in Upper Canada." Therefore, Cochrane was informing Monroe that he had issued orders to the naval forces under his command "to destroy and lay waste such towns and districts upon the coast as may be found assailable." (His orders appear to be issued only to naval forces and to apply to coastal towns — not to the army or to inland cities.) But in keeping with the convention of the times, Cochrane nonetheless closed with the words, "I have the honor to be, sir, with much consideration, your most obedient humble servant."

In his response of September 6, Monroe expressed "the greatest surprise" that Cochrane would cite American actions as grounds for retaliation when the British throughout the war had engaged in a "system of devastation ... contrary to the usage of civilized warfare." Monroe cited atrocities at such places as the River Raisin and among the towns along Chesapeake Bay, and more outrages which were to be added between the exchange of letters (such as the coming attack on Washington). Monroe suggested that such acts had not even been committed during the long years of the Napoleonic Wars. Yet he was also able to advise Cochrane that the United States government had disavowed acts committed by Americans in Canada and had taken action against those involved in the "unauthorized irregularities," and the United States would have been ready to "repair" the British for their losses.

> But in the plan of desolating warfare which your letter so explicitly makes known, and which is attempted to be excused on a plea so utterly groundless, the President perceives a spirit of deep-rooted hostility, which, without the evidence of such facts, he could not have believed existed, or would have been carried to such an extremity.

Monroe then suggested that any reparations would be reciprocal. If the British should

> adhere to such a system of desolation, so contrary to the views and practice of the United States, so revolting to humanity, and repugnant to the sentiments and usages of the civilized world, whilst it will be seen with the deepest regret, it must and will be met with a determination and constancy becoming a free people contending in a just cause for their essential rights and their dearest interests.

Cochrane replied to Monroe's letter on September 19, saying that he must persist in the measures he had adopted. This reveals the character of the leadership with which the American forces contended on August 23, 1814.[18]

Gleig and his unit did not move out from Upper Marlboro until 2 P.M. but they were soon involved with skirmishing with American troops detached from Winder's army at mid-day. When the two antagonists met, the Americans quickly retreated over a bridge into Washington. The British general sent forward a unit of troops to give the impression of an attack aimed at Alexandria.

Meanwhile, President Madison, and Secretaries Armstrong, and Jones returned to Washington ahead of the army as Monroe and Attorney General Rush rode off to watch the road from Upper Marlboro to Bladensburg (northeast of the city). Late that evening, about 11 P.M., Monroe visited the headquarters of General Tobias E. Stansbury at Bladensburg and advised him "to fall forthwith on the enemy's rear, although it was then 12 o'clock at night." Stansbury replied that he had orders "to take a post at Bladensburg, and did not think himself at liberty to leave it." In addition, his troops had just arrived there "after a very fatiguing march" and they should not be marched that night. Monroe then returned to Washington for a brief rest.[19]

Despite Stansbury's reluctance to move his troops for Monroe, he did have them roused from their rest twice during the night and on the second occasion they were marched some distance into new positions. Also during Monroe's visit with Stansbury, there had been some expressions of fear that General Winder had fallen into the hands of the enemy. In fact, Winder had fallen. But the fall was from his horse into a gully during his ride around various camps trying to insure that all was ready to meet the enemy. He only caught a few hours of sleep after four in the morning.

Some time before dawn on Wednesday, the 24th, Gleig and his British friends were up and marching. Now they had turned north from the Woodyard. Gleig described the march as winding

> through the heart of an immense forest and completely overshadowed by projecting branches of trees, so closely interwoven as to prevent a single sunbeam from making its way, even at noon, within the arch.

They did not know that there was not a cloud in the sky. Instead, they enjoyed a coolness that was "extremely pleasant, except for a damp and fetid atmosphere resulting from morning dew." The woods also offered the British the advantage of concealment from American intelligence.

Eventually, the British emerged from the woods and continued for another four miles under greatly changed conditions. Now marching in open country, except for occasional clumps of trees, which they feared could hide American dragoons, the sun beat upon them in full force and dust from the road rose in thick masses to irritate the soldiers' eyes and throats. Gleig later wrote, "I do not recollect a period of my military life during which I suffered more severely from heat and fatigue." He noted that before long, "numbers of men began to fall behind, from absolute inability to keep up." After a march of nine miles, the British stopped by some woods and rested along a small stream as stragglers rejoined their ranks. But soon after resuming the march "some of the finest and stoutest men in the army [were] literally unable to go on."[20]

Indeed, the British march through the woods had kept the American command in ignorance as to its whereabouts. During those same morning hours, Secretary Monroe rode back to General Winder's headquarters at the Washington end of the bridge over the Eastern Branch of the Potomac, many miles from Bladensburg. Here he found President Madison already receiving an irregular flow of reports from dragoons scouring the land to the east of the city. Eventually, there seemed to be some significant reports that the British were marching toward the little town of Bladensburg some few miles northeast of Washington. Monroe offered to ride out in that direction and alert General Stansbury. Madison gave his approval and between 11 A.M. and noon, Monroe joined Stansbury and his exhausted forces overlooking that part of the eastern branch into Bladensburg.

While Monroe was conferring with Madison and Winder, Attorney General Richard Rush had gone to the lodgings of Secretary of War Armstrong. The secretary had just received a message from Winder that affairs were "more and more serious." As Armstrong rode off to Winder's headquarters, Rush went to the White House where he learned that Madison had already gone to meet Winder. By the time Rush reached those headquarters and joined the others, Monroe had already departed for Bladensburg. Shortly, those gathered at Winder's headquarters were joined by Secretary of the Navy Jones and Commodore Tingey, commander of the Washington Navy Yard.

Conferences continued with these government leaders as well as military subordinates who came with messages and left with instructions. Sometime around 10:30 A.M., an express arrived from

Stansbury with confirming news that the British were advancing towards Bladensburg. Immediately, Winder ordered his army in that direction and rode off with his troops. Madison, in Rush's presence, asked Armstrong if he had any advice or plan to offer upon the occasion. The secretary of war replied he had not. He added that as it was to be between regulars and militia, the latter would be beaten. The comments could not have struck Madison as coming from a positive leader. After a few minutes, Armstrong mounted his horse and followed the army to Bladensburg.

President Madison, accompanied now by Attorney General Rush, followed Secretary Jones to the nearby marine barracks. There they met Commodore Barney with his small group of sailors and marines. They were ordered to make all haste with their artillery pieces to Bladensburg. At this point, Madison decided to go to the expected field of battle to be able to give any executive orders which might be necessary. Rush went with the president.[21]

Meanwhile, the hierarchy of the American government gradually began the very perilous choice of gathering in the face of a heavily armed enemy in the vicinity of a bridge which spanned the Eastern Branch of the Potomac and provided the crossing from the town of Bladensburg to a direct route into Washington City.

Monroe was the first of these officials to arrive on the scene, sometime between 11 A.M. and noon of August 24. He found General Stansbury, who had placed his troops on the Washington side of the river. When Stansbury informed Monroe that the enemy was about three miles away, the secretary of state advised the general "to form his troops to receive them, which he immediately commenced. The order of battle was formed on the presumption that his brigade would alone have to meet the enemy in the first instance," Monroe later wrote.[22] For the next hour or so, as new American troops arrived, there was a continual shuffling of men into different positions in an effort to block the British approach across the bridge or on either flank.

When Winder arrived, about noon, he was informed by Mr. Francis Key, of Georgetown, "that he had thought that the troops coming from the city could be most advantageously posted on the right and left of the road near that point," Winder later wrote to the congressional committee. Key then pointed out the proposed positions to General Smith who then made the disposition of the troops. Winder went on to direct other officers to take positions suggested to them by various unknown advisors. Clearly a number of civilians were intruding their personal military theories for setting up the tactical defenses, probably to the disgust of the military leaders supposedly in charge.

Eventually, on the left of the defense line, Winder found General Stansbury in conversation with the secretary of state. Monroe was informing Winder of "their" disposition of troops, when a messenger rode up with news of a victory in the area in which a thousand of the enemy were slain and many prisoners taken. Almost as soon as Winder dispatched this false news to excite the spirit and courage of the American troops, a column of the enemy appeared about a mile distant. Winder immediately ordered still another rearrangement of infantry and gave orders to the artillery to open fire on the British as they made their way toward the bridge.[23]

At this time, Monroe and Winder returned to the road leading back toward Washington and soon met Secretary of War Armstrong. A few minutes later, they were joined by the president and Attorney General Rush. They had only time to confer briefly, get a view of the troop arrangement, observe the approaching enemy, and make a quick exhortation to the troops to stand firm — when, about 1 P.M., the firing of the British brought the forces into battle. The president and his principal civilian aides retired to the rear — and were shortly to be followed by the entire American army.

About 12:30 P.M., the British infantry, which had been using the houses at Bladensburg as cover, began to move down to the river banks to make a crossing at the bridge or wherever they could find a fordable passage across the river. About the same time, the British began firing rockets across the stream into the American positions on the opposite bluff.

Almost at this same instance, Commodore Barney, with his sailors, marines (some of them barefooted), and a few pieces of artillery, arrived on the scene "in a trot." He quickly deployed his men and placed his pieces to look down the road, over the bridge into Bladensburg — and into the enemy troops.

During the deployment of the American troops, Gleig and his British companions approached the scene on the east side of the river and cautiously entered the town of Bladensburg. When the American artillery opened up, they used the town's buildings as cover while General Ross sent out patrols to investigate the possibility of some fordable river crossings. He soon determined to push across the bridge in a frontal assault. It was then that the British preceded the attack with a vigorous use of the relatively new Congreve rockets.

As Gleig later described the scene, the Americans had lined up parallel to the river, with the road, which crossed the bridge, nearly bisecting the center of their lines, with three of four lines of infantry looking across the stream at the approaching red-coated British.

At approximately 1 P.M., the British, in a run, began to swarm over the bridge and fan out on either side once across, and attack the American lines. Other British units had apparently forded the river to the right of the bridge and were beginning to fall on the American left. All along the line Americans gave way and a stream of British began to follow the road up the bluff from the bridge. But they were headed directly into Barney's battery of five guns.

Barney wrote, five days later, to Secretary of the Navy Jones,

> During this period the engagement continued, and the enemy advancing; our own army retreating before them, apparently in much disorder. At length the enemy made his appearance on the main road, in force, and in front of my battery, and on seeing us, made a halt. I reserved our fire. In a few minutes the enemy again advanced, when I ordered an eighteen pounder to be fired, which completely cleared the road; shortly after, a second and a third attempt was made, by the enemy, to come forward, but all were destroyed. They then crossed over into an open field, and attempted to flank our right; he was there met by three twelve pounders, the marines under Captain Miller, and my men, acting as infantry; and again was totally cut up. By this time not a vestige of the American army remained, except a body of five of six hundred posted on a height, on my right, from whom I expected much support, from their fine situation. The enemy from this period never appeared, in

force, in front of us; they pushed forward their sharpshooters; one of which shot my horse under me; who fell dead between two of my guns. The enemy, who had been kept in check by our fire, for nearly half an hour, now began to out-flank us on the right; our guns were turned that way; he pushed up the hill, about two or three hundred, towards the corps of Americans stationed as above described; who, in my great mortification, made no resistance, giving a fire or two, and retiring. In this situation, we had the whole army of the enemy to contend with. Our ammunition was expended, and, unfortunately, the drivers of my ammunition wagons had gone off in the general panic. At this time, I received a severe wound in my thigh; Captain Miller was wounded; Sailing master Warner killed; Acting Sailing master Martin killed; and Sailing master Martin wounded; but to the honor of my officers and men, as fast as their companions and messmates fell at the guns, they were instantly replaced from the infantry.

> Finding the enemy now completely in our rear, and no means of defence, I gave orders to my officers and men to retire. Three of my officers assisted me to get off a short distance, but the great loss of blood occasioned such a weakness that I was compelled to lie down. I requested my officers to leave me, which they obstinately refused; but, upon being *ordered*, they obeyed; one only remained. In a short time I observed a British soldier, and had him called, and directed him to seek an officer; in a few minutes an officer came, and, on learning who I was, brought General Ross and Admiral Cockburn to me.

At this point in Barney's report, there is a colloquy found in a later biography. The first British officer was a Captain Wainwright. On learning the identity of the captive, he went in search of Admiral Cockburn who soon came up in the company of General Ross.

> They were most cordial and attentive, offering sympathy and the immediate help of a surgeon. In tones of marked respect, the British general said, "I am really glad to see you."
> "I am sorry I cannot return you the compliment, General," was Barney's candid reply.
> General Ross smiled and remarked to the British Admiral; "I told you they must be the flotilla men. They have given us the only real fighting we have had today."[24]

Resuming Barney's report to the secretary of the navy, he wrote,

> Those officers behaved to me with the most marked attention, respect, and politeness, had a surgeon brought, and my wound dressed immedi-

ately. After a few minutes' conversation, the General informed me (after paying me a handsome compliment) that I was paroled, and at liberty to proceed to Washington or Bladensburg; as also, Mr. Huffington, who had remained with me, offering me every assistance in his power, giving orders for a litter to be brought, in which I was carried to Bladensburg.

My wound is deep, but I flatter myself not dangerous; the ball is not yet extracted, I fondly hope a few weeks will restore me to health, and that an exchange will take place, that I may resume my command, or any other that you and the President may think proper to honor me with.[25]

When the British army later retreated to their ships, 80 wounded British soldiers were left in Barney's care at Upper Marlboro.

Joshua Barney is a genuine American hero of large proportions. Born in Baltimore in 1759, he was 55 years old when he fought at Bladensburg. He insisted on leaving school at the age of 10 and went to sea with his sister's husband, Captain Drysdale of the sailing ship *Sidney*. Most of their early voyages were to the environs of Ireland. But his first major trial came at the end of 1774 when Barney had become second officer and they were about to sail from Norfolk with a load of wheat bound for Nice, then belonging to the Kingdom of Sardinia, a dependency of Great Britain. But the ship sprang a leak. Back in port, Drysdale lost his first mate following a quarrel. Barney quickly took the job. Then more than half way across the Atlantic, Drysdale died leaving 15-year-old Barney in command of a now badly leaking ship. He made Gibraltar and sought out a commercial house run by a father and son who provided for repairs and then the son accompanied the young captain the remainder of the voyage to Nice.

But Barney had no legal credentials and was a minor. There was much more to the story in Nice, where he was treated with no respect. He and his young business partner then travelled across the southern Alps to Milan to meet with the British consul there. Suffice it to say that the cargo was transferred, and paid for, so that he could refund the Gibraltar loan and sail back to America. But not so fast. His ship was captured by Barbary pirates for a while and when released, he finally made it back to the Chesapeake Bay only to be intercepted by a British man-of-war telling him that his country was now at war with Great Britain.

Some how he cleared that adventure, but still had to report in to his late brother-in-law's ship owner in Baltimore, who immediately inquired, "Who are you?" Barney replied, "I am master of your ship *Sidney*!" When the owner didn't believe him, Barney tossed him documents of this voyage. When read, the owner responded, "*Captain* Barney, welcome home!" During the revolution he was made a prisoner of the British four times and once escaped from the infamous Old Mill Prison in England. At one time he carried the first stars and stripes on a float, shaped like a ship, in Baltimore, and on another occasion he escorted Martha Washington to New York for her husband's inauguration as first President. Between the wars he continued to sail for both the United States and at one time for France. He was truly an amazing mariner, yet remains unknown to Americans today.

It is interesting to compare Gleig's account of this same period of action at Bladensburg, beginning with the British approach to the bridge.

> While we were moving along the street, a continued fire was kept up, with some execution, from those guns which stood to the left of the road, but it was not till the bridge was covered with our people that the two-gun battery upon the road itself began to play.— Then, indeed, it also opened, and the tremendous effect; for at the first discharge almost an entire company was swept down.

Gleig went on to describe the British attack on the American lines and watched them give way and flee "in the greatest confusion." He told of the collapse of the American left, followed after a short resistance by the right and the reserve. Even some cavalry followed the retreat. "The fact is," he wrote,

> with the exception of a party of sailors from the gun boats, under the command of Commodore Barney, no troops could behave worse than they did. The skirmishers were driven in as soon as attacked, the first line gave way without offering the slightest resistance, and the left of the main body was broken within half an hour after it was seriously engaged. Of the sailors, however, it would be injustice not to speak in terms which their conduct merits. They were employed as gunners, and not only did they serve their guns with a quickness and precision which astonished their assailants, but they stood till some of them were actually bayoneted, with fuzes in their hands; nor was it till

their leader was wounded and taken, and they saw themselves deserted on all sides by the soldiers, that they quitted the field.[26]

There is an interesting anecdote by President Madison's black valet regarding Madison's meeting with Barney on the field. A large part of Barney's

> men were tall, strapping negroes, mixed with white sailors and marines. Mr. Madison reviewed them just before the fight, and asked Com. Barney if his "negroes would not run on the approach of the British?" "No sir," said Barney, "they don't

know how to run; they will die by their guns first."[27]

Possibly Barney and his men were more accustomed to a rolling deck which offered no place to hide, than they were to a countryside that gave the soldiers so much land over which to retreat. But for what ever reason they had for making their stand, they demonstrated the only courageous quality which was evident on the American side that day. Six hundred sailors and marines stood against four thousand of the best troops the British could send against them.

32

WASHINGTON ABLAZE

It was mid-afternoon of August 24, 1814. The fighting at Bladensburg was ended. President Madison and much of his cabinet had retreated behind those frightened individuals spreading the alarm of the calamity, which they had left on the bluffs overlooking the Eastern Branch of the Potomac River. Following the government leaders were the fleeing generals and their troops. All that was left behind were the wounded, dying, dead, and captured of both British and American armies.

As for casualties, probably the British suffered most from the naval guns of Commodore Joshua Barney. The American army didn't stay in place long enough to take many casualties.

Nevertheless, the road was now wide open for the advance of the British army into the American national capital. There are numerous accounts of the next hours of shame and depredation. However, among these, first-person witnesses of the burning of the Capitol and the White House are hard to find.

There seems to be a sudden gap in the record from the moment the fighting ceased at Bladensburg, until the fleeing army and the government leaders showed up between Georgetown and places north and west. Yet there are two major stories that are told. One is the afternoon events at the White House. The other was a minor battle of sorts, a little later, at the former home of Albert Gallatin, just to the northeast of the Capitol.

On Tuesday, the 23rd, the day before the battle at Bladensburg, Dolley Madison wrote her sister, Anna Cutts (who had married Supreme Court Justice Thomas Todd), that the president was out looking for the enemy along with cabinet members and generals. She had received two penciled dispatches from her husband.

The last is alarming, because he desires I should be ready at a moment's warning to enter my carriage and leave the city: that the enemy seemed stronger than had been reported, and that it might happen they would reach the city, with intention to destroy it.

Continuing her letter, she wrote, "I am accordingly ready; I have pressed as many cabinet papers into trunks as to fill one carriage; our private property must be sacrificed, as it is impossible to procure wagons for its transportation." And she wanted to wait for James.

Referring to the wagons, and maybe military support, she wrote,

All are gone, even Col. C—, with his hundred men, who were stationed as a guard to the enclosure.... French John [Sioussat, a faithful domestic] with his usual activity and resolution, offers to spike the cannon at the gate, and lay a train of powder which would blow up the British should they enter the house. To the last proposition, I positively object, without being able, however, to make him understand why all advantages in war may not be taken.

Dolley continued the letter on the following day.

Wednesday morning twelve o'clock — Since sunrise I have been turning my spy glass in every direction and watching with unwearied anxiety, hoping to discover the approach of my dear husband and his friends; but alas, I can descry only groups of military wandering in all directions, as if there was a lack of arms, or of spirit to fight for their firesides.

Three o'clock — Will you believe it, my sister? We have had a battle or skirmish near Bladensburg, and I am still here within sound of the cannon! Mr. Madison comes not; may God protect him! Two messengers, covered with dust, come to bid me fly; but I wait for him.... At this late hour, a wagon has been procured; I have had it filled with the plate and most valuable portable articles belonging to the house; whether it will reach its destination, the Bank of Maryland, or fall into the hands of British soldiery, events must determine.

Our kind friend, Mr. Carroll, has come to hasten my departure, and is in very bad humor with me because I insist on waiting until the large picture of Gen. Washington is secured, and it requires to be unscrewed from the wall. The process was found too tedious for these perilous moments; I have ordered the frame to be broken, and the canvass taken out; it is done — and the precious portrait placed in the hands of two gentlemen of New York, for safe keeping. [Jacob Barker and Robert G.L. DePeyster.] And now, I must leave this house, or the retreating army will make me a prisoner in it, by filling up the road I am directed to take. When I shall again write to you, or where I shall be tomorrow, I cannot tell!![1]

Another letter, written by Dolley near the end of 1814 to Mrs. Latrobe, wife of the Capitol architect, is similar, with some differences. Dolley wrote that she

sent out the silver (nearly all) — the velvet curtains and Gen. Washington's picture, the cabinet papers, a few books, and the small clock — left everything else belonging to the public, our own valuable stores of every description, a part of my clothes, and all my servants' clothes, etc. etc., in short it would fatigue you to read the list of *my* losses, or an account of the general *dismay*, or *particular* distresses of your acquaintants. Mrs. Hunter and Mrs. Thompson were the only ladies who stood their ground, I confess that I was so unfeminine as to be free from fear, and willing to remain in the *Castle*. If I could have had a cannon through every window, but alas! those who should have placed them there, fled before me, and my whole heart mourned for my country![2]

There are more details of these "precious moments," which again differ, as written nearly 50 years later by Paul Jennings, the president's Negro valet.

Jennings' account mentioned that around 3 P.M., as the battle was ending in Bladensburg, the servants in the White House were preparing dinner (a rather odd hour) for up to 30 people. A rider from the field of battle galloped up to the House and hurried past the cannons placed on the front lawn and came in to hand a message from the president to Dolley. She was urged to leave, "Now!" Jennings also told of Dolley preparing a wagon with special items to carry away with her, separate from the carriage she would ride in.

At this point Jennings mentions the large painting of George Washington hanging in the East Room. There are differing accounts of what happened next. One is Dolley's letter to her sister-in-law shortly after the event. Another is Jennings' account nearly a half century later. The servant claimed he took down the painting, which is probably true and doesn't really conflict with Dolley's account. The only discrepancy seems to concern who carried the painting from the House, and where was it taken. Dolley never claimed that she took it with her.

Jennings related the stirring scene, with slight variance, attributable to the excitement of the moment and the shading of memory over so many years.

Mrs. Madison ordered dinner to be ready at 3, as usual; I set the table myself, and brought up the ale, cider, and wine, and placed them in coolers, as all the Cabinet and several military gentlemen and strangers were expected. While waiting, at just about 3, as Sukey, the house-servant, was lolling out of a chamber window, James Smith, a free colored man who had accompanied Mr. Madison to Bladensburg, galloped up to the house, waving his hat, and cried out: 'Clear out, clear out! Gen. Armstrong has ordered a retreat!' All then was confusion. Mrs. Madison ordered her carriage, and passing through the dining-room, caught up what silver she could crowd into her old-fashioned reticule, and then jumped into the chariot with her servant-girl Sukey, and Daniel Carroll who took charge of them; Joseph Bolin drove them over to Georgetown Heights; the British were expected in a few minutes.[3]

He also noted that "Mrs. Brown wrote that her mother and sister saw Mrs. Madison in her carriage flying full speed through Georgetown, accompanied by an officer carrying a drawn sword."[4] Much of Dolley's story, Jennings got from her servant Sukey.

Meanwhile, as the president and Attorney General Rush fled from the battle, they agreed that the cabinet should retire to Frederick Town, Maryland (north and a bit west of Washington), if the capital should be captured. They entered the city about the time Dolley left the White House, believed to be about 4 P.M., the president and his small entourage arriving at the home of Dolley's sister and brother-in-law (the Richard Cuttses) on 14th street. Along with Attorney

General Rush and Navy Secretary Jones, and a few others, they dined between 4 and 5 P.M. By then they had been joined by Navy Secretary Jones, General Mason, Charles Carroll, and Tench Ringgold. They then met briefly with Secretary of State Monroe, and possibly Secretary of War Armstrong, at Monroe's home on I Street at what was called the Six Buildings near 21st Street. Only then did they leave the city.[5] It was now after 8 P.M.

It was during these late afternoon hours that the British troops again were on the move from Bladensburg towards the center of the small city proper.

British Lieutenant Gleig's brigade and one other remained on the battlefield until dark. General Ross, accompanied by Admiral Cockburn and a small contingent of the British army, came down what is now Maryland Avenue. Gleig wrote, years later, that they came with a flag of truce hoping to find authorities who would surrender the city and agree to pay a sort of ransom for the city. Barring that, the conquering army would take what they could as spoils of war. First of all, they found no one with whom to treat. Then as they approached the grounds of the Capitol, they were passing a brick house, the home where former Treasury Secretary Albert Gallatin, now commissioner to Ghent, had lived while in Washington. From its windows, sharpshooters (believed to be remnants of Commodore Barney's sailors fired on the advancing British and killed some British soldiers and General Ross' horse. The British escort attacked those who fired from the house with no known killed. Gleig wrote that the house was "reduced to ashes." Nevertheless, that house still stands at Second and Constitution Ave.

The assault from the house irritated Admiral Cockburn and he convinced General Ross to destroy the Capitol building, still a dumpy embryo of its future glory. Gleig justified the burning of the structure, writing that

All this was as it should be, and had the arm of vengeance been extended no further, there would not have been room given for so much as a whisper of disapprobation. But unfortunately, it did not stop here; a noble library, several printing offices, and all the national archives were likewise committed to the flames, which, though no doubt the property of Government, might better have

been spared. It is not, however, my intention to join the outcry, which was raised at the time, against what the Americans and their admirers were pleased to term a line of conduct at once barbarous and unprofitable. On the contrary, I conceive that too much praise cannot be given to the forbearance and humanity of the British troops who, irritated as they had every right to be, spared, as far as possible, all private property, neither plundering nor destroying a single house in the place, except that from which the General's horse had been killed.[6]

Since the British lacked the means of transporting any quantities of booty, they destroyed what could be of value to the vanquished. The lack of transportation went both ways. Yet some of the more far-sighted American government clerks — those not needed on the battle lines — had already procured wagons and carts wherever they could in order to pack them with documents and other valuable belongings from their work places in the various departments. Now they were crowding the streets westward trying to make their way to the Georgetown heights.

Among the more interesting efforts were those of the navy department. A couple of miles south of the Capitol building was the navy yard along the eastern branch of the Potomac, now known as the Anacostia River. Some days prior to the battle, under the direction of Navy Secretary Jones, Thomas Tingey, commandant of the navy yard, had managed to secure transportation for a large number of items that the Americans hoped to place in safety from the enemy. These included

engines, fixtures, shop furniture ... about one hundred tons of cordage, some canvass, considerable quantity of salt petre, copper, iron, lead, block tin, naval and military stores, implements, and fixed ammunition, with a variety of manufactured articles in all the branches; seventeen hundred and forty barrels of beef and pork, two hundred and seventy-nine barrels of whiskey, some plank and timber.

Later, in his report to Congress, the navy secretary stated that he had no means left to transport the sloop *Argus*. He ordered the barges to the Little Falls. There was another crisis brewing on the area's waters that forced the hands of the Americans to send what they could up the Potomac, rather than down past Alexandria. Word had been received that a force of British vessels were making their way up the Potomac past Washington's estate of Mount Vernon, en route to that city. Furthermore, the navy secretary had been warned by General Winder that Fort Washington, on the Maryland side of the river, could not be defended against the passage of the British ships.[7]

But Tingey was severely restricted in his means to obey the secretary's order, lacking sufficient personnel to carry out a salvage operation involving huge quantities of valuable naval stores and even the small shipping remaining in the yard. (Most of the able-bodied naval personnel had been sent to Bladensburg to support the army, leaving blacks and the older navy men to do the security work.) Throughout the afternoon and early evening of the 24th, two of Tingey's trusted subordinates had been trailing the actions of the British on their advance into the city and, by 8 P.M., advised Tingey that the enemy was about to take possession of the city.

In his report to Congress, through Secretary Jones, on October 18, Tingey wrote,

> After receiving repeated contradictory reports, relative to the strength and position of the enemy ... at twenty minutes past eight P.M., I received incontestable proof (by Captain Creighton, and Mr. M. Booth, my clerk, both of whom had been voluntarily active to obtain me positive information) that the enemy was in complete possession of the city, having themselves been within the range of, and exposed to, the fire of his musketry.

A reading of the losses sustained at the navy yard might force a tear or two from an old navy veteran of World War II, 200 years later, despite the great differences in equipment styles and other characteristics so changed by time. Tingey wrote,

> The boats for our conveyance from the yard being stationed according to order, we immediately repaired down the yard, applying fire to the trains leading to the store houses, the principal of which were almost instantly in irresistible flames.
>
> Advancing towards the boats, those to the new frigate Essex, and to the sloop of war Argus were torched, and they also immediately enveloped in a sheet of inextinguishable fire.
>
> From a momentary impulse, and *faint* hope of recovering the new schooner Lynx, I directed her not to be fired, and have the satisfaction to say,

that, by an almost miraculous escape, she is still "ours."

> The frigate Essex's hull, in the shipwright's department, was very near complete, her bottom ready for coppering, and she could have been launched in ten days; her masts and spars were nearly finished, with timber sufficient on the wharf to complete them; all her blocks, dead-eyes, and the major part of her gun carriages, ready; two suits of her heavy sails, and nearly the same quantity of her others, were finished in the sail lofts, ready for bending; her standing rigging, &c. fitted in the rigging loft, and sufficient running rigging in store for her complete equipment; her largest boats nearly ready for launching; all her water casks, and every material of cooper's work, ready to go on board.
>
> The sloop of war Argus lay at the wharf, with all her armament and equipment on board, except her sails, which were in the sail loft, and her provisions in the stores, and therein consumed; and except her powder, which had not been shipped.
>
> A large quantity of timber, plank, knees, &c. were in different parts of the yard, and the seventy-four gun ship timber, stored in the appropriate sheds, all fell prey to the devouring element; also one large and one smaller row galley, both armed, rigged, and prepared for service; and three heavy armed scows, with their guns, &c. on board, also ready.
>
> The buildings destroyed by the fire from the frigate, &c. were the mast shed and timber shed; the joiners' and boat builders' shops, and mould loft; all the offices; the medical store; the plumbers' and smiths' shops, and blockmakers' shop; the saw mill and block mill, with their whole apparatus, tools, and machinery; the building for the steam engines, and all the combustible parts of its machinery and materials; the rigging loft; the apartments for the master and the boatswain of the yard, with all their furniture; the gun-carriage makers' and painters' shops, with all the materials and tools therein at the time; also the hulls of the old frigates Boston, New York, and General Greene.
>
> The storehouses first fired were the provision stores, gunner's and ordnance store, cordage store and sail loft; which, with all their perishable contents, were consumed.
>
> The navy storekeeper's detail issuing store, containing, in its different departments, a large quantity of new canvass, twine, lines, bunting, and colors; together with all our stocks of mathematical instruments, and nautical apparatus, appertaining to navigation; ship chandlery, tools, nails, oils, paints, &c. had escaped through the night the effect of the fire, but was fired by the enemy on the succeeding morning, the twenty-fifth, and entirely

consumed, with all its contents; as were also the coopers' shop, two small frame timber sheds, and that in which our tar, pitch, rosin, &c. were deposited.

The general loss of our papers prevents the possibility of forming a just estimate of the loss in the mechanical departments heretofore enumerated. Of that relative to the stores on hand, in the navy storekeeper's peculiar charge, it is presumed a tolerable accurate estimate may be formed, and will be subject to a future communication, which shall be transmitted as soon as it is possible to effect.

On my return to the yard on the twenty-sixth, I had the mortification to observe, that the provisions which had been laden on board the old gunboat, No. 140, (and with which she had grounded in endeavoring to get out of the branch, on the twenty-fourth) had become a prey to numerous unauthorized persons, some of whom, however, instantly offered to deliver up all in their possession, which was subsequently done, but several barrels are yet to be accounted for. [It would seem better that American neighbors of the yard possess these items, than that they fall into the hands of the enemy.]

A subject of still greater regret is the loss upwards of two hundred barrels of powder, which were wantonly and unauthorizedly taken out of the magazine, and chiefly thrown into the water, the cause of which, however, being under investigation by a court martial, on the corporal of the marine guard then there, I forbear to enlarge on the subject as my feelings would dictate.[8]

There is an odd story related to the destruction in the navy yard. The *Niles Weekly Register*, dated "Saturday, August 27" quoted from a story published in the *National Intelligencer* (of Washington), dated "Aug. 31," followed by another story from the same paper, dated "September 1." The only conclusion is that *Niles* dated their publication a week before they published their articles. The story told of American sailors dumping gunpowder down a well to prevent it from falling into enemy hands. However, the enemy did "capture" the powder in a manner not anticipated. After the British came into the yard and tried to salvage what they could and destroy the rest, they inadvertently tossed some lighted matches down the well. The result was a huge explosion which left a gaping crater in the yard and many dead British soldiers about the grounds.[9]

While the navy yard was being "scuttled," the British army was arriving on Capitol Hill. As noted earlier, Admiral Cockburn and General Ross agreed to torch the Capitol in response to the minor shooting from Gallatin's former home.[10] They also claimed that their action was in response to the burning of the Parliament building in York (now Toronto), Canada. Still, today, the perpetrators of that deed have never been proved, whether Americans, Canadians, or rabble. In any case, what took place in Washington was not done to other capitals across Europe during the Napoleonic Wars.

The Capitol of 1814 was quite unlike the magnificent structure of more recent times. Then, it was just two ugly cubed blocks of stone connected by a wooden walkway. In renewal, the walkway was replaced by the towering dome which covers the giant rotunda — occasionally becoming a solemn memorial room where, on the death of the nation's greatest heroes, they lie in state beginning, oddly enough, with Henry Clay as the first.

The House chamber was then in an elliptical shape. There is an account given, many years later, by a grand niece of Dolley Madison about the British invasion of that chamber.

> Admiral Cockburn, in a strain of coarse levity, mounting the Speaker's chair in the Capitol, went through the form of putting the question: "Shall this harbor of Yankee democracy be burned?" And when the mock resolution was declared unanimous, it was carried into effect, by placing combustibles under the furniture. The temporary wooden structure readily ignited; doors, chairs, the library [of Congress], and its contents in an upper room of the senate wing, everything that could burn, soon disappeared in sheets of flame, illuminating the country for thirty miles around.[11]

The House chamber was later replaced by a beautiful semi-circular chamber in which Clay, after his return from Ghent, was again to sit in the chair of the presiding officer before moving over to the other once ugly block where the newly restored Senate chamber was to hear the voice of Clay and his eloquent contemporaries struggle to prevent a civil war. What wondrous history haunts this old and restored monument of American freedoms.

The events now beginning to unfold in Washington City in 1814 are now 200 years in the past, yet many of the sites remain, albeit in a drastically altered form. Dolley Madison, in flight, went out the north driveway into Pennsylvania Avenue. At 17th Street, the avenue took its slight turn north-westward past 19th street, where, at the northwest corner stood an old house — no longer there — but where the Madisons would live for many months as the White House was rebuilt.

Nearby to the south is now George Washington University — named for that founder whom Dolley knew personally. Dolley continued up the avenue over Rock Creek (now with its lovely park-way crowded with automobiles — unheard of in Dolley's days — and now the route home for thousands of commuters.

Dolley continued west on what is now M Street until she reached a street which was the beginning of the Pike to Rockville, Maryland. It is now Wisconsin Avenue, named for a state not then a part of the Union and then mostly populated by Indians. Dolley's passage up this street was filled with refugees producing a scene of disorder so familiar in all wars.

Continuing up the avenue, in the vicinity of Tennally Town (now simply Tenley Town) at the high point of land, Dolley angled off a bit to the left taking River Road for another mile or so where she and her entourage camped for the night.

It is hard to dwell on a vision of this fashionable first lady melding into the chaotic panorama without trying to place her at the various points so long since changed by a different world. Yet it should be noted that even very old history has a way of leaving footprints in today's world.

There are accounts that say Dolley slept in a tent under guard that night, but one wonders where a tent came from in the hasty departure from the White House. (However, in the account written by Dolley's grand niece, the night was spent "in the house of an acquaintance ... and the long night was passed at the window, gazing at the flames."[12]) In any case, it is doubtful that she got much sleep. Dolley wrote that she feared for James' safety. Yet Dolley's niece wrote that the first lady and James met briefly in Georgetown before she went on up the avenue and the president crossed to the Virginia side of the river near Little Falls. This may be.

Such a meeting was described by the president's valet, Paul Jennings. It was about 8 P.M., and about the time the British were deciding on how to burn the Capitol, when President Madison's small party left for Georgetown and the meeting with Dolley. They all left together with their departure described many years later by Attorney General Rush.

> I have indeed, to this hour, the vivid impression upon my eye of columns of flame and smoke ascending through the night of the 24th of August from the Capitol, President's House, and other public edifices, as the whole were on fire, some burning slowly, others with bursts of flame and sparks mounting high up in the dark horizon. This can never be forgotten by me....
>
> If at intervals the dismal sight was lost to our view, we got it again from some hill-top or eminence where we paused to look at it. We were on horseback, attended by servants, proceeding on the Virginia side of the Potomac, which we crossed at Little Falls, intending to recross at the Great Falls that night or the next morning, so as to be again on the Maryland side, and return to Washington as the movement of the enemy and our own strength might prompt.[13]

What Attorney General Rush was describing, was the result of the British advance of its reserve brigade into the city.

It must have been close to 8 P.M. (about the time the British were preparing to torch the Capitol) when Madison's group headed for Georgetown. His valet, Paul Jennings (who wrote his account of this evening about the time of the American Civil War), stated that the president met his wife in that suburb at a home called Weston. This would be before she went on north to Tennally Town. The president's party then crossed the Potomac River by boat at the Little Falls, with the intention of returning to the Maryland side the next day and making his way to Montgomery Court House, now in Rockville. Jennings wrote that he had walked to Georgetown, leaving the White House about sundown. By the time he was again with the president, that group was waiting for the ferry to Virginia and Jennings continued with them. That night, Madison may have obtained a little rest somewhere in Virginia.

After the Capitol was set aglow by Ross' soldiers, the British moved on up Pennsylvania Avenue, well after the sun was setting, yet bright with so many fires lighting the darkening skies.

The British soldiers didn't reach the White House until well after nine o'clock, hours after Dolley Madison had fled. But the table settings were still there in the state dining room for the 3 P.M. luncheon, which had been prepared by Jennings. The British enjoyed the meal even though the hot food had cooled and the cool food may have melted or was warm. Then this home was also torched to add to the glow in the city's darkness and fear.

By this time, the city was nearly abandoned, except by those hiding in fear within their homes under a British curfew, and the usual looters that always seem to stalk the streets in such circumstances. As for the British troops, they were bivouacked on the grounds where now stand the illustrious Supreme Court Building and the magnificent Library of Congress now grown to be the greatest library in the world.

Early on Thursday, the 25th, a rainstorm patted down some of the fires but British Admiral Cockburn was out early intent on more burning. He was after the offices and presses of the *National Intelligencer*. Though several citizens tried to deny knowledge of the office's location, the Admiral finally found the place. Then some ladies of neighboring houses pled with him not to set the place afire for fear that the conflagration would destroy their homes. Cockburn acquiesced in the burning but had his soldiers wreck the offices and spread type out into the streets. Cockburn insisted on special destruction of the letter C, so the editor could no more use his name to castigate him.

Itching to continue his arsonist campaign, Cockburn next turned to the U.S. Patent Office. However, now guarding this valuable storehouse was its superintendent, Dr. William Thornton, who, years earlier, had submitted the winning design for the U.S. Capitol. Thornton's persuasion convinced Cockburn to stay the hands of his anxious firebugs. Thus was saved "the museum of the arts & that it would be a loss to all the world," as described by Thornton's wife.[14]

Meanwhile, the first family was again on the move. The president re-crossed the Potomac River into Maryland, and made his way beyond the "Montgomery County Court House" in Rockville, and settled in at the Quaker village of Brookeville. There he met with as many of his cabinet members as could assemble.

During this same time, Dolley returned to the Georgetown area with her tiny retinue, including her servant girl, Sukey. They crossed the river on a reciprocal course to James, and ventured two or three miles into Virginia and settled for the night of the 25th at Rokeby, the country home of the Richard Love family. (The house took its name from Sir Walter Scott's Rokeby.) The husband was then absent, engaged with the troops.[15]

Unfortunately, Dolley moved on the next day (the 26th) from this hospitable home. This time, she pushed on to a tavern farther into Virginia. She took a room upstairs until the tavern mistress learned the identity of her "guest." In a fury, she mounted the steps screaming, "Miss [sic] Madison! you come down and go out! Your husband has got mine out fighting, and d--- you, you shan't stay in my house; so get out!" The first lady quietly left and proceeded a few miles farther to take up lodging with a Mrs. Minor. There she stayed the next couple of days.[16]

On the morning of the 25th, as the Madisons were finding shelter miles from the city, the British became fearful that the Americans were re-grouping along the Georgetown Heights, in preparation for a counter assault. But the storm that came from the west was unlike any these troops had ever seen. Lieutenant Gleig described it as well as any:

Whether or not it was their [the Americans'] intention to attack, I cannot pretend to say, because it was noon before they showed themselves; and soon after, when something like a movement could be discerned in their ranks, the sky grew suddenly dark, and the most tremendous hurricane ever remembered by the oldest inhabitant in the place, came on. Of the prodigious force of the wind, it is impossible for one, who was not an eye-witness to its effects, to form a conception. Roofs of houses were torn off by it, and whirled into the air like sheets of paper; whilst the rain which accompanied it resembled the rushing of a mighty cataract, rather than the dropping of a shower. The darkness was as great as if the sun had long set, and the last remains of twilight had come on, occasionally relieved by flashes of vivid lightning streaming through it; which, together with the noise of the wind and the thunder, the crash of falling buildings, and the tearing of roofs as they were stript from the walls, produced the most appalling effect I ever have, and probably ever shall, witness. The storm lasted for nearly two hours without intermission; during which time, many of the houses spared by us were blown down; and thirty of our men, besides several of the inhabitants, buried beneath their ruins. Our column was as completely dispersed as if it had received a total defeat; some of the men flying for shelter behind walls and buildings, and others falling flat upon the ground, to prevent themselves from being carried away by the tempest; nay, such was the violence of the wind, that two pieces of light cannon, which stood upon the eminence, were fairly lifted from the ground, and born several yards to the rear.

Gleig further noted that the storm left the Americans "in as great a state of confusion as our own," and neither side could recover sufficiently to renew a battle. (Actually, most of the American army had retreated to Montgomery County Court House, many miles north of Georgetown.) Under these circumstances, and seeing no advantage in staying in the city as there was nothing new to be gained, General Ross decided to evacuate during the coming night. Therefore, a curfew was imposed at 8 P.M.

In the dark hours of Friday the 26th, the British made their move. Again Gleig described their march.

All the horses belonging to different officers were removed to drag the guns, no one being allowed to ride, lest a neigh, or even the trampling of hoofs, should excite suspicion. The fires were trimmed, and made to blaze brightly; fuel enough was left to keep them so for some hours; and finally, about half past nine o'clock, the troops formed in a marching order, and moved off in the most profound silence. Not a word was spoken, nor a single individual permitted to step one inch out of his place, by which means they passed along the streets perfectly unnoticed, and cleared the town without any alarm being given.

Throughout their march they left small fires and pickets as a rear guard. It was still dark when they arrived at the Bladensburg battlefield. Again Gleig wrote:

When we reached the ground where yesterday's battle had been fought, the moon rose, and exhibited a spectacle by no means enlivening. The dead were still unburied, and lay about in every direction, completely naked. They had been stripped even of their shirts, and having been exposed in this state to the violent rain in the morning, they appeared to be bleached to a most unnatural degree of whiteness. The heat and rain together had likewise affected them in a different manner, and the smell which arose upon the night air was horrible.

Gleig then philosophized about the nature of battle. (He would many years later become an army chaplain.)

There is something, in such a scene as this extremely humbling, and repugnant to the feelings of human nature. During the agitation of a battle, it is nothing to see men fall in hundreds by your side. You may look at them, perhaps, for an instant, but you do so almost without being yourself aware of it, so completely are your thoughts carried away by the excitation of the moment, and the shouts of your companions. — But when you come to view the dead in an hour of calmness, stripped as they generally are, you cannot help remembering how frail may have been the covering which saved yourself from being the loathsome thing on which you are now gazing. — For myself, I confess that these reflections rose within my mind on the present occasion; and if any one should say, that, similarly situated, they would not rise in his, I should give him no credit for a superior degree of courage, though I might be inclined to despise him for his want of the common feelings of a reasonable being.[17]

Gleig, like many of his companions, went to the houses in Bladensburg, now housing American prisoners of war, including Commodore Joshua Barney, still under British guard. Among the wounded soldiers were also numerous British soldiers. They may have been happy to see their fellow soldiers, but were soon to be dismayed, when they learned that they were about to become prisoners of the wounded Americans under Barney's care. Only those British who could walk away were to join their companions for the long all-day march toward their ships anchored in the Chesapeake.

Now the British were beginning to see what their attack on the American capital had cost them in dead and wounded. It wasn't pretty. Even before the evacuation of Washington City, an American, Dr. Hanson Catlett, had obtained permission to cross through the British lines and return to Bladensburg, where he had been during the battle. Catlett was to see to the American wounded. He was to report later on his findings at the site of the battle.

> On our arrival at Bladensburg, the surgeons [British] were ordered to select all the wounded who could walk, (those with broken arms and the like) and send them off immediately. The forty horses were mounted with such as could ride, the carts and wagons loaded, and ninety odd wounded left behind. I estimated their wounded at three or four hundred, besides forty or fifty left in the city. One British surgeon informed me they had buried that day about one hundred on the field; and the men who were sent out next day after the retreat of the enemy, to bury three or four Americans, reported that they also buried fifty of sixty redcoats, or British. I found at Bladensburg Commodore Barney, Captain Miller, of marines, and seventeen odd wounded; though others, who had less opportunity of judging, estimate it at more than double.

In a following note to Congress, Catlett estimated the total strength of the British army at the start of the battle at about 3,540 men. Each side had figured their opponents put nearly 9,000 men on the field. Catlett's estimate was probably closest to the mark.[18]

A report published some days later in the *Niles Weekly Register*, stated that the British had come through Bladensburg so quietly that the American "prisoners" did not even know that their guards had left, still leaving many unburied British comrades on the field. These wounded Americans observed that during the battle, the British "lost many men by fatigue — for they were drove to the charge by the swords of their officers gasping for breath — twelve were buried in one field, that had not a wound." That same account related that when the British had

> reached the bridge, which they crossed in solid column, the artillery opened a fire upon them.... As their men fell, they merely threw them out of the way, and instantly closed up the vacancy without disorder.[19]

So much for the fight between regulars and militia. One final note about the battle: some weeks later a long poem reflecting the shame of the American retreat was published. It was called "The Bladensburg Races."

Now as the British returned to their ships

(again Gleig wrote of their exhausting march in the hot August climate), James Madison learned of the evacuation of the city by the British, and on Saturday the 28th, urged Dolley to return to the city, as he had done. He told her that he had been offered lodging at the home of Attorney General Richard Rush, at one of the "seven houses" at 19th and Pennsylvania Ave. (They did not go there immediately.)

Meanwhile, Dolley started back to the city on Sunday. It wasn't easy. She was now riding incognito and when she reached the long bridge, about a mile wide, now spanned by the 14th Street bridge, she found that the Americans had burned the western end of the bridge while the British had burned the eastern end. It was necessary to take a ferry and the "captain" refused to take just any lady. She had to reveal her true identity to make the crossing. Together again, the Madisons moved into "The Octagon House," the vacated residence of French minister Sérurier. The house, at 19th and New York Avenue, is still a Washington landmark 200 years later.

But there are still a few lesser known incidents relating to this period of activity in the Washington area. As most of the British army returned to their ships in the Bay, there was a smaller British fleet that had made its way up the Potomac River and now menaced the Virginia city of Alexandria. Seven ships, carrying about 125 cannon, were able to sail past Fort Washington, on the east side of the river, only because the fort's commander blew it up prematurely, On the 29th, they positioned themselves facing Alexandria, then stripped of soldiers to defend the place. A delegation of prominent citizens met with the fleet's commander, Captain Gordon aboard the Frigate *Seahorse*, to inquire about the safety of their homes.

On Sunday the 28th, as Dolley re-crossed the Potomac River by ferry, alongside the half-damaged long bridge, it seems she had not been warned of the enemy ships approaching Alexandria a few miles south. With the use of a good spy glass, she might have been able to see their masts. Meanwhile, a deputation from Alexandria's common council, appealed to the commander of the hostile British fleet for terms favorable to the safety of the city. What they received was more atrocious demands from an arrogant enemy.

The redcoats prefaced their demands with the assurance that the city's inhabitants would not be molested "in any manner whatever, or their dwelling houses entered." But they qualified that immediately with a list of six articles almost impossible to fulfill. The first three applied primarily to maritime surrenders:

> Art. 1. All naval and ordnance stores, public or private, must be immediately delivered up.
>
> 2. Possession will be immediately taken of all the shipping, and their furniture must be sent on board by the owners without delay.
>
> 3. The vessels that have been sunk must be delivered up in the state they were, on the 19th of August, the day of the squadron passing the Kettle Bottoms.

(How could the citizens possibly comply with this article with a date five days prior to the Battle of Bladensburg? No ship, once sunk, could possibly be restored immediately to a condition prior to its sinking!)

The next three articles seem to apply to the town merchants, not the citizens in their homes, but would nevertheless be financially ruinous, and again create a condition very difficult to abide:

> 4. Merchandize [sic] of every description must be instantly delivered up, and to prevent any irregularity, that might be committed in its embarkation, the merchants have it at their option to load the vessels generally employed for that purpose, when they shall be towed off by us.
>
> 5. All merchandize that has been removed from Alexandria, since the 19th inst. is to be included in the above articles.

(How could some items possibly be retrieved for surrender?)

> 6. Refreshments of every description to be supplied the ships, and paid for at the market price, by bills of the British government.

A final paragraph is one of those hideous demands by "authority" in which compliance involves every person with utter retaliation if a single person fails to conform.

> 6. [again] Officers will be appointed to see that articles No. 2, 3, 4, and 5, are strictly complied with, and any deviation or non-compliance, on the part of the inhabitants of Alexandria, will render this treaty null and void.

Signed by Gordon.[20]

With further negotiation, the British commander yielded on the demand for re-floating sunken ships.

During this disgraceful episode, authorities from Alexandria warned those of Georgetown, that they were next in line for an unwanted visit by the enemy. But Georgetown leaders said they would fight any attack on them. They were not to be subjected to a similar fate.

When the British completed their plunder, they began a retreat down the Potomac like the fatted calf, taking with them more small confiscated vessels adding to their gun power. They needed it. Angry Americans lined the western bank of the river firing cannon and muskets and anything else they could muster to pelt the retiring ships. The Americans suffered little damage despite being chased by marines landed along the shore to put an end to the sniping. Even the shifting of their ships' ballast, which enabled them to fire their cannon upward to the tops of the river banks, gave them little success. In the long run, of three or four days of harassment, there were almost no American casualties, while the British had a large number of wounded and several killed, including the captain of one of their frigates. Beside the tiny vessels seized by the marauders, their loot consisted mostly of flour, tobacco, and some arms and not much else for their trouble.

The British still in the Chesapeake, were also active in the field of plunder and harassing the settlements along the Bay shores. Among those kept in fear were the inhabitants of Annapolis.[21] Admiral Cochrane, commander of the entire expedition, still had destructive ambitions in mind before leaving the Chesapeake, but much of this accumulating news would be more than a month reaching Henry Clay and his distressed colleagues trying to negotiate a peace treaty in Ghent with the countrymen of these villains.

There was one other political item arising from those disturbing days. A large number of individuals had made complaints about the handling of Washington's defenses under the leadership, or lack thereof, of Secretary of War John Armstrong.

Among them was the vociferous editors of the Georgetown *Federal Republican*. In addition, among the many military men who sent statements to Congress citing their experiences, was a very long letter, dated November 23, 1814, from Major General John P. Van Ness, commander of the District of Columbia militia. He was briefly a congressman from New York in the early 1800s, and the mayor of the District in the early 1830s. He was promoted to major general of the D. C. militia in 1813. While General Van Ness was a respected military officer, militia soldiers were always looked down on since the days of the American Revolution and probably long before those days.

Beginning his recitation of wrongs with the threat to the District as early as June 1813, Van Ness told the congressional committee that Secretary Armstrong readily agreed with him about the necessity of preparing a defense around Washington City, but never followed up with any action to build defenses, order up men to serve or make arms available to them. He stated in his letter,

> After the lapse of some time, not seeing or hearing of any step towards the execution of this project, I several times reminded him of it, and he, as often, still encouraged me, by words, to expect it, whilst he, generally otherwise, appeared rather indifferent, and expressed an opinion that the enemy would not come, or even seriously attempt to come to this District.

Similar comments were made concerning the activities in the summer of 1814 about which he wrote,

> Without any visible steps towards works of defense, either permanent or temporary, either on the land, or the water side, (I never having heard of a spade or an axe being struck in any such operation) or towards forming a rendezvous or camp of regular troops in the neighborhood, to the great anxiety, inquietude, and alarm, of the District and surrounding country; the Secretary generally treating with indifference, at least, if not with levity, the idea of an attack by the enemy.

Van Ness further noted that, "I had occasionally, though seldom, introduced it personally to the President himself," but was referred to the War Department, meaning to Armstrong. He also brought it up with Secretary of State Monroe,

asking him if "it was the intention of Government to abandon and sacrifice the District." Monroe replied that, "So far from that, every inch of ground about it was determined to be contested, and the last drop of blood to be spilt in it its defense."

As the summer days continued and the British began their landings along the eastern shore of the Chesapeake, the conversations continued as before. Again Van Ness called on the secretary to express his apprehensions and stated to him,

> that from their known naval and reputed land force of the enemy, he probably meant to strike a serious blow. His reply was, "oh yes! by G--d, they would not come with such a fleet without meaning to strike somewhere, but they certainly will not come here; what the d---l will they do here," etc. After remarking that I differed very much from him, as to the probable interest they felt in destroying or capturing our seat of Government, and that I believed a visit to this place would, for several reasons, be a favorite object with them, he observed, "no, no! Baltimore is the place, sir; that is of so much more consequence."

As if this failure to prepare for the defense of the capital city was not aggravating enough to Van Ness, he then encountered General Winder on the battlefield at Bladensburg, ready to command his division of District militia, but was told he had no command. He was told that while the militia was "in service," Van Ness, was not! Van Ness went to Armstrong to clarify the issue, but was told it was "an embarrassing case." He then asked President Madison to intervene. That went nowhere either. So, Van Ness wrote a note to Monroe offering to resign his commission (which, of course, he had not the paper in hand). Much later, he received word from Monroe that the president had declined the resignation. However, the depressed Van Ness insisted.[22]

There were to be other complaints striking at other leaders. Many attacked General Winder as lacking the proper skills. In any case, all seemed to place the blame on others rather than absorbing the charges themselves. In a magazine article appearing nearly a century later, a writer quoted remarks from Secretary Armstrong that "The busy and blundering Col. Monroe was responsible for the defeat.... I am in no way responsible for the disgraceful affair." The writer, believed to be an A.K. Hadel, further remarked that

General Winder, under severe censure, made no effort to shift responsibility on any one, which he could easily have done, and had he done so, it might have resulted in preventing the election of James Monroe as the successor of James Madison, but he remained silent and soon severed his connection with the army.

Hadel included some interesting references from British papers when they learned of the "Affair Washington":

The *London Spectator* said; 'Would that we could throw a veil of oblivion over our transaction at Washington. Even the Cossacks spared Paris, but Englishmen spared not the Capital of America.

The *Liverpool Mercury* said: "If the people of the United States retain any portion of the spirit with which they contended successfully for their independence, the effect of these flames will not soon be extinguished."

The *British Annual* said: 'The proceedings of Ross and Cockburn at Washington were a return to the times of barbarism, which would bring a heavy censure upon British character."[23]

Years later, Admiral Cockburn would be the "British jailer of Napoleon Bonaparte en route to his exile on St. Helena." Ross did not survive the war.

33

BRITISH POLICY OF DELAY

Henry Clay was in Brussels when he first heard about the disaster back home. There are two accounts detailing the manner in which Clay received the news. In the *Life of Clay*, by Epes Sargent (1852), there is the following:

The morning after Mr. Clay's arrival in Brussels, upon his coming down to breakfast, his servant, Frederick Cara, whom he had taken with him from the city of Washington, threw some papers upon the breakfast table, and burst into tears. "What's the matter, Frederick?"—"The British have taken Washington, sir, and Mr. Goulbourne [sic] has sent you those papers, which contain the account."—"Is it possible?" exclaimed Mr. Clay. "It is too true, sir," returned Frederick, whining piteously.[1]

The other account came in the form of another minor insult by Clay's negotiating counterparts, British envoy Henry Goulburn. In presenting those papers for Clay's perusal, Goulburn attached a snide note reading, "If you find Brussells [sic] as little interesting as I have done you will not be sorry to have the occupation of reading the latest Newspapers which I have received,"[2] containing accounts of the British capture of Washington City. Clearly, Goulburn enjoyed Clay's distress.

It is possible that the first information he received of the event was a newspaper account in *The Courier* of London of September 27. Its headline read, "WASHINGTON TAKEN AND DESTROYED — AMERICAN ARMY DEFEATED — AMERICAN FLOTILLA BLOWN UP." What an awful way to return from a vacation! Among "The glorious tidings" the paper presented to their English readers was the following:

It was a curious circumstance that when the conquerors entered MR. MADISON'S palace, they found the table laid for a grand supper. The Champaigne [sic] was in coolers — a fine dessert set out on the side-boards, etc. so the British Officers ordered in the supper, and General Ross drank his MAJESTY'S health at the head of the table with the PRESIDENT'S wine.[3]

The account from the *London Gazette* of the same date was no better. It led off with a report from General Ross, dated August 30, and sent to Earl Bathurst. It read:

My Lord — I have the honour to communicate to your Lordship, that on the night of the 24th instant, after defeating the army of the United States on that day, the troops under my command entered and took possession of the city of Washington.[4]

While Ross was brief in detailing his "exertions" in the burning of the Capitol, the "President's Palace," and other buildings, arsenals and bridges, he was lengthy in praising by name numerous British subordinates in the work of destruction.

Nevertheless, in October 1814, Clay was forced to learn the story piecemeal. As much as Clay detested the British since childhood, it is astonishing to note that there is little written evidence of Clay's feelings about this latest British affront. Throughout his life he had been a witness to, or reader of, acts of the British that continually tested his resentment, beginning with the violation of his family's homestead in Virginia during the Revolutionary War. It was followed in his young adult years by the Chesapeake affair and the odious Orders in Council. Within the war, there was the barbarous treatment of the American prisoners of war (including death of his brother-in-law) at the River Raisin, and the British acquiescence to the

Indian gauntlet at Fort Meigs. As he sailed to Europe to make peace with this harsh opponent, he read of the indiscriminate attacks by British soldiers on private homes along Chesapeake Bay. And before this latest act of destruction, he had endured the arrogant intransigence of mediocre envoys at the Ghent peace table.

Doubtless, the full story did not reach Clay for many months and probably years. But even before he was to leave Europe, bits and pieces of the horror certainly reached him through letters from members of the administration in Washington as well as from friends, along with newspapers, often from the British press with its joyous bias. After his return to America, he was privy to any confidential reports sent to Congress. These included those extensive reports now available to history rendered by eye-witnesses to the events. They are now part of the appendix of the *Annals of Congress*, under the title of the "Capture of Washington City," as well as the large volumes of the *American State Papers*. In addition, Clay would certainly hear the emotional personal stories told by those who bore the brunt of the destruction. Surely he heard much in colorful detail while dining with James and Dolley Madison at the Octagon House; stories history has never recorded.

There was only one good piece of news awaiting Clay on his return from his weekend visit. There was a letter from Lucretia, back in Kentucky, telling him that he had been elected again to the next Congress.[5] However, he, Jonathan Russell, and mission secretary Christopher Hughes found that commissioners John Quincy Adams, Albert Gallatin and James Bayard had already learned of the disaster in America's capital. Adams wrote in his *Memoirs* that he could not sleep that first evening after hearing of the news from home.

In the days that followed, Adams wrote of his feelings regarding the British actions both in their military exploits in America and within their dealings with their counterparts at the negotiating table. These appear in his letters to Louisa Catherine, still in St. Petersburg, Russia. In his *Memoirs* were different disclosures. Here, he revealed a growing rancor among his American colleagues. Since learning of the British action in America, it seems they all became more testy.

Though the details of events in Washington City, which reached the envoys, were extremely scarce, the burning of the Capitol and the White House and other public buildings struck an angry cord with the Americans in Belgium. They were quick to compare this additional British atrocity to the fate of several European capitals that had been subjected to occupation by warring armies during the Napoleonic campaigns. Except for Moscow (probably burned by Russians and expanded by French troops), all other seats of government escaped a similar scourge as endured by the Americans.

As Adams wrote his wife, on October 7,

The whole transaction is much more disgraceful to the British than it is injurious to us. The destruction of the Capitol, the President's house, the public offices, and many private houses is contrary to all the usages of civilized nations, and is without example even in the wars that have been waged during the French Revolution. There is scarcely a metropolis in Europe that has not been taken in the course of the last twenty years. There is not a single instance in all that time of public buildings like those being destroyed.

Then reflecting on his impressions of the current war, he told her,

It has indeed been conformable to uniform experience of mankind that no wars are so cruel and unrelenting as civil wars; and unfortunately every war between Britain and America must and will be a civil war.... We must therefore expect that the excesses of war committed by the British against us will be more outrageous than those they are guilty of against any other people, and we must be neither surprised nor dejected at finding them to be so.

Adams also drew a distinction between the ferocity of the British to the Americans, showing a sort of tenderness of the Americans, even in stress. He noted that the British, after their wanton destruction in Washington, so feared

being cut off in their retreat, and their flight so precipitate, that they left their own dead unburied on the fields, and their wounded as prisoners at the mercy of the very people whose public edifices and private habitations they had been consuming by fire. If those wounded prisoners have not been gibbeted on the trees between Bladensburg and Washington, to fatten the region kites, it has not been because the provocation to such treatment was insufficient, but because it belongs to our national character to relent into mercy towards a vanquished and defenceless enemy.[6]

In an earlier letter to Louisa, Adams had told her that, "Mr. Clay is the only one among us who has occasionally entertained hopes that ... peace would be practicable by negotiation here." Adams said, in another letter, "I have no confidence in their sincerity," in reference to the British envoys.[7]

It was more than two weeks after learning of the news from America that we have Clay's feelings on the subject. Writing to Crawford, in Paris, on

October 17, he said,

> I wish, my dear Crawford, it were possible to pass over in silence, & bury in oblivion, the distressing events which have occurred at home. But it would be in vain to attempt to conceal that they have given me the deepest affliction. The enemy, it is true, has lost much in character, at least in the estimation of the impartial world. And the loss of public property gives me comparatively no pain. What does wound me to the very soul is, that a set of pirates and incendiaries should have been permitted to pollute our soil, conflagrate our Capital, and return unpunished to their ships! ... I tremble indeed whenever I take up a late News paper. Hope alone sustains me.[8]

Since the return of Clay, Russell, and Hughes from their tour of Brussels, they were again caught in that exasperating wait on the British for a response to their most recent note presented on September 26. The wait was an irritant that festered under the Americans' skin and this story is told by Adams in his *Memoirs*.

To begin, on October 5, Clay made a suggestion to his colleagues, that they should relate the state of their negotiations to the Emperor Alexander of Russia (now at the Congress of Vienna) and the French government, through U.S. Minister Crawford. It was a simple suggestion. But the suggestion nearly became as complex as the Congress itself—which at this time was in flux and going almost nowhere.

Still, with Clay's suggestion a disturbing animosity rose to the surface. Gallatin asked Adams to draft a letter to Alexander. The next day, Adams showed his draft to Gallatin and proposed to send William Smith (nephew and secretary to Adams) to the emperor in Vienna and at the same time take on the attributes of intelligence operative to obtain for the American mission any valuable information within the Congress. At the mission's two o'clock meeting, Adams read his letter (of which he had also produced a Russian translation for the hands of Count Nesselrode, the Russian foreign minister, also in Vienna). Clay again suggested a similar message through Crawford to the French government, but no more than 20 lines. Gallatin again proposed that Clay author this paper.

On the 7th, fireworks exploded within the mission. Clay wandered into Adams' quarters, where, for the moment, he entertained William Shaler, messenger for the mission. Clay proceeded to read the draft of his paper to be sent to Crawford. When Adams objected to Shaler's presence at the reading, Clay responded that, "He is one of us." The letter was read again at the regular afternoon meeting of all members. There was no conflict over the contents, but a row ensued as to the messenger.

When Russell asked how the letter was to be transmitted, Adams replied that if the mission approved, he would have it carried there by Mr. Smith, because of his acquaintance with certain high ranking individuals posted to the Congress. Both Russell and Clay indicated that they thought Mr. Shaler could take the other message to Crawford.

Now, Adams threw a small wrench into the situation. He mentioned that since he was not

> perfectly satisfied of the propriety of the measure at all, I should send it to Vienna only according to the advice the mission should give me. Mr. Clay said he certainly should give no advice as to the person to be sent.

So, Adams stated that if the mission gave him no advice, he would make the communication "in the regular form, and after my return to St. Petersburg," whenever that might be. "The communication was no measure of mine." And Adams opposed sending information to France at all. If they wanted it, they could ask for it. In his *Memoirs*, he added, "I believed both France and Russia knew as well as we did that England did not intend to make peace with us in this negotiation." At this point, Gallatin must have recalled his own personal efforts described earlier in the year, when he made a mighty effort to secure the good offices of the Russian emperor, while they were both in England, to lean on the British to move toward negotiation.

He would have been delighted to know that about a week earlier, British Prime Minister Lord Liverpool had written the foreign secretary, Lord Castlereagh,

> The Americans have assumed hitherto a tone in the negotiation very different from what their situation appears to warrant. In the exercise of your discretion as to how much you may think proper to disclose of what has been passing to the sovereigns and ministers whom you will meet at Vienna, I have no doubt you will see the importance of adverting to this circumstance, and of doing justice to the moderation with which we are disposed to act towards America. I fear the Emperor of Russia is half an American.[9]

Returning to the controversy between mission members, Adams observed that if France and Russia should receive some notice, so should Sweden. Adams' colleagues thought not. They seemed to believe Sweden was too dependent on England. Then Gallatin suggested that Crawford should only communicate verbally to the French. Clay wanted to leave it at Crawford's discretion, while Russell recommended a private letter to Crawford to present it verbally to the French and then requested Gallatin to draft the letter for Adams to send to Vienna "to be submitted for consideration tomorrow." Gallatin was becoming the writer — as well as the mediator — for the group.

They all met again at 2 P.M. on the 8th. Gallatin's letter draft requested that Adams send the message to Alexander in Vienna, telling him of the status of their negotiations. The messenger was also authorized to collect any information useful to their task in Ghent. Adams asked the mission to name the messenger and brought up the question of paying for the trip — charge it to the mission or the legation to Russia.

Clay and Russell (often arguing together, as Russell was a great admirer of Henry Clay) wanted the messenger to be chosen by Adams since his previous post was aa minister to the emperor of Russia. Again, Adams selected Mr. Smith, who, having been "Secretary of the Legation to Russia, known as such to the Emperor and to Count Nesselrode," along with his assigned task of intelligence acquisition, was the proper person to send. But still Adams insisted on the approval of his choice by the rest of the mission.

Now Clay and Russell threw their own wrench into the controversy. They stated that if they were

called on to recommend a messenger to Vienna, it would be Mr. Shaler, since he had been attached to the mission to serve as "a messenger" (about which Adams contended there was no written evidence). At this point, Gallatin observed that he did not think Shaler was the proper person to fulfill the mission's requirements. He believed Smith's former connection to the Russian legation enhanced his credentials. Gallatin added, "For the other part of the business, it required a person of address and of habits in society, not possessed by Mr. Shaler, though he was a man perfectly confidential and of very good understanding."

When Gallatin offered to edit his letter of authorization leaving in Adams' hands both naming the courier and arranging the method of delivery, Adams responded, saying "I should then send it by the post." Rather stunned, Gallatin answered, "That would not do." At this point it becomes best to quote directly from Adams' *Memoirs*.

> I said I should then ask them to indicate to me the mode by which I should send the letter; I was ready to say to them in writing what I then said verbally. Mr. Clay and Mr. Russell waxed loud, and Mr. Clay very warm. They said they had nothing to do with the appointment of the messenger, that it was my business exclusively, and if I wanted their opinion, they had given it. I said, with much warmth, that they might be assured I was as determined as they were. Each of us must act upon his own responsibility. The proposed measure itself was theirs, and not mine. Its usefulness was, in my own opinion, problematical, but I was ready to acquiesce in their judgment and to execute their charge. I only asked them to name to me the person whom I should send as the messenger, and whoever they named should certainly be sent.
>
> Mr. Clay said, with great heat and anger, that he would give his opinion in writing; that he should be ashamed not to take such a responsibility upon himself; and he added, with a scornful sneer, that he supposed Mr. Crawford would send to ask us how he should perform our request. "A soft answer turneth away wrath"; but I have not always a soft answer at my own command; the next best expedient to check contention is to suppress all angry reply, and I am not always sufficiently master of myself to do that. I was so today. I was silent ... I restrained my feelings, and made no reply.[10]

The dispute was not ended, but, for three or four days, it was suspended, as the British delivered their fourth note (of 15 pages) in response to the Americans' challenges. It came to the U.S. envoys as they dined on Saturday evening, October 8. And it provided Clay and his colleagues with another area in which to vent their anger.

To begin, Adams showed his annoyance when writing Louisa Catherine three days later. The British envoys, he wrote,

> have no other duty as it would seem to perform than that of engrossing clerks. This note is in the same domineering and insulting style as all those that have preceded it, but it contains much more show of argument, falsehoods less liable to immediate and glaring exposure, misrepresentations more sheltered from instant detection, and sophistry generally more plausible than they had thought it worth while to take the trouble of putting into the former notes. The essential part of it is, however, that they have abandoned almost every thing of their previous demands which made it impossible for us to listen to them, and have now offered as their ultimatum an article of a totally different description. You can conceive with what kind if grace they retreat from nine-tenths of their ground when you know that they take care to hint that *at this stage of the war*, their concession must be taken for magnanimity.

Adams went on to write that the British "object of wasting time has now become manifest beyond all possible doubt." He wrote that he had expected the British to break off the negotiations when their terms had been rejected by the Americans, especially considering the present circumstances of the collapse of the Napoleonic regime, and the apparent successes of their attack on Washington. He now felt that the British ministers in London "have not shared in all the delusions of their populace" in regard to their military achievements. From their contacts at the Congress of Vienna, they apparently were aware that "the sensation produced by it upon the continent ... has been by no means credible to them." Locally, Adams added,

> Here we have heard but one sentiment expressed upon the subject — that of unqualified detestation. But here the English are universally hated; the people dare not indeed openly avow their sentiments, but we hear them — "curses not loud but deep."

Adams commented that even some London newspapers had paralleled the British deeds with "the most execrable barbarities of the French revolutionary fury, or by the Goths and Vandals of antiquity." And then they tried to diminish the British "successes" by saying the Capitol "was only *an unfinished building*: the President's house was properly demolished because *the scoundrel* Madison had lived in it."[11]

What was it that the new British note demanded? Principally, added to the note was a proposed article of the prospective treaty. But they posed it in the form of an ultimatum demanding that the two contracting parties would put an end to hostilities with the Indians. It called for both sides to restore to them "all the possessions, rights, and privileges, which they may have enjoyed, or had been entitled to, in 1811." But the Indians also had to desist from their hostilities against the settlers.[12]

The subject of the Indians had never been a part of the original instructions to the American envoys, and transit of messages was so slow, in those days, that a query by the envoys with their superiors in Washington and a return answer could take more than two months. In effect, they had to go it alone in their response.

Loaded with cautious diplomatic language, the bulk of the British note — which as usual, came directly from their superiors in London — was a rehashing of old quibbling about the manner in which the United States obtained the Louisiana Territory and that part of Florida, west of Pensacola, then called West Florida. They charged that Spain never agreed to sell the land to the United States, though the U.S. did not buy it from Spain, who had ceded it to France, the final seller.

They had also inserted a brief paragraph stating that they had never required all of what is today the State of Maine, only that part which would permit a direct route between Halifax, Nova Scotia, and Quebec city, claiming it already belonged to Great Britain.

And they argued again that the proclamations of U.S. Generals Hull and Smith proved that the Americans had intentions of annexing Canada, and that the British had never learned of the disavowal of these proclamations by the U.S. Government, and they refused to recognize any link to their Admiral Cockburn's proclamation justifying plundering the communities along the Chesapeake shores.[13]

The Americans agreed to meet the following afternoon to consult on their response. Bayard was concerned that rejection of the "ultimatum" would give the British grounds for breaking off the negotiations over the Indian issue, and since he didn't want this as a cause, he suggested they have a conference with the British before answering their note. The Americans had also decided to ask the British for a project of a treaty (sometimes appearing in their writings in the French term, "projet").

In this conference, Clay linked the Indian demand to earlier British demands for the U.S. to disarm along the Great Lakes. He adamantly rejected this arrangement because the two articles "would deliver the whole western country up to the mercy of the Indians." There was no further important discussion until Wednesday, October 12.

However, at a meeting on the 10th, Clay and Gallatin called for a brief response — no more than four pages, while Adams was for a note as long as that of the British. He was alone in this proposition. They asked Gallatin to prepare a draft.

On the 12th, Gallatin presented his draft, and Adams read a partial draft he had written — which all opposed. Adams now wrote in his *Memoirs*,

> The tone of all the British notes is arrogant, overbearing, and offensive. The tone of ours is neither so bold nor so spirited as I think it should be. It is too much on the defensive, and too excessive in the caution to say nothing irritating. I have seldom been able to prevail upon my colleagues to insert anything in the style of retort upon the harsh and reproachful matter which we receive. And they appeared to reject everything I had written, and even much of Mr. Gallatin's draft.... Mr. Gallatin's idea is to adopt [the British article] as perfectly conformable to the views we ourselves had previously taken on the subject. Mine is to consider and represent it as a very great concession, made for the sake of securing the peace. But in this opinion I am alone.

Leaving that meeting, Clay took the two drafts to shorten Gallatin's and adopt what he thought proper from Adams' draft. That evening, Adams and Bayard supped together to talk about the negotiations. Adams wrote that Bayard was "extremely friendly and confidential in his manner, and spoke with an open-heartedness which I very cordially returned." He said that Bayard was very

eager to accept the British demands and get them, in return, to produce the "project of accomplishing the peace, or of uniting our whole country in support of the war against our eternal and irreconcilable foe."

On the 13th, when Clay presented his revised draft, Adams wrote, "I disliked it very much in all its parts, but could obtain only that small parts of it should be struck out." They finally settled on a draft, which was then handed to secretary Hughes to prepare a formal copy for their signatures.[14]

The new American note began with an answer to the British argument over the manner in which the Louisiana territory had been obtained, saying that if the United States had not ratified the purchase, that western land would have become a French colony. (That would certainly not have been favorable to Britain in their new war with France.) And it was stated that notice of the cession by France to the U.S. had been communicated to Britain and that "she expressed her satisfaction with it."

Next, they dwelt on the British claim that the U.S. sought to annex Canada through a peace treaty, citing that the U.S. "had been disposed to make peace without obtaining any cession of territory," and the Americans rejected the assertion that the U.S. "gave no proof of a sincere desire to bring the present negotiation to a favorable conclusion." Nevertheless, new instructions from Washington, dated in August (just prior to the attack on that city), gave the American commissioners the power to conclude a peace based "upon a mutual restoration of territory, and without making the conclusion of the peace to depend on a successful arrangement of those points on which a difference had existed." Meaning that the cause of impressment had disappeared with the "maritime pacification of Europe."

As for the British reference to earlier treaties as a basis for new demands for the treatment of the Indians, the Americans cited the treaty of 1783, "which fixes and recognizes the boundary of the United States without making any reservation respecting Indian Tribes."

Then, in highly diplomatic language, the Americans accepted, as a provisional article, the British insistence that the Tribes be placed "precisely, and in every respect, in the same situation as that in which they stood before the commencement of hostilities." But they qualified that acceptance "to the approbation or rejection of the Government of the United States," and having no instructions on this point they cannot be bound by the result by any ratification process and it shall have no effect in any future negotiation.

And finally, the Americans requested "a project of a Treaty embracing all the points deemed material by Great Britain," to which the Americans will then respond with a "counter project."[15]

Before turning over the signed note to the British envoys on the 14th, the U.S. envoys were handed copies of the London *Times* of October 10 and 11, and as noted by Adams in his *Memoirs*,

> containing official accounts of the taking of Machias and other towns in Passamaquoddy Bay, and the destruction of the frigate Adams by the expedition from Halifax ... together with the failure of our attempts to take Michillimackinac, and the taking of Plattsburg by the British Canadian Army.

Only the Plattsburg episode was significant and Adams had the news wrong. The Machias loss was insignificant. As to the destruction of the "corvette" *Adams* (not frigate), in early September, British naval forces landed troops along the present-day Maine coast destroying the *Adams* and demanding the allegiance to King George of the local male residents of the area. The failure at Michillimackinac changed nothing.

Despite the errors in Adams' references, this new revelation sent Clay into another sour mood, about which Adams wrote,

> Mr. Clay, who was determined to foresee no public misfortune in our affairs, bears them with less temper, now they have come, than any of us. He rails at commerce and the people of Massachusetts, and tells what wonders the people of Kentucky would do if they should be attacked.[16]

As part of his letter to Crawford on October 17, quoted from earlier, Clay had this to say about this latest news.

> No consolation is afforded us by the late intelligence from America. It appears that by the unfortunate failure of Chauncey to co-operate with Brown the campaign is lost; and we are compelled every where to act upon the defensive. Drummond, who I thought was caught, will escape, if

he does not take Gains, [defeat that American general] and consequently Chauncey's whole flotilla is seriously menaced.[17]

As so often happens in the early reports of war news, Clay was likely confused as to what actually occurred on this northern front. With the late July retreat by the Americans from Lundy's Lane to Fort Erie in Canada along the Niagara River opposite Buffalo, there was a petty dispute by the generals in charge of the region. In the earlier fighting, Maj. Gen. Jacob Brown, commanding, had been twice severely wounded and had been carried across the river to Batavia to recuperate. He was succeeded by Brig. Gen. Eleazer Wheelock Ripley, who had earlier been speaker of the Massachusetts House of Representatives. But in the army he had quarreled with Brown throughout the campaigning. It appeared to many that Brown was too aggressive, and to others that Ripley was too cautious, thus creating the clash of personalities. Now Ripley crossed the river to get Brown's permission to evacuate Fort Erie and bring all the troops back to Buffalo. Brown was furious, refused, and ordered Ripley to reinforce the fort. The order was carried out — reluctantly, and unknowingly to the British still encamped back at Chippewa.

On July 27, Sir Gordon Drummond, who was the civil and military Governor of Upper Canada, and also the British lieutenant general commanding the British forces in the Niagara area, ordered his troops, newly reinforced by about 1100 men, to march on Fort Erie. A vicious battle ensued on August 14, in which Drummond lost nearly one-third of his force due to an "accidental explosion" of an ammunition dump. Among the British battle losses was a Lt. Col. Drummond. (Relationship to the general is unknown.) The colonel had passed on the general's order to use the bayonet liberally. But it was an American bayonet that pierced a copy of this order, as well as the colonel's body. As the battle was fought, Colonel Drummond commanded his men to offer no quarter and no mercy to his wounded enemies. In one instance, an American officer was severely wounded and asked for quarter. Instead, he was shot dead.

As for the explosion, Benson Lossing, in his massive *Pictorial Field-book of the War of 1812*, recounts, in a footnote, an exception to the accepted version that the explosion was an accident. In 1863, an old veteran of the battle, gave Lossing a letter stating that

> Three or four hundred of the enemy had got into the bastion. At this time an American officer came running up, and said, "General Gaines, the bastion is full. I can blow them all to hell in a minute!" They both passed back through a stone building, and in a short time the bastion and the British were high in the air.

As the remaining British fled the field, they left behind 221 killed, 174 wounded, and 186 prisoners. The American losses were 17 killed, 56 wounded, and 11 missing. Gaines was to write Secretary Armstrong, "It is due to the brave men I have the honor to command that I should say that the affair was to the enemy a *sore beating* and *a defeat*; and it was to us a *handsome victory*."[18]

"Gains," mentioned by Clay in his letter to Crawford, was, in 1814, Maj. Gen. Edmund Gaines. (He was the man who had arrested Aaron Burr in 1807 and sent him by escort to trial in Richmond.) Now in 1814, Gaines, had been called west from Sackett's Harbor by Brown, to take his place in command on the Niagara frontier. He arrived at Fort Erie on August 5, about the same time that Drummond's army reached the scene. As for Clay's comment to Crawford related to Chauncey and Brown, when Brown went west in July, he had urged navy Capt. Isaac Chauncey to sail west from Sackett's Harbor and bring supplies to the general through Fort Niagara, New York, where the river empties into Lake Ontario. However, at this time, and for many weeks to come, the British were in possession of that base. It made little difference, as Chauncey was irked by the "demand" and refused to move until mid August when most of the battles had been fought and Brown was far from the battle sites recovering from his two wounds in Batavia. However, the quarrel between Chauncey and Brown became public and made quite a splash in the press of the day. Near the end of the fighting around Fort Erie, General Gaines was also wounded by a British shell.

These were all new war stories, dating from late July into September, coming from the northern theater of operations, from Lake Huron eastward to the present Maine coast. With the end of major fighting in the Niagara area, though minor skir-

mishes were to continue for weeks, operations along the northern theater almost suddenly shifted eastward to the region of Lake Champlain and cover the comments made by Adams in his *Memoirs*. The American envoys feared that with an anticipated conquest of the lands surrounding Lake Champlain, the British hoped to offer their envoys in Ghent crucial support for a claim to northern Maine in the peace treaty.

Meanwhile, during the early summer months, as many as 11,000 veteran soldiers from the Duke of Wellington's victorious army had been transported from Spain to Canada, following Napoleon's abdication. By early August, they were preparing to sweep south into upper New York state along Lake Champlain against American Maj. Gen. George Izard's 5,000 raw troops. They hoped to follow the course of General Burgoyne of American Revolution days, but with a greater degree of success.

But war secretary Armstrong doubted Izard's reports of the danger as much as he had scoffed at the warnings that British forces might attack Washington later in that hectic August of 1814. He even ordered Izard to march more than 150 miles southwest along the St. Lawrence River to Sackets Harbor (sometimes spelled Sackett's) or even farther to Kingston, Ontario, or Niagara Falls. They were foolish orders.

Izard obeyed on August 29, taking half of his troops westward, leaving the remainder, under Brig. Gen. Alexander Macomb at Plattsburg on the Lake. The Americans had worked diligently to prepare substantial defenses around the town. Within the first week of September, the British under Sir George Prevost, crossed into New York and advanced on Plattsburg. According to author Henry Adams,

> Great Britain had never sent to America so formidable an armament. Neither Wolfe nor Amherst [in the French and Indian War], neither Burgoyne nor Cornwallis [in the Revolutionary War], had led so large or so fine an army as was under command of Sir George Prevost.[19]

The available fleet that the British were capable of placing on the Lake was easily as impressive as their army. Yet the American navy units, under Commander Thomas MacDonough, though smaller in fire power, were superior in leadership. No sooner had Izard started west with his large contingent of American troops, than the British began their march southward in two very strong columns toward Plattsburg. There were estimates that they mustered more than 14,000 capable men. American General Macomb had driven his small force of less than 4,000 able troops to build three forts around the town. He also sent out units northward to harass the British advance with skirmishers and by cutting down trees to block their way. It was quite effective as it took most of September 6 for the enemy to come within sight of Plattsburg on the south side of Saranac River. It was in this position that Sir George (Prevost) sat to wait for the instigation of fighting by the British "fleet" of four ships and 11 gunboats on the lake.

The British fleet, under Capt. George Downie, didn't sail into sight around Cumberland Head and approach the American flotilla, anchored in Plattsburg Bay, until September 11. It appears that the British came up in a column to face the Americans in a broad line often referred to as an admiral's dream in "Crossing the T," from which each ship could pour in broadside shots at the advancing enemy, all hitting a single ship as it came forward. The destruction was devastating to the British and Captain Downie was killed. Nevertheless, the British were eventually able to attack each end of the American line and disable so many of their starboard guns that the latter were quickly losing fire power. But this is where Captain MacDonough showed his ingenuity. With his ships anchored, he had devised a system whereby he was able to pull on the cables and turn (or wind) his ships to bring to bear his larboard broadside guns from the other sides of his vessels. After a battle lasting nearly four hours, the 30-year-old MacDonough was to win the day by unrigging the British ships, which surrendered en masse.

In Lossing's *Field-book* is a footnote quoting a British midshipman, taken prisoner. He wrote,

The havoc on both sides was dreadful. I don't think there are more than five of our men, out of three hundred, but what are killed or wounded. Never was a shower of hail so thick as the shot whistling about our ears. Were you to see my jacket, waistcoat, and trowsers, you would be astonished to know how I escaped as I did, for they are literally torn all to rags with shot and splinters; the upper part of my hat was also shot away. There

is one of the marines who was in the Trafalgar action with Lord Nelson, who says it was a mere *flea-bite* in comparison with this.

Meanwhile, British General Sir George, viewed his mariners' calamity from the shore north of Plattsburg. Another Lossing footnote tells of Prevost's reaction to the British naval disaster. There was an American chaplain, commanding a "Secret Corps of Observation." (Spies?) Prior to the battle, a Colonel Fassett, from Vermont, had crossed the lake to inform General Macomb that more than 10,000 men from that state were coming to the defenses of Plattsburg. The chaplain suggested that the colonel obtain a letter from the Vermont governor verifying this mobilization and then had it placed in the hand of a "shrewd" Irish woman on Cumberland Head. She put it into Prevost's hands. The timid and frightened British commander, with an overwhelming force, and hearing the cheers of the American army on his front, precipitously fled the scene, leaving behind vast stores and many of his own deserters.[20]

William Crawford, in Paris, replied to Clay's letter of October 17, with his own latest views of the action from home. In a letter to Clay dated the 24th, he wrote,

I congratulate you most sincerely upon the favorable issue of the late military and naval operations in the U.S. Some thing of this nature must have been more necessary to you than to me. My mind has been made up all the year for an uninterrupted series of defeats and repulses.

Crawford believed Izard's move to Niagara would end that fighting and yield the safety of Sackett's Harbor. He had more to say about "the naval victory on Champlain," that it

must have been as splendid and decisive in its consequences as that of the last year upon lake Erie. The enemy sought the battle, he must therefore have felt himself superior to our naval hero. The defeat of Genl. Prevot [sic] seems not to be well explained. It is incredible that a militia force should have defeated 10 or 12000 regular troops. McCombs [sic] says that he had but 1500 regulars, & from the representation of the affair they fought in the works only, whereas the enemy appears to have pushed a body of our militia two miles in the rear of the fort, where being joined by the Green Mountain boys they turned like the hunted lion upon their pursuers, and drove them back with immense slaughter. If the Veterans who *conquered*

France, have in the United States suffered themselves to be defeated by Militia, the prosecution of
the war with a view to conquest, must be hopeless
indeed. These Veterans were commanded by generals formed under the *first Captain of this, or any
other age*, [referring to the Duke of Wellington.
who would soon give his superiors in London his
own views on matters] whilst our republican Militia were commanded by men who in most cases
never saw an action.... Ten days ago they [the
British papers] asserted, that they had a decided
Superiority upon lake Champlain, but after the
destruction of their naval force, they have discovered that our fleet was very superior to theirs. I
hope they will discover a real superiority upon
Niagara.

Crawford expected that British General Drummond would be captured.[21] That was not to happen.

Within these days of wrangling in Ghent, both
sets of envoys were getting further battle results
from America. It is assumed they learned of the
events simultaneously, but the only written evidence shows up first in a letter written on October
21, by Goulburn back to his superiors in London.
Clay's first reference to action at Baltimore, is
vaguely mentioned in a letter to Secretary of State
James Monroe on October 26. Goulburn thought
it was a British victory. Clay tied it in with the
victory around Lake Champlain, which took
place only days earlier, as helpful to their negotiations. The connection between the two battles
was soon to have significant consequences on the
negotiations. But the consequences would also be
linked to the blustering at the Congress of Vienna.
In fact, the Americans stated in a joint message
to Secretary Monroe,

> The whole tenor of the correspondence, as well as
> the manner in which it has been conducted on the
> part of the British Government, have concurred to
> convince us that their object has been delay pend-
> ing the settlement of European affairs at the Con-
> gress of Vienna and the anticipated success of
> British arms in America.[22]

Still, such knowledge failed to cool demeanors
within the American delegation at Ghent. Had
they known more, they might have been more affable.

Following the British plunder at the nation's
capital, they terrorized communities along the
Chesapeake shores sweeping in as if to attack Annapolis. British Subaltern Gleig noted that they

stood in so close as to discern the inhabitants flying from their homes: carts and waggons loaded
with furniture hurrying along the roads, and
horsemen galloping along the shore, as if watching
the fearful moment when the boats should be
hoisted out, and the troops quit the vessels.[23]

However, by the evening of September 11, they
had sailed toward the harbor at Baltimore. At
seven the next morning they began landing more
than 9,000 of "Wellington's invincibles," under
the notorious incendiaries General Ross and Admiral Cockburn, on the long promontory of
North Point a dozen miles southeast of the city.
Their march was against only minor resistance
until they had gone nearly seven miles. Even then
the fighting was insignificant, but the skirmish
results were devastating to the British. Two young
Americans, who later lost their lives, managed to
get clear shots at the general, who had earlier announced that he intended to celebrate his expected victory in Baltimore with a sumptuous
Sunday dinner. But by that time, Ross, much like
a fellow officer, was probably soaking in a vat of
wine waiting transportation to England for burial.[24] But, by day's end, under his successor, the
British fought their way closer to the nation's third
largest city.

During that evening, the naval forces that
could approach up the shallow waters of the Patapsco River, hoped to land more troops closer to
the city and attack Fort McHenry from the rear.
At six o'clock the following morning, the long
range guns of the British ships began their deadly
assault on the fort from the river. The shorter
American guns failed to reach the British. The
blasting continued until three in the afternoon,
when it ceased for a while as the British moved
in closer. But not for long, as the American batteries in the fort now found the enemy within
reach and poured in a galling fire. Soon the British
resumed their old position — out of range of the
American guns. Then during the night the siege
resumed with bombs and rocket (described by
Niles Register as "terribly grand and magnificent"
despite its terror). The firing continued till morning when it could be observed from the British
ships down the river that the huge American flag
still waved over the fort's ramparts — so gallantly
as to inspire a poet.

Francis Scott Key, a lawyer from Georgetown,

had gained permission from President Madison to go aboard the British flagship to seek the release of certain Americans (non-combatants) being held prisoners by the British admiral. Key was successful in his mission in securing their freedom after the battle. But as the dawn's early light gleamed over the awful scene, and seeing that star-spangled banner, he was moved to write of his feelings. In 1931, his poem, long since set to the music of an old tavern song, became the national anthem of the United States of America, though described as such for many years prior to its official certification.

It was this same day, the 14th, that Admirals Cockburn and Cochrane, decided that their venture before Baltimore was a failure, and they slowly worked their way back down the Chesapeake seeking less dangerous opposition. At Fort McHenry, only four men were killed and 20 wounded, though overall, the American losses were 20 killed, 90 wounded, and 47 prisoners/missing. Estimates of British losses for the engagement at Baltimore ran between 500 and 700. This battle, along with Lake Champlain, was to have a slowing effect on the prosecution of the war by the British leaders.[25]

But the Americans in Ghent could not know this. From the time Adams wrote on October 14 of his distress about earlier war news from America and Clay wrote to Crawford on the 17th of his concerns, until Crawford's reply to Clay on the 22nd, Adams was to fill his *Memoirs* with accounts of the continuing friction between the American envoys in Ghent over sending emissaries to Vienna and to Paris. Also, during this period, a new set of brief and nearly worthless notes were exchanged between the envoys.

On October 15, Adams showed his irritation over Shaler's position with the mission. He was shown the aide's instructions from Secretary of State Monroe, directing him "to go to the place wherever a Congress might be held for a general peace, and communicate any useful information that he could obtain there to the joint mission and to the government." Adams denied that he had seen the paper before, though both Russell and Shaler claimed they had presented it to Adams and they commented on his response. But Adams said his response was to knowledge that Russell and Clay had given Shaler certain powers

when they were in Gottenburg in April. Adams was probably confused as to what powers they were able to give.

Again, Clay proposed that Shaler be sent to Vienna, but Gallatin thought he should be sent first to Paris to get a passport from Crawford, thus much less apt "to excite suspicion" as to his mission elsewhere. But three days later, following a rude episode between Shaler and another aide over riding in a carriage, it was agreed to cancel his mission anywhere — temporarily. Then Russell observed that the man exhibited "certain indiscretions of vanity in him which showed he was not well qualified for such a mission, and might do more harm than good in it." This judgment was confirmed by Bayard citing Shaler's comments to another person about the contents of the recent note from the British as if he were one of the commissioners. At this point, Clay simply commented that the other person "was such a stupid fellow," as if to say it made little difference what disclosures might be revealed without authority. Then Clay asked for a vote on whether or not Shaler should go to Vienna.

It is now best to quote directly from Adams' *Memoirs*. In Adams' words,

> I asked him [Clay] for his vote first. He said it was for Mr. Bayard to answer first. I asked Bayard, who answered, *No*. Mr. Russell and Mr. Gallatin answered the same. Mr. Clay then declined answering at all, but said he had not changed his opinion. I can now comprehend why the responsibility of sending Shaler to Vienna was to have been put upon me alone, and why Shaler was to have been fastened upon me as the man, without any one of my colleagues appearing to have recommended him to me.

It fell to Adams to notify Shaler of the postponement.

Later that evening, Russell mentioned to Adams, in private, that he had been dissatisfied with their last note to the British. Adams replied that he too was dissatisfied and had offered another draft. He now asked Russell why he had not given his support to Adams. Russell answered that he had expected Clay to object to the wording (relative to the Indian question), but when Clay had said nothing, Russell did not think it his business. Adams mentioned his recent conversation with Bayard. Russell stated that "Bayard always talked about keeping a high tone, but when it came to the point he was always on the conceding side."

And finally, on October 22, the British members submitted their fifth note in reply to the American note of October 13. This time it was quite brief. They announced that they would "waive the advantage" of "the first *projet* of a treaty." They claimed it had all been stated in their first note. The point of "forcible seizure of mariners" and other British "maritime rights" are no longer applicable since the peace in Europe. They said "a discussion of fisheries is unnecessary" and they "expect the northwestern boundary will extend from the Lake of the Woods to the Mississippi [River] (the intended arrangement of 1803) will be admitted without objection." And they went on to say they expected to treat on the basis of *uti possidetis* (possession of the land conquered by the end of the war).

Using a modern slang phrase, the Americans might have said, "That's easy for you to say." It wasn't easy for these envoys, and they were soon to split badly over a response concerning the fisheries and British demands to navigate on the Mississippi. As for *uti possidetis*, they had just received confirmation from Washington to treat of the basis of the *status ante bellum* (as matters were prior to the war). So the American reply was a flat rejection of *uti possidetis*. They stated they had no authority to cede any part of the territory of the U.S. Of course, they were irked at the British refusal to return a sample *projet* of a treaty, but now proposed a simultaneous exchange of drafts. The U.S. note of three paragraphs was returned in two days.

But it was the issues of fisheries and navigation of the Mississippi that divided them deeply. Adams, from Massachusetts, was convinced that his constituents would howl loudly if they no longer had the rights to fish off Newfoundland and then dry their nets on the Canadian shores as before. Though it fails to appear in Adams' accounts of the ensuing arguments, Clay certainly saw the British navigation of the Mississippi, and associated ramifications, as a great interference into the internal affairs of the United States. When based on the treaty of 1783, that river was a boundary line between the U.S. and Spain (and later, briefly, with France). But since the Louisiana

Purchase, that river fell completely within the sovereignty of the United States. As to a line between The Lake of the Woods and the source of the river, they simply do not touch when considering that the fairly well established boundary between the U.S. and Canada went westward on the 49th parallel and never reached the source of the river. Clay thought British adventures on the internal river would permit mischief.

By October 30, Gallatin and Adams began working on a draft of a treaty (their "projet"). Gallatin proposed to renew

> two articles of the Treaty of Peace of 1783, the stipulation for our rights to fish, and dry and cure fish, within the waters of the British jurisdiction, and the right of the British to navigate the Mississippi.

Needless to say, Clay objected to the navigation and was prepared to "leave the matter of the fisheries as a nest-egg for another war," according to Adams. Clay believed it would give the British "a privilege far more important than we should secure in return," Adams added. But Clay was alone in his argument. He also believed the fisheries could be left unmentioned in the treaty, but Adams believed this would be tantamount to abandoning this previous right.

The next day, as they resumed their discussion, they received the sixth note from the British — as "dilatory and evasive" as before. Adams' note of the day: "Mr. Clay is losing his temper and growing peevish and fractious."[26]

The note was seven short paragraphs which said almost nothing, except that they asserted that their previous notes were their "projet," and they now awaited the American *counter-projet*.[27]

It was now November, with nearly three months of negotiations which had gone almost nowhere. In exasperation, Adams wrote Louisa Catherine on November 4, telling her of the extravagant ends to which British newspapers accounted for their activities, in and out of Ghent — even when they had not left the city. Adams noted that

> They have sent us, or dreamt of our being sent, like fire-ships loaded with combustibles, to Vienna, to blow up the Congress there, and spread a conflagration of universal war again all over Europe. One day they have prostrated us at the feet

of the British plenipotentiaries, repenting in the dust, and crying for mercy.

Adams was then to reiterate to his wife what the group had written to Monroe,

We see plainly enough that we shall have no peace but by the failure of the British forces in America to accomplish the objects for which they were sent, and by the failure of the British government to give the law to all Europe at Vienna. Should they succeed in America, we shall have no peace, because our country will never submit to the terms they would dictate. Should they succeed in Vienna, we shall have no peace, because they will prefer war with us, to peace upon any terms.

But within days, Adams wrote to Crawford that, "It is from Vienna and not from America that the balance of peace or of war will preponderate."[28]

Still, they had one more British note in their hands. This time the Americans took much longer to put together a major draft of a prospective treaty. Not only was it a larger project, it brought together the points of contention between them. Clay and Russell wished to tell the British that they "would proceed no further unless they agreed to *Status ante-bellum.*" Next they decided to reply on all points, but divided on the length of the reply and whether to present a formal draft of a treaty. They concluded on the latter presentation.

Of course, the contents again raised the dispute over the navigation of the Mississippi, and Clay insisted that "since Louisiana had become a State, it was part of her sovereignty which the United States could not grant." But Gallatin answered that the British navigation rights

had been stipulated in the treaties of 1783 and 1784. Clay argued that the United States "had been released from it by the war, he saw no reason for renewing it upon them by treaty now. He considered it as a privilege much too important to be conceded for the mere liberty of drying fish upon a desert.

With vision, Clay cited the expectation that "the Mississippi was destined to form a most important part of the interests of the American Union." It was only eight years since the return of Lewis and Clark from their great expedition from St. Louis, on the west bank of the Mississippi, to the far northwest corner of the future boundary of the country—a region that would bring a later dispute between the two nations to the verge of war.

During these early days of November, Adams insisted on securing American rights of the fisheries for his New England constituents, while Clay remained adamant and almost ferocious in his objection to the British rights on the river within U.S. sovereign jurisdiction. He threatened refusal of signing the treaty. Yet Gallatin continued to propose several drafts, but each balanced denial of British navigation rights to denial of fishing rights to Americans—which was fought for by Adams. Surmounting this divisive issue became the substance of every meeting. Adams proposed one version stating that the fisheries were "a part of our national independence, that it could not be abrogated by the war, and needed no stipulation for its renewal." Gallatin again argued that the same could be said for the navigation of the Mississippi. Clay opposed mentioning it all.

Eventually, they would come to terms and produce a *projet* of many pages, in substance, a complete treaty draft containing an introduction, followed by 15 major articles. The introduction stated the purpose of the proposed treaty and named the members of each negotiating delegation.

While stated in more diplomatic language, the articles were in brief:

Article 1. "There shall be peace" between and throughout the two nations and all prisoners of war shall be set at liberty, all territory taken by either side shall be restored, and all private property and documents shall be restored to their rightful owners.

Article 2. Following joint ratification, all hostilities will cease and all items taken by naval vessels in foreign waters thereafter shall be restore to their proper owners.

Article 3. Commissioners shall later be appointed by each country to work out the undetermined boundaries in the general area of Passamaquoddy, the river St. Croix, and the Bay of Fundy.

Article 4. Commissioners shall later ascertain, by survey, and map the lands in what is now northern Maine, and boundaries shall be fixed.

Article 5. These commissioners shall also establish boundary lines in the Great Lakes regions where "doubts have arisen what was the middle of said rivers, lakes, and water communications," etc.

Article 6. In addition, these commissioners are to require to be surveyed and marked the boundaries "between Lake Huron and Lake Superior to the most northwestern point of the Lake of the Woods.

Article 7. The above commissioners are authorized to appoint and pay agents to carry out the work of these articles.

Article 8. The boundary line from the Lake of the Woods westward is to be the 49th parallel.

Article 9. The United States agrees to cease all hostilities with tribes or nations of Indians who had warred against them and restore "all the possessions, rights, and privileges, which they may have enjoyed or been entitled to in 1811 previous to such hostilities," provided that they desist from all hostilities against the United States." The British agree likewise.

Article 10. Neither nation shall employ Indians in any future mutual war.

Article 11. Each nation shall exclude non-naturalized citizen in their naval or commercial services prior to an unspecified date. nor shall any person "be demanded or taken out of any ship or vessel" belonging to the other nation.

Article 12. In the event of the neutrality of either nation, when the other is at war with a third nation, the protection of the neutral ship shall be observed and the cargoes shall not be seized.

Article 13. In a very long article, the British shall pay indemnities to all U.S. citizens "for all losses and damage sustained by them during the late war between Great Britain and France, prior to the commencement of the present war," along with other specific features, such as "the destruction of unfortified towns, and pillage or destruction of private property, and the enticement and carrying away of negroes contrary to the known and established rules and usages of war between civilized nations.

Article 14. Provides that no person residing in the other nation may "be prosecuted, molested, or annoyed" for taking part against the other party.

Article 15. Determines the manner of ratification and exchange of documents.

The long note accompanying their *projet* cited observations on several issues not in the draft. But first, the Americans expressed surprise that the British considered their note of October 21 as "containing the *projet* of a treaty," and also that they stated in that same note "that they had no other propositions to offer than those contained in that note." And these two propositions referred to fixing the boundary from the Lake of the Woods to the Mississippi and settling other boundaries on the basis of *uti possidetis*.

Before responding to these issues, the Americans mentioned the fisheries issue, stating that

they are not authorized to bring into discussion any of the rights or liberties which the United States have heretofore enjoyed in relation thereto. From their nature, and from the peculiar character of the treaty of 1783, by which they were recognized, no further stipulation has been deemed necessary by the Government of the United States to entitle them to the full enjoyment of all of them,

suggesting that it was a closed case.

Next, they advised that they had "explicitly declined treating on the basis of *uti possidetis*," but only on the "principle of mutual restoration of territory." In addition, they are willing "to extend the same principle to the other objects of dispute between the two nations."

They continued in some detail, and in more diplomatic words, about having later commissioners treat on the various boundary matters, which must take into consideration the changed dynamics resulting from the acquisition of the large land mass of the Louisiana territory, and in other areas based on the current lack of knowledge about regions un-surveyed or mapped. In addition, the Americans made brief comments about the articles on impressment of seamen, blockades, and more complicated references regarding indemnities going back several years prior to the war, and then included further references to retaliations growing out of the British Orders in Council over many years.

And finally, they express the

full expectation of receiving ... their explicit answer respecting all the articles embraced in it, and a *projet* also reduced to specific propositions and embracing all the objects which they intend to bring forward.[29]

It was a firm declaration that enough backing and filling had passed, and it was now time to act on agreeing to a treaty!

Hughes copied the documents and gave them to the British on the 10th.

34

WELLINGTON INSERTS HIMSELF

About the same time as the American envoys were trying to stir some life into the dreary negotiations at Ghent, the British leaders were having some stimulating correspondence with the Duke of Wellington in Paris. Lord Liverpool, the British prime minister, hoped to entice the duke into accepting command of all their forces in America, hoping also that he would coerce the United States into an ignominious surrender of large chunks of territory as well as yield to a number of other odious accommodations favorable to the former mother country — even possibly a return to colonial status.

These British dreams were not likely to happen, but it is evidence of how far afield they were in their expectations, or at least in their desires. Especially since they were having problems, about which the Americans would have rejoiced had they known of them. At the Congress of Vienna, Great Britain was having trouble attempting to control the procedures. They wanted the results to be determined by the "Four" major powers — themselves, Russia, Prussia, and Austria. But since the abdication of Napoleon and his exile to the island of Elba, and the restoration of the Bourbon monarchy, the French wanted equal recognition in the affairs of the conference.

Already, Lord Castlereagh, the British foreign secretary, was finding the talks proceeding sluggishly, and now he was under pressure to return to London for the opening of Parliament set for early November. He found Russian Czar Alexander determined to annex most of Poland into his already huge country. Prussia wanted Saxony and possibly some of the French lands to the west of the Rhine River. To thwart the ambitions of these continental powers, Castlereagh was willing to re-store much of what France held prior to their bloody revolution and empire under Napoleon. For these reasons, the British supported French entrance into the power forum to join with Austria in a three to two imbalance of power. Nevertheless, the English insisted on retaining some islands they had taken from the French in the Caribbean.

Meanwhile, in England, Lord Liverpool was trying to deal with the recalcitrant American envoys in Ghent while continuing to fight a costly war in America. He also faced, with growing concern, the massive expense of the American war that Parliament was about to take up in their early session. However, Liverpool still thought they could win the war overseas with the proper man in charge. There was Wellington, the greatest general of his times, sitting in Paris as the country's ambassador to the newly crowned King Louis XVIII. If the duke could be persuaded to go to America, the British would certainly have their great victory.

There was another factor involving Wellington. Liverpool was receiving private messages from a number of sources that Wellington was in grave danger of assassination or kidnapping. Liverpool wrote the duke urging him to quit Paris, and offered two or three options by which he could leave without too many questions. One means was to go to Vienna to give added support to Castlereagh. Another was to come home to London for conferences. But it was Liverpool's grandiose idea to have Wellington go to America with another large army to conquer in America, or at least obtain a peace favorable to the British. As he wrote Castlereagh on November 4, "It was quite essential to remove him from Paris."[1]

That same day, Liverpool wrote the Duke of the latest rumors as to Wellington's safety. He gave his thoughts on grounds for leaving Paris and then stated,

> The other idea which has presented itself to our minds is, that you should be appointed to the chief command in America, and that you should go out with full powers to make peace, or to continue the war, if peace should be found impracticable, with renewed vigour.

Yet there was another side of the coin:

> The more we contemplate the character of the American war, the more satisfied we are of the many inconveniences which may grow out of the continuance of it. We desire to bring it to an honorable conclusion.

He added that they were willing to place the decision "entirely in your hands."[2]

Wellington replied on November 9, with some braggadocio,

> I am quite clear, that if you move me from hence, it must be to employ me elsewhere. You cannot, in my opinion, at this moment decide upon sending me to America. In case of the occurrence of anything in Europe [and here, he was far sighted], there is nobody but myself in whom either yourselves or the country, or your allies, would feel any confidence.... I have already told you and Lord Bathurst that I feel no objection to going to America, though I don't promise to myself much success there.

In this long letter, Wellington presented his views on the overall situation in the American war. At the top of his analysis, he declared,

> That which appears to me to be wanting in America is not a General, or General officers and troops, but a naval superiority on the Lakes. Till that superiority is acquired, it is impossible, according to my notion, to maintain an army in such a situation as to keep the enemy out of the whole frontier.

He then defended the action of Sir George Prevost, citing the failure of the navy to support him at Plattsburg. (Even in those days, and that country, the army people supported the army against the navy.) And again he boasted about his standing should he go to America, "There will always remain this advantage, that the confidence which I have acquired will reconcile both the army and the people in England to terms of which they would not now approve."

And finally, he put it all out on the line.

> In regard to your present negotiations, I confess that I think you have no right from the state of the war to demand any concession of territory from America. Considering every thing, it is my opinion that the war has been a most successful one, and highly honourable to the British arms; but from particular circumstances, such as the want of the naval superiority on the Lakes, you have not been able to carry it into the enemy's territory, notwithstanding your military success, and now undoubted military superiority, and have not even cleared your own territory of the enemy on the point of attack. You cannot then, on any principle of equality in negotiation, claim a cession of territory excepting in exchange for other advantages which you have in your power....
>
> Then if this reasoning be true, why stipulate uti possidetis? You can get no territory; indeed the state of your military operations, however credible, does not entitle you to demand any; and you only afford the Americans a popular and credible ground which, I believe, their government are looking for, not to break off the negotiations, but to avoid to make peace. If you had territory, as I hope you soon will have New Orleans, I should prefer to insist upon cession of that province as a separate article than upon the uti possidetis as a principle of negotiation.[3]

Wellington certainly did not write as one addressing his superiors.

Within days, Liverpool's cabinet subordinate, Earl Henry Bathurst, secretary of war and the colonies, must have received the latest American note, along with their *projet*, dated November 10. However, Goulburn's cover letter, also dated the 10th, mentions that he received the papers from the Americans "last night at 10 P.M." On the 13th, he wrote Bathurst again saying he had written his letter on Friday. Friday was the 11th. Probably London did not receive Goulburn's packet until two days after receiving Wellington's military analysis. In a return letter to the duke, written on the 13th, Liverpool stated that he was still waiting to hear from the Americans. Most of this is rather unimportant, except to illustrate how much time was required in those days to get a communication from place to place, thereby coloring ones impressions and responses to matters that may be important.

In this case, Liverpool must have been stunned by Wellington's words, enough so as to color his response to Goulburn and the Americans. In other words, had Wellington's letter followed some time after Goulburn's, Liverpool might have replied to the American note with a heavier hand than he now did.

Goulburn's cover letter began with a reference to the Louisiana boundary. Now, nearly two centuries later, our focus on the boundary of Louisiana would be of the state, just south of Arkansas and east of Texas. But in those days, the Louisiana that Goulburn addressed was the vast territory west of the Mississippi River.

> To accede to the proposition which the Americans have made of discussing the boundary of Louisiana might be considered as a recognition by us of their right to occupy the country; and to accede to it with the reservation proposed as the country beyond the Stony Mountains would be to abandon to their encroachment the northwestern coast of America, on which they have already made some settlements.

Of course, we know the "Stony Mountains" as the "Rocky Mountains." Only eight years after the return of Lewis and Clark from that northwest coast, the British were showing their concern over land which would become a later diplomatic issue — the Oregon Territory, claimed under the U.S. battle cry of "Fifty-four forty or fight."

But Goulburn went on in his letter to refer to the American projet as "far too extravagant to leave any doubt upon our minds as to the mode in which it could be combated." He wanted to object to most of the articles presented to them, and said that to state their reason, "though not difficult, would be voluminous." So, they asked for instructions, not knowing, or probably even guessing that Liverpool was now in a mood to back down in their continuing pressure to delay negotiations or squeeze what they could from Americans.

Goulburn's only other pertinent comment was that they had no intention of making any reference to the maritime questions, saying, "We have thought that it would be more advisable in the present state of Europe not to agitate them ... [but] if the question is to be mentioned, it must be decided entirely in favour of Great Britain."[4] There was no gesture of reciprocity.

With their most recent note en route to England, Adams wrote Louisa Catherine, still in St. Petersburg, saying that a London paper was forecasting the rupture of the negotiations within a fortnight. During that fortnight, as the Americans now waited for the next reply from their British counterparts, there was a strange absence of activity. Adams wrote nothing in his *Memoirs* (or diary) for those two weeks. None of the other American commissioners added anything of importance in letters about their work in Ghent. The Congress of Vienna was making no substantial progress. And the war in America was dormant.

Adams did write several letters to his wife and to others as the British cabinet dealt with the latest message from the Americans, messages from Wellington, and the lack of diplomatic activity in Vienna. There was activity there in Austria, but it was mostly involving parties and other extracurricular affairs — as indeed it was in Ghent in a more subdued fashion.

To quote from a rather recent biography of Castlereagh, he had few experts to assist him, but,

> Contemporaries were puzzled and amused by the presence of his half-brother, Charles, whose flamboyance, indiscretions and scrapes made an odd contrast to the cool-headed Castlereagh. Lord Apsley tried to save British face at Vienna by explaining that Charles was, after all, Irish. But the British delegation was at least proof against the Austrian secret police; waste-paper baskets were carefully cleaned out. feminine seduction avoided, and the biggest scoop of the secret agents was apparently a glimpse of Castlereagh himself practicing a new Viennese dance with the aid of a chair. Even the endless festivities, which Castlereagh found a terrible waste of time, had their dangers, for when diplomats were not listening to indiscretions, they were trying to gauge the political significance of the dancing partners chosen by the leading personalities. The Tsar dancing a polonaise with Lady Castlereagh was indeed a matter of moment, while Metternich [the Austrian chancellor] seems to have drawn political advantage as well as personal satisfaction from the social round which often delayed more serious business. The politicians had also to be constantly on their guard against the camaraderie of the monarchs, especially under the inspiration of the Tsar, and it must have been a constant source of relief to Castlereagh that the Prince Regent was not present in this intoxicating atmosphere. As for himself, he was somewhat out of place amid this tinsel finery, but his "glacial good manners," his perfect dress sense (in sharp contrast to that of Lady Castlereagh), and his general distinction carried him through the social ordeal without much apparent difficulty.[5]

Or as one of Bayard's correspondents in Vienna quoted a recently deceased subordinate negotiator, "le Congrès danse, mais il ne marche pas."[6]

Meanwhile, in Ghent, as the American envoys "rested on their oars," so to speak, they could only stew in deep frustration over the lack of progress in their work. Were it possible to have any of the correspondence of the other members of the American delegation, their views would shine the same light as that provided in Adams' writings, for they were intimate with, and approving of, all the matters he expressed in his continuing letters.

Adams wrote his wife of their subdued extracurricular affairs. He told of the local weekly entertainment, "half concert, and half ball," which he found "tedious," but the "younger part of our company" attended on a regular basis. This surely included Clay, but also Adams noted that "Mr. Gallatin and James [his son] never miss," and "have become intimately acquainted with the whole troop."

Adams' description of their activities is as tantalizing as that of the Vienna atmosphere. He stated that the concerts

> consisted almost entirely of the scarlet coated gentry from Hanover and England, who are not more favorites of ours than they are of the inhabitants of the country. They are scarcely ever admitted into the good company of the place in private society.

As for the theatrical exertions, Adams wrote,

> The company is, for French players, without exception the worst I ever saw. There is but one tolerable actor, and not one actress in the whole troop. Occasionally they have had one good singer, male, but he had a figure like Sancho Panza, and one female, but she was sixty years old and had lost her teeth ... the standards of the stage are the veriest histrionic rabble that my eyes ever beheld.[7]

In another letter to Louisa Catherine, a few days earlier, on November 11, Adams wrote on more serious business,

> All the letters from England concur in stating that the popular sentiment for continuing the war is a perfect frenzy. The *Times* blubbers that all the laurels of Portugal, Spain, and France, have *withered* at Plattsburg, and threatens damnation to the ministry if they dare to make peace with Madison and his faction. We are even told that Master Bull calls for a more vigorous administration to put down the Yankees, and that that model of public

and private virtue, Wellesley, is to replace such sneaking prodigals of the nation's blood and treasures as Castlereagh and Liverpool.[8]

Wellesley, of course, was now the Duke of Wellington.

Adams wrote of impressions on past events, such as the consequences of the war in America. Writing to a friend in London, Adams referred to the British attacks in America as a

> Fraternal rage — it is civil war. The Capitol, a legislative and judicial palace, a public library and a chapel were blown up, we are told, by way of retaliation. What was Lewiston bombarded for? What was Georgetown, Frederickstown, Frenchtown and Havre de Grace destroyed for? What were the wounded prisoners at the river Raisin butchered in cold blood for? Was it for retaliation? Those things were not indeed translated into all the languages of Europe, and sent by special messengers to every court, and therefore the indignation of mankind has not marked so strongly their feelings as it did to greet the messengers who come to proclaim the destruction of the Capitol — I forbear.[9]

To another friend, Levett Harris, American consul in St. Petersburg, he wrote of subsequent battles won and lost, and then added,

> The defence of Baltimore has given us little more to be proud of, than the demonstration against it has afforded to our enemy. Prevost's retreat from Plattsburg has been more disgraceful to them, than honorable to us, and Wellington's veterans, the fire-eater Brisbane and the firebrand Cockburn, have kept the rawest of our militia in countenance by their expertness in the art of running away.... Left by a concurrence of circumstances unexampled in the annals of the world to struggle alone and friendless against the whole colossal power of Great Britain, fighting in reality against her for the cause of all Europe, with all Europe coldly looking on, basely bound not to raise in our favor a helping hand, secretly wishing us success, and not daring so much as to cheer us in the strife — what could be expected from the first furies of this unequal conflict but disaster and discomfiture to us.... This too is the moment which she has chosen to break through all the laws of war, acknowledged and respected by civilized nations. Under the false pretence of retaliation Cochrane has formerly declared the determination to destroy and lay waste all the towns on the sea coast which may be assailable. The ordinary horrors of war are mildness and mercy in comparison with what the British vengeance and malice have denounced upon us.[10]

To Louisa Catherine, in that November 15 letter, he also mentioned Cochrane's formal declaration to destroy and lay waste towns, adding that the action was

> required by Sir George Prevost to do so ... [yet] Prevost himself at the same time in his expedition to Plattsburg issued a proclamation forbidding every such excess, and declaring that they were not making war upon the American people, but only against their government. Whitbread [a member of the British Parliament] called upon the ministers to account for the inconsistency between Prevost's proclamation and his alleged requisition to Cochrane; but they gave him no answer. The real cause was that Prevost was entering that part of the country to conquer it, and the government intended to keep it. So they tried there the system of coaxing the people. On the sea coast, which they do not expect to keep, they meant merely to plunder and destroy. The retaliation was nothing but a pretext.[11]

In a letter to William Crawford on November 17, Adams expanded on his thoughts regarding retaliation as a pretext, which most likely also expressed the views of his colleagues. Adams referred to Whitbread and other pro–American members of the British Parliament as suggesting that their countrymen do not possess all the facts on the subject. And, he added, some of the Paris papers present the same falsehoods. On this basis, Adams proposed that the French papers be used to present abstracts of the truth "to the public in Europe, with reference to dates, which would point the argument of retaliation, directly against the enemy.... Make the principle recoil upon themselves." His suggestion was based on his conception that "the British have ever since the commencement of the war such entire possession of all the printing presses in Europe, that its public opinion has been almost exclusively under their guidance."

Adams added a further reflection on France's part in the negotiations in Vienna, noting that, under Talleyrand, the French have exerted such a profound "influence in the affairs of Europe without which this continent would be little more than a British colony."[12]

In a long letter, the following day, to his wife, he wrote much in the same vein, but more on his expectations for the Congress of Vienna to fail in its present demands against France and the demands of acquisitions by other States. Then on the 20th, Adams summed up most of his feelings in a very long letter to Secretary of State James Monroe. He began with reference to a situation which had rankled the American envoys for some time. It was the British reluctance to provide "passports for vessels to convey our dispatches" as well as for American citizens who wished transit to the U.S. They had been waiting in vain since September 7 for a response to their application. It even

> precluded our government from transmitting to us any instructions subsequent to their knowledge of the important changes in the affairs of Europe which had so essential a bearing upon the objects of our negotiation. The circumstance was the more remarkable, because the British plenipotentiaries had in one of their notes made it a subject of reproach to the government of the United States, that they had not furnished us with instructions after being informed of the pacification of Europe,

despite having told those same envoys on August 9 that the Americans had received instructions dated at the close of June.

> But this had altogether escaped their recollection; so that while Admiral Cockburn was writing you that his superior officer had decided that there was no further occasion for our government to instruct us until they should receive dispatches from us, the British government was taking it for granted that we had received no instructions and was charging it as an indication that the American government was not sincerely disposed to peace.

Adams went on to comment on the "British pretensions and demands" since their very first meeting and exchange of notes, that they expected that their military operations in America, combined with successes in Vienna, would enable them to raise

> their demands at their own discretion. Failure on either, or even on both sides, would still leave them with a certainty of a peace as favorable as they could have any reasonable pretence to require. They have accordingly confined their plenipotentiaries to the task of wasting time.

Adams also noted that since the Prince Regent's speech to Parliament, "Lord Liverpool has avowed ... that their demands and proposals are to be regulated by circumstances, which implies that they are not yet prepared to conclude," and that one of the British "ministerial papers announces that the negotiation is not to succeed, and that their plenipotentiaries are very shortly to return to England," though Adams had his doubts on this subject. Adams added that

> The popular sentiment throughout Europe has been, and still is, that the United States must sink in the present struggle against the whole power of Great Britain. And such is the British ascendancy over all the governments of Europe, that even where the feelings of the people incline to favor us, they dare not yet unequivocally express them.... We shall have no valuable friends in Europe until we have proved that we can defend ourselves without them. There will be friends enough, if we can maintain our own cause by our own resources.

It was a sad commentary on the prospects of American success in Ghent.

As the Americans continued to wait for a British response to their note and *projet* of November 10, Adams again wrote Louisa Catherine on the 22nd. Oddly, he wrote more to her than to Monroe, on the touchiness of the British on *etiquette* in the matter of who should first present a text of a proposed treaty. The British spoke of an advantage in receiving the initial draft, and they wiggled away from providing one when the Americans suggested they return one simultaneously. Adams thought it incongruous that they would play on this issue for so long. He called it "nothing but devices for wasting time" and "an absurdity." He went on to cite a previous experience he had negotiating a treaty of commerce with the Prussians some years earlier. The first thing they did after their appointment was to send him a project of a treaty. "They never hinted at any question of etiquette."[13]

While still waiting action from the British, Adams continued his letter writing. On the 23rd, he wrote his beloved and wise mother, Abigail Adams, back in Boston. With her, he brought forward a new and ugly situation with which she was actually in closer proximity than her illustrious son. Throughout the war, the New England Federalists had opposed the Madison administration's war effort in so many ways — refusing to help financially, or to send troops to fight, and in their pro–British views in newspapers among the most prominent acts suggesting treason. Early in 1814, several radical leaders including Harrison Gray Otis (president of the Massachu-

setts senate) and Josiah Quincy (who had led in the coercion charge against Clay in 1812/3) agitated for separation of New England from the rest of the Union.

Now in late 1814, these and other men had called for a convention to be held in Hartford, Connecticut, in December, to discuss such moves. Though Adams was a Federalist from Massachusetts, he deplored their actions. So, too, did commissioners Jonathan Russell, a graduate of Rhode Island's Brown University, and James Bayard, the Federalist from Delaware, who had withheld his vote for president in the House that gave the 1801 election to Democrat/Republican Jefferson. Of course, Clay and Gallatin were staunch supporters of the administration having been important leaders in the war effort.

Adams voiced his thoughts on this dark episode when he wrote his mother.

> It is a mortifying circumstance to one who feels for the honor and interest of our country to find a British Prime Minister boasting in Parliament, as the Earl of Liverpool has done, that the infamous outrages of their troops in America has been much more vindicated and justified by Americans in American newspapers, than they have in England itself. Still more of humiliation did I feel at his assertion that the people of the district of which they have taken possession, people of the state of Massachusetts, had manifested a disposition to become British subjects. I still indulge the hope that he has magnified into an expression of popular sentiment the baseness and servility of a few individual sycophants, who may have intended merely to save their property from plunder by paying court to the British commander. Deeply as the sordid spirit of faction had degraded my native state, I will not yet believe that the lofty sentiment of independence has been extinguished in the souls of any considerable portion of my countrymen, or that they have sunk low enough in the scale of creation willing to become subjects of Great Britain.[14]

On November 25, Adams revealed another diplomatic incident in a letter to his wife. This time it was that the American envoys had just learned that the contents of some of their early dispatches back to America had been sent to Congress by President Madison and were "*immediately* published, together with the instructions of the government to us. Mr. Monroe writes that they were producing the best effects, by uniting the sentiments of all parties in support of the war."[15]

Monroe's letter also gave the envoys permission to negotiate on the basis of *status ante bellum*.

The publications would raise hackles among the British in London and Ghent. In London, Lord Liverpool expressed his wrath in a letter of November 26, to Wellington still in Paris.

> Mr. Madison has acted most scandalously in making this communication at the time he did; and his letter to the Congress, which conveys the papers, contains a gross falsehood [not named]. We have no means of knowing what are the instructions which have been transmitted to the American Commissioners by the *Fingal*, but we sent an answer to their last note and projet on Monday [the 21st], and a few days will therefore inform us whether we are likely to have peace, or whether the American government will have advanced new pretensions in consequence of the clamour which they have excited throughout the country on account of the demands brought forward by us in the month of August.[16]

Within days of Liverpool's letter, the documents were also published in the British papers. Remember, these were documents of negotiations through August, now appearing late in November.

Continuing in his letter to Louisa Catherine, Adams noted that on the previous evening the Americans met with their counterparts at one of the local entertainments, where they provided these British with their first information of the publications. "They expressed much astonishment at the publication of dispatches pending a negotiation, and Mr. Goulburn, who is of an irritable nature, could not contain his temper." Adams wrote on that Gallatin believed it would cause the break in negotiation, but Adams felt relieved that if so, it was "an act of our government, in which we had no share, the blame will be none of ours."[17]

In his *Memoirs*, Adams related that he had told Goulburn,

> that the nature of our Government and the character of the war had made it absolutely necessary, and that the American Government, from the nature of the propositions made in the first British note to us, had every reason to suppose the negotiation was ended. We had, at the time when that note was sent to us, been fully convinced that it would have been ended in a very few days.[18]

And he added one further note of information in his letter to his wife, that

> The Massachusetts legislature have appointed twelve delegates to meet others from the rest of the New England states, on the 15th of December, at Hartford in Connecticut, to organize a separate system of defense, and a new confederacy of their own. This is a dangerous measure, but I hope it will not have all the pernicious effects to be apprehended from it.[19]

So it was here that the status of negotiations stood on November 26, when the British note arrived from London in response to the American draft of a treaty projet delivered into the British hands on November 10.

Now with the end of that fortnight lull of activities (of which no one was probably aware) the British note managed to re-ignite the negotiating antagonisms despite conceding to certain American demands. The contents of the British "advisory" stunned Goulburn and company. But it also, unexpectedly, caused a major rift in the previously harmonious quality of the American team.

The Americans had expected the British would, at least, write up their own idea of a projet of a treaty. What they got was their treaty draft returned with marginal alterations and propositions to each of the 15 articles. Taking them in numerical order, many changes were of a minor character, such as inserting dates or a modification of language.

Thus it was with Article 1, on the establishment of peace, except that the British appended a brief paragraph at the end of the document relating to the return of prisoners of war.

Article 2, regarding the notification of the end of hostilities to all concerned government officials, military posts, and naval stations and ships at sea, following the ratification of the treaty.

Article 3, relating to boundaries along the New England coast (a single American paragraph stating that the issues should be dealt with by a subsequent commission) was completely re-written and in a more complicated arrangement.

Articles 4, 5, and 6 dealt with boundary issues in southern New England (4), the Great Lakes (5), and from Lake Superior to the Lake of the Woods (6).

On each of these, the British added minor dates and words, and then appended paragraphs advising on conflicts between subsequent appointed commissioners.

Article 7, on payments and services of all the appointed commissioners, was accepted almost in toto by the British.

Article 8, relating to the extension of the boundary between the U.S. and Canada to be at the 49th parallel westward from the Lake of the Woods, brought out an entirely new substitute paragraph that was to cause the split in the American mission. In it, the British demanded access from Canada

> by land or inland navigation, into the territories of the United States to the river Mississippi, with their goods and effects, and merchandise, and ... have and enjoy the free navigation of the said river.

Article 9, dealing with restoration of rights and privileges of the Indians prior to the war (providing the Indians would make peace) was approved completely by the British.

It was on Articles 10 through 14 where the British showed their stubbornness. They noted in the margins for each, "Inadmissible." Briefly, these were as follows: Article 10 stated that the two countries would not employ Indians as allies in any future war; Article 11 referred to impressment of seamen; Article 12 referred to blockades; Article 13 discussed indemnities; Article 14 dealt with the legal protection of individuals within either country who had opposed that nation's war effort.

Article 15, dealing with ratification of the treaty, was approved with very minor changes. The British added a paragraph to be inserted after Article 2 with reference to the early exchange of prisoners of war.[20]

Though the London authorities gave way to several American proposals, the overall tone was disagreeable to both sides in Ghent. Unknown to the Americans, Goulburn had told his superior, Earl Bathurst in London,

> You know that I was never much inclined to give way to the Americans.... I confess I shall be much surprised if the Americans do not, by cavilling and long debate upon every alteration proposed by us, contrive to keep us in suspense for a longer time than under present circumstances is desirable.

But he added a further comment which would have delighted the Americans, especially Clay, had they known of it. On the subject of the fisheries, he wrote,

> I think that we might have argued the exclusion of the Americans from them ... but having once brought forward the subject, having thus implied that we had (what Lord Castlereagh seemed really

to have) a doubt of this principle, having received from the American plenipotentiaries a declaration of what they consider to be their right in this particular, and having left that declaration without an answer, I entirely concur in your opinion that we do practically admit the Americans to the fisheries as they enjoyed before the war, and shall not without a new war be able to exclude them.

He noted that his two colleagues disagreed with his assessment.[21]

On receipt of the British answer, Adams wrote in his *Memoirs*, "They have rejected all the articles we had proposed on impressment, blockade, indemnities, amnesty, and Indians." Though they appeared to have abandoned their demands for an Indian boundary, British military control of the Great Lakes, and *uti possidetis*, they clapped on a new condition that they would not be bound by their latest "terms hereafter, if the peace should not be made now."[22] Despite these demands, the Americans felt peace was at hand, though they were not ready to agree to everything. It was alterations of Article 8 that now re-kindled Clay's animosity.

After two days study of the British response and drafts of answers, Adams wrote, with regard to Article 8,

> Mr. Clay positively objected. Mr. Gallatin proposed to agree to it, proposing an article to secure our right of fishing and curing fish within the British jurisdiction. Mr. Clay lost his temper, as he generally does whenever this right of the British to navigate the Mississippi is discussed. He was utterly averse to admitting it as an equivalent for a stipulation securing the contested part of the fisheries ... that the navigation of the Mississippi ... was an object of immense importance

and opposed granting it as an equivalent for the fisheries.[23]

Gallatin tried to convince him of how denial of the fishing rights would be received by those New Englanders "now pushing for a separation from the Union and for a New England Confederacy," to say that their interests would be sacrificed. Clay responded, probably heatedly (though Adams does not say so),

> That there was no use in attempting to conciliate people who never would be conciliated; that it was too much the practice of our Government to sacrifice the interests of its best friends for those of its bitterest enemies.[24]

As to the problem to the west, Clay argued that the present British proposal,

> Demanded not only the navigation of the river, but access to it through our territories generally, from any part of their dominions and by any road, and without any guard, even for the collection of duties.

Thus,

> It would give the British access to our country in a dangerous and pernicious manner. It would give them the trade with the Indians in its full extent, and enable them to use all the influence over those savages which had already done us so much harm.[25]

By and large, the arguments that continued revolved about linking the two issues as equals and taking their basis from the Treaty of 1787 in which the United States diplomatically won their independence from Great Britain. Bayard stated that, "The rights secured by the Peace of 1783 ... were certainly permanent, and not to be forfeited by a subsequent war."[26] Therefore, Clay thought the rights of the fisheries were also not to be disturbed. But the matter of the rights on the Mississippi River, within that treaty, were altered by the acquisition of the Louisiana Territory, which changed the river from a boundary line between the U.S. and Spain, into an internal waterway with no more external claim than an equivalent claim to some internal waterway in any other country. He spoke of countering with demands for access along the St. Lawrence River.

As for British trade with the Indians, Adams replied that by restoring their rights as they were in 1811 (as they had agreed to in one of the articles) the British inherently retained such trade. As for duties, a stipulation could be added on that matter. But Adams also observed in his *Memoirs* that since the British had asked for a stipulation to be written into the treaty regarding the navigation of the Mississippi, they must have believed they had lost that privilege. Nevertheless, he did not want to sign a treaty with such a stipulation regarding the fisheries.

After all this squabbling on November 28, a vote was taken on "Gallatin's proposal to offer an article making navigation equivalent for the fisheries ... it was determined that it should." Surprisingly, Clay agreed. On the following day, when the commission met, "It was now on all sides good-humored," Adams wrote. They sat to review Gallatin's draft of the new article, "Closing with the request for a conference," with the British envoys. Again they took a night to re-work Gallatin's draft, and all but Russell were to write new ones which were presented to each other on the last day of November.[27]

In the new proposals, since the U.S. had waived a claim for indemnities for losses during the war, Gallatin wanted to insert provisions for indemnities for American vessels seized by the British at the start of the war, before they had adequate time to return home. Adams wanted to send a deposition "respecting the sale by their officers in the West Indies of negroes seduced from their masters in our Southern States by promises of liberty" (fact of which had been noticed in both houses of Parliament as part of the instructions to the American envoys). The other Americans objected, saying that "the charge as made in Mr. Monroe's instructions to us had more weight without this proof than it would with it." It was not sent.

The revised note to the British was agreed to and given to Mr. Hughes to prepare the final draft. The members signed it at three that afternoon and it was delivered to the British with the request for a conference. That evening, on Adams' return from the theater, he was informed by Gallatin that the British had agreed to the conference and had appointed noon on December 1 for the meeting to be "at the Chartreux, their own home."[28] They were about to embark on a new phase in the negotiations.

35

TREATY OF GHENT

The two sets of commissioners came to the conference on December 1 with entirely different expectations. It was to be a day of much tension but considerable progress. The British arrived believing that a treaty could now be signed based on their newest demand that the Americans accept their alterations to the treaty projet — or else they would not be bound by any of their "conciliatory" proposals. The Americans came to the table in a bit of a foul humor with the realization that several issues needed more consultation. And Adams, in particular, was annoyed at the British suggestion that the meeting be held at their domicile, whereas he considered it the Americans' time to choose a location.

Nevertheless, the Americans were present at the appointed time. Almost all of the following account of this day's conference is taken from Adams' *Memoirs*, the principal source on the three hours of discussions. While this is Clay's story, it is well to remember that though his writings reveal little at this time, he was a strong participant sitting at the bargaining table. We have Adams' brusque comments about his colleagues, particularly Clay, but none by Clay in defense, for we have no private diary or letters to his wife. How his private comments may show any later personal antagonism, might possibly be found when Clay served as President John Quincy Adams' secretary of state beginning in 1825, and when more of his papers are preserved.

Though the Americans had given the British envoys their latest note — to be sent to London — Adams began the discussions by noting that,

> We had agreed to many of the alterations proposed by them to the projet of a treaty ... that we had consented to waive the articles as to which they

had objected, with the exception of part of one of them,

this being Article 8.[1]

They all then agreed to examine each article in turn for comments. Beginning with Article 1, relating to the restoration of any territory conquered by either side during the war, the British immediately began to pick away at making claims for lands they had occupied during the war, while the Americans insisted on the return of all territories to pre-war status.

The British started with a claim to Moose Island in the Bay of Fundy, and quickly expanded their intended grasp by mentioning other places. Gallatin argued that if each place were going to be haggled over, it would only raise new disputes. A silence fell over the British, and the Americans could not interpret their attitude as acquiescence or continued rigidity — so Adams dropped that subject and went on to Article 2.

This article referred to the period required for the cessation of hostilities in relation to the ratification of the treaty by both sides. The American note had prescribed the cessation of hostilities as the date on which the treaty was signed. The British preferred to use the date of ratification.

With today's information technology, the final ratification would have been transmitted instantaneously, but in 1814–15 any such news needed weeks to transit the ocean by slow sailing vessels to notify the other nation of a ratification, and still more time to reach fighting ships at sea. It was quite complicated and was not resolved at this conference. Even the mode of ratification differed between the two countries. Adams observed that the "peace would be made six weeks or two months before it could be ratified," at least by

America. On the other hand, the British commented that they had an advantage whereby "ratification of the treaty would indeed be in England a mere formality, for they had authority to bind their Government; their full power promising to ratify what they should do."[2] Indeed, British ratification depended solely on the approval by the prince regent.

To this, Gallatin reminded the other side that in the United States, "ratification of treaties was by our Constitution reserved to the President and the Senate, and required the consent of two-thirds of the latter." Again the Americans agreed to accept the article as drawn up by the British, that is, cessation of hostilities set as the date of ratification, "finding it preferable to our own" version, though each nation would likely ratify on a different date.[3]

On the articles relating to the appointment of three commissioners to ascertain boundaries, the British preferred two commissioners each and, in the event when there was no agreement, the decision was to be made by "a friendly sovereign." The Americans agreed to this. But in the British response to the American projet on Article 3, the British seemed to be excluding Moose Island, in Passamaquoddy Bay, from judgment by the commissioners, and thereby win that piece of territory. Gallatin objected and included another island in that bay for consideration by any commission. The British accepted this change. Adams wrote, "This removed one of the great remaining obstacles to the peace."[4]

As to filling in the blanks of places where the commissioners were to meet, this point was carried easily. The British suggested Montreal and St. Johns. Gallatin, apparently knowing the geography, proposed to substitute for both of the above, St. Andrews, New Brunswick, a lovely little town on Passamaquoddy Bay. For an American site, Albany, New York, was named. These listings pertained to decisions to be rendered in post-treaty conferences on different articles. The British acquiesced on the locations.[5]

Again, it was Article 8 which provoked the "greatest obstacle" toward agreement. The British, according to Adams' *Memoirs*,

> now proposed a line due west, in the 49th parallel of latitude, with an additional clause, that the British shall have the free navigation of the Missis-

sippi, and free access to it through our territories generally, with their goods, wares, and merchandise.

Adams pointed out that this consisted of two parts. As to the boundary line, he observed that it was based on the Treaty of 1783, and that it bore "a peculiar character, and that it was not liable, like ordinary treaties, to be abrogated by a subsequent war" and therefore the Americans were not authorized to bring them into discussion.[6]

Adams noted that the navigation of the Mississippi also stood on the Treaty of 1783. With this said, he asserted that the issue of the fisheries fell within the same principle. If the British insisted on a new stipulation, the Americans were reluctant to agree to the river navigation without an equivalent given by the British, and for this, the Americans had prepared an article to provide for both — such as navigation of the St. Lawrence. The British were taken by surprise.[7]

Gallatin proceeded to remind the British that if they considered the rest of the article (reference to the 49th parallel of latitude) as an equivalent, "the lands there were of so little value, and the period when they might be settled was so remote" the Americans had no objection to striking out the whole of the eighth article. It is not clear if this viewpoint had previously been discussed privately with the rest of the American mission.

In any case, Goulburn replied that, "It was of no use to them at present, but it might eventually be of some advantage to them. It was a provision for futurity rather for the present time." But he thought "the equivalent must be found in the concessions of Great Britain in the other articles." Gallatin answered "that there was no concession of Great Britain in any of the other articles."

By striking the whole of the 8th article, Goulburn now recognized that the British would lose their claim for navigation of the Mississippi, and noted that the claim was part of their first note presented in August. Gallatin then cleverly observed that the British note of September 21 expressly stated that it contained "the *whole* of their demands," and that claim was not mentioned in it. Adams' *Memoirs* do not reveal any resolution to this issue at this sitting, as the envoys next turned to the question of indemnities.

The British were even less inclined to agree to anything on this subject. While the Americans had offered "to waive all claims for them ... excepting for vessels which had been in British ports when the war had commenced and had been there seized." They noted that the United States had granted British vessels six months to clear American ports.

Adams then wrote in his *Memoirs*,

Dr. Adams and Mr. Goulburn have but a feeble control of their temper. Adams began by an argument, as if he had been in Doctors' Commons, He said that he had examined the section of the law we had sent, and it appeared to him not to *make out a case* for a claim near so strong as our note had stated it; that it only gave authority to the President to give passports to British vessels to depart. Why, this was no more than what the King had power to do in England at all times.

Adams wrote that they were "nettled at the question," as they explained that the American ships had been seized, condemned and given to the party who had made the seizure.

Then the British argued that such indemnities were unprecedented, but came away from that argument losers when Gallatin cited similar attempts by France to gain the same results, and therefore not unprecedented. "'Aye,' said Goulburn, with a coarse and insulting tone; 'but we do not admit Bonaparte's construction of the law of nations.'"[8]

The only mention of Clay in Adams' *Memoirs* in this day's account was when Goulburn asserted that they had hoped to sign a treaty that day without again referring home to their superiors. Clay replied, "We made no question that you would sign the treaty, if we agreed to it in your own terms."[9] Clay would never agree so simply to give in to the British envoys.

Adams put it a bit differently in a letter written the following day to his wife in Russia. "They were very desirous of signing the treaty upon the terms they have now offered, but they manifested it in their usual manner by airs of arrogance and intimated threats." He added that,

We are sure that nothing less than great disappointment both in Europe and America could have brought them down to their present terms, and we are sufficiently apprized that the smallest turn of affairs would make them immediately renew all their most insolent demands and advance others still more extravagant. We, however, are not altogether such creatures of sunshine and of rain. We must adhere to our principles through good and evil fortune.[10]

Undoubtedly, the spirits of the two groups of envoys were reversed from that in which they had entered the day's conference. Though the British came to the table expecting submission by the Americans and found them adamant in opposition, the Americans came to the table soured by the latest British note and came away with the feeling that they had overcome a certain demeanor of British intransigence, and more importantly, that now a treaty was a possibility.

The British left the conference with a request that its substance should be kept secret for at least 24 hours, so that "their messenger might have a start of that time, to carry the first news to the Government" since "there was so much commercial speculation upon the transactions." The Americans "assented," though they could easily have wondered why the advantage went only to the British.

When the Americans met on December 2, for their private meeting, they, too, decided on a secrecy injunction among the ministers, with the exception of secretary Hughes, who was often called on to make copies of the documents.

But there was an odd twist in the denial of information to staff among the Americans. There was an aide named Bentzon who was leaving the next morning for London. Bentzon was the son-in-law of John Jacob Astor. Adams' *Memoirs* relate that during the war a British ship-of-war had broken up one of Astor's settlements at the mouth of the Columbia River on the Pacific Coast (Astoria). Astor had a ship in Canton, China, and wished to return it to that Oregon coast as soon as he heard of the signing of a peace treaty in order to re-settle the post. This would have to be a remarkable achievement to beat a British return to the port. Mr. Shaler also objected to the secrecy injunction, complaining that it intimated that the envoys had lost confidence in him.[11]

Without revealing a particular article under consideration, Adams also told Louisa Catherine that he had been unhappy about an agreement made with his colleagues, saying he thought they gave to the

article a construction much more limited than I do. They were therefore not so averse to accepting it as I was. They thought it amounted to little or nothing. I thought it meant so much that I offered then to reject it even at the hazard of breaking off the negotiation upon it, if they would concur with me. They preferred accepting the article, because they understood the meaning differently from me. Though I have no doubt the British government understand it as I do, yet as my colleagues are all intelligent men, their construction of the article may be the right one, and if so the concession was certainly a mere trifle, and it would have been wrong to risk a rupture by rejecting it. I finally agreed with them in accepting the article, with adopting their opinion of its meaning. It was therefore natural that I should think the concession much greater than they did, and by concurring with them I acquiesced in their judgment rather than adhere inflexibly to my own.

Here was another example of these great minds differing, yet coming to a satisfactory conclusion when the right or wrong choice of action was unknown. In any case, Adams added to his wife that they were "at this moment in the greatest and most trying crisis of the negotiation" ... and until "last Sunday, I never indulged a hope of peace."[12] In another letter to his wife, four days later, Adams expressed the opinion of the rest of the Americans that they would finish their work before the end of the year, though he doubted it.

As usual, there was another wait of more than a week before the next meeting with the British envoys fresh with another note from their London superiors. Unknown to the Americans, this new letter from Lord Bathurst, dated December 6, recognized that the negotiations had narrowed to "two points on which there exist any material difference." But Bathurst added a tiny distinction on claims for territory to be restored based on the *status quo ante bellum*. He wrote of claims that existed prior to the war and therefore he insisted on the terms "Belonging to" as that tiny deviation.[13]

So it was when the next conference between the two sets of envoys was agreeably held at the lodgings of the Americans on December 10. At once, according to Adams, the British member, "Lord Gambier opened by observing that the first thing to be done was to settle the protocol of the first meeting, [on December 1] which Mr. Baker had drawn up, and which he then read." A number of minor alterations were agreed to by both sides.

Nevertheless, responding to Bathurst's letter, Goulburn was quick to object to phrasing in the first article dealing with the possession of islands in Passamaquoddy Bay separating present day Maine from New Brunswick. The British wanted to retain the words "belonging to" as applied to territory to be restored with the termination of the war. Adams suggested that the Americans be permitted to consult privately before replying. It was an example of several "minor" matters that were to be battled over in the following two hours, as opposed to the "major" issues over which the war had been declared and fought over, and since negotiated to some conclusion during long tedious hours. They would soon return to the claims issue.

In the interim, the British turned to a larger problem — the puzzle of working out equivalents over the British demands for transit from Canada to the Mississippi River and navigation down its extent to New Orleans, along with identifying the westward boundary at the 49th parallel or from the Lake of the Woods. This was to be played against the American demands for rights of "taking, drying, and curing, fish within" so called "British waters" along the Atlantic coast.

Again, without knowing of Bathurst's letter, the Americans found the British were now linking the Mississippi navigation question as an equivalent to their agreement of setting the 49th parallel as the national boundary between the United States and Canada all the way from the Lake of the Woods to the Pacific Ocean.

Bathurst's letter admitted that the British "were no longer entitled" to "free access to and navigation of the Mississippi ... under the Treaty of 1783," but he now tried to link that claim to the boundary referring to the 49th parallel as a "favourable arrangement" to the United States.[14]

When Gambier tried to peddle this extravagance, Adams quickly observed

> that it was no increase in territory, but rather a diminution of territory to the United States. The line proscribed by the Treaty of 1783 was from the northwest corner of the Lake of the Woods to the Mississippi, due west.... A line due west from the Lake of the Woods, it had been found, did not touch the Mississippi. But by terms of the treaty we were entitled to a line due west from the northwest corner of the lake, and that was north of 49; by accepting that parallel we really gave up some of our territory, perhaps a degree of latitude.

Dr. Adams thought that might be a matter of controversy, but agreed to leave that part of the article as it stood. But the British could not agree on how the wording of the article should stand. Gallatin expressed some uncertainty about the parallel's true surveyed placement, but Clay said he had no doubt that the line would touch the lake.[15]

There was still another part in Bathurst's letter pertaining to the American claim to continue the "liberty" of the fisheries. However, after a two hour session, the British failed to bring this issue to the table. When the British left, the Americans continued for another hour in consultation, which at times, became rather heated.

They decided to stand by their wording for the Moose Island issue and that "modification of the eighth article, [was] altogether unnecessary." And they discussed the reasoning behind the British arguments and how they should deal with them in their next meeting. Then they agreed to meet at eleven on the 11th in Adams' chambers.

This meeting did not start till noon. Russell began by opposing direct conferences with the British, with good reason, stating that it was better for the Americans to have their comments in writing, because their views were always sent back to London, and it was best to have their views in writing rather than paraphrased and colored by the British envoys. In agreement, Adams noted that "We have not advanced a step in our conferences." While Gallatin was certain the British were "now evidently desirous of peace," Adams was doubtful and told his *Memoirs*,

> My anxiety was much greater than it had been at any period of the negotiation, infinitely greater than when their demands had been so extravagant that we were sure of being supported by our country in rejecting them. When I saw them abandoning everything of any value in their demands, and stubbornly adhering to hairs, merely, as it seemed to me, to keep the negotiation open, I could not but deeply distrust their intentions. They clung to atoms involving principles which they had abandoned as applied to everything important.[16]

Gallatin was struck by the "extraordinary thing that the question of peace or war now depended solely upon two points, in which the people of the State of Massachusetts alone were interested — Moose Island and the fisheries within British jurisdiction." Adams suggested "that was the very

perfidious character of the British propositions," and Russell called it "a disaffected part of the country."[17]

Of course, Clay carried a strong antagonism towards that state's disinclination to support the war cause, and said, "He would do nothing to satisfy disaffection and treason; he would not yield anything for the sake of them" and "he had no doubt but three years more of war would make us a warlike people, and that then we should come out of the war with honor." He was for playing *brag* with the British. "They had been playing *brag* with us throughout the whole negotiation; he thought it was time for us to begin to play brag with them." (Clay had become quite skilled at *Brag*, an old English card game akin to poker.) Adams had forgotten how to play but Bayard reminded them that "You may lose the game by bragging until the adversary sees the weakness of your hand," and then he told Adams privately that, "Mr. Clay is for bragging a million against a cent."[18]

Adams then posed some hypothetical examples of Moose Island being a part of Kentucky or Delaware. Bayard, from the latter, laughed, saying, "Delaware could not afford to give up territory." And Gallatin said it should be defended regardless of what state it belonged to.[19]

In further conversation, they agreed to their earlier firm negotiating stand, but also agreed to hold one more conference before reverting to written responses. There followed a discussion relating to restoration of territory and its relation to the Indian article long since agreed to. But it brought forth another tirade from Clay in which he stated that he would never sign a treaty "including the British right to trade with the Indians, so help him God." Adams added in his *Memoirs* that Clay

> said this in the harsh, angry and overbearing tone which I perhaps more than others, ought to excuse, as the involuntary effusion of a too positive temper. It always offends me in him; but I took no notice of it this day.

Of course he did so in his writings. Both Gallatin and Bayard commented that "every one of us must act according to his own sentiments," but Adams wrote that

> Clay stalked to and fro across the chamber, repeating five or six times, "I will never sign a treaty

upon the status ante bellum with the Indian article, so help me God!" Mr. Russell declared himself against proposing it to-morrow, and I again urged to propose it. Mr. Clay then said he should object to the conference altogether. We came to no express decision, but Mr. Bayard and Mr. Gallatin did not support me in the resolution to make the proposal, so that Mr. Clay actually beat again a majority by outbragging us.

There was still further discussion, in a better humor, between Clay and Adams on supporting this Indian article, but now as to who made the majority when it was first signed, Clay saying it was Adams' article since he signed first, but Adams countering that there was no majority until Clay signed.

Clearly the tension of these exasperating dealings with the British was beginning to ravel the nerves of these men.

When the envoys met at the British residence at noon on the 12th for three hours, Adams immediately noted that

the differences yet to be adjusted were only two, and of so small amount in point of interest that they could hardly be subjects worthy in point of two such nations as the United States and Great Britain to contend about.

He then stated that the Americans could not consent to cede any part of the State of Massachusetts ... without the consent of the state." He went on to remind the British that they had agreed to the principle of "status ante bellum" and that they had taken military possession of Moose Island in Passamaquoddy Bay during the war, inferring that it should therefore be returned to the United States.

Then, still quoting the American Adams,

Mr. Goulburn and Dr. Adams immediately took fire, and Goulburn lost all control of his temper. He has always in such cases a sort of convulsive agitation about him, and the tone in which he speaks is more insulting than the language that he uses. He said that if there could be no cession of territory without the consent of the State, there could be no safety for Great Britain in treating with the United States at all.[20]

But then in a more sober mood, Goulburn began to recite occasions prior to the war during which the Canadian/British authorities exercised jurisdiction over the islands, such as the courts of

Nova Scotia calling on residents of the islands to serve on their juries. And he noted that, following the Treaty of 1783 and up to 1798, they also maintained some jurisdiction. These discussions went on for some time before the conferees turned back to article 8.

While the Americans had agreed to recognize the British "rights," through the Treaty of 1783, to navigate the Mississippi, they in turn, expected the British to recognize their rights to fish, etc. in British-Canadian coastal waters. But now, based on the continuing part of Bathurst's December 6 letter to his subordinates (to deny that Americans had such "rights"—maybe a "privilege" which could be taken away), the British envoys resisted the American claims. Yet it had been Adams' father who had negotiated the rights in the 1783 treaty. The elder Adams had insisted that they had carried those fishing rights as part of their heritage as Englishmen prior to the Revolution and had not lost them when given independence. John Quincy was not about to permit his father's work to be undone.

Various new drafts were presented by both sides on both the navigation and the fisheries issues, but they only sparked more bluster, and Dr. Adams, as might be expected, raised the specter of rupturing the negotiations or, at least, again referring them back to London.

All that was settled after three hours was that the protocol of the day's talks was, "that the Plenipotentiaries met, and, after much discussion upon the subjects yet unadjusted, adjourned."[21]

Again back at their own apartments, after three o'clock, the Americans tried to come to some sense of how to reply to the British at the next meeting. Already, Bayard had been convinced by Goulburn that the British had a very strong claim to keep control of the Passamaquoddy islands.

As Adams went to work on a draft of a reply, Gallatin "advised the young gentlemen to go and dress for the ball, and we continued to discuss the subject [the negotiations] among ourselves until seven o'clock." Nevertheless, Gallatin (and probably Clay) and the various aides and Gallatin's son did attend the ball where "Hail Columbia" was played in honor of the Americans.

On the day of the ball, Gallatin's son, James, made an interesting entry in his diary. While some of James' diary writings have been called untrue, the 17-year-old wrote of a letter to his father from the Duke of Wellington, who not only advised his superiors in London, but had also written a praiseworthy comment to Albert Gallatin. As told by James, Wellington wrote,

> Pray do not take offence at what I say. In you I have the greatest confidence. I hear on all sides that your moderation and sense of justice, together with your good common sense, places you above all the other delegates, not excepting ours. The Emperor Alexander has assured me of this. He says we can place absolute reliance in your word. I have always had the greatest admiration for the country of your birth. You are a foreigner with all the traditions of one fighting for the peace and welfare of the country of your adoption.

James added, "Father, I think, was pleased. He is a foreigner and is proud of it."[22]

On November 28, James had also begun to quote from another letter from the Duke to his father, but when Albert saw the son trying to copy it, he "took it off the table and burned it." But James had quoted the Duke as writing,

> As I gather, Mr. Madison as well as Mr. Monroe gave you full power to act without even consulting your colleagues on points you consider of importance. I now feel that peace is shortly in view. Mr. Goulburn has made grave errors and Lord Castlereagh has read him a sharp lesson.[23]

It's hard to believe even Wellington would have participated in such an indiscretion.

On December 13, before the Americans met at eleven in Adams' chamber, he took time to write his wife again. Despite the internal arguments within his little group, Adams still wrote that,

> Our harmony has been as cordial as perhaps ever existed between five persons charged with so important and so difficult a trust. But it is the temper in the British notes and in the conferences on the part of two of the British plenipotentiaries which brings mine to the severest of trials. You know all the good and all the evil of my disposition; but cannot know the violence of the struggle to suppress emotions produced by the provocations of overbearing insolence and narrow understandings. They have, however, been suppressed.

Adams' letter continued with a cute little observation.

> After the last two conferences we are apparently farther from the conclusion than we were before them. The British plenipotentiaries present to us articles sent to them ready drawn from England, and when we ask what they mean, what the object of them is, they answer they cannot tell; the article was sent them from England, we must construe it for ourselves. If we propose the alteration of a word, they must refer it to their government. If we ask for an explanation, they must refer it to their government. It is precisely the French caricature of Lord Malmesbury. "My Lord, I hope your Lordship is well this morning" ... "Indeed, Sir, I do not know, but I will send a courier to my Court to inquire." And thus all we have obtained from the two conferences of three hours each is, another courier to the Court to inquire.[24]

So, another note goes to London.

But meanwhile, the mission had another meeting in Adams' chamber at eleven, on the 13th, to peruse each other's draft of a reply to the previous day's encounter with the British envoys. Using Adams' *Memoirs* as the source for details of this meeting leaves a large question. The discussion seems to center on how to answer the British demands on "two points" without naming them. It's hard to believe they no longer spoke of the navigation of the Mississippi, but only of (1) claims to the islands of Passamaquoddy Bay and particularly Moose Island, and (2) the fisheries as if they were equivalents.

The various drafts differed considerably and spoke of trying to win both points, win one and sacrifice the other, or even give way on both. For example, Adams wrote of Clay's proposition,

> Mr. Clay was for persisting in the rejection of both the British demands, but with the determination finally to yield both. He thought that by insisting equally upon both we should most probably obtain a concession upon one.

The strongest argument in either direction came from Bayard, who had become convinced that the British claims for Moose Island were better than the Americans' claim, and certainly wanted no rupture of the negotiations over that tiny matter. But Adams felt that the very fact that the British would discuss the islands was proof of their uncertainty as to the ground on which they stood. Clearly, the negotiations were narrowing down to finite points, with no surety they would be resolved.

The two-hour discussion then wandered into how any of these actions would be received at home — both in England and America. Meeting again briefly at three o'clock, they decided to talk more on the morning of the 14th before still another conference with their opponents. That evening they dined with the British envoys. As Adams wrote,

> The party was more than usually dull, stiff, and reserved. Mr. Goulburn attempted to be courteous, and told me he hoped I should pay a visit to England after we have finished here. I said I certainly should, if they would permit me.

Adams — as well as Clay and Gallatin — would spend many months in England following their work in Ghent. At the dinner, Clay would not discuss Gambier's questions on the fisheries.[25]

Again at eleven, on the 14th, the mission met in Adams' chambers. Their haggling this day continued with preparing a response to the British on the fisheries issue. It had narrowed down to whether the United States retained "rights" to the fisheries, assured by the Treaty of 1783 when they became an independent nation broken off from the British Empire, or whether they must now bargain for the "liberty" of the fisheries since, as the British claimed, they no longer had that "privilege" as abrogated by declaring war. It was all so very sticky over such minor wordings to continue fighting a war.

Adams now felt that all his companions had agreed to argue the point with the British, only to surrender to them, if need be. He summed it up in a long paragraph in his *Memoirs*.

> Mr. Clay said he did not wish to make up his mind upon the subject until it should be absolutely necessary. He said we should make a damned bad treaty, and he did not know whether he would sign it or not; but he could draw, in five minutes, an article agreeing to negotiate concerning the Mississippi and the fisheries without impairing our claim to them by the Treaty of 1783. He drew an article accordingly, which I read, and told him I had no other objection to it than that it would be instantly rejected by the British Plenipotentiaries. I further said that they were wrong not to give it up now, and sign the treaty without another reference to England, as well as without my signature. I could not sign it, because I could not consent to give up that point. But if I were of their opinion, I would make sure of the treaty now. They were setting everything afloat by another reference, and it was arrant trifling to be cavilling about a point upon which they had resolved ultimately to yield.

They preferred making one more attempt, the note was adjusted and given to secretary Hughes to make a copy to hand to the British later in the day. And of course, they were informed that evening, by the British secretary, that it was being sent to London. Adams remained apprehensive as to its reception.

Adams' *Memoirs* were to be blank from the evening of the 14th until eight days later — on the 22nd.[26]

In the interim, in a letter to Louisa Catherine, on December 16, Adams began with an amusing reference using a paraphrase of his parents' salutations to each other calling each other their "Best Friend." Noting a conversation between Clay and Goulburn at the recent dinner together,

> Mr. Clay remarked that Mr. Goulburn was a man of much *irritation*. *Irritability*, said I is the word, Mr. Clay, irritability; and then fixing him with an earnest look, and the tone of voice between seriousness and jest, I added "like somebody else that I know." Clay laughed, and said "Aye, that we do; all know him, and none better than yourself." And Mr. Gallatin, fixing me exactly as I had done Mr. Clay, said emphatically, "that is your *best friend*." "Agreed," said I. "*but one*" — and we passed on in perfect good humor to another topic.[27]

It was in this same letter that Adams continued by revealing his general impressions of the working personalities of his companions at arms. It becomes an important analysis, particularly of Clay, since so little appears in his personal writings. I will quote it all.

> Of the five members of the American mission the Chevalier [Bayard] has the most perfect control of his temper, the most deliberate coolness, and it is the more meritorious because it is real self-command. His feelings are as quick, and his spirit as high as those of anyone among us; but he certainly has them more under government. I can scarcely express to you how much both he and Mr. Gallatin have risen in my esteem since we have been here, living together. Mr. Gallatin has not quite so constant a supremacy over his own emotions; yet he seldom yields to an ebullition of temper, and recovers from it immediately. He has a faculty, when discussion grows too warm of turning off its edge by a joke, which I envy him more than all his other talents, and he has in his character one of the most extraordinary combinations of stubbornness and of flexibility that I ever met within man. His greatest fault I think to be an ingenuity sometimes intrenching [sic] upon ingenuousness.

Our next personage in the sensitive scale is Mr. Russell. As the youngest member of the mission, he has taken the least active part in the business, and scarcely any at the conferences with the British plenipotentiaries. He is more solitary and less social in his disposition than the rest of us, and after living with us two months, left us and took separate lodgings for some trifling personal convenience or saving of expense. He nevertheless bears his proportion of all the entertainments that we give. But he has a high sense of his personal dignity, and sometimes takes offense where none is intended to be given. This has never happened upon any circumstance connected with the business of the mission, for he has never entered into the discussions which we have had among ourselves; but we have seen manifestations of his temper in the occurrences of social intercourse, as well in our particular circle, as in our relations with the people of the country. There has, however, never been anything like a misunderstanding between him and any of us. In the conduct of our business he has the greatest deference for the opinions of Mr. Clay.

The greatest diversities of sentiment and the most animated mutual oppositions have been between this last gentlemen and *your* best friend [Adams himself]. They are unquestionably the two members of the mission most under the influence of that irritability which we impute to Mr. Goulburn; and perhaps it would be difficult to say which of them gives way to it the most. Whether Mr. Clay is as conscious of this infirmity as your friend, whether he has made it as much the study of his life to acquire a victory over it, and whether he feels with as much regret after it has passed every occasion when it proves too strong for him; he knows better than I do. There is the same dogmatical, overbearing manner, the same harshness of look and expression, and the same forgetfulness of the courtesies of society in both. An impartial person judging between them I think would say that one has the strongest, and the other the most cultivated understanding; that one has the most ardency, and the other the most experience of mankind; that one has a mind more gifted by nature, and the other a mind less cankered by prejudice. Mr. Clay is by ten years the younger man of the two, and as such has perhaps more claim to indulgence for irritability. Nothing of this weakness has been shown in our conferences with the British plenipotentiaries. From two of them, and particularly from Mr. Goulburn, we have endured much; but I do not recollect that one expression has escaped the lips of anyone of us that we would wish to be recalled.[28]

As both sets of commissioners awaited a reply from London, Adams noted that "we partake of balls, concerts and plays as often as we desire." Again he was to write his wife on Tuesday the 20th. This time he mentioned "the leaky vessels" pertaining to speculation on the status of the negotiations, and even the betting values as to a conclusion. He quoted such a story from a London paper, that a treaty had already been signed. In this case, the paper pointed the accusing finger at an aide of the American mission. Adams suspected that the party might be Bayard's private secretary, Mr. Milligan.

Yet during this time, the authorities in London were busy penning another reply for their envoys to pass on to the Americans. In a dispatch from Lord Bathurst to his subordinates in Ghent, they were advised that the Moose Island controversy could be placed into a post-treaty negotiation, but they would insist on a conclusion of the issue within a set period of years.

Then came some startling directions which the Americans would love to have seen — but didn't.

> With respect to the discussion which has grown out of the latter part of the 8th Article, the Prince Regent regrets to find that there does not appear any prospect of being able to arrive at such an arrangement with regard to the fisheries as would have the effect of coming to a full and satisfactory explanation of the subject.
>
> As this appears, however, now to be the only remaining point on which any difficulty exists, he is unwilling to protract, by a prolongation of the discussion, the period when the war between his Majesty and the United States may be happily terminated. You will therefore present a note, in which, after referring to the language held by you on this subject from the very commencement of the negociation, in which you stated explicitly that the British Commissioners did not intend to grant gratuitously to the United States the privileges formerly granted by treaty to them of fishing within the limits of the British sovereignty, and of using the shores of the British territories for purposes connected with fisheries, you will state that, as there does not appear any prospect of agreeing upon an Article wherein that question may be satisfactorily adjusted, you are authorized to accept the proposition which the Commissioners of the United States proposed in the Protocol of the 1st of December, wherein they expressed their readiness to omit the 8th Article altogether.[29]

During the day, on Thursday, December 22, the Americans received the formal reply from the British envoys. When Gallatin saw that the British referred again "to their declaration of the 8th of August, that Great Britain would not hereafter grant the liberty of fishing, and drying and curing fish, within the British jurisdiction, without an equivalent," he thought it necessary "to write a note again referring to our construction of the Treaty of 1783, and to our right to the fisheries under it." Adams opposed this noting that "we had twice stated it, and in terms peculiarly strong in our last note."

When Clay saw the note, Adams noted that he "manifested some chagrin. He still talked of breaking off the negotiation, but did not exactly disclose the motive of his ill humor, which was, however, easily seen through. He would have much preferred the proposed eighth article, with the proposed British paragraph, formally admitting that the British right to navigate the Mississippi, and the American right to the fisheries within British jurisdiction, were both abrogated by the war."

Following these quick early observations, the Americans again met in the evening for a more considered discussion, wherein "Clay continued in his discontented humor," and tried to enlist others to his view. He was sure of Russell's vote to continue the talks with the British, and thought Gallatin and Bayard were "Too eager for peace." When he asked Adams to join him, Adams told him,

> No; it was now too late. I had offered to break off on the Indian article, which he had not chosen to do. There was nothing now to break off upon. "Well," said he, "will you be of the same opinion to-morrow?" "Perhaps not" said I; "but you can easily ascertain by asking the question again tomorrow." Gallatin and Bayard, who appeared not to know where it was that Clay's shoe pinched him, were astonished at what they heard.

Then Russell called for a vote for another conference with the British for the 23rd. Only Clay voted against it.[30]

Again, the British arrived at the Americans' dwelling at noon on the 23rd. When all were seated, Adams informed them that the Americans had agreed to accept the latest proposal "from London" and that this conference was called

> to make the final arrangements for the conclusion of the treaty, and should be ready to sign it whenever it would be agreeable to them. Lord Gambier

expressed his satisfaction that the negotiation had been brought to this favorable result, and we proceeded to make the definitive amendments for completing the treaty.[31]

But it wasn't that simple.

It was astonishing that there was so much left to form a treaty. Already those earlier articles relating to impressment of seamen, British boundary claims including all of the Great Lakes, indemnities, and Indian issues had been disposed of by striking them out altogether. Now the two sides had agreed to be silent on the matter of navigation of the Mississippi and the fisheries. What had they argued about for nearly five months?

Of the remaining issues, first, there was the cessation of hostilities in relation to the ratification of the treaty, which was to be prepared by each side in triplicate, but only one could bear the official British seal. And the British now demanded that there be no alteration of the contents by the American Senate. Gallatin said that would be no ratification. Nevertheless, the British insisted on that wording. There was consent on the wording which excepted the claim on Moose Island (such a minor issue over which a war might continue). There was a question of restoration of ships captured after the cessation of hostilities. There was wording regarding the release of prisoners of war when peace was restored, and a long and sticky argument over the costs of caring for those prisoners. (The issue of the prisoners was to become a major problem for three of the Americans before Clay was to return home.)

Over the manner of payment for the maintenance of prisoners, Adams made an interesting observation in his *Memoirs*.

> There is nothing that more distinctly characterizes the temper and spirit of the British Plenipotentiaries in this negotiation than this artifice to filch a profit of fifteen or twenty percent upon a sum of perhaps fifty thousand pounds sterling, and their inflexible adherence to it.[32]

There were two additional late propositions brought forward by the British at one of the early December conferences which have not been noted because, in the end, they went nowhere. But in this very late meeting they tried again to push them through. One was inclusion of an article opposing slave trade. While these Americans opposed the trade, they thought the subject had no place in this treaty. The same attitude was held about an article seeking a statement on the use of courts of the other nation. The Americans stood firm in rejecting these two unnecessary articles.

Despite the lack of major issues to be settled, the conference lasted three hours. As Adams reported, it "terminated by an agreement that we should met at three o'clock to-morrow afternoon, at the house of the British Plenipotentiaries, for the purpose of signing and sealing the six copies of the treaty." Yet very few of these late-day issues had concerned the commissioners during the many months of negotiations. The final document was not to look at all like the projet the Americans had handed the British back in October.

It was all rather weird. They probably felt it was a dream. How could this British agreement have happened so suddenly? There is a letter in the papers of the Duke of Wellington dated December 28, 1814, from British Prime Minister the Earl of Liverpool to George Canning, a future prime minister, then in Lisbon, Portugal. In it Liverpool provides some answers to the question. However, the Americans probably never saw this letter, since Wellington's papers were not published till after Clay's death.

Liverpool noted that Wellington was agreeable to taking command of the British army in America, but only reluctantly and had advised his government otherwise. Liverpool wrote that Wellington

> was particularly solicitous for peace, being fully satisfied that there was no vulnerable point of importance belonging to the United States which we could hope to take and hold except New Orleans, and this settlement is one of the most unhealthy in any part of America.

Liverpool noted further that putting more U.S. east coast towns under contribution "would be in vain," and that "continuance of the war for the purpose of obtaining a better frontier for Canada would, I am persuaded, have been found impracticable." But probably of a more important consideration, "We could not overlook the clamour which has been raised against the property-tax, and the difficulties we shall certainly have in continuing it for one year, to discharge the arrears of the war."

Continuing, Liverpool wrote Canning,

The question therefore was whether, under all these circumstances, it was not better to conclude the peace at the present moment, before the impatience of the country on the subject had been manifested at public meetings or by motions in Parliament, provided we could conclude it by obliging the American Commissioners to waive all stipulations whatever on the subject of maritime rights, by fulfilling our engagements to the Indians who were abandoned in the Treaty of 1783, and by declining to revive in favour of the United States any of the commercial advantages which they enjoyed under former treaties. As far as I have any means of judging, our decision is generally approved.

Liverpool added one further comment which was probably a major factor.

> The negotiations at Vienna are not proceeding in the way we could wish. Not that I think there is any chance of their leading to hostilities, but a great irritation will, I fear, remain; and this consideration itself was deserving of some weight in deciding the question of peace with America.[33]

On the conclusion of the joint conference of December 23, the British stated that their secretary, Mr. Baker, would be prepared to head for England on Christmas eve and then follow that mission with a voyage to the United States with the English ratification. They agreed to let Clay's private secretary, Mr. Carroll, travel with Baker. And in a private meeting among the Americans it was agreed that a dispatch should be written to Secretary of State Monroe to go with the copies of the treaty. Adams spent the evening composing a draft of such a letter.

So, it was now December 24, 1814, an historic day that few today celebrate. Adams began the day by writing letters to his secretary of state and to his "Dear and Honored Mother": his salutation to Abigail Adams. But first, the two sets of envoys met at four o'clock at the home of the British with their triplicate sets of the final treaty, and reviewed them. They found minor errors and differences — such as the American notation of the earlier treaty of peace of 1783 as "seventeen hundred and eighty-three," whereas the British copies had it "one thousand seven hundred and eighty-three." This difference also applied to the date of the signatures, which were now appended to the six documents. The ceremony was completed by 6:30 P.M.[34]

According to James Gallatin's diary of December 24,

> The treaty was signed to-day in the refectory of the monastery. Later on there was a solemn service in the cathedral; it was most impressive. We all attended as well as the intendant, all the officers and the high officials of Ghent.[35]

Nowhere in Adams' writings, or those of any other of the envoys, is there any description of the appearance or apparel of any of the commissioners. However, there are two paintings created after the event, in which the men are shown wearing military-style uniforms. One of the paintings, done more than a century later, depicts Clay, standing alone in white knee britches and blue morning coat, a small sword at his left hip. In 1972, at the home of Clay's great-granddaughter, Henrietta Clay, the author was told the story of the painting by its 80-year-old artist, a Mr. George Welsh, Henrietta's only other guest of the evening. He related obtaining from the U.S. State Department a copy of the uniform Clay posed in. He had such a uniform tailored and used a tall young man to stand for the likeness until a print of Clay's head, taken from some old source, was imposed to complete the work. That painting now hangs in Transylvania University — once a place Clay called "home" as a law professor.

Returning to Adams' letter to his mother, he reminded her that he was under "orders" from President Madison to go to London as a part of a mission to negotiate a treaty of commerce, and that he now intended to request Louisa Catherine to join him from her long stay in St. Petersburg, Russia. He also requested that his mother send out his two sons, George and John, to London. In addition, he told her that the peace they had concluded

> is for our government, our country and the world to judge. It is not such as under more propitious circumstances might have been expected, and to be fairly estimated must be compared not with our desires, but with what the situation of the parties and of the world at and during the negotiation made attainable. We have abandoned no essential rights, and if we have left everything open for future controversy, we have at least secured to our country the power at her own option to extinguish the war.[36]

And finally, to his *Memoirs*, Adams confided,

> I cannot close the record of this day without an humble offering of gratitude to God for the conclusion to which it has pleased him to bring the negotiation for peace at this place, and a fervent prayer that its result may be propitious to the welfare, the best interests, and the union of my country.[37]

36

POST-WAR CONTENTIONS

Like so many times in life, in all ages, when it seems that certain special events would produce a feeling of euphoria and exhilaration, there, too, are occasions when the opposite may pervade the scene. So it was within the immediate circle of the American envoys who had just completed nearly five months of exasperating verbal conflict with irritating enemy negotiators to bring an end to a troubling and unhappy war. Now that was all in the past, and all should be celebrating the release of tension with a vision of peace and tranquility for the future.

But emotions within this little group of American diplomats were strung tight as a watch band. And Henry Clay was the catalyst for most of the ensuing arguments. He now vigorously questioned the control of the mission's voluminous collection of official papers.

In the confusing weeks following the signing of the Treaty of Ghent, Henry Clay and three of his colleagues were now required to fulfill the remainder of their diplomatic instructions. They had been ordered to negotiate a treaty of commerce with their recent adversaries. They were to remain in Europe for this work, in fact, go to London, the hotbed of hostility to Americans. John Quincy Adams was to become the new American minister to the Court of St. James, the diplomatic headquarters of their most recent enemy. Albert Gallatin was to join Clay in the next negotiation project between the two antagonists now at peace. Jonathan Russell was to travel to Stockholm, where he would present his credentials as the American minister to Sweden. And a very ill James Bayard was to go home and die.

But these affairs were not to transpire immediately. And in these coming weeks there were odd happenings, including two major historic battles, both seemingly arising out of a time when peace had been restored. (However, one of these famous battles was not to be fought until many weeks into the Americans' next diplomatic assignment.) Also waiting to become a fact was the ratification of the peace treaty by both contending nations.

Among the "odd happenings" were Clay's own comments in letters on consecutive days. On Christmas day, Clay wrote a letter to Secretary of State James Monroe rendering his thoughts on how the treaty might be received at home. He summed it up by stating that,

> The terms of this instrument are undoubtedly not such as our Country expected at the commencement of the War. Judged of however by the actual condition of things, so far as it is known to us, they cannot be pronounced very unfavorable. We lose no territory, I think no honor. If we lose a particular liberty in the Fisheries, on the one hand, (which may be doubted) we gain, on the other, the exemption of the Navigation of the Mississippi from British claims. We gain also the right of exemption from the British practice of trading with the Indians. Judged of by another standard, the pretensions of the enemy at the opening of the negotiation, the condition of the peace certainly reflect no dishonor on us.

But additionally, Clay made the odd assertion that he hoped to leave Europe on the first of April, and mentioned that he was returned to Congress and expected an "Extra Session" in the spring, to deal with the state of peace, and expected to be back in Washington by May 20.[1] However, this didn't seem to provide any time to negotiate a treaty of commerce, as his original instructions called for, especially since he said he expected to spend the next three months seeing Paris and London. Yet a letter signed on December 28 by all five Americans shows that Clay knew full well that he would be spending time in Europe during the next many weeks negotiating a commerce treaty.

This private letter from Clay to Monroe was to go along with two other brief letters between them in which Clay recommended the mission's secretary, Christopher Hughes, and Clay's own aide, Henry Carroll, for future diplomatic posts.[2] Though not found, it is certain that the other envoys also sent similar letters back to Washington. Among these was probably notice of William Shaler, whose name is found with Stephen Decatur's on documents in 1815 settling disputes with the Dey of Algiers over demands for tribute from American commercial vessels sailing along the North African coast.

One other piece of correspondence appears in the papers of the U.S. envoys. On December 28, they passed a note to the British that they had been vested with the "full powers" to negotiate a treaty of commerce. But so like their previous responses to new information from the Americans, they could only reply that their powers had expired and "they are unable to return an answer," but they would transmit the Americans' note to their government.[3]

Now it was these pieces of papers accumulating in the possessions of the Americans that were to cause a very nasty colloquy within the mission. Gallatin presented the group with a "minute" to "determine the disposition of the books, maps, and other papers," but suggested that the papers be packed for the use of the new London mission. Clay countered that they "ought to be sent by the *Neptune* to the Department of State." Then Adams, writing of the episode in his *Memoirs*, noted that

> there came the question about the papers. Mr. Clay was very earnest to have them with him in the *Neptune*, because he had no copies of them at all, and he thought they ought to be deposited in the Department of State, where he could have access to them hereafter.[4]

It was all quite confusing since the *Neptune* was not expected to sail to America for several weeks, and the papers most likely would be of use to the London mission.

Adams responded to Clay's suggestion that with a former mission and precedent, he (Adams) felt the custody would "devolve upon me ... and I should take charge of them accordingly." With that, Adams wrote,

> Mr. Clay immediately kindled into a flame, and said that he should, both physically and morally, revolt at any such pretension, that because I happened accidentally to be in possession of the papers I should assert a right to keep them.

Adams continued to write in his *Memoirs* that it was not because he possessed them and that he would be willing to surrender them at any time, but still considered himself entitled to keep them and got Gallatin to say he was of the same opinion. There was a brief discussion about the disposition of papers of previous missions.

But Clay again contended that "he did not pay any regard to the precedent of the former mission, and he knew nothing about the usage." Thereupon, Russell called for a vote, but Adams argued that he did not consider it

> as a point to be decided by a vote. Mr. Clay seemed to consider this as arrogating a superiority over the other members of the mission, as a claim of prerogative, at which he was excessively indignant and again charged that Adams being named first was merely accidental. As nothing was about to be resolved, Gallatin proposed that the subject be left for a further discussion. It lay untouched until Friday, the 30th.[5]

Meanwhile, on the 28th, they hosted a dinner of 22 that included the British envoys and much of the elite of the city and even the Commander-in-Chief of the Hanoverian troops of the city and the Commander-in-Chief of the English troops. There was much music including "Hail Columbia" and "His Britannic Majesty." Adams toasted the intendant as "The Sovereign Prince of the Netherlands," where Ghent lay, not then in Belgium. In return, he gave "The Congress of Ghent."[6] And it seemed "A good time was had by all."

The argument over the papers resumed on the 30th and became even more heated. This time Clay said he had no copies of the papers and "did not like the trouble of copying," and again mentioned that they should be put on the *Neptune* where he could have access to them. Adams was somewhat vague as to the papers in his possession, and they discussed the future disposal of different papers originating from different sources — from the British envoys, State Department instructions, etc. Gallatin again asserted that it would be ridiculous to return to the Department of State papers that originated there. (Though this, of course, was certainly an important depository for history to have available.) When Bayard asked Gallatin what had happened to the papers of the previous mission, Gallatin said he had them and that they were in his trunks aboard the *Neptune*.

As the discussion continued, Adams asked Clay if he (Adams) had an equal right to the papers as did Clay. "He admitted he did." Then Adams said, "I would deliver up the papers to any person named to me in writing by a majority of the mission and authorized to give me a receipt for them; the papers which I should deliver being specified." That settled the matter for this day, but it was to be dragged out for nearly a week more, as Clay prepared a letter to conform to Adams' request.[7]

A note drawn up by Clay on the 30th only rankled Adams further. Very formally, Clay wrote,

> According to the resolution which was adopted by a majority of the Board of American Commissioners, this day assembled at their Hotel, we request you to have packed up all books, maps, and other articles which have been purchased, at the public expense, for the use of the mission; as also all the original notes, papers, and communications which have been received by the American Commissioners from the British Government, from the British Plenipotentiaries, and from other persons; and cause the said books, maps, and other articles, and notes papers and communications to be transmitted to the Neptune, at the public expense, to be carried to America and deposited with the Department of State.

It was signed by Bayard, Clay and Russell, certainly a majority of the mission, but only with those three in the meeting. It was handed to Adams the next day by Clay. Happy New Year![8]

On January 2, 1815, Adams responded, again in a very formal letter, noting what he thought was the sense of what the request for disposing of the materials entailed. He wrote,

> I expressed my willingness to deliver all the papers in my possession, which should be *specified* to me by a majority of the Mission, to any person *to be named by them* with authority to give me a receipt for them, and on receiving from him such receipt. I conceived this to be indispensable to my own justification for putting the papers permanently out of my hands.

He went on to state that his motive for specified papers was that some from the State Department should not be sent back there and for the motive for identification for the person to receive the papers was to make sure that it would be "a person perfectly confidential."

Continuing, Adams was particularly annoyed that the note was signed by three members of the mission when he believed that it should have been considered by all five, thus giving him a chance to make any exceptions.

> You will perceive, Gentlemen, that I cannot consider the paper signed by you, and presented by Mr. Clay, as the act of a Majority of the Mission; since it was signed without consultation with the whole mission upon its content; although all the members of the mission were here, and might have been consulted — I deem this circumstance so important in point of principle, that I have thought it my duty to answer your Letter in writing.

He suggested a later meeting.[9]

The final collision in this affair was to take place at two o'clock, on January 6, in Gallatin's new chambers at the hotel where they had removed from their lodgings through the course of the negotiations with the British. The meeting was a hurried matter since all were busy packing to leave Ghent on the morrow for a variety of destinations. Adams reviewed his thoughts as stated in his letter.

When Adams said he expected that he would have had an opportunity to make objections to Clay's draft,

> Mr. Clay said that a majority of the mission had expressed their opinions at the meeting; and Mr. Bayard said I had refused to put it to the vote, and had said that I knew very well what the vote would be. I immediately denied ever having said so. I admitted that at the previous meeting I had declined putting it to vote.

Adams went on to tell them that he had changed his opinion somewhat from their first confrontation on the subject but added that he did not know how any vote would go, especially Bayard's opinion. Both Bayard and Gallatin thought they had papers from the mission to St. Petersburg in their trunks aboard the *Neptune*. For the moment, Clay "was now set at his ease," Adams wrote.[10]

Then Clay re-stirred the pot, by telling of Lord Gambier's views on handling state papers. Gallatin said that Gambier "might not know much about it" and Bayard "said he considered his authority as nothing or next to nothing." Still persisting on getting an answer, Clay wanted to know if Adams had come to a final conclusion on the disposition of the papers. He suggested it might be proper to send to Monroe copies of the letters between the mission members. Adams said, "Certainly," but that he had not decided what to do with the papers, that the time was not yet appropriate for such a decision, since they might still be needed in their next mission.[11]

Now it becomes best to tell the rest of the story in Adams' own words as written in his *Memoirs*.

> Mr. Clay said there was the principle and the modus. As to any right of mine to keep the papers, he could not reason about it. He could not think or speak of it with patience. There was nothing in the nature of our Government, nothing in the nature of the mission, that gave any color to it. If it had been asked as a matter of courtesy, he was willing to show all suitable respect to the first-named member of the mission. But a privilege! a prerogative! he could never acknowledge or submit to it; that as to specifying the papers, that could not have been done by him, because they were in my possession; that there was no necessity for naming the person to whom I should deliver them. I might take them on with me to Paris, and give them to any other member of the mission who would return by the Neptune, or I might send them by Mr. Smith, who would probably go to the Neptune from hence. He was desirous of parting in friendship with everybody; we had here transacted our business together, he hoped to the satisfaction of our country, and he did not wish to go away with any heartburnings between any of us.
>
> All this was said in an acrimonious and menacing tone. I said it was not improbable I should return to the United States in the Neptune myself.

Adams then wrote that he would deliver the papers to anyone authorized by a majority of the mission, but

> the paper I had received was not an act of the majority, it was the act of three members. "And although," said Mr. Clay, "those three members form a majority."
>
> "Certainly," said I; "an act of the greater number without consulting the other members is not an act of the majority."
>
> Clay now lost all the remnant of his temper, and broke out with "You *dare* not, you *cannot*, you

SHALL not insinuate that there has been a cabal of three members against you; no person shall impute anything of the kind to me with impunity." Clay then mentioned other examples of papers signed by fewer than all members of a mission, and added, "As it was addressed to you, and known to be against your opinion, it was not necessary to consult you."

> I replied, "What I *dare* say, I have dared to say in writing. Gentlemen may draw from it what inferences they please; I am not answerable for them. I am perfectly satisfied that your letter and my answer should be transmitted to our Government, and I assure you that if you do not transmit them, I shall."

Then Adams added,

> On my reply to the dare not and cannot and shall not, Mr. Clay cooled down, and said that if I had not come to a final determination, he should wish that our letters might not be transmitted to the Government, that if I should go home in the Neptune, there need be no further question upon the subject; that it would cast some dishonor on us all to say anything to the Government about it; that it would look as if we had fallen to a scramble after a few books and papers."
>
> I said that if such was his desire, I was perfectly willing that the Government should not be informed there had been any such question among us, and to say no more about it.[12]

With Clay's quick temper, it was as close as he might have come to call for his second duel. Indeed, he was to fight a second duel several years later, with U.S. Senator John Randolph, when serving in Adams' presidential cabinet.

As a sidebar to this angry exchange of views, it is interesting to know what was to happen 10 years hence (not otherwise to be told in this account of Clay's early career). In 1824, the presidential election was to pit Henry Clay, John Quincy Adams, William Crawford, and Andrew Jackson (who, within days of this Ghent controversy, was to become a national hero for a wasted battle). But in that 1824 election, Jackson won the greatest popular vote as well as the most electoral votes. Adams was second, and Crawford was third. Clay finished fourth. But when none received a majority, the 12th Amendment of the Constitution (not altogether logically) prescribed that in this circumstance, the House of Representatives would choose from the top three candidates, thus disqualifying Clay, then again Speaker, and therefore presiding officer of the body making the final choice for president. Each state had a single vote.

In the election that ensued, one might wonder after the exchange at Ghent, how Clay might react with the power of great influence over the election. He never hesitated. He used that influence, and his personal Kentucky vote, to elect Adams to the White House, despite Jackson's new prestige and collection of votes. The net result of Adams' election to the presidency was that "Old man eloquent" — as Adams was later to be remembered — selected Clay to be his secretary of state (an office that had become the virtual stepping stone to the presidency). There arose from this action a furious diatribe of accusations by the Jackson supporters that Adams and Clay had engaged in a "corrupt bargain." However, despite their Ghent differences, Adams had learned well of Clay's ability to deal with a harsh diplomatic environment. All he knew of Jackson was his distant military successes. Logic was all on the side of this appointment. This time they worked well together.

Now that peace had been restored among the peacemakers, they were preparing to disperse. Several of the aides had already departed. On Christmas day, Henry Carroll had left Ghent with Anthony St. John Baker, a recent British aide (and former aide to Augustus Foster, the British minister to the U.S. before the war), each with copies of the treaty. Their journey to the English Channel was impeded by a minor carriage accident along the way (a valid reason for the multiple copies of the document). However, they were soon in London, where the British ratification merely required the approval of the prince regent (in the absence of the old, mentally deranged King George III). On January 2, 1815, these two aides were again on the high seas aboard British sloop of war *Favorite*, enroute with the treaty copy bearing the British seal.

Meanwhile, the worthy mission secretary, Christopher Hughes, hoping to be the first to bear the news of the treaty to his country, also left Ghent on Christmas Day but went by a longer route to Bordeaux, in southwestern France. After an exhausting, uninterrupted 30 hour ride to Paris, the American minister there, William Crawford, urged him to extend his brief visit before completing his journey. Thus, he didn't arrive in Bordeaux until New Year's Day. Though he expected to board the *Transit* the following day, it was not until the 5th when he boarded and was at sea the following day.[13]

In Hughes' case, he wrote a very informative letter to his former superiors back in Ghent quoting from American newspapers to which he had access on his arrival in the French port. He told them that word from the U.S., as late as the end of October, left the nation believing that "All hopes of peace being completely destroyed in the minds of the Nation a vigorous system of preparation for a long & severe War was commenced," and he noted the efforts in Congress to fulfill such needs. Among these was notice that the government was purchasing 20 or 30 schooners to be sent out under commands of Joshua Barney (of Bladensburg honor), Oliver Hazard Perry (of Lake Erie glory), and David Porter (of multiple successes in the Atlantic).

Then Hughes referred to "The New England Convention," now known as the Hartford Convention. It had received very little notice in Ghent, but was big news back in the States. Its importance is shown in Henry Adams' mammoth history of the Madison administration. By his account in a chapter of more than 20 pages, the convention had its "birth" about October 17, 1814, when Massachusetts Governor Caleb Strong read published dispatches from Ghent as late as August 20, which noted the excessive British demands of cession of lands in present-day Maine along with the abandonment of the American rights to the fisheries.[14]

Despite the fact that the American commissioners refused to submit to these demands, Strong and his supporters wanted to blame the Madison administration and his envoys for everything wrong with the war (a political illness that has infected many American wars for the next two centuries). Strong went so far as to write a Massachusetts member of Congress that he thought the British demands "were reasonable!"

Thus, on October 17, the Massachusetts legislature invited all New England states to join in a conference for the purpose of "looking to the restoration of peace and to the establishment of a new Federal compact comprising either the whole or a portion of the actual Union." It was a virtual call for secession that was followed in greater degree by the South 46 years later — but this time with a happier ending.

As with so many controversial agitations tossed out for the public's action, there were strong viewpoints from several directions which tamed the action. Even within the crowd that pushed the project, there were "leaders" who hesitated and wanted slower action. One of these was a George Cabot, who was chosen as the head of the state's delegation. He even went so far as to utter an often thought expression by those who do not like the trend of agitators, "Why can't you and I let the world ruin itself its own way?" Later, in reply to a young friend asking what he was to do at Hartford, Cabot said, "We are going to keep you young hot-heads from getting into mischief."[15] There was even a call for delaying any decision until the following June. The net result of these differences slowed the convention process, held mostly in secret, until late December, when a committee's recommendations noted that "A severance of the Union by one or more States against the will of the rest, and especially in time of war, can be justified only by absolute necessity."[16]

The convention's document finalized on January 5 proposed measures to the general government which more specifically called for surrendering "a reasonable portion of the taxes collected within said States," and for the empowerment of these states to assume their own military defense. But it also carried a suggestion that if the U.S. Government declined the "arrangement," a new convention should be called to meet in Boston on June 15. The convention's final report still had to clear the various state legislatures, which were now only Connecticut, Massachusetts and Rhode Island.[17] While the legislators did not give their approval to the final report until late January, it was early February when messengers were not appointed and started to Washington.

Now with a sense of urgency diluted, the messengers, carrying the convention's official report to Washington, believed in their hearts that their threat, along with an expected British capture of New Orleans, would topple the Madison administration.

But all of this was unknown to the American envoys anxious to leave Ghent and enjoy a time to relax, visit Paris, London — and Geneva — before

further work. Henry Clay and James Bayard left early on January 7, and may have arrived in Paris late on January 8. From this date until late in March, there are scraps of information in their papers revealing how they used their time. Jonathan Russell also spent some time in Paris, and was still there in late March. Albert Gallatin, with his son, James, left Ghent on January 12, and probably made a brief visit to Paris, but the two of them were anxious to go on to visit the father's old home and birthplace in Switzerland where he still had many old friends. They arrived in Geneva on January 20 and spent a month visiting family and a very old friend and famous lady of letters, Madame de Staël. One other little tidbit from James' diary was their visit to a home in Ferney, the home of Voltaire, whom James' father met as a child, and now James was delighted to have the opportunity to sit in Voltaire's favorite chair.

Meanwhile, Adams remained in Ghent for a couple of weeks. Shortly after the signing of the treaty, he had written Louisa Catherine, still in St. Petersburg, urging her to make preparations for leaving that city to join him in Paris. He advised her in taking leave of any official personages and their mutual friends in the Russian capital, and to note that she was only taking a leave of absence, since her husband had not yet been recalled as the U.S. minister to the Czar. Adams' wife finally left St. Petersburg on February 12.

During these waiting days in Ghent, Adams related a practice that still endures to this day. When the envoys quit their lodging at the Hotel Lovendeghem, their ex-landlords gathered up anything they could find relating to their recent "exalted" guests, including furniture, to sell at public auction. As Adams put it in his letter to his wife,

> The good people of the place consider the Congress of Ghent as an epoch of so much importance in the history of their city, that they have given extravagant prices for some of our relics. I am told that an old inkstand, which was used at the conference, was sold for thirty francs, though it was not worth as many sous. The worst part of the joke was that they put off quantities of bad wine, as if it had been ours. We did not leave a bottle for sale.[18]

Well, maybe the townspeople were right in their estimate of the conference's importance to the

city's history. Other than the peace treaty ema-
nating from their town, it has obtained no other
historic glory despite major 20th century battles
being fought in this region.

Adams left Ghent on the morning of January
26, and again wrote his wife the next day from
Brussels, Belgium. It was a letter of self-introspec-
tion, writing colorfully about his "inertness" causing him to stay in one place too long. He referred
to the fact that in his stay in St. Petersburg, he
hardly left the city, nor did he stray from Ghent,
and now was nearly a month longer there than
were his companions. He wrote also of his dis-
taste for Sweden on his second visit there en route
from Russia (the first being more than 30 years
earlier). His latest objection was derived from
Sweden's current leaning toward Great Britain for
their support in claiming control over Norway.[19]

When Adams finally reached Paris on February
4, to join his Ghent associates, he wrote his
mother, on February 21, in the same nostalgic
tone. This time he wrote of visiting old haunts of
his 1785 tour of the city and finding fine old familiar buildings now in disrepair, maybe an unusual circumstance 200 years ago when change
was slow, unlike the rapid transformations so
many years later. In this letter, he also began describing his social life in that colorful city, and it
would continue throughout his stay in Paris. Already, he had been introduced to King Louis
XVIII by U.S. Minister William Crawford (Adams'
old friend of Senatorial days). The social whirl
also included visits with the Marquis de La Fayette, the great explorer Alexander Humboldt, and

Dupont de Nemours (scientist and ancestor of the
great American chemical firm), and even Madame
de Staël (recently arrived from her visits with the
Gallatins in Switzerland). But most of Adams'
writings in his *Memoirs* for the next month were
heavy with accounts of evening visits at the opera
and theater. He practically made himself a silent
and amusing critic of the performances.[20] One
disappointing feature of his sojourn to Paris was
the troubling health of both Crawford and Bayard. From Bayard's papers we have a note of February 28, that he was quite anxious to return to
America (though it was soon learned that President Madison wanted Bayard to replace Adams
as minister to Russia).

Then, beginning with the first of March the
news suddenly exploded upon the senses, as best
it could in the days long before the means of modern communications, arriving by word of mouth,
many-days-old letters, and week-old newspapers.
On March 1, the Gallatins arrived from their Swiss
sojourn. On March 7, Adams wrote that he had
been informed by Gallatin that Napoleon had escaped from Elba and had landed at Cannes, in
southern France, "with 1,200 men and four cannon." Still, at that evening's theater, the audience
shouted out "Vive le Roi."

On March 11, Adams wrote in his *Memoirs* that
a Mr. Erving had brought him the glorious news
that, "The British had been totally defeated before
New Orleans, and forced to re-embark, with the
loss of their General Pakenham, and he says the
game is up with these people."[21] What had happened?

37

BATTLE FOR NEW ORLEANS[1]

Strangely, this event, a victorious but futile one-day battle, is remembered in history with more interest than the five-month diplomatic struggle that ended the war of 1812. Much of the story of the battle and the preceding activity is described in Benson Lossing's wonderfully detailed *Pictorial Field-Book of the War of 1812*, published during the Civil War. A significant account from the British viewpoint is told by that British subaltern, George Gleig. We last heard from him as he and his fellow soldiers left Baltimore in defeat in September 1814. And we have more information derived from Andrew Jackson's *Correspondence*, as well as more details from Henry Adams' monumental *History of the Madison Administration*.

Though this is principally a biography of Henry Clay, much of the next part of this study is about Andrew Jackson and his part in this phase of the War of 1812. The relationship between these two giants of the early 19th century is also paramount to understanding the quarter of century that followed after Clay's return home from Ghent and his ensuing political battles with "The Hero," Clay's term for his antagonist. They were to run against each other for the presidency two times — in 1824 and 1832.

As Gleig and his fellows plundered the shores of Chesapeake Bay until late October, the irascible Andrew Jackson, recently commissioned a major general in the regular army, was making preparations to defend the Gulf coast of the United States. When we last encountered "Old Hickory" in the summer of 1814, he was well recovered from wounds received from the Benton brothers in their "street brawl" inside a Nashville hotel corridor, and his later clashes with the Creeks at Fort Mims and the Red Sticks at Horse-shoe Bend in Alabama. In his history, Henry Adams related numerous episodes in the late months of 1813 and early 1814 wherein Jackson's militia, on short-term enlistments, were often reluctant to fight. But when they did, the stories repeatedly noted there were few American casualties while they wiped out large camps and villages of Creek Indians of all ages and sexes, almost in the mode of genocide. Adams gave one telling account of Jackson's treatment of obstreperous militia who fostered mutiny. Early in 1814, a private refused to obey an officer and threatened to shoot any man who arrested him. Jackson immediately called a court-martial, tried and sentenced the man, and he was shot as an example.[2]

By July 1814, most of the Alabama Creeks had been subdued, with many of their hostile survivors (the Red-sticks) fleeing to Spanish Pensacola, Florida, rapidly falling under the domination of their British "guests." Under the subsequent Indian treaty, the pro–American Creeks surrendered most of their lands, which consisted of nearly one half of the present state of Alabama.

Now with command of the 7th Military District, Jackson moved south to his new headquarters based in the tiny village of Mobile, Alabama, almost at the same time that the British army under General Ross was attacking Washington City. In an order from London in late July 1814, which Ross may never have received, he was told, when his operations in the Chesapeake were completed, to sail with "his whole force to Jamaica, where he would join an expedition then preparing in England to rendezvous at Cape Negril on the west coast of Jamaica about November 20."[3]

Jackson reached Mobile at the end of August

and learned more about the duplicity between the Spanish authorities and the British in Pensacola. Though it was Spanish territory, the British enemies of America were running things.

During these early fall days, Lt. Col. Edward Nichols, the British commander in Pensacola, was making every effort possible to gather forces which he hoped to use in his future conquests. He sent out messages appealing for allies among southern Indians, disenchanted residents of the region who had earlier held allegiance to France or Spain, to slaves, and even pirates based in the Louisiana bayou country. This latter was a big mistake. Nichols sent a letter to a French pirate who now claimed a loyalty to the United States — Jean Lafitte — who in turn passed the message to Louisiana Governor William C.C. Claiborne, though the governor had plotted to wipe out the pirates' stronghold in Barataria near the estuary of the Mississippi. Nevertheless, Claiborne sent a copy to Jackson. In these letters, Nichols had revealed the future British design on New Orleans. Claiborne and Jackson were becoming steady correspondents. But among their early letters, several times Jackson supported Claiborne's decision to have little to do with the pirates.

Meanwhile, by mid–September, Jackson, expecting an attack on Mobile, put a small detachment of 130 men into Fort Bowyer, now Fort Morgan, at the mouth of Mobile Bay, to thwart the British who came on with four ships, more than 1,300 men, and nearly 100 pieces of artillery. During the four-day engagement, four Americans were killed and four more wounded. The British lost 162 killed and one of their ships. In the interim, Jackson's appeal to Tennessee brought forth about 2,000 men to fight for "Old Hickory." The British seemed to have no idea that these forces were lining up against them, and still believed their own plans were a complete mystery to the Americans.[4]

In some respects the British were accurate, in that Jackson did not put New Orleans at the top of his priorities. He saw Pensacola as the place where mischief was being cultivated, and in mid–October he made an assault on Pensacola, without authorization from Washington. In fact, Jackson was told not to attack Spanish Pensacola in an order sent too late by the new temporary secretary of war, James Monroe (taking that office after

Armstrong's disaster at Bladensburg). And Jackson knew, without word from Washington, that he was off on his own when he wrote to Monroe on October 26, "As I act without the orders of the government, I deem it important to state to you my reasons for the measure I am about to adopt." He then cited his reasons and added,

> I feel a confidence that I shall stand justified to my government for having undertaken the expedition. Should I not I shall have the consolation of having done the only thing in my own opinion which could give security to the country by putting down a savage war, And what to me will be an ample reward for the loss of my commission.[5]

The attack began after November 2, when Jackson sent a brusque letter to the Spanish governor of Pensacola, Gonzalez Manrique, by an escorted messenger, who was fired upon from the fort. The mission returned to Jackson who sent a new letter the next day, followed by an exchange of several more surly letters by both leaders. Jackson occupied the town on November 7, and the British blew up a fort as they departed for Appalachicola the next morning. The action resolved very little, but did run the British away — temporarily.

Of course, Jackson was softly admonished for his indiscretion by the president and secretary of state. Even Armstrong, who usually supported Jackson, and was often at odds with Madison and Monroe, gave Jackson the back of his hand when he wrote,

> The general's attack and capture of the town on the 7th of November, 1814, was to say the least of it decidedly ill-judged, involving at once an offence to a neutral power, and probable misapplication of both time and force as regarded the defence of New Orleans.[6]

Nevertheless, Jackson remained in command over the American forces along the Gulf coast, and was soon convinced that he was needed in New Orleans. As he left Mobile on November 22, along a route which a century and a half later would be an afternoon drive on Interstate 10, his march was almost simultaneous with the adventures of Gleig and his comrades in the British fleet recently arrived from the Chesapeake. They had departed in a fleet of 70 or so sailing ships. Their next port was Jamaica, where in late November, another fleet from Europe was to join them.

In an interesting note about their stay in Jamaica, Gleig mentions that news of their rumored destination (New Orleans) was spread far and wide. When the local commanding admiral died, his successor, a captain, allowed "a Jew merchant" to read his official dispatch, who in turn was paid for passing on the information to American authorities. Yet it was pretty well known, as early as Gallatin's July visit to London, that New Orleans was a target. Another odd comment by Gleig was that after they left Jamaica with only 50 sail, and sailed up along the Gulf coast, it was cold and there was sleet in late November.[7] It coincided with Jackson's comments, in a letter to Monroe, that his journey to the Crescent City was under 10 days of "incessant" rain.

In Jackson's venture, on arrival just north of New Orleans, he was entertained on December 1 at the home of a wealthy bachelor, whose Creole hostess was used to Napoleon's decorated generals. She was to describe her guest of honor as

a tall, gaunt man, very erect, ... with a countenance furrowed by care and anxiety. His dress was simple and nearly threadbare. A small leather cap protected his head, and a short Spanish cloak his body, whilst his ... high dragoon boots [were] long innocent of polish or blacking.... His complexion was sallow and unhealthy; his hair iron grey, and his body thin and emaciated like that of one who had just recovered from a lingering sickness,

all of which may have been quite true. "But a fierce glare ... [lighted] his bright hawk-like eye." But then she told the bachelor, "You asked me to receive a great General. I make your house combe il faut, and prepare a splendid déjeuner, ... all for ... an ugly old Kaintuck flat-boatman."[8] But what New Orleans needed was a fighter, not a glamour boy.

Jackson entered the city the next day, finding it essentially defenseless. The legislature was deeply divided with no union, harmony nor confidence. "The people, alarmed and distrustful, complained of the Legislature; that body, in turn, complained of the governor; and Claiborne complained of both the Legislature and the people." Both finances and armaments were scarce. The militia was small, but the storehouses were filled with valuable merchandise, causing the merchants to prefer surrender than loss of their property.[9]

It seemed there were no forces available to Jackson to thwart any enemy attack. However, fortunately for Jackson, but unknown to the British, there were a variety of small groups of men willing to fight — but they were not visible as a fighting force to any British spies. They were approaching New Orleans in groups of 50 men to as many as 4,000 from as far away as Kentucky and Tennessee and Georgia. Most were the often-scorned militia.

For the next few days, Jackson and aides explored the region to mark out places of defense including a study of the possible enemy approaches by way of the Mississippi River. It was along these lines that the general posted a battery of artillery here and another there. On December 9, he learned that the British fleet had been spotted approaching south of Gulfport and Biloxi, Mississippi, headed towards Lakes Borgne and Pontchartrain. Though believing this a feint with the real attack to come elsewhere, Jackson's naval aide, at this time, Daniel T. Patterson, arranged a set of gunboats on Lake Borgne to block the British advance. Here we have the account of British Lieutenant (or subaltern) Gleig.[10]

Gleig wrote of sailing from Negril Bay, on the western shores of Jamaica, on November 26 and arriving off Mississippi on December 10 completely unaware that the Americans had any knowledge of their approach. They were soon disabused of this thinking. His account of the succeeding clash, was prefaced by an interesting description of the importance of New Orleans as the outlet of so much of American export originating in the Ohio valley and the lower Mississippi. He could not include in this sketch how much more important this port would become in later years with the gigantic growth in the Louisiana Territory (now less than 10 years after its exploration by Lewis and Clark).

Gleig's companions entered Lake Borgne late on the 13th and found the Americans lined up in five gunboats to oppose the British. However, the British placed 1,200 men on more than 50 armed barges and advanced on the tiny American squadron containing a total of 182 men and 23 guns. While the British won the day, they were stalled and lost about 300 men killed or wounded compared to six Americans killed and 35 wounded. The British followed by landing an army of troops on some of the swampy lands in the area. They were not going away — yet.

Meanwhile, Jackson, with the help of some prominent citizens of the city, organized a parade of his skimpy militia down the city streets to the Old Spanish Cathedral, where, on December 18, the gathered throng heard stirring speeches aimed at whipping the populace into a fighting mood. The people might have turned against Jackson, but they did not even later when he declared martial law. Instead, according to Lossing, they celebrated with American, French, Spanish national anthems (though, of course, the former was not yet the "Star Spangled Banner," just getting its verses into print and unconnected to any music).

Jackson's speech was delivered by Edward Livingston, a member of the local Committee of Safety. From an old distinguished New York family, Edward was the younger brother (by 18 years) of Robert Livingston (one of the five men who drafted the Declaration of Independence, who swore in Washington as the first president, and later helped Robert Fulton construct the first steamboat — named Clermont for the Livingston family estate). Edward had served with Jackson in early Congresses, was mayor of New York, moved to Louisiana where he authored the state's legal code, became Jackson's military aide, supported him for president, and finally succeeded Henry Clay as secretary of state when Jackson succeeded John Quincy Adams as president.[11]

For the next few days, following the rousing reception for the general, Jackson waited for word from his outposts of any British landing. And he was gratified by the arrival of several assorted American military units of a few hundred men upward to 1,800 Tennesseans under Brig. Gen. John Coffee who had fought with Jackson several months earlier in the hotel brawl against the Benton brothers.

But back to Gleig and his invading companions, about December 13, a very large contingent, under heavy rains, went ashore at a place he called Pine Island, a barren place incapable of furnishing fuel for fires and no refuge from the storm, without tents or huts. When the rains ceased, Gleig noted, "a severe frost set in; which congealing our wet clothes upon our bodies, left little animal warmth to keep the limbs in a state of activity," with some of the soldiery dying in their sleep from

the frost and cold. It was no easier for the sailors of the fleet who spent four days rowing back and forth to the ships to put more men ashore by the 21st.

But the British were further deceived when so-called American deserters came into camp to inform the British that there were not 5,000 soldiers in the entire state, and that the principal inhabitants had left the city. They spoke of "Jackson as an able man; but as one so hated on account of his tyranny and violence, that not an inhabitant of the State would adhere to his standard, after they beheld the British flag fairly unfurled."[12] It still appeared to the British that it might be a bloodless conquest of rich booty flowing through this important port, outlet for so many goods coming down the Ohio and Mississippi Rivers. In addition, they assumed that many Indian tribes, relieved of their lands and forced into desperate living conditions, would now come to the support of the British.[13] There certainly was no love among them for Jackson and they would readily have supplied the British with spies, if only the British would trust them.

At 9 A.M., on December 22, subaltern Gleig, under Col. Thornton (his superior officer at Bladensburg), in turn now under Gen. Keane, began a difficult maneuver in more heavy rain by open boats, some holding more than 70 men each, transferring more than 1,500 men from Pine Island to Bays de Cataline, a distance of 80 miles. Of nearly 100 boats, most carried smaller units, but none enjoyed the cramped and exhausting passage described in detail by the rain-drenched subaltern. The move was not completed until early on the 23rd when they made their way up a narrowing bayou. The rain subsided but was followed "by a keen frost, and northerly wind as sharp and cutting as any mortal would desire to face," Gleig wrote. After a full day and night of utter misery, the British worked their way through bogs and tall reeds until they reached firmer ground and habitation around sugar-cane fields and finally the shore of the "mighty Mississippi River," some 10 miles from the tiny city.[14] Now the soldiers believed they would have several days of rest and waiting for growing support from troops still being rowed ashore from the ships.

But the word of their advance toward New Orleans reached Jackson at 106 Royal Street in the present day French Quarter. For among the sugar-cane fields on which the British camped was the plantation of Louisiana militia Major General Jacques Phillippe de Villeré. In the general's absence, his son, Major Gabriel Villeré and two friends were quietly enjoying a repast on their mansion's large veranda, when British soldiers suddenly appeared on the grounds. The three Americans were soon prisoners of war. But their incarceration didn't hold and in their escape, they rushed into the city and directly to Jackson's headquarters to alert the Americans of the arrival of the British so near at hand. Jackson had thought he had that area watched. Nevertheless, he was quick to act and declared, "By the Eternal, they shall not sleep on our soil!" At 2 P.M., he gathered his staff and told them, "Gentlemen, the British are below. We must fight them tonight. I will smash them, so help me God!"[15]

In the quiet evening of December 23, 1814, as Gleig and his British companions rested on the grounds of the sugar-cane fields, disturbing noises suddenly brought them to attention. The British had thrown out sentries forward of their position that stretched along a narrow strip of land (less than a mile wide) between the river and a grove of trees in what was called a cypress swamp. The sound that startled them was the pounding hoofs of a troop of American dragoons galloping down the levee road alongside the river. These were quickly followed by a couple hundred infantry. The American intrusion lasted only minutes and almost as quickly, the American horsemen withdrew.

Gleig wrote of the incident, "I cannot deny that it produced a curious effect upon us. Not that we experienced the smallest sensation of alarm. We held them in too much contempt to fear their attack." Though not counting on a renewed attack, any future danger they thought would be incited by themselves. Yet they became more cautious. As darkness descended they relaxed with cigars.

But a renewal of action was in store, and it was not initiated by the British. It came from the river. Gleig noted,

Instead of the deep silence which five minutes ago had prevailed in the bivouac, a strange hubbub of shouts, and questions, and as many cries, rose up the night air; nor did many minutes elapse, ere first one musket, then three or four, then a whole

platoon, were discharged ... flash, flash, flash, came from the river; the roar of cannon followed, and the light of her broadside displayed to us an enemy's vessel at anchor near the opposite bank, and pouring a perfect shower of grape and round shot into the camp.

The volleys came from the American schooner *Carolina*.[16]

In effect, the *Carolina* had signalled an American attack of mounted troops and infantry that made the surprise visit on the British camp. After a couple hours of close-order combat, Gleig's group found their line had been pushed back on the right and they realized that Americans were behind them.

Our close order was lost; and the contest became that of man to man. For myself, I did what I could, cutting and thrusting at the multitudes about me, till at last I found myself fairly hemmed in by a crowd, and my sword-arm mastered. One American had grasped me round the waist, another, seizing my wrist, attempted to disarm me, whilst a third was prevented from plunging his bayonet into my body, only by the fear of stabbing one or other of his countrymen. I struggled hard, but they fairly bore me to the ground.... I expected nothing else than instant death; but at the moment when I fell, a blow upon the head with the butt-end of a musket dashed out the brains of the man who kept his hold upon my sword-arm, and it was freed, and I intuitively made a thrust at the man who wielded it. The thrust took effect, and he dropped dead beside me.

Gleig found that the hand that saved him was that of his close subaltern companion — Charlton, a fictional name for this officer spoken of frequently by Gleig.

Meanwhile, fresh British troops arrived on the scene to permit their escape. Gleig estimated that the Americans brought about 1,500 men to the field against a mere 100 British before support arrived. About one in the morning, there was a renewed American attack ending in an entirely different fashion. The British gave way as this small American unit attacked, and was soon surrounded and became British prisoners — which, Gleig noted, "consisted entirely of members of the legal profession. The barristers, attorneys, and notaries of New Orleans having formed themselves into a volunteer corps.... It is probably needless to add," Gleig continues, that the circumstance was productive of no trifling degree of mirth amongst us; and to do them justice, the poor lawyers, as soon as they recovered from their first alarm, joined heartily in our laughter.[17]

Not long afterward, a fog covered the field bringing a halt to the battle with both armies holding their original positions. Though it may have been considered a draw, the Americans lost 24 men killed, 15 wounded, and 74 were taken prisoner. By contrast, the British lost 46 men killed, 167 wounded, and 64 taken prisoners. Jackson reported that "I expect the enemy is pretty sore today."[18] The next day, the 24th, was quiet around New Orleans, but celebration took place across the ocean in Ghent as the Treaty of Peace was signed.

Meanwhile, Jackson was busy organizing his battle line with young men from some of the best families of the city. Hoping for glory and renown on the battlefield, they were given spades and axes and put to work raising the wall of the Rodriguez Canal by as much as three more feet. Instead of wounds these natives of New Orleans came away with blistered hands. Their civilian parents in New Orleans mistrusted Jackson and rumors circulated that in defeat, he would allow their city to suffer the fate of Moscow under Napoleon.

As the digging continued along the American lines, a new and unexpected "guest," named Jean Lafitte, began to make his mark. This "retired pirate" had learned the art of entrenching from Napoleon's engineers. He now called for an extension of the American battle line into the cypress grove saying it could be penetrated by men on foot.[19] Though hated among the citizens of the city, Lafitte had managed to reason with Jackson that he could bring guns and powder, along with men, to lend added support in the coming clash against the British.

On the British side, the sullen mood of disappointment in their effort on the 23rd, and their melancholy duty of burying their dead on the 24th, were washed away on Christmas Day with the arrival of Lt. Gen. Sir Edward Pakenham, the 37-(or 38)-year-old "Hero of Salamanca" in Spain. This well-liked brother-in-law of the Duke of Wellington (married to Pakenham's sister) quickly reorganized the British force now under his command and revived the spirit of his troops.

On the 26th, both armies tried to enhance their positions and add to their numbers in men and guns. At dawn on the 27th, the British began a bombardment on the American lines as well as against the *Carolina* across the river. It didn't take long before the ship was in great danger and the crew abandoned her only moments before a British shell caused the vessel to die in a mammoth explosion, leaving only the *Louisiana* protecting the Americans' right flank. Immediately that crew, in small boats, set to work pulling the warship up the river toward the city and safely away from the British shelling. The day continued with sporadic shelling by both armies.

That evening Gleig and his friends hoped for a quiet rest. Instead, the Americans, standing in relays at their heavy guns and with their muskets, pattered the British camp throughout the night causing Gleig to write that "the entire night [was] spent in watching, or at best in broken and disturbed slumbers, than which nothing is more trying, both to the health and spirits of an army." He noted that at night the sentries of European armies sit within 20 yards of each other without molesting the other. Yet "The Americans entertained no such chivalric notions. An enemy was to them an enemy, whether alone, or in the midst of five thousand companions" and "to us it appeared an ungenerous return to barbarity."[20]

Through these encounters, the Americans had a distinct advantage. Most were backwoodsmen from Kentucky and Tennessee, where they were brought up using the marvelous Kentucky long rifles for engaging Indians to defend life and property and hunting animals for food and clothing. They may have been untrained militia, but they were expert sharp-shooters.

During the next several days, both contending generals ordered up naval guns and artillery pieces and occasionally used them against their opponent. What heavy guns Jackson could procure, had to come from troops as far north as Tennessee and Kentucky — still slowly en route. Pakenham had to plead with the testy Admiral Cochrane to release guns (and sailors) from his ships far off beyond Lake Borgne and transfer them through the swamps to the British lines. The British even managed to dig deeper some of the local canals and open dikes in the levees to the Mississippi to afford waterways to float barges carrying the guns to the British positions. The British got the better of one such duel by forcing the *Louisiana* to be pulled out of range to do harm to them.

On the 28th, with the *Carolina* gone and the *Louisiana* escaping up the river (temporarily), the British, now confident and optimistic under General Pakenham, moved forward about three miles before encountering the Americans, sheltered and hard to see behind that freshly raised parapet erected by the sons of New Orleans, who probably did not realize the security they bestowed on their countrymen (though it was called "contemptible" by the British). The well-protected American infantry along with their well-established artillery men were about to give the hardcore British regulars a lesson in warfare. It was an expensive class for the invaders. While the Americans lost nine killed and eight wounded, the British lost, in all, about 150 men.

In the attack that ensued, the British advanced in two columns. The left column, under a galling fire from the Americans batteries (both from the battle line and from the *Louisiana*, now back in support from the river), was quickly brought to a quick halt as they came close to panic. The right column, next to the woods and swamp, advanced and forced the Americans to fall back — momentarily. But then, to Gleig's astonishment, Pakenham, seeing the whole scene and fearing a disaster, ordered a "retrograde movement." As Gleig wrote,

> Without so much as one effort to force through them, was a British army baffled and repulsed by a horde of raw militiamen, ranged in line behind a mud-wall, which could have hardly protected them from musketry, far less from round-shot; there was not a man among us who failed to experience both shame and indignation, when he found himself retreating before a force for which he entertained the most sovereign contempt.[21]

Lossing described the British action a bit differently as they were ordered to seek shelter in the little canals.

> Away they ran, pell-mell, to those places of refuge, and in mud and water almost waist-deep ... concealing themselves in the rushes which grew on the banks of the canal. It was a humiliating position for "Wellington's veterans" in the face of a few rough backwoodsmen, as they regarded Jackson's troops.

They would meet again.

On this same day, Jackson and his men were cheered by the arrival "of a band of rough-looking armed men" on the run all the way from Fort St. John on Lake Pontchartrain. These were Lafitte's Baratarian pirates under his subordinate Dominique You. They were experienced gunners and quickly took a place behind American artillery pieces about to greet the British troops.[22]

The next few days were spent by both armies in strengthening their positions and there are few details of any action except for an account by Gleig. He noted that on the morning of the 30th he was assigned to a "piquet" about half way between the two contending forces. They spent the dark hours, as had their predecessors, without any fire against the "piercingly cold" day. But as dawn arrived, they felt safe enough to light two fires. He wrote,

> It seemed as if the American artillery-men had waited for some such object to direct their aim, for the smoke had hardly began to ascend, when there played upon us, from a battery of five guns, as perfect a storm of grape-shot as ever whistled past the ears of men so situated; and in five minutes the fires were abandoned.

There followed a skirmish, which Gleig described in some detail, lasting nearly five hours as the two sides battled each other in the growing daylight — achieving virtually nothing. The British had two men wounded but continuing into the night of the 31st, the Americans moved forward a couple heavy guns with a range to strike into the midst of the main British camp.[23]

It was now New Year's day 1815. A thick fog hung over the battle lines. The British army woke to band music. It was coming from behind the American lines. As Gleig wrote:

> Two or three tolerably full bands began to play, which continued to entertain both their own people and us till broad daylight came in. Being fond of music, — particularly of the music of a military band, I crept forward beyond the sentries, for the purpose of listening to it. The airs which they played were some of them, spiritless enough, — the Yankees are not famous for their good taste in anything; — but one or two of the waltzes struck me as being peculiarly beautiful; the tune, however, which seemed to please themselves the most, was their national air known among us by the title of "Yankee doodle"; for they repeated it at least six times in the course of their practice.

Jackson had agreed to have a formal parade and party in recognition of the day, and women were invited. The party was not to last.

Looking beyond the American lines, the British soldiers could see

a crowd of white tents [which] shewed themselves, not a few of which bore flags at the top of their poles. The American camp, in short, exhibited at least, as much pomp and circumstance of war, as modern camps are accustomed to exhibit; and the spirits of its inmates were continually in a state of exhilaration by the bands of martial music.

By contrast, Gleig continued,

The British army lay there without tents, without works, without show, without parade, upon the ground. Throughout the whole line not more than a dozen huts were erected, and these, which consisted only of pieces of plank, torn from the houses and fences near, furnished but an inefficient protection against the inclemency of the weather.... It was impossible not to be struck with the contrast which the conditions, and apparent comforts, of the invading and defending hosts presented.[24]

Suddenly, according to Gleig in his other book,

Our batteries opened, and the face of affairs was instantly changed. The ranks were broken; the different corps dispersing, fled in all directions, whilst the utmost terror and disorder appeared to prevail. Instead of nicely-dressed lines, nothing but confused crowds could now be observed; nor was it without much difficulty that order was finally restored.

But he added, "Oh, that we had charged at that instant!"[25]

They did not charge, but both sides used the entire day in an artillery duel — until the British ammunition began to run short. After all, their supplies still had to be transported 70–80 miles from their fleet lying well beyond Lake Borgne. To protect the newly placed guns, the British had built low mounds of earth and hogsheads filled with sugar, expecting them to shelter the guns as might cotton bales. Again, the British were to learn a lesson — these were not the same. Once hit, the sugar would melt away into the mud around them. The day was simply another with the exchange of artillery shots. No lines changed position. But most of the British soldiers had not slept for nearly 60 hours and their rations, like their ammunition, were running short. They finally "retired, not only baffled and disappointed,

but in some degree disheartened and discontented. All our plans had as yet proved abortive."[26]

Over the next few days, Jackson strengthened his main line along the Rodriquez Canal and established two more lines in support behind it. But Jackson was not satisfied. He wrote Secretary of War/State Monroe that arms he was expecting still had not arrived. "All we hear of them is that they are on the river, And that the man who has been intrusted with their transportation, has halted on the way for the purpose of private speculations." He followed with a statement that seems to ring true centuries later.

Depend upon it this supineness, this negligence, this *criminality*, let me call it, of which we witness so many instances in the agents of Government, must finally lead, if not corrected, to the defeat of our armies, and to the disgrace of those who superintend them.

He recognized that he had had "good fortune not to have been expected, and which furnishes no safe foundation for future hope." He further noted in his message to Monroe, that General Adair (the senator who resigned making way for 29-year-old Clay to serve an unexpired term in 1807) had arrived with his detachment of Kentuckians — with only one third bearing arms.[27] To this Jackson was heard to say, "I don't believe it. I have never seen a Kentuckian without a gun and a pack of cards and a bottle of whisky in my life."[28]

For the next early days of January 1815, both sides worked feverishly to enhance their positions. Pakenham, thwarted and probably embarrassed by his lack of progress against the raw backwoods Americans, developed a scheme he thought might work and give his army a chance to win their way into that nearby city filled with food, clothing, and much more in wealth. His army had even come to this place with people who would take over the civilian administration of the "conquered" city so near their grasp.

With the reluctant aid of Admiral Cochrane, Pakenham devised a complicated attack plan whereby the British would bring large boats from the fleet, far off beyond Lake Borgne, drag them through the swamps and then float them through the canal on the Villeré plantation, through a cut in the levee into the Mississippi, cross it, and attack a lightly held force under American General

David Morgan. (Morgan had only about 500 ill equipped and untrained militia.) Once the maneuver was completed, involving the capture of Morgan's guns, the British would fire across the Americans' right flank. Meanwhile, a frontal attack would smash Jackson's lines at the Rodriquez Canal. All of this was to be done in the darkness of the early hours of January 8. But a few things went wrong with Pakenham's plan.

To begin with, some of his navy's boats were too large for the shallow canal and when the muddy sides sank into the canal, the large boats blocked the transit of smaller one. And these had to be dragged through thick mud. The cut in the levee to permit the flow of the river to fill the canal didn't work. The flow of the river had subsided to a point where little water passed inland. While about half of the small boats reached Colonel Thornton commanding this operation, only half of his 1,500 men boarded the boats, but not until daylight had arrived and his crossing was under heavy fire from Morgan's line as well as from the *Louisiana* still hovering about.

Meanwhile, quite upset over the operations' late start, Pakenham had arranged for two columns to move forward, in darkness, when Thornton's guns would be the signal to initiate the main assault. A column on the British right, under Maj. Genl. Sir Samuel Gibbs, was to attack the area held by Jackson's long-time friend General Coffee in a strong position bordering the swamp. On the British left, Maj. Genl. John Keane was to carry his attack along the levee and into the right side of the American army.

In the days preceding the battle Jackson did all he could to prepare for the British assault. In less than a mile width for the battle field, he had more than 5,000 men — practically a man for every foot of ground. However, they were strategically arranged. A series of batteries of heavy guns behind four lines of infantrymen left no gaps for the British to penetrate. As one line of men fired their long muskets, or Kentucky rifles, the next line would move up and take their place until the fourth line was succeeded again by a return of the first line. It was a constant. Furthermore, the American infantry could lie flat on the ground behind the newly-build parapet so that only their heads — behind their guns — were exposed. And Jackson had admonished them to take careful aim

at the white cross belts over the red British tunics. In retrospect the outcome hardly need be told. It was easy to see — at least for Americans — how the venture would turn out.

And now Jackson took a brief nap. About one in the morning, he was woken by a message from his subordinates across the river announcing that the British were preparing to cross the river and that they wanted more support. Jackson informed the messenger that the main enemy attack would come in front of him. He then roused his aide telling them, "Gentlemen, we have slept enough."[29]

As Thornton's units crossed the river, they had not anticipated the river's fast flow and they landed nearly a mile below their planned debarkation point. As they began their firing, on the far side of the river, Pakenham ordered a rocket to be fired signaling the advance of the main body against Jackson's prepared positions. Not only was it now broad daylight, the heavy fog had dissipated revealing the bright red coats of the British troops marching in orderly columns to — disaster.

The advanced British units were to carry facines and ladders to help them cross the canal and climb up the sides of the parapet. That unit went up front with few supplies and had to go back for more. It really made little difference. Those tools were not to come into any significant usage. By the time any of Pakenham's brigades reached the canal they had been cut to pieces by artillery or musketry.

As Lossing described the scene:

> Steadily on marched Wellington's veterans, stepping firmly over the dead bodies of their slain comrades until they had reached a point within two hundred yards of the American lines, behind which, concealed from the view of the invaders, lay the Tennesseeans and Kentuckians four ranks deep. Suddenly the clear voice of General Carroll rang out, *Fire!* His Tennesseeans arose from cover, and, each man taking sure aim, delivered a most destructive volley on the foe, their bullets cutting down scores of the gallant British soldiery. The storm ceased not for a moment; for when the Tennesseans had fired they fell back, and the Kentuckians took their places, and so the four ranks, one after another, participated in the conflict. At the same time round, grape, and chain shot went crashing through the ranks of the British, making awful gaps, and appalling the stoutest hearts. The line began to waver, and would have broken but

for the cool courage and untiring energy of the officers.[30]

Leading the desperate challenge was none other than General Pakenham — but not for long, as his horse was shot from under him about the time the general was wounded in his bridle arm. He mounted a pony of one of his aides only to be wounded again, but continued to advance. Within moments he suffered a mortal wound. About the same time, both of his subordinate generals, Gibbs and several other leading officers received killing wounds and General Keane suffered a severe neck wound. Pakenham's last order was to Maj. Gen. John Lambert, newly arrived from the fleet with a new brigade, to throw forward the reserve. But the new commander was wise enough to see a debacle in progress, and instead called for a retreat.

It was only 8:30 in the morning when the American infantry ceased to fire, having lost an enemy that was now stumbling backward over their own dead and dying. The artillery continued to follow the decimated British until two in the afternoon.

The scene that remained on the field brought from Jackson his personal view.

> I never had so grand and awful an idea of the resurrection as ... [when] I saw ... more then five hundred Britons emerging from the heaps of their dead comrades, all over the plain rising up, and ... coming forward ... as prisoners.

When he learned that his losses were seven men killed and six wounded, he said, "The unerring hand of providence shielded my men."[31] The American army still had the unpleasant task of dealing with the maimed and slain of the British army lying on the field in front of Jackson's line. Of the British losses, Benson Lossing (writing during the American Civil War) reported 700 killed, 1,400 wounded, and 500 taken as prisoners of war.[32] All of these casualty figures were to be revised upward, not so much for the Americans, but the British losses may never be known. But they were awesome — some were well over 2,500 dead and nearly an equal number in wounded.

Nevertheless, the British disaster was not complete. While their main attack fell apart over the Rodriquez Canal, the British fortunes were rising across the river as Thornton's men launched their assault against American Brig. Genl. David B. Morgan. The results were a mixed bag of confusion. First of all, Morgan's forces were mostly ill trained and equipped militia, many Kentuckians. About a third of his forces were sent forward to meet the British under Col. Thornton (Gleig's old commander), but the British quickly thrust their way forward and, quoting Lossing: "put the Kentuckians to flight, who ran in wild confusion, and could not be rallied." The Americans quickly fled the field in some disarray. As the British advanced, they were soon notified of the disaster occurring on the east side of the river and realized they had to save themselves and urgently retreated to their boats and returned across the river to the main British camp — to join their beaten redcoat companions where their big decision was trying to decide how to leave the field with some semblance of order and honor.

When Jackson initially learned that his American forces on the opposite shore had fallen back in panic placing his right flank in jeopardy of being enfiladed from the opposite shore, he was furious. Hours later he expressed himself in typical "Jackson eloquence" on January 9, when he wrote acting Secretary of War Monroe of that engagement. Writing of the British troops,

> *These* having landed were hardly enough to advance against the works of General Morgan; and what is strange and difficult to account for, at the very moment when their entire discomfiture was looked for with a confidence approaching to certainty, the Kentucky reinforcements, ingloriously fled, drawing after them, by their example, the remainder of the forces; and thus yielding to the enemy that most fortunate position. The batteries which had rendered me, for many days, the most important service, though bravely defended, were of course now abandoned; not however, until the guns had been spiked.[33]

It is interesting to note that as quickly as his comments regarding the Kentuckians could fly overseas, they were met by a peevish Henry Clay by this time in London — to be noted later.

While this chapter is principally the story of the Battle for New Orleans, there continued to be much aftermath. For several days there were flags of truce and correspondence between the two commanding generals, Jackson and the surviving British commandeer, Maj. Genl. John Lambert, regarding the disposition of wounded and dead.

Jackson could not be sure for some time whether or not the British still had sufficient forces to renew their attempt to reach the city, until finally the invaders began to withdraw through the swamps and slowly return to their ships and make their way toward home — England. As with General Ross, after their Baltimore fiasco, and now after this fight, more British generals went home in vats of wine.

Subaltern Gleig was badly wounded in the battle and was unconscious for a while after trying to scale the American parapet during the January 8 British debacle. He was carried away by companions and was on his way back to England before he was able to resume his writing. It was mid January before the crippled British army returned to their ships. As they headed home they learned that peace had been restored.

38

LAST DAYS IN EUROPE

Hard upon this astonishing news of the American victory at this unnecessary battle for New Orleans, as it reached the Ghent commissioners in Paris early in March, daily reports of Napoleon's escape from Elba and his rapid advance toward the French capital soon competed with word of the ratification of the peace treaty by the United States Senate on February 17. This latter news was to stir Henry Clay from his respite into action.

Again, much of the story of these events, particularly in Paris, comes from the *Memoirs* and *Writings* of John Quincy Adams, and a little from Clay, Gallatin's son, James, and even a few letters from Jonathan Russell.

It was on March 1, 1815, that the Gallatins arrived in Paris from their sojourn in Switzerland. It was noted earlier that while they were in the senior Gallatin's old homeland, they had met the celebrated Madame de Staël. Now in Clay's early days in Paris, it was his time to meet this well-traveled lady. At a party given by an American banker to celebrate the peace between the United States and Great Britain Clay was introduced to her and they had a long and animated conversation.

"Ah!" said she, "Mr. Clay, I have been in England, and have been battling your cause for you there." — "I know it, madame; we heard of your powerful interposition, and we are grateful and thankful for it." — "They were very much against you," said she: "so much so, that they at one time thought seriously of sending the duke of Wellington to command their armies against you!" — "I am very sorry, madame," replied Mr. Clay, "that they did not send his grace." — "Why?" asked she, surprised, — "Because, madame, if he had beaten us, we should have been in the condition of Eu-

rope, without disgrace. But, if we had been so fortunate as to defeat him, we should have greatly added to the renown of our arms."

The next time he met Madame de Staël was at a party at her own house, which was attended by the marshals of France, the duke of Wellington, and other distinguished persons. She introduced Mr. Clay to the duke, and at the same time related the above anecdote. He replied with promptness and politeness, that if he had been sent on that service, and had been so fortunate as to have been successful over a foe so gallant as the Americans, he would have regarded it as the proudest feather in his cap."[1]

Clay was not known for attending many parties. Yet much was about to happen in his world. It was on the 7th when the flood of astonishing news began. Adams wrote in his *Memoirs* that he had gone to visit his old colleague, James Bayard, and "found him very ill, with a severe cough and some fever, his throat is much ulcerated." He followed with a note that while on his visit, Clay, Gallatin, and others arrived. But that it was Bayard who "first mentioned to me that Bonaparte was in France," and continued by writing that "The proclamation of the King, declaring him a rebel and traitor, is in the Moniteur of this morning." Nevertheless, Adams continued his near nightly visit to a theater where he heard the crowds shouting "Vive le Roi" as if nothing or no one were afoot.[2]

Within the ensuing week, Adams continued his visits to the theater but also wandered the Paris streets near the Tuileries trying to grasp the accuracy of all the rumors he heard of the advance of the former emperor and the moves of the current French government to counter the "rebel's" march toward the capital. The crowds continued to shout out their support for their king and many young men indicated their willingness to march against Napoleon. During another of Adams' visits with an old friend (a Mr. Erving) on March 11 he was informed that "the British had been totally defeated before New Orleans, and forced to re-embark, with the loss of their General, Pakenham, and he says the game is up with these people." Meaning the British?[3]

By Wednesday, the 15th, Adams reported that the theater was

> almost empty.... The public spirit in Paris now is confident and sanguine. It does not appear that Napoleon had advanced from Lyons. He is undoubtedly there, very weak; and formidable forces are marching from all quarters against him. It is ascertained that a part of the troops, as well as of the highest officers, are faithful to the King, and Napoleon's soldiers will probably desert him in the end.

On his return to his lodgings that evening Adams found a letter from his wife (and their son, Charles) in Berlin on the way from St. Petersburg, Russia, to join John Quincy in Paris.[4]

On Saturday the 18th, Adams, along with Gallatin, paid another visit to Bayard and found him "very much reduced but evidently much better" than on the last visit. This time, Bayard presented him with papers announcing the American ratification of their peace treaty by the U.S. Senate, and more news of the victory at New Orleans.

The treaty ratification process in 1815 is revealed in Adams' *Memoirs*. In England the treaty was simply ratified by the British Prince Regent and then shipped off to the United States in the corvette *Favorite* from Plymouth on January 3, 1815, arriving in New York on February 9 and in Washington on the 14th. The U.S. Senate ratified it on the 17th. President Madison issued a proclamation on the 18th stating that the war had ended. The ratified treaty was in New York by the 22nd and on its way again on the *Favorite* arriving again in Plymouth on March 11 after a speedy 17-day passage.

> The American ratification was received by Lord Castlereagh in the evening of 13th March, and the event was immediately communicated by him to

the Lord Mayor of London, and received after ten at night,[5]

opening the way for great celebrations, which Adams does not mention. But it was when this news reached Paris that Henry Clay was moved to leave for London.

On Sunday, the 19th, another friend of Adams told him that Marshal Ney was with Napoleon's troops and that the former emperor would be in Paris the next day — "the King of Rome's birthday." Again Adams went out to stroll

> by the Tuileries and the Place du Carrousel, where a great concourse of people was assembled. The King was going out to review the troops, who are to march out to-morrow morning to meet Napoleon. No appearance of anything like defection to the royal cause was discernible, but the countenances of the attendants at the Tailors marked dejection. Mr. Crawford told me yesterday that a person

... told him that when...

> the officers of the garrison of Paris attempted to prevail upon the troops to cry, "Vive le Roi!" the soldiers would say, "Oh, yes! 'Vive le Roi' and laugh." They had not a hope the soldiers would fight.

Nevertheless, the King and his aides attempted to rally the populace with pamphlets and leaflets — but on the morrow, the King and his family fled northward.[6]

Henry Clay had made his own departure from Paris on that Sunday, the 19th. Clay had work to do in London. As did Adams and Gallatin — for all three of them still had instructions to negotiate a treaty of commerce with the British. As Clay made his way alone to England, Adams remained in Paris observing the upheaval in the French capital. It's interesting to see how his estimates of the situation were so far removed from reality.

On the same day that Clay left for England, Adams wrote his mother, the great former First Lady, Abigail Adams, trying to tell his story of the startling events in France. He wrote,

> I am afraid you will think I am sporting with credulity when I assure you that now, at the moment when I am writing, the impression almost universal throughout Paris is, that within six days he (Napoleon) will enter this city as a conqueror, without having spent and ounce of gun-powder

on his march. I have not yet brought myself to that belief.... At the first news of his landing I considered it as the last struggle of desperation on his part. I did not believe that he would be joined by five hundred adherents, and fully expected that he would within ten days pay the forfeit of his rashness with his life.

Adams wrote further,

In the mean time nothing is seen or heard here but manifestations of attachment and devotion to the King and the House of Bourbon. In the streets, at all the public places, in all the newspapers, one universal sentiment is bursting forth of fidelity to the King, and of abhorrence and execration of this firebrand of civil and foreign war.... I do not believe that he will enter Paris without bloodshed; nor even that he will reach Paris at all.... At the same time I must admit that the facts have hitherto turned out so contrary to all my expectations that my confidence in my own judgement is shaken.[7]

On the 21st, Adams was again writing home — this time to his father, the second President, and he noted that on the evening he had written his mother, Napoleon slept at Fontainebleau on the outskirts of Paris. The younger Adams went on to describe the strange events transpiring in the French capital.

Two days after Clay's departure, Adams wrote his father, former President John Adams, to tell him that at one o'clock in the morning of the 20th, "the King and royal family left the Tuileries, and took the road to Lille," and that night,

Napoleon slept at Fontainebleau.... Yesterday a detachment of Napoleon's advance guard entered the city amidst the acclamations of the same multitude which has been for the last fortnight making the atmosphere ring with the cries of *Vive le Roi*. They took possession of the Tuileries, where the three-colored flag is now waving in triumph, and last evening the walls of all the public places were covered with the proclamation of Napoleon ... addressed to the people and to the army, pasted over the proclamations scarcely dry for Louis 18, declaring Napoleon Bonaparte a traitor and rebel, and commanding all civil and military authorities, and even every individual citizen, to seize and deliver him to a court martial. I saw in the garden of the Palais Royal, a huge bonfire of all the proclamations, indignations, execrations, addresses, verses and appeals to the people and army against the Corsican monster and tyrant, which had been loading the columns of the arches the preceding fortnight, and many of which had been stuck up

there the same morning, probably by the identical hands which were now with shouts of thunder committing them to the flames.

He noted that even the newspapers, in a single day "metamorphosed" their allegiance from the king to the emperor.[8]

Additionally, he wrote his father that

Napoleon holds out the olive branch to them [the other powers in Europe] in the remark that the French must forget that they have been the masters of other nations, but he holds not the sword in the declaration that foreign nations must not be suffered to intermeddle in the affairs of France.

Therefore, Adams added in his letter to his father, "the settlement of European affairs at the Congress of Vienna cannot be considered as definitive."[9]

All of these events were intruding into the life of Henry Clay in London anxiously hoping to break through the reluctance of the British government to sit down and talk about commerce. As during the lonely days he spent in Gottenburg, Sweden, in April and May 1814, Clay could only write to anyone he could think of (though no family letters are found) and in each he voiced his wish to be on the high seas making his way back to America. As he now awaited the arrival of his old colleagues of Ghent days, only two of them would join him in London. Russell would unhappily go to Sweden to serve as the U.S. minister. Bayard and Crawford would remain on the sick list and eventually sail together on the *Neptune* for America. It was Gallatin and his son who would be first to join Clay in London. Adams would not follow until late in May when he was satisfied that he was appointed and had instructions to be minister to the British Court of St. James.

A couple of days after his arrival in London on March 21, Clay wrote to William Crawford, back in Paris, to say he had "experienced no difficulty whatever in getting horses from Paris to Calais, or in any other respect." He made note of the failure of a bank bill to pass the U.S. Senate and also the news that the peace treaty was "received with great joy, manifested in illuminations, etc." One of his corespondents told him that the Senate had approved the treaty unanimously — which was surprisingly correct.

In this same letter to Crawford, Clay noted that

the loss of the British in their New Orleans expedition is estimated at 4000. Jackson's account of the assault of the 8th. of Jan. does not essentially vary from that of the British. But for the cowardice of the Militia (and I am mortified to add a portion of my Countrymen) on the right bank of the Mississippi. Jackson states that the whole of Thornton's corps would have been captured. [See endnote 10 regarding Jackson's comment.]

But Clay had other comments to Crawford which might seem strange when compared with today's opinions of Napoleon. Clay wrote,

> If we are to credit the papers of this morning the denoument [sic] of the astonishing scenes began [sic] in France before I left it has occurred, and Napoleon is again quietly seated on the throne. Wonderful age! wonderful man! wonderful nation!

Yet one must recall that Clay had that frightful memory of British troops devastating his childhood home and then there were numerous British atrocities that haunted his early legislative speeches. Britain's orders in council, impressments of seamen and support of Indian atrocities against western settlers all motivated Clay to champion war against Great Britain. The decrees and edicts of Napoleon's government always seemed of lesser urgency to Clay. He went on to write Crawford,

> The mind is not sufficiently tranquillized to speculate on the consequences of this great event. European peace is out of the question, but who will be the parties to the new War? Will they make a war upon him, or he on them? Is the same career to be run of Blockades, decrees, orders in Council, captures, confiscations and burnings?

Was Clay having a bleak vision of a return to the trappings of war thought to have been so recently put to rest? Clay was to use these same phrases in a letter two days later to Secretary of State James Monroe.

But finishing up his letter to Crawford he noted that he was "extremely anxious to hear from poor Bayard. I hope he has recovered." He also told Crawford that he was to see Lord Castlereagh tomorrow and he hoped to be able to estimate how much longer he would be detained in Europe.[10]

In his letter to Monroe, Clay even indicated his indifference to a commerce treaty noting that such a treaty, is "in my judgment ... of little importance, except on one or two points now that the peace of Europe is again threatened assumed [sic] (to assume?) a new character." Additionally, he revealed his diplomatic talent observing that

I think War between this country and France inevitable. Napoleon must do something. He now gives employment to that military the loss of whose employment estranged them from the King and continued their attachment to him. He will strike for Belgium; and the pride, the hopes and mistaken interests of England all combine to urge her to attempt to retain (?) it. Already the Mails are stopped. And the foolish cry for war every where resounds.

(And then he repeats the quote of blockades, etc. from his letter to Crawford.)

As Clay waited for companionship, the activities of the Gallatins were colorfully told by James in his diary — despite the father's admonition to the son "not to record any gossip in my diary — to confine it as much as possible to interesting facts." So he does!

On their journey back to Paris from Switzerland, they stopped at Fontainebleau on February 28, the day before coming into the capital. James wrote,

> I was shown the apartment that Napoleon gave to the Pope when he made him prisoner. The Pope would not allow a divorce between King Jerome and his wife; that was one of the reasons he brought him to Fontainebleau, as he himself wanted to divorce Josephine....

The next day he wrote, "Oh, beautiful Paris! I am so glad to get back...."

A day later, James noted that "his Majesty wished for an interview unofficial [with Albert]. It is a delicate matter, as father feels, until he has been to London that his mouth is closed." Meanwhile,

> We lodged in a quiet little hotel in the Rue de Monsieur. Father will not spend any money unnecessarily as his expenses are paid by his Government. His strong idea is that the representative of a republic should not make any show or be ostentatious, saying, "It is only the vulgar *nouveaux riches* that do that."

Were these the personal principles of Gallatin or a sometimes very frugal former secretary of the treasury?

There was not much on the "interview" on the following day, except that the king, speaking to Albert privately as they stood by a window, said he hoped the "American" would be sent there as the next minister to France, suggesting that he had been French before belonging to America.

But much would transpire before that could happen.

In that same day's entry, James noted that the "great artist" Monsieur David had asked Albert to permit James to pose for him for "Cupid." The diary, printed in 1904, contains a full page copy of the painting, *L'Amour et Psyche*"— James and a young woman together in the nude. But later James explains they posed separately and we can not be sure from his writing that they ever met. James later reveals that the model "must be very pretty, only seventeen. We are not to pose together."

The next few days provide brief accounts of the approach of Napoleon on Paris, "Great consternation," "The Emperor is marching on Paris, gathering men on his way," "All sorts of wild reports: one does not know what to believe," and by the 16th

> The Emperor marching steadily on to Paris — acclaimed everywhere. Father says the Royal Family will leave Paris in a few days. He has private information, but has not told me any details. I walk about all day. Bands of young men shouting, "Vive l'Empereur." It is very exciting.

And on the 19th (the day that Clay left Paris) Albert told James that the Royal Family would leave Paris that night and advised James to remain indoors. The next day the father gave the son an American flag to hang from the balcony for protection in case of trouble. And James saw the emperor arrive as thousands cheered. And James wrote, "People seem mad with joy. What turncoats the French are!" On the 24th James went to the opera — attended also by Napoleon. "The scene was superb. For fully twenty minutes the audience yelled when the Emperor appeared, I yelled too. He is fat, looks very dull, tired, and bored." Even James was to settle down and do more posing and visit the high spots of the capital.

The excitement did not end there. On March 29, James tells his diary that the Emperor requested an interview with his father, "purely on some financial matters. It places him in a most awkward position; he regrets he did not leave for England sooner." James did not attend the audience on the 30th.

> Father was not at all pleased with his interview. He says the Emperor was brusque — that his

speech is most vulgar.... I had better quote father's own words: "The Emperor first asked my advice on important financial matters, to which I gave my frank opinion. He then began to question me about Canada, also the slave trade. I replied, 'Sire, my position is such that on these subjects my lips are at present sealed.' He abruptly said, 'Then why did you come here!' Bowing, I answered, 'I obeyed your Majesty's command out of respect for the ruler of France, but as an envoy from the United States to England I am not my own master.' The Emperor, turning his back on me, walked to a window; I having backed out of the room, so ended our interview."

The following day, James wrote, "We are leaving to-morrow for London. Father thinks it is wiser."

They did not leave Paris until April 3, with stops in Rouen, where James visited the cathedral where Joan of Arc was burned. They reached le Havre and James noted that they "embarked at once on the 7th for a very rough passage on "a miserable little packet! Only one cabin, and horrid odours of onions frying. I have gone under." They reached Dover on the 9th and arrived in London on the 10th.[11]

Within days James wrote that,

> I am very busy now as I have all sorts of documents to copy and file. I also go with father to take notes. All settling of negotiations is at present entirely carried out by him, so the work is very heavy. Lord Castlereagh is most gracious, even friendly.

He added, "that I have been enjoined not to record any gossip in my diary — father doesn't like gossip or tittle-tattle, saying it is only fit for idle women." But for some reason, on April 12, he wrote that "Clay arrives in a few days." He was already there.

A few days prior to the arrival of the Gallatins on April 10, an oft-called "melancholy, or unfortunate" episode near Plymouth, in Devonshire, occurred involving American prisoners of war, and it thrust Clay and Gallatin into its whirlpool.[12]

Of course, Clay and Gallatin were in London to negotiate a treaty of commerce with the British, not deal with a military disturbance of any size. On April 16, the two American envoys met with British foreign secretary Lord Castlereagh hoping he would take up the subject of commerce. Writing Bayard on April 28, Clay described the meeting with the Englishman. Instead, Castlereagh began by discussing the Dartmoor affair and proposed

that in order to investigate its causes thoroughly one of us together with one of the British commissioners who negotiated the treaty of Ghent, should proceed to the spot and collect & report the real facts of the case, promising that if the British officers had acted improperly, that they should be punished. We declined going, it being inconvenient to both Mr. G. and myself, and indeed not falling within our duties; but we advised Mr. Beasley [Reuben G.] to co-operate in the joint investigation proposed, and recommended him to appoint for that purpose C. King, an intelligent young man, son of Rufus King, who happened to be here. The story of the Dartmoor incident is best and succinctly told by Benson Lossing in his mammoth treatment in his *Pictorial Field-book of the War of 1812.*

In connection with the release of captives, a circumstance occurred at a depot for prisoner in England which caused great exasperation on the part of the American people. That depot was situated on Dartmoor, a desolate region in Devenshire [near Plymouth] where it was constructed in 1809 for the confinement of French prisoners of war. It comprised thirty acres, inclosed within double walls, with seven distinct prison-houses, with inclosures. At the time of the ratification of the treaty of peace, there were about six thousand American prisoners there, including twenty-five hundred impressed American seamen, who had refused to fight in the British Navy against their countrymen, and were there when the war broke out in 1812. Some had been there ten or eleven years. The place was in charge of Captain T.G. Shortland, with a military guard. That officer was charged with much unfeeling conduct toward the prisoners, accounts of which reached America, from time to time, and produced great irritation in the public mind.

There was much delay in the release of the Dartmoor prisoners. It was nearly three months after the treaty of peace had been signed before they were permitted to know the fact. From that time [March 20, 1815.] they were in daily expectation of release. Delay caused uneasiness and impatience, and there was evidently a disposition to attempt an escape. Symptoms of insubordination appeared on the 4th of April, when the prisoners demanded bread instead of hard biscuit, and refused to receive the latter. On the evening of the 6th [April], so reluctantly did the prisoners obey orders to retire to their quarters, that, when some of them, with appearance of mutinous intentions, not only refused to retire, but passed beyond the

prescribed limits of their confinement, they were fired upon, by orders of Captain Shortland, for the purpose of intimidating all. This firing was followed by the soldiers without the shadow of an excuse, according to an impartial report made by a commission appointed to investigate the matter. Five prisoners were killed and thirty-three were wounded. The act of the soldiers was regarded by the Americans as a wanton massacre; and when the British authorities pronounced the act "justifiable homicide," the hottest indignation was excited. But time, the great healer, has interposed its balm, and the event appears in history as one of the inevitable cruelties of ever-cruel wars.[13]

Certainly not the feeling in 1815! It is interesting to note here that Lossing was writing at the beginning of the American Civil War and such treatment of prisoners of war on both sides roused great indignation that lasted into the twentieth century. A committee report in the *Annals of Congress* lists seven killed, thirty dangerously and thirty slightly wounded followed by the names of each and the form of their wound. Among them were several amputations of limbs.

The report by King and his associate, Francis Seymour Larpent, was considerably more detailed and with it were interviews with scores of witnesses to the event. In some of the testimony, Mr. Beasely was cited as not well liked by the Americans. When their report was given to Clay and Gallatin, on April 26, they sent copies to the new U.S. minister to G.B., John Quincy Adams, still in Paris waiting for instructions from Monroe. Copies also were given by Castlereagh to the prince regent, who thought the foreign secretary provided a fine response, but not at all satisfactory to the Americans. The Americans sent their own observations to their government.

This closed Clay's responsibility for dealing with the Dartmoor tragedy. And he now hoped to get on with the commerce treaty. However, in that first meeting with Castlereagh, in which the Dartmoor episode took precedence — in the Lord's comments — the idea of a treaty of commerce was finally broached.

Yet all that came out of this conference was the suggestion that Clay and Gallatin meet with two of their old Ghent adversaries — Goulburn and Dr. Adams — along with a Mr. Frederick J. Robinson, vice president of the Board of Trade. But Castlereagh and his high British government leaders were caught up in another outside interference. This time it was Bonaparte.

As the British government wrestled with the problem of a renewed confrontation with Napoleon, Clay was again on the waiting list for what Castlereagh called an "interview." On April 15, Clay wrote to Bayard saying he had already seen and conversed with Castlereagh twice, but nothing was happening in the discourses. And again he expressed his long-growing desire to go home.

> I have not yet been able to ascertain whether I can procure a passage from Liverpool for America.... My anxiety to return is extremely great, and I fear particularly a long passage if I should not be able to take advantage of the Easterly winds which are now beginning to prevail.[14]

The next day, now joined by Gallatin, they met with Castlereagh to discuss the subject of a commerce treaty.

There is another letter of April 28 to Bayard in Clay's papers that again goes over the above details but not another letter until May 10 to Jonathan Russell, now unhappily in Sweden. Yet in the interim, Albert Gallatin's teenage son, James, seemed to sum up quite succinctly the subjects wanting discussion in talks for a commerce treaty — such as

> Colonial policy; regulating traffic with Canada; opening the St. Lawrence River to us; impressment and blockade in times of war; trade with West Indies and Nova Scotia; trade between India, Europe and the United States.[15]

It wasn't to be that simple. Not all of these issues were pursued, and others came up. And the haggling was endless.

In that letter of May 10, to Jonathan Russell, Clay wrote that in their last meeting with Castlereagh, he told the Americans

> that four or five days would be necessary for them to prepare for the interview (re: commerce) which we consented should take place. Thus matters remained for more than three weeks, without our receiving any notice that they were ready for the interview. Having been invited to dine with Lord C. on Sunday next, we thought the opportunity a good one to give a hint of our intention to wait no longer, and declined accepting it on the ground that we had fixed our departure to a preceding day.

Later, Mr. Robinson came to Clay and expressed regret at the delay and offered to meet with the Americans the next Thursday, which they agreed to.

Clay continued in this letter to Russell writing that

> the prospect of renewed War in Europe, on which the Allies appear to be resolved renders it extremely desirable that the Impressment question should be arranged, and perhaps renders it eligible to prevent collisions by settling some other disputed points of a Commercial nature.

Clay wanted to leave that week for Plymouth to join Bayard and Crawford already prepared to sail on the *Neptune*. At the end of this letter, Clay told Russell that Adams was still in Paris.

But there is a strange conclusion to this letter begun on May 10. Nearly two months later, Clay finished it on July 1 stating that "a Commercial Convention ... is to be signed on Monday next," July 3.[16] He follows that with what is about a half page printed out in his papers detailing the results of the negotiations. Later, the appendix of the *Annals* carries no more than a half dozen pages dealing with the official results.

But then one can look at the *Memoirs* of John Quincy Adams who left Paris on May 16, arrived in London on May 25 and then goes on for nearly 50 pages with his accounts of the hectic negotiations for this rather minor treaty of about five articles which were to serve the commerce for these two nations for only four years. The hassling that Adams describes sounds more like that which they endured in negotiating the very crucial importance of the peace treaty. Again the Americans encountered the same arrogance, changes to agreements already made, and demands of a special equivalent for any new privileges the American might wish in their world-wide commerce that touched British interests. It was a wonder that these men kept good graces. And throughout the ordeal — for that it was — Clay urgently wanted to join Bayard and Crawford on the *Neptune* to return to America. (It left without Clay and Gallatin.) Yet he was so frequently stalled that it was the old phrase — "He missed the boat."

While Clay waited to complete that letter to Russell, Adams remained in Paris and the Gallatins did a bit of sightseeing and touring the blue-blood estates in the area. At one of these James Gallatin wrote,

> I have been to two balls and a rout. What a funny thing the latter is. You crawl up the staircase, bow to your hosts at the top, and crawl down again with your clothes torn off your back. They call that pleasure. We dine to-morrow with the Duke of Wellington.[17]

Within a month the duke was going to be busy with "Boney" [Bonaparte]!

Also as Clay waited for Adams' arrival, he and Gallatin composed a very long dispatch to their superior back home, Secretary of State James Monroe. On May 18 they summarized their meeting with Castlereagh which began with the Dartmoor comments and finished with a discussion of the expected talks about commerce. This was followed by a review of their diplomatic encounters with their British counter envoys — and these frequently were quite counter to their expectations. In this report, the Americans cataloged the issues up for discussion and followed these with the summary responses that would keep them in verbal battles for the next half-dozen weeks. Each subject was again digested in their later writings.

Still "in the waiting room" the two Americans heard from Castlereagh on May 23. The Englishman reported that he had presented the King-Larpent report to the prince regent, who

> has commanded me to express through you to the Government of America, how deeply He laments the Consequences of this unhappy Affair. — If anything can tend to relieve the distress which His Royal Highness feels on this occasion, it is the consideration that the conduct of the Soldiers was not actuated by any spirit of Animosity towards the prisoners, and that the Inactivity of the Officers may be attributed rather to the Inexperience of Militia forces, than to any Want of Zeal or Inclination to afford that liberal protection which is ever due to Prisoners of War.

The letter goes on to quote the regent's suggestions that the behavior of the soldiers was due "to a want of Steadiness in the Troops and of exertion in the Officers." Castlereagh went on to note that it was the desire of the prince "to make a Compensation to the Widows & Families of the Sufferers," etc.

The wording is so similar to that used on so many occasions over the years when political leaders really want to stay aloof of charges of incompetence in the acts of their subordinates. In this event, the next day Clay and Gallatin acknowledged receipt of the note and stated again that it was outside their jurisdiction, but notice of the regent's feelings would be sent to America.

At last Adams arrived in London on May 25. Typically of Adams' practice of thorough details, in his *Memoirs* he designed a chart of his passage from Dover to London noting miles per day, numbers of horses, costs, and even the names of innkeepers, and describing the countryside as he recalled it from travels with his father many years earlier.

On the 26th, Adams met with Clay (Gallatin was not present) for a briefing on the current status of the treaty negotiations. Later in the day he wrote to Castlereagh announcing his "arrival with a public commission, and requiring him to appoint a time for me to call on him." He received a reply on Sunday the 27th and was invited to dine with him the next Tuesday. That same Sunday evening, Gallatin visited and gave Adams a project for the treaty.

When Adams finally met with Lord Castlereagh, Adams was late for the appointment and was made to wait. They discussed many aspects of the peace treaty which now seemed to require further regulations and rules, etc. Adams brought up the issue of impressment saying that the U.S. would no longer allow British sailors to serve on American warships, but Castlereagh countered with the fact that the U.S. was using British sailors who had become naturalized, while the British never recognized that a British sailor could give up his British allegiance. It went on like this on the subjects of boundaries, the refusal of the British naval commander in America to return captured American slaves to their owners, and other issues. A subject on which Adams had not yet become involved was "Dartmoor," brought up by Castlereagh. Adams told him that he had been counselled on the matter by his friends and thought British Captain Shortland should have been tried. Of course, Castlereagh was completely opposed to this. But Clay and Gallatin were not even present at these "chats."

Following these initial talks with Castlereagh, Adams was in London for a full two weeks before he was able to present his diplomatic credentials to the prince regent at the end of a general levee, on June 8. In the interim, he wrote in his *Memoirs* of dining out frequently, always arriving late and finding himself (or with Clay and Gallatin) as first arrivals. The conversations were mostly about the intents of Bonaparte (as the French emperor was called in England). There were also a couple more meetings with Castlereagh and other times with the British delegation appointed to treat on commerce (Robinson along with, Goulburn and Dr. Adams from the Ghent days). But nothing was accomplished in any of these meetings. Even the meeting with the prince was desultory. He did not know that Adams was the son of the second U.S. president and earlier the first U.S. minister to Great Britain — and that this new minister had been with his father in those days.[18]

It's a bit odd that Adams, in his *Memoirs*, mentions nothing about being called on by an aide to Castlereagh, to make some "small contribution" to those who rendered services to him in making possible the meeting with the prince regent. But such an encounter appears in one of the biographies of Clay written during his lifetime — and apparently with his approval. In Sargent's *Life of Henry Clay* published in 1853 (and edited by Horace Greeley after Clay's death) there appears the following story:

> Lord Castlereagh offered to present him [Clay] to the prince-regent. Mr. Clay said he would go through the ceremony, if it were deemed necessary or respectful. Lord Castlereagh said, that having been recognised [sic] in his public character by the British government, it was not necessary, and that he might omit it or not, as he pleased. Mr. Clay's repugnance to the parade of courts prevented his presentation, and he never saw the prince. He met, however, with most of the other members of the royal family.
>
> A few days after his interview with Lord Castlereagh, the keeper of the house at which Mr. Clay lodged, announce a person who wished to speak with him. Mr. Clay directed him to be admitted; and, on his entrance, he perceived an individual, dressed apparently in great splendor, come forward, whom he took to be a peer of the realm. He rose and asked his visiter [sic] to be seated, but the latter declined, and observed that he was the first waiter of my Lord Castlereagh! "The first waiter of my Lord Castlereagh!" exclaimed Mr. Clay; "well, what is your pleasure with me?" — "Why, if your excellency pleases," said the man, "it

is usual for a foreign minister, when presented to Lord Castlereagh, to make to his first waiter a present, or pay him the customary stipend"; at the same time handing to Mr. Clay a long list of names of foreign ministers, with the sum which every one had paid affixed to his name.

> Mr. Clay thinking it a vile extortion, took the paper, and, while reading it, thought how he should repel so exceptionable a demand. He returned it to the servant, telling him that as it was the custom of the country, he presumed it was all right; but that he was not the minister to England, Mr. Adams was the minister, and was daily expected from Paris, and he had no doubt, would do whatever was right. "But," said the servant, very promptly, "if your *excellency* pleases, it makes no difference whether the minister presented be the present minister or a special minister, as I understand your excellency to be; — it is always paid." Mr. Clay, who had come to England to argue with the master, finding himself in danger of being beaten in argument by the man, concluded it best to conform to the usage, objectionable as he thought it; and, looking over the paper for the smallest sum paid by any other minister, handed the fellow five guineas, and dismissed him.

It was not until Wednesday, June 7, that the three-member teams from both nations met to begin talks. They briefly quibbled over very minor errors in the initial drafts of credentials. Then the first subject came up — that of opening U.S. trade with India. This swiftly became confused with the British linking of trade with India to mention trade with the East Indies and with the current exclusive rights of the East Indies Company under a treaty of 1794 and even comments about the West Indies. It was enough to anger any negotiators, but it was not enough for the British. They immediately asked for some sort of equivalent — such as Canadian fur trade with Indian tribes living in the United States. Of course, the Americans stated they had no instructions on this matter. And all along Clay was making it clear that he wanted to leave for Plymouth and the *Neptune* by Monday June 12.

On the Sunday before Clay's hoped-for-departure from London, both delegations dined with the top British leaders with their prime minister (Lord Liverpool) seated between Clay and Gallatin, and Castlereagh between Clay and Adams. Meanwhile, most of the conversation centered on Bonaparte. Castlereagh observed to Adams that he had never seen the emperor but would like to have met him. The only comment about the commerce talks came from Robinson who told Clay that their counter-project (called projet in Adams' papers) would be sent to the Americans on Wednesday. Clay told Adams that he and Gallatin "had agreed to stay until that time."[19] The British reply came to Adams' abode late Friday the 16th.

By now the British were thinking entirely of Bonaparte. For it was on this day that the emperor was aligning his forces just south of Brussels, Belgium (then being called The Netherlands), near a little place called Waterloo. As to the counter-project, Adams noted, "It is in every respect so different from what Mr. Clay and Mr. Gallatin had expected, and led me to expect, that I think it useless to pursue the negotiations any further."[20] He took it immediately to Clay and Gallatin—not at home.

Early on the morning of Saturday, the 17th, Clay and Gallatin were at Adams' place with the British proposals. Adams noted in his *Memoirs* of this date that

> There were three points upon which Messers. Clay and Gallatin, upon the results of their conferences with the British Plenipotentiaries before my arrival, had concluded to enter upon a formal negotiation: 1. the intercourse between the United States and Canada; 2. the mutual abolition of discriminating duties, and placing the commercial relations between the two counties on the footing of the most favored nation; and 3. the East India trade.... Mr. Clay said that he had been deceived by the British Plenipotentiaries upon all three. Their counter-projet now offered us a Canadian article, which would give them access to trade with the Indians in our territory. They limited to their European dominions the offer to treat us as the most favored nation, and they limited the intercourse to be secured to us with India to four places, and to two years from the ratification of the treaty, with high pretentious of liberality in granting so much, and a formal notification that they gave us the two years only for the Government of the United States to be prepared to give an equivalent for the continuation of the privilege. Mr. Clay said that if he had imagined it would come to such a projet as this, he never would have entered into this negotiation, and he was for asking immediately a conference with the British Plenipotentiaries, stating to them that we had entirely misunderstood their intentions, and informing them that we do not think it worth while to proceed any further with them in the business.

However,

Mr. Gallatin was averse to making an acknowledgment that he had been deceived, but for meeting the British Plenipotentiaries, proposing alterations to their counter-projet, and bringing them to a definite answer before breaking off.

The others agreed to meet later that day. Only Robinson was available and all agreed to meet on Monday, the 19th. As the talks resumed on Monday, Adams noted that he

> took no part in the discussion; the whole business is conducted with so much precipitation, and the reference is so continual to the conferences which had taken place before my arrival, upon the substance of which the ideas of the two parties are so widely different, that I have not felt it safe or prudent to enter into the debates, and have been entirely silent. It became perfectly clear to me this day that upon no one of the three points for which the negotiation was commenced is there any likelihood of our coming to an agreement with the British Plenipotentiaries. Their counter-projet presents the article relating to the intercourse with Canada so drawn that it would indirectly give them the trade with Indians within our territories, and it does not admit us to navigate the river St. Lawrence even down to Montreal.

Then the dialog got a bit nasty when Clay said they were not talking about a ship but

> scarcely even a boat navigation that we asked. It was little more than the mere floating of rafts to be taken down in exchange for gewgaws [decorative trinkets of no value] from Europe. Dr. Adams was piqued at this term geegaws, and said that if our people liked those geegaws, no doubt they would give their lumber and flour in exchange for them. The doctor appeared offended, too, at our proposal to omit the article altogether. Mr. Gallatin urged, with force, that if the navigation to Montreal was denied us, the article would be of no benefit to us whatever.

Of course, Dr. Adams found a way to refute this line of argument, saying,

> that was no reason for leaving it out; because if the benefit to us was not in that article, it might be in some other, or in the whole treaty. The proposition of placing the two nations respectively on the footing of the most favored nation was confined by the British projet to the territories in Europe on the British part.

Then the British cited examples of other countries getting special treatment because they had colonies. They replied that the nations having colonies themselves were now allowed the indirect trade with India, and that by placing us on the footing of the most favored nation, it would in point of fact give us for nothing the indirect trade for which we had been informed that an equivalent would be required.

But the Americans responded that they had no colonies.

There remained for discussion an article about equalization of duties, but it ran into complaints about wording and the British requested a "more precise draft of the article." At dinner that evening, Gallatin was able to provide a new draft for the British. As the Americans talked about their day,

> Mr. Clay and Mr. Gallatin again expressed the inclination to sign an article limiting us to the direct trade with India, notwithstanding our instructions, on the ground that the British Government, having since the date of our instructions, allowed to their own subjects other than the East India Company a direct trade with China, had no longer the same motive for allowing the trade to us.

It was at his gathering that they first heard of the commencement of hostilities at Waterloo.[21]

On June 22, word of the battle on the continent was received after some hints earlier that Wellington had been beaten. Now, as reported to the Americans by Castlereagh, all was a "splendid and a complete victory of the Duke of Wellington and Marshal Blücher over the French army, commanded by Bonaparte in person, on Sunday last, the 18th." Adams wrote the next day of riding "'round the streets to see the illuminations for the great victory of the 18th. They were not general, nor very magnificent."

Over the next few days, they agreed on the equalization of duties and bounties, retreated from demands for Canadian fur trade with Indians in the United States and noted that they had no authority to discuss navigation of the St. Lawrence. They relinquished the demand for an equivalent for trade in the East Indies. Through all of this the title of a treaty was changed to "a convention."

By July 2 all was agreed to by the two countries — but not so between the American envoys. Adams was adamant and even threatened the signing of the documents unless the duplicate copies were signed in the manner he felt was proper — that the document for each nation was headed by the names of its delegation. He got his way and on July 3, 1815, it was a done deed.

And away went Henry Clay with Albert Gallatin and son following in his wake as best they could. They were on their way to Liverpool to take passage on any ship available. From Birmingham, on the 8th, Clay wrote one of the delegation's aides, John Todd, that in his rush, "I wait for no man." From Liverpool on the 14th he wrote his poor lonely wife, Lucretia, that he expected to board the *Lorenzo* (a ship of unknown type or nationality) for the fastest voyage home he could find.[22] Their ship did not leave until July 23.

Now there was a long period when Clay and the Gallatins in effect were out of sight. We might now take time to look at what was happening to their companions in diplomacy during these days — and later. John Quincy Adams, of course, was stuck with the unpleasant job of minister to Great Britain (the so-called "Court of St. James," but later became the sixth American president.

Bayard and Crawford, both ill, departed Plymouth, England, on June 18, 1815, and after a voyage of 43 days on the *Neptune*, they landed near Wilmington, Del., on August 1. A quote from a Washington newspaper states,

> The news of this arrival produced the most affecting spectacle. The last accounts from Europe respecting the health of Mr. Bayard had caused great anxiety more especially in the minds of those who were acquainted with him as a private citizen.... As soon as it was known that Mr. Bayard was aboard the *Neptune*, though very ill, the assemblage burst into loud huzzas.... In the evening he was brought from the *Neptune* to his house having been confined in his bed seventy days.

Yet a mere four days later that paper, quoting from another, stated, "Illustrious Bayard, a victim of love of country, is no more among men." Then from a private letter from an unknown woman of Wilmington, "Bayard is gone! Last evening about 8 o'clock he was released from suffering 'such' he said, 'as no mortal could imagine and which I hope has not been in vain.'"[23]

Returning home, Crawford held cabinet posts until 1824 when he joined Adams, Clay and Jackson running for president. None had a plurality in the electoral vote. As required by the constitution, only the top three names went to the House of Representatives where the election would be determined by the states, each voting as a unit. Finishing fourth, Clay was eliminated, but as Speaker of the House he would preside over the event. Since Crawford had been ill for some time, the election settled between Adams and Jackson.

Since Jackson had obtained both the largest popular and the electoral vote, his supporters assumed he would therefore be the winning candidate. However, by the nature of the spread of votes by the states voting as a unit, and the influence of the presiding officer, the election went to John Quincy Adams.

As Adams selected his cabinet, he chose Clay to be his secretary of state — a natural choice after their in-depth association in the diplomatic struggle with the British at Ghent. But Jackson's supporters charged it was "a corrupt bargain," and it was to haunt Clay the rest of his life.

So, lagging behind his diplomatic companions, Clay, along with the two Gallatins, arrived in New York on September 1, after 41 days at sea. Clay stayed long enough to be feted at a "superb entertainment on the 5th at "Tammany Hall." Among the 30 toasts, the two returning envoys were toasted as "Our two distinguished guests." Clay himself rendered a toast to "The 8th of January," the date of Andrew Jackson's victory at New Orleans.[24]

Again quoting from the *National Intelligencer*, Clay's toast at a Philadelphia banquet on September 12, honored "The genuine patriotism which, rising above sectional influence, looks to the interest, the honor, and the glory of the whole."[25]

Next on Clay's slow journey home was a visit to Washington. Nothing is known of his reaction to the sight of the devastated city, but seeing the ruin of the old chamber of the House of Representatives and the burned-out shell of the White House must have been wrenching.

Yet again, he was celebrated by the officials of the city of Washington, apparently not quite in the manner they wished. The *National Intelligencer* reported on September 19 that Clay had arrived in the city on the 16th but that

> his determination to leave for home on the 18th prevented his being honored by a public dinner and induced the Mayor of the City to convene a special meeting of the City Council at which the

resolutions here presented were adopted unanimously.

Among the resolutions was "That the services rendered to the nation by the negotiators of the Treaty of Peace, entitle them to the respect and gratitude of their country." But what Clay wanted most was simply to go home.

Apparently, the dinner was not given, since Clay's response to the resolutions is by letter in which he again expressed his thoughts that "the issue of the negotiation was owing to the determined spirit of resistance of our military and naval forces.... A great object of the war has been attained in the firm establishment of the national character." Clay then went on to note that, "wherever I have been since my return, is attended with the melancholy reflection that one of my colleagues unhappily can no longer participate in the congratulations of our country." Of course, he referred to the now-beloved, American first, James A. Bayard.

Continuing his journey to Kentucky, on September 28, from "Beamers town," Ohio, Clay wrote to Gallatin in Washington regarding their expenses while abroad.

Clay arrived in Lexington, Kentucky, by October 5 where the celebrations resumed in the most friendly atmosphere, and were to continue for days.

Clay, a young man of 37, was acclaimed as a hero throughout his country. Yet his best years were still ahead of him. He had already served as Speaker of the House of Representatives and as a commissioner to treat for peace, but much lay in the future.

Following his service abroad, he would again sit in the chair of the Speaker — but in a much smaller chamber in what was called the "Old brick capitol," from 1815 to 1819. It sat on grounds now occupied by the the U.S. Supreme Court until the original Capitol building was sufficiently restored to bring Congress back to its new chambers. Under his Speakership he would champion legislation for the American System, the Missouri Compromise, and internal improvements such as roads and canals. His incumbency as Speaker ranks second in longevity only to that of Sam Rayburn of Texas.

He sought unsuccessfully the office of president in 1824, against his companion in diplomacy John

Quincy Adams, the hero of New Orleans Andrew Jackson, and the earlier president pro-tem of the Senate William Crawford. He ran again in 1832 against Jackson, but again lost. He failed to secure the Whig nomination in 1840 when William Henry Harrison — the general he endorsed so highly early in the War of 1812 — won the nomination and the election, only to die one month into office. Clay won the nomination again in 1844 but lost to four-year Speaker, James K. Polk. In 1848 he lost the nomination to Zachary Taylor, a little-known general during the War of 1812 who came to fame in the Mexican War — a war opposed by Clay and in which he lost a son. Strangely, the two candidates who blocked Clay's nomination in the primary elections both died while in office.

Adding to his diplomatic prestige, Clay served skillfully under President John Quincy Adams working on relations with the Latin American nations as they struggled for independence. His most distinguished days were those of his return to the U.S. Senate where he is recognized as the author of the Great Compromise of 1850.

The U.S. Senate in 1957 was called upon to name the five greatest previous senators. Clay was among them, along with Daniel Webster, John C. Calhoun, Robert M. LaFollette, and Robert A. Taft. But one of the senators voting on that occasion told the author personally that if they had been required to vote for the single greatest senator in the total history of that body, it would have been Henry Clay of Kentucky.

* * *

In October 1815, Henry Clay, home from his diplomatic labors abroad and basking in the adulation of his friends, was honored at a sumptuous banquet in Lexington. In response to many toasts Clay rendered a very thoughtful summary of America's part in his war — the War of 1812. Again praising the work of his colleagues at Ghent he remarked that

> they could not do otherwise than reject the demands made by the other party, and if their labours finally terminated in an honorable peace, it was owing to causes on this side of the Atlantic, and not to any exertion of theirs — Whatever diversity of opinion may have existed as to the declaration of the war, there were some points on which

all might look back with proud satisfaction. The first related to the time of the conclusion of the peace. Had it been made, immediately after the treaty of Paris [May 30, 1814, when Napoleon was sent to Elba], we should have retired humiliated from the contest, believing that we had escaped the severe chastisement with which we were threatened, and that we owed to the generosity and magnanimity of the enemy, what we were incapable of commanding by our arms.... We should have retired unconscious of our own strength, and unconscious of the utter inability of the enemy, with his whole undivided force, to make any serious impression upon us. Our military character, then in the lowest state of degradation, would have been unretrieved.

Fortunately for us, G. Britain chose to try the issue of the last campaign. And the issue of the last campaign has demonstrated, in the repulse before Baltimore, the retreat from Plattsburgh, the hard fought actions on the Niagara frontier, and in that most glorious day, the 8th of January, that we have always possessed the finest elements of military composition, and that a proper use of them only was necessary to ensure for the army and militia a fame as imperishable as that which the navy had previously acquired.

We fought the most powerful nation, perhaps in existence, singlehanded and alone without any sort of alliance. More than 20 years had Great Britain been maturing her physical means, which she had rendered as efficacious as possible, by skill, by discipline, and by actual service. Proudly boasting of the conquest of Europe, she vainly flattered herself with the easy conquest of America also. Her veterans were put to flight or defeated, while all Europe was gazing with cold indifference, or sentiments of positive hatred of us upon the arduous contest. Hereafter no monarch can assert claims of gratitude upon us, for assistance rendered in the hour of danger and difficulty.

There was another view of which the subject of the War was fairly susceptible. From the moment that Great Britain came forward at Ghent with her extravagant demands, the War totally changed its character. It became, as it were, a new war. It was no longer an American war, prosecuted for redress of British aggression upon American rights, but became a British war, prosecuted for objects of British ambition, to be accomplished by American sacrifices. And what were those demands? Here, in the immediate neighborhood of a sister state, and territories, which were to be made in part the victims, they must have been felt & their enormity justly appreciated. They consisted of the erection of a barrier between Canada and the United States, to be formed by cutting off from Ohio and some of the territories, a country more extensive than Great Britain, containing thousands of freemen, who were to be abandoned to their fate, and creating a new power, totally unknown upon the continent of America: Of dismantling of our fortresses, and naval power on the Lakes, with the surrender of the military occupation of those waters to the enemy, and of an *arrondissement* for two British Provinces. These demands, boldly asserted, and one of them declared to be a *sine qua non*, were finally relinquished. Taking this view of the subject, if there be loss of reputation by either party, in the terms of the Peace, who has sustained it?

The immediate effects of the war were highly satisfactory. Abroad our character, which at the time of its declaration, was in the lowest state of degradation, was raised to the highest point of elevation. It was impossible for any American to visit Europe without being sensible of this agreeable change, in the personal attentions which he receives, in the praises which are bestowed on our past exertions, and in the flattering predictions which are made as to our future prospects. At home a government which, at its formation, was apprehended by its best friends and pronounced by its enemies to be incapable of standing the shock of war, is found to answer all the purposes of its institution. In spite of the errors which had been committed (and errors had undoubtedly been committed) aided by the spirit and patriotism of the people, it is demonstrated to be as competent to the objects of effective war, as it had been before proven to be to the concerns of a season of peace. Government has thus acquired strength and confidence.

Our prospects for the future are of the brightest kind. With every reason to count upon the permanence of peace, it remains only for the government to determine upon military and naval establishments adapted to the growth & and extension of our country and its rising importance, keeping in view a gradual but not burthensome increase of the Navy. To provide for the payment of the interest, and the redemption of the Public Debt, and for the current expenses of Government. For all these objects, the existing sources of revenue promise not only to be abundantly sufficient, but will probably leave ample scope to the exercise of the judgment of Congress, in selecting for repeal, modification or abolition, those which may be found most oppressive, inconvenient or unproductive.[26]

It was an outline of hope for the future and one that is relevant for the twenty-first century.

APPENDIX:
TREATY OF GHENT, 1814

Treaty of Peace and Amity Between His Britannic Majesty and the United States of America.

His Britannic Majesty and the United States of America, desirous of terminating the war which has unhappily subsisted between the two Countries, and of restoring upon principles of perfect reciprocity, Peace, Friendship, and good Understanding between them, have for that purpose appointed their respective Plenipotentiaries, that is to say, His Britannic Majesty on His part has appointed the Right Honourable James Lord Gambier, late Admiral of the White now Admiral of the Red Squadron of His Majesty's Fleet; Henry Goulburn Esquire, a Member of the Imperial Parliament and Under Secretary of State; and William Adams Esquire, Doctor of Civil Laws: And the President of the United States, by and with the advice and consent of the Senate thereof, has appointed John Quincy Adams, James A. Bayard, Henry Clay, Jonathan Russell, and Albert Gallatin, Citizens of the United States; who, after a reciprocal communication of their respective Full Powers, have agreed upon the following Articles.

ARTICLE THE FIRST.

There shall be a firm and universal Peace between His Britannic Majesty and the United States, and between their respective Countries, Territories, Cities, Towns, and People of every degree without exception of places or persons. All hostilities both by sea and land shall cease as soon as this Treaty shall have been ratified by both parties as hereinafter mentioned. All territory, places, and possessions whatsoever taken by either party from the other during the war, or which may be taken after the signing of this Treaty, excepting only the Islands hereinafter mentioned, shall be restored without delay and without causing any destruction or carrying away any of the Artillery or other public property originally captured in the said forts or places, and which shall remain therein upon the Exchange of the Ratifications of this Treaty, or any Slaves or other private property; And all Archives, Records, Deeds, and Papers, either of a public nature or belonging to private persons, which in the course of the war may have fallen into the hands of the Officers of either party, shall be, as far as may be practicable, forthwith restored and delivered to the proper authorities and persons to whom they respectively belong. Such of the Islands in the Bay of Passamaquoddy as are claimed by both parties shall remain in the possession of the party in whose occupation they may be at the time of the Exchange of the Ratifications of this Treaty until the decision respecting the title to the said Islands shall have been made in conformity with the fourth Article of this Treaty. No disposition made by this Treaty as to such possession of the Islands and territories claimed by both parties shall in any manner whatever be construed to affect the right of either.

ARTICLE THE SECOND.

Immediately after the ratifications of this Treaty by both parties as hereinafter mentioned, orders shall be sent to the Armies, Squadrons, Officers, Subjects, and Citizens of the two Powers to cease from all hostilities: and to prevent all causes of complaint which might arise on account of the prizes which may be taken at sea after the said Ratifications of this Treaty, it is reciprocally agreed that all vessels and effects which may be taken after the space of twelve days from the said Ratifications upon all parts of the Coast of North America from the Latitude of twenty three degrees North to the Latitude of fifty degrees North, and as far Eastward in the Atlantic Ocean as the thirty sixth degree of West Longitude from the Meridian of Greenwich, shall be restored on each side:— that the time shall be thirty days in all other parts of the Atlantic Ocean North of the Equinoctial Line or Equator:— and the same time for the British and Irish Channels, for the Gulf of Mexico, and all parts of the West Indies:— forty days for the North Seas for the Baltic, and for all parts of the Mediterranean — sixty days for the Atlantic Ocean South of the Equator as far as the Latitude of the Cape of Good Hope.— ninety days for every other part of the world South of the Equator, and one hundred and twenty days for all other parts of the world without exception.

ARTICLE THE THIRD.

All Prisoners of war taken on either side as well by land as by sea shall be restored as soon as practicable after the Ratifications of this Treaty as hereinafter mentioned on their paying the debts which they may have contracted during their captivity. The two Contracting Parties respectively engage to discharge in specie the advances which may have been made by the other for the sustenance and maintenance of such prisoners.

ARTICLE THE FOURTH.

Whereas it was stipulated by the second Article in the Treaty of Peace of one thousand seven hundred and eighty three between His Britannic Majesty and the United States of America that the boundary of the United States should comprehend "all Islands within twenty leagues of any part of the shores of the United States and lying between lines to be drawn due East from the points where the aforesaid boundaries between Nova Scotia on the one part and East Florida on the other shall respectively touch the Bay of Fundy and the Atlantic Ocean, excepting such Islands as now are or heretofore have been within the limits of Nova Scotia, and whereas the several Islands in the Bay of Passamaquoddy, which is part of the Bay of Fundy, and the Island of Grand Menan in the said Bay of Fundy, are claimed by the United States as being comprehended within their aforesaid boundaries, which said Islands are claimed as belonging to His Britannic Majesty as having been at the time of and previous to the aforesaid Treaty of one thousand seven hundred and eighty three within the limits of the Province of Nova Scotia: In order therefore finally to decide upon these claims it is agreed that they shall be referred to two Commissioners to be appointed in the following manner: viz: One Commissioner shall be appointed by His Britannic Majesty and one by the President of the United States, by and with the advice and consent of the Senate thereof, and the said two Commissioners so appointed shall be sworn impartially to examine and decide upon the said claims according to such evidence as shall be laid before them on the part of His Britannic Majesty and of the United States respectively. The said Commissioners shall meet at St Andrews in the Province of New Brunswick, and shall have power to adjourn to such other place or places as they shall think fit. The said Commissioners shall by a declaration or report under their hands and seals decide to which of the two Contracting parties the several Islands aforesaid do respectely belong in conformity with the true intent of the said Treaty of Peace of one thousand seven hundred and eighty three. And if the said Commissioners shall agree in their decision both parties shall consider such decision as final and conclusive. It is further agreed that in the event of the two Commissioners differing upon all or any of the matters so referred to them, or in the event of both or either of the said Commissioners refusing or declining or wilfully omitting to act as such, they shall make jointly or separately a report or reports as well to the Government of His Britannic Majesty as to that of the United States, stating in detail the points on which they differ, and the grounds upon which their respective opinions have been formed, or the grounds upon which they or either of them have so refused declined or omitted to act. And His Britannic Majesty and the Government of the United States hereby agree to refer the report or reports of the said Commissioners to some friendly Sovereign or State to be then named for that purpose, and who shall be requested to decide on the differences which may be stated in the said report or reports, or upon the report of one Commissioner together with the grounds upon which the other Commissioner shall have refused, declined or omitted to act as the case may be. And if the Commissioner so refusing, declining, or omitting to act, shall also wilfully omit to state the grounds upon which he has so done in such manner that the said statement may be referred to such friendly Sovereign or State together with the report of such other Commissioner, then such Sovereign or State shall decide ex parse upon the said report alone. And His Britannic Majesty and the Government of the United States engage to consider the decision of such friendly Sovereign or State to be final and conclusive on all the matters so referred.

ARTICLE THE FIFTH.

Whereas neither that point of the Highlands lying due North from the source of the River St Croix, and designated in the former *Treaty of Peace* between the two Powers as the North West Angle of Nova Scotia, nor the North Westernmost head of Connecticut River has yet been ascertained; and whereas that part of the boundary line between the Dominions of the two Powers which extends from the source of the River st Croix directly North to the above mentioned North West Angle of Nova Scotia, thence along the said Highlands which divide those Rivers that empty themselves into the River St Lawrence from those which fall into the Atlantic Ocean to the North Westernmost head of Connecticut River, thence down along the middle of that River to the forty fifth degree of North Latitude, thence by a line due West on said latitude until it strikes the River Iroquois or Cataraquy, has not yet been surveyed: it is agreed that for these several purposes two Commissioners shall be appointed, sworn, and authorized to act exactly in the manner directed with respect to those mentioned in the next preceding Article unless otherwise specified in the present Article. The said Commissioners shall meet at se Andrews in the Province of New Brunswick, and shall have power to adjourn to such other place or places as they shall think fit. The said Commissioners shall have power to ascertain and determine the points above mentioned in conformity with the provisions of the said *Treaty of Peace* of one thousand seven hundred and eighty three, and shall cause the boundary aforesaid from the source of the River St Croix to the River Iroquois or Cataraquy to be surveyed and marked according to the said provisions. The said Commissioners shall make a map of the said boundary, and annex to it a declaration under their hands and seals certifying it to be the true Map of the said boundary, and particularizing the latitude and longitude of the North West Angle of Nova Scotia, of the North Westernmost head of Connecticut River, and of such other points of the said boundary as they may deem proper. And both parties agree to consider such map and declaration as finally and conclusively fixing the said boundary. And in the event of the said two Commissioners differing, or both, or either of them refusing, declining, or wilfully omitting to act, such reports, declarations, or statements shall be made by them or either of them, and such reference to a friendly Sovereign or State shall be made in all respects as in the latter part of the fourth Article is contained, and in as full a manner as if the same was herein repeated.

ARTICLE THE SIXTH.

Whereas by the former *Treaty of Peace* that portion of the boundary of the United States from the point where the fortyfifth degree of North Latitude strikes the River Iroquois or Cataraquy to the Lake Superior was declared to be "along the middle of said River into Lake Ontario, through the middle of said Lake until it strikes the communication by water between that Lake and Lake Erie, thence along the middle of said communication into Lake Erie, through the middle of said Lake until it arrives at the water communication into the Lake Huron; thence through the middle of said Lake to the water communication between that Lake and Lake Superior": and whereas doubts have arisen what was the middle of the said River, Lakes, and water communications, and whether certain Islands lying in the same were within the Do-

minions of His Britannic Majesty or of the United States: In order therefore finally to decide these doubts, they shall be referred to two Commissioners to be appointed, sworn, and authorized to act exactly in the manner directed with respect to those mentioned in the next preceding Article unless otherwise specified in this present Article. The said Commissioners shall meet in the first instance at Albany in the State of New York, and shall have power to adjourn to such other place or places as they shall think fit. The said Commissioners shall by a Report or Declaration under their hands and seals, designate the boundary through the said River, Lakes, and water communications, and decide to which of the two Contracting parties the several Islands lying within the said Rivers, Lakes, and water communications, do respectively belong in conformity with the true intent of the said Treaty of one thousand seven hundred and eighty three. And both parties agree to consider such designation and decision as final and conclusive. And in the event of the said two Commissioners differing or both or either of them refusing, declining, or wilfully omitting to act, such reports, declarations, or statements shall be made by them or either of them, and such reference to a friendly Sovereign or State shall be made in all respects as in the latter part of the fourth Article is contained, and in as full a manner as if the same was herein repeated.

ARTICLE THE SEVENTH.

It is further agreed that the said two last mentioned Commissioners after they shall have executed the duties assigned to them in the preceding Article, shall be, and they are hereby, authorized upon their oaths impartially to fix and determine according to the true intent of the said *Treaty of Peace* of one thousand seven hundred and eighty three, that part of the boundary between the dominions of the two Powers, which extends from the water communication between Lake Huron and Lake Superior to the most North Western point of the Lake of the Woods;— to decide to which of the two Parties the several Islands lying in the Lakes, water communications, and Rivers forming the said boundary do respectively belong in conformity with the true intent of the said *Treaty of Peace* of one thousand seven hundred and eighty three, and to cause such parts of the said boundary as require it to be surveyed and marked. The said Commissioners shall by a Report or declaration under their hands and seals, designate the boundary aforesaid, state their decision on the points thus referred to them, and particularize the Latitude and Longitude of the most North Western point of the Lake of the Woods, and of such other parts of the said boundary as they may deem proper. And both parties agree to consider such designation and decision as final and conclusive. And in the event of the said two Commissioners differing, or both or either of them refusing, declining, or wilfully omitting to act, such reports, declarations or statements shall be made by them or either of them, and such reference to a friendly Sovereign or State shall be made in all respects as in the latter part of the fourth Article is contained, and in as full a manner as if the same was herein revealed.

ARTICLE THE EIGHTH.

The several Boards of two Commissioners mentioned in the four preceding Articles shall respectively have power to appoint a Secretary, and to employ such Surveyors or other persons as they shall judge necessary. Duplicates of all their respective reports, declarations, statements, and decisions, and of their accounts, and of the Journal of their proceedings shall be delivered by them to the Agents of His Britannic Majesty and to the Agents of the United States, who may be respectively appointed and authorized to manage the business on behalf of their respective Governments. The said Commissioners shall be respectively paid in such manner as shall be agreed between the two contracting parties, such agreement being to be settled at the time of the Exchange of the Ratifications of this Treaty. And all other expenses attending the said Commissions shall be defrayed equally by the two parties. And in the case of death, sickness, resignation, or necessary absence, the place of every such Commissioner respectively shall be supplied in the same manner as such Commissioner was first appointed; and the new Commissioner shall take the same oath or affirmation and do the same duties. It is further agreed between the two contracting parties that in case any of the Islands mentioned in any of the preceding Articles, which were in the possession of one of the parties prior to the commencement of the present war between the two Countries, should by the decision of any of the Boards of Commissioners aforesaid, or of the Sovereign or State so referred to, as in the four next preceding Articles contained, fall within the dominions of the other party, all grants of land made previous to the commencement of the war by the party having had such possession, shall be as valid as if such Island or Islands had by such decision or decisions been adjudged to be within the dominions of the party having had such possession.

ARTICLE THE NINTH.

The United States of America engage to put an end immediately after the Ratification of the present Treaty to hostilities with all the Tribes or Nations of Indians with whom they may be at war at the time of such Ratification, and forthwith to restore to such Tribes or Nations respectively all the possessions,

rights, and privileges which they may have enjoyed or been entitled to in one thousand eight hundred and eleven previous to such hostilities. Provided always that such Tribes or Nations shall agree to desist from all hostilities against the United States of America, their Citizens, and Subjects upon the Ratification of the present Treaty being notified to such Tribes or Nations, and shall so desist accordingly. And His Britannic Majesty engages on his part to put an end immediately after the Ratification of the present Treaty to hostilities with all the Tribes or Nations of Indians with whom He may be at war at the time of such Ratification, and forthwith to restore to such Tribes or Nations respectively all the possessions, rights, and privileges, which they may have enjoyed or been entitled to in one thousand eight hundred and eleven previous to such hostilities. Provided always that such Tribes or Nations shall agree to desist from all hostilities against His Britannic Majesty and His Subjects upon the Ratification of the present Treaty being notified to such Tribes or Nations, and shall so desist accordingly.

ARTICLE THE TENTH.

Whereas the Traffic in Slaves is irreconcilable with the principles of humanity and Justice, and whereas both His Majesty and the United States are desirous of continuing their efforts to promote its entire abolition, it is hereby agreed that both the contracting parties shall use their best endeavours to accomplish so desirable an object.

ARTICLE THE ELEVENTH.

This Treaty when the same shall have been ratified on both sides without alteration by either of the contracting parties, and the Ratifications mutually exchanged, shall be binding on both parties, and the Ratifications shall be exchanged at Washington in the space of four months from this day or sooner if practicable. In faith whereof, We the respective Plenipotentiaries have signed this Treaty, and have hereunto affixed our Seals.

Done in triplicate at Ghent the twenty fourth day of December one thousand eight hundred and fourteen.

GAMBIER. [Seal]
HENRY GOULBURN [Seal]
WILLIAM ADAMS [Seal]
JOHN QUINCY ADAMS [Seal]
J. A. BAYARD [Seal]
H. CLAY. [Seal]
JON. RUSSELL [Seal]
ALBERT GALLATIN [Seal]

Chapter Notes

Chapter 1

1. Mrs. Mary Rogers Clay, *The Clay Family*. Part Second: The genealogy of the Clays. [Filson Club Publications, No. 14] (Louisville, 1899), 65ff.

2. Lewis Peyton Little, *Imprisoned Preachers & Religious Liberty in Virginia* (Lynchburg, Va., 1938), 214.

3. Ibid., 217.

4. Ibid., 338.

5. Ibid., 218.

6. Calvin Colton, *The Life and Times of Henry Clay* (New York, 1846), 1:18.

7. Hon. Zachary F. Smith, *The Clay Family, Part First: The Mother of Henry Clay* [See note1.] 29–30. (Further references to his work — Part First — will be cited as *Clay Family*.)

8. Henry Clay papers, Manuscripts Division, Library of Congress. (Further references to Henry Clay papers from this collection at the Library of Congress will be cited as Clay Papers. Meanwhile, a very large collection of his papers is found in those of his son, Thomas J. Clay and will be cited as T. J. Clay Papers. All additional material taken from the manuscripts Division of the Library of Congress will have the added initials MSS-LC.)

9. Henry P. Johnson, *The Yorktown Campaign and the Surrender of Cornwallis, 1781* (New York, 1881), 37–38.

10. *Clay Family*, 14–19: John S. Littell, *The Clay Minstrel* (New York, 1842), 72. Clay, Speaking of the Tarleton episode, states that the graves of his father and grandfather were desecrated. But probation of the wills of both of Henry Clay's grandfathers reveal they died prior to his birth. Other records in Clay Papers, MSS-LC, relating to a friendly suit over disposition of George Hudson's late property show that Clay's Hudson grandmother died in "May or June 1781," therefore probably in May, just before Tarleton's raid.

11. *Clay Family*, 28.

12. Clay Papers, MSS-LC. The land suit, dated September 1784, refers to Elizabeth Watkins, indicating her marriage to Henry Watkins earlier than this date. (See Littell, *Clay Minstrel*.)

13. Nathan Sargent (also known as Oliver Oldschool), *Life of Henry Clay* (Philadelphia, 1844), 1n.

14. Colton, *Life*, 1:19.

15. John Frost, *Clay* (Philadelphia, 1853), 17–18.

16. Richmond *Virginia Gazette*, April 13, 1791.

17. Joseph Morgan Rogers, *The True Henry Clay* (Philadelphia, 1904), 22.

18. Colton, *Life*, 1:20.

19. Frost, *Clay*, 23.

20. Clay letters to Benjamin B. Minor, May 3, 1851, in appendix of *Decisions of Cases in Virginia by the High Court of Chancery*, ed. B. B. Minor (Richmond, Va., 1852), xxxii–xxxvi.

21. Richmond *Virginia Gazette and General Advertizer*, August 21, 1793.

22. *Writings of George Washington*, ed. John C. Fitzpatrick (Washington, D.C., 1940), 33:71–72.

23. Colton, *Life*, 25.

24. *Virginia Gazette and General Advertizer*, August 5, 1795.

25. Francis J. Brooke, *A Family Narrative* (Richmond, 1849), 10–13.

Chapter 2

1. Colton, *Life*, 51.

2. Peter, Robert, *History of Fayette County Kentucky* (Chicago, 1882), 736–37.

3. Railey, William E., "History of Woodford County," *Register Kentucky Historical Society,* vol. 19, no. 55 (Frankfort, Ky., January 1921) 99.

4. "Journal of Moses Austin, 1796–7," ed. George P. Garrison, *The American Historical Review*, vol. V. no. 3 (New York, April 1900), 525–26. Austin was a poor writer. Garrison made minor punctuation changes for publication in the *Review*, but in this text still more spelling and punctuation changes have been made to provide cleaner reading.

5. George Washington Ranck, *History of Lexington, Kentucky* (Cincinnati, 1872), 14. Pages 1–15 contain an interesting and detailed account of the mound builders. See also Peter, *Fayette County*, 40–53.

6. Ranck, *Lexington*, 19; Peter, *Fayette*

County, 223–24; Lexington (Ky.) *Lexington Reporter*, July 29, 1809.

7. Peter, *Fayette County*, 61–64.

8. Ibid., 264.

9. J. O. Harrison, "Henry Clay: Reminiscences by His Executor," *Century Magazine*, vol. 33, no. 2 (New York, December 1886), 178–79.

10. George D. Prentice, *Biography of Henry Clay* (New York, 1831), 9.

11. Lexington (Ky.) *Kentucky Gazette*, April 25, 1798.

12. Ibid., February 28, 1799.

13. Ibid., August 1 and 15, 1798; Washington (D.C.) *Washington Mirror*, August 18, 1798.

14. *Kentucky Gazette*, November 28, 1798.

15. Ibid., August 5, 1816.

16. Prentice, *Clay*, 23–25.

17. E. D. Warfield, *The Kentucky Resolutions of 1798* (New York, 1894), 76; *Washington Mirror*, November 17, 1798.

18. Charles Kerr, *History of Kentucky* (Chicago, 1923), 3:5.

19. Archibald Henderson, "The Transylvania Company, A Study in Personnel; II. The Hart Brothers; Thomas, Natahaniel, and David," *The Filson Club History Quarterly*, vol. 21, no., 3 (Louisville, Ky., July 1947), 228–41.

20. Warfield, *Kentucky Resolutions*, 70–71.

21. John Breckinridge's instructions for John Payne (plantation overseer) in master's absence, October 18, 1806, Breckinridge Family Papers, MSS-LC.

22. Cassius Marcellus Clay, *The Life of Cassius Marcellus Clay* (New York, 1186), 87.

23. Prentice, *Clay*, 18.

24. L. F. Johnson, *History of Franklin County, Ky.* (Frankfort, Ky., 1912), 11–12 and 44; *Washington Mirror*, August 28, 1799. This newspaper spells the farmer's name as "Field," rather than "Fields," as Johnson does.

25. *Kentucky Gazette*, August 17, 1801.

26. Prentice, *Clay*, 12–13; Colton, *Life*, 84.

27. Ibid., 13–14 and 85; and "Henry Clay's Personal anecdotes, incidents, etc.," *Harper's Magazine*, vol. 5 (New York, August 1852), 393–94.

28. Prentice, *Clay*, 14–16; Colton, *Life*, 86.

29. Colton, *Life*, 96.

30. Prentice, *Clay*, 16–18.

31. Colton, *Life*, 39.

32. Prentice, *Clay*, 29–30.

33. Ibid., 19.

34. Calvin Colton, *The Last Seven Years of Henry Clay* (New York, 1856), 266–67.

35. Colton, *Life*, 96.

36. Rogers, *Henry Clay*, 36–37; Lexington, *Republican Leader*, April 6, 1902.

37. Ranck, *Lexington*, 211.

38. Peter Harvey, *Reminiscences and Anecdotes of Daniel Webster* (Boston, 1876), 217.

39. William W. Story, ed., *Life and Letters of Joseph Story* (London, 1851), I:423.

Chapter 3

1. *Kentucky Gazette*, February 9, 1801.

2. *National Cyclopedia of American Biography*, 13:2–3.

3. *Kentucky Gazette*, July 10, 1800.

4. *The Presidential Counts* (New York, 1877), 16–18.

5. Alexander Hamilton to Gouverneur Morris, December 29, 1800 and to James A. Bayard, August 6, 1800, *The Works of Alexander Hamilton*, ed. Henry Cabot Lodge (New York, 1904), 10:401 and 387.

6. "Papers of James A. Bayard, 1796–1815," ed. Elizabeth Donnan, *Annual Report of the American Historical Association for the Year 1913*. vol. II (Washington, 1915). Details of the election are described by Bayard, 131–36. Bayard's efforts to get Jefferson's authorization are described in the footnotes, 128–29. Bayard's letter to President John Adams, February 19, 1801, 130.

7. Frankfort (Ky.), *The Palladium*, December 25, 1802.

8. *Kentucky Gazette*, February 1, 1803.

9. Ibid., February 14, 1803.

10. Much of the story of the Louisiana Purchase has been summarized from the very detailed accounts from Henry Adams, *History of the United States of America* (New York, 1890), 1:334–98. Adams' account is outstanding by virtue of his extensive research into official archives of the United States, Great Britain, France, and Spain.

11. *The Writings of Thomas Jefferson*, collected and edited by Paul Leicester Ford (New York, 1897), 8:58.

12. Charles R. Staples, *The History of Pioneer Lexington (Kentucky), 1779–1806* (Lexington, Ky., 1959), 181–82 and 185.

13. Henry Clay to William Taylor, July 23 and August 10, 1802, and March 1, 1803, *The Papers of Henry Clay*, Vol. I, 1797–1814, ed. James F. Hopkins (Lexington, Ky., 1939), 84–85 and 98. All references from this work are Volume 1 unless otherwise noted.

14. William Littell, *The Statute Law of Kentucky* (Frankfort, Ky., 1811), 3 (1802–07):30.

15. Humphrey Marshall, *The History of Kentucky* (Frankfort, Ky., 1824), 2:374.

16. Joseph Howard Parks, *Felix Grundy* (University, La., 1940), 22. See also *Kentucky Gazette*, January 23 and 30, 1806.

17. Parks, *Grundy*, 22

18. Daniel Mallory, *The Life and Speeches of the Hon. Henry Clay* (New York, 1844), 1:18–19.

19. *Palladium*, November 12, 1803.

20. H. Adams, *History*, 1:424.

21. Summarized from the first six chapters of H. Adams, *History*, vol. 2.

22. Clay to Breckinridge, November 21, 1803, Breckinridge Family Papers, MSS-LC.

23. *Palladium*, November 26, 1803.

24. Thomas Todd to John Breckinridge, December 1, 1803, Breckinridge Papers, MSS-LC.

25. Ibid.

26. Prentice, *Clay*, 28. Also Clay to Breckinridge, December 30, 1803, Breckinridge Papers MSS-LC. Prentice, writing in 1831 or earlier, states that the attempt to remove the capital from Frankfort took place in the 1805 legislative session. This date has consistently been used by later biographers. However, Clay refers to this attempt in his 1803 letter to Breckinridge and reference to it is also contained in the *House Journal* of that session. It does not appear in later Journals or letters. It is assumed Prentice gave the date based on someone's memory rather than on documentation.

27. James K. Hosmer, *History of the Louisiana Purchase* (New York, 1902), 165–74.

28. Clay to Breckinridge, December 30, 1803, Breckinridge Papers, MSS-LC.

29. Breckinridge to Jefferson, September 10, 1803, Breckinridge Papers, MSS-LC.

30. Clay to Breckinridge, December 30, 1803, Breckinridge Papers, MSS-LC.

31. John Clay to H. Clay, July 6, 1804, T. J. Clay Papers, MSS-LC.

32. Clay to Breckinridge, (ca.) October 1, 1804, and John Clay to H. Clay, December 1, 1804, Clay, *Papers*, 152 and 159.

33. James Brown to H. Clay, March 12, 1805, Clay Papers, MSS-LC.

34. *Kentucky Gazette*, March 15, 1803, and December 13, 1805.

35. Kerr, *Kentucky*, 4.

36. Edward Stanwood, *A History of the Presidency from 1788 to 1897* (New York, 1912), 82–84.

37. Joshua W. Caldwell, *Sketches of the Bench and Bar of Tennessee* (Knoxville, Tenn., 1898), 54–55 and 60.

38. Kentucky, *Journal of the House of Representatives of Kentucky*, November 4–5, 1804.

39. Ibid., November 13–15, 1804.

40. Jack Jouett to Breckinridge, December 24, 1804, Breckinridge Papers, MSS-LC.

41. Kentucky, *Journal*, various days in November and December 1804.

42. *Kentucky Gazette*, December 8, 1804.

43. Prentice, *Clay*, 27.

44. Kentucky, *Journal*, several days in December 1804.

45. James Brown to Clay, March 12, 1805, Clay Papers, MSS-LC.

46. W. Moore to Breckinridge, January 23, 1805, Breckinridge Papers, MSS-LC.

47. *Kentucky Gazette*, January 29, 1805.

48. Henry Innes to Breckinridge, December 20, 1804, Breckinridge Papers, MSS-LC.

49. Breckinridge was advised by Robert H. Grayson in a letter dated November 18, 1804. Breckinridge suggested Grundy be named a U.S. Commissioner in a letter to Albert Gallatin, April 25, 1805. Gallatin informed Breckinridge that the post was filled in a letter dated July 11, 1805. All of these are in Breckinridge Papers, MSS-LC.

50. James Brown to Clay, October 31, 1805, Clay Papers, MSS-LC.

51. Kentucky, *Journal*, November 4, 1805.

52. Marshall, *Kentucky*, 374.

53. William Stevenson to Breckinridge, January 5, 1806, Breckinridge Papers, MSS-LC.

54. Kentucky, *Journal*, November 21–23, 1805.

55. Ibid., December 1805.

56. Dr. Samuel Brown to James Brown, December 13, 1805, James Brown Papers, MSS-LC.

57. Mallory, *Life*, 2:61.

58. Innes to Breckinridge, December 24, 1805, Breckinridge Papers, MSS-LC.

59. Ibid., William Russell to Breckinridge, March 1, 1806.

60. Ibid., F. L. Turner to Breckinridge, December 20, 1805.

Chapter 4

1. Robert Peter, *Transylvania University: Its Origin, Rise, Decline, and Fall*, [Filson Club Publication, No. 11] (Louisville, Ky., 1896), 88–89.

2. *Kentucky Gazette*, January 6, April 15 and 19, May 13, June 7 and 14, 1806.

3. Breckinridge to Clay, March 19, 1806, typed copy in Indiana Historical Society — William H. Smith Collection, Indianapolis, Ind.

4. *National Intelligencer*, Washington, D.C., August 15, 1806.

5. Washington (D.C.), *National Intelligencer*, August 15, 1806.

6. Ibid.

7. John Wood to Clay, October 9, 1806, Clay Papers, MSS-LC.

8. Technically, Marshall was not one of the midnight appointees because he was named to the court prior to passage of the judiciary bill that gave Adams the authority to fill an expanded court system with new judges. But Marshall is generally included because Adams' appointees were almost exclusively Federalists who received their posts in the closing days of the President's term and Marshall fits in this mold.

9. *National Cyclopedia*, 2:412.

10. W. M. Paxton, *The Marshall Family* (Cincinnati, 1885), 81.

11. Two books are quite detailed on the history of the Spanish Conspiracy. Thomas Marshall Green, author of *The Spanish Conspiracy* (1891), was related ancestorily to the Marshalls and rendered their viewpoint in his history. The other account, by Temple Bodley, in the form of an "Introduction" to reprints of *Littell's Political Transactions in and Concerning Kentucky*, Filson Club Publication, no. 31 (Louisville, Ky., 1926), is written with more objectivity and is based on more recent research.

12. These accounts are drawn from the *National Intelligencer*, August 15, 1806, which reprinted in full the first serialization of "The Spanish Conspiracy" in Frankfort (Ky.) *Western World*, July 6, 1806.

13. Bodley, *Littell's*, xxxi–xxxv.

14. *Western World*, September 13, 1806.

15. Andrew Jackson, a former U.S. Senator from Tennessee, had killed Charles Dickinson in a duel earlier in the year. Following Burr's visit, Jackson issued a proclamation, October 4, 1806, "to the militia of Tennessee, calling for volunteers for an expedition against the Spaniards." Miss Leslie Henshaw, "The Aaron Burr Conspiracy in the Ohio Valley," *Ohio Archeological and Historical Society Publications* (Cincinnati, 1919), 127.

16. *National Intelligencer*, September 26, 1806.

17. John Wood to W. S. Hunter, June 22, 1809, Innes Papers, MSS-LC.

18. *Western World*, September 20, 1806.

19. Ibid., November 1, 1806.

20. *National Cyclopedia*, 13:56–57.

21. Joseph Hamilton Daveiss, "View of the President's Conduct Concerning the Conspiracy of 1806," reprinted in *Quarterly Publication of the historical and Philosophical Society of Ohio* (Cincinnati, 1917), 12, nos. 2 and 3: 69–96.

22. Clay to Dr. R. Pindell, October 15, 1828, Clay, *Correspondence*, 206–07.

23. R. T. Coleman, "Jo Daveiss, of Kentucky," *Harper's New Monthly Magazine* (New York, 1860), 21 (June–Nov.): 341–56.

24. *Kentucky Gazette*, July 19, 1803.

25. Adams nominated Daveiss on December 8, 1800, and he was confirmed by the Senate on the 12th, *Journal of the Executive Proceedings of the Senate* (Washington, 1828), 1 (1789–1805):357–58.

26. Kentucky House of Representatives, *Journal*, November 3, 1806.

27. *Kentucky Gazette*, November 6, 1806.

28. *Western World*, November 8, 1806.

29. Burr to Clay, November 7, 1806, Clay Papers, MSS-LC.

30. Clay, *Correspondence*, 207.

31. James Parton, *The Life and Times of Aaron Burr* (New York, 1861), 50n. Burr's biography, here is summarized from the early chapters of Parton's book.

32. *Western World*, November 8, 1806.

33. *Kentucky Gazette*, November 17, 1806.

34. Ibid.

35. Kentucky House of Representatives, *Journal* (1806), 35–36.

36. Ibid., 59–62.

37. Ibid., 63.

38. Ibid., 67–68.

39. *Palladium*, November 27, 1806.

40. Burr to Clay, November 27, 1806, Clay Papers, MSS-LC.

41. Kentucky House of Representatives, *Journal* (1806) 86, 96–114.

42. John Breckinridge to Polly Breckinridge, July 25, 1806; and to Joseph Cabell Breckinridge, August 30, 1806, Breckinridge Papers, MSS-LC; and to Thomas Jefferson, October 21, 1806, Thomas Jefferson Papers, MSS-LC.

43. Burr to Clay, December 1, 1806, T. J. Clay Papers, MSS-LC.

44. *Western World*, December 18, 1806. These proceedings were also reprinted in the *National Intelligencer*, January 5 and 12, 1807.

45. *National Intelligencer*, January 5, 1807

46. *Western World*, December 18, 1806.

47. *National Intelligencer*, January 5, 1807.

48. William Flavius McCaleb, *The Aaron Burr Conspiracy* (New York, 1903), 188.

49. Ibid., 191, and *National Intelligencer*, January 2, 1807.

50. *Western World*, December 18, 1806.

51. Ibid.

52. *Kentucky Gazette*, December 15, 1806.

53. Ibid., and *Western World*, December 18, 1806.

54. Ibid.

Chapter 5

1. Clay to Thomas M. Prentice, February 15, 1807, Clay, *Correspondence*, 14–15; Hopkins in Clay, *Papers*, I:281n, says date may be correct but he believes Clay's letter was written to William Prentice. He took information from a typed copy of the Historical and Philosophical Society of Ohio, Cincinnati, Ohio.

2. William Plumer, *Diary*, pt. 2:583–84, William Plumer Papers, MSS-LC.

3. *Ibid.*, 612–13.

4. Clay to Joseph M. Street, December 17, 1806, *Annals of Ohio* (Des Moines, Iowa, April 1909), 5:71–72.

5. William H. Safford, *The Blennerhassett Papers* (Cincinnati, 1864), 470.

6. Margaret Bayard Smith, *The First Forty Years of Washington Society* (New York, 1906), 10–11.

7. Plumer, *Diary*, 546–47, Plumer Papers, MSS-LC.

8. Ibid., 745–46.

9. Ibid., 606.

10. Clay to Dr. Pindell, October 15, 1828, Clay, *Correspondence*, 208.

11. Clay to Col. Thomas Hart, February 1, 1807, typed copy, Smith Collection, Indiana Historical Society.

12. Plumer, *Diary*, 790–91, Plumer Papers, MSS-LC.

13. Ibid., 625–28.

14. Ibid., 628.

15. *Annals of Congress*, 9th Cong., 2nd sess., 30.

16. John Quincy Adams, *Memoirs of John Quincy Adams*, ed. Charles Francis Adams (Philadelphia, 1874), 1:444–45.

17. Plumer, *Diary*, 750–53, Plumer Papers, MSS-LC.

18. Ibid., 857, and *Annals*, 9th Cong., 2nd sess., 52 and 76.

19. William Cranch, *Reports of Cases in the Supreme Court of the United States*, 2nd edition (New York, 1812), 4:171–75.

20. A. C. Quisenberry, *The Life and Times of Hon. Humphrey Marshall* (Winchester, Ky., 1892), 107.

21. Plumer, *Diary*, 535–36, 659, 671–72, and 801, Plumer Papers, MSS-LC. and Clay, *Clay Family*, 70.

22. Plumer, *Diary*, 698, Plumer Papers, MSS-LC.

23. Ibid., 700–01.

24. John Adams to Dr. Benjamin Rush, February 2, 1807, Alexander Biddle, *Old Family Letters*, Series A (Philadelphia, 1892), 129.

25. *Annals*, 9th Cong., 2nd sess., 39–43.

26. Aaron Burr to James Wilkinson (in cipher), July 29, 1806, General James Wilkinson, *Memoirs of My Own Times* (Philadelphia, 1816), 316.

27. Ibid., 317.

28. Ibid., Appendix LIX, Second Deposition of Isaac Briggs, Isaac Briggs Papers, MSS-LC.

29. Plumer, *Diary*, 729–30, Plumer Papers, MSS-LC.

30. Ibid., 731–32 and 754.

31. Ibid., 815–20 and 844–49.

32. Dunbar Rowland, *Third Annual Report of the Director of the Department of Archives and History of the State of Mississippi*, October 1, 1903 to October 1, 1904 (Nashville, Tenn., 1905), Appendix III, 101.

33. Clay to Innes, January 16, 1807, Clay, *Papers*, 270.

34. Clay to Prentice, February 15, 1807, Clay, *Correspondence*, 14.

Chapter 6

1. Clay to Prentiss, February 15, 1807. Clay, *Correspondence*, 14–15.

2. Document dated July 16, 1807, T. J. Clay Papers, MSS-LC.

3. *Western World*, March 5, 1807, and *Kentucky Gazette*, January 14, 1808.

4. Albert James Pickett, *History of Alabama* (Charleston, S.C., 1851), 2:213–28. These pages contain a detailed and interesting account of Burr's capture and journey to Richmond. Pickett personally interviewed Mr. Hinson, Lieutenant Gaines, and his brother (who was ill at Ft. Stoddert), and a member of the posse that escorted Burr to Richmond.

5. Cranch, *Reports*, 126.

6. Washington Irving to Mrs. Hoffman, June 4, 1807, Pierre Munroe Irving, *Life and Letters of Irving* (New York, 1882), 1:150–51.

7. Open letter from Samuel Swartout to Brig. Gen. James Wilkinson, October 21, 1807, *Virginia Gazette*; Safford, *Blennerhassett*, 459n–60n.

8. Safford, *Blennerhassett*, 268–71.

9. Most of the description of Burr's trial has been summarized from a variety of sources. Some of the best accounts are found in Parton, *Burr*, 458–512; McCaleb, *Burr Conspiracy*, 310–60; and Nathan Schachner, *Aaron Burr* (New York, 1937), 396–441.

10. Clay to Caesar Augustus Rodney, December 5, 1807, Rodney Family Papers, MSS-LC.

11. Prentice, *Clay*, 34.

12. Summarized from Parton, Schachner, and others named in note 9.

13. Winfield Scott, *Memoirs of Lieut.-General Scott* (New York, 1864), 11–19.

14. Summarized from H. Adams, *History*, 4:1–26.

15. Jefferson to James Maury, April 25, 1812, Thomas Jefferson, *The Works of Thomas Jefferson* (New York, 1905), 242.

16. Coleman, "Daveiss," *Harpers Monthly*, 21:352.

17. Kentucky, *Journal*, January 5, 1808, 28–29, and January 23, 1808, 84.

18. Ibid., January 11, 1808, 44–46.

19. Ibid., January 6, 1808, 33.

20. Ibid., January 12, 1808, 51.

21. Ibid., January 6, 1808, 33.

22. Ibid., January 12, 1808, 51.

23. Ibid., January 15, 1808, 62.

24. Ibid., January 18, 1808, 72.

25. Thomas Hart Clay, *Henry Clay* (Philadelphia, 1910), 46–47.

26. Kentucky, *Journal*, January 26–February 19, 1808, 96–216.

27. *Western World*, February 25, 1808.

Chapter 7

1. *Lexington Reporter*, June 11, 1808 (reprinted from the *Kentucky Gazette*).

2. *Western World*, June 30, 1808.

3. *Lexington Reporter*, June 18, 1808.

4. Ibid., June 11, 1808.

5. *Kentucky Gazette*, June 21, 1808.

6. *Lexington Reporter*, July 2, 1808.

7. Ibid., July 9, 1808.

8. James Brown to Clay, September 1, 1808, T. J. Clay Papers, MSS-LC. Also, Clay, *Correspondence*, 16–17.

9. Kentucky, *Journal*, December 12, 1808, 3.

10. Prentice, *Clay*, 24.

11. Kentucky, *Journal*, December 15, 1808, 30–31.

12. Ibid., January, 3, 1909, 93.

13. Lewis Collins, *History of Kentucky* (Covington, Ky., 1881), 477; Quisenberry, *Humphrey Marshall*, 100–01; H. Blanton to Patrick U. Major, June 3, 1879 (folder 82 at Kentucky Historical Society, Frankfort, Ky.).

14. Bernard Mayo, *Henry Clay: Spokesman of the New West* (New York, 1937), 338.

15. Clay to Marshall and Marshall to Clay, January 4, 1809. Both notes now in Clay Papers, MSS-LC. They were also reprinted in *Lexington Reporter*, January 26, 1809, and *Kentucky Gazette*, January 31, 1809. Both Clay and Marshall had written "Frankfort" before the date at the top of their notes and then inked over it to remove appearance of negotiating the duel on Kentucky territory.

16. Clay to Thomas Hart, Jr., January 4, 1809, Clay Papers, MSS-LC. It is claimed in Quisenberry, *Humphrey Marshall*, 103, that "the pistols with which this celebrated duel was fought belonged to Col. Joseph Hamilton Daveiss, and are not (1889) in the possession of a member of the family living in Harrodsburg, Ky."

17. Kentucky, *Journal*, January 5, 1809.

18. Duel rules, January 19, 1809, Clay Papers, MSS-LC. Reprinted in *Kentucky Gazette*, January 31, 1809.

19. Duel description, Ibid.

20. Quisenberry, *Humphrey Marshall*, 103n.

21. Dr. Frederick Ridgley to Thomas Hart, Jr., January 19, 1809, Clay Papers, MSS-LC.

22. T. H. Clay, *Clay*, 550–51.

23. *Appleton's Cyclopaedia of American Biography* (New York, 1898), 2:308.

24. Katherine Helm, *The True Story of Mary, Wife of Lincoln* (New York, 1928), 3 and 71–72.

25. *Kentucky Gazette*, March 21, July 11, August 8, October 31, November 7 and 28, 1809.

26. Kentucky, *Journal*, January 4, 1809, 120.

27. Story by George E. Kelley in a Louisville paper, 1896.

28. U.S. *Senate Journal*, 11th Cong., 2nd sess., February 6, 1810, 435.

29. *Kentucky Gazette*, March 6, 1810.

30. Clay to George Thompson, March 14, 1810, Clay Papers, MSS-LC.

31. Allen C. Clark, *Life and Letters of Dolly Madison* (Washington, 1914), 93.

32. Clay to John Watts, March 4, 1810, Clay, *Papers*, 456.

33. *National Intelligencer*, February 23, 1810.

34. *Annals*, 11th Cong., 2nd sess., 579–82.

35. H. Adams, *History*, 5:191–98.

36. James Brown to Clay, February 26, 1810, Clay Papers, MSS-LC.

37. *Annals*, 11th Cong., 2nd sess., 644.

38. Ibid., 663–64.

39. Ibid., 626–30.

40. *Kentucky Gazette*, May 15, 1810.

41. Clay to James Monroe, November 13, 1810, Monroe Papers, MSS-LC.

Chapter 8

1. Clay to Rodney, August 6, 1810, Rodney Papers, MSS-LC.

2. *Annals*, 11th Cong., 3rd sess., 1258.

3. Ibid., 43–63.

4. Extract of a letter from Washington to the editors of the *Baltimore American & Commercial Daily Advertizer*, January 2, 1811, published as an extract in the *Kentucky Gazette*, January 29, 1811.

5. *Annals*, 11th Cong., 3rd sess., 65–66.

6. Ibid., 67 and 79.

7. Ibid., 83 and 1259–60.

8. Ibid., 1262.

9. Ibid., 369–70.

10. Ibid., 370–77.

11. Ibid., 525.

12. *Annals*, 11th Cong., 3rd sess., 1258.

13. Ibid., 107, 127, 937–38, 151–52, 963–64.

14. H. Adams, *History*, 5:331.

15. Albert Gallatin to John Badollet, July 29, 1824, microfilm of Gallatin Papers, MSS-LC. Originals at New York Historical Society.

16. Gallatin to William Crawford, January 30, 1811, *Annals*, 11th Cong., 3rd sess., 123–25.

17. Ibid., 132–50.

18. Ibid., 175–208.

19. Ibid., 209–19.

20. Ibid., 346–47.

21. J. Q. Adams, *Memoirs*, 64. Adams wrote on November 26, 1825, "Mr. Clay said that he wrote the speech of Vice President George Clinton which he delivered in Senate upon giving the casting vote against the renewal of the old Bank of the United States. He said it was perhaps the thing that gained the old man more credit than anything else that he ever did. He had written it, but under Mr. Clinton's dictation, and he never should think of claiming it as his composition."

22. Extract of a letter to the editors of the *Baltimore Whig*, February 15, 1811, reprinted in *Philadelphia Aurora*, February 22, 1811.

23. From *Richmond Enquirer*, reprinted in *Philadelphia Aurora*, March 20, 1811.

24. Irving, *Life*, 1:272.

25. Smith, *Forty Years*, 84–85.

26. Irving, *Life*, 263.

27. Gallatin to Madison, March 4, 1811, Gallatin Papers, MSS-LC.

28. Monroe to Madison, March 23, 1811, *The Writings of James Monroe*, ed. Stanislaus Murray Hamilton (New York, 1901), 5 (1807–1816):181–82.

29. Madison summed up his conversation with Smith in 19 pages, which he endorsed "(Quere: if necessary to become public). Memorandum as to R. Smith. April 1811." Madison Papers, MSS-LC.

30. Robert Smith to Samuel Smith, March 1811, Samuel Smith Papers, MSS-LC.

31. William Duane, editor of the *Philadelphia Aurora*, had published an anti–Administration address and editorialized in support of it and Smith.

32. Clay to Rodney, April 29, 1811, Gallatin Papers, MSS-LC.

Chapter 9

1. Clay to Rodney, April 29, 1811, Gallatin Papers, MSS-LC.

2. Duc de Cadore to General John Armstrong, August 5, 1810, *State Papers and Publick Documents of the United States* (Boston, 1817), VII:468–70.

3. *National Intelligencer*, January 31, and February 2, 1811.

4. *American State Paper: Foreign Relations* (Washington, D.C., 1832), 3:471–99.

5. Jefferson to William Henry Harrison, February 27, 1803, *Writings of Thomas Jefferson*, ed. Andrew A. Lipscomb (Washington, D.C., 1903), 10:368–73.

6. William Henry Harrison to William Eustis, August 6, 1810, *Messages and Letters of William Henry Harrison*, ed. Logan Esarey, [Vol. VII of Indiana Historical Collection, *Governors Messages and Letters*] (Indianapolis, Ind., 1922), 1 (1810–11):456–57.

7. Benson J. Lossing, *The Pictorial Field-book of the War of 1812* (New York, 1868), 191–93. Lossing's book comes close to being the Bible of the histories on the War of 1812. Many years after that war Lossing travelled to all of the major sites of land battles and interviewed hundreds of survivors of the war. The account of Harrison's meeting with Tecumseh is retold in a letter from Harrison to Eustis, August 22, 1810, in Harrison, *Messages and Letters*, 1:459–63. Following that letter is a reprint of Tecumseh's speeches of August 20 and 21 which Harrison included in his letter to Eustis, 1:463–69.

8. *Kentucky Gazette*, July 23, 1811.

9. Ibid., October 8, 1811, The *Gazette's* reprint was from the Cincinnati *Liberty Hall* of September 25, 1811, when that paper quoted from a letter from Fort Wayne dated September 6. The letter stated that the notice appeared in the *National Intelligencer* with no date given. The original source was a letter from Harrison to Eustis, July 18, 1810, found complete in Harrison, *Messages and Letters*, 1:446–47. The British agent mentioned in the quote was not "Ellicott," but rather Mathew Elliot. Even Harrison's letter to Eustis had spelled the name with one "t."

10. Clay to Rodney, August 17, 1811, Rodney family Papers, MSS-LC.

11. Bayard to Rodney, December 22, 1811, "James Asheton Bayard Letters, 1802–1814," *Bulletin of the New York Public Library*, 4 (1908):232.

12. Nathan Sargent, *Public Men and Events* (Philadelphia, 1875), 125.

13. Lemuel Sawyer, *Biography of John Randolph* (New York, 1844), 12.

14. William Plumer, *Memorandum of Proceedings in the United States Senate, 1803–1807*, ed. Everett Somerville Brown (New York, 1923), 269.

15. Sawyer, *Randolph*, 42.

16. Sargent, *Public Men*, 130.

17. Edward Hooker, "Diary of Edward Hooker," *Annual Report of the American Historical Association* (Washington, D.C., 1897), 1 (1896):927.

18. *Annals*, 12th Cong., 1st sess., 330–31.

19. Benjamin Franklin Perry, *Reminiscences of Public Men* (Philadelphia, 1883), 53.

20. John A. Harper to Plumer, December 2, 1811, Plumer Papers, MSS-LC.

21. Clay, *Papers*, 1:594.

22. *Annals*, 12th Cong., 1st sess., 11–15.

23. Rep. (Rev.) Samuel Taggart to Rev. John Taylor, November 7, 1811, "Letters of Samuel Taggart," *Proceedings, American Antiquarian Society* (Worcester, Mass., 1924), New Series, v.33, Pt. 2:361. (Hereafter cited as N.S., 33/2:361.)

24. Reprint from *Baltimore Whig* in *New York Evening Post*, November 19, 1811.

25. Reprint from Lexington *Reporter* in *New York Evening Post*, December 12, 1811.

26. *Annals*, 12th Cong., 1st sess., 376–77.

27. Felix Grundy to Andrew Jackson, November 28, 1811, Andrew Jackson, *Correspondence*, ed. John Spencer Bassett (Washington, 1926), 1:208.

28. William Lowndes to his wife, December 7, 1811, Mrs. St. Julien Ravenel, *Life and Times of William Lowndes* (New York, 1901), 90.

29. *Annals*, 12th Cong., 1st sess., 414–417.

30. Ibid., 422.

31. Ibid., 422–27.

32. Ibid., 441–55.

33. Ibid., 456–67.

34. Ibid., 476–83.

35. *Richmond Enquirer*, December 24, 1811.

36. *Annals*, 12th Cong., 1st sess., 491.

37. Ibid., 525–45.

38. *National Intelligencer*, December 31, 1811.

39. *Annals*, 12th Cong., 1st sess., 588–89.

40. Charles Humphreys to Clay, May 4, 1812, RG 107, Letters Received, (6) C-303, National Archives, Washington, D.C.

41. James B. Swain, *The Life and Speeches of Henry Clay* (New York, 1843), 1:15–21. While Swain's copy of Clay's speech differs in some order and even phraseology from all other reprints (including that in the *Annals*, 12th Cong., 1st sess., 596–606), his is the only one to present Clay's words as spoken in the first person and is, therefore, the reference used here.

Chapter 10

1. *Annals*, 12th Cong., 1st sess., 616.

2. Ibid., 707.

3. Ibid., 735–37.

4. Ibid., 743–44.

5. Ibid., 876.

6. Swain., *Life*, 22–32.

7. *Annals*, 12th Cong., 1st sess., 999.

8. Clay to James Morrison, December 21, 1811, Clay Papers, MSS–Duke University.

9. Bayard to Rodney, December 22, 1811, *Bulletin, NYPL*, 4:232–38.

10. Josiah Quincy to Harrison Gray Otis, Samuel Eliot Morison, *Life and Letters of Harrison Gray Otis, Federalist 1765–1848* (Boston and New York, 1913), 2:34.

11. Taggart to Taylor, December 28, 1811, *Proceedings, AAS*, n.s., 33/2:371–72.

12. Sir. Augustus John Foster to Richard Wellesley, December 11, 1811, Great Britain, Public Records Office, Foreign Office 5, Vol. 77, photostats in MSS-LC. (Hereafter cited as FO 5:77 or other volume number.)

13. Ibid., November 25, 1811.

14. Ibid., November 29, 1811.

15. Ibid., December 11 and 18, 1811.

16. Ibid., December 20, 1811.

17. Ibid., January 30, 1812.

18. Ibid., January 16 and 31, 1812, vol. 84.

19. Ibid., February 2, 1812.

20. Ibid., January 31, 1812.

21. Ibid., January 11 and 16, 1812, vol. 77.

22. Harper to Plumer, February 17, 1812, Plumer Papers, MSS-LC.

23. James Bayard to Andrew Bayard, January 25, 1812, Bayard, *Report, AHA*, 2 (1913):189–90.

24. Sir. Augustus John Foster, *Diary*, February 11 and April 15, 1812; Foster, *Notes on the United States of America*, 1:4 and 149, Augustus Foster Papers, MSS-LC.

25. Bayard to Andrew Bayard, January 25, 1812, Bayard, *Report, AHA*, 2 (1913): 189–90.

26. Harper to Plumer, February 6, 1812, Plumer Papers, MSS-LC.

27. Grundy to Jackson, February 12, 1812, Jackson, *Correspondence*, 216.

28. Henry Dearborn to Gallatin, March 29, 1812, Gallatin Papers, MSS-LC.

29. Taggart to Taylor, February 24, 1812, *Proceedings, AAS*, n.s., 33/2:385.

30. Bayard to Rodney, January 26, 1812, *Bulletin, NYPL*, 4:233.

31. From *Baltimore Sun*, quoted in *Philadelphia Aurora*, January 31, 1812.

32. *Aurora*, January 25, 1812.

33. Ibid., January 30, 1812.

34. *National Intelligencer*, January 28, 1812.

35. Gallatin to Clay, January 21, 1812, *Annals*, 12th Cong., 1st sess., 929.

36. *Annals*, 12th Cong., 1st sess., 1041.

37. *Lexington Reporter*, February 4, 1812.

38. Clay to editor, February 9, 1812, Ibid., February 12, 1812.

39. Clay to editor, February 28, 1812, Ibid., March 7, 1812.

40. Foster to Wellesley, FO 5:84, February 26, and March 6, 1812.

41. Madison to Jefferson, March 6, 1812, James Madison, *Letters and Other Writings of James Madison* (Philadelphia, 1865), 2 (1794–1815):530.

42. Jefferson to Madison, March 26, 1812, Jefferson Papers, MSS-LC.

43. Jefferson to Hugh Nelson, April 2, 1812, Ibid.

44. H. Adams, *History*, 4:176–77. Much of the account of the Henry episode is rewritten from Adams' description in his history published in 1890. By 1895 he had found evidence that some of his "facts." were wrong. He wrote a paper of correction entitled, "Count Edward de Crillon," *The American Historical Review* (New York, 1896), 1 (October 1895):51–69.

45. Foster, *Notes*, 110–11, Foster Papers, MSS-LC.

46. Ibid., 112; and Elbridge Gerry to Madison, January 2 and 3, 1812, Madison Papers, MSS-LC.

47. H. Adams, *History*, 6:177–78; and Foster, *Notes*, 113, Foster Papers, MSS-LC.

48. H. Adams, *History*, 6:178–81; and *American Historical Review*, 1 (October 1895):51–69.

49. Harper to Plumer, March 11, 1812, Plumer Papers, MSS-LC.

50. *Annals*, 12th Cong., 1st sess., 1182.

51. Ibid., 1184.

52. Dolley Madison to Mrs. Anna Cutts, March 20, 1812, Dolly Madison, [She used the spelling, "Dolley"], *Memoirs and Letters of Dolly Madison*, ed. Lucia B. Cutts (Boston and New York, 1826), 76; and Abijah Bigelow to Mrs. Bigelow, March 18, 1812, "Letters of Abijah Bigelow, Member of Congress, to His Wife, [Hannah], 1810–1815, *Proceedings, AAS*, 40:331. Bigelow wrote, "There is much trouble at the white house as we call it, I mean the President's." This clearly proves that the building had acquired that identification prior to the burning by the British in August 1814.

53. Abijah Bigelow to Mrs. Bigelow, March 22, 1812, *Proceedings, AAS*, 40:333.

54. *Annals*, 12th Cong., 1st sess., 1204–05; 1217–18; and 1225–27.

Chapter 11

1. Clay to James Monroe, March 15, 1812, Monroe Papers, MSS-LC.

2. Bayard to Rodney, March 16, 1812, *Bulletin, NYPL*, 4:236.

3. Foster, *Diary*, March 20, 1812, Foster Papers, MSS-LC.

4. Foster to Robert Stewart, 2nd Marquis of Londonderry, better known as Viscount Castlereagh, April 1, 1812, FO 5:85, Pt.3. On March 31, 1812, Foster learned from dispatches from his Government that Castlereagh had succeeded Lord Wellesley (resigned February 18) as Secretary for Foreign Affairs on February 28, 1812. Thus his official correspondence to that office was now directed to a new superior.

5. *National Intelligencer*, March 24. 1812.

6. Wellesley to Foster, Dispatches No.

1 and No. 2 of January 28, 1812, Draft in FO 5:83. Also Great Britain, Foreign Office, *Papers Presented to Parliament in 1813* (London, n.d.), 314–323. Also Great Britain, Foreign Office, "Instructions to the British Ministers to the United States, 1791–1812," ed. Bernard Mayo, *Report AHA* 3 (1936):340.

7. Foster to Castlereagh, April 1, 1812, FO 5:85, pt.3.

8. Louis Sérurier to Le Duc de Bassano [Hugues Bernard Maret], March 22, 1812, French Document no. 49, *Correspondence Politique, Etats Unis*, vol 67, pt. 3, item 184, Archives des Affaires Étrangères, Paris. Bassano became the French Minister of Foreign Affairs on April 17, 1811.

9. Ibid., March 23, 1812.

10. *Annals*, 12th Cong., 1st sess., 1234–35.

11. Foster to Wellesley, February 27, 1812, FO 5:84.

12. Foster, *Diary*, March 25, 1812, Foster Papers, MSS-LC.

13. Clark, *Dolly Madison*, 127; and Foster, *Diary*, March 29, 1812, Foster Papers, MSS-LC.

14. Dolley Madison to Anna Cutts, March 27, 1812, Clark, *Dolly Madison*, 130.

15. James Bayard to Andrew Bayard, May 2, 1812, Bayard, *Papers*, 196.

16. Foster, *Diary*, March 30, 1812, Foster Papers, MSS-LC.

17. Gallatin to Jefferson, March 10, 1812, Albert Gallatin, *The Writings of Albert Gallatin*, ed. Henry Adams (Philadelphia, 1897), 1:517.

18. The entire account of this hearing of the Foreign Relations Committee is from a memo dated March 31, 1812, Samuel Smith papers, MSS-LC.

19. *National Intelligencer*, April 2, 1812.

20. Madison to Jefferson, April 3, 1812, *Madison*, 2 (1794–1815):530–32.

21. Foster, *Diary*, March 31, 1812, Foster papers, MSS-LC.

22. Edmund Quincy, *Life of Josiah Quincy* (Boston, 1874), 256.

23. *Annals*, 12th Cong., 1st sess., 1587.

24. Ibid., 1587–98, for this long debate.

25. Foster, *Diary*, April 1, 1812, Foster Papers, MSS-LC.

26. Foster to Castlereagh, April 2, 1812, FO 5:85.

27. Ibid., April 3, 1812.

28. *Annals*, 12th Cong., 1st sess., 1602–05.

29. Ibid., 1616.

30. Ibid., 1255–66.

Chapter 12

1. James Madison to Thomas Jefferson, April 24, 1812, Madison Papers, MSS-LC.

2. *National Intelligencer*, April 9, 1812.

3. Sérurier to Bassano, April 9, 1812, Archives des Affaires Étrang res, Paris; and H. Adams, *History*, 6:200–01.

4. Foster to Castlereagh, April 23, 1812, FO 5:85, pt. 2, no. 26.

5. *National Intelligencer*, April 14, 1812.

6. Foster to Castlereagh, April 23, 1812, FO 5:85, pt. 2, no. 26.

7. Foster, *Diary*, May 13, and April 8, 1812, Foster Papers, MSS-LC.

8. The Monroe draft of the editorial, published in the *National Intelligencer*, April 14, 1812, is in the Franklin D. Roosevelt Library, Hyde Park, N.Y.

9. Joseph Gales, "Recollection of the Civil History of the War of 1812," (by a Contemporary), *National Intelligencer*, September 12, 1857.

10. Henry Adams, *Life of Albert Gallatin* (Philadelphia, 1879), 460–61.

11. New York *Evening Post*, April 1 and 3.

12. Madison to Jefferson, April 24, 1812, Madison, *Letters*, 2:534.

13. Foster to Castlereagh, April 2, 1812, FO 5:85, pt. 2, no. 21.

14. Madison to Jefferson, April 24, 1812, Madison, *Letters*, 534.

15. Foster to Castlereagh, April 23, 1812, FO 5:85, pt. 2, no. 26.

16. Foster, *Diary*, April 4, 15, and 17, 1812, Foster Papers, MSS-LC.

17. Foster to Castlereagh, April 21, 1812, FO 5:85, pt. 2, no. 25.

18. Foster, *Diary*, April 21–22, Foster Papers, MSS-LC.

19. *Annals*, 12th Cong., 1st sess., 1326.

20. *Niles Weekly Register*, April 25, 1812, 130.

21. *National Intelligencer*, April 23, 1812.

22. *Annals*, 12th Cong., 1st sess., 1354–62.

23. Ibid., 1375 and 227.

24. H. Adams, *History*, 6:207–9.

25. The New York Republicans had by now accepted the Federalists' term for their party — "Democrats."

26. Foster to Castlereagh, April 24, 1812, FO 5:85, pt. 3.

27. Rutherford to Morris, May 2, 1812, Gouverneur Morris, *The Diary and Letters of Gouverneur Morris*, ed. Anne Cory Morris (New York, 1888), 2:539.

28. *National Intelligencer*, May 24, 1812 (quoted from Albany *Register*).

29. *Annals*, 12th Cong., 1st sess., 1425.

30. Harper to Plumer, May 13, 1812, Plumer Letters, MSS-LC.

31. Foster to Castlereagh, May 15, 1812, FO 5:86, pt. 1, no. 35.

32. Foster, *Diary*, May 19, 1812, Foster Papers, MSS-LC.

33. *Niles*, May 23, 1812, 192–93.

34. Ibid.

35. Ibid., June 27, 1812, 276.

36. Ibid.

Chapter 13

1. *Annals*, 12th Cong. 2nd sess., 565.

2. Swain, *Clay*, 40.

3. *Annals*, 13th Cong. 1st. sess., 254.

4. Adams, *Gallatin*, 457–58.

5. Adams, *Memoirs*, I, 377.

6. Bayard to Rodney, March 22, 1812, *Bulletin, NYPL*, 237.

7. Bayard to Madison, April 14, 1812, Bayard, *Papers*, 195.

8. Epes Sargent, *The Life and Public Services of Henry Clay* (Auburn, N.Y., 1852 edition), 44–45.

9. Edwin Williams, *The Statesman's Manual* (New York, 1849), 178.

10. Richard Hildreth, *The History of the United States of America* (New York, 1852), 6:298.

Chapter 14

1. Sérurier to Bassano, May 27, 1812, Adams, *History*, 6:217.

2. Ibid.

3. Foster to Castlereagh, May 23, 1812, FO 5:86, pt.1.

4. *Kentucky Gazette*, June 9, 1812.

5. Foster to Castlereagh, June 6, 1812, FO 5:86, pt.1, no. 41.

6. Duc de Bassano's report to Napoleon, March 10, 1812, ASP:FR, 458. This was published March 16, 1812, in the French newspaper *Moniteur*, and Castlereagh sent a copy of the paper to Foster.

7. Castlereagh to Foster, April 10, 1812, FO 115. Also Great Britain, "Instructions," *Report AHA*, 3 (1936):360.

8. Madison, *Writings*, 9:272–73; Also, Madison Papers, MSS-LC.

9. Foster to Castlereagh, June 6, FO 5:86, pt. 1. no. 41

10. Foster to Monroe, June 4, 1812, ASP:FR, 3:461. At the beginning of this note to Monroe, Foster wrote, "I have perceived an article in the public prints stated to be extracted from an English newspaper, and purporting to be an official declaration of His Royal Highness, the Prince Regent." Comparing the wording Foster gave Monroe on the 4th to the official document, that arrived some days later, the sentence structure differs but the meaning is unaltered.

11. Foster to Castlereagh, June 6, 1812, "Private and Secret," FO 5:86, pt.1.

12. Sargent, *Life*, 41.

13. Ibid.

14. *Annals*, 12th Cong., 1st sess., 1451–68.

15. Robert C. Winthrop, *Memoir of Henry Clay* (Cambridge, Mass., 1880), 6.

16. *Annals*, 12th Cong., 1st sess., 1468–70.

17. Hugh Garland, *Life of John Randolph of Roanoke* (New York, 1859), 1:299–303.

18. *National Intelligencer*, June 18, 1812.

19. Ibid., July 2, 1812.

20. Cheves to Clay, July 30, 1812, Colton, *Correspondence*, 18–19.

21. *Annals*, 12th Cong. 1st Sess. 1624–29.

22. Ibid., 1630–32.

23. Ibid., 1546–54.

24. *Annals*, 12th Cong. 1st Sess. 1638. From a statement by Rep. Samuel Taggart preceding a speech of his printed in the *Alexandria Gazette*, June 24, 1812, which he had prepared to make in the House during debate on the war bill.

25. Ibid., 1630–33.

26. Foster, *Diary*, June 3, 1812.

27. Foster to Castlereagh, June 6, 1812, "Private and Secret," FO 5:86, pt.1.

28. *Annals*, 12th Cong. 1st Sess. 1633–37.

29. Benjamin Rush to John Adams, June 2, 1812, Richard Rush, *Letters of Benjamin Rush*, ed. L. H. Butterfield (Princeton, N.J., 1951), 2:1137.

30. Thomas Worthington to his wife, June 7, 1812, Frank Theodore Cole, "Thomas Worthington," *Ohio Archeological & Historical Publications* (Columbus, Ohio, 1903), 10:354. Cole used Worthington's private memoir by Mrs. Sarah Peter, Governor Worthington's daughter. (For bibliographical citation, see Henshaw.)

31. Foster to Castlereagh, June 6, 1812, "Private and Secret," FO 5:86, pt. 1.

32. Richard Rush to his father, Benjamin Rush, June 20, 1812, H. Adams, *History*, 6:229.

33. *Lexington Reporter*, July 1, 1812.

34. Clay to Jesse Bledsoe, published in the *Lexington Reporter*, June 27, 1812.

35. Quincy, *Quincy*, 255. Quincy lived 1772–1864.

36. *Annals*, 12th Cong. 1st Sess. 1546.

37. Ibid., 1576.

38. Article in Boston's *Repertory & General Advertiser*, June 26, 1812, reprinted in *National Intelligencer*, July 2, 1812, along with Clay's response.

39. Clay's response to comments from Boston paper, *National Intelligencer*, July 2, 1812.

40. *Kentucky Gazette*, August 4, 1812.

Chapter 15

1. Clay to Monroe, July 29, 1812, Monroe Papers, MSS-LC.

2. *Lexington Reporter*, July 1, 1812.

3. Harrison to William Eustis, April 14, 1812, Harrison, *Messages and Letters*, 2:33.

4. Ibid., June 3, 1812, 59.

5. Ibid., May 27, 1812, 56–57.

6. Tecumseh's speech to the Indians at Massassinway, May 15, 1812, Harrison, *Messages and Letters*, 2:51.

7. Harrison to Eustis, July 7, 1812, Harrison, *Messages and Letters*, 2:66.

8. Ibid., July 9, 1812, 71.

9. Harrison to Governor Scott, July 14, 1812, Harrison, *Messages and Letters*, 2:73.

10. William Wells to Harrison, July 22, 1812, Ibid., 2:77.

11. James Freeman Clarke (Grandson of William Hull), *History of the Campaign of 1812, and the Surrender of the Post of Detroit*, 417: Printed together in a single volume with — Mrs. Maria Campbell (Hull's daughter), *Revolutionary Service and Civil Life of General William Hull, Prepared from His Manuscripts* (New York, 1848).

12. Dearborn to Eustis, July 1, 1812, H. Adams, *History*, 6:307.

13. Eustis to Dearborn, July 9, 1812, Ibid., 308.

14. Dearborn to Eustis, July 28, 1812, Ibid., 310–11.

15. William Hull, "A Proclamation," July 15, 1812, *Documents Relating to the Invasion of Canada and the Surrender of Detroit, 1812*, selected and edited by Ernest A. Cruikshank (Ottawa, 1912), 58–59.

16. Harrison to Eustis, August 12, 1812, Harrison, *Messages and Letters*, 2:85–89; also, Moses Dawson, *A Historical Narrative of the Civil and Military Services of Major-General William Henry Harrison* (Cincinnati, 1824), 277.

17. *Lexington Reporter*, August 15, 1812.

18. Clay to Monroe, August 12, 1812, Monroe Papers, MSS-LC.

19. *Lexington Reporter*, August 15, 1812.

20. Robert B. McAfee, *History of the Late War in the Western Country* (Bowling Green, Ohio, 1816), 119–20.

21. *Kentucky Gazette*, August 18, 1812.

22. Jared Sparks, *Journal*, April 19–30, 1830, Harvard University.

23. Clay to Eustis, August 22, 1812, National Archives, RG107, Letters Received, (6) C-448.

24. *Lexington Reporter*, August 29, 1812.

25. "Extract of a letter [dated Detroit, August 8, 1812] from Ohio to a friend in Kentucky," *Kentucky Gazette*, August 29, 1812.

26. Harrison to Eustis, August 28, 1812, Harrison, *Messages and Letters*, 2:98.

27. Clay to Monroe, August 25, 1812, Monroe Papers, MSS-LC.

28. Clay to Eustis, August 26, 1812, National Archives, RG107, Letters Received (6) C-453.

29. Captain Heald (Commander of the garrison at Fort Dearborn) to Eustis, October 23, 1812, Cruikshank, *Documents ... Detroit*, 225–26.

30. Hull to Eustis, August 26, 1812, Ibid., 186.

31. *Niles*, 3:39.

32. Maj. Gen. Isaac Brock to Hull, August 15, 1812, Cruikshank, *Documents ... Detroit*, 144.

33. Andrew C. McLaughlin, *Lewis Cass* (Boston and New York, 1900), 77.

34. Lewis Cass to Eustis, September 10, 1812, Cruikshank, *Documents ... Detroit*, 220.

35. Brock to Sir George Prevost, August 16, 1812, Ibid., 156.

36. Clay to Monroe, September 21, 1812, Monroe Papers, MSS-LC.

37. Monroe to Clay, August 28, 1812, Clay Papers, MSS-LC.

38. Madison to Dearborn, August 9, 1812, Madison Papers, MSS-LC.

39. Dolley Madison to I. Winston, August 31, 1812, Dolley Payne Madison Papers, MSS-LC.

40. Jefferson to Madison, November 6, 1812, Jefferson Papers, MSS-LC: also Jefferson, *Writings*, ed. Ford, 9:370.

41. *Richmond Enquirer*, October 23, 1812.

42. Monroe to Clay, August 28, 1812, Clay Papers, MSS-LC.

43. Monroe to Clay, September 17, 1812, Clay Papers, MSS-LC.

44. Ibid.

45. Clay to Monroe, September 21, 1812, Monroe Papers, MSS-LC.

46. Harrison to Winchester, August 27, 1812, William H. Harrison Papers, MSS-LC.

47. Winchester narrative from the *National Intelligencer*, September 16, 1817.

48. Harrison to Eustis, August 28, 1812, Harrison, *Messages and Letters*, 2:98–100.

49. Lossing, *Field-book*, 324.

50. Harrison to Clay, August 29, 1812, Clay Papers, MSS-LC.

51. Harrison to Clay, August 30, 1812, Ibid.

52. Monroe to Clay, September 17, 1812, *Ibid.*

53. Harrison to Eustis, September 3, 1812, Harrison, *Messages and Letters*, 2:108–110.

54. Ibid.

55. Elias Darnell, *A Journal Containing an Accurate and Interesting Account of the Hardships, Suffering, Battles, Defeat, and Captivity of Those Heroic Kentucky Volunteers and Regulars Commanded by General Winchester in the Years 1812–13* (Philadelphia, 1854), 20.

56. Richard M. Johnson to Madison, September 18, 1812, Madison Papers, MSS-LC.

57. Harrison's General Order, September 19, 1812, Harrison, *Messages and Letters*, 2:141–42.

58. Eustis to Harrison, September 17, 1812, Ibid., 2:136.

59. Eustis to Shelby, September 17, 1812, Ibid., 2:135–36.

Chapter 16

1. Clay to Monroe, Sept. 21, 1812, Monroe Papers, MSS-LC; and Clay to Rodney, Dec. 29,1812, Historical Society of Pennsylvania; Hopkins, *Clay Papers*, 1:150–51; and Clay to [William Taylor], Nov. 20,1812, H. Clay Papers, MSS-LC.

2. Hamilton to Rodgers, June 18 and 22, 1812; Rodgers to Hamilton (three messages), June 21, 1812, microfilm of "Correspondence of Navy Captains to and from the Secretary of the Navy," National Archives, Washington, D.C.

3. Perry, *Reminiscences*, 53–54.

4. Reprinted in *Lexington Reporter*, September 26, 1812, from *New York Public Advertiser*.

5. Lossing, *Field-book*, 443.

6. Ibid., 444.

7. Quoted in Elliot Snow, *On the Decks of "Old Ironsides"* (New York, 1932), 108–09, from Moses Smith, *Naval Scenes in the Last War* (n.p., n.d.).

8. Lossing, *Field-book*, 444.

9. *Lexington Reporter*, September 19, 1812.

10. Captain Dacres' report to Vice Admiral Sawyer, September 7, 1812, Lossing, *Field-book*, 445n.

11. *Lexington Reporter*, September 19, 1812. Reprinted from *Boston Gazette*, August 31, 1812.

12. *Niles*, November 7, 1812, 156; and January 23, 1813, 324.

13. H. Adams, *History*, 6:379.

14. Dearborn to Maj. Gen. Van Rensselaer, September 2, 1812, Cruickshank, *The Documentary History of the Campaign Upon the Niagara Frontier in the Year 1812* (Welland, Ontario, Canada, 1902), 1, pt. 1:232.

15. Van Rensselaer to Brig. Gen. Smyth, October 5, 1812, Cruickshank, Ibid., pt. 2:34.

16. Jefferson to Madison, November 6, 1812, Jefferson Papers, MSS-LC; and Jefferson, *Writings*, ed. Ford, 9:370.

17. *Annals*, 12th Cong., 2nd sess., 11–16.

18. Timothy Pickering to Edward Pennington, July 12, 1812, *Documents Relating to New-England Federalism, 1800–1815*, ed. Henry Adams (Boston, 1905), 389.

19. Statement by Rufus King in *Life and Correspondence of Rufus King*, ed. Charles R. King (New York, 1898), 5(1907–16):264–71. This statement provides a full account of this meeting and King's views.

20. King to Christopher Gore, September 19, 1812, Ibid., 276–77.

21. King to Christopher Gore, September 19, 1812, 277–81; and R. King to William King, October 23, 1812, 288, Ibid.

22. John T. Sullivan (as told to him in a series of letters from his father, William Sullivan), *The Public Men of the Revolution, Including Events from the Peace of 1783 to the Peace of 1815* (Philadelphia, 1847), 351.

23. Foster, *Diary*, May 15, 1812.

24. *Niles*, December 5, 1812, 224.

Chapter 17

1. *Annals*, 12th Cong. 2nd Sess., November 10, 1812, 146–48.

2. Ibid., November 21, 1812, 167 and 173.

3. Harper to Plumer, November 21, 1812, Plumer Papers, MSS-LC.

4. *Morning Courier and New York Enquirer*, October 18, 1845. In response to a *History of the War of 1812*, written by Charles Jared Ingersoll and published in 1845, Stewart wrote, on October 10, 1845, a caustic criticism of Ingersoll's book. It covered four columns in the October 18 issue of this New York newspaper. It contains some known inaccuracies, such as the statement that Calhoun's suggestion for an entertainment came after the House had once voted down the 74's, though in fact the House did not consider the issue until after the entertainment. Other errors are also apparent in his accounts of a still later Navy ball as well as his charges against the Administration's orders for the Navy early in the war.

5. *National Intelligencer*, November 28, 1812.

6. Harper to Plumer, January 4, 1813, Plumer Papers, MSS-LC.

7. Monroe to Crawford, December 3, 1812, Monroe Papers, MSS-LC. This letter in the Manuscripts Division of the Library of Congress is torn down the entire right side. Yet it is clear from a reading that the torn edge can be no more than would allow a very short name following "I wish to confer with you and Mr.," such as "Clay." Also, since Crawford was then the temporary presiding officer of the Senate, it is logical that the other party to the conference would be the presiding officer of the House of Representatives. In addition, Monroe's July-to-September personal correspondence with Clay reveals a close confidence and trust between the two men. No other name fits the situation so well.

8. Gallatin to Jefferson, December 18, 1812, H. Adams, *Gallatin*, 470.

9. Crawford to Monroe, September 9, 1812, Monroe Papers, MSS-LC.

10. Monroe to Jefferson, June 7, 1813, Monroe, *Writings*, 260.

11. Monroe to Jefferson, June 7, 1813, Monroe Papers, MSS-LC.

12. Monroe to —, October 16, 1812, *Bulletin NYPL*, Vol. VI, 1902, 211.

13. Jefferson to William Duane, October 1, 1812, Jefferson Papers, MSS-LC; also, Jefferson, *Writings*, ed. Ford, 367.

14. Monroe to Jefferson, June 7, 1813, Jefferson Papers, MSS-LC.

15. Monroe Papers, MSS-LC.

16. *Annals*, 12th Cong. 2nd sess., 218–235.

17. Ibid., 235–40.

18. Jonathan Roberts, "Memoirs of a Senator from Pennsylvania: Jonathan Roberts, 1771–1854," *Pennsylvania Magazine of History and Biography*, Vol. 62 (Philadelphia, 1938), 245.

19. *Annals* 12th Cong., 2nd sess., 241–56.

20. Ibid., 254.

21. Roberts, "*Memoirs*," 244–47.

22. *Annals*, 12th Cong., 2nd sess., 298.

23. Ibid., 298–304.

24. Ibid., 311.

25. Ibid., 315–21.

26. Ships were designated by class determined by a fixed number of guns (cannon). They sometimes carried more than their class designation.

27. *Niles*, January 2, 1813, 285.

28. *National Intelligencer*, December 10, 1812.

29. Lemuel Sawyer to the Editors of the *New York Courier & Enquirer*, October 21, 1845, as reprinted in *Niles*, October 25, 1845, 119.

30. Taggart to Rev. John Taylor, December 21, 1812, *Proceedings AAS*, 416.

31. Edward Coles to James Gallatin,

November 22, 1845, microfilm Albert Gallatin Papers, MSS-LC.

32. Taggart to Taylor, December 8, 1812, *Proceedings AAS*, 412–13.

33. *New York Courier and Enquirer*. October 18, 1845.

34. Monroe to Jefferson, June 16, 1813, Monroe, *Writings*, 268–69.

35. *Annals*, 12th Cong., 2nd sess., 392.

36. Ibid., 436–37, and 449–52.

37. Clay to Rodney, December 29, 1812, Hopkins, *Clay Papers*, 751.

38. Clay to Monroe, December 23, 1812, Ibid., 748–49; and DNA RG107 Letters Received (7) C41.

39. Harper to Plumer, December 22, and November 21, 1812, Plumer Papers, MSS-LC.

40. John Pierce's Memoirs, *Proceedings, Massachusetts Historical Society*, Vol. 30, Boston, October 1905, 377.

41. *National Intelligencer*, January 19, 1812, reprinted from *Alexandria Gazette*.

42. Clay to Rodney, December 29, 1812. Hopkins, *Clay Papers*, 751.

43. Harper to Plumer, January 4, 1813, Plumer Papers, MSS-LC.

44. *National Intelligencer*, January 12, 1813.

Chapter 18

1. Clark, *Memoirs*, 147.

2. Dearborn to Smyth, October 21, 1812, Cruickshank, *Niagara*. Vol. I, Part II, 152.

3. Ibid., 193–94; also, *Niles*, Vol. 3, November 28, 1812, 203.

4. Cruikshank. *Niagara*, 134.

5. *Niles*, Vol. 3, December 5, 1812, 216–17.

6. Lossing, *Field-book*, 428n.

7. *Niles*, December 19, 1812, 254.

8. Smyth to Dearborn, December 8, 1812, Cruikshank, *Niagara*, 288.

9. Extract of a letter from Canandaigua, N.Y., December 5, 1812, printed in the *New York Gazette*, December 15, 1812.

10. Porter to *Buffalo Gazette*, December, 8, 1812, reprinted in *National Intelligencer*, December 24, 1812.

11. *National Intelligencer*, January 2, 1813.

12. Monroe to chairmen of Congressional Military Committees, "Exploratory Observations," December 23, 1812, Monroe, *Writings*, Vol. V, 1807–16 (New York, 1901), 227–241.

13. *Annals*, 12th Cong. 2nd Sess., 466, 470–71, and 481.

14. Ibid., 467.

15. Ibid. 475.

16. Ibid. 510–11.

17. Ibid. 540–580 and 600n.

18. Taggart to Taylor, January 17, 1813, *Proceedings, AAS*, 418.

19. Quincy, *Quincy*, 296.

20. *Annals*, 12th Cong. 2nd Sess. 659n.

21. *National Intelligencer*, February 6, 1813.

22. *Annals*, 12th Cong. 2nd Sess. 659–76, and Swain, *Life*, 33–54. The phrase,

"Seamen's Rights and Free Trade," was a slogan used frequently in newspapers throughout the war.

23. Harper to Plumer, January 8, 1813, Plumer Papers, MSS-LC.

24. J. Roberts to M. Roberts, February 14, 1813, "Memoirs," *PMHB*.

25. Quincy, *Quincy*, 299–300.

26. From the *Boston Messenger*, reprinted in the *Georgetown Federal Republican and Commercial Gazette*, February 5, 1813.

27. Gallatin to Madison, January 4, 1813; and Crawford to Madison, January 3, 1813, Madison Papers, MSS-LC.

28. Gallatin to Madison, January 4 and 7–8, 1813, MSS-LC.

29. *National Intelligencer*, January 12, 1813.

30. Adams, *History*, vol. VI, 428; and Bayard to Rodney, January 17, 1813, *N.Y.P.L. Bulletin* Vol. 4, 1900, 239.

31. Plumer to Harper, January 19, 1813, Plumer Papers, MSS-LC.

32. Harper to Plumer, January 28, 1813, Plumer Papers, MSS-LC.

Chapter 19

1. *Annals*, 12th Cong. 2nd Sess, 850.

2. Ibid., 862.

3. Randolph's speech, January 13, 1813, *Annals*, 12th Cong. 2nd Sess., 800

4. *Annals*, 12th Cong. 2nd Sess., 864–66.

5. *Niles*, January 9, 1813, 296–7.

6. Madison's annual message, read in the Senate, November 4, 1812, *Annals*, 12th Cong. 2nd Sess., 13.

7. *Annals*, 12th Cong. 2nd Sess., 932.

8. H. Adams, Vol. VI, 453–4.

9. *Niles*, January 23, 1813, 325.

10. *Niles*, January 23 and 30, 1813, 335 and 347. Also *National Intelligencer*, January 21 and 26.

11. *Niles*, February 13, 1813, 384.

12. Harrison to Eustis, October 13, 1812, Harrison, *Messages and Letters*, 2:177.

13. Ibid., October 15, 1812, 2:180.

14. Ibid., January 4, 1813, 2:294.

15. William Atherton, *Narrative of the Suffering & Defeat of the Northwestern Army, Under General Winchester* (Frankfort, Ky., 1842), 14.

16. Darnell, *Journal*, 41. Much of the following description is summarized from a blending of the accounts by the two soldiers, Atherton and Darnell.

17. Harrison to Eustis, December 12, 1812, *Massages and Letters*, 2:242

18. Ibid., January 6, 1813, 2:302.

19. Monroe to Harrison, 26 December 1812, Ibid., 265.

20. Monroe to Harrison, January 17, 1813, Ibid., 313.

21. John Armstrong, *Notices of the War of 1812* (New York, 1836), Vol. I, 67–69. Armstrong gives a two-page quote of Col. Allen's address.

22. Darnell, *Journal*, 47. A footnote at this point in Darnell's book reads as follows: "A Frenchman who lived in this vil-

lage said, when the word came the Americans were in sight, there was an old Indian smoking at his fireside. The Indian exclaimed, 'Ho, de Mericans come; I suppose Ohio men come, we give them another chase'; (alluding to a recent approach to the village by General Tupper from Hull's road.) He walked to the door smoking, apparently very unconcerned, and looked at us till we formed the line of battle, and then rushed on them with a mighty shout! He then called out 'Kentuck, by God!' and picked up his gun and ran to the woods like a wild beast."

23. Harrison to Monroe, January, 20, 1813, Harrison, *Messages and Letters*, 316–17.

24. Charles J. Ingersoll, *Historical Sketch of the Second War Between the United States of America and Great Britain* (Philadelphia, 1845), Vol. I, 134.

25. Dr. Lyman C. Draper, *Biographical Field Notes*, Bulletin No. 4, Vol. 5, The Historical Society of Northwestern Ohio (Toledo, October 1933), Note No. 84.

26. The Rev. Thomas P. Dudley, one of the survivors, *Battle and Massacre at Frenchtown, Michigan, January 1813* (Historical Collections, Michigan Pioneer and Historical Society, Lansing, Mich., 1894), Vol. XXII, 437–8.

27. Dawson, *Narrative ... of Harrison*, 456.

28. Atherton, *Narrative*, 42.

29. Armstrong, *Notices*, 200.

30. Talcott E. Wing, "History of Monroe County, Michigan," in *Michigan Historical and Pioneer Collections*, IV (Lansing, 1883), 320.

31. *Niles*, June 5, 1813, 223.

32. Atherton, *Narrative*, 53.

33. Reprint from *Kentucky Gazette*, *Niles*, April 10, 1813, 98.

34. *National Intelligencer*, March 9, 1813.

35. Affidavit of Medard Labbardie, February 11, 1813, *ASP MA*, I, 371.

36. Affidavit of Dr. John Todd, M.D., May 3, 1813, *ASP MA*. I. 373.

37. Dudley, *Battle*, 440.

38. Affidavit of Albert Ammerman, April 21, 1813, *ASP MA*, I, 374.

39. Judge Daroche's narrative of Captain Hart's massacre, accompanying a letter of D. S. Bacon to Hon. R. McClelland, March 29, 1858, "Report of the Pioneer and Historical Society of the State of Michigan," (Lansing, 1886) VIII, 644–5. Also in the same publication, an account based on recollections of P. Lecuyer to Maj. Charles Larned, March 9, 1818, 646–7.

40. Dr. Todd, *ASP MA*, I, 373.

41. These news reports were from various issues of the *National Intelligencer* over a period of nearly two months.

42. *Niles*, February 27, 11.

43. Thomas Harris, *The Life and Services of Commodore William Bainbridge* (Philadelphia, 1837), 15.

44. *Niles*, December 19, 1812, 254

45. Ibid., December 26, 1812, 269.

46. Ibid., May 8, 1813, 163.

Chapter 20

1. *Annals*, 12th Cong., 2nd sess., 1116–17.

2. Sérurier to Bassano, March 2, 1813, Irving Brant, *James Madison: Commander in Chief 1812–1836* (Indianapolis and New York, 1961), 6:147.

3. *Annals*, 12th Cong., 2nd sess., 1167–68.

4. The inaugural scene as described by "An Old Virginia Farmer," from the *Alexandria Gazette* reprinted in *Poulson's American Daily Advertiser*, Philadelphia, March 13, 1813.

5. *Annals*, 12 Cong. 2nd Sess., 122.

6. Ibid., 122–3,

7. An extract from Mrs. William Seaton's "A Biographical Sketch" of her husband, in Clark, *Dolly Madison*. 149.

8. *Georgetown Federal Republican*, March 5, 1813.

9. Gouverneur Morris to Mr. Parish, March 6, 1813, Morris, *Diary*, II: 548.

10. Clark, *Dolly Madison*, 149.

11. Ibid.

12. *National Intelligencer*, March 9, 1813.

13. *Georgetown Federal Republican*, March 12, 1813.

14. Monroe's official instructions to the three commissioners, April 15, 1813, *ASP FA*, 30:695.

15. Adams, *Gallatin*, 410.

16. Gallatin to Madison, March 5, 1813, Microfilm of Gallatin Papers, MSS-LC.

17. H. Adams, *History*, 6:41. The enclosed quote is from Gallatin's letter to Nicholson, May 5, 1813.

18. Bayard's diary, October 21, 1813, Bayard, *Papers*, ed. Donnan, 476.

19. Monroe, *Writings*, ed. Hamilton, 5:267–8.

20. Bayard to Monroe, April 7, 1813, Bayard, *Papers*, ed. Donnan, 204.

21. Monroe's instructions to the Commissioners, Bayard, Papers, ed. Donnan, 204–26 (includes five confidential paragraphs not in *ASP-FA*), April 15, 1813.

22. Two letters from Monroe to the Commissioners, April 27, 1813, Bayard, *Papers*, ed. Donnan, 215–16.

23. Monroe, *Writings*, ed. Hamilton, 5:251.

24. Richard Rush to John Adams, June 6, 1813, "Some unpublished correspondence of John Adams and Richard Rush, 1811–1816," *Pennsylvania Magazine of History and Biography* (Philadelphia, 1836), 60:437.

25. Clay to [James Taylor], April 10, 1813, University of North Carolina Southern Historical Collection, reprinted in Clay, *Papers*, ed Hopkins, 782–3.

26. Agreement between H. Clay and John Fisher, April 28, 1813, T.L Clay Papers, MSS-LC.

Chapter 21

1. Lossing, *Field-book*, 699n.
2. *Niles*, April 10, 1813, 102.

3. Lossing, *Field-book*, 668.

4. Ibid.

5. *Niles*, April 24, 1813, 133.

6. Ibid., May 8, 1813, 163–4.

7. Ibid., May 15, 1813, 177.

8. Ibid., June 12, 1813, 238; and Lossing, *Field-book*, 589.

9. Ibid., June 5, 1813, 229–30; and Lossing, 501.

10. Statement of Maj. Joseph Grafton, September 18, 1815, *Niles*, November 18, 1815, 161–62.

11. Ibid., June 19, 1813, 259.

12. Chauncey to the Secretary of the Navy, June 4, 1813, Ibid., June, 19, 1813, 259.

13. Harrison to Armstrong, May 13, 1813, Harrison, *Messages and Letters*, 2:443–4.

14. From a written address of Thomas Christian, a volunteer in Colonel Dudley's regiment, read about June 20, 1874, by Leslie Combs, another survivor of the battle, to the Western Reserve and Northern Ohio Historical Society, Tract no. 23, published by the Society (Cleveland, Ohio, 1877), 6.

15. Col. William Stanley Hatch, *A Chapter of the History of the War of 1812* (Cincinnati, Ohio, 1872), 113–4.

16. Description by man named English, Ibid., 116n.

17. *National Intelligencer*, January 28, 1813.

18. This depiction is a blend of quotes from Col. Hatch, *History*, 146; and Benjamin Drake, *Life of Tecumseh* (Cincinnati, Ohio, 1841), 180–2.

19. Dr. Lyman C. Draper, Biographical Field Notes (No. 145), The Historical Society of Northwestern Ohio, *Quarterly Bulletin* (Toledo, Ohio), Vol. 5, No. 4, October 1933.

20. Drake, *Tecumseh*, 180–2.

21. Clay to Martin D. Hardin, May 26, 1813, original in Chicago Historical Society Library; copy published in *Papers*, ed. Hopkins, 1:799.

22. Timothy Pickering to his wife, May 24, 1813, from Charles W. Upham, *The Life of Timothy Pickering* (Boston, 1873), IV:224–5.

23. *Annals*. 13th Cong., 1st sess., 106; and Ingersoll, *Historical Sketch*, I:206.

24. *Annals*, 13th Cong., 14–17.

25. Ibid., 109.

26. Ibid., 119.

27. Ibid., 121–153.

28. Daniel Webster to Moody Kent, June 12, 1813, *The Writings and Speeches*, 16:25–6.

29. The story of the battle between the *Chesapeake* and the *Shannon* is a blend from Lossing, *Field-Book*, 701–711; and H. Adams, *History*, VII:292–301. Most of it comes from Lossing.

30. *Niles*, July 10, 1813.

Chapter 22

1. *Annals*, 13th Cong., 1st sess., 83–87.

2. Harvey, *Reminiscences ... Webster*, 317–8.

3. Ingersoll, *Historical Sketches*, I:64.

4. Webster, *Writings and Speeches*, 14:3–7.

5. Charles W. March, *Reminiscences of Congress* (New York, 1850), 35–36.

6. Webster, *Writings and Speeches*, 14:3.

7. Daniel Webster, *Works of Daniel Webster* (Boston, 1853), 6th Edition, I:xxxviii.

8. Webster to Charles March, June 10, 14, 19, 1813, Webster, *Writings and Speeches*, 16:20–21.

9. Webster to Edward Cutts, Jr., May 26, 1813, Ibid., 16:14.

10. Webster to James Hervey Bingham, June 4, 1813, Ibid., 17:233–4.

11. *Annals*, 13th Cong., 1st sess., 199–200.

12. Ibid., 252.

13. Ibid., 266.

14. Ibid., 302.

15. Ibid., 311.

16. Webster to March, June 21, 1813, *Writings and Speeches*, 16:22.

17. Ibid., June 22, 1813.

18. Daniel Webster to Ezekiel Webster, June 28, 1813, Ibid., 17:236.

19. *Georgetown Federal Republican*, June 30, 1813. King Log is from an Aesop Fable which tells of frogs asking Jupiter for a king. The god tossed them a log which the frogs accepted until they found it would not move. They asked Jupiter for another king and were sent a stork which devoured the frogs — thus illustrating the difference between an inert ruler and tyranny. The mention of an eighty-year-old may refer to Gerry who, however, was only 69 at the time. The mention of "potter's clay" and the individual who might get in "the direct line of succession by acting the part of the Duke of Gloucester," probably refers to Henry Clay, and suggests the part possibly played by Gloucester of killing the two princes in the Tower of London clearing the way for the seizure of the throne by Richard III.

20. Monroe to Jefferson, *Writings*, 271–73.

21. Dolly Madison to Edward Coles, July 2, 1813, Clark, *Dolly Madison*, 153–54.

22. *National Intelligencer*, July 7, 1813.

23. Ingersoll, *Historical Sketches*, I:287–88.

24. *Annals*, 13th Cong., 1st sess., 312.

25. Extract of Clay's letter in *Lexington Reporter*, June 26, 1813, sent to William W. Worsley, editor, June 17, 1813, Clay, *Papers*, ed. Hopkins.

26. *Annals*, 13th Cong., 1st sess., 441–42.

27. Russell to Monroe, June 30, 1812, *ASP-FR*, 3:615.

28. *Annals*, 13th Cong., 1st sess., 435.

29. "Extract of a letter from a Lady in Norfolk to her friend in New York," dated July 1, 1813, as reprinted in *Niles*, July 24, 1813, 334.

30. "Extract of a letter from Capt. Cooper of the Cavalry, to Lieut. Gov. Charles K. Mallory, July 10, 1813," Ibid.

31. "Extract of a letter to a gentleman in Charleston, June 30, 1813," Ibid.

32. *Annals*, 13th Cong., 1st sess., 498.

33. Ingersoll, *Historical Sketches*, I:123.

34. Ibid., I:126.

35. *Lexington Reporter*, August 7, 1813, quoted from *National Intelligencer*.

36. *Annals*, 13th Cong., 1st sess., 499.

37. Mrs. Smith to Mrs. Kirkpatrick, July 20, 1813, Smith, *First Forty Years*, 89–91.

38. Ingersoll, *Historical Sketches*, I:126.

39. *Annals*, 13th Cong., 1st sess., 500–04.

40. Ibid., 490–92.

Chapter 23

1. Benjamin Latrobe to Clay, August 15, 1813, Hopkins, *Clay Papers*, 1:818–19. Also in Latrobe Letterbook, 588–90, owned by Mrs. Ferdinand C. Latrobe, Baltimore, Md.

2. Ibid. (Letterbook), Latrobe to Clay, August 24, 1813, 612, and September 5, 1813, 634–35.

3. Agreement between Robert Grinstead and Allen Davis and Clay, September 17, 1813, Hopkins, *Clay Papers*, 1:825. Also in Fayette County Circuit Court file 412. (1818).

4. Bill of sale, September 13 1813, Ibid. (Hopkins), 824–25.

5. *Kentucky Gazette*, August 31, 1813.

6. Clay to Gov. Isaac Shelby, August 22, 1813, Ibid. 1:819. Also in Archibald Henderson, *Isaac Shelby, Revolutionary Patriot and Border Hero*, The North Carolina Booklet, XVIII (July, 1918), 33.

7. Harrison to Shelby, July 20, 1813, Harrison, *Messages and Letters*, 1:492–93.

8. Shelby's call for men, July 31, Ibid., 1:504.

9. Shelby to Harrison, July 31, 1813, Ibid., 1:508–09.

10. Harrison to Maj. George Croghan, July 29, 1813, Ibid., 1:502.

11. Croghan to Harrison, July 30, 1813, Ibid., 503.

12. Harrison to Croghan, July 30, 1813, Ibid., 503.

13. Croghan to the editor of the Cincinnati *Liberty Hall*, August 27, 1813, Ibid., 1:527–28.

14. Harrison to Eustis, August 4 1813, Ibid., 510–13.

15. Harrison to Eustis, August 4, 1813, and Croghan to Harrison, August 5, 1813, Ibid., 514–16.

16. Croghan to Harrison, August 3, 1813, Ibid., 509.

17. Harrison to Armstrong, August 4, 1813, Ibid., 1; 512.

18. Thomas Hart Benton to Clay, August 23, 1813, Clay Papers, MSS-LC.

19. John Armstrong to Jackson, January (should have been February) 5, 1813, Jackson, *Correspondence*, 1:275.

20. Jackson to Armstrong, March 15, 1813, Ibid., 1:291–92.

21. Jackson to Madison, March 15, 1813, Ibid., 1:294.

22. Jackson to David Holmes, April 24, 1813, Ibid., 1:306.

23. Benton's account related in "Addresses on the Presentation of the Sword of General Andrew Jackson to the Congress of the United States. (Washington, D.C., February 26, 1855). Reprinted in William M. Meigs, *The Life of Thomas Hart Benton* (Philadelphia, 1904), 72.

24. Benton to Clay, June 22, 1813, Clay Papers, MSS-LC.

25. Jackson to Benton, July 19, 1813, Jackson, *Correspondence*, 1:310.

26. Benton to Jackson, July 25, 1813, Ibid., 1:313.

27. James Parton, *Life of Andrew Jackson* (New York, 1860), 368.

28. Jackson to Benton, July [28 or later], 1813, Jackson, *Correspondence*, 1:314.

29. This account of the Jackson-Benton affair is summarized from "Thomas H. Benton's Account of his Duel with Jackson," written from Franklin, Tenn., September 10, 1813, Jackson, *Correspondence*, 1:317–18; and Coffee's account in Parton, *Jackson*, 391–95. Parton, writing in 1860, states that "I received it from an old friend of all the parties, who heard General Coffee tell the story with great fullness and care, as though he were giving evidence before a court."

30. Meigs, *Benton*, 79–80.

31. Lossing, *Field-book*, 519.

32. Ibid., 520.

33. *Niles*, October 9, 1813, 5:98.

34. Lossing, *Field-book*, 524.

35. David C. Burnell, *Travels and Adventures of David C. Burnell* (Palmyra, N.Y., 1831), 109–118.

36. Lossing, *Field-book*, 527.

37. Ibid., 528.

38. Ibid., 530. Also, Harrison, *Messages and Letters*, 539.

39. See text for endnote 31 of Chapter 24 for comment by a London newspaper on Perry's victory on Lake Erie.

40. Ibid. (Lossing), 531.

41. *Lexington Reporter*, September 25, 1813.

42. Tecumseh's speech was in Harrison's hands by October 11, 1813, and was published in *Niles Register*, November 6, 1813, 174.

43. Major John Richardson, *War of 1812* (no place, 1842), 119–21.

44. *Niles*, October 30, 1813, 149.

45. Lossing, *Field-book*, 546n.

46. Harrison to Ohio Governor Meigs, September 27, 1813, *Niles*, 117.

47. Harrison to Armstrong, October 9, 1813, Harrison, *Messages and Letters*, 562.

48. Ibid., 564–65.

Chapter 24

1. Latrobe to Clay, November 2, 1813, Hopkins, *Clay Papers*, 834–36. (Latrobe Letterbook), 675–77.

2. William Jones to Clay, November 4, 1813, *National Archives Naval Records Collection*, Miscellaneous Letters Received, 1813, 7:23.

3. Clay to Thomas Bodley, December 18, 1813, *Kentucky Historical Society*, also Clay, *Papers*, 841–42; Clay to John H. Barney, November 30, 1813, Clay papers, MSS-LC; and Clay to Rodney, December 11, 1813, Rodney family papers, MSS-LC, also, Clay, *Papers*, 839–40.

4. Much of this story from Parton, *Jackson*, 417–18.

5. The entire account of Jackson's battles with the Creeks has been summarized from Parton, *Jackson*, 421–44.

6. Clay to Rodney, December 11, 1813, Rodney family papers, MSS-LC; also, Clay, *Papers*, 839–40.

7. James Wilkinson to John Armstrong, November 3, 1813, Cruikshank, *Niagara Frontier*, III, Pt. IV:126. Also Wilkinson, *Memoirs*, III: App.38.

8. Ibid., 140–41.

9. Ibid., 122.

10. Clay to Thomas Bodley, December 18, 1813, *Kentucky Historical Society*; also, Clay, *Papers*, 841–42.

11. *Annals*, 13th Cong., 2nd sess., 538–44.

12. Ibid., 2031–32.

13. Ibid., 2056–58.

14. Rocellus Sheridan Guernsey, *New York City During the War of 1812–15* (New York, 1889), 370.

15. Harrison to Armstrong, December 21, 1813, Harrison, *Messages and Letters*, 610–11.

16. John O'Fallon to unknown, December 17, 1813, J. Thomas Scharf, *History of St. Louis City and County* (Philadelphia, 1883), 1:344.

17. David Buell to Ezra Buell, November 25, 1813, Augustus C. Buell, *History of Andrew Jackson* (New York, 1904), 1:280.

18. Ingersoll, *Historical Sketches*, 1: 189.

19. Ibid., 190–91.

20. *New York Evening Post*, December 24, 1813.

21. Ibid.

22. Clay to Dr. William Thornton, December 24, 1813, Clay, *Papers*, 844. Also in Buffalo Historical Society.

23. From a "Private Correspondent in Washington," *Charleston (S.C.) Courier*, January 7 and 13, 1814. The story of the carriage ride was reprinted from the *Baltimore Federal Gazette*.

24. *National Intelligencer*, December 28, 1813.

25. Jeremiah Mason to Mrs. Mason, December 29, 1813, *Memoir and Correspondence of Jeremiah Mason* (Cambridge, Mass., 1873), 74.

26. *ASP-MA*, 1:484.

27. Madison's "Copy of note on General McClure's letters," December 29, 1813, Madison papers, MSS-LC.

28. *Niles*, January 1, 1814, 300–01.

29. Wilkinson to Prevost, Cruikshank, *Niagara Frontier*, IX:153.

30. Mrs. William Winston Seaton, "A

Biographical Sketch," on her husband, in, Clark, *Dolly Madison*, 157–58.

31. *London Times*, November 12, 1813.

32. These three letters were communicated by President Madison to Congress, January 7, 1814. They are: Lord Castlereagh to Monroe, November 4, 1813; Lord Cathcart to the Count De Nesselrode (in French), 1 September, 1813; and Monroe to Castlereagh, January 5, 1814. All are in *ASP-FR*. 621–23.

33. Memo from Monroe to Madison, undated, Monroe, *Writings*, 277–81.

34. Madison to the four commissioners, National Archives, M36, R2.

35. March, *Reminiscences*, 43–44.

36. *Annals*, 13th Cong., 2nd sess., 1057.

37. March, *Reminiscences*, 45.

38. Ibid., 42–43.

39. *Annals*, 13 Cong., 2nd sess., 1057.

40. *National Intelligencer*, January 5, 1814.

41. *Niles*, February 5, 1814, 380.

Chapter 25

1. Clay to the editor, January 27, 1814, *Lexington Reporter*, February 5, 1814.

2. Quotes from instructions to Peace Commissioners, *ASP-FR*, III. on January 28, 1814, 701–02; April 15, 1813, 695–700; June 23, 1813, 700–01; January 1, 1814, 701.

3. Monroe to Commissioners, April 15, 1813, Bayard, *Papers*, 2;205. This reprint of instructions to Gallatin, Adams, and Bayard includes only the five confidential paragraphs omitted in *ASP*. Confidential paragraphs missing from *ASP* are found in Bayard, *Papers*, April 15, 1813, 204–06; June 23, 1813; 226–229; January 18, 1814, 263–265. The full text of the January 28, 1814, instructions is also found in Clay, *Papers*, 857–862.

4. Monroe to Gallatin and Bayard, June 23, 1813, Bayard, *Papers*.

5. Monroe to original Mission, January 1, 1814, *ASP-FR*, III:271.

6. Monroe to the new peace Mission, confidential paragraph, January 28, 1814, Bayard. *Papers*. 263–64.

7. *ASP-FR*, III:702.

8. Monroe to Mission, January 28, 1814, Bayard, *Papers*, 264.

9. *ASP-FR*, III:702.

10. Monroe to Mission, January 28, 1814, Bayard, *Papers*, 265.

11. Ibid.

12. David Parish to Clay, January 28, 1814, Thomas J. Clay Papers, MSS-LC.

13. Clay to Monroe, February 13, 1814, Monroe Papers, MSS-LC.

14. Clay to Monroe, February 23, 1814, Ibid.

15. *Niles*, February 19, 1814, 410.

16. Clay to Monroe, February 14, 1814, Monroe Papers, MSS-LC.

17. Monroe to Clay, February 18, 1814, Ibid.

18. Clay to Monroe, February 23, 1814, Ibid.

19. Joseph B. Nones papers, American Jewish Historical Society, Brandeis University.

20. Amos Kendall, *Autobiography of Amos Kendall*, edited by his son-in-law, William Stickney (Boston, 1872), 93–114.

21. Lucretia Clay to Henry Clay, March 10, 1814, Clay, *Correspondence*. 24–25.

22. In about 1817, Theodore suffered some sort of accident. The author has been unsuccessful in learning the nature of this episode. But a family doctor predicted the boy would eventually become insane. This, in fact, happened when Theodore was in his late 20s. He was to live till 1870 as a patient at a local Lexington hospital. At the time of his death, the *New York Times* carried his obituary (May 10, 1870).

In a personal note relating to these boys, Thomas, who married Marie Mantelle, was the great grandfather of Henrietta Clay. In 1972, while browsing in the shelves of the University of Kentucky library, the author found a pamphlet written by Miss Clay. I learned that she still lived in Lexington. I called her and spent a delightful evening with her and a painter friend of hers talking about my subject. She showed me personal items that had belonged to her illustrious great great grandfather. The artist showed me copies of a painting he did of Henry Clay at the signing of the Treaty of Peace at Ghent on Christmas Eve 1814. He had obtained the characteristics of the uniform worn on the occasion by Clay, had a copy of it tailored and a model pose in it for the painting, and then substituted a copy of Clay's "head" for the portrait. The original painting hangs in the library of Transylvania University in Lexington.

23. Kendall, *Autobiography*, 115–18.

24. Nones Papers.

Chapter 26

1. Nones, *Fascicle* 13, Papers, Brandeis University Library.

2. Clay and Russell to Adams, April 14, 1814, Adams Papers, MSS-LC, and Bayard, *Papers*, 284.

3. Bayard to Andrew Bayard, March 19, 1914, Bayard, *Papers*, 281.

4. Clay to Crawford, April 14, 1814, Crawford Papers, MSS-LC.

5. Crawford to Clay, April 8, 1814, Clay Papers, MSS-LC.

6. Clay to Monroe, April 23, 1814, Monroe Papers, MSS-LC; also Bayard *Papers*, 287–88.

7. Clay to Russell, May 1, 1814, Bayard, *Papers*, 290

8. J. Q. Adams, *Memoirs*, 642.

9. Clay to Russell, May 4, 1814, Clay *Papers*, 893–4.

10. Bayard to Clay & Russell, April 20, 1814, Clay Papers, MSS-LC.

11. Gallatin to Clay, April 22, 1814, Clay Papers, MSS-LC.

12. *The* (London) *Times*. April 15, 1814.

13. Ibid., April 27, 1814.

14. Ibid., May 17, 1814.

15. Ibid., May 18, 1814.

16. Ibid., May 20, 1814.

17. Ibid., June 2, 1814.

18. *The* (London) *Courier*, May 21, 1814.

19. Clay to Russell, May 1, 1814, Bayard, *Papers*, 288–90

20. Clay to Bayard and Gallatin, May 2, 1814, Russell Papers, Brown University; and Bayard, *Papers*, 290–93.

21. Clay to Gallatin, May 2, 1814, Gallatin Papers, micro, MSS-LC; also H. Adams. *Gallatin*, 508–10.

22. George B. Milligan to Bayard, May 10, 1814, Bayard *Papers*, 293–94.

23. Clay to Crawford, May 10, 1814, Clay, *Papers*, 896–99.

24. Russell to Clay, May 8, 1814, Clay, *Papers*, MSS-LC; Clay to Bayard and Gallatin, May 16, 1814, Gallatin Papers, microfilm, MSS-LC.

25. Clay to Russell, May 16, 1814, Russell Papers, Brown University.

26. Russell to Clay, May 22, 1814, Russell Papers, Brown Univ.

27. Clay to Russell, May 27, 1814, Ibid.; also Clay, *Papers*, 925–26.

28. Russell to Clay, Ibid., Russell Papers and Clay *Papers*, 924–25.

29. Adams, *Memoirs*, II:603.

30. Ibid. 634.

31. Lord Henry Bathurst to Bayard and Gallatin, May 16, 1814, Bayard, *Papers*, 306–07.

32. Clay to Russell, May 31, 1814, Russell Papers, Brown Univ.

33. Clay to Russell, May 31, 1814, and Clay to Adams and Russell, May 31, 1814, Ibid.: also Bayard, *Papers*, 298–99.

34. Clay to Russell, May 27, 1814, Russell Papers, Brown Univ.

35. Adams, *Memoirs*, June 2–11, 639–43.

36. Ibid., June 11, 1814, 644.

37. Nones papers, Brandeis Univ.

38. This correspondence is in *ASP, Naval Affairs*, II:460–63.

39. Nones Papers.

Chapter 27

1. J. Q. Adams to Louisa Catherine Adams, June 25, 1814, *Writings of John Quincy*, ed. Worthington Chauncey Ford (New York, 1915), V:51.

2. Adams. *Memoirs*, II:644–46.

3. J. Q. Adams to L. C. Adams, June 25, 1814, Asams, *Writings*, V:50–51.

4. Adams, *Memoirs*, II:647.

5. J. Q. Adams to L. C. Adams. June 25 1814, Adams, *Writings*, V:51.

6. Adams, *Memoirs*, II:650.

7. Ibid., 651.

8. Adams, *Writings*, V:52.

9. Crawford to all the Commissioners, May 13, 1814, Gallatin Papers, micro., MSS-LC.

10. Ibid., May 24, 1814.

11. Ibid. May 28, 1814, and Lafayette to Crawford, May 26, 1814, enclosed. These documents are also in Clay *Papers*, 926–28.

12. Bayard, *Papers*, 507–13.

13. James Gallatin, June 18, *The Diary of James Gallatin*, ed. Count Gallatin (New York, 1924), 24–25.

14. Gallatin to Czar Alexander, June 19, 1814, Gallatin Papers, micro., MSS-LC.

15. Crawford to Clay, June 10, 1814, Clay Papers, MSS-LC.

16. Clay to Crawford, July 2, 1814, Crawford Papers, MSS-LC.

17. J. Q. Adams to L. C. Adams, July 2, 1814, Adams, *Writings*, V:55.

18. Adams, *Memoirs*, II:655.

19. Ibid., II:656.

20. Bayard, *Papers*, 514; and J. Gallatin, *Diary*, 27.

21. J. Q. Adams to L. C. Adams, August 1, 1814, Adams, *Writings*, V:533.

22. Ibid., Adams to Russell, March 8, 1816, Adams, *Memoirs*, II:533.

23. J. Q. Adams to L. C. Adams, July 12, 1814, Adams, *Writings*, 59.

24. Carl Schurz, *Life of Henry Clay* (Boston and New York, 1887), I:102–05.

25. J. Q. Adams, *Memoirs*, II:656–57.

26. J. Q. Adams to L. C. Adams, July 12, 1814, Adams, *Writings*, V:61.

27. J. Gallatin, July 15, 1814, *Diary*, 27.

28. J. Q. Adams to L. C. Adams, July 22, 1814; and L. C. Adams to J. Q. Adams, June 10, 1814, Adams, *Writings*, V:66 and footnote.

29. J. Q. Adams to L. C. Adams, July 22, 1814, Adams. *Writings*, V:66.

30. Adams, *Memoirs*, II:659.

31. J. Q. Adams to L. C. Adams, July 12 and 19, 1814, Adams, *Writings*, II:59 and 64–65.

32. Ibid., August 5, 1814, II:71; also Bayard, July 31, 1814, *Papers*, 514.

33. J. Q. Adams to L. C. Adams, August 12, 1814, Adams, Adams, *Writings*, V:73n.

34. Ibid. August 1, 1814, V:70 and footnote.

35. Adams, *Memoirs*, II:656–59.

36. Crawford to Clay, August 4, 1814, Clay *Papers*, Supplement, 1992, 34.

Chapter 28

1. J. Gallatin, *Diary*, 27.

2. Adams, *Memoirs*, III:3–4.

3. *Dictionary of National Biography* (London, 1889), s.v. Gambier, James, XX:393–95; and Lady Chatterton, *Admiral Lord Gambier* (London, 1861), II:214–18.

4. Adams, *Memoirs*, III:15.

5. Bayard, *Papers*, 350.

6. Adams, *Memoirs*, III:15.

7. Bayard to Richard Henry Bayard, October 27, 1814, Bayard, *Papers*, 350.

8. Bayard to Crawford, August 16, 1814, Ibid., 315–16.

9. *Dictionary of National Biography*, XXII:283–85, s.v. Adams, William.

10. Bayard, *Papers*, 350.

11. J. Gallatin, August 8, 1814, *Diary*, 28.

12. Liverpool to Castlereagh, Bradford

Perkins, *Castlereagh and Adams* (Berkley, Calif., 1964), 59.

13. An original copy of Clay's "Journal of Ghent Negotiations," in the hand of Christopher Hughes, August 7–10, 1814, is in Crawford Papers (National Archives, M221, R20). Another copy was sent to Secretary Monroe. But for easier reference, it is also found in Clay, *Papers*, 952–59, for August 7–10, 1814, and 968–70, for August 19, 1814. For future citations from this journal, see the pages from Clay, *Papers*. This particular citation is found on pages 952–3.

14. Adams, *Memoirs*, III,5.

15. Ibid., and Clay *Papers*, 953.

16. Clay, Ibid.

17. Clay, Ibid., 954.

18. Adams, *Memoirs*, III:6.

19. Clay, *Papers*, 954–55.

20. Ibid., and Adams, *Memoirs*, III:7.

21. Monroe to the Commissioners, June 25 and 27, 1814, *ASP-FR*, III:703–04.

22. Ibid., June 27, *ASP-FR*, III:784–5.

23. Clay, *Papers*, 955.

24. Ibid., and enclosure with Henry Goulburn to Earl Bathurst, August 9, 1814, *Supplementary Despatches, Correspondence, and Memoranda of Field Marshall Arthur Duke of Wellington* (London, 1862), edited by his son, the Duke of Wellington, IX:177–78.

25. Commissioners to Monroe, August 12, 1814, *ASP-FR*, III:706.

26. Adams, draft of a dispatch to Monroe, August 11, 1814, Adams, *Writings*, V:80.

27. This account of the talks of August 9, is taken from Adams, *Memoirs*, III:8–10.

28. Clay to Monroe, August 18, 1814, Monroe Papers, MSS-LC. Also in Clay, *Papers*, 964–5.

29. Ibid.

30. Goulburn to Bathurst, August 9, 1814, Wellington, *Despatches*, IX:177–78.

31. British Commissioners to Castlereagh, August 9,1814, Massachusetts Historical Society, *Proceedings* (Boston, 1915), 48:141–44. Also Castlereagh, [Lord, Robert Stewart 2nd Marquess of Londonderry], *Letters and Despatches of Lord Castlereagh* (London, 1848–53), X:67.

32. Adams, *Memoirs*, III:10.

33. Ibid., 11, and Clay, *Papers*, 957.

34. Adams, Ibid., 11.

35. Ibid.

36. Ibid., 11–12.

37. Ibid., 12.

38. Ibid., 12–13; along with comments by Clay in his journal, *Papers*, 957–8.

39. J. Gallatin, *Diary*, 28.

40. J. Q. Adams to L. C. Adams, August 9, 1814, James, *Writings*, V:74.

41. Bayard to Crawford, August 16, 1814, Bayard, *Papers*, 315.

42. Commissioners to Monroe, August 12, 1814, *ASP-FR*, III:706.

43. Bayard to Robert Harper, August 19, 1814, Bayard *Papers*, 317–18.

44. J. Gallatin, August 12, 1814, *Diary*, 29.

45. Clay to Monroe, August 18, 1814, Monroe Papers, MSS-LC, 36; also Clay, *Papers*, 963.

46. Ibid., *Papers*, 965–6.

47. Adams to Monroe, August 17, 1814, Adams, *Writings*. V:84 and 87.

48. Clay to Monroe, August 18, 1814, Monroe Papers, MSS-LC, 36; also Clay, *Papers*, 967.

49. Adams, *Memoirs*, III:14.

50. J. Q. Adams to L. C. Adams, *Writings*, V:83–4.

51. Ibid., 89.

52. Adams, *Memoirs*, III:15–6.

53. Clay to Monroe, August 18, 1814, Monroe Papers, MSS-LC, 36; also Clay, *Papers*, 966.

Chapter 29

1. J. Q. Adams to L. C., Adams, August 23, 1814, Adams, *Writings*, 90.

2. Castlereagh to the Earl of Liverpool, August 28, 1814, Wellington, *Despatches*, IX;192.

3. The story of this conference of August 19, 1814, is a blend of accounts taken from the following sources: Adams, *Memoirs*, 17–20; Clay, Journal of August 7–10, and 19, 1814 in Clay *Papers*, 952–9 and 962–70; Crawford, Papers, MSS-LC; Bayard to Harper, August 19–20, 1814, Bayard, *Papers*, 318; Castlereagh to the British Commissioners, August 14, 1814, Castlereagh's *Despatches*, II:86–91; and the American Commissioners to Monroe, August 19, 1814, *ASP-FR*, III: 708–09.

4. Adams, *Memoirs*, 17–8.

5. These accounts are a continuation of those noted in endnote no. 3 except that the dialog about the line from Lake Superior to the Mississippi is from Clay's Journal, *Papers*, 970.

6. Ibid., 19; and Clay, Journal.

7. *ASP-FR*. III:709.

8. Adams, *Memoirs*, 19–20.

9. J. Q. Adams to L. C. Adams, August 23, 1814, Adams, *Writings*, 90.

10. Adams, August 19, 1814, *Memoirs*, 20.

11. Bayard to Harper, August 19, 20, 1814, Bayard, *Papers*, 318.

12. Bayard to Levett Harris, August 28, 1814, Bayard, *Papers*, 327.

13. Adams, August 19, 1814, *Memoirs*, 20.

14. Clay to Monroe, August 18–19, 1814, Monroe Papers, MSS-LC.

15. This is a continuation of the accounts related in endnote 5.

16. J. E. D. Shipp, *Giant Days, or the Life and Times of William H. Crawford* (Americus, Ga., 1909), 123–24.

17. Gallatin to Monroe, August 20, 1814, Adams, *Writings* I, 637–640. Hill's part in the planned expedition was cancelled.

18. H. Adams, *Gallatin*, 524.

19. Goulburn to Earl Bathurst, August 21, 1814, Wellington, *Despatches*, IX;189.

20. Adams, August 21, 1814, *Memoirs*, 21.

21. Ibid., August 23, 1814, 21–22.

22. Goulburn to Bathurst, August 23, 1814, Wellington, *Despatches*, IX:189–190.

23. Adams, August 24, 1814, *Memoirs*, 22–23.

24. Adams, Draft of response to British Commissioners, August 24, 1814, Adams, *Writings*, IV:95–6.

25. Americans to British, August 24, 1814, *ASP-FR* III:711–2 and Bayard's unsent draft, *Papers*, 322,

26. This account of the note to the British and the suggestions of the American envoys is built upon three sources. They are the official note of August 24, 1814, *ASP-FR*, III:711–13; Bayard's draft, Bayard, *Papers*, 320–25; and Adams' draft, *Writings*, 93–101.

27. Adams, *Memoirs*, III:33.

28. Adams, August 26, 1814, Adams, *Writings*. 103–04.

29. Summarized from Lossing, *Fieldbook*, 816–21.

Chapter 30

1. Memorandum of Conferences for Saturday, August 27, 1814, Bayard, *Papers*, 338.

2. Bayard to Levett Harris, August 28, 1814, Ibid., 327.

3. Clay to Goulburn, September 5, 1814, Clay, *Papers*, 973.

4. Adams, August 26 and 27, *Memoirs*, III:23.

5. J. Q. Adams to L. C. Adams, August 26, 1814, Adams, *Writings*, III:103.

6. Adams, *Memoirs*, III:23–24.

7. Adams to William H. Crawford, August 29, 1814, Adams, *Writings*, III:105–06.

8. Adams, August 31, 1814, *Memoirs*, III:24.

9. This message to Bathurst was wrongly dated the 24th, since it included the American response of the 25th to last note from the British.

10. Goulburn to Earl Bathurst, August 24,1814, Wellington, *Despatches*, IX:190.

11. Goulburn to Castlereagh, August 26, 1814, Ibid.. 193.

12. Castlereagh to Goulburn, August 28, 1814, Ibid., 196.

13. Castlereagh to Earl Liverpool, August 28, 1814, Ibid., 192–93.

14. Earl Liverpool to Castlereagh, September 2, 1814, Ibid., 214.

15. Goulburn to Bathurst, September 2, 1814, Ibid., 217.

16. This long description of the conversation with Goulburn is in Adams long letter to Monroe, September 5, 1814, Adams, *Writings*, V:110–120; and Adams, September 1, 1814, *Memoirs*, III:24–30.

17. Adams, *Memoirs*, III:30–1. In July 1972, the author spent an evening with Henrietta Clay, great-granddaughter of Henry Clay. During the visit, she removed from her dining-room wall and

showed me the small painting of flowers that her illustrious ancestor had won by his gambling skills.

18. James Gallatin, September 3, 1814, *Diary*, 30.

19. British commissioners to the American envoys, September 4, 1814, ASP-FR, III:713.

20. Adams, September 5, 1814, *Memoirs*, III; 31.

21. James Gallatin, September 5, 1814, *Diary*, 30–1.

22. J. Q. Adams, to L. C. Adams, September 9, 1814, Adams, *Writings*, III:120–21.

23. Events of September 5–8, 1814, are from Adams, *Memoirs*, III:31–3.

24. American Commissioners to the British, September 9, 1814, *ASP, FR*. III, 715–17.

25. J. Q. Adams to Abigail Adams, September 10, 1814, Adams, *Writings*, III, 131.

26. Adams to Lafayette, September 11, 1814, Ibid., 134–5.

27. Adams, September 10, 1814, *Memoirs*, III, 33–4.

28. Ibid., 35–36.

29. Goulburn to Bathurst, September 16, 1814, Wellington, *Despatches*, I, 266.

30. J. Q. Adams to L. C. Adams, September 13, 1814, Adams, *Writings*, III:136.

31. Adams to Crawford, September 14, 1814, Ibid., 140–1.

32. Adams, September 20, 1814, *Memoirs*, 36–7.

33. James Gallatin, September 15, 1814, *Diary*, 31.

34. British Commissioners to the Americans, September 20, 1814, *ASP, FR*, III, 717–8.

35. Adams, September 20–24, 1814, *Memoirs*, III:38–40.

36. J. Q. Adams to L. C. Adams, September 27, 1814, Adams, *Writings*, III: 145–7.

37. Adams, *Memoirs*, III:41–2. Webster defines Clay's use of "cant" as "The insincere use of pious phraseology."

38. American to British ministers, *ASP, FR*, III:719–21.

39. Adams., September 25–30, 1814, *Memoirs*, III:41–5.

Chapter 31

1. Lossing, *Field-book*, 1009n.

2. Gallatin to Monroe, August 20, 1814, *Writings*, I:637–40

3. Attorney General Richard Rush to Richard M. Johnson, Chairman of the House Committee of Inquiry, October 15, 1814, *ASP-Military Affairs*, 541.

4. Gallatin to Monroe, June 13, 1814, *Writings*, I:627–9.

5. Summary of comments from several cabinet members to the House Committee of Inquiry, various dates, *ASP-MA*, 538–41.

6. Lossing, *Field-book*, 918n.

7. W. H. Winder to the House Committee of Inquiry, *ASP-MA*. 543–5.

8. General John P. Van Ness to the House Committee of Inquiry, Ibid. 580–1.

9. William Jones to the House Committee on Inquiry, *ASP-MA*, 540.

10. Monroe to the House Committee of Inquiry, *ASP-MA*, 536.

11. Monroe to George Hay, September 7, 1814, New York Public Library, *Bulletin* (1902), VI:217.

12. Monroe to Armstrong, August 18, 1814, *Writings of Monroe*. V:289.

13. Monroe to Madison, August 20, 1814, *ASP-MA*, 537.

14. Monroe to House Committee of Inquiry, *ASP-MA*, 536; and George Robert Gleig, *A Subaltern in America; Comprising His Narrative of the Campaigns of the British Army, at Baltimore, Washington, Etc., Etc., During the Late War* (Philadelphia, 1833), summarized 6–16.

15. Monroe to the House Committee of Inquiry, November 13, 1814, *ASP-MA*, 338.

16. Dr. Hanson Catlett to the House Committee about mid November 1814.

17. Gleig, *The Campaigns of the British Army at Washington and New Orleans, in the Years 1814–1815 (London, 1836)*, 108–09.

18. Cochrane to Monroe. August 18 and September 19, 1814, and Monroe to Cochrane, September 6, 1814, to House Committee of Inquiry, *ASP:FR, III*, 693–4.

19. Monroe to House Committee, November 13, 1814, *ASP:MA*, 536.

20. Gleig, *Campaigns*, 114–8.

21. Rush to House Committee of Inquiry, October 15, 1814, *ASP:MA*, 542.

22. Monroe to House Committee of Inquiry, November 13, 1814, *ASP:MA*, 536.

23. Winder's lengthy report to the House Committee of Inquiry, September 26, 1814, *ASP:MA*, 557.

24. Ralph D. Paine, *Joshua Barney* (New York, 1924), 371.

25. Barney to Secretary Jones, August 29, 1814, *ASP:MA*, 579–80.

26. Gleig, *Campaigns*, 125–6.

27. Paul Jennings, *A Colored Man's Reminiscences of James Madison* (Brooklyn, 1865), 9–10.

Chapter 32

1. Clark, *Dolly Madison*, 164–6.

2. Dolley Madison to Mrs. Latrobe, December 3, 1814, Clark, *Dolly Madison*, 166–7.

3. Jennings, *Colored Man's Reminiscences*, 10–11.

4. Clark, *Dolly Madison*, 167.

5. Ibid., 170.

6. Gleig, *Campaigns*, 131.

7. Navy Secretary William Jones, to the House Committee of Inquiry, October 3. 1814, *ASP-MA*, 575.

8. Commandant Thomas Tingey, via Secretary Jones, to the House Committee

of Inquiry, October 18, *ASP-MA*, 577–8.

9. *Niles*, August 27, 1814, 446.
10. Ibid., 446.
11. *Memoirs and Letters of Dolly Madison*, edited by her Grand Niece (Port Washington, N.Y., 1886), 104.
12. Ibid., 108.
13. Ibid., 170–1.
14. From Mrs. Thornton's diary, Clark, *Dolly Madison*, 176.
15. Ibid., 169.
16. Ibid., 168–69.
17. Gleig, 141–47.
18. Dr. Hanson Catlett to the House Committee on Inquiry, *ASP-MA*, 384–5.
19. *Niles*, August 27, 1814, 443.
20. Ibid., 444.
21. Gleig, *Campaigns*, 156–63.
22. General John P. Van Ness to the House Committee on Inquiry, *ASP*, November 23, 1814, 580–3.
23. A. K. Hadel, "A Review of the Battle of Bladensburg," Part II, *Maryland Historical Magazine*, I, No. 3, September 1906, pp. 201–204.

Chapter 33

1. Sargent, *Life ... Clay*, 1852, 52.
2. Goulburn to Clay, October 3, 1814, Clay, *Papers*, I, 982.
3. *The Courier*, of London, September 27, 1814.
4. *London Gazette Extraordinary*, September 27, 1814.
5. Adams, *Memoirs*, September 29, 1814. 43.
6. Adams to his wife, October 7, 1814, Adams, *Writings*, 153–5.
7. Ibid., October 5, 1814, and Adams to Crawford, October 26, 1814, *Writings*, 152.
8. Clay to Crawford, October 17, 1814, *Papers*, 988–9.
9. Liverpool to Castlereagh, September 27, 1814, H. Adams, *Gallatin*. 516.
10. Adams, *Memoirs*, 46–50: and Liverpool to Castlereagh, September 27, 1814, Wellington, *Despatches*, IX:290–1.
11. Adams to Louisa Catherine, October 11, 1814. Adams, *Writings*, 155–8.
12. British to American Commissioners, *ASP-FR*, 721–23.
13. British Commissioners to the Americans, October 8, 1814, *ASP-FR*. 721–3.
14. Adams, October 9–13, *Memoirs*, III, 50–52.
15. American Commissioners to the British, October 13, 1814, *ASP-FR*, 723–4.
16. Adams, October 14, 1814, *Memoirs*, III, 50–53.
17. Clay to Crawford, October 17, 1814, *Papers*, I, 988–9.
18. Summarized from Lossing, *Field-book*, 831–35.
19. H. Adams, *History*, 1986 reprint, 978.
20. Summary from Lossing, *Field-book*, 859–875.

21. Crawford to Clay, October 24, 1814, Clay *Papers*, 992–93.
22. American Commissioners to Monroe, October 25, 1814. Clay, *Papers*, 995.
23. Gleig, *Campaigns*, 169.
24. Lossing, *Field-book*, 946. Lossing relates the death of British officer Sir Peter Parker and notes that he was sent home "preserved in spirits."*
25. The story of the attack on Baltimore is summarized from *Niles*, September 24, 1814, VII: 23–25: Lossing, 945–59; and Gleig.
26. Adams, *Memoirs*, October 30–1, 1814, VII. 60–61.
27. British Commissioner to the Americans, October 31, 1814, *ASP-FR*, 726.
28. Adams to L. C. Adams, November 4, 1814, *Writings*, 177–8; and to Crawford, November 6, 1814, 181.
29. American commissioners to the British, November, 10, 1814, *ASP-FR*, III: 735–41.

Chapter 34

1. Liverpool to Castlereagh, November 4, 1814, Wellington, *Despatches*, IX:405.
2. Liverpool to Wellington, Ibid., 406–7.
3. Wellington to Liverpool, November 9, 1814, Ibid., 425–6.
4. Goulburn to Bathurst, November 10, 1814, Ibid., 427.
5. C. J. Bartlett, *Castlereagh* (London), 1966, 138.
6. Erick Bollman to Bayard, December 20, 1814, Donnan, *Bayard Papers*, 360. Bollman had been implicated with the "Burr affair," (see chapter 5) but had subsequently gone to England to advocate a British retreat from impressment of seaman, and was now in Vienna seeking to establish a steamboat venture on the Danube. In his correspondence with Bayard, he was passing on information he obtained from a confidant, Baron Reinhart, an aide to Tallyrand.
7. Adams to L. C. Adams, November 15, 1814, Adams, *Writings*, V:188–9.
8. Adams to L. C. Adams, November 11, 1814, Ibid., 182.
9. Adams to George Joy, November 14, 1814, Ibid., 185.
10. Adams to Levett Harris, November 15, 1814, Ibid., 187–8.
11. Adams to L. C. Adams, November 15, 1814, Ibid., 191.
12. Adams to Crawford, November 17, 1814, Ibid., 192–5.
13. Adams to L. C. Adams, Ibid., 203–4.
14. Adams to Abigail Adams, November 23, 1814, Ibid., 207–8.
15. Adams to L. C. Adams, Ibid., 212.
16. Ibid., footnote to above letter, Liverpool to Wellington, November 26, 1814, taken from Wellington, *Despatches*, IX:456.
17. Ibid., 213–4.
18. Adams, November 24, 1814, *Memoirs*, III:69.

19. Adams to L. C. Adams, Adams, *Writings*, V:215.
20. *ASP-FR*, III:735–41.
21. Goulburn to Bathurst, November 25, 1814, Wellington, *Despatches*, IX: 452–3.
22. Adams, *Memoirs*, November 27, 1814, III:70.
23. Ibid., 71.
24. Ibid., 72.
25. Ibid., 73.
26. Ibid., 73.
27. Ibid., 75.
28. The above story is told almost entirely from Adams' *Memoirs*, 71–8.

Chapter 35

1. (A copy of the final draft of the Treaty will be found in the appendix.) The next several paragraphs are summarized from Adams, *Memoirs*, III:79–90. Quotes from other sources will be so noted.
2. Adams, *Memoirs*, III; 82–3.
3. Ibid., 83.
4. Ibid., 84.
5. Ibid.
6. Ibid.
7. Ibid., 85.
8. Ibid., 87–9.
9. All of the above account of the conference of December 1, 1814, is from Adams, *Memoirs*, 79–90.
10. Adams to L. C. Adams, Adams, *Writings*, V:224.
11. Ibid., 90–1.
12. Ibid., 222–3.
13. Bathurst to the British envoys, December 6, 1814, Castlereagh, *Letters*, IX: 214.
14. Ibid., 215.
15. Adams, *Memoirs*, III:94–5.
16. Ibid., 99–100.
17. Ibid., 101.
18. Ibid., 101–2.
19. Ibid., 101–2.
20. Adams, *Memoirs*, III:103–4.
21. Ibid., 108–112.
22. James Gallatin, *Diary*, December 12, 1814, 34–5.
23. Ibid., 34.
24. Adams to L. C. Adams, December 13, 1814, Adams, *Writings*, V:236.
25. Ibid., 113–6.
26. Ibid., 118–9.
27. Ibid., 237–8.
28. Ibid., 238–9.
29. Bathurst to the British Commissioners, December 19, 1814, Castlereagh, *Despatches*, X:221–2.
30. Adams, *Memoirs*, III:120–2.
31. Ibid., 122.
32. Ibid., 122–4.
33. All of Liverpool's letter to George Canning, is from December 28, 1814, Wellington, *Despatches*, IX:513–4.
34. Ibid., 124.
35. James Gallatin, *Diary*, 35.
36. Adams, *Writings*, V:247–8.
37. Adams, *Memoirs*, III:127.

Chapter 36

1. Clay to James Monroe, December 25, 1814, Clay, *Papers*, 1007–8.

2. Ibid., December 26, 1814, 1009.

3. American envoys to British envoys, December 28, 1914, and British to Americans, December 30, 1914, Ibid., 1009–10 and 1012–13.

4. Adams, *Memoirs*, III:129–30.

5. Ibid., 130–1.

6. Ibid., 131.

7. Ibid., 133–4.

8. Note from Clay, Bayard, and Russell to Adams, December 30, 1814, Clay, *Papers*, 1012.

9. Adams to Bayard, Clay, and Russell, January 2, 1815, Adams, *Writings*, V:258–60; and Clay, *Papers*, II:1–2.

10. Adams, *Memoirs*, III:140.

11. Ibid., 140–1.

12. This long colloquy between Clay and Adams is in Ibid., 140–4.

13. Copies of two letters from Christopher Hughes to American Commissioners, January 6 and 9, 1815, Clay, *Papers*, 2:5–6.

14. All of the following account of the Hartford Convention is summarized from H. Adams, *History*, VIII:287–310.

15. George Cabot to Timothy Pickering and to a young friend, H. Adams, Ibid., III:291–2.

16. Ibid., 296.

17. Ibid., 298.

18. Adams to L. C. Adams, January 17, 1815, Adams, *Writings*, III:268.

19. Adams to L. C. Adams, January 27, 1815, Adams, *Writings*, III:274–5.

20. Adams writing in many pages of his *Memoirs*.

21. Adams, *Memoirs*, III:167.

Chapter 37

1. This chapter provides only a brief account of the Battle of New Orleans, as Henry Clay was not involved in the events in any direct way.

2. H. Adams, *History*, II:253.

3. H. Adams, *History*, II:311,

4. Lossing, *Field-Book*, 1017–9.

5. Jackson, *Correspondence*, II:82–3.

6. H. Adams, *History*, II: 330.

7. Gleig, *Subaltern*, 188.

8. Marquis James, *The Life of Andrew Jackson* (New York) 1940, 201; quoted from Alexander Walker, *Jackson and New Orleans* (1856), 13 and 15.

9. Lossing, *Field-book*, 1023–4.

10. Gleig published two books, one in Philadelphia in 1833 referenced under the heading of "Subaltern," etc. and the other in London in 1836 called "Campaigns." There are some odd disconnections in which he covers the same events entirely differently, particularly in detailing the episodes during the battle for New Orleans. For instance, in one book he refers to action on December 24, 1814, which is not at all like that of the same date in the other book. In one he refers to a companion officer as Gray, and in the other book he writes of Charlton (who turns out not to be the real name of his companion. They are definitely different individuals, since one is killed and the other goes on to higher service ranks). I have had to make use of these accounts as best I can. I have concluded that the writing in "Subaltern" is his true story, whereas the story of the "Campaigns" is something of a fictional account describing events in other soldiers' lives.

11. *Biographical Directory of the United State Congress, 1774–1961*, U.S. Government Printing Office (Washington, D.C.), 1226.

12. Gleig, *Subaltern*, 206.

13. Gleig, *Campaigns*, 266–8.

14. Gleig, *Subaltern*, 207–9.

15. James, *Jackson*, 217–8.

16. Gleig, *Subaltern*, 219–21.

17. Gleig, *Subaltern*, 218–27.

18. James, *Jackson*, 227.

19. Ibid., 229.

20. Gleig, *Campaigns*, 313–4.

21. Gleig, *Subaltern*, 234–5.

22. Lossing, *Field-book*, 1037–8.

23. Gleig, *Subaltern*, 238–43.

24. Gleig, *Subaltern*, 244–7.

25. Gleig, *Campaigns*, 325–6.

26. Ibid., 326–7.

27. Jackson to Monroe, January 3, 1815, *Correspondence*, 130.

28. James, quoted in *Jackson*, 240, from Augustus C. Buell, *A History of Andrew Jackson* (New York, 1904).

29. James, *Jackson*, 241.

30. Lossing *Field-Book*, 1046.

31. James, *Jackson*, 247, quoted from James Parton, *Life of Andrew Jackson* (1859–60), II, 208. And Jackson to Col. Robert Hays, January 26, 1815, Jackson, *Correspondence*, 153.

32. Lossing, *Field-book*, 1049.

33. Jackson to Monroe, January 9, 1815, *Correspondence*, 137.

Chapter 38

1. Sargent, *Life*, 23.

2. J. Q. Adams, *Memoirs*, March 7, 1815, III:165.

3. Ibid., 167 and 170.

4. Ibid. 170.

5. Ibid., 173–4.

6. Ibid. 172–3.

7. J. Q. Adams to Abigail Adams, 19 March 1815, Adams, *Writings*, III:290–3.

8. J. Q. Adams to John Adams, 21 March, 1915, Ibid., III:195–6.

9. J. Q. Adams to his father. April 21, 1815, Ibid., III:295–8.

10. Clay to Crawford, March 23, 1815, Clay, *Papers*, 2:10–12. In most of his comments about Castlereagh in his correspondence, Clay omitted the letter "g" in the Lord's name. A footnote to this letter regarding Andrew Jackson's reference to the debacle on the east side of the Mississippi at the battle for New Orleans, is the following: "Among those who had fled was a small detachment of Kentucky militia, which was singled out for especially severe censure in Jackson's official report of the battle." Jackson's Comment rankled Clay.

11. All of James Gallatin's accounts are from, *The Diary of James Gallatin*, New York, 1924, February 28–April 10, 1815, 63–69.

12. Most of the official accounts of this episode are found In the appendix of the first session of the 14th Congress, in the *Annals*, 1st sess., 14th Cong. App.; 1506–1601, where the story is related in great detail, and where it was called "The Massacre at Dartmoor Prison."

13. Lossing, *Fieldbook*, page unknown.

14. Clay to Bayard, April 13, 1815, 2: 18–9.

15. James Gallatin, April 16, 1815, *Diary*, 70.

16. Clay to Russell, May 10 (July 1), 1815, *Papers*, 23–6.

17. James Gallatin, May 9, 1815, *Diary*, 73.

18. Adams, June 8, 1815, *Memoirs*, V: 213–6.

19. Ibid. 2:19–20.

20. Adams, Memoirs. V:221.

21. Ibid., Comments by J. Q. Adams over the 17th to 20th of June, 1815. Memoirs, V:221–6.

22. Clay to John Payne Todd, July 6, and Lucretia Clay, July 14, 1815, Clay, Papers, 2:59–60.

23. Bayard, *Papers* n.384.

24. A footnote in Clay, *Papers*, 2:61, quoted from the *National Intelligencer*, September 11, 1815.

25. Clay, *Papers*, 2:62.

26. Address by Clay at a public dinner in his honor in Lexington, Ky., October 7, 1815, Colton, *Life*, I; app. 4.

BIBLIOGRAPHY

Books

Adams, Henry. *History of the United States of America*. New York: Scribner's, 1921.

_____. *The Life of Albert Gallatin*. Philadelphia: J. B. Lippincott, 1879.

Adams, Henry, and John Quincy Adams. *Documents Relating to New-England Federalism*. Boston: Little, Brown, 1905.

Adams, John Quincy, and Charles Francis Adams. *Memoirs of John Quincy Adams, Comprising Portions of His Diary from 1795 to 1848*. Philadelphia: J. B. Lippincott, 1874.

_____, and Worthington Chauncey Ford. *Writings of John Quincy Adams*. New York: Macmillan, 1914.

Anonymous. *Presidential Counts*. New York, 1877.

Armstrong, John. *Notices of the War of 1812*. New York: G. Dearborn, 1836.

Atherton, William. *Narrative of the Suffering & Defeat of the North-Western Army, Under General Winchester Massacre of the Prisoners, Sixteen Months Imprisonment of the Writer and Others with the Indians and British*. Frankfort, KY: Printed for the author by A. G. Hodges, 1842.

Bartlett, C. J. *Castlereagh*. New York: Scribner, 1967.

Bayard, James A. *The Papers of James A. Bayard, 1796–1815*. Edited by Elizabeth Donnan. Vol. 2, Annual Report of the American Historical Association for 1913. Washington, D.C., 1915.

Biddle, Alexander. *Old Family Letters*. Philadelphia: J. B. Lippincott, 1892.

Brant, Irving. *James Madison: Commander in Chief 1812–1836*. New York: Bobbs-Merrill, 1961.

British Commissioners. *Proceedings, Massachusetts Historical Society*. Boston, 1915.

Brooke, Francis T. *A Family Narrative*. Richmond, VA: MacFarlane & Fergusson, 1849.

Buell, Augustus C. *History of Andrew Jackson*. New York: Scribner's, 1904.

Burnell, David C. *Travels and Adventures of David C. Burnell*. Palmyra, NY, 1831.

Caldwell, Joshua W. *Sketches of the Bench and Bar of Tennessee*. Knoxville, TN: Ogden, 1898.

Campbell, Maria, and James Freeman Clarke. *Revolutionary Services and Civil Life of General William Hull Prepared from His Manuscripts*. New York: D. Appleton, 1848.

Castlereagh. [Lord, Robert Stewart 2nd Marquess of Londonderry], *Despatches of Lord Castlereagh*. London, 1848–53.

_____. *Letters and* Chatterton, Georgiana. *Memorials Personal and Historical of Admiral Lord Gambier*, G.C.B. London: Hurst and Blackett, 1861.

Clark, Allen C. *Life and Letters of Dolly Madison*. Washington, D.C.: W. F. Roberts, 1914.

Clay, Cassius Marcellus. *The Life of Cassius Marcellus Clay. Memoirs, Writings, and Speeches, Showing His Conduct in the Overthrow of American Slavery, the Salvation of the Union, and the Restoration of the Autonomy of the States ...* Vol. I. Vol. I. Cincinnati: J. F. Brennan, 1886.

Clay, Henry, and Calvin Colton. *The Private Correspondence of Henry Clay*. Cincinnati: H. W. Derby, 1860.

_____, and Daniel Mallory. *The Life and Speeches of the Hon. Henry Clay*. New York: Van Amringe and Bixby, 1844.

_____, and James B. Swain. *The Life and Speeches of Henry Clay*. New York: Greeley & McElrath, 1843.

_____, James F. Hopkins, and Robert Seager. *Papers*. [Lexington]: University of Kentucky Press, 1959.

Clay, Thomas Hart, and Ellis Paxson Oberholtzer. *Henry Clay*. Philadelphia: G. W. Jacobs, 1910.

Collins, Lewis, and Richard H. Collins. *History of Kentucky*. Covington, KY: Collins, 1882.

Colton, Calvin, and Henry Clay. *The Life and Times of Henry Clay*. 2 vol. A. S. Barnes: New York, 1846.

_____, and Thomas B. Stevenson. *The Last Seven Years of the Life of Henry Clay*. New York: A. S. Barnes, 1856.

Cranch, William, and R. L. Batts. *Reports of Cases Argued and Adjudged in the Supreme Court of the United States*. New York: Printed by C. Wiley, 1812–1817, 1812.

Cruikshank, E. A. *The Documentary History of the Campaign Upon the Niagara Frontier in the Year 1812*. Welland: Tribune, 1902.

Cruikshank, Ernest A. *Documents Relating to the Invasion of Canada and the Surrender of Detroit, 1812*. Ottawa: Government Printing Bureau, 1912.

Dawson, Moses. *A Historical Narrative of the Civil and Military Services of Major General William H. Harrison and a Vindication of His Character and Conduct as a Statesman, a Citizen, and a Soldier*. Cincinnati: M. Dawson, 1824.

Drake, Benjamin. *Life of Tecumseh and of His Brother the Prophet with a Historical Sketch of the Shawanoe Indians*. Cincinnati: E. Morgan, 1841.

Frost, John. *Life of Henry Clay: The Statesman and the Patriot, Containing Numerous Anecdotes with Illustrations*. Philadelphia: Lindsay & Blakiston, 1853.

Gallatin, James. *The Diary of James Gallatin*. Edited by Count Gallatin. New York: Scribner, 1924.

_____, and Henry Adams. *The Writings of Albert Gallatin*. Philadelphia [etc.]: J. B. Lippincott, 1879.

Garland, Hugh A. *The Life of John Randolph of Roanoke*. New York: D. Appleton, 1859.

Gleig, G. R. *A Narrative of the Campaigns of the British Army at Washington and New Orleans Under Generals Ross, Pakenham, and Lambert, in the Years 1814 and 1815 with Some Account of the Countries Visited*. London: J. Murray, 1826.

_____. *A Subaltern in America; Comprising the Narrative of the Campaigns of the British Army, at Baltimore, Washington, &C., &C., During the Late War.* Philadelphia: E. L. Carey & A. Hart, 1833.

Great Britain, Foreign Office. *Papers Presented to Parliament in 1813.* London, n.d.

Green, Thomas Marshall. *The Spanish Conspiracy.* Cincinnati: R. Clarke, 1891.

Guernsey, R. S. *New York City and Vicinity During the War of 1812–15, Being a Military, Civic and Financial Local History of That Period.* New York: C. L. Woodward, 1889.

Hamilton, Alexander, and Henry Cabot Lodge. *The Works of Alexander Hamilton.* New York: G. P. Putnam's, 1904.

Harris, Thomas. *The Life and Services of Commodore William Bainbridge.* Philadelphia: Carey, Lea & Blanchard, 1837.

Harrison, William Henry. *Messages and Letter of William Henry Harrison.* 2 vols. (1800–1811). Edited by Logan Esarey. Indianapolis, Indiana Historical Commission, 1922.

Harvey, Peter. *Reminiscences and Anecdotes of Daniel Webster.* Boston: Little, Brown, 1877.

Hatch, Col. William Stanley. *A Chapter of the History of the War of 1812.* Cincinnati, Ohio, 1872.

Helm, Katherine. *The True Story of Mary, Wife of Lincoln.* New York: Harper, 1928.

Henderson, Archibald. *Isaac Shelby, Revolutionary Patriot and Border Hero, The North Carolina Booklet, XVIII* (no place) July, 1918.

Hildreth, Richard. *The History of the United States.* Vol. 6. New York: Harper, 1852.

Hosmer, James K. *History of the Louisiana Purchase.* New York: D. Appleton, 1902.

Indiana, and Logan Esarey. *Governors Messages and Letters.* Indianapolis: Indiana Historical Commission, 1922.

Ingersoll, Charles J. *Historical Sketch of the Second War Between the United States of America and Great Britain.* Philadelphia: Lea and Blanchard,1845.

Irving, Pierre Munroe. *The Life and Letters of Washington Irving.* New York: G. P. Putnam's, 1882.

Jackson, Andrew. *Correspondence.* Edited by John Spencer Bassett. Vol. 1. Washington: Carnegie Inst., 1926.

James, Marquis. *The Life of Andrew Jackson.* New York: Garden City, 1940.

Jefferson, Thomas, and Paul Leicester Ford. *The Works of Thomas Jefferson.* New York: G. P. Putnam, 1904.

_____, Andrew A. Lipscomb, and Albert Ellery Bergh. *The Writings of Thomas Jefferson.* Washington, D.C.: 1903.

Jennings, Paul. *A Colored Man's Reminiscences of James Madison.* Brooklyn: G. C. Beadle, 1865.

Johnson, Henry P. *The Yorktown Campaign and the Surrender of Cornwallis, 1781.* New York, 1881.

Johnson, L. F. *History of Franklin County, Ky.* Frankfort, KY: Roberts, 1912.

Kendall, Amos. *Autobiography of Amos Kendall.* Boston, 1872.

Kerr, Charles, William Elsey Connelley, and E. Merton Coulter. *History of Kentucky.* Chicago: American Historical Society, 1922.

King, Rufus, and Charles R. King. *The Life and Correspondence of Rufus King Comprising His Letters, Private and Official, His Public Documents, and His Speeches.* New York: G. P. Putnam, 1894.

Lee, Sidney. *Dictionary of National Biography.* London: Smith, Elder, 1895.

Littell, John S. *The Clay Minstrel, or, National Songster: To Which Is Prefixed a Sketch of the Life, Public Services and Character of Henry Clay.* Philadelphia: Turner & Fisher, 1842.

Littell, William. *The Statute Law of Kentucky.* Vol. 3. Frankfort, Ky., 1811.

_____, George Nicholas, James Wilkinson, and Temple Bodley. *Reprints of Littell's Political Transactions in and Concerning Kentucky and Letter of George Nicholas to His Friend in Virginia; Also General Wilkinson's Memorial.* Louisville: J. P. Morton, 1926.

Little, Lewis Peyton. *Imprisoned Preachers & Religious Liberty in Virginia.* Lynchburg, VA: J. P. Bell, 1938.

Lossing, Benson J. *The Pictorial Field-Book of the War of 1812.* New York: Harper, 1868.

Madison, Dolley, and Lucia Beverly Cutts. *Memoirs and Letters of Dolly Madison, Wife of James Madison, President of the United States.* Boston: Houghton, Mifflin, 1886.

Madison, James. *Letters and Other Writings of James Madison.* Vol. 2. Philadelphia: J. B. Lippincott, 1865.

_____. *The Writings of James Madison.* Edited by Gaillard Hunt. New York, London: Putnam, 1908.

Marshall, Humphrey. *The History of Kentucky.* In Two Volumes. Frankfort: Henry Gore, 1812.

Mayo, Bernard. *Henry Clay, Spokesman of the New West.* Hamden, CT: Archon Books, 1937.

McAfee, Robert B. *History of the Late War in the Western Country.* Bowling Green, Ohio, 1816.

McCaleb, Walter Flavius. *The Aaron Burr Conspiracy: A History Largely from Original and Hitherto Unused Sources.* New York: Dodd, Mead, 1903.

McLaughlin, Andrew Cunningham. *Lewis Cass.* Boston: Houghton, Mifflin, 1900.

Meigs, William Montgomery. *The Life of Thomas Hart Benton.* Philadelphia: J. B. Lippincott, 1904.

Minor, Benjamin B., ed. *Decisions of Cases in Virginia by the High Court of Chancery.* Richmond, VA: J. W. Randolph, 1852.

Monroe, James, and Stanislaus Murray Hamilton. *The Writings of James Monroe, Including a Collection of His Public and Private Papers and Correspondence Now for the First Time Printed.* New York: G. P. Putnam's, 1898.

Morison, Samuel Eliot. *The Life and Letters of Harrison Gray Otis, Federalist, 1765–1848.* Boston: Houghton, Mifflin, 1913.

Morris, Gouverneur. *The Diary and Letters of Gouverneur Morris.* Edited by Anne Cory Morris. 2 vols. New York, 1888.

The National Cyclopedia of American Biography. Clifton, NJ: J. T. White, 1980.

Paine, Ralph Delahaye. *Joshua Barney, a Forgotten Hero of Blue Water.* New York: Century, 1924.

Parks, Joseph Howard. *Felix Grundy, Champion of Democracy.* University: Louisiana State University Press, 1940.

Parton, James. *The Life and Times of Aaron Burr.* New York: Mason, 1860.

_____, Abraham Lincoln, and Robert Todd Lincoln. *Life of Andrew Jackson.* New York: Mason, 1860.

Parton, W. M. *The Marshall Family.* Cincinnati, 1885.

Perkins, Bradford. *Castlereagh and Adams: England and the United States, 1812–1823.* Berkeley: University of California Press, 1964.

Perrin, William Henry. *History of Fayette County, Kentucky. With an Outline Sketch of the Blue Grass Region*, by R. Peter, Illustrated. Chicago: Baskin, 1882.

Perry, B. F., and Hext McCall Perry. *Reminiscences of Public Men, by Ex-Gov. B. F. Perry.* Philadelphia: J. D. Avil, 1883.

Peter, Robert, and Johanna Peter. *Transylvania University Its Origin, Rise, Decline, and Fall.* Louisville, KY: J. P. Morton, 1896.

Pickering, Octavius, and Upham, Charles W. *The Life of Timothy Pickering.* Boston, 1873.

Pickett, Albert James. *History of Alabama, and Incidentally of Georgia and Mississippi from the Earliest Period.* Charleston [S.C.]: Walker and James, 1851.

Plumer, William, and Everett Somerville Brown. *William Plumer's Memorandum of Proceedings in the United States Senate, 1803–1807.* New York: Macmillan, 1923.

Prentice, George D. *Biography of Henry Clay.* New York: J. J. Phelps, 1831.

Quincy, Edmund. *Life of Josiah Quincy.* Boston: Little, Brown, 1874.

Quisenberry, Anderson Chenault. *The Life and Times of Hon. Humphrey Marshall: Sometime an Officer in the Revolutionary War ... Senator in Congress from 1795 to 1801.* Winchester, KY: Sun, 1892.

Ranck, George Washington. *History of Lexington, Kentucky.* Cincinnati: R. Clarke, 1872.

Ravenel, Harriott Horry. *Life and Times of William Lowndes of South Carolina, 1782–1822.* Boston: Houghton, Mifflin, 1901.

Richardson, Major John. *War of 1812* (no place), 1842.

Rogers, Joseph M. *The True Henry Clay.* Philadelphia: J. B. Lippincott, 1904.

Rowland, Dunbar. *Third Annual Report of the Director of the Department of Archives and History of the State of Mississippi, from October 1, 1903, to October 1, 1904, with Accompanying Historical Documents Concerning the Aaron Burr Conspiracy.* Jackson, MS: Department, 1905.

Rush, Richard. *Letters of Benjamin Rush.* Edited by L. H. Butterfield. Princeton, N.J., 1951.

Safford, William H. *The Blennerhassett Papers.* Cincinnati: Moore, Wilstach & Baldwin, 1864.

Sargent, Epes. *The Life and Public Services of Henry Clay.* Auburn, NY: Derby & Miller, 1852.

Sargent, Nathan. *Life of Henry Clay.* Philadelphia: R. G. Berford, 1844.

_____. *Public Men and Events from the Commencement of Mr. Monroe's Administration, in 1817, to the Close of Mr. Fillmore's Administration, in 1853.* Philadelphia: J. B. Lippincott, 1875.

Sawyer, Lemuel. *A Biography of John Randolph, of Roanoke, with a Selection from His Speeches.* New York: W. Robinson, 1844.

Schachner, Nathan. *Aaron Burr: A Biography.* New York: A. S. Barnes, 1937.

Scharf, Thomas. *History of St. Louis City and County.* Philadelphia: L. H. Everts,1883.

Scott, Winfield. *Memoirs of Lieut.-General Scott, LL.D.* New York: Sheldon, 1864.

Shipp, J. E. B. *Giant Days, or the Life and Times of William H. Crawford.* Americus, Ga., 1909.

Smith, Margaret Bayard, and Gaillard Hunt. *The First Forty Years of Washington Society, Portrayed by the Family Letters of Mrs. Samuel Harrison Smith (Margaret Bayard) from the Collection of Her Grandson, J. Henley Smith.* New York: Scribner's, 1906.

Smith, Z. F., and Mary Katharine Rogers Clay. *The Clay Family Part First; The Mother of Henry Clay, by Hon. Zachary F. Smith ... Part Second; The Genealogy of the Clays.* Louisville, KY: J. P. Morton, printers to the Filson Club, 1900.

Snow, Elliot. *On the Decks of "Old Ironsides."* New York, 1932.

Sparks, Jared. *Jared Spark's Journals.* Harvard University, 1830.

Stanwood, Edward. *A History of the Presidency, from 1788 to 1897.* Boston: Houghton Mifflin, 1912.

Staples, Charles R. *The History of Pioneer Lexington (Kentucky) 1779–1806.* Lexington, KY: Transylvania, 1939

Story, William Wetmore. *Life and Letters of Joseph Story, As-sociate Justice of the Supreme Court of the United States, and Dane Professor of Law at Harvard University.* Boston: C. C. Little and J. Brown, 1851.

Sullivan, William, and John T. S. Sullivan. *The Public Men of the Revolution. Including Events from the Peace of 1783 to the Peace of 1815.* Philadelphia: Carey and Hart, 1847.

Walker, Alexander. *Jackson and New Orleans. An Authentic Narrative of the Memorable Achievements of the American Army, Under Andrew Jackson, Before New Orleans, in the Winter of 1814, '15.* New York: J. C. Derby, 1856.

Warfield, Ethelbert Dudley. *The Kentucky Resolutions of 1798: An Historical Study.* New York: G. P. Putnam's, 1887.

Washington, George, and John Clement Fitzpatrick. *The Writings of George Washington from the Original Manuscript Sources, 1745–1799.* Washington: Government Printing Office, 1940.

Webster, Daniel, and Edward Everett. *The Writings and Speeches of Daniel Webster.* Boston: Little, Brown, 1903.

Wellington, Arthur Wellesley of, and Arthur Richard Wellesley of Wellington. *Supplementary Despatches and Memoranda of Field Marshal Arthur, Duke of Wellington...: India 1797–1805.* London: Murray, 1860.

Wilkinson, James, and Abraham Small. *Memoirs of My Own Times.* Philadelphia: Printed by Abraham Small, 1816.

Williams, Edwin. *The Statesman's Manual.* New York, 1849.

Wilson, James Grant, and John Fiske. *Appletons' Cyclopaedia of American Biography.* New York: D. Appleton, 1887.

Winthrop, Robert C. *Memoir of Henry Clay.* Cambridge: J. Wilson, 1880.

Periodical Articles

Adams, Henry. "Count Edward de Crillon," *American Historical Review,* Vol. 1 (October 1895).

Anonymous. "Henry Clay's Personal anecdotes, incidents, etc.," *Harper's Magazine,* Vol. 5 (August 1852).

Austin, Moses. "Journal of Moses Austin, 1796–7," *American Historical Review,* Vol. 5, No. 3 (April 1900).

Bayard, James A. "James Asheton Bayard Letters, 1802–1814," *Bulletin of the New York Public Library,* Vol. 4 (1908).

Bigelow, Abijah. "Letters of Abijah Bigelow, Member of Congress, to His Wife, [Hannah], 1810–1815." *Proceedings of the American Antiquarian Society.* Vol. 40, New Series.

Christian, Thomas. Address read at *Western Reserve and Northern Ohio Historical Society.* Cleveland, Ohio (1877).

Clay to Joseph Story. *Annals of Ohio,* Vol. 5. (April 1909).

Coleman, R. T. "Jo Daveiss of Kentucky," *Harper's Magazine,* Vol. 21 (June-Nov. 1860).

Daroche, Judge. "Narrative of Captain Hart's Massacre." *Report of the Pioneer and Historical Society of the State of Michigan.* Lansing, Mich., 1886. Vol. VIII.

Daveiss, J. H. "View of the President's Conduct Concerning the Conspiracy of 1806," *Quarterly Publication of the Historical and Philosophical Society of Ohio,* Vol. 11, 1917, Nos. 2 and 3.

Great Britain, Foreign Office. "Instructions to the British Ministers to the United States, 1791–1812." Edited by Bernard Mayo. Vol. 3. *Annual Report of the American Historical Association for 1936.* Washington, 1936.

Harrison, J. O. "Henry Clay: Reminiscences by His Executor," *Century Magazine,* Vol. 33, No. 2 (Dec. 1886).

Hadel, A. K. *A Review of the Battle of Bladensburg.* Pt. II. Maryland Historical Magazine, I, No. 3, September 1906

Henderson, Archibald. "Isaac Shelby, Revolutionary Patriot and Border Hero," *North Carolina Booklet,* XVIII, July 1918.

_____. "The Transylvania Company, A Study in Personnel; II. The Hart Brothers: Thomas, Nataniel, and David," *The Filson Club History Quarterly*, Vol. 21, No. 3 (Louisville, July 1947).

Henshaw, Miss Leslie. "The Aaron Burr Conspiracy in the Ohio Valley," *Ohio Archeological and Historical Society Publications*, 1919.

Hooker, Edward. "Diary of Edward Hooker," *Annual Report of the American Historical Association*. Vol. 1, 1896. Washington, 1897.

Niles Weekly Register (many volumes)

Ohio. Bulletin No. 4, Vol. 5. Toledo, Oct. 1933. Ch.19 n.25 Dudley, The Rev. Thomas P. "Battle and Massacre at Frenchtown, Michigan, January 1813." *Michigan Pioneer and Historical Society*. Lansing, Mich., 1894. Vol. XXII.

Pierce, John. "Memoirs," *Proceedings, Massachusetts Historical Society*, Vol. 30. Boston, October 1905.

Railey, William E. "History of Woodford County," *Register, Kentucky Historical Society*, Vol. 19, No. 15 (Jan. 1921).

Roberts, Jonathan, "Memoirs of a Senator from Pennsylvania: Jonathan Roberts, 1771–1854," *Pennsylvania Magazine of History and Biography*, Vol. 62. Philadelphia, 1938.

Rush, Richard, to John Adams. "Some Unpublished Correspondence of John Adams and Richard Rush, 1811–1816." *Pennsylvania Magazine of History and Biography*, Vol. 60.

Taggart, Samuel. "Letters of Samuel Taggart," *Proceedings of the American Antiquarian Society*, Vol. 33, New Series, Part 2.

Wing, Talcott E. "History of Monroe County, Michigan." *Michigan Historical and Pioneer Collections*. Lansing, Mich. (1894) Vol. IV.

Newspapers

Baltimore (Md.) *American and Commercial Daily Advertizer*.
Baltimore (Md.) *Whig*.
Cincinnati (Ohio) *Liberty Hall*
Frankfort (Ky.) *Palladium*.
Frankfort (Ky.) *Western World*.
Georgetown (D.C.) *Federal Republican and Commercial Gazette*
Lexington (Ky.) *Kentucky Gazette*.
Lexington (Ky.) *Reporter*.
Lexington (Ky.) *Republican Leader*.
London *Times*.
London Courier.
London *Gazette Extraordinary*.
New York *Courier and Enquirer*.
New York *Evening Post*.
New York *Gazette*.
New York *Times*.
Philadelphia (Pa.) *Aurora*.
Philadelphia (Pa.) *Poulson's American Daily Advertizer*.
Richmond *Virginia Gazette (and General Advertizer)*.
Richmond *Enquirer*.
Washington (D.C.) *National Intelligencer*.
Washington (Ky.) *Mirror*.

Government Documents

American State Papers: Foreign Relations (ASP-FR), Vol. III, Washington, 1832.

American State Papers: Naval Affairs (ASP NA). Vol. II, Washington, France, Archives des Affaires Étrangères, *Correspondence Politique, Etats Unis*.

Great Britain, Public Records Office, Foreign Office 5. [Photostats, MSS-LC.]

Kentucky Historical Society.

Kentucky, House of Representatives, *Journal*.

National Archives, Record Group 107, "Letters Received," (6) C-303.

National Archives, "Correspondence of Navy Captains to and from the Secretary of the Navy."

National Archives, Naval Records Collection.

State Papers and Publick Documents of the United States, Vol. VII, Boston, 1817.

U.S. Congress, *Annals of Congress*.

U.S. Congress. *Biographical Directory*. 1961.

U.S. Congress, Senate, *Journal*.

U.S. Congress, Senate, *Journal of the Executive Proceedings of the Senate*.

Manuscripts

H. Blanton, Kentucky Historical Society, Frankfort, Ky.
Breckinridge Family Papers, Library of Congress.
Isaac Briggs Papers, Library of Congress.
James Brown Papers, Library of Congress.
Henry Clay Papers, Library of Congress.
Henry Clay Papers, Duke University.
Thomas J. Clay Papers, Library of Congress.
Augustus Foster Papers, Library of Congress.
Albert Gallatin Papers. New York Historical Society. (Microfilm of the originals are in Library of Congress.)
Harry Innes Papers, Library of Congress.
Thomas Jefferson Papers, Library of Congress.
James Madison Papers, Library of Congress.
James Monroe Papers, Library of Congress.
Joseph B. Nones Papers, Brandeis University.
William Plumer Papers, Library of Congress.
Caesar Rodney Papers, Library of Congress.
Rodney Family Papers, Library of Congress.
Jonathan Russell Papers, Brown University
Samuel Smith Papers, Library of Congress.
William H. Smith Collection, Indiana Historical Society. Indianapolis, Ind.

INDEX